an introduction to
HUMAN RESOURCE MANAGEMENT

NICK WILTON

KU-792-298

Los Angeles | London | New Delhi
Singapore | Washington DC | Melbourne

Los Angeles | London | New Delhi
Singapore | Washington DC | Melbourne

SAGE Publications Ltd
1 Oliver's Yard
55 City Road
London EC1Y 1SP

SAGE Publications Inc.
2455 Teller Road
Thousand Oaks, California 91320

SAGE Publications India Pvt Ltd
B 1/I 1 Mohan Cooperative Industrial Area
Mathura Road
New Delhi 110 044

SAGE Publications Asia-Pacific Pte Ltd
3 Church Street
#10-04 Samsung Hub
Singapore 049483

Editor: Kirsty Smy
Development editor: Gemma Shields
Production editor: Sarah Cooke
Copyeditor: Gemma Marren
Proofreader: Audrey Scriven
Indexer: Silvia Benvenuto
Marketing manager: Alison Borg
Cover design: Francis Kenney
Typeset by: C&M Digitals (P) Ltd, Chennai, India
Printed and bound in Great Britain by Bell
   and Bain Ltd, Glasgow

Library of Congress Control Number: 2015960210

British Library Cataloguing in Publication data

A catalogue record for this book is available from
the British Library

ISBN 978-1-4739-1571-8
ISBN 978-1-4739-1572-5 (pbk)
ISBN 978-1-4739-5419-9 (pbk & interactive ebk) (IEB)

At SAGE we take sustainability seriously. Most of our products are printed in the UK using FSC papers and boards.
When we print overseas we ensure sustainable papers are used as measured by the PREPS grading system.
We undertake an annual audit to monitor our sustainability.

an introduction to

HUMAN RESOURCE MANAGEMENT

PRAISE FOR THE PREVIOUS EDITIONS

'A highly accessible book for all students with broad coverage of a wide range of HRM topics. The combination of research and practice results in an interesting insight into HRM. The new interactive ebook is a great addition.'
Wendy Yellowley, Principal Lecturer HRM, University of Hertfordshire

'This book has become an established text, combining insights and examples that bring something fresh to the study of HRM. With its comprehensive format, it's an all-rounder and a staple on my bookshelf. Undoubtedly a rich resource for students and lecturers of HRM.'
Dr Shirley Barrett, Lecturer, International Business, Ulster University Business School

'This is engaging and comprehensive in its coverage of HRM theory and practice. It is a 'must go to' text for both undergraduate, postgraduate, MBA and CIPD HRM students and HRM academics.'
Dr Kate Black Senior Lecturer, Newcastle Business School, Northumbria University

'This is an excellent introductory text that goes well beyond most conventional HR texts. Nick Wilton not only successfully outlines the rationale and operation of HRM but adopts a critical perspective on the study and practice of HRM by integrating state of the art academic research with contemporary "real world" challenges, debates and practical cases. This text is instructive, engaging and will provide students with a comprehensive understanding of the challenges and potential for HR to contribute to both organisational performance and individual well-being.'
Dr Timothy Bartram, (Joint) Editor in Chief of the Asia Pacific Journal of Human Resources and Associate Professor, School of Business, La Trobe University, Australia

'This is an excellent textbook that combines research and practice in a very readable and interesting way! It does a great job of covering all the major topics in HRM and each chapter is filled with outstanding learning features.'
Randall S. Schuler, Distinguished Professor, HRM, Rutgers University

'Well written and crafted in a format that meets the needs of international students for whom English is not a first language. Inclusion of end-of-chapter case studies and self-test questions can be utilized for group work and the overall layout is most helpful to busy lecturers crafting their sessions. I will certainly be recommending this as a key resource for next academic year's students.'
Mrs Jillian Ashley-Jones, Faculty of Business, Environment & Society, Coventry University

'This comprehensive text covers a range of HRM topics in a clear and well-organized way. Contemporary and critical issues are considered and future/emerging ideas are also addressed. The text is highly interactive and encourages students to apply ideas and develop their understanding of concepts through a number of case studies and other activities. Each chapter is supplemented by a number of helpful additional readings and website materials and is suitable for students at senior undergraduate and postgraduate levels.'
Mr Martin Dowling, School of Management, University of St Andrews

'This book is an excellent resource for students of human resource management. It provides a comprehensive and critical perspective on the theoretical and practical aspects of HRM.'
Professor Peter Wimmer, Business and Management, University of Applied Sciences, Augsburg

'A very good source for basic concepts. Especially suitable for students who are just being introduced to HRM.'
Dr Alhajie Khan, Human Resource Management & Industrial Relations, Keele University

'With clear outlines and key learning goals this book provided a whole picture on what to expect after reading a book. Discussions at each chapter helped students to explore and analyze issues. National and international context as well as HRM in practice in other organizations really helped understanding of the subject in many contexts.'
Professor Hyun Jeong Kim, College of Business Administration, Inha University

SUMMARY OF CONTENTS

CONTENTS

15 Current Trends and Future Challenges in HRM 406

LIST OF FIGURES

LIST OF TABLES

ABOUT THE AUTHOR

NICK WILTON is Academic Director, Employability and External Engagement, for the Faculty of Business and Law at the University of the West of England, Bristol. He is also a Principal Lecturer in HRM, Senior Fellow of the Higher Education Academy and Chartered Member of the CIPD. His teaching covers HRM, Human Resource Development, Sociology of Work and International Management. His current research interests focus on graduate employability, the relationship between higher education and the labour market and the changing nature of careers.

PREFACE

As the title suggests, this book provides an introduction to the management of people in work organisations, or as it is now most commonly known, human resource management (HRM). It seeks to outline the purpose and operation of HRM activities in the 'real world', whilst situating practice in the context of associated debates and controversies played out in the parallel field of academic study. It adopts a critical perspective on the study and practice of HRM to provide the reader with an understanding not only of the potential for HRM to contribute to both improved organisational performance and individual well-being in the workplace, but also why it very often fails to achieve either of these positive outcomes.

What certain universal models of HRM claim to offer is a means by which organisations can maximise the contribution of workers to the achievement of strategic objectives through the implementation of specific formulations of HR practices. Recent developments in markets, labour markets and economies, however, tend to put significant pressure on managers not to think in a long-term strategic manner about how best to use their human resources, but to use workers in a more instrumental manner for short-term gain. In other words, whilst the rhetoric and theory of HRM tend to emphasise strategic investment in employees, the operational reality is such that employees are often treated in a way that is unlikely to maximise employee commitment and motivation. Nonetheless, whilst acknowledging the wide range of approaches that organisations can adopt to managing their workforce, the subtext of this book is that a strategic approach to HRM – well designed, properly implemented and executed, and which has, as a core precept, the ethical treatment of employees – can contribute to both the short- and longer-term success of the enterprise. Underpinning this subtext, however, is how difficult this is to do in practice.

This book is aimed at students across the academic spectrum, whether studying on a specialist HRM programme of study, a generalist business and management programme or studying HRM as part of a programme in an ostensibly unrelated discipline (such as engineering or humanities). This intention is reflected in the central theme running through the book that the management of people is not the preserve of HR specialists but an area of interest and concern for all organisational actors. Ultimately, managing a firm's human resources has always been the responsibility of all managers, but recent developments in HRM have tended to result in line managers and supervisors adopting ever-greater responsibility for the way in which their teams and departments perform. People management skills, including the ability to communicate effectively and to motivate, develop and engage others, are increasingly viewed by organisations as *the* critical set of competencies required by managers at all levels. Subsequently, students aspiring to become managers in the future – or those currently working as managers – need to appreciate how HRM practices and processes work in reality and the assumptions, associated debates and inherent problems associated with such practice. The intention of this book is, therefore, not to provide a detailed 'how-to' of HRM in practice, rather to introduce the HR practices and issues in contemporary HRM within their wider environmental and organisational context.

THE STRUCTURE OF THE BOOK

Each chapter in this book seeks to present a critical review of its subject and to provide both practical and theoretical insight. The book is divided into three sections.

HRM in context

The principal purpose of this section is to situate HRM in both its theoretical and environmental context. The first chapter introduces HRM, both as an organisational function and as an academic discipline, and a number of important themes and concepts that recur throughout the book. Chapter 2 discusses the relationship between HRM and the individual worker through a discussion of the employment relationship and how HRM can manage the component elements of this relationship. The subsequent three chapters each discuss a 'layer' of the context of HRM: the organisational and strategic context; the labour market context; and the wider national and international context.

HRM in practice

This section introduces five core areas of HRM: people resourcing; performance management; reward; learning and development; and employee relations. Each chapter seeks to present a critical perspective on contemporary practice in the specific functional area of HRM. Whilst each chapter discusses a discrete area of HRM, a recurring theme is the importance of considering their inter-relationship when making decisions about organisational policy and practice.

Contemporary issues in HRM

The final section introduces a number of contemporary issues in HRM. Whilst the issues discussed here – equality and diversity; career development; workplace discord; and employee well-being – are by no means new concerns, they represent areas where contemporary trends in practice or context have 'moved the goalposts' for management or represent notable areas of both innovative and poor practice. The final chapter revisits a number of important issues in contemporary HRM that have been introduced elsewhere in the book, such as the use of new technology, knowledge management and HR outsourcing, but which warrant further discussion because they represent both important challenges and opportunities for management and provide an indication of the future direction of HRM.

HOW TO USE THIS BOOK AND ITS ONLINE RESOURCES

An Introduction to Human Resource Management, third edition, is supported by SAGE Edge, which offers a wealth of online resources for both students and lecturers. Access these features at **https://edge.sagepub.com/wilton3e**

For students

Learning Objectives remind you of what you have learned in each chapter of the book and aid revision

Action Plans for each chapter help you track what material you have revised and effectively plan your studies

Glossary Flashcards featuring terms from the book to help you get to grips with HRM terminology and revise for exams

Author Videos from Nick Wilton provide an introduction to key topics at the start of selected chapters

Video Links highlight real world examples of HRM

Interactive Multiple Choice Questions allow you to test your knowledge of each chapter

 Free Selected SAGE Journal Articles from each chapter are available to further develop your understanding

 Extended Case Studies provide you with further examples to aid your studies

 Useful Weblinks direct you to resources that will deepen your understanding of chapter topics

For lecturers

Instructor's Manual containing additional case studies, tutor's notes and exercises to support your teaching

PowerPoint Slides featuring figures and tables, learning objectives and key concepts from each chapter

Further Video links have been compiled in one easily accessible place for easy upload into your University's learning environment

Lecturer Testbank offering a wide range of assessment questions, complete with model answers

HOW *AN INTRODUCTION TO HUMAN RESOURCE MANAGEMENT* WILL SUPPORT YOUR LEARNING

This third edition of **An Introduction to Human Resource Management** offers a range of learning resources in the text and online designed to aid your understanding of the key issues and ideas discussed in each chapter.

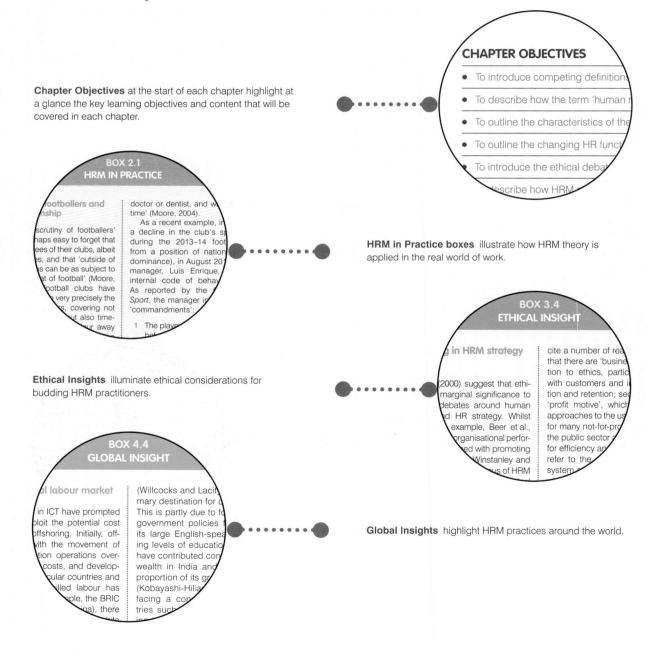

Chapter Objectives at the start of each chapter highlight at a glance the key learning objectives and content that will be covered in each chapter.

CHAPTER OBJECTIVES

- To introduce competing definition
- To describe how the term 'human r
- To outline the characteristics of the
- To outline the changing HR funct
- To introduce the ethical deba
- describe how HRM

BOX 2.1
HRM IN PRACTICE

ootballers and
nship

scrutiny of footballers'
haps easy to forget that
ees of their clubs, albeit
s, and that 'outside of
s can be as subject to
at of football' (Moore,
ootball clubs have
very precisely the
s, covering not
ut also time-
ur away

doctor or dentist, and w
time' (Moore, 2004).
As a recent example, i
a decline in the club's s
during the 2013–14 foot
from a position of nation
dominance, in August 20
manager, Luis Enrique,
internal code of beha
As reported by the
Sport, the manager i
'commandments':

1 The playe

HRM in Practice boxes illustrate how HRM theory is applied in the real world of work.

Ethical Insights illuminate ethical considerations for budding HRM practitioners.

BOX 3.4
ETHICAL INSIGHT

g in HRM strategy

(2000) suggest that ethi-
marginal significance to
debates around human
d HR strategy. Whilst
example, Beer et al.,
rganisational perfor-
ed with promoting
Winstanley and
us of HRM

cite a number of re
that there are 'busine
tion to ethics, partic
with customers and i
tion and retention; se
'profit motive', which
approaches to the us
for many not-for-pro
the public sector
for efficiency an
refer to the
system

BOX 4.4
GLOBAL INSIGHT

l labour market

in ICT have prompted
loit the potential cost
ffshoring. Initially, off-
ith the movement of
tion operations over-
costs, and develop-
ular countries and
illed labour has
ple, the BRIC
a), there

(Willcocks and Lacit
mary destination for
This is partly due to f
government policies
its large English-spea
ing levels of educatio
have contributed co
wealth in India and
proportion of its g
(Kobayashi-Hilla
facing a con
tries such

Global Insights highlight HRM practices around the world.

Research Insights analyse real research into HRM practice.

BOX 5.9
RESEARCH INSIGHT

M practices in

ssible to transfer HRM
n the country in which
nother is a key issue of
ional human resource
NCs, the degree to
ferring HRM prac-
can mean the
dvantage and
his can be
for

equality, weak unce
power distance. Swis
terised as reflecting lo
more masculine and
of uncertainty avoidan
the cultural characteris
countries is, therefore
lenge to the effecti
management prac
in respect of h
practices and
The re

BOX 6.1
UNDERSTAND

mand

nt or technology to
kforce skills.
n of work
by introducing
he demarcation

of individual
to address

shifting towards fle
outsourcing certain
- Relocate operations
local labour force ch
the availability of che
workers.
- Seek to improve inc
performance and
by introducing p
and performan
greater emp
making

Understand boxes guide your knowledge and
understanding of key practices and examples in HRM.

BOX 7.7
AGEMENT SKILLS AND ATTRI

pitfalls of

have been subject
ns, often associated
that they are con-
, line managers can
st be perceived as
egations of bias,
(whether of the
rent manag-
respond

dysfunctional beha
For example, Brown
that even well designe
result in employee wo
Many of the prob
management respons
are crystallised in the
extent that appraisa
resource activity t
(Redman, 2006
are not convi
als can

Management Skills and Attributes boxes in the 'HRM in
Practice' section to highlight the critical skills that managers
need to be effective in enacting practice.

Summary Points recap key concepts covered in the chapter to aid your revision.

Self-Test Questions and **Case Study Questions** help you check your understanding of HRM principles and revise for exams.

End of chapter **Case Studies** offer a more in-depth look at HRM across a variety of organisations.

Useful Reading provides you with a mix of articles, books and reports to further your study and guide your revision.

USEFUL READING

dynamic behind
Pacific Journal of

that HRM – where
behaviours and
organisational
mocracy and
d with the

Paauwe, J. (2
Achievements, met
Journal of Managem
This article provi
development of HRM
over the past three
debates and contr
therefore acts as
panion piece fo
the next two

FURTHER ONLINE READING

ssed for free on the
tps://edge.sagepub.

aarden, J. and Brosseau,
merce firms: Innovations
ntinuities with the 'old',
, 24 (5): 443–70.

J. (2006) HR and
ties in Australian

organisations, *Asi*
Resources, 44 (2): 24

Verreynne, M.-L., Par
Employment systems
analysis, *International S*
405–31.

Wright, C. (2008) Rei
agement: Business
the limits to profess
1063–86.

Further Online Reading gives you free access to scholarly journal articles selected to reinforce your learning of key topics in each chapter.

Glossary Terms are bolded in the text and allow you to quickly reference new terms and get a handle on HRM terminology.

360-degree appraisal/feedback A form of p
appraisal which collects feedback from
of sources, typically superiors, subordina
and internal/external customers, to provi
holistic view of whole job performance.
Appraisal See **Performance appraisal**.
Arbitration Intervention in an industrial dispu
the parties to the dispute appoint a third
to evaluate the evidence and make a deci
resolve the dispute.
Assessment centre Often used for highly
posts (such as places on graduate trai
schemes); these are extended sele
ich involve a combination of
le interviews, such

ACKNOWLEDGEMENTS

My deepest thanks, as always, to Joanna, Martha and Erin for taking all this far less seriously than I do. Thanks also to Kirsty Smy, Gemma Shields and Robin Lupton at SAGE Publishing, colleagues at Bristol Business School, the reviewers of previous editions and early versions of this book and all those who adopted the second edition and/or said positive things about it.

The author is grateful to those who granted permission to reproduce copyright material.

THANKS FROM THE PUBLISHER

The publisher would like to thank the reviewers for providing feedback and suggestions to help shape this new edition:

Svala Guðmundsdóttir, Assistant Professor in HRM, University of Iceland

Lorraine Quinn, Senior Lecturer, University of the West of Scotland

Sabine Raeder, Prof. Dr., University of Oslo

Alan J. Ryan, Principal Lecturer in HRM, De Montfort University

Tessa Wright, Senior Lecturer in Human Resource Management, Queen Mary University of London

Wendy Yellowley, Principal Lecturer, University of Hertfordshire

Yu Zheng, Lecturer in Asian Business and International HRM, School of Management, Royal Holloway University of London

PART ONE
HRM IN CONTEXT

PART MAP

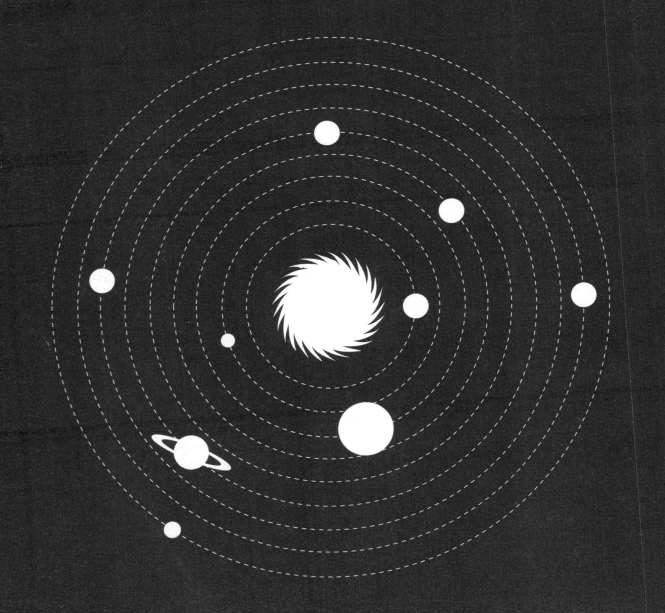

The purpose of the five chapters that make up the first section of this book is twofold. First, the chapters introduce a wide range of concepts, theories and models that are critical to a sound understanding of contemporary human resource management. Second, it seeks to situate people management in its wider social, political and economic context. In short, these chapters set the scene for those that follow in order to provide a backdrop against which HRM practices and associated controversies can be assessed.

Like many aspects of organisational activity, the means by which organisations manage their employees – for example, how they seek to motivate and reward staff, how they recruit and develop required labour and how firms deal with conflict – are often taken for granted and unquestioned. However, how people are managed in the modern workplace is underpinned by a wide range of theoretical constructs, such as those that seek to understand how people are motivated, that have developed since the advent of industrial capitalism. Therefore, an understanding of these theories and how they translate into HRM practice is critical for understanding what firms do, why they do it and the impact of these practices on both employees and the organisation itself. Furthermore, implicit in the discussion of HRM throughout this book – as set out in these opening chapters – is a consideration of the experience of work and employment and of the relationship that exists between workers and their employer. An understanding of this relationship is critical to an appreciation of how firms can translate HRM practices into improved individual performance at work and thus into improved organisational performance. These chapters seek to discuss these relationships and stress how the complexity of human interaction makes the management of people problematic.

Each chapter in this section plays a specific role in this 'scene-setting'. The first chapter introduces HRM, both as an organisational function and as an academic discipline, and a number of important themes, concepts and contemporary developments in HRM practice that are referred to throughout the book. Chapter 2 discusses the relationship between HRM and the individual worker through a discussion of the employment relationship and how HRM seeks to manage the component elements of this relationship. It introduces some key concepts – such as employee engagement and the psychological contract – that underpin much discussion of how HRM can 'add value' to business performance, a predominant concern in both HRM research and practice. The subsequent three chapters each discuss a 'layer' of the internal and external context of HRM. First, Chapter 3 sets out the organisational and strategic context of HRM, principally the different approaches an organisation can adopt to designing an overarching approach to people management, as well as the debate regarding how exactly HRM acts to influence organisational performance. Chapter 4 then outlines the labour market context of HRM, discussing, in particular, key trends that act to influence the supply of and demand for labour, and how firms respond to change through the organisation of work. Finally, Chapter 5 has as its central theme the notion that HRM practices do not exist in a vacuum and are shaped by the legal, political, social and economic environment in which they develop. Considered in the context of the process of globalisation, this chapter seeks to set out how HRM differs across borders, the factors that shape management practice and the challenges these differences present for firms that do business internationally.

By the end of this section, the reader should have an appreciation of the different meanings of HRM, the key controversies associated with its recent development and the role it can play in contributing to organisational success, as well as an understanding of the theoretical and environmental context in which people are managed in contemporary work organisations.

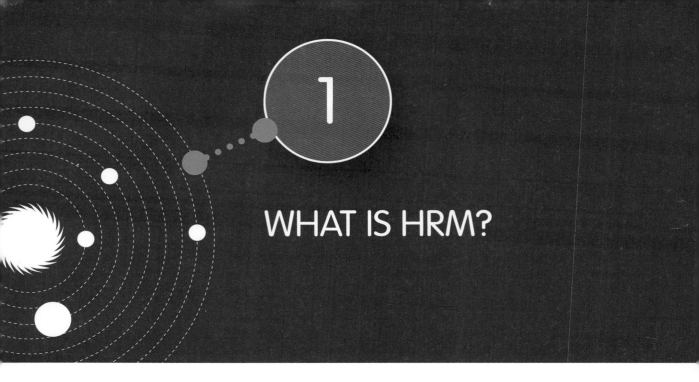

1

WHAT IS HRM?

CHAPTER OBJECTIVES

- To introduce competing definitions of HRM

- To describe how the term 'human resource management' came to be so widely used

- To outline the characteristics of the 'high-commitment' variant of HRM

- To outline the changing HR function and the growing role of line managers in HRM

- To introduce the ethical debates surrounding HRM

- To describe how HRM practices might differ in small and medium-sized enterprises.

INTRODUCTION

Human resource management (HRM or simply HR) is the term commonly used to describe all those organisational activities concerned with recruiting and selecting, designing work for, training and developing, appraising and rewarding, directing, motivating and controlling workers. In other words, HRM refers to the framework of philosophies, policies, procedures and practices for the management of the relationship that exists between an employer and worker. The purpose of this chapter is to introduce the broad area of managerial activity referred to as HRM, to explore the alternative meanings attached to the term and its relevance to today's work organisations. The chapter outlines how people management has developed over the past three decades from a largely administrative, operational function to an area of management often viewed as central to organisational viability and sustained competitive advantage. It also introduces a number of running themes that reoccur throughout the book and represent key challenges for contemporary HRM, including ethical issues associated with people management and international differences in HRM practice.

HRM comprises a number of discrete but overlapping areas of managerial activity. Part Two of this book focuses on the following five broad functions of HRM, central to managing the workforce:

1 *People resourcing* – ensuring optimal staffing for current and future business needs through activities that include human resource planning, recruitment, selection, induction, talent management, succession planning and the termination of the employment relationship (including managing retirement and redundancy).

2 *Managing performance* – managing individual and team performance and the contribution of workers to the achievement of organisational goals, for example, through goal-setting and performance and development reviews or appraisals.

3 *Managing reward* – designing and implementing reward and pay systems covering individual and collective, financial and non-financial reward, including employee benefits, perks and pensions.

4 *Human resource development* – identifying individual, team and organisational development requirements and designing, implementing and evaluating learning and development interventions.

5 *Employment relations* – managing employee 'voice', communication and employee involvement (EI) in organisational decision-making, handling union–management relations (including industrial action and collective bargaining over terms and conditions of employment), managing employee welfare and handling employee grievance and discipline.

Other tasks and activities that come under the remit of HRM include workforce administration, health, safety and employee well-being, and equality and diversity management. HRM is also likely to be involved in wider strategic and operational managerial activity such as change management and employer branding. In some of these areas, HRM specialists play a central and leading role and in others they are more likely to fulfil an advisory capacity to support managers in other areas of the business. For example, in filling a job vacancy, HR specialists in large organisations are likely to provide support in designing job specifications and advertisements, ensuring legal compliance (for example, with equal opportunities legislation) and assisting with or advising on the selection process. HRM professionals might be generalists responsible for all HR processes in a firm or, more likely in larger organisations, they might specialise in one or more specific areas, for example reward, training or diversity. Importantly, HRM encompasses not only those activities that are the responsibility of designated HR departments or specialists but also those activities that are carried out by managers in all areas of the business who are responsible for the management of co-workers.

COMPETING DEFINITIONS OF HRM

The term 'human resource management' is typically used in one of the two following ways:

● To describe any approach to managing people, as in Boxall and Purcell's definition: 'HRM includes anything and everything associated with the management of employment relationships in the firm' (Boxall and Purcell, 2003: 1). In other words, it is the contemporary 'umbrella' term used to denote the activities associated with people management in work organisations.

- To describe a distinctive approach to managing people that is significantly different from traditional personnel management practices (as outlined later in this chapter) through its ability to contribute to both organisational performance and to engender employee commitment to the organisation (hence sometimes referred to as high-commitment HRM). Such an approach to HRM offers management, theoretically at least, the prospect of enhanced organisational performance whilst simultaneously improving workers' experience of employment (the 'mutual gains' perspective). In the words of Storey (2007: 7), it is a specific 'recipe' for the management of people. Price defines HRM in this way, as 'a philosophy of people management based on the belief that human resources are uniquely important in sustained business success. An organisation gains competitive advantage by using its people effectively, drawing on their expertise and ingenuity to meet clearly defined objectives. HRM is aimed at recruiting capable, flexible and committed people, managing and rewarding their performance and developing key competencies' (2007: 32).

This book takes a broad, inclusive perspective on HRM as referring to all aspects and approaches to the management of people and, therefore, not 'solely with a high-commitment model of labour management or with any particular ideology or style of management' (Boxall and Purcell, 2003: 1). The reason for this is that by focusing exclusively on the distinctive model of HRM it is rather easy to lose sight of the fact that the majority of organisations do not adhere to such a sophisticated model of labour management (Bacon, 2003). The intention of this book is to consider the wide range of approaches that organisations can adopt for the management of people. HRM is therefore defined as an area of managerial activity with the *potential* to be formulated along the lines of Price's definition but acknowledging a wider array of management styles and associated practices.

THE EMERGENCE OF HRM

Despite taking an inclusive approach in this book, in order to understand the significance of HRM in contemporary firms it is important to discuss in greater depth its more specific meaning, as it helps explain why and how the term 'human resource management' came to be so widely used. The term 'personnel management' has historically been used to denote the area of managerial activity, most usually a distinct department, that is principally concerned with administering the workforce (for example, in respect of payroll and contractual issues), providing training, ensuring legal compliance (for example, in the area of health and safety) and managing collective industrial relations between the firm and trade unions.

In many firms, personnel management has traditionally been constituted as a support function, existing on the periphery of organisational and strategic decision-making, which held a relatively lowly operational status (Redman and Wilkinson, 2006). In the mid-1980s, however, patterns of innovative forms of people management began to emerge that held more strategic ambitions (Storey, 2007). Subsequently, over the course of the past three decades, people management has gradually developed and, whilst acknowledging that in many firms HRM remains marginalised and primarily an administrative function, for many firms its scope is rather wider today than in the past. Torrington et al. (2008) suggest that rather than representing a revolution in people management practices, the emergence of HRM represents an evolution towards more effective practice. Similarly, Watson (2009) stresses that HRM is not some new, or even recent, managerial or academic 'fad' or some novel or groundbreaking invention that is peculiar to modern circumstances. It is a profoundly commonsensical notion that would be sensibly taken up by people in charge of any human enterprise in which work tasks are undertaken and where there is a concern for that enterprise to continue into the future as a viable social and economic unit. (2009: 8–9)

In other words, HRM is the latest manifestation of ongoing attempts to allocate work tasks within a social group and to compel each member of that group to make best use of their individual knowledge, behaviours and capabilities for the greater good. Lengnick-Hall et al. (2009) suggest that whilst much of the literature addressing more strategic approaches to HRM have been written in the last 30 years, its origins can be traced back to 1920s America when more progressive employers were exploring ways to achieve competitive advantage through 'unity of interest [between employer and employee], cooperation and investment in labour as a human resource' (Lengnick-Hall et al., 2009: 64). A historical perspective on the development of people management practices is presented in Chapter 2.

Box 1.1 shows Storey's model of HRM, which emphasises the potential for 'people' to be a key strategic asset in the contemporary firm and the key prescriptions in how they should be managed to maximise their performance.

Along similar lines, Sisson (1990) suggests that the distinctive notion of HRM has four critical dimensions: an integration of HR policies with business planning; a shift in responsibility of HR issues from personnel specialists to line managers; a shift from the collectivism of management–trade union relations to the individualism

---

BOX 1.1
UNDERSTAND

The HRM model

Beliefs and assumptions

- That it is the human resource which gives competitive edge.
- That the aim should not be mere compliance with rules, but employee commitment.
- That therefore employees should, for example, be very carefully selected and developed.

Strategic qualities

- Because of the above factors, HR decisions are of strategic importance.
- Top management involvement is necessary.
- HR policies should be integrated into the business strategy – stemming from it and even contributing to it.

Critical role of managers

- Because HR practice is critical to the core activities of the business, it is too important to be left to personnel specialists alone.
- Line managers are (or need to be) closely involved both as deliverers and drivers of the HR policies.
- Much greater attention is paid to the management of managers themselves.

Key levers

- Managing culture is more important than managing procedures and systems.
- Integrated action on selection, communication, training reward and development.
- Restructuring and job redesign to allow developed responsibility and empowerment.

Source: reproduced with permission of Cengage Ltd from J. Storey (ed.) (2007) *Human Resource Management: A Critical Text* (3rd edn). London: Thomson, Figure 1.1, p. 9

of management–employee relations; and an emphasis on employee commitment. Both of these formulations echo earlier work by Guest (1987), who suggested four key elements of HRM: employee commitment; workforce flexibility; quality (both in terms of required worker attributes and of their performance); and the strategic integration of HRM policies and practices.

PEOPLE MANAGEMENT

Taken together, such models indicate a number of key features of HRM that represent a distinctive approach to people management. First, HRM is not simply the concern of HR specialists but requires the involvement of both senior and line managers in successfully developing and implementing policies and practices to maximise individual performance. Second, workers perform more effectively when committed to the goals of the organisation, rather than simply complying with its rules, and this can be achieved both by aligning the needs of employees and the firm and by the internalisation of organisational values through the management of culture. Third, HR practices and policies such as those in the areas of selection, development and reward should be integrated both with the overall strategy of the firm and each other. In relation to this last point, Caldwell (2002) suggests that the 'advanced' personnel policies associated with HRM pre-dated the development of HRM itself but that its importance lies in advocating HR policies and practices that are integrated with one another and are mutually reinforcing. In summary, HRM in its specific sense is concerned with ensuring that:

- HRM philosophies, policies and practices are supportive of wider organisational strategy
- the organisation has the right calibre or quality of employee to operationalise this strategy through the adoption of appropriate techniques for selection and recruitment, appraisal, development and promotion
- line managers are committed to executing these HRM policies and practices
- employment systems are flexible enough to allow adequate adaptation to changing organisational context.

The greater contemporary focus on people as a source of competitive advantage is also evident in the corporate literature of firms across diverse industry sectors that lay claim to a heavy reliance on their human resources to deliver strategic objectives, as well as seeking to position or 'brand' themselves as desirable organisations in which to work. A selection of such corporate statements is presented in Box 1.2.

HARD AND SOFT VARIANTS OF HRM

High-commitment or high-performance HRM, as outlined above, is often associated with management practices that focus on the 'human' element in managing people and the notion of 'soft HRM' (Guest, 1987). Soft HRM has its emphasis on developing and investing in human capital, nurturing employee loyalty and providing well-rewarded and satisfying work. This approach prioritises a positive employer–employee relationship based on mutual trust, developed through employee participation (EP) and involvement in organisational decision-making, worker empowerment, collaboration and teamworking and a stakeholder approach where the interests of all groups are equally valued. This model of HRM views the organisation as pluralist, where the differing needs of the organisation and individuals are acknowledged and addressed. This approach is also referred to as 'collaborative HRM' (Gooderham et al., 1999). An alternative approach to HRM tends to emphasise the 'resource' element in the management of labour. This 'hard' (Guest, 1987) or 'calculative' (Gooderham et al., 1999) approach emphasises the instrumental use of labour to meet business objectives. This model views the employment relationship as unitarist, where the

BOX 1.2
HRM IN PRACTICE

The rhetoric of HRM and the importance of people to organisational success

Nissan – 'The power comes from inside'

'This simple phrase familiar to every Nissan employee conveys a powerful truth. Any company is only as strong as the people who bring it to life. Companies do not create products, deliver services or solve problems; people do'.

Virgin Atlantic – 'The people that make up Virgin Atlantic, make Virgin Atlantic'

'This isn't a company that just talks about putting employees first or glibly claims that our people are our greatest asset. This is a company that simply wouldn't exist without the energy, the determination, the wit and the wisdom of our people'.

Sainsbury's – 'A great place to work'

'Our success rests upon our 161,000 colleagues providing great service to our customers every day. Motivated colleagues are fundamental to our continued success, so we're committed to giving our people the opportunity to be the best they can be'.

Shangri-La Hotels – 'Are you Shangri-La?'

'We are family. We share something powerful – our genuine care and respect for others. It takes a very special kind of person to work at Shangri-La. Someone with an eye for detail and the skills to perform. Someone with an attitude to deliver and a passion to delight'.

Walmart – 'The most important part of our business – people. Just like you'.

'Our associates are the heart of our business – all 2.2 million of them. Our people make the difference, and their hard work and dedication have made us what we are today. Our people work hard to save customers money in new and better ways each day'.

Lego – 'Succeed together'

'The role of the LEGO People Promise is to enable execution of the business strategy and build the long-term health of the company. It defines why people should choose and commit the best of themselves to the organisation, clarifies the "give" and the "get" of the employee "deal" and provides a common point of reference for employee management'.

needs and interests of the organisation and individuals are one and the same. Hard HRM is often associated with exploitative practices such as intensive working, low pay, low levels of job security and, subsequently, low levels of employee commitment. However, hard and soft approaches to HRM are not mutually exclusive as organisations can use 'soft' practices in an instrumental manner.

The distinction between soft and hard HRM raises the issues of ethics in people management and the extent to which the objectives and needs of a business should take primacy over the needs of its workforce. The question of ethics in HRM is a running theme of this book and later chapters will consider the ethical issues surrounding particular elements of HRM activity, such as employment flexibility and reward systems. Box 1.3 provides an introductory discussion into this ever-more important area of both HRM and wider business and management.

PATTERNS OF HRM PRACTICE

As stated previously, the definition of HRM adopted in this book is rather broader than a narrow 'high-commitment' approach. This is because for many employees this vision of people as a 'top agenda item' and a highly valued organisational asset might

BOX 1.3
ETHICAL INSIGHT

Should people be treated as 'resources'?

Ackers (2006) suggests that the advent of HRM in the 1980s presented an opportunity for UK managers to demonstrate their concern for employees, particularly given that at the time both trade union and government regulation of the employment relationship in the country were declining. The language of HRM tends to emphasise the importance of the human resource and its role in uniting individual and organisational needs, addressing both employees' desire for 'social justice' (equity and fairness of treatment) and business imperatives. Indeed, much discussion of HRM assumes that high performance HRM practices are good for workers and that managers are 'the primary actors in the employment relationship, responsible for designing and implementing the appropriate HRM practices to produce gains for both employees and employers' (Janssens and Steyaert, 2009: 145). However, research suggests that the reality is somewhat different from the rhetoric of 'mutual gains' (Legge, 1995a). Evidence shows limited take-up of HRM practices that might lead to such shared benefit, especially in the absence of trade unions, and suggests that the focus of labour management in the UK tends to remain on cost reduction and short-termism, leading to the poor treatment of workers.

Even where high-commitment HRM is practised there are ethical concerns about the model of the employment relationship upon which it is based. Within much HRM theory there is the implicit assumption that business needs should take primacy over human considerations, and where the needs of workers are met it is simply because of a convergence of the two. This is most obviously played out in the changing role of HR professionals, where as a consequence of their growing importance in strategic decision-making they are compelled to prioritise business needs over employee welfare. Indeed, the very term 'human *resource*' can be said to promote the treatment of workers not as both a means and

an end, but as a means alone (Crane and Matten, 2006). In other words, workers are regarded as simply a factor of production, not as legitimate organisational stakeholders worthy of ethical treatment as an end in itself. Inkson (2008) makes the important point that the adoption of the standardised term 'human resources' to refer to people at work, even if only as a metaphor, leads both managers and employees to accept the notion of people as passive commodities, rather than active agents, and to behave accordingly.

Nonetheless, often a business case is made for the 'ethical' treatment of workers: for example, the positive effect that it can have on employee commitment, engagement and, consequently, performance. However, for many, the idea that business self-interest is sufficient to guarantee the ethical treatment of workers is flawed, not least because as business needs change the imperative to treat employees well might recede. The unitarist assumption of common interest and mutual benefit in much HRM theory and practice can subsequently be questioned (Boselie et al., 2009). The idea that organisations are harmonious 'families' where managers make decisions for the good of all stakeholders is problematic given the primacy of business needs, and, arguably, only where managers accept a plurality of interest groups with divergent needs will employee welfare be adequately considered as a first-order concern.

Even in firms where 'soft' HRM practices are firmly embedded and good treatment of employees is evident there remains controversy regarding managerial attempts to manipulate organisational culture and instill the values of the firm in their employees as a means of improving performance. This unease centres on the extent to which employees act as 'willing slaves' through 'extensive cooperation or complicity with living the "brand values" consciously generated by senior executives and management consultants' (Storey, 2007: 5). Abbott (2015) goes as far as to suggest that HRM, when focused on developing employee conformity to a specified organisational culture and the willing acceptance of managerial authority, bears a closer relation to the practices of political totalitarianism rather than democracy.

The question of ethics and corporate social responsibility (CSR) are critical concerns for twenty-first-century work organisations. For this reason, ethics in HRM forms a central concern of this book and each chapter raises questions about the relationship between management practice and the ethical treatment of people in the workplace.

Questions

1 To what extent do you consider it to be the role of business enterprises to commit to the ethical treatment of workers beyond what is required by legislation?

2 How would you construct a 'business case' argument for ethical considerations in formulating HRM policies?

3 How could this business case be critiqued?

not ring true in their everyday working lives. The high-commitment rhetoric – that employees should be positively nurtured by an organisation in order for them to become more 'engaged' in their activities and, therefore, more productive – does not necessarily match the reality of HRM practice in many firms.

Despite many firms re-labelling their personnel departments as HR departments, this often represents 'old wine in new bottles': a re-labelling rather than a fundamental reinvention of the function (Legge, 1995a). Storey (2007) suggests that whilst there is extensive evidence of the adoption of individual practices associated with HRM, evidence for the widespread integration of these practices is more limited. Successive surveys of HR practice in the UK have shown that the strategic role and function of HRM continue to be limited. For instance, the Workplace Employee Relations Survey (WERS) 2004 (Kersley et al., 2006) reported that, despite firms often having claimed to have adopted a strategic approach to HRM this often amounted to little more than the 'pick and mix' adoption of specific HRM practices that were not strategically integrated with either each other or any overarching human resource strategy. The subsequent WERS survey in 2011 (van Wanrooy et al., 2013) found little evidence of change in the proportion of firms adopting a formal strategic plan for employee development, job satisfaction or employee diversity and only a small increase in the proportion of firms adopting a strategic approach to recruitment.

WERS

The evidence suggests therefore that most organisations adopt HR practices associated with good practice in a piecemeal or incomplete manner, despite often compelling evidence that more strategic approaches and the coherent adoption of practices associated with high-commitment HRM can yield positive improvements in workforce productivity and, therefore, organisational profitability. Moreover, if we accept the importance of people to organisational performance, the fact that successive studies (for example, Guest and Baron, 2000; Guest and Conway, 2004; CIPD, 2015a) have found a widespread lack of consideration for employee issues is concerning. The integrated HRM models described by Guest, Storey and Sisson appear, therefore, to represent, at best, an aspiration rather than a workplace reality in many organisations and present a significant challenge and a major competitiveness issue for both UK employers and the government (Box 1.4).

When discussing the extent to which UK firms have adopted HRM, a further proviso is also necessary. Many of the claims for HRM and its emergence in the 1980s were a reflection of the role of sophisticated HR policies and practices in blue-chip multinational companies, and subsequent HRM literature has tended to focus on the development of people management practices in large work organisations. It is important, however, to understand HRM within small and medium-sized enterprises (SMEs). SMEs are increasingly important to the European economy as they

BOX 1.4
HRM IN PRACTICE

HRM and the 'productivity puzzle'

CIPD (2015a) reported on research exploring the productivity puzzle facing the UK – that whilst levels of employment have grown strongly in recent years, overall productivity of the British economy has not grown at an equivalent rate, not least in comparison to other developed economies. This means that neither businesses nor the UK economy are yielding the benefits of growing employment and, subsequently, pay growth for UK workers remains slow. In other words, whilst businesses have increased their staff numbers in response to demand for their products and services, they have failed to increase the output of their employees – their productivity – at the same rate.

At the heart of this puzzle is what the UK Commission for Employment and Skills (UKCES, 2015) refer to as the 'black box' of workplace productivity: the question of how employers turn skilled workers and tools into the products and services that customers value. The CIPD are clear that the management of people, and the practices to do so, have the potential to unlock this latent and untapped productivity, benefiting all economic stakeholders – the government, employers and employees. In particular, the institute calls for employers and the government to enact and support initiatives that promote cooperative working and investment in workforce development and that seek to engender trust and employee engagement. In other words, CIPD advocates a form of 'best practice' HRM of the sort outlined at the outset of this chapter,

as part of 'a shift in focus towards increasing the value generated by the workforce and how work is organised. This will require a renewed focus on the way people are managed and developed to deliver "smarter", more productive working' (People Management, 2015b). Moreover, the CIPD argue strongly that workforce productivity is not solely the concern of employer and employee and that the role of government is vital for economic and social prosperity. Mark Beatson, CIPD Chief Economist, states:

> Decisions over how we fund vocational and further education and support small businesses to raise their game and get more out of their people are just as critical to our future prosperity as investments in transport, infrastructure and technology and need to be given more attention by government and businesses. (People Management, 2015b)

Despite the potential benefits of firms investing in their staff, however, it would seem firms remain either sceptical about such benefits or seek to create efficiencies elsewhere, ignoring workforce productivity in favour of, for instance, keeping pay at a low level. The CIPD research found that only 41 per cent of businesses considered increasing productivity to be a priority and one-third do not measure productivity at all.

Source: CIPD (2015a) *Productivity: Getting the Best Out of People*, London: CIPD; UKCES (2015) *Growth through People: Evidence and Analysis*, London: UKCES

---

make up both an increasing proportion of firms and a growing source of employment, particularly for highly qualified workers (Stewart and Knowles, 2000). Despite this growing importance, Cassell et al. (2002) suggest that there is both a lack of research into HRM practice in SMEs and an inference within management literature that SMEs should simply learn from the practices of large firms. Box 1.4 discusses some of the assumptions often made about people management in SMEs and the research that has sought to explore the reality behind those assumptions.

 Further online reading The following article investigates an approach to HRM which has been adopted in small to medium-sized UK e-commerce firms to explore the assumption that such firms are more likely to adopt radically new and innovative management practices. The authors find the dominant approach falls somewhere between radical 'new' innovations and enduring continuities with 'old' people management techniques.

Dietz, G., van der Wiele, T., van Iwaarden, J. and Brosseau, J. (2006) HRM inside UK e-commerce firms: Innovations in the 'new' economy and continuities with the 'old', *International Small Business Journal*, 24 (5): 443–70.

BOX 1.4
RESEARCH INSIGHT

HRM in small and medium-sized enterprises

Dundon et al. (1999) argue that most commentators on the employment relationship in small firms tend to adopt one of two polarised perspectives. The first has been described as 'small is beautiful' and suggests that SMEs are characterised by informal, cooperative and harmonious relationships between owner–managers and employees (Goodman et al., 1998). The small firm is therefore typified by low incidence of conflict and informal communications, characteristics that are assumed to negate the need for collective representation of workers by trade unions. Such firms gain the cooperation of their staff and develop a good working relationship between management and workers 'despite paying little explicit attention to people management issues and having few formalised practices for managing them' (Goodman et al., 1998: 548).

The second perspective suggests that this portrayal of harmonious relations serves to obscure exploitative practices in small firms that characterise them as '*Bleak House*' (Sisson, 1993: 207) and their employee management practices as 'ugly' and 'bad' (Guest and Hoque, 1994: 3). Rainnie (1989) suggests that such organisations are typified by poor working conditions, authoritarian management, poor safety conditions and little involvement of staff in the running of the business. These 'black hole' organisations (Guest and Conway, 1999) – a term used to describe firms that have little in the way of formal individual or collective structures and practices for the purposes of employee management – are

typically small establishments, often privately owned, operating in labour-intensive sectors such as hotel and catering (Guest and Conway, 1999). Wilkinson (1999) argues that a lack of overt conflict in small firms may simply represent the fact that employee dissatisfaction is more likely to be manifest in individual expressions such as absenteeism and high turnover, rather than collective action.

However, conclusions drawn on the HRM practices of SMEs based on either of these two polarised perspectives are likely to be too simplistic. Wilkinson (1999, quoting Ram, 1991: 601) claims 'workplace relations in SMEs may be "complex, informal and contradictory rather than simply either harmonious or autocratic"'. Indeed, Cassell et al. (2002) found considerable diversity among a sample of SMEs (also, Kotey and Slade (2005) and Storey (1995), in a study of the take-up of HRM practices, found that whilst larger firms were more likely to have adopted such practices, the success of their implementation was greater in smaller organisations). Therefore, given the sheer number and diversity of SMEs and evidence for a wide variety of approaches to HRM, it is perhaps not helpful to assume that they conform to one stereotype or the other and that there is no simplistic optimum approach to HRM for small firms to adopt, not least because the most effective practice will inevitably vary as firms grow (Drummond and Stone, 2007; CIPD, 2015b). Verreynne et al. (2011) do, however, present evidence that suggests that better performing small firms are those who adopt integrated clusters of employment and management practices that engender trust, fairness and employee participation and communication.

HRM AND A CHANGING ORGANISATIONAL CONTEXT

The supposed shift in the way workers are viewed by senior managers can be at least partially linked to relatively recent changes to the external business environment that have reduced the impact of traditional sources of competitive advantage (such as technology or machinery) and increased the significance of new sources – particularly a firm's workforce – that need to be exploited to promote organisational adaptability and innovation (Pfeffer, 1994). This is most obviously the case for firms competing in sectors of the economy where organisational success relies heavily on the ingenuity, creativity, skills and knowledge of their workforce, such as information and communication technology (ICT), business consultancy and pharmaceuticals. It is of no surprise, therefore, that the shift from personnel management to HRM has coincided with a set of perceived changes in the nature of advanced capitalist economies associated with globalisation and rapid advancements in ICT that are connected to the emergence of the 'post-industrial society' (Bell, 1973) or knowledge economy (Kinnie et al., 2006). Organisational success in such an economy relies on the commercialisation of the knowledge possessed by its workers and for firms to acquire and develop employee capabilities through increasingly sophisticated means of management (Davenport et al., 2006). However, it should also be acknowledged that these competitive pressures, particularly developing patterns of globalisation and the emergence of new economic powers such as Brazil, India, China and Russia, are at the same time compelling managers to cut costs, often leading to the more instrumental use of labour. Developments in the labour market context of HRM are discussed further in Chapter 4 and patterns of globalisation in Chapter 5. Chapter 15 specifically addresses the issue of knowledge management and how HRM can facilitate the development and sharing of employee knowledge as a source of competitive advantage.

The movement from collectivism to individualism in the management of the employment relationship is also reflective of contextual change. In the last three decades there has been a marked decline in trade union membership, representation and collective bargaining over pay and conditions in the UK, especially in the private sector. The reasons for this trend are complex, encompassing changing political attitudes towards unionism, increased global competition, changes in social attitudes towards increased self-interest, economic restructuring (notably the accelerated shift from a manufacturing to a service-based economy) and legislation that has placed greater restrictions on union activity. HRM itself can be viewed both as a cause and consequence of the decline in workplace collectivism. The decline in trade union power and influence opened up a space in which managerial prerogative over decision-making could be asserted more emphatically and the adoption of anti-union strategies associated with US management used as a lever to further marginalise or substitute for the presence of unions. As a result of this changing landscape, management saw greater opportunities to implement more flexible, individualised arrangements for employees. For example, there has been a marked increase over recent years in individualised performance-related pay (PRP) and performance targets, non-representative methods of employee communication and greater individual responsibility for career development. Individualised HRM practices partly reflect, therefore, a desire among organisations to alter the employment relationship to make it more flexible by dismantling workforce solidarity and mechanisms for the expression of shared worker interests. This is discussed in more detail in Chapter 10.

It is important to recognise that the concept of high-commitment or high-performance HRM is underpinned by a particular set of assumptions reflective of the cultural context in which it developed, specifically the USA and, latterly, the UK. Given patterns of globalisation and the growth in both size and scope of multinational corporations (MNCs), it is important to recognise that the specific ideas and practices associated with HRM are not necessarily universally applicable. Box 1.5 provides an introduction to another running theme central to this book, that of the international context of HRM. Chapter 5 develops this discussion of cultural influence on people management.

BOX 1.5
GLOBAL INSIGHT

HRM and national difference

It is important to recognise that the approach to people management specifically referred to as HRM embodies a Western perspective on the employment relationship and the means by which employees can be a source of added value to an organisation. In particular, much of the rhetoric and reality of HRM reflects its origins in the USA, to the extent that Guest (1990) referred to HRM as a '*manifestation of the American dream*' and Gooderham and Brewster (2003: 16) suggest that the growing influence of HRM in Europe (particularly the UK) reflects the '*Americanization of personnel management*'. As Price (2007) suggests, US corporations have dominated world trade for much of the twentieth and into the twenty-first century and, therefore, it is not surprising that North American business methods and ideology have been widely promoted and adopted, first in some Western European countries, notably the UK, and then in other countries further afield.

Whilst much of the discussion in this book reflects this Western perspective, each chapter outlines how HRM practices vary throughout the world. In particular, it outlines how the social, cultural and institutional context in which people management practices develop are reflected in how employees are recruited, managed and rewarded. For example, in the USA, people management techniques have tended to reflect a psychological perspective with an emphasis on improving worker motivation. This has led to a focus on the individual, on analysing employee needs and responding through the manipulation of rewards systems and job design which, in turn, reflect American cultural values of individualism and self-determination. In (continental) Europe, however, people management has evolved more from sociology resulting in a greater focus on the collective workforce and understanding organisations as social systems within a broader economic and political context. Therefore, rather than focusing on the individual employee's relationship with the employer, there is greater concern for the collective employment relationship between government, unions and management. The focus of managerial activity is on industrial democracy and joint regulation of the employment relationship, reflective of cultural values reflecting workforce solidarity and low tolerance for inequality (Schneider and Barsoux, 2008).

As well as divergent views on managing the employment relationship, von Glinow et al. (2002) note that the status of the HRM function varies across countries, according to, for example, the average size of organisations, ownership patterns, the credibility that the HR function has in that country and where power tends to reside within firms. For example, in the UK power within firms tends to reside with the finance function, which has implications for the extent to which people are viewed as investment or cost and, therefore, the strategic influence afforded to HR managers.

The extent to which HR responsibilities are entrusted to line managers – as 'required' under high-performance HRM – also varies between countries (Lucas and Curtis, 2006). For example, Larsen and Brewster (2003) report that devolution to line managers in the UK and Ireland was low compared to other EU countries, particularly Denmark and Finland. The extent of devolution in a country tends to reflect the institutional framework within which organisations operate: for example, the complexity of employment legislation that determines the extent to which an employer needs decisions to be made by HR specialists rather than line managers. However, relatively recent studies have noted a growing international trend towards greater devolution, for example, Kulik and Bainbridge (2006) (in Australia) and Mesner Andolsek and Stebe (2005) (across 20 European countries).

Further online reading The following article draws on the perspectives of both employees and managers, and explores the relationship between HR practices and capabilities and organizational performance. It not only helps to understand the HR issues specific to small firms but also provides a backdrop to subsequent discussions of the relationship between HR and performance.

Verreynne, M.-L., Parker, P. and Wilson, M. (2011) Employment systems in small firms: A multilevel analysis, *International Small Business Journal*, 31 (4): 405–31.

THE CHANGING HR FUNCTION

As the high-commitment perspective on HRM has developed since the 1980s so has the role of HR managers and specialists. The HR profession has undergone a significant transformation reflecting the increased responsibility placed upon it to deliver improvements in worker performance; a 'mission' at odds with the traditional outsider status of the personnel function. In line with the movement of HRM to centre stage in its perceived ability to contribute to the sustained competitive advantage of the firm, the HR function in some organisations has shifted from a predominant emphasis on operational issues to a more strategic focus (Francis and Keegan, 2006).

Stanton and Coovert (2004) suggest that the activities of the HR function can be divided into three broad, interlocking functional areas:

1 *Administrative* – HR professionals ensure the organisation's compliance with regulatory structures (including organisational policy and employment law) as they relate to personnel activities such as recruitment and dismissal.

2 *Financial* – HR professionals research, recommend and manage the organisation's use of monetary rewards and perquisites.

3 *Performance* – HR professionals develop, deploy and maintain organisational policies and practices that allow workers to create the greatest possible value with the available 'human capital' (for example, training, performance management, talent management).

PERFORMANCE MANAGEMENT

The greater HR focus on strategic issues emphasises the importance of the last of these three areas of activity and stresses the contribution of HRM towards the achievement of organisational objectives through the innovative design and implementation of value-adding policies and practices. A survey of senior HR practitioners (CIPD, 2003a) supports the impression that HRM is becoming a more prominent aspect of organisational strategic decision-making. The survey found that almost three-quarters of respondents reported that the influence of HR practitioners on senior colleagues had increased in recent years. Seventy per cent also reported that their CEO believes HR has a key role to play in achieving business outcomes. The Accenture *High-Performance Workforce Study 2006* reports that:

 for years, HR leaders have been asking for 'a seat at the table' – to be taken seriously in the executive suite as a key contributor to the overall direction and mission of the business ... judging from the results of our study, HR leaders' wish has been granted: In a large majority of companies participating in our survey, the HR head is viewed as a strategic partner to the business, and in most companies he or she reports directly to the chief executive officer or head of the overall enterprise. (Accenture, 2006: 1)

The growing influence of HRM within organisations is also reflected in the changing role of HR practitioners and the need for HR practitioners to go beyond an administrative role and to critically reflect on the contribution of HR activities to overall business success and to develop more effective mechanisms to provide people-added

TABLE 1.1 *A typology of HR roles*

Strategic partner	Incorporating the roles of change agent, business expert, strategic HR planner and manager of organisational 'knowledge'
Functional expert	Emphasising concern for administrative efficiency and the design of HR policies and interventions
Employee advocate	Addressing the needs of an organisation's current workforce
Human capital developer	Preparing employees to meet future challenges
Leader	Incorporating leadership of the HR function itself, working collaboratively with other areas of the business and being effective in the preceding four roles

Source: adapted from Ulrich, D. and Brockbank, W. (2005) *The HR-Value Proposition*, Boston MA: Harvard Business School Press. Reprinted with permission.

value. In other words, the HR department should operate as a '*business within a business*' (Ulrich et al., 2008). HR professionals are encouraged to continually update their professional knowledge and skills and gain greater understanding of wider business processes in order to increase their influence on corporate strategic decision-making. This perspective of the role of HRM in the organisation clearly fits with that espoused in Box 1.1 and reflects the growing complexity of the HR function by suggesting that it is now concerned with a combination of people and process-related activities and strategic and operational functions.

Ulrich and Brockbank (2005) identify five distinct roles that HR professionals should adopt to respond to the changing business context, combining effectiveness in the present with preparing for the future (Table 1.1).

This role profile suggests that HRM practitioners should seek to reconcile the interests of all stakeholders in the organisation, addressing the welfare and development needs of workers and the strategic imperatives of senior management, providing support for line managers and ensuring external compliance on issues of corporate governance. The role of the HR specialist is, therefore, multifunctional, acting as both a facilitator and leader of the strategic direction of the firm. However, Ulrich and Brockbank's typology has been criticised for assuming that the needs of all these stakeholders can be balanced by the HR function, especially as evidence suggests that the strategic and financial imperatives of the firm often override concern for employee welfare. Legge (1978, 1995b) argues that the HR function experiences a fundamental 'role ambiguity' associated with being part of 'management' whilst also being expected to be representative of employees' interests. CIPD (2003a) found that HR practitioners are more likely to aspire to involvement in the strategic dimensions of Ulrich's typology rather than the operational roles, such as employee advocate. The same survey also found, however, that operational activity still dominates the work of HR practitioners, suggesting that the short-term, day-to-day imperatives of HRM continue to supplant longer-term considerations.

Central to Ulrich's typology is the notion of business partnering. The CIPD (2004: 6) suggest business partnering involves 'executing business strategy, meeting customer needs and becoming overall champions of competitiveness in delivering value'. The business partners are HR professionals who work closely with business leaders or line managers, usually embedded in a particular business unit, to influence strategy and enable strategy implementation. CIPD (2015c) note that the role of HR business partners varies widely between organisations, depending on organisational size, sector, business priorities and culture, but activities that HR business partners are likely to be involved in may include:

- organisational and people capability building
- longer-term resource and talent management planning
- using business insights to drive change in people management practices
- advising on the people implications of organisation change, making recommendations
- intelligence gathering of good people management practices internally and externally, so they can raise issues of which executives may be unaware.

CIPD suggest, however, that HR business partnering focuses on processes that support business strategy whereas the next evolutionary step for HR requires it to become 'insight driven' with an 'increasing emphasis on examining the business's fitness for purpose, now and in the future … on supporting an organisation to do what is needed to drive performance that lasts – encouraging strategic vision and using shared purpose to drive sustainable performance' (CIPD, 2011d: 6). To do this, they suggest that HR needs to develop expertise across three domains of organisational insight:

1 *Organisational savvy* – an appreciation of how the interplay of hard and soft factors enables or derails business success, including an understanding of the impact of people, culture and leadership, and of change dynamics.

2 *Business savvy* – a deep understanding of the core value-drivers and a deep appreciation of what makes the business successful, or prevents its success.

3 *Contextual savvy* – an understanding of both market trends and forces, but also how broader demographic, macroeconomic and societal factors are affecting business now and in the future.

Ulrich's latest contribution to the debate about what HR is and what it needs to be is to focus not on the roles to be fulfilled but on the importance of relationships. To this end, Ulrich (2015) proposes a number of principles that underpin the development of successful relationships between different aspects of an HR function including sharing a common purpose, respecting differences and caring for those in different parts of the function.

Further online reading This article examines how HR managers interpret the role of 'business partners' and 'internal consultants' and assess the extent to which this results in greater self-esteem and organisational status and contributes towards identity as a member of a unitary HR 'profession'.

Wright, C. (2008) Reinventing human resource management: Business partners, internal consultants and the limits to professionalization, *Human Relations*, 61: 1063–86.

Devolution of HRM responsibility to front line managers

There are a number of factors that continue to facilitate a movement away from an administrative model of people management. In particular, there is evidence of a growing trend to devolve at least some operational responsibility for HR issues to front line managers (as defined in Box 1.6). For example, line managers are now more likely to have greater responsibility for conducting performance appraisals, identifying training requirements for subordinates, providing coaching and mentoring and dealing with grievances and disciplinary matters.

Marchington and Wilkinson (2008) suggest that part of the reason for devolution of responsibility is a response to long-running criticism by line managers of the contribution of HR specialists to organisational performance. They suggest that this criticism generally takes four forms:

1 HR specialists are out of touch with commercial realities and do not fully understand the needs of managers, customers and the business itself.

2 HR constrains the autonomy of line managers to make local decisions that would benefit the business.

3 HR specialists are unresponsive, slow to act and hinder the firm's ability to respond quickly to unfolding circumstances.

4 HR specialists tend to promote policies that are difficult to put into practice or are inappropriate for the workplace.

Guest and King (2004) argue that recent developments in HRM have seen HR managers become more closely aligned with management and increased devolution of the employee champion role to line managers. Therefore, HR professionals act in an advisory capacity, ensuring that those with direct supervisory responsibility are equipped to make appropriate decisions through 'ownership' of HRM initiatives. In other words, line managers and HR specialists work in partnership to manage the workforce (Ulrich, 1998). This reflects a growing body of research that shows that line managers are increasingly perceived as key to the successful implementation of HR practices and the relationship between line managers and subordinates has a significant influence on individual performance (Purcell and Ahlstrand, 1994; Hope Hailey et al., 2005; Purcell and Hutchinson, 2007a; Harney and Jordan, 2008). Ulrich (1997) suggests that line managers must have ultimate responsibility for HR processes and outcomes, and whilst they have always also been people managers to some degree, the growing emphasis on the strategic dimension of HRM in contributing to corporate performance has elevated this role to the extent that some argue that HRM responsibilities should be of equal importance to line managers' day-to-day functional responsibilities.

BOX 1.6
UNDERSTAND

Who are front line managers?

- Responsible for an employee or work group to a higher level of management.
- Normally lower management.
- Employees who report to them do not themselves have any managerial or supervisory responsibility.

- Often promoted from within.
- Unlikely to have a formal management education.

Source: CIPD, 2009g

Despite the apparent strength of this trend, however, the research evidence concerning devolution of HR responsibility to line managers does not always suggest business benefits. On the one hand, line managers are more likely to be able to determine appropriate HR solutions by virtue of their better understanding of operational complexities and being 'closer' to workers. Whittaker and Marchington (2003) report that line managers were both prepared and willing to take on additional HR responsibilities, particularly where they related explicitly to the development of their team. However, devolution of HRM activities has also been shown to have created frustration and role conflict for managers, especially where they have inadequate resources or time to fulfil these obligations (McConville, 2006). Considered from a political perspective,

HR managers might not want to relinquish responsibility for certain elements of HRM (Harris et al., 2002) but, equally, line managers might be reluctant to take on new responsibilities. Recent research (Boury and Sinclair, 2012) suggests confusion among 4,000 UK line managers about the strategic role of HRM and a continued reluctance to take on people management responsibilities.

There are also concerns that line managers often do not possess the skills (IRS, 2000) or are not provided with adequate training and HR support to fulfil this additional responsibility. This might result in HR issues not receiving adequate attention or being handled poorly or inconsistently (Renwick, 2003). Indeed, there are concerns that despite the importance of integrated HR systems in many models of HRM, the decentralisation of HR activities to line managers might lead to differently applied policies and practices. Significant devolution can lead to the limited integration of HR policies and strategy through their differential application in different parts of the organisation, particularly where support from HR specialists is lacking. In contradiction, however, Caldwell and Storey (2007) suggest that the greater empowerment of line managers in HR process might actually have an integrative effect, bringing together a variety of elements of people management under the individual manager.

Further online reading The following article presents research evidence on the trend within Australian organisations to devolve people management activities to line management and the differing views of HR and line managers about the extent to which they consider it likely to yield positive results.

Kulik, C. T. and Bainbridge, H. T. J. (2006) HR and the line: The distribution of HR activities in Australian organisations, *Asia Pacific Journal of Human Resources*, 44 (2): 240–56.

Outsourcing and HRM

Recent years have also seen a notable trend towards the greater outsourcing of HR administration, leaving HR professionals to focus on more strategic concerns related to business performance. For example, Scott (2008) reported that the UK retail arm of Barclays Bank, which employs 32,000 people in the UK, outsources its recruitment for permanent staff (up to senior management level) to a specialist third-party service provider. The CIPD (2009c) also suggest that an increasing number of firms are exploring the use of HR shared service centres (either in-house or outsourced) to provide routine HR administration services, such as recruitment, payroll and training, to all parts of the business. Income Data Services (IDS, 2006a) reported that, as part of a wide-reaching review of the organisation's effectiveness, the UK National Trust has overhauled its HR function with a view to placing greater accountability on line managers for people issues and delivering more cohesive and cost-effective HR support. This has been enabled by the establishment of a shared service centre to handle all lower-level HR transactions and the greater use of ICT (for example, in recruitment) allowing field-based (HR) advisors to focus on helping the business with strategic planning and more complex casework. Box 1.7 provides a recent example of how the UK government has sought to use outsourcing as a key means by which to reduce public sector spending.

The increasing use of ICT in HRM

The movement away from a transactional focus within HRM departments is increasingly enabled and supported by the use of new technology (Lengnick-Hall and

BOX 1.7
HRM IN PRACTICE

HR outsourcing at the UK Ministry of Defence

In March 2012, *People Management* magazine reported that the human resource function (along with a number of other back office functions, including finance) of the UK Ministry of Defence (MoD) was to be managed by outsourcing firm, Serco, as part of a deal to make savings of £71 million over the firm's four-year contract (*Personnel Management*, 2012a). Under the contract, Serco will not only manage these functions, but also seek to 'radically transform' how such support services are delivered in the department, partly through the creation of a shared service centre and through building on 'private sector best practice' in the shape of cost-cutting, efficiency gains and innovation.

Despite assurances over the maintenance of terms and conditions for employees that will be transferred from the MoD to Serco, trade unions representing MoD staff have expressed concern over jobs and pay cuts, and over the manner in which the deal was done with unions claiming that they were not consulted over the arrangements.

The outsourcing deal with Serco represents the latest attempt at the MoD to cope with a significant funding shortfall, due to both spending cuts across the public sector and overspending at the department. Job cuts at the Ministry since mid-2010 will ultimately see its workforce reduced by 36,000 employees and the final number of redundancies may run to tens of thousands more as the MoD seeks to 'plug a £38bn budget black hole' (*The Guardian*, 2012a).

Moritz, 2003; Martin, 2005; Parry and Tyson, 2007). For example, firms are making ever-greater use of company intranets and the Internet for the purposes of recruitment, the management of the internal labour market and for employee development, in the form of e-Learning. At a basic level, e-HR can assist in carrying out the administrative functions of the role, potentially freeing up HR specialists for more strategic concerns. However, e-HR is also seen as possessing the potential to be 'transformational', for example, through its ability to contribute to more effective strategic decision-making. Therefore, technological developments not only present challenges for HR professionals in respect of how they are changing the way workers do their jobs but also in how HR specialists themselves work (Stanton and Coovert, 2004). For example, line managers and employees themselves are increasingly able to undertake basic HRM transactions (for example, updating their personal details or booking training courses) via 'self-service' portals on their desktop computers.

Overall, Caldwell (2003) suggests that the personnel function has become increasingly fragmented as a result of outsourcing, the use of HR consultants, the use of shared service centres and e-HR and the devolution of responsibility to line managers (Valverde et al., 2006). Whilst the increasingly strategic focus within HRM and recognition of its value in contributing to competitive advantage have led to the elevated status of HR professionals, continued fragmentation of the function over the longer term may present challenges. For example, the devolution of HR responsibility and growing use of ICT might not always lead to the liberation of HR specialists from operational concerns for more strategic work and might actually have the effect of marginalising HRM specialists. In one sense, therefore, contemporary developments in HRM can be seen as somewhat contradictory in that whilst managers increasingly profess the value of their human resources, the HR function is increasingly seen as an area ripe for cost-cutting (as in the MoD example in Box 1.7), as businesses evaluate the option of managing without a formal, centralised HR function (Morley et al., 2006). Others, however, view the increasing use of HR consultants as reflecting the increased importance of HRM, in that HR concerns are seen as important enough to warrant such investment. Chapter 15 further considers the future of the HR function and provides a more detailed discussion of the implications of outsourcing, shared service centres and e-HR.

SUMMARY POINTS

- HRM can be understood as the contemporary term used to describe all activities associated with the management of people. An alternative, more specific, meaning of HRM is as a novel approach to people management based on the view that people represent a key strategic asset to work organisations and should be managed as such.

- The main concern of high-commitment or best practice HRM is to design and operationalise integrated systems of HR policies and practices that serve both individual and organisational needs. Such models have emerged in response to a range of changes in the context of organisations over the last three decades.

- Adoption of high-commitment approaches to HRM in the UK, especially in a 'full-blown', highly integrated form, is patchy and many employers fail to live up to this best practice model. However, such thinking remains very influential, especially among larger employers.

- HRM can be understood as having 'hard' and 'soft' variants. The former emphasises the use of human resources in an instrumental manner and is often associated with low pay, low job security and poor terms and conditions of employment. The latter emphasises the positive treatment of workers in order to develop employee commitment.

- Contemporary models of HRM represent the individualisation of the employment relationship, commensurate with the declining involvement of trade unions in managing the collective workforce.

- There have been a number of developments in the HR function associated with the perceived movement from an operational to a more strategic focus for HR specialists. These include the greater use of shared service centres, the adoption of e-HR systems, greater line manager responsibility for HRM and increased outsourcing of HR activities.

SELF-TEST QUESTIONS

1 Outline the two competing definitions of human resource management.

2 What are the characteristics of high-commitment HRM that differentiate it from traditional approaches to personnel management?

3 What changes in environmental context contributed to the emergence of HRM in the 1980s?

4 What are the differences between hard and soft variants of HRM?

5 What are the central issues concerning ethics in HRM?

6 What are the causes and implications of the individualisation of the employment relationship?

7 What specific roles do HR professionals fulfil according to Ulrich and Brockbank's (2005) typology?

8 In what ways does the formulation of HRM activities differ internationally?

9 What trends have led some commentators to suggest increasing fragmentation of the HR function?

TEST YOURSELF

Want to know more about this chapter? Review what you have been learning by visiting:
https://edge.sagepub.com/wilton3e

- Print out or download the chapter summaries for quick revision
- Test yourself with multiple-choice questions
- Revise key terms with interactive flashcards

CASE STUDY

Challenging times at the Redfield and Clifton Building Society

The organisation

The Redfield and Clifton (R&C) Mutual Building Society – a form of bank found in the UK and elsewhere that is owned by its customers, rather than shareholders – is one of Britain's oldest and largest financial institutions with an explicit focus on personal and business banking and the provision of financial services, such as home and life insurance, current accounts, credit cards, loans and mortgages. The R&C has approximately 8 million customers and assets of around £140 billion, is one of the UK's largest mortgage lenders and savings provider and has around 600 branches and approximately 11,000 employees.

Despite the global credit crunch and recession that began in 2007, R&C has performed solidly over recent years, expanding its customer base and offering a wider range of financial products. In part, this growth has been a result of customers switching their banking to such 'narrow' banks – those that simply take deposits and provide basic financial services – and moving away from those banks with an investment banking arm and which have been blamed for causing the financial problems of the last few years and required government bailouts to continue to operate.

The firm emphasises three core values for the manner in which it conducts its business: integrity, customer focus and stability. The focus on these core values stems directly from the 'wisdom' of the founder of the Redfield Co-operative – the precursor to the R&C. In recent marketing activity, R&C has played heavily on these traditional values in promoting their services as in direct contrast to the less reliable 'fast buck' banks which many consumers still view with suspicion and hostility.

The market context

Despite the recent difficulties in the financial services sector, retail banking remains a very competitive industry, especially given that many of the banks that were originally bailed out by the government as 'too big to fail' are now offering products and pricing guarantees which cannot be matched by those lacking such government subsidy. The challenge for financial institutions such as the R&C is, therefore, to deliver products and services that provide long-term value for its customers to ensure that it can continue to thrive in this hyper-competitive market.

Despite great play being made of its long history and tradition, R&C has recently embarked on an ambitious modernisation process designed to improve both customer service quality and the efficiency and effectiveness of its business processes in order to reduce overheads and allow greater downward flexibility in the 'pricing' of its products. Through such change, R&C senior management aims to grow its business sustainably whilst maintaining its reputation as a safe haven for savings and investment.

Part of the current business strategy is to purchase 150 branches from a larger bank, which was formed when two bailed-out banks merged (to create Bad Bank), which the government has subsequently insisted be broken up in the interests of competition. This process of expansion is, however, taking place at a time when consumer confidence in the financial services industry is at an all-time low, with even R&C's customer surveys indicating a deep suspicion of the industry and of 'bankers' in general (which the company takes to mean all those who work within the sector). Moreover, recently introduced regulation has made the controls on the selling of banking and insurance products much stricter.

Senior management at R&C view the current market conditions as challenging but also note that greater consumer awareness of the differences between different types of financial services providers is an opportunity to gain market share. For this reason, they are keen to have the new branches assimilated into R&C as quickly as possible and 'new and improved' customer service provision rolled out to coincide with a rebranding exercise, seeking to reinforce R&C's reputation with the slogan 'We care about your money'.

The workforce at Redfield & Clifton

As part of the purchase, R&C has made a promise to employ all those staff previously employed by Bad Bank (a very different type of financial service provider with the marketing slogan 'Let your money have some fun'), at least for the 12 months following completion of the takeover. In addition, R&C have recently recruited 500 new members of staff in response to a recent customer satisfaction survey that found dissatisfaction with the time spent queuing in branch and difficulty in getting appointments with advisors. These new employees will be spread throughout the branch network.

As the 'face' of the R&C, customer-facing staff in the branch network – including those in the newly acquired branches – have a central role to play in the continued success of the organisation and form a crucial dimension of its new marketing strategy. These employees have been identified as critical to marking-out R&C as 'not like other banks' and are to be exemplars of its recently unveiled core values:

- integrity
- prudence
- customer focus
- constancy.

Branches are staffed by a range of employee roles from Customer Service Representatives who can perform transactions and deal with general enquiries about products, through to Customer Account Managers, Mortgage Consultants and Senior Financial Consultants who provide more bespoke financial planning advice on a range of products and services.

At the same time as the firm increasing the number of branch-based, customer-facing staff, it has sought to reduce the headcount at its head offices in Bristol. So far, the firm has sought to do this through allowing employees on fixed-term contracts to leave the firm, not replacing leavers where possible and some internal restructuring to broaden responsibilities among its workforce. Through these means the firm has reduced its central workforce by between 5 and 10 per cent, although there has been some disquiet among staff about work intensification. The firm also made significant payroll savings by scaling back its use of sub-contractors, particularly among those staff responsible for the firm's IT infrastructure and its online banking services.

The crisis

In the same month as the R&C went national with its marketing blitz with a widely shown advertisement portraying its roots in Victorian Bristol (showing Joseph Redfield as a taciturn but benevolent money lender) it suffered a catastrophic failure in its online banking service. A rudimentary upgrade to its security systems caused the shutdown of its online banking provision, meaning that its 2.7 million current account and credit card customers were unable to access their money, pay bills or have direct debit payments made for four days.

The days following the online shutdown saw recriminations fly. The finance director blamed the Head of IT – it was clearly a failure of her systems – and the head of IT blamed the director of HR – it was all his fault for allowing the IT team to be cut to the bare bones. The director of HR, in turn, blamed the finance director for assuming that success would come by cutting costs. The marketing director simply cried about the fact that his advertising campaign was likely to have been a waste of time.

The technical problem was eventually resolved at immense expense to the firm, not least the cost of having to sub-contract an army of IT specialists who were in the position to name a price for their service. Several of these specialists were previously long-term sub-contractors at R&C and, subsequently, could drive an extremely hard bargain.

Out in the branches, the fall-out from the failure of the online banking service was felt acutely, not least because of the fact that staff had to deal with queues of angry customers, some of whom were determined to take their custom elsewhere. The meager compensation the company offered to disgruntled customers did little to appease them, but in light of the estimated £30 million fine likely to be levied by the Financial Services Authority, such limited recompense was all the firm could afford (or so the finance director told the board).

Questions

1 What are the specific challenges facing the R&C – both external and internal to the organisation – in respect of its management of people?

2 How do you think the firm needs employees to behave in their work and interactions with customers in order to make its current business strategy a success?

3 What problems might be presented by a large number of new staff, both those being transferred from Bad Bank and new recruits, entering the business at a critical time for the business?

4 How do you think the key HRM activities of recruitment and selection, training and employee reward might contribute to the ongoing success of the firm?

USEFUL READING

Journal articles

Abbott, K. (2015) The totalitarian dynamic behind HRM's democratic façade, *Asia Pacific Journal of Human Resources*, 53 (2): 204–20.

This article explores the assumption that HRM – where it is concerned with shaping employee behaviours and values consistent with those of a desired organisational culture – is associated with (workplace) democracy and suggests instead that it is more closely aligned with the social control associated with totalitarianism.

Boselie, P., Brewster, C. and Paauwe, J. (2009) In search of balance – managing the dualities of HRM: an overview of the issues, *Personnel Review*, 38 (5): 461–71.

This short article introduces a special edition of *Personnel Review* that is concerned with managing the dualities in HRM. The article provides a useful summary of the development of the HR field of academic study and discussion of the complexity of the concept and practice of HRM today. It also examines a number of concepts and ideas discussed in this and subsequent chapters.

Inkson, K. (2008) Are humans resources? *Career Development International*, 13 (3): 270–9.

This short article provides a thought-provoking discussion of the issues associated with the use of the metaphor 'human resources' to refer to people at work and presents a number of alternatives to its use.

Paauwe, J. (2009) HRM and performance: Achievements, methodological issues and prospects, *Journal of Management Studies*, 46 (1): 129–42.

This article provides a concise summary of the development of HRM as an academic field of study over the past three decades. It introduces a range of debates and controversies in the field of HRM and therefore acts as both a useful backdrop and companion piece for much of the discussion in this and the next two chapters.

Purcell, J. and Hutchinson, S. (2007) Front-line managers as agents in the HRM-performance causal chain: Theory, analysis and evidence, *Human Resource Management Journal*, 17 (1): 3–20.

This article reports on extensive research concerned with the role of front line managers in the causal chain between HRM and organisational performance. In particular, the article stresses the importance to employee commitment and job satisfaction of line manager leadership and their local implementation of HR practices.

Winstanley, D. and Woodall, J. (2000) The ethical dimension of human resource management, *Human Resource Management Journal*, 10 (2): 5–20.

The article introduces a range of issues associated with ethics in HRM. It provides an outline of previous work in the area and the frameworks by which ethics can be applied to HRM, stressing the importance of developing 'ethical sensitivity' among HRM professionals and managers, particularly in professional education, training and development.

Books, book chapters and reports

Caldwell, R. and Storey, J. (2007) The HR function: Integration or fragmentation? in J. Storey (ed.), *Human Resource Management: A Critical Text* (3rd edn), London: Thomson.

This book chapter critically explores contemporary developments in HRM and addresses two fundamental questions about the changing HR function. First, it evaluates the impact of new models of HR delivery, including outsourcing and self-service e-HR systems. Second, it assesses changes to the role of HR professionals themselves, with a particular focus on the concept of 'business partnering'.

CIPD (Chartered Institute of Personnel Development) (2011) *Next Generation HR: Insight-driven*, London: CIPD. Available at: **www.cipd.co.uk/hr-resources/research/next-generation-hr-insight-driven.aspx** (accessed 9 September 2015).

The report discusses the evolution of the HR function beyond one that is largely process-driven towards one that is insight-driven; that is, concerned with, and responsible for, the strategic health of the organisation and which actively works towards its 'future proofing'. Drawing on insights from senior HR leaders, the report introduces some interesting ideas about how HR can fulfill its strategic potential and the capabilities it must develop to do so.

Renwick, D. (2009) Line managers, in T. Redman and A. Wilkinson (eds), *Contemporary Human Resource Management* (3rd edn), Harlow: FT Prentice–Hall.

This comprehensive book chapter explores the developments connected to the increasing use of line managers in HRM. It provides international comparisons on the extent of devolution of responsibility, its impact in different contexts and the pitfalls and challenges associated with this trend.

UKCES (UK Commission for Employment and Skills) (2015) *Growth through People: Evidence and Analysis*, London: UKCES.

This useful report provides a summary of the key labour market trends subsequent to the global recession and their impact on employers, workers and government. It provides a concise summary of key trends in skills, pay and workplace productivity and proposes a number of critical employer and government actions, particularly in the area of workforce development, in response to these trends. It provides useful background reading for subsequent chapters on the drivers for HR activity.

FURTHER ONLINE READING

The following articles can be accessed for free on the book's companion website **https://edge.sagepub.com/wilton3e**:

Dietz, G., van der Wiele, T., van Iwaarden, J. and Brosseau, J. (2006) HRM inside UK e-commerce firms: Innovations in the 'new' economy and continuities with the 'old', *International Small Business Journal*, 24 (5): 443–70.

Kulik, C. T. and Bainbridge, H. T. J. (2006) HR and the line: The distribution of HR activities in Australian organisations, *Asia Pacific Journal of Human Resources*, 44 (2): 240–56.

Verreynne, M.-L., Parker, P. and Wilson, M. (2011) Employment systems in small firms: A multilevel analysis, *International Small Business Journal*, 31 (4): 405–31.

Wright, C. (2008) Reinventing human resource management: Business partners, internal consultants and the limits to professionalization, *Human Relations*, 61: 1063–86.

Want to know more about this chapter? Visit the companion website at: **https://edge.sagepub.com/wilton3e** to access practice questions, videos and selected journal articles to further enhance your study.

HRM AND THE INDIVIDUAL

CHAPTER OBJECTIVES

- To outline the dimensions of the employment relationship

- To define the concept of the 'psychological contract' and its relevance to HRM theory and practice

- To provide a brief historical overview of people management theory and practice

- To discuss the mechanisms organisations can utilise to control their workforce

- To outline determinants of individual performance in work organisations

- To introduce motivational theory that underpins HRM practice

- To introduce a conceptual framework to help understand how HRM can contribute to improved individual performance at work

THE PSYCHOLOGICAL CONTRACT

INTRODUCTION

Central to the strategic purpose of HRM is the management of individual worker performance to maximise its contribution to the achievement of organisational objectives. In order to achieve this aim, HRM has a variety of practices at its disposal to ensure that individuals have the ability, motivation and opportunity to perform effectively. The intention of this chapter is to provide a backdrop against which we can better understand the rationale for the HRM practices discussed in subsequent chapters by outlining the assumptions and theory that underpin them.

Guest (2002) suggests that there are two broad streams of literature on HRM. The first presents a critical analysis of the HRM phenomenon and its possible role in the exploitation of workers (reflecting 'hard' HRM as discussed in Chapter 1). The second is concerned with the relationship between HRM and corporate performance (further discussed in Chapter 3). Guest notes, however, that both streams largely neglect worker reactions to HRM practices and stresses the importance of understanding worker responses to these practices. Guest identifies a positive association between workers' reports of the presence of certain HR practices and their work and life satisfaction and, therefore, some support for the view that worker attitudes and behaviours represent a key linkage in the relationship between HRM and individual and organisational performance. Guest argues, therefore, that 'in developing HR practices to enhance performance, organisations ... need to consider explicitly the response of workers' (2002: 354). Wright and Nishii (2007) suggest that HRM practices can be understood in three ways: *intended* (as 'designed' at an organisational level); *actual* (as implemented at a local level); and *perceived* (as understood by employees). Given that there is likely to be a difference between intended, actual and perceived HRM practices, this presents a significant problem for management, not least in seeking to minimise the 'distance' between intended practices and how they are perceived. In light of this, the critical questions for managers are *why* certain types of HR practices might be associated with improved individual performance, and *how* are HR practices mediated by the individual in a way that is conducive to organisational success?

With these questions in mind, and before we consider in Chapter 3 specific formulations of HR practices and their contribution to individual and organisational performance, it is necessary to consider in detail the relationship that HRM seeks to manage. Chapter 1 suggested that HRM can be understood as the contemporary umbrella term for those activities involved in managing the employment relationship. An awareness of the multi-dimensional nature of this relationship is essential to understanding the various functions that HRM fulfils within work organisations, and the problems faced in managing a resource that is unpredictable, temperamental, wilful and that has commitments and pursuits other than work.

The chapter will introduce some of the concepts and theory through which to understand the mechanics of HRM practices and provide a number of the reference points necessary to explain why organisations are paying ever-greater attention to the implementation of sophisticated HR policies and practices, and the challenges they face in managing people.

Further online reading This article argues that HRM literature tends to pay limited attention to workers' reactions to HRM, suggesting that an understanding of how employee reactions mediate the HRM–performance relationship can pay dividends for both employer and employee.

Guest, D. (2002) Human resource management, corporate performance and employee wellbeing: Building the worker into HRM, *Journal of Industrial Relations*, 44 (3): 335–58.

WHAT IS THE EMPLOYMENT RELATIONSHIP?

At its most elemental, the employment relationship is simply the economic exchange of an individual's labour for reward of some description, otherwise referred to as the wage–effort bargain or 'a (fair) day's work for a (fair) day's pay'. In order to fully understand the role of HRM in contemporary organisations, however, a more sophisticated understanding of the relationship is necessary; one that emphasises that it is multi-dimensional, with socio-political, legal and psychological elements in addition to its essentially economic function. In the first instance, it is important to recognise the variety of forms of labour that can be 'purchased' in this economic exchange. Most obviously, work can take the form of physical or mental ('thinking') labour, but it can also be emotional ('the act of expressing organisationally-desired emotions during service transaction', Morris and Feldman, 1996: 987) or aesthetic (manifest in 'looking good' or 'sounding right', Nickson et al., 2003).

Table 2.1 summarises the various elements of the employment relationship, which will be discussed in more detail in the sections that follow. The table indicates the complexity of the relationship between employer and employee and stresses that the nature of the employment relationship in any instance reflects more than the explicit terms and conditions laid out in a contract of employment. It is important, therefore, to recognise that all employment relationships can be considered unique. For example, whilst a group of similarly employed workers might be subject to the same or similar terms and conditions of employment, their assumptions and expectations about their employer are likely to differ to some degree and they might therefore be motivated to work to differing extents. This might reflect differential management treatment, length of service and future period of engagement, previous employment experience, individual work ethic and personal values and beliefs. The nature of the employment relationship might also reflect different 'modes' or ways of working, for example where, as is increasingly the case, workers are 'employed' by one organisation but work in another or across a variety of different organisations. The increasing demand for workers to be 'flexible' in how, where and when they carry out their duties will also alter the nature of the relationship. Equally, the employer might have different preconceptions about the capabilities and the value of each of their employees and treat them differently (for example, giving preferential treatment to 'favourites' or more valued employees). For this reason, Schein (1980) suggests that there are three 'types' of contract in the employment relationship: the formal (economic and legal); the informal (reflecting the social norms in the workplace – the organisational 'culture' – and in wider society, about how people should treat each other); and the psychological (the implicit 'contract' made up of unspoken expectations and obligations).

TABLE 2.1 *The constituent elements of the employment relationship*

Economic	Often referred to as the wage–effort bargain, reflecting the notion of work as an exchange of 'effort' for a 'wage' of some description. This 'effort' can be physical, mental, emotional, skilled, unskilled and so on. The 'wage' typically refers to a financial payment but can also include non-financial incentives, benefits and perks
Socio-political	The employment relationship is also one of power and authority. Typically, the balance of power in this relationship resides with the employer who possesses the 'power to command' the worker who, in turn, has an 'obligation to obey' (Kahn-Freund, 1977, cited in Williams and Adam-Smith, 2005). However, in certain labour market circumstances, where an individual possesses sufficient 'labour market' power, they may exert greater leverage over the terms under which their labour is engaged
Legal/ contractual	This refers to both the legal status of the employment contract as binding on both parties and to the series of contractual and statutory employment obligations by which the parties must abide
Psychological contract/social exchange	The employment relationship is also a psychological transaction that establishes an implicit and unwritten set of beliefs and assumptions about what each party expects of the other and what they perceive their own obligations to be

The employment relationship is constructed in a specific context and is under constant influence from factors both within and outside of organisations that transform the conditions under which labour is engaged and the way in which an individual worker experiences employment. These include the organisational, political, legal, social, technological and economic conditions that will vary both geographically and over time. The contextual factors shaping the employment relationship are explored in detail in Chapters 4 and 5. Suffice to say, reflecting these multiple dimensions and changing contexts, most employment relationships can be both ambiguous and contain a host of contradictions.

THE EXPLICIT CONTRACT OF EMPLOYMENT

ACAS

The most obvious manifestation of the employment relationship is the individual contract of employment that represents the legal rights and obligations of the two parties to the contract. The contract of employment is defined by the UK Advisory, Conciliation and Arbitration Service (Acas) as 'an agreement between two parties enforceable by law ... a contract of service [that] comes into being when an employee agrees to work for an employer in return for pay' (2009d: 1). The terms of a contract can be 'express' (those that are explicitly agreed between the parties, either in writing or orally) or 'implied' (those that are not explicitly agreed but would be taken by the parties to form part of the contract).

Expressly agreed terms can emanate from a variety of sources, most obviously the contract itself (which may refer to associated documents such as a company handbook or collectively incorporated terms, such as a trade union agreement), as well as the letter of appointment and written or oral statements made by the employer and accepted by the employee. These terms vary in content depending on the individual, the job, the employing organisation, the sector and the country. In the UK, certain information must be included in the contract as a statutory requirement, such as rate of pay, hours of work, length of engagement if not 'permanent', entitlement to holiday and sick pay and the notice period for termination of the contract. The nature of the employment relationship is therefore shaped in the first instance by these express terms of employment and how these have been determined (for example, by negotiation between the parties or unilaterally imposed by management). These terms and conditions are likely to reflect the power balance in the employment relationship and the importance of the relationship to the employing organisation, both of which reflect the 'labour market power' of the individual. For example, employees who possess scarce skills or knowledge and, subsequently, are of greater value to the employer, will be able to negotiate more favourable terms and conditions.

The contract is also subject to statutory terms that are imposed by the statutory law that applies in a given country (in the UK, an Act of Parliament or other Statutory Instrument). For example, the contract might be subject to legislation that protects against discrimination at work, that guarantees minimum standards of employment, such as a national minimum wage or entitlement for maternity or paternity leave, and that provides protection against unfair termination of employment. Contractual terms cannot be worse than the minimum provisions laid out in legislation, but may be better (for example, the length of paid maternity leave). In addition to the explicitly stated terms and conditions of employment contained in the contract of employment, in the UK, both parties are subject to *implied duties* under common law. Table 2.2 provides some examples of implied duties for the employer and employee. Terms of employment can also be implied where they are too obvious to mention or where the parties assumed they

TABLE 2.2 *UK common law duties of employer and employee*

Implied duties of employees	Implied duties of employers
Be ready and willing for work and to cooperate with others	Provide a reasonable opportunity for employee to work
Perform competently in their duties	Pay the agreed wages (and not make unauthorised deductions)
Take reasonable care in the conduct of their work (and avoid damage to employer's property)	Provide a secure, safe and healthy environment
Obey reasonable orders and not disrupt business on purpose	Obey the law and not require employees to break the law
Be trustworthy, honest and behave with integrity	Treat all employees in a courteous and polite manner

would be incorporated at the time the contract was entered into, such as where they are necessary to make the contract workable (for example, that an employee employed as a driver will hold a valid current driving licence) or they reflect the well-established custom and practice of the business or industry.

The contract of employment therefore represents an accumulation of rights and responsibilities for both parties and constitutes the explicit and implied 'rules' under which labour is employed. These rights and responsibilities are the result of a range of processes, including:

- the means by which the individual terms and conditions of employment are determined and altered, for example: renegotiation of contractual terms; pay increases; unilateral changes to company policy; or outcome of grievance and disciplinary procedures
- the means by which the collective (i.e. workforce) terms and conditions of employment are determined and altered, for example: collective bargaining between employers and trade unions; dispute resolution processes (for example, the arbitration decision of a third party); employee negotiation or consultation in decision-making; or unilateral management pronouncement
- the law-making process, including case law and legal precedents
- the evolution of organisational custom and practice.

These rules, and the procedures designed to both determine and enforce these rules, play a vital role in regulating the employment relationship on behalf of both parties. They define roles and accountabilities, set the boundaries for behaviour and establish standards of expected performance in relation to the contract. For employees, rules help to ensure consistency and fairness of treatment by providing a formal structure for the relationship, thus guarding against arbitrary management practice (so long as the procedures and rules are adhered to). In this sense, rules help to address the power imbalance in the employment relationship and avoid or restrain conflict. Box 2.1 shows how rules can also act to protect an organisation's investment in its staff.

However, there are numerous problems associated with the regulation of the employment relationship. Whilst it is generally desirable for both employees and managers to establish the exact terms under which an employer is engaging labour (for example, the hours of work), extensive systems of formal rules can be inflexible, overly bureaucratic and time-consuming, and can act as a significant impediment to the achievement of organisational objectives, in particular by restricting the capacity of organisations to cope with rapid change.

Alternatively, informal rules such as organisation custom are open to misinterpretation and hold the potential for confusion or abuse of workplace arrangements. Moreover, where rules are perceived by employees to be unreasonable, or where they are imposed contrary to the views of those who must comply with or enforce them, they are unlikely to be effective and, at worst, can undermine performance. Tensions between different sets of rules can also exist. For example, workplace custom may contravene legislation. Workplace rules and the procedures for dealing with contravention of these rules are discussed in further detail in Chapter 13.

BOX 2.1
HRM IN PRACTICE

The rules of the game – footballers and the employment relationship

With the intense media scrutiny of footballers' exorbitant wages, it is perhaps easy to forget that players are simply employees of their clubs, albeit often millionaire employees, and that 'outside of the military, few occupations can be as subject to rules and regulations as that of football' (Moore, 2004). Most professional football clubs have extensive rulebooks that dictate very precisely the conduct required of their players, covering not only issues of fitness and health, but also time-keeping, appearance and their behaviour away from football. In effect, these rulebooks reflect the level of investment in human capital (in transfer fees and wages) that the modern-day footballer represents and a desire by their clubs to protect that investment. This is over and above, the rules for professional conduct set down by the professional bodies that govern football and other professional sports, nationally and internationally (O'Leary, 2012).

A football club's human resource – its players, as well as the manager and coaching staff – clearly represent its prime source of competitive advantage, in a sporting sense, and it therefore makes sense for clubs to control the conduct of their employees and, in turn, seek to maximise their performance and achieve their potential. The employment relationship for professional footballers can be understood, therefore, on the basis that, in return for high levels of remuneration, footballers afford their clubs the right to tell their players 'where to live, what to wear, what to eat, what to drink, when to see the doctor or dentist, and what to do in their spare time' (Moore, 2004).

As a recent example, in an effort to address a decline in the club's sporting performance during the 2013–14 football season (albeit from a position of national and international dominance), in August 2014, the FC Barcelona manager, Luis Enrique, introduced a strict internal code of behaviour for his players. As reported by the Catalonian newspaper, *Sport*, the manager introduced ten disciplinary 'commandments':

1 The players must be at training an hour before it begins.
2 Alcohol is prohibited during meals.
3 Players must be home by midnight in the 48 hours before a game.
4 An act of serious indiscipline may result in being sacked.
5 Players must always be respectful in their public statements.
6 Financial penalties will range between 1,000 and 6,000 €.
7 Players must wear official club clothing on trips and events.
8 Players must be responsible on social networks.
9 It is prohibited to participate in risky activities, including riding a motorbike, jet skiing, climbing and diving.
10 The fines levied for indiscipline will be given to charity.

Unitarist and pluralist perspectives on the employment relationship

When considering the nature of the employment relationship, there are a number of theoretical perspectives or frames of reference that can be adopted that reflect the extent to which employers and employees share common interests and objectives, whether conflict is inevitable between the parties and the balance of power between the parties. Chapter 10 discusses in detail these theoretical perspectives and their influence over how firms manage the collective employment relationship that exists between an employer and its workforce. However, it is important here to briefly outline what is meant by two key perspectives: unitarism and pluralism.

> *Unitarism* represents the viewpoint that organisations are 'families' or 'teams' where managers and workers share common objectives and in which conflict or dissent among employees is deviant behaviour. A unitarist ideology underpins both authoritarian and paternalistic approaches to people management, the former reflecting the view that employees should obey managers simply because of the position that they hold and the latter reflecting a view of the firm as akin to a family where members look after one another.

> *Pluralism* reflects the viewpoint that organisations are made up of various interest groups, most notably managers and workers, who have conflicting but equally legitimate interests and therefore conflict is both inevitable and natural. A pluralist ideology can underpin approaches to management that are consultative under which the legitimate interests of diverse groups are recognised and emphasis is placed on negotiated decision-making.

Implicit in each perspective of the employment relationship is a view of power in the employment relationship. Under unitarism the view is that power should reside in the hands of management by virtue of their position of authority as organisational decision-makers. Under pluralism, power is viewed as being more distributed and the balance of power within organisations can shift from one group to another depending on circumstances or the issue at hand.

Further online reading This article reports on a study of the employment relationship in three medium-sized firms. In particular, it provides an interesting insight into the interaction between employment regulation, managerial prerogative and employee action as a result of their perceptions of the nature of the psychological contract.

Atkinson, C., Mallett, O. and Wapshott, R. (2014) 'You try to be a fair employer': Regulation and employment relationships in medium-sized firms, *International Small Business Journal*, 1–18.

THE PSYCHOLOGICAL CONTRACT

THE
PSYCHOLOGICAL
CONTRACT

A problematic and often controversial element of the employment relationship is the psychological contract. Related to social exchange theory (Blau, 1964) which stresses the inherent dynamism and complexity of social relationships, the psychological contract has been defined as 'a set of unwritten reciprocal expectations between an individual employee and the organisation' (Schein, 1978: 48), and 'the perceptions of the two parties, employee and employer, of what their mutual obligations are towards each other' (Guest and Conway, 2002: 1).

BOX 2.2
ETHICAL INSIGHT

Ethics and the employment relationship

Berkley and Watson (2009) suggest ethics and corporate social responsibility work at multiple levels in work organisations, beginning with the accountability of individual employees and managers for their conduct in carrying out work-related activities, to the responsibility of corporations towards their employees and wider communities. The authors suggest, however, that whilst employees represent one of the most important organisational stakeholders, they are 'consistently ignored when considering the scope of ethical decisions' (2009: 275) despite being among those most affected by the unethical behaviour of those in more senior positions.

The central ethical issues surrounding HRM and the employment relationship concern the rights and duties of employees. On the employer side, areas of ethical decision-making include employees' rights for 'fair' pay, 'good' and safe working conditions, freedom from discrimination and bullying and the right to due process in, for example, the handling of promotion or employee discipline. Berkley and Watson (2009) also note, however, that given that the relationship is reciprocal, employees also owe due ethical consideration to their employers. Ethical duties of the employee include taking responsibility for the health and safety of colleagues and compliance with the law and contract of employment. Evidently, many of these rights and duties are often enshrined in national employment legislation (as in Table 2.2) and, therefore, ethical behaviour is often seen only in terms of legal compliance. Some rights and duties, however, fall outside the coverage of specific legal frameworks and, therefore, become wider issues of explicit ethical decision-making, not least where the law is open to interpretation, relies on management discretion in its application or is under-developed in protecting the basic human rights of workers. This last point is of particular concern to the activities of multinational corporations operating in developing countries where employee protection legislation is often limited. The ethical dilemmas faced by MNCs are discussed further in Chapter 5.

Entering into an employment relationship creates 'moral hazards' for both parties or, put another way, costs that are not included in the contract of employment. These hazards are associated with the 'asset specificity' associated with the employment relationship – that is, the fact that 'employees "invest" time and effort in developing assets specific to a particular employer' (Crane and Matten, 2006: 265). From the perspective of the employee, these hazards can include social and financial dependency on a firm if employment is over a long period and the 'investment' involved in relocation to take a new position or in undertaking self-funded training. For the employer, the hazards include the threat of skilled or knowledgeable employees being poached by competitors and an inability to control all of their employees all of the time, with the implication that firms can be damaged by poor productivity, conduct or performance. Given that employees tend to represent the weaker and more dependent part of the employment relationship, the moral hazards tend to be greater for workers than their employers when entering into the contract of employment.

Both parties, therefore, have a vested interest in developing an employment relationship that is based on mutual ethical behaviour, not least because doing so can help minimise the risk associated with such hazards. For employees, acting ethically can help to ensure both the long-term survival of the firm and their place within it. For employers, the ethical behaviour of employees is likely to positively impact upon individual and organisational performance, not least in the manner in which they conduct their work and interactions in the workplace. Indeed, many of the benefits of a positive psychological contract – employee commitment, trust and engagement – can develop directly from an employment relationship founded on ethical principles. Moreover, recent research finds a positive association between socially responsible HRM – policies and practices designed to recruit, support and reward socially responsible workers – and individual performance and behaviour at work (Shen and Benson, 2014).

Further online reading This research article finds that the adoption of socially responsible HRM (SRHRM) – practices that promote, support and reward the socially responsible behaviour of employees – can yield positive improvements in task performance and extra-role helping behaviour. These findings suggest an imperative for firms to invest in corporate social responsibility (CSR) directed towards employees as a means of both furthering their CSR agenda and also to positively impact on employee behaviour and organisational identification.

Shen, J. and Benson, J. (2014) When CSR is a social norm: How socially responsible human resource management affects employee work behavior, *Journal of Management*, 1–24.

At the heart of the concept of the psychological contract is the idea that employers and employees have an understanding about the nature of the employment relationship that goes beyond what is written or implied in the contract of employment or other explicit manifestations of the employment relationship (for example, job descriptions). As opposed to terms and conditions that are largely closed to interpretation and unambiguous, the psychological contract is constructed of subjective, often unarticulated beliefs, expectations and obligations that are subject to constant change. Consequently, it is a key source of conflict between employers and employees, particularly as the psychological contract is played out with neither party ever fully knowing the intentions and beliefs of the other; as such, the extent to which this constitutes a 'contract' in the true sense of the word has been questioned.

The psychological contract between an employing organisation and the individual begins to take shape even before the explicit employment contract is established. On the basis of claims made in job advertising or in the recruitment process, applicants will begin to form associations, make assumptions and construct expectations about employment at the organisation. Subsequently, formal policies and practices and informal social cues either reinforce or lead to a reassessment of these beliefs. The development of a positive psychological contract, therefore, involves the ongoing alignment and realignment of organisational and individual needs and part of the role of HRM is the management of expectations, ensuring that employees are aware of the expectations placed upon them and also ensuring that what employees can expect of the organisation is clearly transmitted.

As employees are increasingly recognised as a key organisational asset, the management of the psychological contract becomes paramount in monitoring and shaping employee attitudes and expectations. In particular, the psychological contract can be viewed as a mediating factor that translates HRM policies and practices into individual performance (Katou and Budhwar, 2012), as the 'state' of the psychological contract informs the actions of the employee on a day-to-day basis, particularly whether to work to their potential or withhold effort. Figure 2.1 outlines the way in which the psychological contract is shaped by organisational 'inputs' such as HR policies and practices, the behaviour and actions of line managers and senior managerial leadership, in the broader context of individual attributes – such as age (Adams et al. 2014), level of education, work status (Chambel and Alcover, 2011), tenure (Conway and Coyle-Shapiro, 2012; Payne et al., 2015) and contractual basis of employment (Callea et al., 2014) – and organisational characteristics – such as sector, competitive strategy, size (Atkinson et al., 2014) and work culture (Restubog et al., 2015). These inform the three key elements of the psychological contract that constitute its 'state': an employee's sense of fairness in the way they are treated by their employer; the degree of trust they have in that employer; and their belief that the employer will deliver on the implicit deal between them (Guest and Conway, 1997; Guest, 1998). For example, Guest and Conway (2002) find that employee voice in organisational decision-making can have a positive impact on employee trust and, therefore, organisations should engage and involve employees to build and maintain a positive psychological contract. In addition, O'Donohue and Nelson (2009) posit an ethical dimension to the psychological contract whereby a positive psychological contract is likely to be sustained where an organisation's activities are perceived by the employee as congruent with both the individual's values and beliefs and the prevailing ethical climate of the firm.

Understanding the psychological contract allows us to appreciate why the management of people presents a problem for organisations. Unlike the explicit contract of employment, the psychological contract is subject to constant change. For example, management might decide to outlaw a customary privilege informally enjoyed by workers or renege on a particular promise. In such cases, workers will then interpret management actions and redefine the relationship in a positive or negative fashion. The instability of the psychological contract and the considerable scope for misinterpretation frequently result in violation or breach of the psychological contract (Robinson and Rousseau, 1994). These violations are likely to lead to negative adjustments in employee behaviour (Shanawaz and Goswami, 2011; Eckerd et al., 2013) and will have a cumulative impact on the employment relationship that, ultimately, may result in either employee resignation or dismissal. Short of leaving the organisation, employees are likely to respond to breaches of the psychological contract by adjusting work inputs (effort) to take account of perceived lowered outputs (rewards).

One of the central problems in 'managing' the psychological contract is that of *multiple agency*. Employees have formal or informal exchanges with a wide variety of organisational 'agents' (such as managers at varying levels) and, therefore, maintaining consistent messages across the organisation is problematic. A key

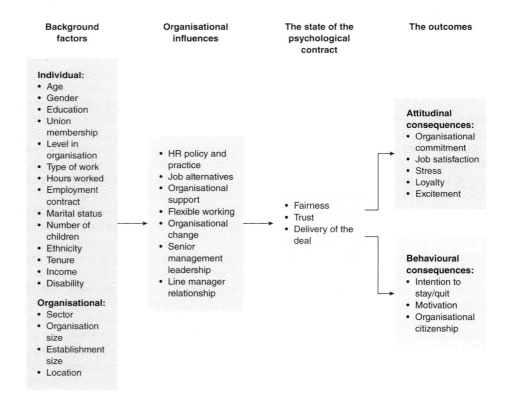

FIGURE 2.1 Components of the psychological contract (from D. Guest and N. Conway (2004) *Employee Well-being and the Psychological Contract*, reproduced with the permission of the publisher, the Chartered Institute of Personnel and Development, London, www.cipd.co.uk)

element in the management of the psychological contract is therefore to ensure clear communication between employers and employees in explaining the rationale behind managerial actions and providing a mechanism through which employees can voice their opinions and grievances. One way to maintain consistency of attitude and behaviour across an organisation is the establishment and management of organisational culture. This is discussed further in Chapter 7.

Employee engagement and the psychological contract

The concept of the psychological contract is closely linked to the more recently coined notion of *employee engagement*. Employee engagement is defined as:

 a combination of commitment to the organisation and its values plus a willingness to help out colleagues. It goes beyond job satisfaction and is not simply motivation. Engagement is something the employee has to offer: it cannot be 'required' as part of the employment contract. (CIPD, 2009a: 1)

Alternatively, Schaufeli et al. (2002: 74) define engagement as a 'positive, fulfilling, work-related state of mind that is characterised by vigour, dedication and absorption', and suggest that such engagement is not momentary or specific to a particular task but 'persistent and pervasive'. Robinson et al. (2004) suggest that the behaviours demonstrated by the engaged employee include a belief and pride in the organisation, a desire to work to make things better and an understanding of business context and the 'bigger picture'. Given these definitions, there is no doubt that a state of engagement among its employees is desirable for an organisation (Gruman and Saks, 2011).

Both the psychological contract and employee engagement represent a means of understanding the connection between the way people are managed and both individual and business performance (Simpson, 2009). In particular, a positive psychological contract and high levels of engagement contribute to the creation of beneficial behavioural and attitudinal employee outcomes such as job satisfaction, organisational commitment, increased motivation and lowered intention to quit (Guest and Conway, 2004; Saks, 2006; Chambel and Alcover, 2011). Moreover, both 'states' have been associated with the development of higher levels of organisational citizenship behaviour – the discretionary behaviour that is beneficial to the organisation and work team performance through the willingness of employees to 'go that extra mile' for a colleague, client or customer (Decktop et al., 1999).

Theoretically, therefore, through the development of a positive psychological contract via particular configurations of HR policies and practices, organisations can elicit greater discretionary effort from employees, increase levels of engagement and unlock hidden potential. For example, Farndale et al. (2011) report that employee perceptions of trust, equity and fairness of treatment regarding HRM practices are important in developing positive employee behaviours and attitudes, such as employee commitment. However, creating an engaged workforce is problematic and 'organisations must work to engage an employee, who in turn has a choice about the level of engagement to offer the employer' (Robinson et al., 2004: 1). Robinson et al. (2004) suggest that a sense of feeling valued and involved at work represents the strongest driver of engagement, which is, in turn, reflective of the extent to which employee voice is listened to in decision-making, the provision of opportunities for employees to develop their jobs and organisational concern for employees' health and well-being.

The changing psychological contract?

Much of the interest in the psychological contract originates in the need for organisations to search for more innovative people management practices in the context of economic and organisational restructuring, heightened international competition and changing labour market dynamics (Cullinane and Dundon, 2006). These broad developments have had significant implications for the nature of the employment relationship, and the way in which individuals experience work and careers (discussed in more detail in Chapter 4). In particular, as a result of the need for organisational flexibility and adaptability, the 'traditional' employment relationship based on an exchange of job security in return for loyalty and commitment is argued to have been replaced by 'new deals' in employment (Adamson et al., 1998), whereby firms offer opportunities for the accumulation of skills and experience (not a 'job' but the opportunity to enhance one's employability) in return for a temporary provision of service.

As a result, employment is experienced in a highly fragmented and individualised manner, there is less dependency between the parties to the employment relationship, and career development becomes the sole responsibility of the individual. Rousseau (1989) uses the term transactional psychological contract to reflect such a relationship based on short-term mutual instrumentality in contrast to the traditional relational psychological contract. CIPD (2009b) suggest that the 'new' psychological contract is made up of employee commitments such as assurances to work hard, to develop new skills and update old ones and to be flexible, in exchange for employer promises to provide pay commensurate with performance, opportunities for training and development, and interesting and challenging work. Cartwright and Holmes (2006) argue that this shift represents a significant problem for managers in that such a psychological contract develops mistrust and cynicism among employees, associated with a loss of meaning attached to their work, which can have negative consequences for employers in the form of reduced commitment and engagement among the workforce.

In addition, there has been a significant change over recent years in the composition of the labour market, both in terms of the diversity of the labour supply (for example, in terms of age and ethnicity) and in the flexible ways in which organisations employ labour. This, therefore, presents an increasingly complex set of relationships for managers to manage as each group of workers holds different expectations about the terms of their relationship with an employing firm. Moreover, where firms operate in more than one country then management need to be mindful of cross-cultural differences in the nature of the relationship between employer and employee (Box 2.3). Chapter 5 explicitly examines the international context of HRM and the influence of both institutional and cultural factors. Where appropriate, each chapter will consider different practices, elements and themes associated with HRM in an international context.

Further online reading Drawing on empirical research, this article develops the transactional and relational categorisations of the psychological contract and identifies multiple types of psychological contract based on different employer and employee obligations. It provides a useful aid in understanding the complexity of managing the employment relationship in different settings.

Janssens, M., Sels, L. and van den Brande, I. (2003) Multiple types of psychological contracts: A six-cluster solution, *Human Relations*, 56 (11): 1349–78.

BOX 2.3
GLOBAL INSIGHT

National differences and the psychological contract

The forces of globalisation, intensified competition and rapid technological innovation have all contributed to changes in organisational form, the functioning of the labour market and the nature of the employment relationship itself. Whilst some commentators suggest that the process of globalisation is contributing to a convergence of approaches to the management of labour, others argue that many of the assumptions behind HRM are based on a Western perspective on the employment relationship, reflecting a particular set of cultural values, such as specific attitudes to authority or 'risk', and institutions, e.g. the approach to regulation adopted by a particular nation state.

From this perspective, particular HRM practices developed in a particular cultural context might not represent appropriate approaches to the management of labour in different settings. For example, Lucas et al. (2006) suggest that there might be international differences in the perception of the psychological contract, such as in the extent to which employees respond to violations of the contract. In support of this perspective, Westwood et al. (2001) found that by Western standards the psychological contract among a sample of Hong Kong junior and senior managers was one-sided. They reported that a strong sense of duty and obligation in Chinese culture is reflected in a strong perception that employees are more obliged to their employer than the employer is obliged to them. Subsequently, Thomas et al. (2003) report that cross-cultural employment relationships – where managers represent one cultural profile and employees another – are likely to be more difficult to manage as a result of systematic differences in interpretation and motivation between the parties. Therefore, organisations managing across cultures need to pay specific attention to the formation of the psychological contract, and how this contract operates and is subsequently acted upon.

A BRIEF HISTORY OF PEOPLE MANAGEMENT

Whether we adopt a revolutionary or evolutionary perspective on HRM as a distinctive approach to the management of people, it is useful to place it in the context of changing assumptions about how workers can be controlled and motivated. In early capitalism, entrepreneurs and business owners were faced with a workforce that was thought to be ill disciplined and inherently indolent. Guided by the principles of control employed in the armed forces, people management was conceived in an authoritarian manner and founded upon the principles of coercion and punishment. In the mid-nineteenth century, managers in emerging industries, such as the railway companies, adopted highly sectional bureaucracies as a mechanism of control with the emphasis on the rigid adherence to chain of command and the strict demarcation of roles and responsibilities (McKenna, 1980).

The origins of modern personnel management and HRM lie, however, in the late nineteenth century with social reformers looking to address the exploitation of workers by factory owners, and the appointment of managers concerned with worker welfare (Torrington et al., 2008). For example, in the UK a group of industrialists (often Quakers, for example, Cadbury's at Bourneville in the Midlands of England) adopted a 'paternalist' attitude towards their workforce and concerned themselves with meeting the social and moral needs of workers by providing subsidised housing, education and improved working conditions. Although the imperative for this treatment was more a product of Christian morality than a search for increased efficiency or productivity, and although these ideas were implemented in the context of strict worker discipline and control, such approaches presaged the influence of social psychology in management thinking discussed later in this chapter.

Since then, the management of people has undergone an at least partially evolutionary process reflecting the increasing application of 'scientific' principles to the problems of motivation and control, and a developing understanding about what makes people 'tick' and the way in which work organisation and management practice can contribute to organisational performance. This section briefly outlines a number of key developments in people management to place the current manifestation of HRM in its historical context.

Scientific management

One of the earliest attempts to apply the principles of rationality to the management of people and organisation of production is that of scientific management or Taylorism (after its innovator, Frederick Winslow Taylor). At around the turn of the twentieth century, Taylor (1856–1917), an American engineer in iron and steelmaking, identified and sought to remedy a range of inefficiencies that were seen to be restricting industrial output. Taylor and his counterparts were facing a rapidly changing industrial system in which the number of large-scale workplaces was growing rapidly, but where output was hindered by high levels of labour turnover and strong solidarity among the workforce.

Taylor identified that power and control in factory production processes were held almost exclusively by workers, in that they organised their own work, worked at their own pace, used their own tools, hired their own 'crews' and possessed far greater skill and knowledge of production than did their supervisors. As a result of this control, aided by management's ignorance of the system of production, Taylor believed that workers restricted their output or, in his words, 'soldiered', either because they were inherently lazy ('natural soldiering') or in a calculated manner to maximise staffing levels ('systematic soldiering'). Subsequently, Taylor sought to rationalise the labour process and impose a new logic that would allow managers to regain control of the shopfloor, rigorously applying the detailed division of labour advocated by the social philosopher, Adam Smith (1723–90). The approach established by Taylor has been one of the central tenets of industrial society for the best part of a century and his ideas remain both highly influential in job design and in the wider management of labour, and a contentious source of academic debate. It is, therefore, worth laying out Taylor's ideas in some detail. Buchanan and Huczynski (1997) suggest that there are five principles to scientific management:

1 A clear division of tasks and responsibilities between management and workers.
2 Use of scientific methods to determine the best way of doing a job.
3 Scientific selection of the person to do the newly designed job.
4 The training of the selected worker to perform the job in the way specified.
5 Enthusiastic cooperation with the workers to ensure that the work is performed in accordance with scientific management principles, and this being secured by the use of economic incentives.

Taylor's ideas were both radical and controversial and his system, where implemented, resulted in dramatic increases in output, cost savings and efficiency. It also led to the creation of new departments, or areas of managerial activity, such as quality control and personnel, as these functions were removed from the control of workers (for example, the recruitment and selection of workers). Taylor's ideas reflected a simple model of worker motivation that equated humans to machines: a means of production that responded to financial reward as the primary inducement to work. However, the deskilling, routinisation and standardisation at the heart of Taylor's system effectively removed the 'meaning' from work for those carrying it out. As such, subsequent critiques of Taylorism argue that if workers are treated as though money was their sole motivator, then they will act accordingly, with no attention to quality and no pride in their achievements, little loyalty or commitment to the employer and, ultimately, gaining little fulfilment from work (Grey, 2007). Despite later attempts to humanise scientific management, Taylorism is still largely viewed as a divisive and exploitative system of work organisation associated with poor employee relations outcomes.

BOX 2.4
RESEARCH INSIGHT

Work organisation and control in call centres

Taylor et al. (2002) contrast two general types of call centre work and workflows:

1 *Quantity-oriented* call centres are characterised by simple and routinised customer interaction, 'hard' quantitative targets, strict script adherence, tight call-handling times, a high percentage of operator time spent on the phone, high call volumes and low level of operator discretion.

2 *Quality-oriented* call centres are characterised by more complex and individualised customer interaction, 'soft' or qualitative targets, flexible or no scripts, relaxed call-handling times, prioritisation of customer satisfaction, low call volumes and high levels of operator discretion.

The researchers sought to explore the perceptions of operators in each of these types of call centre regarding the degree to which they had control over key aspects of their work. Prior research has identified that employees engaged in 'quality-oriented' work experienced such work more positively than those in 'quantity-oriented' work (Frenkel et al., 1998) as a result of having higher degrees of discretion, being subject to lower levels of control and regimentation and being able to work more creatively and use their initiative (for example, in problem-solving for customers). Taylor et al. (2002) found, however, that even in organisations where workflows emphasise quality (the 'high-end' of the call centre industry), significant numbers of workers reported an absence of control over key aspects of their job, for example, the pace of work, breaks from work, work planning and targets. Such control is technological, as well as bureaucratic and normative (Bélanger and Edwards, 2013). Moreover, they found evidence of attempts to quantify in detail qualitative aspects of operators' work (for example, their conformity to prescribed call conventions such as call 'opening' and 'closure'), and that operators in all call centres found the work repetitive. Therefore, whilst it is important to note the variety of work undertaken in a call centre environment, Taylor et al. suggest that even optimistic accounts of employee experience in such work – particularly, in respect of control – show it to be more uniform and that even where the nature of the work tends towards a requirement for greater discretion and autonomy, management seek to find new means of control or fall back on old ones.

Further online reading

Taylor, P., Mulvey, G., Hyman, J. and Bain, P. (2002) Work organization, control and the experience of work in call centres, *Work, Employment and Society*, 16 (1): 133–50.

It would be amiss to discuss Taylorism without adding at least a footnote about Fordism. To a great extent, Taylor's ideas reached their full potential for worker control when allied to the innovations of Henry Ford (1863–1947). The detailed division of labour advocated under Taylorism led to greater worker specialisation in simpler tasks which, when allied to single-purpose machines and the moving assembly line, enabled the development of a system of mass production and mass worker control. By combining Taylor's principles of rationalisation and standardisation to new technology, Ford was able to build control into the technology and the production process itself; the single-purpose machinery, designed to be used by unskilled workers after minimal training, allowed no room for human error or innovation, and the moving assembly line eliminated the potential for 'soldiering'.

Scientific management provides a backdrop to the development both of people and production management over the twentieth century and is still alive and well in the twenty-first, despite continued criticism of the alienating and dissatisfying effects of deskilling in the organisation of work (Braverman, 1974). In his book *The McDonaldization of Society*, George Ritzer (2007) outlines the use of Taylor's principles in the fast-food industry and recent research in the call centre industry demonstrates the modernisation of Fordism in a truly contemporary setting, referring to the 'assembly line in the head' and the technological control of worker effort (Taylor and Bain, 1999).

The human relations movement

Grey (2007) suggests that the story of organisational behaviour often follows a simple narrative in which scientific management is most often cast as the bad guy and the human relations movement as the good guy, the 'human' response to Taylor's unethical system of control. However, Grey suggests that this story rather over-simplifies the evolutionary relationship between the two and in particular wrongly promotes the human relations movement as the search for a corrective remedy to scientific management.

The origin of the movement was a set of experiments on productivity improvement that took place at the Hawthorne plant of Western Electric Ltd between 1924 and 1932, led by a researcher called Elton Mayo. One perspective on the human relations movement is that these experiments prompted a revision or rejection of the Taylorist notion of workers as economically motivated automatons and prompted greater recognition of workers' social needs and interests. In particular, the Hawthorne experiments are credited with the discovery of the importance of informal groups within organisations and their ability to either work with or against management through means other than coercion. The alternative viewpoint plays down this benevolence that has come to be associated with the experiments, by suggesting that, like Taylor, they sought to address a pressing management need in the USA of the 1920s. In this case, the problem was how to respond to the problems of scientific management (for example, absenteeism, turnover and worker sabotage) by presenting management in a less confrontational manner, and to establish more sophisticated 'levers' for managerial control.

Regardless of our reading of history, what the Hawthorne experiments signified to management was that social interaction and the experience of working in a tight-knit group could be a significant source of motivation at work. The experiments concluded that the 'latent' effort that informal work groups 'irrationally' withhold could be released by the right kind of management. The identification of informal norms of behaviour and discipline that had evolved in the groups under study revealed the divergence of worker and management aims and the imperative for management to channel worker 'sentiment' so that it parallels management's concern for efficiency. As such, a key function of management is the 'social engineering' of group objectives and behaviours towards the achievement of organisational aims, as well as engendering a close supervisor relationship to mediate between the demands of the company and the desires of the group. Human relations, therefore, arguably bears the same instrumental rationality of scientific management despite tactical differences; whilst scientific management sought to control workers by avoiding human relationships, human relations seeks to achieve the same objective through cultivating these relationships.

Neo-human relations

In considering scientific management and the human relations movement we have been introduced to two different conceptualisations of the human at work. The principles of scientific management were based upon the notion of a rational-economic person whereas human relations emphasised the notion of the social being. The neo-human relations movement (Grint, 2005) that emerged in the 1940s and 1950s introduced an alternative perspective and the idea of the self-actualising person. This approach rejected some of the ideas associated with the early human relations movement, in particular, that humans are easy-to-control social beings. The theories associated with neo-human relations emphasise 'self-actualisation' and the achievement of one's full potential through work as the most effective motivator. For example, Maslow's (1954/1970) hierarchy of needs suggests that there are five sets of instinctive human needs and that as an individual satisfies one set of needs they will move to the next. Self-actualisation is the highest level of need (above physiological, safety, love and esteem needs). Whilst this model was not directly concerned with work itself, it follows that when individuals satisfy their basic requirements through work (for example, financial reward can satisfy physiological and safety/security needs), organisations should look to the next in order to elicit greater motivation as individuals seek to satisfy higher level needs. One implication of this hierarchy is that for low-paid workers, financial reward is likely to be of greater significance than for those who are better-paid and who can 'afford' to seek the satisfaction of alternative needs. Similarly, Herzberg (1966) suggests that there are two sets of work characteristics that might serve as sources of worker satisfaction or motivation:

- *Hygiene factors* are prerequisites for high productivity or motivation (for example, pay and working conditions); they cannot motivate greatly alone, but can act as 'dissatisfiers' when absent.

- *Motivation factors* represent the fulfilment of symbolic and psychological needs (for example, recognition of achievement, intrinsic job interest and a sense of belonging and purpose); when added to hygiene factors they can motivate people to perform well.

Herzberg's typology suggests, for example, that whilst financial reward needs to be set at an appropriate level that meets employee expectations, paying above this level will not result in appreciably greater worker motivation. Higher levels of motivation tend to be associated with work that is satisfying and intrinsically rewarding, with worker autonomy and opportunities for social interaction. Neo-human relations, therefore, rejects the fragmentation and deskilling of jobs advocated by Taylorism. The difference between Taylor's conception of the worker and that presented by the neo-human relations movement is best outlined by the two opposing assumptions made about people at work suggested by McGregor (1960):

- Theory X – people have an inherent dislike of work and coercion is necessary for compliance. They have limited ambition and have security as a priority.

- Theory Y – people respond better to self-control and exercise self-discipline at work and it is possible to provide organisational goals to help workers achieve self-actualisation.

Scientific management is founded upon an assumption that humans conform to Theory X and, as such, management is required to control workers closely to maximise productivity. Over the past two to three decades, however, Theory Y has dominated thinking in HRM and, in particular, has become synonymous with Post-Fordism. In broad terms, whereas the emphasis of Fordism is on mass production and product standardisation, Post-Fordism denotes business systems focused on producing smaller numbers of customised products for niche markets, reflecting the notion of 'flexible specialisation' (Piore and Sabel, 1984). In terms of employment, Post-Fordism is used to describe flexible working arrangements, high skill, job variety, autonomy, empowerment and the promotion of a team ethos. Theoretically, at least, it is the antithesis of Fordism and reflects work design and management practices that seek to both motivate and control through responding to the social and psychological needs of workers, as a means of improving organisational performance. These ideas were heavily influenced by Japanese management techniques that came to dominate managerial discourse in the 1980s as Western firms sought to compete with the high levels of productivity achieved in firms such as Toyota and Nissan by replicating as far as possible their practices and processes.

MANAGERIAL CONTROL

TOYOTA JOB SECURITY

Within this brief summary of the key developments in people management we can discern a number of clearly defined mechanisms for worker control. Friedman (1977) suggested that organisations may choose between two 'logics of control' for the management of people at work, depending upon the nature of product and labour markets, which draw upon opposing perspectives both of the psychological contract and of the power relationship between employer and employee:

● Direct control that emphasises a low-trust relationship between management and employees, strict supervision and task specification; such a control strategy reinforces the subordination of labour to capital and is clearly evident in scientific management.

● Responsible autonomy that is associated with a high-trust, high-commitment relationship where workers have a degree of discretion and responsibility for their work; this is likely to be an appropriate strategy by which to manage highly skilled professionals or knowledge workers who require and respond positively to greater degrees of independence.

Edwards (1979) developed this analysis by identifying two 'structural' strategies for control:

1 Technical control, where control is built into machinery and technology, a strategy which clearly relates to Fordist production processes.

2 Bureaucratic control, concerned with control via the demarcation of responsibility, the construction of internal labour markets and career structures. To a certain degree, such strategies of control are inherent in all work organisations.

We can add to these typologies the notion of social (or normative) control that refers to the informal mechanisms that regulate individual behaviour within a social group (whether a team, department or entire organisation) to ensure compliance with a set of explicit or implied rules. This control can either be through the individual internalisation of the norms and values of the group (for example, via a deeply embedded corporate culture) or the use of positive or negative sanctions. In relation to these control strategies, Handy (1976), referring to organisations in their broadest possible sense (i.e. not only work organisations), identifies three types of psychological contract:

1 *Coercive*, where the contract is not entered into freely (e.g. prisons) and where the majority are dominated by a minority who exercise control by rule and punishment with the emphasis on conformity.

2 *Calculative*, where the contract is entered into freely but control is maintained by management and power is expressed in terms of their ability to give desired rewards to the individual.

3 *Cooperative*, where the individual tends to identify with the goals of the organisation and strive for their attainment through individual effort. Effort is based on the degree to which the individual has an input in determining the company's goals.

This last point of classification is key to understanding the theory that underpins high-commitment models of HRM. These models advocate the use of particular configurations of HRM policies and practices to engender commitment of the individual to the achievement of organisational goals in order to unlock the worker's discretionary effort. Arguably, this discretionary effort would likely remain untapped under more coercive forms of management and, therefore, management must seek to develop an employment relationship based on mutuality and employee commitment to elicit and exploit this greater effort. As the CIPD (2007a: 1) note, 'whatever controls or sanctions the organisation employs it will still lie within the employee's power to either give or withdraw discretionary behaviour. It is therefore discretionary behaviour that drives performance and makes the differences between organisations that are "OK" and those that are "great"'. As under control via 'responsible autonomy', the notion of employee empowerment is important here. Put simply, employee empowerment means giving workers greater opportunity to contribute to organisational success through more autonomous working and a voice in organisational decision-making. Empowerment, therefore, can partly be seen as an organisational attempt to increase employee commitment to the goals of the organisation by ceding a degree of managerial power. We return to the notion of empowerment in Chapter 10.

THE COMPONENTS OF INDIVIDUAL WORK PERFORMANCE

Implicit in the evolution of people management is the development of perspectives on how worker performance can be improved. A contemporary understanding of individual performance is provided by Boxall and Purcell (2003) who suggest that individual performance is a function of ability, motivation and opportunity or, alternatively, P = f (AMO). This performance equation is useful in identifying the key points at which HRM can intervene to improve individual performance. The following sections discuss each of these components in turn and how HRM can contribute to their development.

Ability

'Ability' denotes a range of individual attributes or competencies that affect a person's capability to carry out a specified job role, such as their knowledge, skill, attitude, behaviour, or, most likely, a combination of these factors. In one sense, this dimension of performance is associated with what people know and think, what they can do and how they behave because of how they feel (Le Doux, 1996, cited in Gibb, 2002). A range of factors can influence an individual's ability to perform a particular role, such as their personality, prior education and previous life and work experience, and a number of HRM activities are relevant to ensuring an organisation has a ready supply of adequately able labour. Most obviously, learning and development activities represent a key means by which workers can acquire required skills but equally important are those activities which should ensure that employees recruited into the organisations are those most capable of performing the required tasks or responding to the development opportunities provided. In respect of attitudes and behaviours, a positive psychological contract is important in developing the organisational citizenship behaviour central to maximising individual effectiveness. In Chapter 4, we discuss the changing requirements for many jobs and the 'abilities' being sought by employers (for example, recent years have seen an increasing emphasis placed on interpersonal skills in service sector and managerial employment).

Motivation

JASON FRIED
TED TALK

Motivation can be understood both as the individual's choice to perform a particular task, as well as the level and persistence of effort given to that task (Boxall and Purcell, 2003). The role of HRM in maximising employee motivation is to design jobs, practices, processes and an environment to stimulate workers to perform to their potential in a direction desired by the organisation. An understanding of motivational theory is useful in explaining the rationale behind specific HRM practices discussed in later chapters, and their value in motivating employees and unlocking their discretionary effort.

In broad terms, theories of motivation can be classified as either *content* or *process* theories. *Content theories* of motivation focus on the factors that motivate people, for example, the role of financial incentive, recognition, status, job satisfaction and achievement. The ideas of Taylor, Mayo, Maslow, Herzberg and McGregor constitute content theories of motivation as they are concerned with specific types of financial and non-financial reward, whether explicitly or implicitly. In contrast, *process theories* focus on the process of motivation and the internal decision-making mechanism by which individuals decide upon the level of effort to exert in a given situation.

Content theories of motivation are related to the economic notion of agency in the employment relationship where one party (the principal) delegates work to another (the agent). The 'principal–agent problem' is concerned with how the principal (the employer) can align the desires and goals of the agent (employee) with their own. Understood in this way, employee motivation to perform to the level desired by the employer is dependent on the extent to which business and employee interests are aligned. In order to motivate workers, therefore, HRM is concerned with reconciling the divergent interests and mixed motives of employers and employees and ensuring sufficient levels of mutuality in the relationship to maintain stability of performance. For example, increased motivation will result where an employee's 'need' for financial reward is matched or exceeded by that offered by the employer. In very broad terms, scientific management, human relations and neo-human relations highlight the three broad groups of motivators: economic reward, social relationships and intrinsic satisfaction. Agency theory tends to stress the value of monetary rewards in shaping employee behaviour at work in that it argues that extrinsic reward matters most to employees, albeit acknowledging that it is not the only motivator.

Expectancy theory is a process theory of motivation that focuses on the decision-making process involved in determining an individual's desire to perform. Georgopoulos et al. (1957) suggest that employee motivation to perform effectively depends on the individual's specific needs and the expectation of fulfilling those needs through productive behaviour. Vroom (1964) produced a systematic formulation of an expectancy theory of work motivation. He labelled the value a worker places on a particular outcome (e.g. an end-of-year bonus) its valence (V), and used the term 'subjective probability' for the expectation (E) that particular behaviour will lead to the achievement of that objective. Subsequently, the 'force' of motivation (F) is expressed as a function of expectancy and valence (or, $F = E \times V$). In short, expectancy theory suggests that people will be motivated to reach a goal if they believe in the worth of that goal and they can clearly understand what they need to do in order to achieve it.

Expectancy theory relates closely to the psychological contract in that ongoing motivation at work is affected by employee expectations and whether these are perceived as being met on an ongoing basis. Expectancy theory also stresses that firms cannot motivate employees unless they have rewards that they value. Setting employees impossible goals will more likely frustrate rather than motivate, and unrewarded goals may be ignored. Under this analysis, motivation to work is the result of a calculated, instrumental decision-making process that has significant implications for the design of reward systems and performance management. For example, if an ambitious employee is promised a promotion for achieving particular sales targets, they will be motivated to achieve this objective. If, however, they value financial reward over promotion, then the force of motivation might be weaker.

Opportunity

Finally, individual performance is partly a function of 'opportunity to succeed'. This suggests that performance does not take place in a vacuum: it is embedded in a wider organisational context. The 'opportunity' to perform effectively is provided by a working environment that provides the necessary support for employees to achieve their potential. This support consists of both the formal and informal structures of the firm, including factors such as the quality of available resources and channels of communication. In particular, 'opportunity' under 'high-commitment' HRM refers to the extent to which employees are empowered to contribute to organisational decision-making. We can also consider the degree of job influence and discretion afforded to a worker as providing the 'space' whereby they can exhibit the behaviours associated with high performance, such as organisational citizenship behaviour (Snape and Redman, 2010).

A CONCEPTUAL FRAMEWORK FOR UNDERSTANDING HOW HRM CAN CONTRIBUTE TO IMPROVED INDIVIDUAL PERFORMANCE

The sum of this discussion is that, in order to be effective, organisations should aim to hire, develop and retain 'motivated capability': not simply the right 'mix' of skills, knowledge and abilities required by the firm but people with the 'can do' and 'will do' attributes relevant to their particular job (Boxall and Purcell, 2003: 138). A recent model that seeks to explain how HRM can enhance organisational performance and

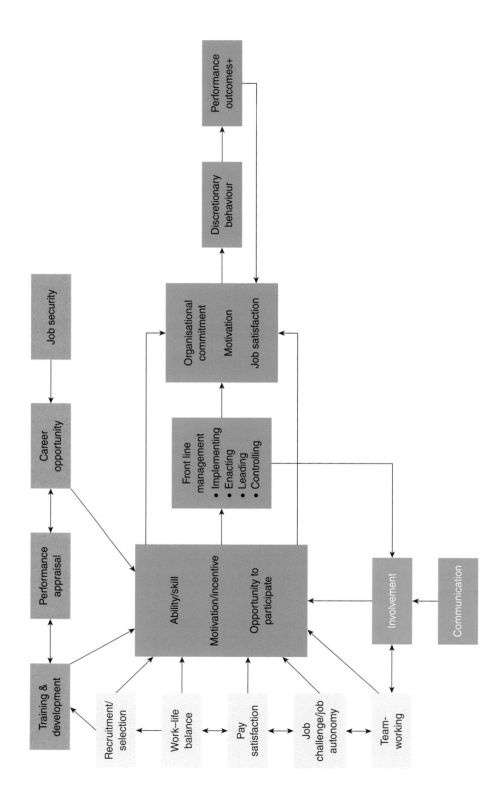

FIGURE 2.2 The Bath People and Performance Model (from J. Purcell, N. Kinnie, S. Hutchinson, B. Rayton and J. Swart (2003) *Understanding the People and Performance Link: Unlocking the Black Box*, reproduced with the permission of the publisher, the Chartered Institute of Personnel and Development, London, **www.cipd.co.uk**) 'This model was developed by Bath University for the CIPD.'

that builds upon the AMO formula is the Bath People and Performance Model (Purcell et al., 2003). This model (Figure 2.2) suggests that HR practices in themselves do not generate people-added value but can only create the building blocks of good performance (ability, motivation and opportunity). The degree to which these building blocks develop into improved individual performance is mediated by a number of factors. The most important of these are the activities and behaviour of line managers in implementing and enacting HR practices, which, in turn, determine the extent to which these practices translate into job satisfaction and employee commitment to the firm and its objectives. As noted above, satisfaction and commitment, in turn, elicit discretionary behaviour which is essential to improved individual and, subsequently, organisational performance. Moreover, Innocenti et al. (2011) find that employee trust in their line manager has an important mediating effect between HRM practices, particularly those aimed at motivating workers, and individual behaviour and attitudes.

In seeking to explain how HR can contribute to improving individual performance, this model emphasises the importance of implementing a set of integrated, mutually reinforcing HR practices which all managers in the firm should take responsibility for implementing and which are informed by the express needs of both the workforce and organisation itself. In one sense, this model represents where we are today in seeking to understand how best to manage people at work. However, whilst this model is one formulation of the link between people and performance, the degree to which such a link exists is a central theme of HRM research and is highly contentious. This is discussed in more detail in Chapter 3.

SUMMARY POINTS

- The challenge of demonstrating the value of HRM as a managerial activity that can impact positively on individual and organisational performance lies in the problematic nature of managing people at work.

- The employment relationship is multifaceted with economic, socio-political, contractual and psychological dimensions. HRM is ultimately concerned with the management of this relationship to elicit improved individual performance at work.

- The employment relationship is 'governed' by a range of rules and procedures for their enforcement. These rules can be explicit or implied and emanate from a wide range of sources including legislation, workplace custom and practice, and individual or collective negotiation between management and workers.

- The psychological contract represents the unwritten and often unexpressed expectations that an individual employee and the organisation hold of each other. This concept is important to understanding the role of HRM in eliciting employee commitment to the aims of the organisation and unlocking discretionary effort.

- Over time, management has devised a range of practices, tactics and strategies for managerial control and worker motivation that continue to constitute a range of influences on HRM practice and choices in how organisations manage different groups of workers.

- The theory and underpinning assumptions of scientific management (or Taylorism), human relations and neo-human relations are important in understanding and critiquing contemporary developments in people management.

- Individual work performance can be understood as a product of ability, motivation and opportunity. HRM plays a significant role in maximising individual performance through intervention in each of these three elements.

SELF-TEST QUESTIONS

1 What are the key dimensions of the employment relationship and how does each contribute to an understanding of the role of HRM in managing this relationship?

2 What do you understand by the term the 'psychological contract'?

3 It has been argued that the psychological contract has changed over recent years. How would you characterise these changes and why have they taken place?

4 Why have the principles of scientific management been criticised in respect of their impact on workers?

5 How does McGregor's Theory X and Theory Y of motivation relate to the historical evolution of people management?

6 What approaches can a work organisation adopt to control its workforce?

7 What are key differences between content and process theories of motivation?

8 What is meant by the 'opportunity' dimension of the AMO formula?

TEST YOURSELF

TEST YOURSELF

Want to know more about this chapter? Review what you have been learning by visiting:
https://edge.sagepub.com/wilton3e

- Print out or download the chapter summaries for quick revision
- Test yourself with multiple-choice questions
- Revise key terms with interactive flashcards

CASE STUDY

Control and motivation in a call centre environment

Buffalo Insurance is part of a larger insurance group and operates a medium-sized call centre in an urban area of North-West England. The area experiences relatively high levels of unemployment and these 'loose' local labour market conditions are typically favourable to employers. Whilst there are a number of other call centres in the area competing for workers, overall, such workplaces experience lower labour turnover in this region compared to other UK areas. The Buffalo Call Centre employs approximately 220 members of staff split into two groups depending on which types of customer service they are involved in: either the *sale of insurance policies* or *claims handling*. Previously, Buffalo senior management had attempted to train employees to be multi-skilled so they could work across the two departments. However, following a rise in customer complaints about claims handling

and a fall in sales, the division of departments was established with workers being trained in a limited range of skills and breadth of knowledge.

To all intents and purposes, the two departments operate completely independent of each other and employees interact only in the shared canteen. This division is reinforced through the office layout, with each department working on separate floors of a purpose-built facility. Each department is similarly organised into teams. Currently, there are 12 teams of eight employees in each department and each team is organised in *three* layers of seniority: *team leaders*, *senior CSRs (Customer Service Representatives)* and *junior CSRs*.

In both departments the senior and junior CSRs work entirely on the phones. However, the role of the team leader differs quite significantly in each. In broad terms, the role of the team leader in the sales department is to act as a 'motivator' for their team; leaders are often to be found walking between the desks, reminding individual CSRs of their sales targets and how close they are to achieving these targets. Team leaders also tell members how they are performing in relation to other teams and berate under-achievers. Some team leaders encourage CSRs to pin pictures above their monitor screens of items (such as cars and mobile phones) that they aspire to own to act as an incentive when pressing for sales.

Approximately 40 per cent of an individual team leader's salary and 25 per cent of a CSR's salary is dependent on the achievement of team targets and subsequently both team leaders and CSRs have a vested interest in maximising sales. This pay system occasionally leads to significant pressure being put on individuals both to attend work when ill (no allowance is given for team member absence) and to 'not let the side down' (particularly from the senior CSRs who have more to lose than their junior colleagues from poor team performance). Automatic call distribution means that CSRs are prompted to spend as little time on individual calls as possible, particularly where a sale does not seem likely, and to push hard for completion.

On the *sales floor* each team has a highly visible electronic 'sales board' upon which each employee's targets and achievements are displayed, which allows individual and team performances to be assessed and compared. At the end of each month, the most successful team is awarded, at the discretion of the sales manager, a sizeable additional bonus. The 'winning' team leader also wins an all-inclusive short 'city break'.

In the *claims handling department*, CSRs have to be more knowledgeable about the details of the insurance policies that the sales team are selling. They therefore spend more time than their sales colleagues in training to ensure that they are up-to-date in their product knowledge and that they develop the problem-solving skills necessary to handle complex claims. Senior and junior CSRs perform slightly different functions in handling claims. Junior colleagues act as the front line of customer service but are able to refer difficult queries to their more senior colleagues. The team leader in the claims department spends a considerable amount of time on the phone handling difficult calls, complaints or unusual queries. Many of the complaints emanate from customers who, upon making a claim, report having been mis-sold a product that does not serve their purposes.

The work of the junior CSRs in claims handling is incentivised on an individual basis: 20 per cent of their pay is dependent on a qualitative assessment of two aspects of their work. First, senior CSRs are asked to rate each junior on the basis of 'unnecessary referrals' (i.e. calls that the junior has referred but should have been able to handle themselves). Second, each CSR is subjected to 'silent listening' and call recording by the management team to assess the quality of customer service.

Senior CSRs are assessed purely on the basis of 'silent listening' and call monitoring via recording and playback. The performance of team leaders in the department is incentivised using six-monthly bonuses based both on an overall assessment of their team's performance and following a performance appraisal. On average, pay for claims handlers is reported to be 20 per cent lower than for the sales team.

A recent employee attitude survey conducted by Buffalo's HR department has found that job satisfaction, whilst still unacceptably low, is higher among workers in the claims handling department than in the sales department. It also shows, however, that a large minority of employees in the sales department report high levels of job satisfaction. The survey also found that employee turnover is one-third higher among the sales team.

Questions

1 Which form(s) of labour are both the CSRs and team leaders involved in at Buffalo?
2 What forms of control are evident at the Buffalo call centre?
3 How might the findings from the employee attitude survey be interpreted?
4 How would you describe the way in which each group of workers is motivated?
5 How can the motivational theory discussed in this chapter be applied in this case?

USEFUL READING

Journal articles

Cullinane, N. and Dundon, T. (2006) The psychological contract: A critical review, *International Journal of Management Reviews*, 8 (2): 113–29.

This article provides a critical overview of the concept of the psychological contract. It outlines the origins of the concept, a number of theoretical and empirical limitations and, despite these limitations, how it has become absorbed into mainstream HRM literature.

Grant, D. (1999) HRM, rhetoric and the psychological contract: A case of 'easier said than done',

The International Journal of Human Resource Management, 10 (2): 327–50.

This article illustrates the importance of employee expectations to the formulation of the psychological contract and how these expectations are influenced by management rhetoric. Drawing on case study research, the author reports on how a failure of management to match their 'promises' to reality can lead to a number of negative implications for organisational performance.

Guest, D. (2004) The psychology of the employment relationship: An analysis based on the psychological contract, *Applied Psychology*, 53(4): 541–55.

In this article, Guest outlines how the psychological contract provides a useful conceptual framework by which to understand the contemporary employment relationship and how a range of studies have adopted the psychological contract to study aspects of employment relations.

Macey, W. H. and Schneider, B. (2008) The meaning of employee engagement, *Industrial and Organizational Psychology*, 1: 3–30.

Drawing on a diverse range of literature, this article provides a useful review of the meaning of employee engagement, the variety of ways the notion has been conceptualised and defined and how at different times engagement has come to refer to psychological states, traits and behaviours, alongside their causes and consequences.

Payne, S. C., Culbertson, S. S., Lopez, Y. P., Boswell, W. R. and Bargee, E. J. (2015) Contract breach as a trigger for adjustment to the psychological contract during the first year of employment, *Journal of Occupational and Organizational Psychology*, 88 (1): 41–60.

This article provides a useful insight on the early development of the psychological contract for new employees by reporting on research to investigate how much and in what direction the psychological contract changed during the first year of employment and the extent to which change was a function of a psychological contract breach.

Thomas, D. C., Au, K. and Ravlin, E. C. (2003) Cultural variation and the psychological contract, *Journal of Organisational Behavior*, 24: 451–71.

This article stresses the influence of cultural differences in shaping perceptions of the psychological contract. In particular, it identifies both cognitive and motivational mechanisms through which the 'cultural profile' of individuals influences the formation of the psychological contract, perceptions of violation and responses to perceived violations.

Books, book chapters and reports

Grey, C. (2007) *A Very Short, Fairly Interesting and Reasonably Cheap Book about Studying Organisations*, London: Sage.

This book is a highly readable introduction to organisations and management. Of particular relevance to the discussion in this chapter are the chapters on 'Bureaucracy and scientific management' and 'Human relations theory and people management'.

Purcell, J., Kinnie, N., Hutchinson, S., Rayton, B. and Swart, J. (2003) *Understanding the People and Performance Link: Unlocking the Black Box*, London: CIPD.

This report presents findings of extensive research conducted in 18 organisations over a three-year period. Based on interviews with employees, this research led to the development of the People and Performance Model, which stresses the importance of mediating factors that transform HRM practices into improved individual and organisational performance.

FURTHER ONLINE READING

The following articles can be accessed for free on the book's companion website **https://edge.sagepub.com/wilton3e**:

Atkinson, C., Mallett, O. and Wapshott, R. (2014) 'You try to be a fair employer': Regulation and employment relationships in medium-sized firms, *International Small Business Journal*, 1–18.

Guest, D. (2002) Human resource management, corporate performance and employee wellbeing: Building the worker into HRM, *Journal of Industrial Relations*, 44 (3): 335–58.

Janssens, M., Sels, L. and van den Brande, I. (2003) Multiple types of psychological contracts: A six-cluster solution, *Human Relations*, 56 (11): 1349–78.

Shen, J. and Benson, J. (2014) When CSR is a social norm: How socially responsible human resource management affects employee work behavior, *Journal of Management*, 1–24.

Taylor, P., Mulvey, G., Hyman, J. and Bain, P. (2002) Work organization, control and the experience of work in call centres, *Work, Employment and Society*, 16 (1): 133–50.

This article (summarised in Box 2.4) reports on research to examine the relationship between work organisation and employee experience in a number of call centres. The authors challenge the optimistic accounts of positive worker experience in the quality-oriented workplaces, particularly in respect of worker control and discretion.

Want to know more about this chapter? Visit the companion website at: **https://edge.sagepub.com/wilton3e** to access practice questions, videos and selected journal articles to further enhance your study.

3

HRM, STRATEGY AND PERFORMANCE

**DEVELOPING
STRATEGIC HRM**

CHAPTER OBJECTIVES

- To outline key considerations in the formation of HR strategy

- To outline and critique competing models of HRM strategy formation: best fit, best practice and the resource-based view

- To outline evidence for the positive contribution HRM can make to organisational performance

- To highlight the controversies surrounding claims of the impact of best practice HRM on organisational performance.

INTRODUCTION

Having explored in the previous chapter how people management practices might act to exert influence over individual workers, whether through motivating them to improved performance, controlling behaviour in the workplace or through engendering commitment to the goals of the organisation, this chapter considers management decision-making regarding the overarching approach an organisation might take to the management of its workers. In particular, it explores the approaches a firm might take to determining an appropriate philosophy for people management and the strategic framework within which decisions over specific HR policy and practices are made.

Tyson (1995: 3) defines human resource strategy as 'a set of ideas, policies and practices which management adopt in order to achieve a people management objective'. In simple terms, therefore, HR strategy can be viewed as the overall approach and means an organisation adopts towards the management of workers, including both formal and informal policies and practices, and the 'critical goals' to be achieved through such an approach (Boxall and Purcell, 2003). From this perspective, the notion of strategy can be viewed both as *process* – the ways in which labour is managed – and *outcome* – the objectives of such an approach (for example, sustained competitive advantage or, simply, short-term organisational viability). It is important to make a distinction between the operational and strategic elements of HRM. The former represents the policies and practices adopted to manage workers whilst the latter refers to the underpinning philosophy behind these practices. Tyson (1995) suggests that there are distinctive philosophies of people management that are manifest in different HRM strategies. These philosophies result in different types of psychological contract between employer and employee, which constitute the reasons why people might work for a chosen organisation and determine their level of performance. If competitive advantage is understood as a set of organisational capabilities or resources leading to superior performance relative to that of its competitors (or in relation to prior performance) and we accept the consensus view that people can be just such a resource, then HR strategy is the process of defining and enacting appropriate systems that maximise people-added value.

The purpose of this chapter is to outline the process of HRM strategy formation and the different 'models' that firms can adopt in this process. It also seeks to outline the debate regarding the claims of a link between particular HRM practices (or configurations of practices) and improved organisational performance. As indicated in the previous chapter, a primary factor that is said to differentiate HRM from personnel management is the emphasis placed upon strategic integration and its key role in enhancing organisational performance. A central tenet of explanations of how HRM can increase people-added value is, therefore, the extent to which HRM systems are constructed in a coherent manner and the extent of congruity between HRM and organisational strategy. Whilst some texts make a distinction between HRM and strategic HRM (SHRM), Storey (2007: 59) argues that the prefix is not really required because the function is supposed to be inherently strategic when used in its specific, rather than generic, sense. In this chapter, therefore, no distinction is made between HRM and SHRM.

THE STRATEGY-MAKING PROCESS

Before we consider the different approaches an organisation might adopt in developing an appropriate HR strategy, it is important to note that the concept of strategy is far from straightforward and that there are a number of competing perspectives on the process of strategy formation. In particular, there are two key dimensions along which different approaches to strategy-making vary: first, the extent to which this process is deliberate and the result of long-term planning are emergent and subject to change; second, whether it is internally or externally focused and the extent to which elements of the organisational context are seen as influential. On the basis of these two dimensions, four broad schools of thought on strategy formation have evolved (Whittington, 2001):

The classical approach to strategy-making stresses the importance of a long-term, formal and analytical planning process, including a comprehensive assessment of both the external environment and internal resources of the firm. This assessment enables senior management to evaluate and choose from a range of strategic choices in order to maximise profit through matching internal plans to external context and then implementing these plans through line management. This approach tends to separate out operational practices (such as HRM or marketing) from higher-level strategy formation, the former simply being the means by which business strategy is enacted. This approach tends to be criticised for over-simplifying the strategy-making process and, given its long-term focus, being too inflexible to deal with a complex and changeable business context.

Alternatively, the evolutionary approach suggests that strategy should be formulated to respond to the unpredictability of a competitive environment by taking its lead from an organisation's immediate market context, and that rationally planned strategies can, at best, only deliver temporary advantage designed as they are to fit one particular set of circumstances.

The processual approach also stresses complexity and uncertainty but goes further than the evolutionary approach by emphasising that the process of strategy-making tends to be fragmented, adaptive and largely intuitive and, subsequently, strategy emerges incrementally rather than fully formed. This approach is underpinned by a view of the work organisation as consisting of numerous interest groups with conflicting goals that can influence strategic implementation and need to be taken into account in its formation. Therefore, the strategy formation process involves a range of contributors, in addition to senior management, and its focus is on the internal 'politics' of the firm. The processual perspective views strategy as emerging patterns of action that enable the achievement of business objectives, rather than as conscious, fully formed managerial plans.

Finally, the systems approach to strategy formation emphasises that organisations are able to plan ahead but that strategic choices are shaped not only by market context but also the cultural and institutional interests of broader society, including its political and legal framework. Therefore, the systems approach emphasises that strategic 'decision-makers are not detached, calculating individuals interacting in purely economic transactions but members of a community rooted in a densely interwoven social system' (Golding, 2007: 41). Here, the focus is on the wider external context of the firm beyond its competitive environment.

The significance of this brief discussion is that the central debates over the nature of strategy and strategy-making apply equally to HR strategy. Different approaches to HR strategy formation tend to reflect a particular resolution of the contentions outlined above, particularly the extent to which an internal or external focus is adopted and the significance given to particular environmental factors and organisational stakeholders.

DIMENSIONS IN HR STRATEGY FORMATION

Before addressing the three main theoretical approaches to the formation of HR strategy, it is important to consider some fundamental questions that underpin different HR strategies. Chapter 2 outlined the need for organisations to hire, develop and retain 'motivated capability'. Fundamental to HR strategy, therefore, are the assumptions that managers make about how worker effort can be directed in a productive manner – 'motivated' in the broadest sense of the word – and how required 'capability' can be realised. In addressing the means by which management can address these two fundamental issues we can draw on two useful typologies.

The first typology suggests that in formulating HR strategy managers have a broad choice between adopting a *control* or *commitment* (or resource-based) approach to the management of people (Walton, 1985). A control-based HR

HR BEST PRACTICE,
GOOGLE

strategy is predicated upon the close monitoring and management of employee role performance, employing both direct and bureaucratic forms of control, and tends to reflect a cost-minimisation business strategy where employees are viewed as a variable cost. Subsequently, managers are likely to follow an HR strategy and adopt practices as instruments to closely control all aspects of work in order to secure a high level of labour productivity, as under scientific management (see Chapter 2 for discussion). Required labour is typically sourced from the external labour market and management will invest little in workforce development. Alternatively, a commitment-based HR strategy is grounded in the view of human resources as an organisational asset, rather than cost. The emphasis here is on responsible autonomy and the quality of the employment relationship where worker 'control' and motivation are a product of a positive psychological contract and the internalisation of organisational values. Such an approach promotes employee commitment and loyalty, and motivation is derived from a sense of belonging, good line management relationships, high financial reward and job design that emphasises intrinsic job satisfaction and worker interest. The influence of human relations and neo-human relations (see Chapter 2) is apparent in such an approach. To a degree, these positions or philosophies represent two extremes on a continuum and an organisation is likely to adopt a mix of the two approaches or different approaches for different groups within the organisation.

Bamberger and Meshoulam (2000) offer an alternative typology that posits two main dimensions of HR strategy: 'locus of control' and 'acquisition and development'. In determining the *locus of control*, management must decide on the degree to which HR strategy is focused on monitoring employees' compliance with *process*-based standards, as opposed to developing a psychological contract that nurtures positive social relationships, encourages mutual trust and respect, and focuses on *outcomes*. These two alternatives clearly mirror those discussed above. The emphasis on processes prioritises close worker control to ensure that workers follow a pre-determined best way of carrying out a task, emphasising rules, procedures and supervision. Alternatively, a focus on outcomes implies a more 'hands-off' approach to managerial control where the concern is not with how a job gets done but more on the final product or service that is delivered. This is not to say that the process is unimportant; rather workers have greater discretion and are 'empowered' to determine the best course of action. *Acquisition and development* refers to the choice that management must make about where the organisation acquires its required human resources and the extent to which the HR strategy prioritises the development of internal human capital, through a 'strong' internal labour market (prioritising employee retention and investment in its employee development), or focuses on the external labour market and neglects employee retention in favour of deskilling jobs to enable the recruitment of low-cost workers. This is referred to as the 'make or buy' dimension of HR strategy. This discussion of the characteristics of organisational labour markets is developed in Chapter 4.

These models give us a sense of the range of considerations that management must take into account when formulating HR strategy or that can influence its emergence. However, it is important to stress that the repeated use of the word 'choice' in relation to strategy is perhaps a little misleading. Organisations are not likely to have an infinite range of options in the type of strategy they adopt, and different firms in different sectors have only 'degrees of freedom' in strategic decision-making (Boxall and Purcell, 2003: 35). In particular, the notion of 'strategic choice' might exaggerate the ability of managers to make decisions and take action independent of the environmental context (Colling, 1995). Thompson and McHugh (2002) suggest that a firm's choice of HR strategy is governed by variations in organisational form, size and scope, competitive pressures and the stability of labour markets, mediated by the extent to which workers have the power to resist particular strategies through collective (trade union) organisation. Even customer and supplier networks can act to constrain and exert influence over the HR choices that firms are able to make (Harney and Jordan, 2008). Subsequently, Kochan et al. (1984: 21, cited in Hyman, 1987: 29) suggest that 'strategic decisions can only occur when the parties have discretion over their decision: that is where environmental constraints do not severely curtail the parties' choice of alternatives'. As noted above, strategic decisions are not necessarily based on the output of rational calculation but can often emerge as a result of the dynamic interplay of organisations and their market contexts. Boxall and Purcell (2003) suggest therefore that managers do not make strategic decisions irrespective of external and internal factors and that strategy is likely to be both planned and emergent. In this sense, adopting a strategic approach to HRM is about more than having a formal, pre-determined 'strategy' and involves adopting a strategic orientation to deal with contingencies that may arise.

BOX 3.1
RESEARCH INSIGHT

Strategic choice in the hotel sector

Much discussion of approaches to HRM in the hotel sector focuses on the extent to which managerial decisions are unavoidably reactive and 'forced' by the often unpredictable nature of demand in the sector or whether management in the sector is able to act in a more strategic, longer-term manner. For HR professionals, the question is whether their role is essentially about 'being there' to cope with and respond to immediate operational problems or whether there is scope for strategic 'choice' in how HRM is configured and conducted.

Most of the UK hotel industry operates in a high-volume, low-cost product market and attempts to generate profits from increasing market share. Subsequently, the dominant 'model' of HR strategy is one of process-based control with a focus on the external labour market as a source of required labour. Such control is often achieved through the use of Taylorised working practices reflecting a high degree of specialisation, minimal training and a close monitoring of performance. Wage costs are minimised by the use of non-standard employment and sub-contracting.

Belying this apparent homogeneity of HR practice, a number of studies have, however, suggested that a more contingent perspective is necessary to fully understand approaches to

HRM in this highly diverse sector as employer responses to the pressures and tensions of the industry tend to be unpredictable (Hoque, 1999, 2000; Wilton, 2006). Many hotels in the UK have high levels of operational complexity, both serving highly variable product markets and competing in 'tight' labour markets, that tends to inform a 'hard' cost-minimisation 'strategy', a reactive, unitary management style and the instrumental use of labour. Better firms might adopt an ambiguous strategy attempting to balance the need for strict control over labour costs and the maintenance of standards. Hotels that operate in the more stable commercial or high-end marketplace tend to be in a better position to adopt a proactive strategy of quality enhancement and associated HRM practices and are likely to be compelled to do so by ever-rising customer expectations (Davidson et al., 2011). Therefore, whilst HR strategies that emphasise outcome-based control and a longer-term commitment to labour are very much the exception, environmental context is not all-powerful in determining approaches to HRM, and management in some hotels do act in a more 'strategic' manner.

Source: adapted from Wilton (2008). This discussion box can be used in conjunction with the case study at the end of this chapter.

PERSPECTIVES ON HR STRATEGY

Within the HRM literature, three broad theoretical perspectives on strategic HRM are often presented: best fit, best practice and the resource-based view (RBV). The following discussion outlines each of these three approaches and identifies the benefits and drawbacks associated with each.

Best fit

The 'best fit' or 'contingency' approach to HR strategy formation advocates a close match between HR and business strategy and the use of a set of HR policies and practices that are strategically integrated with each other and with the goals of the organisation. This approach suggests that business performance will improve when HR practices mutually reinforce the firm's approach to the marketplace. In other words, HR strategy should be inextricably linked to the 'formulation and implementation of strategic corporate and/or business objectives' (Forbrun et al., 1984: 34).

Schuler and Jackson (1987) suggest that the adoption and implementation of different competitive strategies requires a unique set of responses from workers, or 'needed role behaviours' (for example, teamworking, risk-taking, innovation and knowledge-sharing), and, consequently, a particular HR philosophy as well as strategy, policies, practices and processes to stimulate and reinforce this behaviour (Schuler, 1989, 1992). As an example, if a firm adopts a business strategy centred on high-quality service delivery, HR strategy, policies and practices need to encourage a concern for quality among employees by developing and rewarding such attitudes and behaviour. In essence, therefore, the best fit approach to HR strategy formation is concerned with matching employee role behaviour with the company's mission, values and goals through the vertical alignment of competitive and HR strategy. In this spirit, Boswell (2006) refers to the need for organisations to create a clear 'line of sight' to enable employees to understand not only the firm's strategic goals but also the behaviours and actions necessary to accomplish these goals. Some models of HR strategy formation depict the environment as a mediating factor in determining HRM strategies (for example, Bamberger and Philips, 1991) and rather than HR strategy formation being simply about matching HR strategy and business strategy, account must also be taken of the wider external context.

Further online reading This article introduces a matching model of HRM using a framework integrating competitive strategies and HRM based on the importance of considering 'needed role behaviours', cost constraints and market conditions when determining appropriate approaches to managing people.

Schuler, R. (1989) Strategic human resource management and industrial relations, *Human Relations*, 42 (2): 157–84.

Clearly, to promote specific behaviours requires a consistency in the message delivered through HR practices and processes and, therefore, the emphasis within a best fit approach is on the integration of all HRM activities in such a way that they are mutually supporting and contribute to the achievement of organisational objectives. Subsequently, in determining the best fit between business and HR strategy and HR policies and practices, consideration needs to be taken of both vertical integration (or external fit) – HR activities should be aligned both with competitive strategy and (under particular analyses) the organisation's stage of development and context – and horizontal integration (or internal fit) – the need to ensure that individual HR practices and policies are designed to fit with and support each other as a coherent set. This consistency of HR practices should be evident to the single employee, across all employees and over time. Properly formulated, HR strategy should emphasise the 'positive bundling' of complementary practices and the avoidance of 'deadly combinations' where the positive effects of different HR practices might be cancelled out.

A number of models that seek to connect HR and corporate strategy can be discerned in the literature advocating a broad best fit approach to the formation of HR strategy. *Competitive advantage models* of best fit stress the importance of directly connecting HR strategy to an organisation's approach to its market. Most notably, Schuler and Jackson (1987) draw on Porter's (1985) three key bases of competitive advantage – cost leadership, differentiation through quality and service and a focus on 'niche' markets – suggesting that these are best served by HR strategies focused on cost-reduction, quality enhancement and innovation respectively. The needed role behaviours that HR practices and policies should promote under each of these strategies are presented in Table 3.1.

An alternative perspective suggests that organisations should adopt an HR strategy appropriate for their stage of organisational development or life cycle. Golding (2007) proposes that two key questions for HR strategists here are: 'How can HR strategy secure and retain the type of human resources that are necessary for the organisation's continued viability as the market develops?', and, 'Which HR policies and practices are more likely to contribute to sustainable competitive advantage through an organisation's life cycle?' For example, in the start-up phase, the emphasis of HR

TABLE 3.1   *HR strategies and needed role behaviours*

Innovation strategy	Quality-enhancement strategy	Cost-reduction strategy
High degree of creative behaviour	Relatively predictable behaviour	Relatively predictable behaviours
Longer-term focus	More long-term or intermediate focus	Short-term focus
Relatively high levels of cooperative and interdependent behaviour	Modest amount of cooperative and interdependent behaviour	Primarily autonomous activity
Moderate concern for quality	High concern for quality	Modest concern for quality
Moderate concern for quantity of output	Modest concern for quantity of output	High concern for quantity of output
Equal degree of concern for process and results	High concern for process (how goods or services are made or delivered)	Primary concern for results
Greater degree of risk-taking	Low risk-taking activity	Low risk-taking activity
High tolerance of ambiguity and unpredictability	Commitment to the goals of the organisation	High concern for stability

Source: adapted from Schuler and Jackson, 1987

strategy might be on flexibility to foster entrepreneurialism and enable the firm to grow. During the growth stage, the emphasis would move to the development of more formal HR policies and procedures reflecting the increased size and complexity of the firm. In maturity, the focus may move to cost control and, in decline, to rationalisation with downsizing and redundancy implications.

There are a number of assumptions that underpin this contingency approach to HR strategy formation. First, best fit assumes an essentially unitarist relationship between management and labour in that both parties share common interests, principally the success of the organisation, and employees can therefore be expected to express the behaviours intended by management. As discussed in the previous chapter this is by no means guaranteed. Second, it presupposes that the most effective means of managing employees will vary from organisation to organisation. In other words, there is no one best way to manage labour. In broad terms, best fit also assumes that operational considerations such as HRM should be largely dictated by corporate strategy, reflecting the classical approach to strategy-making. However, this is not necessarily always the case and, therefore, the link between business and HR strategy can be assessed using a proactive–reactive continuum (Kydd and Oppenheim, 1990). In a reactive relationship, the HR function is subservient to corporate and business-level strategy, and organisational-level strategies ultimately determine HR policies and practices. A proactive relationship indicates that HR specialists contribute to higher-level strategic decision-making and competitive strategy is at least partly shaped by HR considerations. Alternatively, Torrington et al. (2008) identify five degrees of 'fit' between organisational strategy and HR strategy. In the *separation* model, there is no vertical integration or relationship between organisational and HR strategy. The *fit* model is consistent with the reactive and top-down relationship outlined above. The *dialogue* model indicates a two-way relationship where HR and organisational strategy inform one another (although this may be limited to passing information up from the HR function to senior management). The *holistic* model recognises employees as a key source of competitive advantage and not simply as the means by which to implement organisational strategy, suggesting a critical role for HR strategy in determining the strategic direction of the firm. Finally, the *HR-driven* model places HR as the key strategic decision-maker within the organisation.

CRITICISMS OF BEST FIT APPROACHES TO HRM

The idea that organisations can pick an HR strategy 'off the shelf' to fit its broadly defined approach to the market or stage in the organisational life cycle is subject to a number of criticisms. As noted above, in its 'purest' form, best fit largely casts the role of HRM as subservient to 'product market logic' and HR strategy as reactive to the competitive strategy of the firm. This is likely to diminish the extent to which HRM is able to fully contribute to competitive advantage in a proactive and innovative manner. In particular, it fails to adequately consider the internal context of the firm and the unique characteristics and practices that might provide a key source of competitive advantage. Moreover, the unitarist assumption that underpins best fit and the importance placed on aligning HRM practices with competitive strategy can lead to managerial practices that fail to consider employees' interests. This can result in the instrumental utilisation of labour to meet organisational objectives, reflective of hard HRM, and a failure to consider the goals and interests of all stakeholders.

Despite particular models acknowledging the influence of context on HR strategy formation, the best fit approach has also been criticised for failing to adequately reflect the complexity of the relationship between HR strategy, competitive strategy and organisational environment. In particular, an over-emphasis on external markets as the primary environmental concern may also lead to limited recognition of societal and cultural influences, for example, social norms, legal requirements and labour market requirements of different groups of workers. Detailed consideration of these issues is likely to be of particular importance for organisations operating across national cultures (Lucas et al., 2006).

Finally, in line with criticisms of the classical approach to strategy-making, the rigid approach of best fit is charged with failing to adequately stress the importance of 'dynamics' and the need for HR strategy to be flexible to meet changing environmental and competitive conditions. The underlying assumption that there can exist a logical, linear relationship between business-level strategy and HR strategy is questionable given the evidence that strategy formulation is often informal, politically charged and subject to complex contingency factors (Boxall and Purcell, 2003).

Whilst a tight fit might be appropriate in stable market conditions, for organisations competing in turbulent markets the benefits of best fit are likely to be relatively short-lived as the market changes. This highlights the strategic tension between performing in the present and preparing for the future that needs to be resolved when determining an appropriate strategy at any one point in time. In order to be effective, therefore, a matching approach to HR strategy formation is most useful when it recognises the complex nature of organisations, emphasising an evolving relationship between HRM strategy and business strategy with a strong focus on the continuous re-evaluation of both vertical and horizontal integration (Delery and Doty, 1996). A firm's strategic goals are also likely to be plural, combining both financial and operational dimensions, adding to the complexity of the relationship between organisational objectives and HR strategy. Subsequently, 'multiple fits' are likely to be required to ensure HR practices support all desired outcomes, and HR strategy should be segmented according to different groups of workers and business divisions, especially where there is an international dimension to a firm's activities.

Best practice

**BEST PRACTICE
HR TIPS**

In contrast to best fit, best practice or universalist HRM represents a prescriptive approach to people management. In essence, best practice HRM refers to the high-commitment or high-performance HRM outlined at the beginning of Chapter 1 (i.e. that which is distinct from personnel management). There are a number of perspectives on what constitutes best practice and whilst models tend to vary in their degree of prescription and their specific emphasis (for example, employee commitment, involvement in decision-making or the development of human capital), they tend to be based on the assumption that all firms, irrespective of competitive strategy and environment, will see performance improvements if they implement particular HR policies and practices in a strategic manner.

In broad terms, the best practice approach advocates enhancing knowledge, skills and competence through effective recruitment, selection and investment in training, motivating and generating desired employee behaviour through both financial and non-financial reward and sympathetic job design, and providing opportunities for employees to contribute to organisational decision-making. At the heart of best practice, therefore, is the strategic investment in human resources to generate a range of universally desirable organisational and employee outcomes including improved individual and organisational performance, greater organisational adaptability and cost-effectiveness, greater employee engagement and commitment, lower levels of employee absenteeism and turnover, and improved job satisfaction.

In other words, best practice HRM is argued by its advocates to play a key role in generating sustained competitive advantage. For example, one of the most commonly cited models of best practice HRM is presented by Pfeffer (1998), who argues that firms can generate competitive advantage by addressing seven areas of people management: employment security; selective hiring; self-managed teams or teamworking; high pay contingent on company performance; extensive training; reduction in status differences (between managers and workers); and information-sharing. Pfeffer's model stresses the importance to corporate performance of cooperative relationships between co-workers and between workers and managers based upon mutual gains for each party. The framework is underpinned by the premise that if all employees feel valued, are kept informed of organisational developments and receive investment in the form of training and development, they will perform to a high standard, especially where reward is contingent upon this performance.

Rather like best fit, a key theme in best practice HRM is the importance placed on the implementation of integrated and complementary bundles of HR practices (MacDuffie, 1995). This is exemplified in one of the most recent best practice models, that of the High Performance Work System (HPWS) (Appelbaum et al., 2000; Ashton and Sung, 2002) (Figure 3.1).

The central precept of the high performance workplace is that whilst the *individual* techniques it advocates are not new (they are common to many best practice models and to a degree represent 'common sense good practice', DTI, 2005), when used *together* each practice has a far more powerful effect on employee and organisational performance than when used independently. As such, HPWS emphasises coherent *clusters* or *bundles* of practices that, when in place, result in mutual gains for the employee and employer: high employee commitment and job satisfaction; low stress (as a result of employee performance resulting from the exercising of discretionary effort rather than compulsion); and enhanced organisational performance. This rationale lies at the heart of many models of best practice: that these bundles of practices create the reinforcing

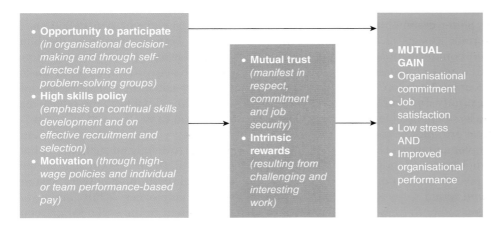

FIGURE 3.1 High Performance Work System Model (adapted from E. Appelbaum, T. Bailey, P. Berg and A. L. Kalleberg (eds), *Manufacturing Advantage: Why High Performance Work Systems Pay Off*. Copyright © 2000 by Cornell University. Used by permission of the publisher, Cornell University Press)

HPWS

conditions that support employee motivation, given that employees have the necessary knowledge and skills to perform their jobs effectively (Stavrou and Brewster, 2005).

ISSUES ASSOCIATED WITH BEST PRACTICE APPROACHES TO HRM

There are, however, significant questions to be addressed about the extent to which best practice models of HRM are universally applicable. Arguably, the most fundamental consideration regarding the appropriateness of HR practices and policies to a specific firm is affordability. The significant investment in employees advocated by many best practice models may not be affordable or justifiable in all firms, even within the same sector. Furthermore, models of best practice tend to disregard the influence of contextual factors on HR strategy, for example the organisation's strategic goals, differences in national context (Box 3.2) and industry sector. Arguably, best practice HRM is most applicable in sectors in which the exploitation of advanced technology and the creativity and ingenuity of the workforce are paramount to organisational success, or where firms compete on the basis of service or product quality. MacDuffie (1995) suggests that there are three organisational 'conditions' the presence of which might warrant the implementation of a best practice approach to HRM:

1 Employees possess knowledge and skills that managers lack.
2 Employees need to be motivated to apply those skills and knowledge through discretionary effort.
3 The organisation's business strategy can only be achieved when employees contribute such discretionary effort.

This clearly suggests that for some organisations (for example, those operating in highly competitive markets, with tight financial controls and low profit margins), best practice HRM is likely to be considered an expensive luxury. Ethical considerations aside, a cost-reduction, hard HRM may be more appropriate in firms, for example, employing low-skilled or unskilled workers, where Taylorised work design removes a reliance on discretionary effort and control-based strategies are adequately effective to satisfy organisational goals (Grugulis and Stoyanova, 2011).

Some commentators also argue that there are significant contradictions in certain aspects of best practice, most notably that between employee flexibility and commitment. As discussed in detail in the following chapter, organisational attempts to increase labour flexibility can often have negative implications for job security. Therefore, whilst best practice rhetoric advocates the utilisation of skills flexibility and employee-friendly forms of working-time flexibility, the reality may be less beneficial for employees. Therefore, in addition to the theoretical and practical critiques of best practice, there are also questions surrounding management's implementation of best practice HRM and its potential to deliver mutual gains to both employers and employees. For example, Danford et al. (2005) report that, despite a positive impact on organisational performance, High Performance Work Systems were found to be associated with limited gains for employees. Whilst employees reported both high skills and high levels of commitment to the organisation, competitive pressures on the firms led to job insecurity, stress and low participation in decision-making among workers. Similar findings were evident in a review of recent research (van de Voorde et al., 2012) that found evidence to support the 'mutual gains' perspective on HPWS when employee well-being was measured according to happiness and the quality of social relationships, but not when measured according

BOX 3.2
GLOBAL INSIGHT

Best practice HRM in international context

A specific criticism of universal formulations of HRM is that they fail to take account of differences in national context, specifically differences in employment law, cultural and societal norms, management style, power relationships, the extent of worker representation and wider economic systems. For example, national culture influences attitudes towards job and career mobility, acts to shape appropriate pay systems and determines the importance of hierarchies within organisational structures (Edwards and Rees, 2006) that can run counter to prescribed practices. 'High-commitment' HRM tends to denote Western best practice, often with specific applicability to the Anglo-Saxon traditions of the UK and USA. The extent to which highly prescriptive variants of HRM are appropriate outside of the Western business world is, therefore, questionable. Similarly, Eastern approaches to management might not have universal applicability in the West. For example, it has been pointed out that Japanese social and institutional structures have been important in facilitating particular practices in Japan, and which render them not readily transferable (Oliver et al., 1996). Delbridge et al. (2011: 486) suggest, therefore, a need in HRM research to give 'sufficient weight … to the historical, institutional, economic, and social contexts of … organizations and their practices'.

Critics of universalist management practice argue therefore that there is a need to recognise cultural divergence, for 'thinking locally' (Tayeb, 1992) and to adopt a contingent approach to strategy formation in acknowledgement of national differences, as reflective of a 'contextually based theory of human resources' (Paauwe, 2009). Some argue, however, that the importance of national culture is often overstated (Martin and Beaumont, 1998). The most recent international studies on the impact of geographic context on the relationship between HRM and improved business performance (Stavrou et al., 2010) suggest, however, that context is an important factor in mediating the impact of HRM. The authors suggest that 'no perfect, or universal set of best practices exists, rather a combination of "best practice" and "best fit" depending on bundle [of HRM practices] and region' (Stavrou et al., 2010: 950), suggesting some degree of adaptation, where what might be considered best practice HRM in one context is exported to another. The influence of national culture and institutions on HRM is discussed further in Chapter 5.

to its impact on health and well-being of employees (albeit as a parallel outcome to improved organisational performance, rather than a consequence).

RECONCILING BEST FIT AND BEST PRACTICE

Boxall and Purcell (2003) suggest that the debate between contingency and universal approaches to HRM can be reconciled by taking the perspective that there are some more effective ways of carrying out generic HR processes which all firms would be wise to follow (best practice) but that a surface layer of specific HR policies and practices tend to be heavily influenced by context and are therefore contingent (best fit). In other words, managers should focus on 'homegrown' rather than universal good practice.

A framework that strikes a balance between best fit and best practice is the Harvard model of HRM or the Map of HRM Territory (Beer et al., 1984) as shown in Figure 3.2. Reflecting a best fit perspective, Beer et al. (1984: 25) stress that 'an organisation's HRM policies and practices must fit with its strategy in its competitive environment and with the immediate business conditions that it faces'.

However, the model also recognises a wider range of situational factors that can be influential in HR strategy and a variety of stakeholders' interests that should be acknowledged. Beer et al. suggest, therefore, that business strategy should not become the dependent variable (as under a 'pure' best fit approach) and that, in the long run, creative HRM policies and practices can beneficially influence these factors. The stakeholder, developmental approach that the Harvard model takes to HRM allies it to the notion of soft HRM discussed in Chapter 1 (Boselie et al., 2009).

The resource-based view (RBV) of the firm

One of the central criticisms of the best fit approach to HR strategy formation is that it fails to sufficiently consider the internal context of the firm, particularly the unique characteristics and practices that might generate competitive advantage. Alternatively, the best practice approach is criticised for being overly prescriptive and failing to take account of organisational diversity. The resource-based view contrasts with both these perspectives by adopting a contingent approach to HR strategy formation, focusing on the internal organisational resources of the firm rather than its external context. Under this view, it is the array of a firm's resources, including its workforce, and their organisation that give a firm its uniqueness and which can be a significant source of sustainable competitive advantage. RBV suggests that any features of a firm with value-creating properties, for example, in-house knowledge or technology, culture, skilled personnel or networks, are considered as 'strategic assets' that can be a source of advantage if they are scarce, valuable, organisation-specific and difficult to imitate. In this sense, RBV recognises the HR function as a key 'strategic' player in developing

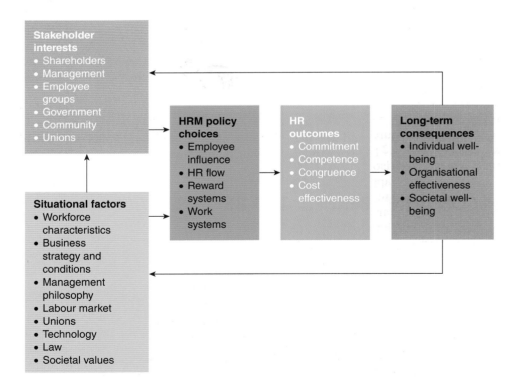

FIGURE 3.2 Harvard framework for HRM (Beer et al., 1984; reproduced with permission from the author, M. Beer)

sustainable competitive advantage, and employees as key assets in developing and maintaining this advantage (Wright et al., 2001).

There are two potential sources of competitive advantage in HRM that need to be considered. The first is *human capital advantage*, which is a function of the people a firm employs and can be generated through the recruitment and retention of 'valuable' people (for example, those with scarce skills). The second is *organisational (human) process advantage*, which is a function of the complex social processes that evolve in organisations over time and which can be difficult for competitors to imitate. HR strategy should therefore inform the design and implementation of HR practices and policies by which each form of advantage reinforces the other, creating an organisation constructed of 'better people with better processes'.

Under RBV, the question for management in strategy formation is how to develop valuable, firm-specific characteristics, exploit them for strategic purposes and create barriers to their 'imitation' or 'erosion' by competitors. The circumstances in which an organisation develops are unique and, by taking advantage of opportunities to learn and develop, firms can build up unique clusters or 'bundles' of human and technical resources over a period of time which constitute value-adding capabilities or competencies. 'Buying' this unique organisational learning can often be a reason for organisational takeovers (Aguilera and Dencker, 2004).

The focus under RBV is not only on developing employees' behaviour to align with competitive strategy but also on developing the skills, knowledge, attitudes and competencies that underpin desired behaviour to have a longer-term impact and which determine a firm's ability to learn faster than its rivals and to adapt its behaviour more productively. Work organisations are socially complex entities and successful firms develop strong clusters of human and social capital over time – reflecting the firm's particular historical learning or 'path dependency' – that can act as a natural barrier to imitation by competitors. Organisational routines and processes are deeply embedded in a firm's emergent 'social architecture' and can constitute valuable combinations of human and non-human resources that are difficult to replicate. Moreover, given the complex interaction between formal and informal, social and technical organisational processes and practices, there is an inevitable ambiguity about what elements of a firm contribute to improved performance. This ambiguity can again constitute a barrier to imitation.

Barney (1991, 1995) and Barney and Wright (1998) provide the VRIO framework to identify the characteristics – value, rarity, inimitability and organisation – that organisational resources should possess if they are to provide sustained competitive advantage. Table 3.2 presents the ways in which HRM might contribute to developing these characteristics.

The practical application of RBV hinges upon defining, developing and exploiting a company's core competencies (Hamel and Prahalad, 1994) or 'core capabilities' (Leonard, 1998), which are superior to those of their competitors. Leonard suggests that competitive advantage may arise from four groups of organisational attributes or core capabilities:

1 employee knowledge and skill
2 physical technical systems – both individual technical competence and that accumulated in physical systems built over time
3 managerial systems – a firm's systems of education, rewards and incentives which guide and monitor the accumulation of employee knowledge
4 values and norms – determine what kinds of knowledge are sought and nurtured and what kind of activities are tolerated and encouraged.

Both Leonard, and Hamel and Prahalad suggest firms are only partially idiosyncratic and there are many aspects of organisations which simply enable participation in an industry sector but do not make a firm distinctive or account for superior performance. These are referred to as 'table stakes' (Hamel and Prahalad, 1994) or 'enabling' capabilities (Leonard, 1998). These include the minimum HR policies and practices required by each firm to play the competitive 'game' and these will vary by sector and are dependent on the activities of competitor firms. For example, companies competing in a particular sector might tend to adopt particular reward strategies. The ubiquity of HR policies renders such practices 'table stakes', and it is only where organisations innovate and develop novel ways of doing things that HR practices can become a source of competitive advantage. It is also important to recognise that, given the inherent dynamism in organisational context, over the course of time core competencies that were once sources of competitive advantage become 'table stakes' as other organisations replicate these practices and processes, thus making them industry norms. As such, organisations must identify, implement and nurture new value-adding capabilities, whether these are people, practices or processes. Therefore, whilst the resource-based view advocates an internal focus, its effectiveness is inextricably linked to the external context of the firm and its approach to its market. Buller and McEvoy (2012: 53) stress, therefore, that the specific HRM practices and their configuration in a specific firm will be 'unique, complex and dynamic … because each firm's environment and requisite strategy are also unique, complex and dynamic'.

TABLE 3.2 *The VRIO framework and the role of HRM in developing competitive advantage*

Value	HRM should help the organisation to create value, both through improving efficiency and by explicitly meeting the needs of customers
Rarity	HRM should seek to develop and exploit rare characteristics of human resources
Inimitability	HRM should develop and nurture characteristics that cannot be easily imitated by competitors (for example, through creating and sustaining a particular culture)
Organisation	HRM should ensure that human resources are appropriately organised to add value and to capitalise on their rarity and inimitability with an emphasis on integrated, coherent systems of HR practices ('positive bundles') to enable employees to reach their potential

Further online reading This research article discusses research findings that show a positive and longitudinal relationship between a human resource management practices and performance in SMEs. In particular, it presents evidence to support the importance of 'bundling' of HRM practices and also the differential impact of different areas of HRM practice and different measures of performance.

Sheehan, M. (2014) Human resource management and performance: Evidence from small and medium-sized firms, *International Small Business Journal*, 32 (5): 545–70.

In relation to employees, RBV suggests that sustained competitive advantage stems from both tacit and explicit knowledge within the firm and the ability of employees to learn faster than their rivals. Therefore, organisations would appear to gain more added-value from adopting RBV where the context is unpredictable; for example, in the high technology sector where new product development and the ingenuity of its employees are central to sustained competitive advantage, and the emphasis is on creating the future, rather than reacting to it.

BOX 3.3
RESEARCH INSIGHT

RBV, strategic HRM and small firms

In Chapter 1 it was suggested that much research into HRM practice tends to focus on larger employers and an inference within management literature that SMEs should simply learn from the practices of these large firms (Cassell et al., 2002). However, research into HRM in SMEs tends to suggest that such equivalence is not always useful because SMEs, unlike larger competitors, are typically characterised by HRM practices that are ad hoc, informal and driven by a need to minimise cost and they are unlikely to have a professional HR 'presence' (Cardon and Stevens, 2004). In an international review of the research on HRM practice in small firms, Mayson and Barrett (2006) find that this informality, and an accompanying lack of strategic or long-term thinking in HR decision-making, presents a problem for the growth and competitiveness of smaller firms because it fails to recognise the value of employees, and fails to realise the benefits of adopting complementary HR practices. In other words, despite informality of HRM in small firms being associated with the positive characteristics of flexibility and adaptability, for growing firms this can yield 'diminishing returns'.

Mayson and Barrett (2006) suggest, therefore, that rather than adopting HR practices that are convenient, easy to use, minimise cost and respond to pressing needs of their market or labour market context (as in the case of the hotel sector in Box 3.1), a more strategic approach to HRM can be a source of sustained competitive advantage (see also, Ait Razouk, 2011), not least in fast-growing and entrepreneurial businesses. Sheehan (2014), for instance, presents data that show significant positive returns to human resource investment among SMEs, in terms of profitability, innovation and lower labour turnover, and that the contribution of this investment increases over time. Moreover, whilst individual practices can be beneficial to a number of measures of performance, the data show both the value of implementing practices as bundles and that training and development has the most significant association across a range of measures.

Mayson and Barrett (2006) argue that the resource-based view is particularly applicable to small firms, especially where the 'unique or idiosyncratic nature of employees' skills and knowledge, management structure, and skills and orientations of the owner–manager are likely to be difficult to imitate by competitors' (2004: 452). Therefore, focusing on developing these unique resources through the development of vertically and horizontally integrated HR practices, rather than adopting a short-term concern for their cost, may contribute not only to the long-term survival of such firms, but also their growth. However, not all research is so positive about the impact of more formal, strategic HRM in SMEs. De Grip and Sieben (2009) report that the adoption of more advanced HR systems, whilst delivering better wages for workers, has no impact on productivity. Moreover, Storey et al. (2010) suggest a link between greater formality of HRM in SMEs and lower self-reported job quality among employees.

ISSUES ASSOCIATED WITH RBV

Again, however, RBV is subject to a number of criticisms. For example, McKenna and Beech (2008) suggest that such an approach tends to be too introspective, giving insufficient attention to the socio-political and economic context in which the organisation operates. Moreover, not all work organisations seek competitive advantage, and therefore the terminology of RBV is perhaps not appropriate when referring to, for example, public sector organisations. Indeed, as indicated above, RBV is likely to have most resonance in firms where innovation is central to competitive advantage and market context is particularly unpredictable and complex.

Similar to best practice models, RBV can also inadequately recognise the pluralism of work organisations and the potential for conflict between employers and

Ethical decision-making in HRM strategy formation

Winstanley and Woodall (2000) suggest that ethical issues have been of marginal significance to the unfolding academic debates around human resource management and HR strategy. Whilst some models of HRM (for example, Beer et al., 1984) suggest that, alongside organisational performance, HRM should be concerned with promoting individual and societal well-being, Winstanley and Woodall argue that the contemporary focus of HRM on strategic fit and best practice ignores this ethical dimension by focusing solely on HRM's contribution to organisational performance and shareholder value. Although employee well-being might be a by-product of best practice, it is not typically a primary consideration and, therefore, organisational commitment to ethical practices (or practices that have the side effect of employee well-being) is likely to waver according to changing market conditions and their perceived impact on the bottom line. A particular problem of best practice approaches to HRM is that they are underpinned with an assumption of unitarism that tends to ignore the tension in the employment relationship, assuming that the different interests of employer and employee can be managed to pursue organisationally defined goals. However, it is often the case that organisations fail to address the needs of all stakeholders and the needs of employees are more likely to be subjugated to those of shareholders.

Winstanley and Woodall (2000) propose, however, that the ethical treatment of workers is worthy of equal consideration as performance objectives when designing HRM strategies and policies. They cite a number of reasons for this: first, they argue that there are 'business' reasons for paying attention to ethics, particularly enhanced reputation with customers and improved employee motivation and retention; second, they point out that the 'profit motive', which drives many instrumental approaches to the use of labour, is not appropriate for many not-for-profit work organisations such as the public sector and charities (although the need for efficiency and productivity remain); finally, they refer to the argument that the 'wider economic system and ultimately the business organisations within it exist to service human and societal needs rather than the opposite' (2000: 6). This last argument is perhaps the most compelling and raises some important questions about whether work organisations should exist and operate purely to serve their shareholders or should be accountable to a wider range of social stakeholders, including those people that work within them.

As the importance of corporate social responsibility to both company image and financial performance has developed over the past two decades, there is a strong argument that the most effective way of creating an ethical or socially responsible firm is not simply by imposing a CSR agenda from above but to actively involve employees at all levels in developing this agenda, to ensure both a deeply held concern for ethical behaviour and employees' buy-in and commitment to it (Maclagan, 2007; Nord and Riggs Fuller, 2009). Indeed, in seeking to ensure that employees behave in an ethical manner in carrying out their work, it would seem sensible to begin by treating them as legitimate stakeholders worthy of ethical treatment themselves.

employees. As such, whilst a firm's human resources might possess the capabilities necessary for competitive advantage, they might not choose to exercise them fully in pursuit of organisational objectives. Proctor and Rowlinson (2011) suggest that, in the debate over how HRM can result in improved organisational performance, RBV presents problems of both operationalisation and generalisation across firms.

 Further online reading This article explores the challenges facing strategic HRM and potential directions for future study and practice. In particular, it explores the mediating factors that might link HRM and firm performance.

Becker, B. E. and Huselid, M. A. (2006) Strategic human resource management: Where do we go from here?, *Journal of Management*, 32 (6): 898–925.

ORGANISATIONAL PERFORMANCE

A key element of the process of strategy formation is the monitoring and evaluation of its effectiveness. Under classical approaches to strategy formation, the predominant measure of organisational performance and effective strategic decision-making is financial outcomes, such as productivity or profitability (Prowse and Prowse, 2010). However, increasingly, organisations adopt a wider range of indicators to assess the impact of policy change or the need for such change, partly to acknowledge the role and contribution of employees in achieving high performance. One model that provides a range of potential measures of organisational performance is the balanced scorecard (Kaplan and Norton, 1992). The balanced scorecard is based on the premise that for an organisation to be successful it must satisfy the requirements of key stakeholders, principally investors, customers and employees. Kaplan and Norton suggest, therefore, that firms should identify objectives, measures, targets and initiatives to address four key elements of business performance (Box 3.5).

BOX 3.5
UNDERSTAND

The balanced scorecard

1 *Financial perspective* – 'To succeed financially, how should we appear to our shareholders?'

   Measures of performance include profitability, growth, market share, risk or cashflow.

2 *Customer perspective* – 'To achieve our vision, how should we appear to our customers?'

   Measures of performance reflect the 'value' proposition that underpins the organisation's position in the market and might refer to service or product quality, price, customer relationships, customer retention and loyalty and response times.

3 *Internal business process perspective* – 'To satisfy our shareholders and customers, what business processes must we excel at?'

This perspective might refer to the efficiency of 'formal' business processes reflected in productivity, process response speed and wastage or 'informal' processes that are important to performance, such as knowledge-sharing among employees.

4 *Learning and growth (or people) perspective* – 'To achieve our vision, how will we sustain our ability to change and improve?'

   Assessing performance under this perspective requires an evaluation of the extent to which employees are motivated, equipped with the competencies and subject to work processes that enable them to do their jobs effectively now and in the future.

Box 3.6 provides an example of the balanced scorecard concept in practice. Barclays – the global financial service provider – use their scorecard to connect the firm's mission to become 'the "Go-To" bank for all our stakeholders' to broad objectives or outcomes across five dimensions of performance.

The balanced scorecard recognises the impact that key HR activities can have on business performance, by emphasising the importance of providing employees with opportunities for personal development and growth, mechanisms to allow

BOX 3.6
HRM IN PRACTICE

Balanced scorecard for Barclays

The Barclays' Balanced Scorecard provides an example of how such a scorecard seeks to connect a set of diverse organizational concerns with specific outcomes that help the firm to establish its success to addressing each area. Barclays uses the Balanced Scorecard to set out a series of five areas of priority which it seeks to address over a five-year period. The firm refers to these priorities as the 5Cs: Customer & Client; Colleague; Citizenship; Conduct; Company. The scorecard provides guidance for employees at Barclays to understand the strategic priorities of the firm as well as what success in each area looks like at a strategic level. This company scorecard is thus translated into the strategic planning in each business unit and function, as well as the setting of individual performance objectives, linking activity at a local and individual level to that of the wider organization.

The table below shows how the dimensions of performance associated with the '5Cs' translates into specific desired outcomes. Against each of these outcome statements are specific organisational commitments to which stakeholders can hold the firm accountable, associated metrics and strategic initiatives to achieve these aims. As such, the scorecard presents a statement of intent across a range of activities and targets, progress towards which can

BARCLAYS BALANCE SCORECARD

be objectively measured and on which the firm will report.

As an example of how these statements might then influence actual practice, in the area of 'Colleagues' (that aspect of the scorecard concerned with people management). Barclays has set itself two broad commitments:

1 'Sustained engagement of colleagues' score (from 74 per cent in 2013 to 87–91 per cent in 2018).
2 Percentage of women in senior leadership (from 21 per cent in 2013 to 26 per cent in 2018).

To achieve these objectives the company has implemented a series of strategic initiatives, including:

- Launching company 'Purpose and Values', to be embedded into all HR processes including recruitment, promotion and performance management.
- Developing leaders through the Barclays Leadership Academy and Barclays Global Curriculum.
- Implementing a global diversity and inclusion plan to create a more diverse talent pipeline.

From the above example it is clear to see how a firm might take a 'headline' set of objectives at a strategic level and cascade these through the firm so that connection between individual, group and corporate level activity and performance are linked.

Source: www.home.barclays/about-barclays/balanced-score card.html (accessed 28 September 2015)

Balanced scorecard	Outcome statement
Customer and client	To be the 'Go-To' bank for their customers and clients
Colleague	Barclays colleagues (employees) are fully engaged To 'create a diverse and inclusive environment where colleagues can fulfill their potential'
Citizenship	Barclays 'positively impact the communities in which we operate'
Conduct	Barclays' 'products and services are designed and distributed to meet clients' needs' To act with integrity in everything the firm does
Company	To 'create sustainable returns above the cost of equity' Understand and effectively manage risk, and continuously improve control

employees to contribute to the achievement of organisational objectives and measures to assess employee attitudes, behaviours, knowledge and skill. The balanced scorecard is often presented as a set of broad strategic objectives in each area that connect to specific operational targets and performance indicators to which departments and individuals contribute.

HRM AND PERFORMANCE

The acid test of HRM strategies, policies and practices is the extent to which they impact upon organisational performance. As noted in Chapter 1, the claims made for the positive impact of HRM on business performance have been a primary factor in raising the profile of the HR function, and Kinnie et al. (2006: 27) note that 'research into the links between HR policy and organisational performance has become one of the main areas, some would say the main area, of study in the field of human resource management'.

Much of the initial interest in HRM in the 1980s resulted from the so-called 'excellence movement' which posited that innovative HR practices as part of a wider recognition of the importance of people to competitive advantage were characteristic of highly successful blue chip organisations (for example, Peters and Waterman, 1982). This was reinforced by the emerging literature on the positive impact of Japanese work organisation on employee commitment, loyalty, discretionary effort and, ultimately, continuous performance improvement. Since then numerous studies have sought to provide evidence of a link between HRM and organisational performance. CIPD (2006a) suggest that there are strong theoretical grounds to suggest a link between HRM and performance, and a number of studies show a clear connection between HRM and organisational performance or 'health', particularly those investigating the impact of best practice configurations (see Table 3.3). These studies suggest that particular combinations of HRM practices can give quantifiable improvements in organisational performance when measured in a variety of different ways.

Further online reading This article places the notion of the HPWS in a broader context of the development of a high skill national economy and sets out the core features of such systems with a particular focus on the managerial 'governance' processes. In particular, it stresses the importance of developing high levels of employee performance in understanding how intended practices connect to employee responses and organisational outcomes.

Boxall, P. and Macky, K. (2007) High-performance work systems and organisational performance: Bridging theory and practice, *Asia Pacific Journal of Human Resources*, 45: 261–70.

However, despite the substantial and growing volume of research dedicated to establishing a clear people–performance link, Purcell (1999: 26) suggests that the high-commitment HRM discourse has led to 'extravagant claims on the universal applicability of the best practice model, implying one recipe for successful HR activity', despite insufficient evidence for the strength of these claims. Critique of the positive claims made in many studies tends to focus on a number of perceived flaws in the research itself. Marchington and Wilkinson (2005: 72) suggest that it is difficult to draw generalised conclusions from these studies because of methodological differences between them, such as the nature and type of HR practices examined, the measures of performance used, the sector in which the studies have taken place, the methods of data collection and the respondents from whom information has been sought. Similarly, Becker and Gerhart (1996) note variation in what constitutes best practice across different studies and the number of HR practices included in the analyses, and Hyde et al. (2006) and Proctor and Rowlinson (2011) report little consistency in the results of the empirical studies that claim an HRM–performance link. Wall and Wood (2005) suggest that whilst studies examining the HRM–performance link open up a 'promising line of enquiry', the methodological limitations of these studies render claims of decisive proof of this link premature, and more large-scale, long-term research is required (Boselie et al., 2005).

TABLE 3.3 *Examples of studies reporting a link between HRM and performance*

Author(s)	Principal findings
Arthur, J. B. (1994)	In a study of US steel 'minimills' those who adopted a 'commitment' HR strategy had higher productivity, lower wastage rates and lower employee turnover than those who adopted 'control' strategies
Huselid (1995)	High-performance work practices had a significant impact on both employee outcomes (labour turnover and productivity) and long-term measures of corporate financial performance
MacDuffie (1995)	The adoption of team-based work systems and high-commitment HR practices (including performance-related pay and extensive training) within flexible production systems, were associated with improved productivity
Delaney and Huselid (1996)	HRM practices, such as employee participation in decision-making, incentivised pay systems and selective hiring, were positively associated with perceived firm performance
Koch and McGrath (1996)	'Positive and significant' effects on labour productivity were shown for organisations that utilise more sophisticated HR planning, recruitment and selection strategies in a sample of US business units
Welbourne and Andrews (1996)	Correlation shown between company survival and the value placed on employees by the firm and the implementation of employee reward based on organisational performance
Youndt et al. (1996)	HR systems focused on human capital enhancement were directly and positively related to multiple dimensions of operational performance, including employee productivity, in the context of high-quality manufacturing strategies
Huselid et al. (1997)	The effective delivery of high-quality operational and strategic HRM activities enhanced firm performance
Ichniowski et al. (1997)	In a study of US steel production lines, the use of a set of innovative work practices (including incentive pay, teamworking, flexible job assignments, employment security and training) achieve substantially higher levels of productivity than lines with the more traditional approach (characterised by narrow job definitions, strict work rules and hourly pay with close supervision)
Patterson et al. (1997)	Key elements of best practice HRM (acquisition and development of skilled people, job design stressing autonomy and flexible problem-solving) associated with improved productivity and profitability
Becker and Huselid (1998)	Implementation of bundles of high-performance HRM practices were positively correlated with differences in organisational performance, using a variety of measures. including profit, market value and staff turnover
Appelbaum et al. (2000)	Implementation of practices associated with High Performance Work Systems resulted in both higher employee job satisfaction and firm performance

Author(s)	Principal findings
Hutchinson et al. (2000)	Where implemented in a coherent and complete manner, bundles of HRM practices were positively associated with superior organisational performance but their impact was mediated by a range of factors, particularly environmental context
Black and Lynch (2001)	Implementation of progressive people management practices, including greater employee voice in decision-making, profit-sharing and incentive-based compensation, associated with higher labour productivity
Batt (2002)	Quit rates were lower and sales growth higher in a sample of US call centres where HR practices emphasised high skills, employee participation in decision-making and teamworking
West et al. (2002)	Strong associations between HR practices, specifically the extensiveness and sophistication of appraisals, training and teamworking, and patient mortality in a sample of 61 acute hospitals in England
Ahmad and Schroeder (2003)	Implementation of Pfeffer's best practice model of HRM resulted in increased organisational performance, mediated by employee commitment (generalisable across countries and industries)
Gould-Williams (2003)	Bundles of HR practices (reflecting Pfeffer's model) led to superior organisational performance in public service organisations in the UK
Laursen and Foss (2003)	'Complementarities' or integrated bundles of HRM practices positively associated with levels of innovative performance
Wright et al. (2003)	HR practices and the resultant organisational commitment significantly related to operational measures of performance (including quality and productivity), lower operating cost and increased profitability
Sels et al. (2006)	Greater use of high-performance work practices associated with increased productivity among small businesses in Belgium and an overall positive effect of profitability, despite increased labour costs
Subramony (2009)	In exploring the results of 65 studies, the author reports that bundles of HRM practices aimed at enhancing specific workforce characteristics – employee empowerment, motivation and skill levels – impact on various business outcomes to a greater extent than their constituent individual practices
Heffernan et al. (2009)	Drawing on a survey of 2,000 high-performing firms in Ireland, a positive relationship was found between HRM systems, the creation of a climate of creativity, innovation, collaboration and learning and, ultimately, organisational performance
Jones et al. (2010)	Evidence drawn from a Finnish retail firm, collected from a wide range of data sources, suggests that a 'participatory' HRM environment is associated with improved business performance
Katou and Budhwar (2010)	Among a sample of Greek manufacturing firms, organisational performance was seen to depend on effective HRM policies to develop the required skills, attitudes and behaviours commensurate with business strategy
Chand (2010)	A model of HRM that approximates to best practice was found to be positively correlated with improved service quality, customer satisfaction and firm performance in a study of hotels in India
Elorza et al. (2011)	In a study of Spanish SMEs, evidence indicated that an HRM system that sought to address the three dimensions of the AMO formula resulted in higher employee commitment, lower absenteeism and higher productivity
Sheehan (2014)	Positive impact of HRM practices, both individually and as bundles, on firm performance, measured in a variety of ways, among a sample of small to medium-sized enterprises

Further online reading This article critically discusses the research that claims to have established a link between HRM practices and firm performance. It proposes a number of ways forward in seeking to establish such a link more conclusively.

Wall, T. D. and Wood, S. J. (2005) The romance of human resource management and business performance, and the case for big science, *Human Relations*, 58: 429–62.

Fleetwood and Hesketh (2006) also argue that despite a large volume of empirical research claiming to establish an HRM–performance link, it remains under-theorised and the literature fails to establish adequately what this link (often referred to as the 'black box') might be and, subsequently, how certain we can be of these findings. In seeking to better theorise the HRM–performance link, a number of studies have sought to explore not only the specific HRM practices associated with improved firm performance, but also the process or mechanisms by which they do so (Chow, 2012). For instance, Boselie et al. (2001) find that employee satisfaction, motivation, retention, social climate and employee involvement in decision-making are all important mediators in the relationship between HR practices and firm performance. Chow (2012) suggests that organisational culture and

---

BOX 3.7
RESEARCH INSIGHT

HPWS in practice

Danford et al. (2005) conducted research into two major UK multinationals in the aerospace industry to explore the incidence of HR practices associated with High Performance Work Systems and the employment outcomes associated with these practices. In particular, they sought to explore the claims of Appelbaum et al. (2000) that clusters of HR practices associated with HPWS result in greater employee commitment, job security, trust, job satisfaction and employee participation, and lower levels of workplace stress.

The research found a high incidence of practices associated with HPWS in the two employers, including semi-autonomous teamworking, job rotation, **on-the-job** and **off-the-job learning**, formal consultation practices and employee share ownership. The research also found that employee commitment to the firms was high, evident in the high proportion of workers who felt loyal to their employer, were proud to tell people who they worked for and were willing to work harder to help their firm succeed. Moreover, at both firms, a high proportion of both manual and non-manual workers reported an increase in skill,

responsibilities and flexibility as a result of HPW practices.

However, the research found that the mutual gains associated with HPWS were limited, despite a significant adherence to HPWS principles. For example, despite extensive mechanisms for participation in decision-making, a large majority of employees felt that they were hardly ever, or never, consulted over future plans for the workplace or on staffing levels and redundancies. Workers also reported an increase in workload and work-related stress associated with greater pace and intensity of work. In the context of widespread recent job losses at both firms and the wider aerospace industry and despite a relatively high proportion of highly qualified workers feeling their jobs were safe, a very low proportion of manual workers at both firms felt their jobs were secure. Subsequently, whilst HPW practices might contribute to improved organisational performance, the consequences for workers were more variable. The researchers suggest that these limited mutual gains result from the necessity for managers to incessantly cut costs to remain competitive in an intense global marketplace. These demands result in a downward pressure on costs and lead times, alongside a need to improve quality.

effective implementation by line managers are key factors in translating high-performance HRM practices into improved performance. Similarly, implementation of practices at the local level, and employee perception of these practices, were found to be important predictors of intra-firm performance variance in large firms (van de Voorde et al., 2010).

Guest et al. (2003) and Batt and Banerjee (2012) raise, however, the problem of causality in establishing a link between HRM and performance and Guest et al. pose the question of whether HRM leads to improved organisational performance or, alternatively, whether better performing and, therefore, wealthier organisations are more likely to be able to invest in high-commitment approaches. In relation to the HPWS literature, Danford et al. (2005) suggest that much of the evidence to date for the positive impact of HPWS on workers is contradicted by studies which show that such practices tend to be associated with downsizing (Osterman, 2000), a worsening of employees' work–life balance (White et al., 2003), and a failure to adequately consider employees' views. They attribute problems with HPWS not necessarily to the practices that are advocated but to the inadequate or partial implementation of the bundles of practices that lead to one-sided gains. As Ramsay et al. (2000) argue, advocates of high-performance best practice models should take care when proclaiming the assumption that everyone gains from managerial innovation. Paauwe (2009) suggests the need for a more balanced approach to HRM research that pays greater attention to the concerns and well-being of employees, as part of both a broader appreciation of the stakeholders of HRM and a multi-dimensional perspective on performance beyond the dominant managerialist focus on profitability, efficiency and so on.

SUMMARY POINTS

COMPETITIVE STRATEGY

- The HR strategy-making process is complex and its relationship with wider business strategy formation and the dynamic context in which many firms operate is problematic.

- Organisations can take a number of different approaches to HR strategy formation, reflecting the differing extents to which an internal or external focus is adopted and the significance given to particular environmental factors and organisational stakeholders.

- The elevated status of the HR function over recent years has much to do with claims of a link between best practice HRM and organisational performance, reflecting the view that firms should configure HR policies and practices regardless of organisational contingencies.

- Alternatively, a best fit approach stresses the importance of matching HRM strategy and practices with the firm's competitive strategy and the context in which it operates.

- An increasingly influential perspective on HR strategy formation is the resource-based view, which suggests that rather than subjugate HRM to competitive strategy and organisational environment, or adopt prescribed practices, businesses should adopt practices that help them to exploit their unique, inimitable internal resources to produce people-added value.

- A significant body of research claims to support the link between best practice HRM and organisational performance based on a range of indicators including profitability, productivity, organisational survival and staff turnover.

- Equally, however, sceptics argue both that the claims of this research are exaggerated and that the link between HRM and performance is inadequately theorised.

SELF-TEST QUESTIONS

1   What are the dimensions along which the four contrasting perspectives on strategy formation differ?

2   What are key differences between control and commitment strategies utilised in the management of people? What employment practices do they tend to be associated with?

3   Explain the 'make' or 'buy' element of HRM strategy formation.

4   Briefly outline the underpinning philosophy of the best fit approach to HRM.

5   What are the key elements that tend to constitute best practice approaches to HRM?

6   What does the VRIO framework suggest is the role of HRM in contributing to sustained competitive advantage under the resource-based view?

7   What are key criticisms levelled at the many studies claiming a clear link between HRM and organisational performance?

TEST YOURSELF

TEST YOURSELF

Want to know more about this chapter? Review what you have been learning by visiting:
https://edge.sagepub.com/wilton3e

● Print out or download the chapter summaries for quick revision

● Test yourself with multiple-choice questions

● Revise key terms with interactive flashcards

CASE STUDY

Approaches to HRM in the hotel sector

The Mercury Hotel

As outlined in Box 3.1, HRM in the hotel sector is strongly influenced by the variability of customer demand, particularly in those establishments serving the seasonal tourism industry. The hotel sector is also heavily dependent on the external labour market as staff turnover is typically high and, therefore, a ready supply of both skilled and unskilled labour is often required to meet customer demand. This high turnover often results in problems of skills shortages in key operational areas, such as among waiting or kitchen staff. However, as Box 3.1 suggests, whilst the hotel industry context often acts to constrain managers' choice in HRM strategy, policies and practices, evidence suggests a variety of approaches to staffing and managing the workforce. The following case studies contrast the employment practices adopted in two 'similar' hotels operating in the same city.

The Mercury is a franchise establishment of a large US hotel chain. It is 4-star rated and mainly serves the commercial market, catering for business clients, including the hosting of conferences and seminars. It has almost 300 guestrooms, is located in the centre of a large UK city and directly employs more than 200 members of staff. Two-thirds of employees are employed full-time on 39-hour contracts with working patterns varying from week to week. Any hours worked beyond this are paid as overtime. The remaining third of employees are part-time (up to 25 hours per week). This structure appears to provide a balance between the need for flexibility in predictably busier periods throughout the year and as cover for short-term increases in demand. Management also make extensive use of return staff, mainly students who live in the area during term time or holiday periods to provide a further element of labour flexibility. Such employees are seen as a ready supply of trained labour but who have no claim to minimum hours, who can be shed with limited notice and who are most willing to work unsociable hours. Further, shortfalls in labour supply are met either by contracted or non-contracted casuals or by increasing permanent staff hours at short notice. Contracted casual employees are 'on-call' so that managers can demand that employees work 'as and when required', principally being used for functions such as wedding receptions. Management seek to minimise the potentially damaging effects on service quality by minimising the use of non-contracted casuals and ensuring that, whilst providing a degree of flexibility, most employees are a 'known quantity' and have received at least some training. Moreover, rather than relying solely on numerical forms of flexibility (altering staffing levels in line with demand) The Mercury attempts to meet the challenge of variable demand by training members of staff across a range of different areas; a rudimentary form of skills flexibility. The approach to staffing adopted at The Mercury appears to reflect a compromise between the need for labour flexibility and employee stability, with management attempting not to overly manipulate employee hours simply to meet the direct needs of the organisation.

In terms of employee involvement and communication, formal departmental meetings are held weekly for staff to discuss operational aspects of the hotel. Open staff meetings are held monthly, for both permanent and casual employees, the purpose of which is twofold. First, to pass on information on the performance of the hotel and, second, to act as a forum in which staff can ask questions directly of the general manager. Most importantly, a consultative committee, known as the 'Employee Forum', meets monthly and is chaired by the general and personnel manager. This forum is comprised of elected staff representatives from each department and allows staff to raise issues related to their working environment. It is also where recognition is passed on to staff for good service and employee representatives vote for 'employee of the month'.

Staff turnover is not considered a significant problem at The Mercury within the context of the industry. Management report an annual turnover rate of approximately 35 per cent (the company target is 25 per cent). However, the HR manager claims to do a significant amount of work to reduce this figure, particularly in the recruitment process. For example, department managers receive training in interviewing techniques and ensure that candidates are made aware of the idiosyncrasies and demands of the industry. In addition, staff retention is addressed through ensuring staff development is offered to 'capable' employees and good performance is rewarded and recognised. Turnover is mainly attributed to mistakes made in recruitment and candidates' misconceptions about the industry generally, specifically pay levels and working hours. This is reflected in the fact that departing staff rarely leave to work in other hotels, unless at a higher level, but tend to leave the industry. Absenteeism at The Mercury is considered acceptable. The personnel manager has suggested that an environment in which 'teamworking' has evolved at the hotel and a degree of peer pressure discourages unnecessary absence.

Management at The Mercury consider skills shortages to be a huge problem in the industry, compounded by the highly competitive nature of the local labour market where it is felt that during most of the year employees will be able to leave employment at one hotel and gain employment 'five minutes down the road' in another. The HR manager claims that the inherent skills shortages in the local labour market are not felt as keenly in this hotel as in others because their image as a 'good employer' is useful in attracting and retaining staff. The package of benefits available to staff are described, by management, as 'exceptional' and are claimed to be central in recruiting and retaining high-quality, skilled employees and reducing problems of skills shortages, albeit within the context of moderate levels of staff turnover.

The Luna Hotel

The Luna is located approximately one mile from The Mercury and is part of a large UK hotel chain. It has 201 rooms, is also 4-star rated and employs 128 members of staff. The hotel was subject to a takeover six months ago and is in a period of transition, not least in the way in which HRM is conducted. Again, two-thirds of the workforce is full-time, but the current management are seeking to significantly reduce this figure, having claimed they are overstaffed with permanent employees. They plan not to replace leavers in certain departments or to replace them by offering workers flexible contracts; they express a willingness to rely heavily on casuals and agency staff to plug gaps in the workforce. Even permanent employees are now employed on significantly less favourable terms than prior to the takeover. Management claimed that this provides 'working-time flexibility' for both employer and employee. The number of hours and shift patterns are adjusted and planned on a weekly basis according to business levels, with both parties able to request more or less hours in a given period. No attempt has been made to train employees across a range of tasks to provide greater skills flexibility nor is there any intention to do so, given the stated desire to keep training costs to a minimum.

Employee communication at The Luna is predominantly one-way. General manager's briefings are held for all staff every quarter to inform them about organisational and establishment strategy and managerial decisions. Managerial meetings and communication between heads of department and employees are limited to one-to-one meetings as and when required, instigated by either party, usually to deal with grievance or disciplinary issues. There is no dedicated structure or schedule to these intra-departmental meetings although some departments impose some formality by holding five-minute 'chats' between departmental heads and staff every month. Other departmental managers prefer employees to approach heads of department to raise issues. These one-to-one meetings appear to be the only means of upward communication. There is no other provision for employee consultation, suggestion or participation in decision-making. It appears that even the general manager's briefing is merely a communicative device with little provision for employee feedback.

The hotel has experienced high levels of labour turnover since the takeover, some of which is likely to be as a result of the upheaval caused. Regardless, labour turnover is reported to be both problematic and beneficial at The Luna, depending on the staff involved. On the one hand, employee turnover is considered undesirable because of the costs involved in recruiting new members of staff, especially skilled workers such as chefs and maintenance workers. On the other hand, however, employee turnover is considered a source of employment flexibility and 'natural wastage' of staff viewed as positive, especially where poor performing staff are concerned. The general manager claims that the large labour market in which the hotel operates means that staff are readily available, albeit often lacking required skills. Management copes with this apparent skills shortage by minimising reliance on particular skills or providing rudimentary training. The high level of staff turnover often requires management to adopt expedient approaches to filling vacancies, even in important frontline operational (for example, waiting and front of house) or skilled areas of work. As the HR and training manager suggest, 'When someone leaves just like that … you're in a hole and you have to get someone in, then you can't afford to wait a week of so for references to come through, when you've got a job to fill. You take a chance.'

Questions

1 In what ways does the environmental context of the two hotels constrain or present opportunities for strategic choice?

2 Why do you think the two hotels have contrasting approaches to the management of their employees?

3 From a best fit perspective, which of these hotels would appear to have best tailored its HR policies and practices to its competitive strategy?

4 What elements of best practice HRM has The Mercury Hotel adopted and why might it have done so?

5 Drawing on the resource-based view, what elements of people resources could be exploited to create competitive advantage in the hotel industry?

USEFUL READING

Journal articles

Barney, J. B. and Wright, P. M. (1998) On becoming a strategic partner: The role of human resources in gaining competitive advantage, *Human Resource Management*, 37 (1): 31–46.

This article explores how the resource-based view of the firm and the VRIO framework can help to achieve competitive advantage through more effective use of human resources.

Boselie, P., Dietz, G. and Boon, C. (2005) Commonalities and contradictions in HRM and performance research, *Human Resource Management Journal*, 15 (3): 67–94.

This article provides an extensive and very useful review of empirical research articles on the linkage between HRM and performance published in academic journals between the mid-1990s and 2003.

Buller, P. F. and McEvoy, G. M. (2012) Strategy, human resource management and performance: Sharpening line of sight, *Human Resource Management Review*, 22: 43–56.

This article develops earlier work on the importance of employees understanding both of the goals of the firm and the behaviours necessary to accomplish these goals, and presents a model that seeks to illustrate how HRM practices can effectively align organisational, group and individual factors with a firm's strategy.

Guest, D., Michie, J., Conway, N. and Sheehan, M. (2003) Human resource management and corporate performance in the UK, *British Journal of Industrial Relations*, 41 (2): 291–314.

This article presents research findings from an extensive study of UK firms to explore HRM and performance using a range of subjective and objective measures of performance.

Lengnick-Hall, M. L., Lengnick-Hall, C. A, Andrade, L. S. and Drake, B. (2009) Strategic human resource management: The evolution of the field, *Human Resource Management Review*, 19: 64–85.

This article provides a comprehensive account of the chronological evolution of the field of strategic HRM by exploring seven key themes that have characterised debate and research in this area of study. In doing so, it develops much of the discussion presented in this chapter, including the problems of measuring HRM outcomes and methodological challenges in its study.

Prowse, P. and Prowse, J. (2009) Whatever happened to human resource management performance?, *International Journal of Productivity and Performance Management*, 59 (2): 145–62.

This article covers much the same ground as this chapter but develops the discussion around the evidence of a link between HRM and performance. It also provides a useful recap of some of the discussion in Chapter 1 on the evolution of HRM.

Books, book chapters and reports

Appelbaum, E., Bailey, T., Berg, P. and Kalleberg, A. (2000) *Manufacturing Advantage: Why High Performance Work Systems Pay Off*, Ithaca, NY: Cornell University Press.

This book provides an introduction to High Performance Work Systems and presents research evidence that suggests that specific 'bundles' of HRM practices can result in improved individual and organisational performance.

Boxall, P. and Purcell, J. (2011) *Strategy and Human Resource Management* (3rd edn), Basingstoke: Palgrave Macmillan.

This book provides a comprehensive discussion of the theoretical and practical issues surrounding HRM, strategy and organisational performance.

FURTHER ONLINE READING

The following articles can be accessed for free on the book's companion website **https://edge.sagepub.com/wilton3e**:

Becker, B. E. and Huselid, M. A. (2006) Strategic human resource management: Where do we go from here? *Journal of Management*, 32 (6): 898–925.

Boxall, P. and Macky, K. (2007) High-performance work systems and organisational performance: Bridging theory and practice, *Asia Pacific Journal of Human Resources*, 45: 261–70.

Schuler, R. (1989) Strategic human resource management and industrial relations, *Human Relations*, 42 (2): 157–84.

Sheehan, M. (2014) Human resource management and performance: Evidence from small and medium-sized firms, *International Small Business Journal*, 32 (5): 545–70.

Wall, T. D. and Wood, S. J. (2005) The romance of human resource management and business performance, and the case for big science, *Human Relations*, 58: 429–62.

Wright, P. M., Dunford, B. B and Snell, S. A (2001) Human resources and the resource based view of the firm, *Journal of Management*, 2: 701–21.

Want to know more about this chapter? Visit the companion website at: **https://edge.sagepub.com/wilton3e** to access practice questions, videos and selected journal articles to further enhance your study.

4

THE LABOUR MARKET CONTEXT OF HRM

CHAPTER OBJECTIVES

- To define internal and external labour markets

- To outline the role of HRM as the interface between an organisation and its labour markets

- To identify the changing labour market conditions under which contemporary organisations operate

- To critically evaluate the implications for HRM of the knowledge economy

- To outline how labour market trends are impacting upon how organisations utilise labour and how HRM practices are driving labour market change

- To outline the various ways that firms can respond to different labour market conditions

- To outline the notion of organisational flexibility and how various forms of flexible working practices impact on both employers and employees

APPROACHES
TO LABOUR
FLEXIBILITY

INTRODUCTION

The purpose of this chapter is to provide an assessment of the contemporary labour market context of HRM and the impact of current trends in labour supply and demand on the practices associated with people management. Labour market context inevitably shapes the approach a firm takes to HRM and is one of the key factors in determining an organisation's 'degrees of freedom' in HR strategic formation (Boxall and Purcell, 2003). In particular, the extent to which the demand for labour, both in absolute numbers and in the availability of particular skills, knowledge and expertise, can be met by the available supply is a key constraint on the range of choices that an organisation has when determining an appropriate HR strategy. Over recent years developments in the economic, political, technological and social spheres have significantly altered the composition of the labour supply and the types of labour required by contemporary firms. Subsequently, an understanding of the labour market context of work organisations is essential to appreciate the challenges faced by HRM in the twenty-first century.

This chapter begins by defining what is meant by internal and external labour markets before discussing in detail a range of developments in organisations, the economy and society that have impacted on the supply and demand for labour. With this in mind, it takes a relatively broad perspective on the notion of labour markets and discusses a range of developments that are taking place inside and outside of organisations that impact both on how organisations engage and utilise labour and how individuals experience work and employment. In particular, this chapter discusses the increasingly flexible ways in which organisations employ workers and the implications of flexible working for employees. The chapter concludes with a discussion of 'quality of working life' as an indication of how contemporary developments in work, employment and HRM have impacted upon the experience of individuals in work organisations. As in the previous chapters, the aim is to provide a number of reference points by which we can understand the role of HRM in the contemporary organisation and how it can provide the strategic means to enable firms to cope with uncertainty and add value to business processes. It provides part of the backdrop by which the following chapters on HRM practices and issues can be better understood.

WHAT IS A LABOUR MARKET?

A labour market can be understood as the mechanism through which human labour is bought and sold as a commodity and the means by which labour demand (the number and type of available jobs) is matched with labour supply (the number and type of available workers). As such, the labour market constitutes the systematic relationship that exists between workers and work organisations. In order to achieve its strategic objectives, a fundamental concern for an organisation is to ensure that it has the right people with the right skills, knowledge and attributes in the appropriate positions. The previous chapter outlined two competing approaches a firm might adopt to acquiring required labour, referred to as 'make' or 'buy' strategies. The former refers to configuring HRM activities to fulfil a firm's human resource requirements by developing existing employees and retaining their services over the long term. The latter refers to a strategy of recruiting required labour from outside the firm as and when needed. A 'make' strategy is, therefore, internally focused whilst a 'buy' strategy is externally focused.

The internal labour market

The internal labour market refers to that which exists within a single organisation and represents its internal supply or stock of labour. In its broadest sense, the internal labour market is the mechanism by which existing employees are attributed to particular roles within a firm. The specific characteristics of an organisation's internal labour market are reflective of a number of HR policy emphases, for example, the level of investment in employee training and development, the availability of career development opportunities and the extent to which employee retention and job security are prioritised. Contextual factors, particularly the types of skills, knowledge and attributes required, also act to shape the type of internal labour market that exists within a firm. Depending on its characteristics, an internal labour market can fulfil a number of functions for an organisation. For example, in seeking to retain employees the internal labour market can act as a source of motivation and contribute to a positive psychological contract, through the provision of training and development, career opportunities and good terms and conditions of employment. The operation of the internal labour market can also be understood as a device for managerial control through a process of stratification, division and the detailed allocation of roles and responsibilities. This reflects the bureaucratic approach to control outlined in Chapter 2.

Whilst all organisations have internal labour markets of some description, the 'classical model' of internal labour markets (Grimshaw et al., 2008) is typically associated with a very structured approach to managing the workforce. This includes limiting access to the labour market from outside the firm (often restricted to specific entry points, generally at lower levels) and recruiting to more senior jobs by internal promotion or transfer, often accompanied by in-house training. Such internal structures are notable characteristics of larger organisations that benefit from employee retention and promote the long service of employees both by providing internal opportunities for career advancement and through reducing their ability to move to another firm (for example, through limiting the development of transferable skills in favour of those related to firm-specific technologies and processes).

When understood in this specific sense, then, it is apparent that many firms do not operate a 'strong' internal labour market, especially in the extent to which they offer employees the opportunity to develop careers. In organisations characterised by 'weak' internal labour markets, there are limited prospects for career progression, labour turnover is considered unproblematic or unavoidable, little emphasis is placed on learning and development and the focus is on the external labour market as the principal source of workers, skills and expertise. Alternatively, some organisations will have a strong internal labour market for some employees, for example those that have scarce skills or expertise, but not others.

Whilst the 'classical model' is often a characteristic of best practice models of HRM – as represented by the emphasis on employment security and high levels of investment in training – there is evidence to suggest an erosion of access to strong internal labour markets as a result of increased global competition and market uncertainty. For example, Grimshaw et al. (2008) report that in a series of case study organisations recent changes to organisational context associated with economic restructuring have resulted in a dismantling of the traditional labour market as organisations 'delayer' and 'downsize', resulting in a dislocation of workers from traditional career paths and limited access to training and development. The implications of organisational change and attrition of the internal labour market for careers are further examined in Chapter 12. An example of how the restructuring of internal labour markets in response to wider organisational change can impact on employees is provided in Box 4.1.

The external labour market

For a particular organisation, the external labour market represents its external supply or available stock of labour. Both the types of labour that the firm requires and the potential pool of workers available are determined by the industry sector in which the firm operates, its central activities, its location, size and scope and its competitive and HR strategies. In reality, as labour is not a homogeneous commodity, the external labour market can be understood as a multitude of individual labour markets. For example, a firm's external labour market can be local, regional, national or international and many larger organisations will operate in all of these depending on the type of labour sought and its relative scarcity. For example, a multinational corporation seeking to recruit a senior executive will most likely look to recruit internationally in order to provide themselves with the widest possible pool of applicants, given that the skills, knowledge and experience for such a position are likely to be in relatively short supply and such workers are often highly mobile. Alternatively, for middle management positions the organisation may focus on the national labour market, and to fill administrative or lower-skilled positions may focus on the local labour market. National and local labour markets vary significantly depending on the extent to which governments intervene in the buying and selling of labour through, for example, employment protection legislation, the industry sectors that the labour market supplies and the composition of the labour supply itself. Some of these factors that shape the operation of labour markets and, subsequently, HRM in a particular national context are outlined in Chapter 5.

There is a wide variety of ways in which labour markets can be segmented aside from geography. Labour markets can be analysed according to the distribution of skills, knowledge, educational achievement and occupational group. We can also view the labour market as being segmented according to worker characteristics such as age, gender, ethnicity, disability, cultural background or attitude. It is

BOX 4.1
HRM IN PRACTICE

Women and the labour market in Brazil

Alongside Brazil's transformation into a global economic power following a process of economic liberalisation starting in the late 1980s (Rocha, 2009), a range of forces is acting to alter the composition of the country's labour market. Brazil, therefore, provides a useful insight into how a combination of social and economic change can alter both the supply of and demand for labour.

The Economist (2012) reports that tight labour market conditions creating a shortage of available talent to Brazilian firms are leading employees to look beyond their prejudices, creating more job opportunities for women at all levels of the occupational structure. They report that in 1960, just 17 per cent of women in Brazil worked outside the home, among the lowest levels in Latin America. In 2012, two-thirds of women had jobs, one of the highest proportions in the region, an increase partly due to a fall in average family sizes. Furthermore, large rises in the country's minimum wage, an increase in formal jobs and increasing access to traditionally male-dominated jobs have decreased the gender pay gap for poorly educated men and women. For instance, not-for-profit

schemes designed to increase the employment opportunities for women have resulted in increasing numbers of women developing the required skills and accessing jobs in plumbing, bricklaying and house painting.

These changes in the operation of the Brazilian labour market are being both driven and reinforced by rising educational levels, particularly among women. For example, women constitute 60 per cent of recent university graduates, with many such graduates describing themselves as 'very ambitious'. These developments represent a challenge to entrenched views about the division of labour between men and women in Brazilian society, with an increasing female presence at middle and senior managerial levels, both in the private and public sectors. *The Economist* notes, however, that whilst the labour market in Brazil continues to expand, providing greater opportunities for both men and women, traditional attitudes are relatively easy to ignore. If, however, economic slowdown results in greater competition for jobs, the increasing presence of women in managerial and professional roles might lead to greater overt prejudice and resistance from men who find their opportunities diminished.

important to understand such labour market diversity, not least because the labour market experiences of different groups of workers and their access to particular jobs are likely to be very different, either because of legitimate sources of labour market 'power' accorded by differential human capital, or illegitimate prejudice or entrenched disadvantage. Worker characteristics are also important in assessing the most appropriate way of managing different groups of employees. For example, different occupational groups tend to display different perspectives on motivation, control and career development. Professionals, for example, tend towards career progression outside the confines of a specific organisation, favour autonomous working without close supervision and often adopt a more altruistic orientation to work (Woodall and Winstanley, 1998). Similarly, different generations of workers might display different orientations to work, including different attitudes to 'risk' and uncertainty (Tissen et al., 2010), the extent of employee loyalty to their employer and the value placed on different elements of working life, for example, work–life balance or high pay (Cox and Parkinson, 2003). Understanding labour market diversity is also important because having a workforce that is representative of the society from which it is drawn and ensuring that labour is recruited from the widest possible pool of talent can represent a significant source of competitive advantage. The management of diversity and equality is addressed in Chapter 11.

UNEMPLOYMENT AND UNDEREMPLOYMENT

It is important to acknowledge that unemployed labour represents an integral element of the external labour market. People who are out of work but actively seeking employment, particularly those unemployed over a long period, tell us a great deal about the operation of the labour market. The unemployed or surplus labour in any given market plays a role in determining the cost of employed labour, the terms under which it is engaged and the extent of industrial conflict. For example, where there is a large surplus of labour then this will result in greater competition for jobs, a downward pressure on wages and conditions and a lowered likelihood of employees 'rocking the boat'. Where particular groups are disproportionately affected by unemployment for reasons unconnected to their capabilities (for example, reflecting social group disadvantage) this reflects a distortion of the 'proper' working of the labour market.

There are a number of types of unemployment. Structural unemployment exists where there is a fundamental mismatch between the supply and demand for labour. For example, where demand for particular types of skill is low those in possession of these skills are at a relatively greater risk of being out of work. As such, unemployment can result from a lack of employability and can be addressed through workers retraining or moving to areas where their skills are in greater demand. Unemployment can also be cyclical in that it reflects business or economic cycles. For example, in times of recession the demand for labour in general falls and unemployment rises. Therefore, being out of work is not necessarily associated with one's long-term employability, rather it is linked to a short-term decline in the overall demand for labour. Finally, frictional unemployment reflects a temporary mismatch in the demand and supply of labour that is always present in an economy. For example, a worker might be unemployed whilst looking for a particular type of job but is yet to identify an appropriate existing vacancy. Therefore, even where supply broadly meets the demand for labour, unemployment temporarily persists.

As an adjunct to discussion of unemployment, we also need consider the labour market phenomenon of underemployment. Whilst often used to refer to employment in jobs that do not require the incumbent's possessed skills and knowledge

BOX 4.2
RESEARCH INSIGHT

The informal sector of employment

Much of the discussion in this chapter presupposes employment in the formal economy – that is, work that is both paid and formally declared to the state for the purposes of taxation and coverage by employment protection legislation. However, Jütting and Laiglesia (2009) estimate that the majority (1.8 billion) of the global workforce of 3 billion is in the informal sector and, in many economies, the informal sector is larger than the formal sector (Dibben and Williams, 2012). As such, whilst most workers around the world are paid (either waged or through some type of informal self-employment), even where the work can be considered legal (unlike in the criminal economy) such employment is not subject to the same governance as that in the formal economy. Williams (2014) refers to a range of terms used to described such employment such as 'atypical', 'cash-in-hand', 'hidden', 'irregular', 'non-visible', 'shadow', 'undeclared', 'underground' and 'unregulated'.

In the context of the discussion of HRM, therefore, it is important to recognise the array of meanings attached to the notion of work and employment and to be mindful of the varied context within work is 'managed' and experienced. Even within the EU the extent of informal work is perhaps surprising, varying from almost one-third of GDP in Bulgaria to 8.1 per cent in Luxembourg, suggesting that even among advanced economies the extent and economic contribution of the informal sector is significant (Williams, 2014).

(for example, graduate underemployment is often used to refer to employment of graduates in jobs that do not require the holder to possess a degree), more often it is used to refer to those workers who are in employment but who work fewer hours than they want. In the UK, whilst unemployment has fallen markedly since the economic downturn of 2008, the number of underemployed workers had increased by 47 per cent to 3.1 million workers in 2012 – an increase of almost 1 million (ONS, 2012b).

Further online reading This article provides a useful overview of the concept and extent of the informal economy. It provides a useful counterweight to the discussions of labour markets that present all work as paid and subject to regulatory provision.

Williams, C. (2014) Out of the shadows: A classification of economies by the size and character of their informal sector, *Work, Employment and Society*, 28 (5): 735–53.

LABOUR MARKET CHANGE

The composition of both the labour 'supply' (the availability of labour in general and of specific 'types' of workers) and the 'demand' for labour (the amount and type of labour sought by employers) is influenced by a wide range of factors. Table 4.1 details a number of factors that impact on the supply and demand for labour.

From Table 4.1 it is clear that the labour market is shaped by a range of processes that can be both planned, such as government policy, or largely uncontrolled and unpredictable, such as shifting social attitudes. It is important to note that some elements appear on both sides of the table, stressing the reflexive relationship between the supply and demand for labour. For example, if the government alters the supply of particular 'types' of labour to the market through education and training policies, firms will change their demand strategies to accommodate, take advantage of or neutralise the impact of this changed supply. Box 4.3 shows a clear example of this in relation to the recent expansion of higher education in the UK and the ways in which employers have responded to the increased supply of graduates to the labour market.

TABLE 4.1 *Factors shaping the external labour market*

Labour market supply	Labour market demand
• Changing societal attitudes to work and education (for example, increased acceptance of female participation in the labour market, desire for work–life balance)	• Changes to the external business environment
• Economic conditions (regional, national and international)	• Increases in consumer demand for particular goods or services; changes in consumer taste
• Level of unemployment	• (Cheaper) competition from abroad
• Interest rates, inflation and exchange rates and their impact on the cost of living (for example, rising house prices has meant increasing numbers of families where both parents work)	• Changes in the internal business environment
	• Changes in production or business processes and the organisation of work (for example, as a result of technological investment or innovation)
• Changing demography (for example, falling birth rates, the extent of workforce gendering, life expectancy and associated changes to retirement ages)	• Organisational restructuring
• Migration (and the impact of international agreements on the movement of labour)	• Mergers and acquisition (resulting in possible duplication of labour)
• Government policy – both national and international (e.g. European Union)	• Changing communication and production technologies
• Employment regulation, which affects the ways in which labour can be employed	• Changes in the political context (for example, the extent of employment regulation)
• Level and focus of investment in education and training	• Economic restructuring (for example, shift from manufacturing to service sector)
• Industrial policy (for example, support provided to particular industry sectors)	• Changing skills requirement (for example, resulting from development and diffusion of new technology)
• Wider social policy (for example, level of social security and investment in regional regeneration)	• Regional, national and international economic conditions – inflation, level of unemployment and interest rates

As a further example of the way in which contextual factors can act to shape the formation of labour markets, both within and outside of work organisations, Box 4.5 provides a summary of research exploring how economic reform acts to shape how people access different types of jobs in China through altering social attitudes and challenging entrenched cultural traditions.

Further online reading This article provides an interesting discussion of the relationship between higher education and economic competitiveness and stresses the importance of better understanding the concept of 'graduate skills' and their connection to employment.

James, S., Warhurst, C., Tholen, G. and Commander, J. (2013) What we know and what we need to know about graduate skills, *Work, Employment and Society*, 27 (6): 952–63.

BOX 4.3
UNDERSTAND

The graduate labour market: changing labour market supply and demand

The UK higher education (HE) system has undergone a major transformation over the past three to four decades from a system that catered for a limited number of entrants in the late 1960s and early 1970s (approximately 6 per cent of school leavers) to one that now has a participation rate of over 45 per cent. The shift from an elite to a mass higher education system has been viewed by successive governments as the principal mechanism by which to create an adequate supply of highly qualified workers to fill the expanding number of high-skill jobs in the economy (Keep and Mayhew, 2004), encouraged by employers who claim that more graduates are needed for UK organisations to remain competitive (HM Treasury, 2011). The higher education funding reforms of 2011 that require English students (unlike their peers from other parts of the UK) to bear virtually all of the costs of their higher education through increased personal contribution to university fees have increased the pressure on higher education institutions to deliver more 'employable' graduates to the labour market, through the development of the skills demanded by employers during the course of degree study.

However, employers have responded to the dramatically increased supply of graduate labour in a number of ways, not all of them in line with their calls for a more highly qualified labour supply. Some have created new or modified existing roles to take advantage of the supply of graduates and a number of studies have highlighted the incidence of existing jobs/occupations being 'upgraded'. There is also evidence to suggest that graduates are able to 'grow' ostensibly non-graduate jobs into appropriate work that utilises their skills and knowledge. However, there is a parallel trend for employers to recruit graduates into jobs previously held by non-graduates for which the requirements have not changed, which under-utilise the abilities of the role-holder and which provide no route into graduate-appropriate roles.

Questions

1 What are the implications for both employers and graduates of the expansion of higher education over the last two decades?
2 Why do employers continue to complain about the work-readiness of graduates and a shortage of particular skills?

HM
TREASURY

One of the most influential factors in shaping contemporary national labour markets is the accelerated process of globalisation evident over the last four decades (discussed further in Chapter 5). The growth of global financial networks, production systems and markets, as well as complex patterns of international migration, has created significant interconnectedness between national and regional labour markets. Subsequently, many of the processes outlined in Table 4.1 need be understood both as national and international. For example, changes to the availability of specific forms of labour in one part of the world can influence the relative demand for labour in another. This reflects the developing international division of labour whereby certain regions or nations specialise in particular industrial activity. One of the most newsworthy recent developments in the international division of labour is the widespread offshoring of business activities, mainly customer contact ('call') centres but increasingly back-office functions such as IT, HRM, finance and accounting – referred to as IT outsourcing (ITO) and business processing outsourcing (BPO) – from Western nations to lower-cost countries such as India, South Africa and the Philippines (see Box 4.4).

Increasingly, firms employ a globally distributed workforce or, at the very least, rely on overseas labour at some point in their supply chain. On the one hand, access to a global labour market presents the opportunity for cost savings and provides access to a more diverse labour supply and the ability to situate production close to large or emerging markets. On the other hand, firms are presented with a set of challenges associated with managing a global workforce. Burke and Ng (2006, citing Roberts et al., 1998) identify three major challenges: deployment (getting the right skills to the right place at the right time); the dissemination of knowledge, innovation and effective practice across a geographically dispersed workforce; and the identification and development of talent. The challenges for firms operating across national borders are further discussed in Chapter 5.

BOX 4.4
GLOBAL INSIGHT

Offshoring and the global labour market

As noted above, advances in ICT have prompted companies to seek to exploit the potential cost savings associated with offshoring. Initially, offshoring was associated with the movement of manufacturing and production operations overseas to exploit lower labour costs, and developing technical expertise in particular countries and regions. However, as more skilled labour has become more available in, for example, the BRIC countries (Brazil, India, Russia and China), there is a growing trend towards the offshoring of white collar and knowledge work. As Paton (2007) notes:

> thanks to instant, global communications and an ever more highly qualified pool of graduates [in developing countries] to call on, you are now just as likely to find sophisticated 'knowledge economy' jobs – investment banking, web, software and architectural design, legal services, drug development, tele-radiology and film editing to name but a few – being shunted overseas. (Paton, 2007)

In 2014, the global market size of outsourcing of IT and business processes exceeded $100 billion (USD) with much of this outsourcing being directed overseas.

India, in particular, has benefited considerably from the offshoring activities of Western companies and, by 2008, had captured 65 per cent of global ITO and 43 per cent of global BPO (Willcocks and Lacity, 2009). It remains the primary destination for offshoring (Deloitte, 2014). This is partly due to foreign-investment-friendly government policies from the late 1990s and its large English-speaking workforce with rising levels of education. ITO and BPO services have contributed considerable growth and new wealth in India and account for a significant proportion of its gross domestic product (GDP) (Kobayashi-Hillary, 2007). However, India is now facing a considerable challenge from countries such as South Africa and Mexico, seeking to imitate its success, as well as from the other BRIC nations, particularly China (Oshri et al., 2009). Like other destinations for offshoring, India is also subject to the impact of new technology and developing global competition that shape firms' approaches to organising their global operations. For instance, IBM are reported to be reducing their Indian workforce by 50,000 employees by 2017 in response to developments in, for instance, automation technology.

The impact of offshoring on the labour market in the UK and other advanced economies is the subject of some debate, but it is clear that such activity does act to alter the dynamic between labour supply and demand both nationally and internationally. For example, one reported consequence of an increasing tendency towards the offshoring of certain IT functions by UK firms to India is the stagnation of wages for low-skilled jobs in the UK IT sector (BBC, 2008).

Changing demography of the labour market

WORKFORCE MANAGEMENT STYLE

Labour markets are in a continuous state of change, not least because of long-term demographic trends shaping the composition of the labour supply. Many Western nations and other advanced economies such as Japan have ageing populations as a result of a long-term trend of falling birth rates and lengthening life expectancy. The labour market is, therefore, increasingly composed of older workers, many working beyond retirement out of choice or compulsion, as the supply of new labour market entrants continues to diminish. Over the 25-year period 1985 to 2010, the median age of the UK population increased from 35.4 years to 39.7 years. This pattern is forecast to extend well into the future with the median age of the UK population projected to rise to 42.2 years by 2035 with 23 per cent of the population aged 65 and over. Such recent and projected trends are repeated across the European Union. For example, Germany is reported to be the EU member state with the most aged population, having a median age of 44.2 years in 2010 with 31 per cent of its population aged 65 or over (ONS, 2012a). This trend is, however, most marked in Japan, where it is predicted that by 2050, 37 per cent of the population will be aged 65 or over (GCCIJ, 2010). Coupled with shrinking populations in virtually all industrialised nations, and some developing nations, population ageing presents a significant challenge for both governments and businesses. The implications for HRM of an ageing workforce are further examined in the discussion of managing diversity in Chapter 11.

Further online reading This article presages the discussion in Chapter 11 of the implications for management of an ageing workforce, in particular the treatment of older workers in respect of training and development. It suggests that management behaviour towards older workers has not changed in line with the wider social and labour market context, particularly in respect of the opportunities provided for continued development late into career.

Beck, V. (2012) Employers' views of learning and training for an ageing workforce, *Management Learning*, 45 (2): 200–15.

WOMEN IN THE WORKFORCE

A further influence on labour market composition is the long-term trend of increasing female participation in the workforce. In the UK at the beginning of the twentieth century, around 5 million women worked, making up 29 per cent of the total workforce (Lindsey, 2003). In 2013, the figure had risen to 13.4 million representing 47 per cent of the total workforce (ONS, 2013b). Notably, however, approximately 42 per cent of women's jobs were part-time compared with around one in eight of men's. This rise in female labour market participation has led to a growth in the proportion of dual-career couples and working single parents in the labour force. For example, the proportion of lone parent households that were 'workless' declined from 52 per cent in 1996 to 23 per cent in 2014 (ONS, 2014).

The UK labour market is also more ethnically diverse than ever before, partly reflective of patterns in the international migration of labour. For example, the impact of European Union expansion has increased the supply of migrant labour into many nations, bringing with them diverse experiences and expectations of employment and a wide range of skills, knowledge and capabilities. In the year to September 2014, an estimated 624,000 immigrated to the UK, including 192,000 who came to the UK to study. In the same period, however, an estimated 327,000 people emigrated from the UK. Net migration, the difference between immigration and emigration, was 298,000 in 2014, the equivalent to adding over 800 people a day to the UK population (ONS, 2014).

BOX 4.5
RESEARCH INSIGHT

Economic liberalisation, social ties and labour market activity in China

Huang (2008) provides an interesting example of the way in which multiple aspects of national context act to shape the formation of both internal and external labour markets in Chinese work organisations. In particular, Huang explores how political and economic reform in China over the past two decades has changed processes of job search and acquisition in the Chinese labour market and whether *guanxi* networks continue to play a significant role in the allocation of jobs. *Guanxi* networks are deeply embedded interpersonal ties between two people in Chinese society that have the potential to facilitate the exchange of favours between the parties (Huang, 2008: 468) and have traditionally played a significant role in determining access to jobs in Chinese organisations through the use of personal and family connections. Huang found that the use of *guanxi* networks remains most pronounced in the state sector, reflecting cultural traditions where jobs have long been allocated according to personal and social ties. However, in large corporations, in the private sector, Huang found that the influence of such networks has become 'limited, resisted or eliminated' through the adoption of 'transparent procedures to screen and recruit the most qualified candidates' (2008: 467). Therefore, as China has developed towards a more open economy, its employment practices have begun to shift, partly towards the more performance-driven means of recruiting staff associated with Western firms, resulting in changes to the activities of job seekers.

MIGRATION
OF LABOUR

Economic change and the labour market

Recent developments in the broader economic context of employment are also altering both the demand for and supply of labour. In particular, advanced capitalist economies are argued to have entered an era of post-industrialism (Bell, 1973) associated with the development of a knowledge-intensive firms economy. Watson (2008: 65) defines the post-industrial society as 'a type of economically advanced social order in which the centrally important resource is knowledge, service work has largely replaced manufacturing employment and knowledge-based occupations play a privileged role'. In other words, 'knowledge' has displaced the traditional factors of production such as land and capital (i.e. a firm's physical assets) as the primary source of competitive advantage for firms and nations, and, consequently, investment in human capital is viewed as the foundation for success in a global economy (Thompson, 2004).

The concept of the knowledge economy stresses a break from the past, a transition from the Fordist era with its emphasis on rationality, standardisation and predictability of both labour and markets to Post-Fordism, which stresses economic complexity and uncertainty. The acceleration of a number of long-term processes, principally the rapid development and adoption of ICT and globalisation, has altered not only the context in which organisations operate but also, it is argued, the types of skills, knowledge and qualifications required by workers, stressing the need to produce a workforce that is well educated, highly skilled, innovative and responsive to change to fill the growing number of 'knowledge worker' roles in the economy (OECD, 2006). The notion of knowledge work and workers is further discussed in Chapter 15.

One perceived indicator of a shift towards a knowledge-intensive economy is the relative decline of manufacturing and the growth of the service sector in many Western nations. In the UK, between 1978 and 2014 the proportion of jobs accounted for by the service sector increased from 63.2 per cent to 83.4 per cent and the proportion of jobs accounted for by manufacturing (along with mining and quarrying) fell from 26.4 per cent to 8 per cent. The largest increases in jobs have been in the finance and insurance sector, and distribution, hotels and restaurants. Reflecting this broad shift towards service sector employment, the contemporary workforce is increasingly comprised of professional or knowledge-based occupations such as lawyers, accountants, managers, marketing and advertising executives, scientists, engineers, doctors, ICT specialists and all the employees who support these occupations (Albert and Bradley, 1997). Further evidence for a broad upskilling of the UK workforce is found in the demand for specific types and level of skill (Box 4.6).

For some commentators, these recent occupational changes and data on changing skills levels offer irrefutable evidence of a shift towards a knowledge-intensive economy where increasing proportions of workers are involved in knowledge work and benefit from the enhanced pay and working conditions attached to such jobs. Others, however, contest this perspective of radical 'upskilling', arguing that the growth in the demand for knowledge workers and 'thinking skills' has been overstated (Brown and Hesketh, 2004) and they will continue to comprise a clear minority of workers (Grugulis et al., 2004). Sceptics argue that detailed analysis of job content and skill requirements indicate a far more diverse picture where a significant proportion of jobs created are low skill, highly routinised and low-wage jobs. Wolf (2002) reports, for example, that the single fastest growing job in the 1980s was 'postman' and in the 1990s was 'care assistant'. As Warhurst and Thompson (1998) put it, there is insufficient sensitivity to the heterogeneity of employment in the service sector between '*Mcjobs*' (low-skilled, poorly paid, menial jobs) and '*iMacjobs*' (well-rewarded, knowledge-intensive jobs). They explain the rise in employer requirements for qualifications as representing 'credentialism' – the unnecessary reliance on qualifications to allocate jobs – rather than as evidence of widespread upskilling (Keep and Mayhew, 1997).

MC JOBS

BOX 4.6
UNDERSTAND

The changing requirements for skill

Felstead et al. (2007) report that in the UK from 1986 to 2006 the broad requirement for job skills rose significantly along with increasing job complexity and the requirement for employees to continually develop new and update existing skills.

For example, the proportion of jobs requiring qualifications at level 4 or above (equivalent to a certificate in higher education or higher) for entry rose from 20 per cent in 1986 to 30 per cent in 2006. The proportion of jobs not requiring qualifications fell by 11 percentage points over the same period. On average, jobs in 2006 were also associated with longer periods of training. In 2006, jobs requiring training lasting two years or more accounted for 30 per cent of total jobs in Britain, compared to 22 per cent in 1986. The proportion of jobs requiring less than one month 'to learn to do well' accounted for 27 per cent of the total in 1986 compared to 19 per cent twenty years later. Finally, the proportion of respondents strongly agreeing to the statement 'my job requires that I keep learning new things' has consistently moved upwards during the 1992–2006 period – rising from 26 per cent in 1992 to 30 per cent in 2001 and then to 35 per cent in 2006.

Empirical research appears to suggest that there is increasing skills polarisation within the labour market, where some workers will enjoy the benefits associated with knowledge work and others will be confined to routinised service and production work, reflecting an 'hourglass' economy. It is perhaps pertinent therefore that in 2006 almost equal numbers of jobs required level 4 or above qualifications for entry (29 per cent) as those that required no qualifications on entry (28 per cent) (Felstead et al., 2007).

Further online reading This article provides a critical overview of some of the key debates and developments discussed in this chapter, particularly the contention that the last two decades have seen a fundamental shift in economic structures and labour markets and the implications of change both for employers and employees.

Thompson, P. (2003) Disconnected capitalism: Or why employers can't keep their side of the bargain, *Work, Employment and Society*, 17 (2): 359–78.

Emotional labour

Grugulis et al. (2004) argue that it is not 'thinking' or technical skills which are of increasing importance in the contemporary labour markets but 'person-to-person' skills. This connects to the growing importance of emotional labour as a result of the shift to greater service sector employment. The notion of *emotional intelligence* (EI) has also gained greater currency in recent years. EI is defined as the individual's ability to develop and express a range of skills such as awareness of the emotions of others, self-awareness, empathy and influence (Goleman, 1995). In managerial roles, the increased importance placed on interpersonal skills can be associated with the perceptible shift in emphasis from bureaucratic to charismatic leadership, where authority is based on force of personality rather than status and 'office' (Brown and Scase, 1994).

THE RESTRUCTURING OF INTERNAL LABOUR MARKETS

Associated with wider changes in the demand for and supply of labour resulting from changing economic structures and technological developments, the way that labour is utilised within firms is also changing (Szabó and Négyesi 2005), with considerable implications for how work is experienced. A central theme of this chapter is the reflexive relationship between external and internal labour markets. As such, key changes in the organisation of work are at least partly a result of the changing composition of the labour supply and the wider economic, political, legislative, technological and social processes outlined above.

Further online reading In this article the authors outline the causes and consequences of the shift from patterns of employment associated with industrial societies towards the contingent work that is increasingly associated with employment in a knowledge-based economy.

Szabó, K. and Négyesi, A. (2005) The spread of contingent work in the knowledge-based economy, *Human Resource Development Review*, 4 (1): 63–85.

The flexibility of organisational structure

One implication of the developing organisational context outlined above is that as markets become more unpredictable and dynamic then firms must respond in a commensurate fashion by increasing the flexibility of both their organisational form and workforce. It has become received wisdom that rigid bureaucratic forms of organisation, characterised by vertical hierarchies of authority, centralisation of control and task specialisation, are not adaptable or responsive enough to cope with the demands of twenty-first-century capitalism. Consequently, such structures are being replaced with 'post-bureaucratic forms that are leaner, flatter and consequently more responsive, flexible and focused' (Morris, 2004: 264). New, more appropriate organisational forms are described as 'networked' (Castells, 2000), 'boundaryless' (Grimshaw et al., 2002), 'organic, entrepreneurial [and] tight–loose' (Jacques, 1990: 127). Organisations are also argued to be using autonomous work groups or flexible project teams, associated with the 'unstructured' approaches to management associated with the effective deployment of knowledge workers (Davenport et al., 1996), to replace tight managerial control and strict demarcation between work tasks. The abandonment of traditional organisational form and pursuit of flexibility have been enacted through downsizing, rightsizing, delayering, restructuring and business process re-engineering, involving the centralisation of core competencies and the outsourcing of non-core activities to specialist firms (Blair and Kochan, 2000).

Inevitably, changes in organisational structure have profound implications for workers in terms of job content, employee motivation, job security and organisational commitment, especially given the evidence that employers have often used the 'flexibility' rationale for reorganisation to justify redundancies (Child and McGrath, 2001). Grimshaw et al. (2002) note that, theoretically at least, in flatter, non-hierarchical, networked organisations, workers have greater autonomy, often work together in teams and are able to adapt more quickly to change.

However, one apparent contradiction in this process of restructuring is that delayering (for example, the removal of a hierarchical level of management) tends to undermine the linkage between training and career advancement – key elements in the establishment of a strong internal labour market and in developing employee commitment. In particular, lower-level workers in 'flatter' organisations have experienced a widening of the gap up to the next broad band of mid-management positions and a withdrawal of the training and development opportunities necessary to bridge this gap. Subsequently, the hourglass feature of a skills-polarised external labour market can also be found within internal labour markets, reflecting the same set of 'winner takes all' characteristics where those with access to the 'top' of organisations benefit from preferential terms and conditions of employment compared to those below with no clear path to such positions. As a result of this ongoing rationalisation of organisational structures and associated job insecurity, it is argued that workers in the knowledge economy must develop new 'career' strategies. This is further discussed in Chapter 12.

Further online reading This article presents research evidence that demonstrates the erosion of the 'classical model' of the internal labour market in four large firms as a result of pressures both inside and outside of the organisation. The article reports on implications both for employers and employees.

Grimshaw, D., Ward, K., Rubery, J. and Beynon, H. (2008) Organisations and the transformation of the internal labour market, *Work, Employment and Society*, 15 (1): 25–54.

The flexibility of labour

One key determinant of an organisation's ability to respond effectively to a changing and uncertain business environment is the flexibility and adaptability of its workforce. The notion of Post-Fordism is associated with flexible, adaptable business processes that are able to respond rapidly to changing circumstances, such as variation in consumer demand, which require both individual and collective employee flexibility. Flexibility of labour is reflected in an employer's ability to: recruit or dispose of labour as required; alter labour costs in line with market needs; allocate labour efficiently within the firm; and fix working hours to suit business requirements (Reilly, 1998). Subsequently, employment flexibility can take many forms, as Box 4.7 illustrates.

CIPD (2012a) report that the most common forms of flexible working arrangements in the UK are part-time working, working from home on a regular basis, flexitime, job-sharing and compressed hours (for example, working full-time hours over four days instead of five). To a certain degree, the ultimate objective of

BOX 4.7
UNDERSTAND

Approaches to labour flexibility

Functional flexibility

This is the ability of employees to undertake a range of tasks, either horizontally (employees are multi-skilled to perform a range of tasks at the same organisational level) or vertically (employees have increased managerial or supervisory responsibility). A distinction is made between multi-skilling (providing employees with a range of transferable skills, associated with vertical functional flexibility, empowerment and enhanced terms and conditions) and multi-tasking (expanding the range of tasks and responsibilities of an individual horizontally, associated with work intensification and no commensurate improvement in reward).

Financial (or wage) flexibility

Employee reward is linked to individual, team, department, divisional or organisational performance, through such techniques as individual or team performance-related pay, commission, bonuses and profit-sharing. Wage flexibility seeks to promote individual association with the goals and objectives of the organisation, link individual performance with that of the firm and ensure that wage costs closely match individual and business performance.

Numerical flexibility

This reflects the organisational ability to alter the number of employees it directly employs. Firms seek the ability to hire, fire and re-hire workers with relative ease resulting in insecurely or irregularly employed workers. This form of flexibility is associated with the use of casual, short-term, temporary, agency and self-employed workers and the outsourcing and sub-contracting of certain activities.

Temporal flexibility

This is the organisational and individual ability to vary the number and timing of hours worked, and is associated with non-standard patterns of working that diverge from the 9–5, 38-hour working week. Such arrangements include part-time working, flexi-time, shift work, weekend work, overtime, stand-by and call-out arrangements, annualised hours, term-time working, compressed hours and seasonal working.

Spatial (or locational) flexibility

This refers to flexibility in the 'location' of employment through, for example, home-working, hot-desking or desk-sharing, teleworking and the use of consultants or freelancers. Often this is implemented either to reduce overhead facilities costs to the employer or to respond to the work–life balance demands of workers.

flexible approaches to the utilisation of labour is to minimise labour costs, or, in the words of Fleetwood (2007):

> To have just the right number of suitable skilled and motivated workers to match the needs of the productive system at any point in time and to hire them at wages that reflect their differing productivity and when the productive system does not demand all of them, it does not want them on the premises and does not want to pay for them. (2007: 13)

However, employers claim to introduce flexible working practices for a wide range of reasons (Box 4.8), relating to both improving organisational performance and meeting the needs of workers.

The previous chapter made the distinction between cost-minimisation and quality-enhancement HR strategies, the former with the emphasis on the reduction of labour costs, the latter with an emphasis on developing and maintaining a positive psychological contract as a source of competitive advantage. Under these two broad approaches, the imperative for organisational flexibility can be viewed in different ways. Under the former strategy, the emphasis would likely be on numerical and temporal flexibility, with little concern for the impact on employees themselves (for example, the use of 'hire and fire' policies), and job enlargement by multi-tasking employees. This approach has been referred to as 'flexploitation' (Gray, 2004: 3) and is associated with a reactionary, opportunistic approach to the management of labour. Alternatively, a quality-enhancement approach would place greater emphasis on job redesign and multi-skilling (job enrichment) to increase both employer and employee skills flexibility, employee-friendly approaches to temporal flexibility (for example, flexible start and finish times) and spatial and numerical flexibility which emphasises notions of employee well-being and work–life balance. Indeed, a central tenet of many best practice models of HRM (for example, High Performance Work Systems) is skills flexibility that can contribute to mutual gains for employees (improved job satisfaction through work variety and challenge) and employer (improved individual and organisational performance).

Further online reading This article reports on research undertaken in a sample of Spanish firms that supports the assumption that workforce flexibility is an important mediating variable in translating High Performance Work Systems into improved organisational performance.

Beltrán-Martín, I., Roca-Puig, V., Escrig-Tena, A. and Bou-Llusar, J. C. (2008) Human resource flexibility as a mediating variable between High Performance Work Systems and performance, *Journal of Management*, 34: 1009–44.

However, firms cannot necessarily be so clearly categorised as adopting either a 'hard' or 'soft' approach to employee flexibility given that different forms of flexibility might be appropriate for different workforce segments. Atkinson (1984) provides a useful theoretical model – the flexible firm – that shows the different approaches to labour flexibility that an organisation might adopt depending on the types of labour employed (Figure 4.1).

In Atkinson's model, different forms of flexibility are utilised within the same firm depending on both the utility and value of the employee to the firm and the nature of the employment relationship in each instance.

BOX 4.8
UNDERSTAND

Employer reasons for introducing flexible working practices

- To improve staff retention
- To enhance reputation as an 'employer of choice'
- In response to requests from staff
- In response to government legislation
- To improve work–life balance
- To improve staff morale
- To attract job applicants/widen recruitment pool
- To provide adequate cover for extended opening hours
- To meet seasonal fluctuations in the market

- To stay competitive in the market
- To improve productivity
- To encourage diversity
- To reduce sickness absence/help those returning from long-term sick leave
- To limit overtime costs
- To encourage loyalty
- To address environmental/travel-to-work issues
- To reduce property costs
- To enable a young workforce to pursue their personal interests.

Source: IDS, 2006b. Reprinted by kind permission of Incomes Data Research.

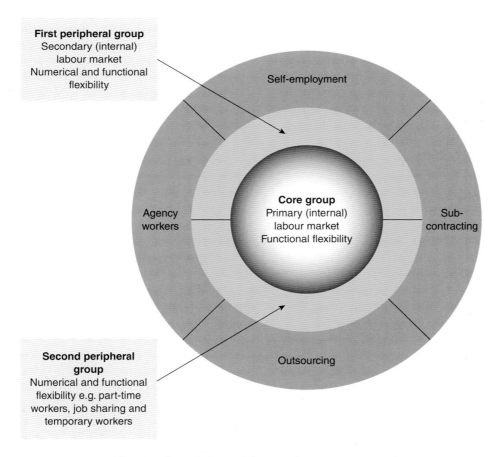

First peripheral group
Secondary (internal) labour market
Numerical and functional flexibility

Self-employment

Core group
Primary (internal) labour market
Functional flexibility

Agency workers

Sub-contracting

Second peripheral group
Numerical and functional flexibility e.g. part-time workers, job sharing and temporary workers

Outsourcing

FIGURE 4.1   The flexible firm (adapted from Atkinson, 1984: 29)

The core worker group is comprised of highly skilled, valued workers whose capabilities might be firm-specific, scarce in the external labour market and are central to the core activities of the firm. Under the resource-based view of the firm, they constitute a unique resource and, therefore, the emphasis is on a strong internal labour market to ensure their retention. Flexibility among this core group lies in their continuous development and deployment of a range of skills and capabilities.

The first peripheral worker group is comprised of employees who possess skills needed by the firm but that are not firm-specific (for example, general ICT skills). The firm offers limited scope for movement to the core and few career prospects, preferring to accept a reliance on the external labour market to fill these posts and tolerating a degree of labour turnover. They provide both functional and numerical flexibility.

The second peripheral group might consist of workers employed under 'non-standard' contractual arrangements and who provide both temporal and numerical flexibility. The final group of employees contains all those workers not directly employed by the firm, such as sub-contractors with skills and knowledge that are only temporarily required by the organisation. Grimshaw et al. (2008) suggest that it is becoming increasingly difficult for labour market participants to predict with certainty their position within a segmented labour market of 'core' and 'peripheral' workers because the boundaries between different groups of employees are being continuously redrawn.

Despite the ubiquity and resilience of the flexible firm as a theoretical model of how organisations have responded to the increased need for flexibility, it has been subject to significant criticism. For example, Pollert (1988) suggests that the model fails to explain what is new about flexible management strategies given that they reflect pre-existing labour market segmentation and disadvantage according to gender and race (those groups most likely to be subjected to the poor terms and conditions of employment of the peripheral groups). Despite this criticism, Proctor and Ackroyd (1998) cite a number of studies that support the continued growth of both functional and numerical flexibility and suggest that Atkinson's model remains helpful in drawing attention to the importance of labour in securing flexibility.

Further online reading Kalleberg discusses some key ways in which employers have sought to restructure their workforces to become more flexible and the consequences of such restructuring for workers and jobs, particularly the extent to which flexibility strategies create workforce division.

Kalleberg, A. L. (2003) Flexible firms and labor market segmentation: Effects of workplace restructuring on jobs and workers, *Work and Occupations*, 30 (2): 154–75.

THE CONTROVERSIES OF FLEXIBILITY

The flexible firm model demonstrates how attempts to create a more adaptive and flexible workforce can have profound implications for the job content, job security and loyalty of different groups of workers. As Conley (2006: 52) suggests, 'flexibility is an amorphous term used to describe many qualitatively different forms of work, and it is sometimes ... employed as a term holding both positive and negative connotations'. Fleetwood (2007) argues that in the context of the employment relationship, flexibility is *for* the employer and *of* the employee, and, subsequently, whilst there are undeniable benefits for labour from certain forms of flexibility – where there are mutual gains to be had from both parties – flexibility cannot be seen as unequivocally good from an employee perspective. This is despite the notion of flexibility often being subsumed under the rhetoric of 'employee well-being' and 'family-friendly policies'. Fleetwood suggests that, in broad terms, flexible working practices can be described as being either 'employer-friendly' or 'employee-friendly' (Box 4.9). Typically, those practices that are employer-friendly have the explicit aim of minimising labour costs reflecting minimal commitment to employees and/or an ability to alter the supply of labour at short notice and subject employees to high levels of insecurity. Practices that are employee-friendly are those that are, in reality, 'family-friendly' or improve 'work–life balance' by allowing a degree of worker discretion in working patterns. Some practices can be considered 'neutral' in particular circumstances in that they are beneficial for both parties.

In respect of employee commitment, flexible working practices present something of a dilemma for employers. Whilst much research identifies employee loyalty as a key source of individual motivation and enhanced performance, employers can be reluctant to demonstrate sufficient degrees of loyalty to those who work for them, even among their core employees and those who fulfil important functions in the organisation (for example, front line staff in the hospitality industry). Moreover, the perpetual insecurity associated with much employment flexibility has significant implications for stress and the alienation of workers, potentially leading to the loss of valuable employees. Evidence from both the UK and USA – labour markets with a significant focus on flexibility – suggests that non-standard

---

BOX 4.9
UNDERSTAND

Categories of flexible working practices

Employer-friendly or employee-unfriendly – sought by employers	Employee-friendly or employer-unfriendly – sought by workers
Temporary working	Flexible start and finish times
(Involuntary) part-time working	Term-time working
Zero hours contracts	(Voluntary) part-time
Overtime	Job-share
Shift working	Compressed working weeks
Annualised hours	Shift swapping
Stand-by and call-out arrangements	Self-rostering
Seasonal work	Time off in lieu
Job-and-finish	Sabbaticals/Career breaks

Source: Fleetwood, 2007

employment (part-time, temporary and fixed-term) disproportionately increased workers' exposure to 'bad job' characteristics, such as low pay, no sick pay provision or access to health insurance, no employer pension scheme and no access to a recognised promotion ladder (Kalleberg et al. 2000; McGovern et al. 2004).

Whilst many of the problems of flexibility tend to be associated with numerical and temporal forms, the impact of functional or skills flexibility on workers is also a contentious issue. Many best practice models of HRM such as the High Performance Work System (outlined in Chapter 3) have multi-skilling as a central component with the dual objectives of both improving organisational performance and enriching jobs. However, a number of studies (for example, Danford et al., 2005) have found that in practice, multi-skilling often means multi-tasking and, therefore, rather than providing employees with job enrichment, functional flexibility is often a form of work intensification contributing to work overload and stress. In contrast, Kashefi (2011) found benefits to be associated with HPWS for standard (i.e. core) workers, including increased skills, participative decision-making and teamworking but which were not available to non-standard or peripheral workers. Similarly, in a study of Taiwanese hotels, Tsai et al. (2009) found that internal (core) employees tended to be subjected to commitment-based approaches to HRM, whereas external (peripheral) workers were managed using control strategies.

Of course, some flexible working arrangements benefit particular groups of workers. For example, where flexible arrangements are structured and predictable – such as fixed part-time hours – employees can arrange patterns of work that are compatible with other responsibilities, such as childcare and study. However, Purcell et al. (1999) suggest that some groups are more likely to benefit than others from flexible working arrangements. Managerial, professional and clerical workers, particularly those with scarce expertise or skills, mainly experience a net benefit (Alonzo and Simon, 2008). For manual and lower-skilled workers, however, flexibility often means insecurity and unpredictability, particularly where working patterns fluctuate according to consumer or employer demand, and can present a barrier to career progression, not least as a result of limited access to training and development opportunities (Tomlinson, 2004). Wilcox and Lowry (2000) refer to workers who often have little choice but to accept insecure work as a result of low levels of job mobility, and who are easy to dispense with, as 'captive and disposable'. The negative impact of flexible working is most pronounced where it reinforces patterns of social exclusion, for example, among migrant workers, women and minority ethnic groups, by undermining opportunities for stable, long-term employment and career progression and creating financial insecurity.

Labour market flexibility and government policy

The organisational dilemma of creating a flexible workforce whilst still attempting to elicit discretionary effort among its employees through the establishment of a positive psychological contract is a micro-version of a wider policy problem. Neo-liberal economic policy argues that economic responsiveness via the flexibility and adaptability of its institutions, including the labour market, is key to prosperity in a turbulent global economy. This puts significant pressure on national governments to minimise the regulation of business practices, including employment protection legislation, to ensure that businesses are best able to respond to changes in market conditions. However, governments also have a responsibility to protect the interests of workers and, therefore, are forced to strike a balance between economic responsiveness and employee protection.

BOX 4.10
ETHICAL INSIGHT

Employment flexibility and the fair treatment of workers

There is clearly an ethical contention at the heart of the debate over flexible working practices. Among the concerns about the impact of flexible working on employees is the perception that by accepting the perpetual insecurity associated with particular forms of flexibility as 'the way things are' work organisations are relieved of their moral responsibility to their workforce. Indeed, the political and economic discourse of flexibility – both of labour and labour markets – that pervades much discussion of economic competiveness can be viewed as creating an 'ethical' climate whereby employers feel enabled to treat people as disposable resources, thus creating a greater sense of precariousness and risk among increasingly large sections of society (Lambert, 2008).

However, Warren (1996: 42) suggests that whilst the 'death of the company as a long-term employment organisation' is a proposal that is pervasive in managerial discourse in both the UK and USA it is not, for example, in Japan, where organisations are viewed as communities, or in continental Europe, where companies are more often run like families. Warren argues that accepting pervasive job insecurity as the norm for the majority of the workforce will result both in increasing social exclusion and lowered morale of those working for the firm, contributing to a decline in citizenship behaviour which can be valuable to organisations. He argues, therefore, that whilst care should be taken not to overburden business with too many responsibilities, companies should be viewed as contributors to the moral order of society; collective citizens whose sole objective is not just to make money but also to be of wider social benefit. Therefore, just as the issue of labour flexibility cuts to the heart of the role of employers and governments in balancing the needs of business and those of employees, it is also at the centre of discussions over the responsibilities of work organisations in society and the obligations that firms have in delivering return on investment to their shareholders or value to taxpayers, whilst adequately providing employees with work that is satisfying, adequately rewarded and which allows them to plan for their futures.

There also exist wider questions over the impact of flexible working on the ethical behaviour of employees. For example, Carey (2011) suggests that the significant growth in the use of contingent employment in social work in the UK carries risks to both the employer and employee. For instance, where flexible employment acts to limit worker access to training and development opportunities, this diminishes opportunities for individuals to progress their careers as well as their ability to adhere to the changing professional codes or ethical guidelines that govern how these workers behave. Similarly, in the private sector, in a reversal of the mutuality and employee commitment that might stem from a positive psychological contract arising from relative security of employment, flexible work that is undertaken not through choice but by necessity might lead to a lack of concern for the ethical treatment of customers and clients.

Questions

1 To what extent do you think a business should be responsible for the employment security of its workforce?

2 Do you think that a business case argument – that job insecurity is damaging both to employee morale and, ultimately, individual performance – is sufficient to encourage businesses to prioritise stability of employment?

3 In what ways might the use of contingent workers potentially compromise the service quality that end users or customers might receive?

This is clearly illustrated in the long-running battle over rights for agency and temporary workers, a key component of a flexible labour market because of the ability of firms to hire and fire such workers and offer them less favourable terms and conditions of employment compared to permanently employed employees. Wintour (2008) reports that May 2008 saw the end of a six-year battle to give 1.4 million temporary and agency workers equal rights (for example, concerning statutory sick pay, pension contributions and holiday entitlement) with Britain's full-time permanent workforce, following a compromise between the Confederation of British Industry (CBI) and the Trade Union Congress (TUC). The trade union lobby argued that the use of cheaper agency and casual workers has undermined the pay and conditions of the full-time workforce whilst the CBI were staunch advocates of the need for continued labour market flexibility. Whilst the government claimed the deal represented the right balance between fairness and flexibility, the chairman of the British Chambers of Commerce condemned the agreement saying that:

> this is a bad deal for the country and a bad deal for business. The success of the UK economy over recent years has been down to our flexible labour market. When the economy is weakening, this is not the time to further reduce flexibility. (Wintour, 2008)

The issue of striking a balance between economic competitiveness and employment protection continues to lie at the heart of discussions about how to reinvigorate the UK economy. On the one hand, many in the current UK government are calling for more power for employers to be able to 'hire and fire' workers as an incentive to create more jobs. On the other hand, opponents to the removal of employment protection argue that employers currently have enough power to dismiss under-performing workers and the removal of such protection will not in itself create more jobs (*Financial Times*, 2012a).

QUALITY OF WORKING LIFE

Many of the employment practices discussed later in this book tend to reflect a best practice approach to HRM which claims to produce mutual gains for both the employee and employer: improving both individual and organisational performance and the quality of working life. However, there is considerable debate about the extent to which recent changes in labour market context, and managerial responses to these changes, have had a positive or negative impact on workers. Quality of working life (QWL) is a rather ambiguous concept with a variety of definitions. In particular we can distinguish between conceptualisations that suggest an objective notion – that 'good quality' work is something external to the individual and is made up of specific and identifiable characteristics – and those that stress its subjectivity – that all individuals have different sets of needs and expectations of work and, therefore, QWL must be defined as such (Eurofound, 2012). Nonetheless, there are a number of job characteristics that can be viewed as 'desirable' whilst still reflecting the essential multi-dimensional nature of QWL. Che Rose et al. (2006) suggest that:

> QWL is a comprehensive construct that includes an individual's job related well-being and the extent to which work experiences are rewarding, fulfilling and devoid of stress and other negative personal consequences ... [The] elements that are relevant to an individual's quality of work life include the task, the physical work environment, social environment within the organisation, administrative system and relationship between life on and off the job. (2006:1)

The European Working Conditions Survey adopts a highly objective conceptu-alisation in assessing change to job quality on an index comprised of earnings, prospects, intrinsic job quality (including level of discretion, work intensity and social and physical environment) and 'working time quality (including duration of working hours, flexibility and scheduling). Table 4.2 outlines a range of elements of QWL both in relation to the job itself and those relating to the wider organisa-tional and labour market context.

TABLE 4.2 *Factors that impact on Quality of Working Life*

QWL factors	Measures of quality
Remuneration including pay, perks and benefits	General (societal) comparability reflecting notions of a 'well-paid' or 'lowly paid' job
	Context-specific comparability (colleagues, organization, sector)
	'Felt fairness' – reward commensurate with level of effort exerted
Opportunities for learning and development	Opportunities to develop new skills
	Opportunities for career progression and advancement
Job security	Contractual arrangements (for example, permanent or temporary employment)
	Level of threat of redundancy
	(Perceived) impact of restructuring
	Access to jobs in internal and external labour market
Job content and the utilisation of skill	Pace and intensity of work
	Appropriate level of 'challenge'
	Variety
	Working hours and flexibility
	Match or 'fit' between worker and job characteristics (e.g. skills possessed and skills utilised)
Working conditions/physical environment	Impact of work on physical and mental well-being
Work–life balance	Delineation between work and home life
	Job allows enough time to pursue other interests and fulfil other commitments
	Acceptability of stress levels
Employee voice	Extent of involvement and influence in organisational decision-making
Control	Degree of autonomy in work organisation
	Extent of task discretion
	Level of surveillance/managerial control
Fair treatment	Equal treatment in organisational and wider labour market context
Management	Managerial style and support
	Leadership
	Recognition of good performance
Workplace relations	Relationship with management and colleagues

Given the complexity of the concept, assessing the impact of recent labour mar-ket change on QWL is problematic. Evidence on one indicator might suggest an improvement in job quality, whereas another might indicate a general deteriora-tion. For example, a key, subjective indicator of job quality for many workers is the

EUROPEAN
WORKING
CONDITIONS

extent of work–life balance, a key determinant of which is working hours. Despite the UK typically being associated with a long working hours' culture, in recent years this has declined and in 2013 men and women in full-time employment worked an average of 36.5 hours in their main job compared to 37.7 hours in 2000 (OECD, 2014), although it must be noted, however, that in the late 1970s, the average was around 35 hours. International comparison shows significant variation. In Holland, for instance, average weekly hours are 30 whereas in Turkey average hours are 47.9 (following by South Africa, South Korea, Mexico, Chile and Greece).

Evidence relating to a number of other trends associated with QWL points, however, towards more complex trends in the quality of working life in the UK over recent years. In respect of job security, CIPD (2013b) report that job tenure – the average length of time an individual stays with an employer – has increased in the UK, particularly among women, in the years 2006–2011 to just over nine years, following a long period of relative stability. However, comparatively, job tenure in the UK still remains among the lowest in the European Union (Portugal has the longest average job tenure at almost 13 years). In the USA, however, average job tenure is significantly lower at between five and six years. Whilst these trends of widespread increases in job tenure may be viewed as a sign of increasing stability of employment, these figures may also demonstrate the impact of economic recession where workers are perhaps faced with fewer alternative employment choices or the impact of an ageing workforce in which older workers are less likely to move employers.

More negatively, a range of studies shows that work is becoming progressively more intense. Green (2006), for example, reported a rise in average work effort throughout the 1990s in the UK, based upon the required speed of work and the necessity to work to tight deadlines, leading to a decline in job satisfaction (Green and Tsitsianis, 2005). Correspondingly, workplace stress is a growing problem for both employers and employees and a powerful indicator of poor job quality. Approximately 15 million working days were lost in the UK in 2013 due to stress, depression and anxiety, with an average of 23 days lost per case (HSE, 2014). This is not, however, simply a UK problem. A Europe-wide survey (Kelly Services, 2005) shows that whilst 20 per cent of British workers face high levels of workplace stress, this was lower than the average of 27 per cent across all of Europe. The issues of stress and employee well-being are discussed in more detail in Chapter 14.

Employee empowerment is considered to be both a key component of high-commitment models of HRM and a centrally important element in employee job preference. It is surprising, therefore, that the proportion of workers reporting a great deal of influence over how to do tasks at work fell from 57 per cent in 1992 to 43 per cent in 2006 (Felstead et al., 2007). Felstead et al. (2007) also reported a growing imbalance between the skills and qualifications of the labour supply and the demand for those qualifications. In 2006, 40 per cent of workers held qualifications at a higher level than was required for entry to the jobs they were doing, up from the figure of 35 per cent recorded in 2001. This widespread under-employment represents a significant source of job dissatisfaction (Rose, 2003).

Whilst this is only a brief discussion of the evidence on a limited number of indicators of QWL, the suggestion of declining job quality is supported by the broader evidence on job satisfaction. Clark (2005) found in a study of job quality in OECD countries that over the course of the 1990s overall measures of job outcomes were either static or falling despite favourable movements in hours of work, wages and job security. In particular, Clark found that satisfaction with *the work itself* (including level of autonomy and what workers actually do in their jobs) had declined sharply in the UK. Again, this is not purely a UK problem. Kelly Services (2005) found that just 47 per cent of workers surveyed in the UK were either happy or very happy with their current position compared with 68 per cent of Scandinavian workers, 61 per cent in France, 53 per cent in both Italy and

Switzerland, 50 per cent in both Russia and Germany, 46 per cent in Spain, 45 per cent in The Netherlands and 35 per cent in Belgium. The survey found that employees were particularly unhappy with the level of salary, health benefits and training opportunities. Commensurately, across Europe, evidence suggests that the proportion of 'poor quality' jobs varies significantly from 7.4 per cent of all jobs in Denmark to over half of jobs in Turkey (Eurofound, 2012).

On the evidence presented here, the current state of quality of working life would appear to make rather cheerless reading for HRM professionals and would seem to reflect a gap between the rhetoric of high-commitment HRM and the reality of worker experience. The Work Foundation (Constable et al., 2009) reports that whilst many organisations accept that there is a link between good quality jobs, employee retention and motivation, evidence suggests that management themselves represent a key barrier to improving the quality of jobs because of, for example, a lack of management skills and assumptions that some jobs simply can't be made more interesting. Similarly, despite a substantial link between employee engagement and a satisfactory balance between work and home lives, access to flexible working that might facilitate such a balance is undermined in many firms by the negative attitudes of line managers towards flexible workers and an inability to effectively manage such workers (CIPD, 2012a). Of course, management practices are only one, albeit significant, factor in determining job satisfaction and creating high-quality jobs. Other factors include the level of state intervention in employment regulation, the extent of trade union influence, technical and organisational change and increasing global competition. Nonetheless, it is clear that there is an imperative for HRM to address both the needs of the firm and the quality of employment in order to improve QWL.

SUMMARY POINTS

EMPLOYMENT RESTRUCTURING, BBC

- The labour market context of contemporary work organisations is highly fluid and unpredictable, shaped by a wide range of economic, social, technological, legal and political factors.

- Changes to the supply of labour, for example, changing demography, education and social attitudes, influence the approach an organisation takes to HRM, particularly employee resourcing and the design of jobs.

- Developments associated with the knowledge economy, such as the intensifying global economy and the rapid development and diffusion of ICT, and its consequences, such as the rapid expansion of higher education, provide the backdrop against which to better understand the range of current challenges and opportunities for HRM.

- Amid the rhetoric claiming the advent of a high-skill economy, much evidence continues to suggest that significant current employment and future job creation is in low-skill areas of the service sector.

- An increasingly competitive and unpredictable global economy is argued to necessitate greater flexibility of both organisational form and labour.

- A number of alternative forms of flexibility are at the disposal of organisations – functional, numerical, temporal, financial and spatial – that have differing implications for managers and employees.

- Changes to the labour market and organisational context of employment have significant repercussions for QWL.

- Evidence suggests that quality of working life is in decline, for example, in respect of work intensification, declining job security, increasing stress, low levels of discretion and autonomy and growing underemployment.

SELF-TEST QUESTIONS

1 What are the characteristics of a 'strong' internal labour market?

2 What are the key demographic changes that are affecting labour markets in many Western nations?

3 What do you understand by the term 'the knowledge economy' and why is it argued that many advanced capitalist nations have entered such a phase in their development?

4 Why do some commentators argue that the notion of a knowledge economy has been overstated?

5 How have businesses responded to the perceived need for increased organisational flexibility? What are the implications of these developments for employees?

6 What are the key approaches that work organisations can adopt to increase the flexibility of labour?

7 Why are some flexible working practices described only as employer-friendly?

8 Provide an assessment of the key developments affecting quality of working life over the past two decades.

TEST YOURSELF

TEST YOURSELF

Want to know more about this chapter? Review what you have been learning by visiting: **https://edge.sagepub.com/wilton3e**

- Print out or download the chapter summaries for quick revision
- Test yourself with multiple-choice questions
- Revise key terms with interactive flashcards

CASE STUDY

Blitzen Engineering and an ageing workforce

The UK, in common with many other advanced economies, has an ageing population, characterised by a declining proportion of young labour market entrants and a growing proportion of workers approaching or exceeding retirement age. This presents a number of challenges to organisations, particularly those who are reliant on an ageing workforce themselves.

Blitzen Engineering is a supplier of specialised automotive components made to the detailed specification of a limited number of prestige car manufacturers. The focus on quality that is the hallmark of their customers has meant ever-greater requirements for high-quality components delivered over ever-shorter timeframes. Given the exacting specification of their products and the high degree of precision necessary in their production,

the importance of skilled engineers to Blitzen cannot be overstressed. Strategically, the skill, knowledge and expertise of these engineers represent a key factor in maintaining existing business and winning new contracts. In other words, the engineers at Blitzen are the core reason why the company has managed to remain highly competitive in the face of growing overseas competition and maintained such prestigious contracts.

A recent staff review at Blitzen has, however, found that the average age of engineering staff was 53. Sixteen of the 25 engineers in the firm were aged between 50 and 60 and one was over 60. No members of the engineering staff were under 30 at the time of the review. Such skewing of the workforce age profile is reflective of the wider UK engineer population (in 2005, 62 per cent of engineering technicians were aged between 45 and 64) and partly reflects an historic reluctance to invest in new technology and associated skills both by employers and government. Within Blitzen there is considerable concern that within five to ten years the vast majority of the engineering department will likely have left the company.

Blitzen has begun to address what it considers to be a potentially catastrophic situation by seeking to recruit a number of engineering graduates, by attending recruitment fairs at local universities and advertising in local newspapers. Managers have, however, been dismayed at the level of interest in engineering jobs expressed by graduates at the recruitment fairs and disappointed by both the number and quality of graduate applicants. This partly reflects a national shortfall in engineering graduates who actually enter the engineering profession to meet the projected increase in demand for such graduates in the UK economy. Many graduates who possess the skills acquired on engineering degrees – particularly, advanced problem-solving and numeracy skills – are highly prized by firms in business services and banking and finance. Consequently, Blitzen is competing in a highly competitive labour market in which the best graduates are often either snapped up by larger engineering employers (because of their ability to pay higher wages and offer more structured graduate development programmes) or high-profile firms in other sectors. In contrast to their experiences in the graduate labour market, the HR manager has recently accepted an invitation to speak at a local further education college and has been surprised at the enthusiasm of many of the students who attended.

Task

You have been asked to advise senior management at Blitzen about how you might go about addressing the labour market problems that they are experiencing and put together one or more strategies for management to consider. In reflecting on these problems, consider what factors are important in ensuring the long-term viability of the company, the interaction between the internal and external labour markets, alternative approaches to sourcing required labour and how the company might best compete in the external labour market.

USEFUL READING

Journal articles

Grugulis, I. and Stoyanova, D. (2011) Skill and performance, *British Journal of Industrial Relations*, 49 (3): 515–36.

This excellent article explores the relationship between skill and performance at multiple levels of economic activity. In particular, it provides useful insight into the problems of defining both of these often taken-for-granted terms.

Morris, J. (2004) The future of work: Organisational and international perspectives, *International Journal of Human Resource Management*, 15 (2): 263–75.

This article places the discussion about changes to working and work in an international context. Whilst acknowledging the impact of new technology and internationalisation on organisational context, it argues that this does not necessarily mean the eradication of traditional forms of work and calls for a more considered, empirically based assessment of change.

Books, book chapters and reports

Brown, P. and Hesketh, A. (2004) *The Mismanagement of Talent: Employability and Jobs in the Knowledge Economy*, Oxford: Oxford University Press.

Drawing on empirical evidence, this wide-ranging text provides insightful critiques of the contemporary job market, education sector and recruitment industry. It particularly focuses on the notion of 'employability' and its influence on policy-makers in the UK in relation to the graduate labour market.

CIPD (2012a) *Flexible Working Provision and Uptake: Survey Report*, London: CIPD

This report summarises the findings from a recent survey of both employees and employers on the provision and uptake of flexible working arrangements and provides some interesting insights into the barriers to and difficulties associated with flexible working.

Constable, S., Coats, D. Bevan, S. and Mahdon, M. (2009) *Good Jobs*, London: The Work Foundation, available at **www.theworkfoundation.com/Reports/226/Good-Jobs** (accessed 9 September 2015).

This report outlines research on employers' perceptions of what constitutes 'good jobs' and the relationship between job quality and employee motivation and organisational performance. The findings suggest increasing agreement that good jobs and organisational success can be mutually supporting goals.

European Working Conditions Surveys (EWCS), available at **www.eurofound.europa.eu/european-working-conditions-surveys-ewcs** (accessed 9 September 2015).

The EWCS has been undertaken every five years from 1990 to provide an overview of working conditions. The detailed reports provide comparative data on trends in key measures of job quality and their impact – a valuable resource to understand how work is experienced and the differential access to good quality jobs across the EU. The reports also provide some useful discussion about the conceptualisation of and measurement of 'job quality'.

Parker, L. and Bevan, S. (2011) *Good Work and Our Times: Report of the Good Work Commission*, London: The Work Foundation.

Drawing on extensive research, this thought-provoking report provides a broad discussion of what constitutes 'good work' and how governments, employers and employees can work together to create more of such work. It provides a very useful accompanying piece to the discussion on quality of working life provided in this chapter.

FURTHER ONLINE READING

The following articles can be accessed for free on the book's companion website **https://edge.sagepub.com/wilton3e**:

Beck, V. (2012) Employers' views of learning and training for an ageing workforce, *Management Learning*, 45 (2): 200–15.

Beltrán-Martín, I., Roca-Puig, V., Escrig-Tena, A. and Bou-Llusar, J. C. (2008) Human resource flexibility as a mediating variable between High Performance Work Systems and performance, *Journal of Management,* 34: 1009–44.

Grimshaw, D., Ward, K., Rubery, J. and Beynon, H. (2008) Organisations and the transformation of the internal labour market, *Work, Employment and Society*, 15 (1): 25–54.

James, S., Warhurst, C., Tholen, G. and Commander, J. (2013) What we know and what we need to know about graduate skills, *Work, Employment and Society*, 27 (6): 952–63.

Kalleberg, A. L. (2003) Flexible firms and labor market segmentation: Effects of workplace restructuring on jobs and workers, *Work and Occupations*, 30 (2): 154–75.

Szabó, K. and Négyesi, A. (2008) The spread of contingent work in the knowledge-based economy, *Human Resource Development Review*, 4 (1): 63–85.

Thompson, P. (2003) Disconnected capitalism: Or why employers can't keep their side of the bargain, *Work Employment and Society*, 17 (2): 359–78.

Williams, C. (2014) Out of the shadows: a classification of economies by the size and character of their informal sector, *Work, Employment and Society*, 28(5), 735–53.

Want to know more about this chapter? Visit the companion website at: **https://edge.sagepub.com/wilton3e** to access practice questions, videos and selected journal articles to further enhance your study.

THE NATIONAL AND INTERNATIONAL CONTEXT OF HRM

CHAPTER OBJECTIVES

- To outline how national culture shapes HRM policies and practice

- To identify the national and international institutions that influence and constrain HRM practices

- To discuss the implications of national difference for the transference of HRM practices within multinational corporations (MNCs)

- To examine the interaction of home and host country characteristics in shaping HRM practice in MNCs

CULTURAL AND INSTITUTIONAL INFLUENCES

INTRODUCTION

The previous chapter outlined a number of key developments in the labour market context of HRM. This chapter extends this focus and outlines the broader political, legal, social, economic and cultural context of work, employment and HRM. Brewster (1995) suggests that organisations operate under four levels of constraint that act to shape HRM policy and practice: international (for example, the activities of the European Union), national (culture and institutions), organisational (for example, the objectives and strategy of the firm) and those directly relating to HRM itself (for instance, the presence of trade unions). This chapter is concerned with the first two of these constraints: those that constitute an organisation's 'outer' context, which, along with 'inner' organisationally specific factors, shape HRM policies and practices (Budhwar and Debrah, 2001) (see Figure 5.1).

Nation states differ in a number of important ways and consequently the challenges faced by managers from country to country are not identical. The purpose

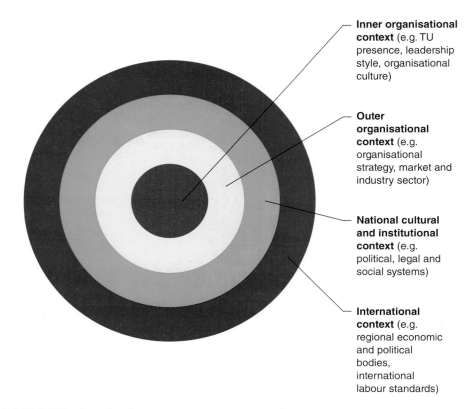

Inner organisational context (e.g. TU presence, leadership style, organisational culture)

Outer organisational context (e.g. organisational strategy, market and industry sector)

National cultural and institutional context (e.g. political, legal and social systems)

International context (e.g. regional economic and political bodies, international labour standards)

FIGURE 5.1   Levels of constraint on managerial activity

of this chapter is to outline how management style, employment practices and the relationship between employer and employee are affected by both the institutional ('hard') and cultural ('soft') dimensions of national business systems. The imperative of understanding how the national and international context of HRM constrains and provides opportunities for HRM is particularly strong in the context of globalisation, the growth of multinational corporations and international cooperation between companies, through partnerships or strategic alliances (Browaeys and Price, 2008) and the trend towards regional integration in the form of transnational economic and political institutions. It is important, therefore, for all managers to understand the cultural assumptions that underpin HRM practices in order to be able to assess what policies are likely to be effective in a given context, for example, when companies are working together or where a firm is operating outside of its country of origin, to identify where difficulties may be encountered and to explain the apparent success or failure of specific approaches to people management.

GLOBALISATION AND THE CHANGING INTERNATIONAL CONTEXT OF HRM

CHALLENGES OF
GLOBALIZATION

Globalisation can be understood as the movement towards a more integrated and interdependent world economy that is fundamentally altering the where and how of material production, distribution and consumption of goods, services and finance (Dicken, 2007). This process is gradually compressing the 'distances' between people and places with the potential (albeit contested) outcome of a single global economy and society in which 'individual places, groups of people and individual societies have lost their significance and power' (Abercrombie and Warde, 2000: 13). This 'convergence' scenario is associated with the ever-increasing speed in the transmission of technologies, products, ideas and management practices beyond the individual nation state, which are gradually breaking down cultural, social and political barriers between nations and eroding economic sovereignty.

There is, however, significant debate over the extent to which globalisation is truly de-emphasising national borders. On the one hand, the activities of MNCs, allied to the growth of supra-national state organisations such as the European Union, are argued to be part of a trend of convergence in economic and political policy, patterns of consumption and management activity. Furthermore, as barriers to labour mobility between countries become more permeable, patterns of international migration are changing the composition of national labour supplies. Subsequently, very few states, if any, have complete economic and political freedom to determine their future destiny without regard to events in the wider world (Kidger and Allen, 2006) and most are subject to significant influence from outside their borders. On the other hand, however, it is clear that both world politics and the emergent transnational business system continue to be largely organised in terms of nation states (Dicken, 2007) and it can be argued that globalisation is actually throwing the cultural and institutional differences between nation states into sharper relief. This is especially the case where MNCs operate across a wide variety of national business systems. Social structures and processes are historically embedded and can, therefore, be slow to change despite the pressures resulting from globalisation. In this respect they can prove to be a considerable impediment to the 'free' activity of MNCs and the transference of HRM practices from one country to another.

THE NATIONAL CONTEXT OF HRM

A nation's economic development depends on the exploitation of its physical resources (such as supplies of raw material for manufacturing or oil and gas reserves) and human resources (the size and composition of its labour force) as well as the systems that have evolved over time to utilise and develop these resources (Edwards and Rees, 2006). These systems include the formal political, educational and legal systems that govern how people live together (institutions), as well as systems of informal social regulation created by socialisation and education, which establishes the values, beliefs and customs that shape people's behaviour towards each other (culture). Nation states, therefore, act as 'containers' of distinctive cultures and institutional frameworks that have a significant influence on all economic activity and, subsequently, the ways in which organisations manage workers. In discussing their influence on HRM, national culture and institutions are sometimes conflated. Tayeb (2005) suggests, however, that the way in which they influence managerial practice is different, culture influencing management informally through the 'internalised socially accepted norms of behaviour' (2005: 45), whilst institutional influence is formal, through rules, regulations and the imposition of sanctions for non-conformity. However, the interaction between a nation's culture and its institutions is bilateral in that the institutions both reflect and reinforce the dominant values and attitudes held by a society. Institutions are viewed as symbols or artefacts of national cultural values that in turn shape the way political and business systems have developed.

NATIONAL CULTURE

Culture can be defined as 'a learned, shared, compelling, interrelated set of symbols whose meanings provide a set of orientations for members of a society' (Terpstra and David, 1991: 6). Culture therefore represents an organised system of values, attitudes, beliefs, assumptions and behavioural meanings that shape how members of a social group relate to each other and to outsiders. The development of culture within a social group helps to reduce complexity and uncertainty, establishing both ways of 'being' and 'thinking' that provide a consistency of outlook and making possible the processes of decision-making, coordination and control within that group. In broad terms, culture can be viewed as a set of responses to the basic questions of how a group sees itself, how it relates to the environment, how it relates to others and how it relates to time (Kluckholn and Strodtbeck, 1961). This is clear in Schein's (1985) definition of culture as a set of shared solutions to universal problems of external adaptation (how to survive) and internal integration (how to stay together) that have evolved over time and are handed down from one generation to the next.

Tayeb (2003) suggests that there is a range of factors that shape national culture, including a country's physical environment, its history and the influence of institutions such as religion, education and mass media. However, nation states and culture are not always synonymous. Culture can transcend national borders and, even within the same nation, different regions or social and religious groups might possess distinctively different cultures. It is therefore important to acknowledge that subcultures exist and that conflict, dissent and variation exist within a distinct national culture. Despite such heterogeneity, Hofstede (2001) suggests that nations are distinctive political entities and social systems with unifying legal, education, labour and employment relations systems and many are small enough to have similar geographic and ecological conditions and to share a common language. These factors influence the way in which people interact with their environment and each other thereby constituting 'a constant thread ... through our lives which makes us distinguishable from others, especially those in other countries: this thread is our national culture' (Tayeb, 2003: 13).

Conceptualising culture

HOFSTEDE ON CULTURE

The most well-known attempt to conceptualise and measure dimensions of national culture in order to assess its subsequent implications for organisations is presented by Hofstede (2001). Using data collected in a survey of 117,000 workers employed by IBM in 40 different countries, Hofstede measured the values and beliefs held by these workers according to four (and later a fifth) identified dimensions along which national culture could be evaluated (Box 5.1) and which shape the relationships between individuals and their colleagues, subordinates, managers and the organisation as a whole. By concentrating on employees of a single firm, Hofstede sought to ensure that organisationally specific factors were controlled for, thus isolating nationality as the key cultural variable yet providing a sufficiently large sample to justify generalising his findings to the wider population. Whilst even Hofstede notes that there was not complete uniformity of 'values' among same-country respondents, the typology of cultural dimensions that resulted from the study provides a useful means by which to make sense of and to contrast national cultural differences, although, as Thomas (2008) warns, categorisation can often lead to oversimplification, replacing complex reality with stereotypes.

On the basis of this typology, Hofstede suggests that the countries that made up his original sample can be grouped into eight cultural clusters united by common cultural characteristics (Table 5.1). It is clear that geography plays a considerable part in the cultural make-up of a particular country as many of the groupings constitute regional 'blocs' (for example, the Nordic group). Hofstede's groups also reflect the level of industrial advancement and also patterns of historic colonialism.

Hofstede's work has been subject to significant criticism. For example, there are grounds to suggest that even a large sample of employees of a single organisation is not sufficiently representative to generalise about the cultural characteristics of

---

BOX 5.1
UNDERSTAND

Hofstede's (2001) dimensions of culture

Individualism (versus collectivism)

This dimension denotes both the extent to which one's self-identity is defined according to individual or group characteristics and the extent to which individual ('loose ties') or group ('close ties') interests and responsibilities predominate in society. In individualist cultures, there is an emphasis on the exercise of individual initiative, personal responsibility and preoccupation with the self and the immediate family. In contrast, in 'collectivist' cultures there exists a broader set of loyalties and dependencies, including the extended family, the wider social network and the firm.

Power distance

Power distance refers to the extent to which power differences within society are accepted and sanctioned and the acceptability of social inequality. In high power distance societies there is an acceptance that managers act in an autocratic, directive manner and that power requires limited legitimisation other than 'rank'. However, latent conflict and mistrust between managers and subordinates can exist. In cultures rated low in power distance, a closer relationship exists between superiors and subordinates, with greater worker involvement in decision-making.

Uncertainty avoidance

This dimension refers to the extent to which risk-taking is encouraged and situations of ambiguity tolerated. In societies ranked low in uncertainty avoidance, there is an acceptance of taking 'each day as it comes', risk-taking is encouraged and people place less importance on following rules. In societies predicated on high uncertainty avoidance greater emphasis is placed on the creation of security, the avoidance of risk and ambiguity and a preference for the long-term predictability provided by rules and established relationships.

Masculinity (versus femininity)

This measure refers to how sharply the social divide between males and females is drawn and the extent of clear differentiation between female and male roles. It also reflects the extent to which traditional male orientations of ambition, autonomy and achievement are emphasised over traditional female orientations of nurturance and interpersonal harmony. High masculinity societies emphasise the acquisition of material possessions as measures of success, whereas in low masculinity countries, job satisfaction tends to take precedence over extrinsic job success along with an emphasis on concern for the environment, quality of life and caring.

Long-term/short-term orientation

This fifth dimension refers to how cultural orientation relates to time. Cultures characterised by a long-term orientation are future-directed, with an emphasis on persistence and thrift and high levels of personal adaptability to change. A short-term orientation is reflective of cultures that emphasise the achievement of quick results, the importance of the 'bottom line' and personal steadfastness and stability.

an entire nation. Moreover, the absence of Eastern European and African nations within the sample acts to undermine the attempt to provide an overarching picture of contrasts in national culture. Notably, McSweeney (2002) provides a forceful critique both of the methodology employed by Hofstede in his original work and the assumptions of cultural homogeneity that underpin his classification. Similarly, Spector et al. (2001) and Fernandez et al. (1997) have called into question the validity of Hofstede's measures of cultural variation. In contrast, however, some studies suggest that Hofstede's dimensions and cultural clusters continue to be appropriate (Ronen and Shenkar, 1985; Smith et al., 1998; Merritt, 2000).

Further online reading This article critiques Hofstede's national culture research and challenges some of the crucial assumptions that underlie his claim to have 'uncovered the secrets of entire national cultures'.

McSweeney, B. (2002) Hofstede's model of national cultural differences and their consequences: A triumph of faith – a failure of analysis, *Human Relations*, 55 (1): 89–118.

Further typologies of cultural variation have been developed by Trompenaars (1994) and Trompenaars and Hampden-Turner (1998), but the most recent attempt to categorise national cultural differences is provided by the Global Leadership and Organizational Behaviour Effectiveness (GLOBE) project which collected data from approximately 17,000 middle managers in 951 organisations across 62 different 'societies' (House et al., 2004). This project developed nine dimensions of cultural variation, based on both management practice and values. Overall, the typology represents an amplification and development of Hofstede's earlier work (Box 5.2). The project also suggested that whilst some forms of leadership tend to be universally and cross-culturally endorsed, leadership styles that value status and individualism may not be appropriate in all cultures.

Implications for HRM

National culture, at least in part, shapes the values, attitudes and behaviour of managers, employees and customers. In particular, the cultural background of senior management in an organisation is likely to 'set the tone' for management practice and directly influence organisational culture. National culture also shapes the nature of the employment relationship in a given context and subsequently how HRM acts to manage this relationship. For example, Kidger and Allen (2006) contrast Anglo-Saxon culture (such as the US and UK) and that found in some Asian countries, such as Japan. They suggest that in Anglo-Saxon culture, reflective of the view that nature can and should be controlled, managers stress their right to manage employees as they see fit, albeit alongside employee groups who also seek control over work organisation. The employment relationship is subsequently perceived as confrontational and low-trust, leading to HRM practices that emphasise close supervision and the formalisation of workplace discipline. This contrasts with the 'Eastern' perspective that is to value harmony with nature and stresses adaptability. This is reflected in attitudes towards personal and work relationships, particularly the importance placed on mutual obligation and the earning of respect. The findings of a survey conducted by the Japanese firm Dentsu (Jacques, 2005) further reinforce this contrast. It found that 68 per cent of Americans and 60 per cent of Britons identified with 'a society in which everyone can freely compete according to his/her will and abilities' compared with just 22 per cent of Japanese.

TABLE 5.1 *National variations in cultural characteristics*

	Anglo	Germanic	Nordic	More developed Asian	Less developed Asian	Near Eastern	More developed Latin	Less developed Latin
Power distance	Low	Low	Low	Medium	High	High	High	High
Uncertainty avoidance	Low–medium	High	Low–medium	High	Low	High	High	High
Individualism	High	Medium	Medium	Medium	Low	Low	High	Low
Masculinity	High	High	Low	Medium	Medium	Medium	Medium	Diverse
Examples	Australia, Canada, Ireland, New Zealand, UK, USA	Austria, Germany, Italy, Israel, South Africa, Switzerland	Denmark, Finland, Netherlands, Norway, Sweden	Japan	India, Pakistan, Singapore, Taiwan, Thailand	Greece, Iran, Turkey	Argentina, Brazil, Belgium, France, Spain	Chile, Colombia, Mexico, Peru, Portugal, Venezuela

Source: adapted from Hofstede, 2001

This reflects the extent of high and low individualism found in the respective cultures. The survey also found that only 15 per cent of Japanese agreed with the proposition that 'it's all right to break the rules, depending on the circumstances', compared with 37 per cent of Americans and 39 per cent of Britons, reflecting the lower degree of risk avoidance in Anglo-Saxon culture.

BOX 5.2
UNDERSTAND

The GLOBE nine dimensions of national culture

- *Institutional collectivism* – the degree to which organisational and societal institutional practices encourage and reward collective distribution of resources and collective action.
- *In-group collectivism* – the degree to which individuals express pride, loyalty and cohesiveness in their organisations or families.
- *Power distance* – the degree to which members of a collective expect power to be distributed equally.
- *Uncertainty avoidance* – the extent to which a society, organisation or group relies on social norms, rules and procedures to alleviate the unpredictability of future events.

- *Gender egalitarianism* – the degree to which a collective minimises gender inequality.
- *Assertiveness* – the degree to which individuals are assertive, confrontational and aggressive in their relationships with others.
- *Human orientation* – the degree to which a collective encourages and rewards people for being fair, altruistic, generous, caring and kind to others.
- *Future orientation* – the extent to which people engage in future-orientated behaviours such as delayed gratification, planning and investing in the future.
- *Performance orientation* – the degree to which a collective encourages and rewards group members for performance improvement and excellence.

Source: House et al., 2004

National culture therefore influences many aspects of HRM, such as the degree to which decision-making is centralised, the importance of hierarchy and the relationships between managers, subordinates and peers. For example, Boisot and Xing (1992) found that due to a strict adherence to bureaucracy, Chinese managers spend more time communicating with senior management but less time communicating with peers compared to US managers. As Hofstede suggests, however, these contrasts are not restricted to geographically distant cultures. Stewart et al. (1994) found that as a result of flatter organisational structures and a greater emphasis on technical as opposed to interpersonal control, German managers were less concerned about gaining cooperation with workers, less focused on direct supervision and expected more technical involvement in tasks than their British counterparts. Part Two of this book looks at specific functions of HRM and provides more detailed discussion of the ways in which national differences impact on HR policy and practice.

Further online reading This article explores the assumption that national culture acts as a constraint on management practice, which the author argues is inconsistent with empirical evidence or requires further exploration and verification.

Gerhart, B. (2008) Cross-cultural management research: Assumptions, evidence and suggested directions, *International Journal of Cross Cultural Management*, 8 (3): 259–74.

BOX 5.3
ETHICAL INSIGHT

Ethics in international context

Recognition of cultural and institutional varia- tion presents a particular problem for ethics in HRM because there are 'persistent, fundamen- tal national differences in terms of how business ethics is defined, debated and judged due to distinctive institutional, legal, social and cultural contexts' (Schneider and Barsoux, 2008: 305). Thomas (2008) suggests, for example, that discrimination in employment against women that is reprehensible in one culture is a normal expression of gender-based roles in another. In particular, cultures vary in the extent to which ethi- cal decision-making reflects an individual, moral judgement or a consensual set of guiding prin- ciples or norms of behaviour. Cultures that adopt the former perspective such as the US tend to place an emphasis on explicit rules to shape behaviour, whereas those cultures that reflect consensual approaches place greater emphasis on informal social control.

These two approaches reflect two moral phi- losophies that can guide managers in making ethical decisions. *Consequential models* of ethical decision-making focus on the outcome or conse- quence of a decision to determine what is ethical based upon the moral doctrine of utilitarianism (that we should always act to produce the greatest good for the greatest number in the decisions that we make). *Deontological (or rule-based) models* hold that human beings have certain fundamental rights and that a sense of duty to uphold these rights is the basis of ethical decision-making rather than a concern for consequences. Individual pref- erence for either of these principles is affected by national culture.

However, even though a manager might adhere to one of these philosophies to make a particular decision, under different cultural con- ditions this might still result in different 'ethical' behaviour. *Cultural relativism* suggests that moral and ethical standards are specific to a particular culture: what is considered unethical in one cul- ture might be quite acceptable in another, even though the same moral principle is being adhered to. At its extreme, the concept of cultural relativism 'declares the international decision-making arena as a moral-free zone where everything goes' (Thomas, 2008: 111).

NATIONAL INSTITUTIONS

As well as the cultural dimension of national context, nation states vary accord- ing to the institutions that constitute the national business system. In broad terms, the economic growth strategy adopted in a particular country tends to rely on a particular production regime which is, in turn, supported by specific national forms of industrial relations, employment regimes, welfare and financial systems. For example, a country might promote economic growth through low- wage mass production or a high-value, high-quality production strategy, both of which require a specific supporting institutional infrastructure. For the latter, this might include regulation that stresses employment security, relatively high wages delivered by centralised, coordinated bargaining between employers and trade unions and government inducements for long-term skill and technological investment, financed through high levels of taxation. It is evident, therefore, that the role of the state, national financial and legal systems, education and train- ing systems and labour relation systems combine to form the distinctive social organisation of a country and provide a 'logic of action' that guides manage- ment practice (Edwards and Rees, 2006). This logic is also shaped by patterns of regional integration. For example, firms operating in the European Union must take account of both national and international context as the EU increasingly acts to influence management practice above and beyond the sovereign nation. The following section details some key elements of the institutional framework that acts to shape HRM.

Political economic system

The prevailing political economic system in a nation provides the ideological framework within which all government and social activity takes place. It is a direct influence on the way in which a nation develops and the specific institutions that seek to enact a particular ideological position. For example, the 'type' of capitalism in operation shapes a range of national political, legal and social welfare processes (Box 5.4). Ideological differences around state intervention in the free operation of markets, whether through public ownership of national assets or through regulation, are often reflected in the party political system, where historically the political 'right' (free market) has been contrasted with the 'left' (social market). Whilst over time the dividing line between parties becomes blurred or redrawn (as with the advent of 'New' Labour in the 1990s, a more centrist version of the UK Labour party), political parties are constrained by national culture in that they must govern according to the fundamental values of that nation. For example, neither the Democratic nor Republican party in the USA would propose to significantly increase government intervention in the operation of the labour market because it would fundamentally contradict the values of individual freedom and self-sufficiency that underpin US culture. The prevailing political ideology of a nation state and the institutional context it shapes act to

---

BOX 5.4
UNDERSTAND

Four models of capitalism

Dicken (2007) identifies four models of capitalism and suggests that the fundamental difference between them lies in their differing conception of the 'proper' role of government in regulating the economy.

- In *neo-liberal market capitalism* (exemplified by the USA) free enterprise in an open market is encouraged and the dominant philosophy is shareholder value and the maximisation of returns to the owners of capital. There is limited or minimal state intervention in the activities of business, including in the treatment of workers, limited rights of recognition for trade unions and the state does not significantly attempt to plan the economy in a strategic manner.
- In *social market capitalism* (such as Germany) a higher premium is placed upon collaboration or social partnership

between economic actors, with a broader identification of stakeholders beyond that of shareholders. This is reflected in the greater emphasis on social welfare – such as employment rights – and the greater regulation of business activity both through direct state intervention and trade union legitimacy and involvement.

- In *developmental capitalism* (reflective of several South-East Asian nations such as Japan or South Korea) the state plays a much more central role, particularly in setting social and economic goals within an explicit industrial strategy, although not normally in terms of extensive public ownership.
- In the *communist–capitalist system* of China a highly centralised political system and the extensive state-ownership of economic activity are combined with an increasingly open capitalist system.

---

significantly influence HRM practices, primarily in the extent to which government intervenes directly in managerial practice through legislation and the type of employment relationship it promotes. For example, cooperation between managers and employees is typically stronger in social market economies.

Government

Shaped by the prevailing political ideology and party political divisions, the policies of the incumbent government in a country are clearly influential in establishing the political, legal and social context of HRM. The state has a number of distinctive roles (including economic manager, legislator and employer) and how the government seeks to fulfil each of these roles influences HRM practice, either directly or indirectly. The direct influence of government might be seen in employment legislation that curtails the ability of managers to act in a particular way (for example, by imposing minimum standards of employment). Indirect influence might stem from its position as the regulator of trade, foreign investment and industry. For example, the government's support for both inward and outward foreign direct investment (FDI) will determine the exposure of domestic firms to foreign management practices and, ultimately, shape the way the state regulates the labour market. (For example, in order to attract investment from overseas MNCs, governments might weaken labour market regulation as an incentive.) The government's position as an employer is influential, particularly in the extent of public ownership of national assets and the degree to which it uses public sector employment practices to set an example to private sector firms.

Other issues affecting management practice are government attitudes to trade unions and the level of intervention in social policy beyond employment, for example, the level and focus of investment in education and training and the provision of social welfare. The stability of the incumbent government and of the wider political system also shapes the context in which management operates.

Economic context

Economic context influences HRM and employment practice in a number of ways. Most fundamentally, the stage of economic development in a country will shape the societal, market and labour market conditions under which management operates. For example, economically advanced nations are characterised by a high degree of urban population concentration and comparatively high levels of education across society, which can act both as a driver and by-product of a more knowledge-intensive economy. Less economically developed nations are characterised by lower levels of education, less concern for welfare and an economy based upon agriculture or manufacturing. Opportunities and constraints for management practice are also associated with the prevailing economic conditions. For example, in times of economic downturn where unemployment is high or rising, the increased supply of labour means that management is in a stronger bargaining position over terms and conditions of employment and is able to manage more autocratically than in situations where labour wields increased power because of its relative scarcity. Subsequently, the extent of the reality or threat of unemployment shapes the relationship between employer and employee. Moreover, economic factors such as inflation, interest rates, unemployment, business cycles and economic forecasts all shape HRM policy and practice.

MANAGING
IN A GLOBAL
ECONOMY

The law and HRM

In brief, national and international labour law constrains the degrees of freedom a company has in determining the substantive content of the employment relationship. More broadly, it shapes the role of the state in employee relations and the relationship between firms and the government. The national legal system can most obviously influence HRM activities through directly outlawing particular activities or imposing minimum standards for the treatment of workers. Labour law can be both individual and collective. Individual employment legislation covers areas such as health and safety at work, maternity and paternity rights, the minimum wage, physical working conditions, pensions, redundancy and dismissal. Collective legislation relates to that which governs industrial relations, for example, the legitimacy of trade union membership and the rights of recognition afforded unions for the purposes of collective bargaining. In this area, legislation can shape employment relations by promoting either competition or cooperation among employers and employees. For example, Germany has a long-standing tradition of co-determination rights for workers and a strong legal position for trade unions that encourages a partnership approach to workforce management. In contrast, only in 1998 were trade unions in the UK given the positive 'right' of recognition by employers to bargain on behalf of their members.

National legal systems can also have an indirect impact on employment management in the extent to which it embodies a 'hands-off' approach to the regulation of markets and competition or provides detailed rules and laws covering issues such as restraint of trade, corporate social responsibility and the environment. National case law also influences employee management through setting precedents for practice. The extent to which legislation is pro-worker or pro-employer reflects the prevailing political ideology, economic conditions, the extent of inequality and poverty in society, the strength of trade unions/employers' associations and the effectiveness of their lobbying of government. For firms operating within the European Union, management practice is also shaped by European-wide legislation in respect of both social and economic policy. Internationally, pressure from bodies such as the International Labour Organisation (ILO) influences the direction and content of national labour law by seeking to impose minimum standards for the treatment of workers and greater rights for employees. Both the ILO and the EU are discussed further below.

Financial systems

The financial system in a given nation – in particular, the relationship between capital supply and demand – shapes the approach that firms take towards the market and ultimately how workers are managed. For example, in a shareholder economy such as the USA, where large companies are typically privately owned by small and large investors, the emphasis for senior management is to deliver short-term return on investment. This is reflected in an emphasis on the bottom line, rather than other measures of organisational performance or 'health'. In a stakeholder economy, such as Germany, substantial investment is provided through long-term relationships between firms and banks, in the form of 'patient capital', rather than simply private shareholders. The emphasis is on the longer term and consideration of a wider range of interest groups in the company, and on the more gradual development of market share and sustainable growth. In Japan this long-term focus is also made possible because of close cooperative relationships between organisations within large corporate networks called *keiretsu* and the involvement of the state in directing industrial activity. In such economies, in connection with other institutional and cultural factors, employees are more likely to be considered as organisational stakeholders whose welfare is a principal concern, rather than simply an organisational resource to be used instrumentally in the pursuit of profit. This ultimately determines HRM practices and the extent to which workers' interests are considered in corporate decision-making.

Trade unions

The status, form and origins of trade unionism shape their power and independence *vis-à-vis* management and their ability to represent the interests of their members. Union characteristics differ across nations. For example, the historic origins of trade unions in the UK in trades or craft guilds has resulted in unions of workers being formed on the basis of occupation or industry, typically independent of employers. In contrast, Japanese unions have been traditionally associated with particular enterprises in a more dependent relationship (similar bodies are typically referred to as employee associations in the UK). The relationship between unions and management also varies across nations. In the UK, reflective of historical class structures, this relationship is traditionally adversarial. In Germany, however, the relationship tends to be more cooperative and consensual and unions are more likely to be considered as equal partners in collective bargaining. It should be noted, however, that mutual antagonism between the parties is likely to exist regardless of the dominant 'type' of relationship, representing the fundamental conflicts of interest between employer and employees. The role and activities of trade unions are heavily influenced by the rights and responsibilities afforded to them under legislation; for example, the right to undertake particular forms of industrial action, the right to recognition by employers for bargaining purposes and the right of individuals to collectively express, promote, pursue and defend common interests ('freedom of association'). Trade unions are discussed further in Chapter 10.

Employers' associations

The power and influence of employers' associations also varies from country to country. In some, employers' associations are typically lobbying groups (for example, the Confederation of British Industry) whose primary purpose is to promote the interests of business. In other countries, however, employers' associations are involved in collective bargaining at a national level with individual unions or confederations of unions. For example, negotiations of pay and other terms and conditions of employment in the German automobile sector take place between a federation of car manufacturers and trade unions, such as IG Metall, to collectively agree employment practice across the entire sector.

Social structures

As well as political and economic institutions, social structures also shape HRM activity. Tayeb (2005: 53) suggests that the 'degree of rigidity of social structures and the relationship between the various social strata are to a large extent reflected in work organisations'.

In many industrial societies, social structures are based upon class differentiation that is sometimes overlaid with other parallel social stratification, such as caste or racial segregation. The degree of entrenchment of class structures varies across nations and is again the result of both social history and government attempts to reduce this differentiation. For example, Tayeb (2005) suggests that class differentials are minimised in Scandinavian countries by social welfare policies to promote equality of opportunity, whereas class differences remain strong in the UK partly because of more limited attempts to address them.

Other dimensions of social structures that can be reflected within organisations are attitudes to the elderly and ageing. For example, in Japan seniority and older workers are respected, whereas in many Western societies youth tends to be lionised and ageing associated with declining ability and performance. Overall, prevailing social structures can be replicated in work organisations in the legitimacy given to discrimination against certain sections of society, often minority groups such as women, homosexuals, minority religions, minority ethnic groups and the elderly. These attitudes are culturally determined norms and tend also to reflect the presence or absence of legislation outlawing such discrimination.

As an example of how institutions and context interact to shape patterns of employment and management practice, Box 5.5 briefly outlines the Indian context of employment and HRM. There is a range of other national examples provided on the companion website, including the UK, Sweden, Germany, Japan and China.

INTERNATIONAL INSTITUTIONS

Alongside national institutions, HRM practices are also influenced by international bodies that act to directly and indirectly shape the conditions under which organisations operate.

International Labour Organisation (ILO)

ILO

The ILO seeks to improve working conditions and eradicate exploitative employment practices through establishing conventions and enacting recommendations to improve worker rights across its 170 member states. ILO conventions outline legal principles that should be present in national legislation but which require ratification by each member state. Recommendations are guidelines on practice to supplement existing conventions or where no convention is warranted. The central objectives and mission of the ILO are outlined in Box 5.6. In particular, the ILO seeks to promote freedom to form trade unions and bargain collectively and actively works towards a ban on forced and child labour.

The ILO's labour code is an important reference point for MNCs who enter into agreements with overseas suppliers. There have been a number of recent examples where the reputation of Western firms has been damaged when they have been found to use overseas suppliers who violate these ILO principles. For example, in June 2008 a BBC documentary revealed how Indian suppliers to the UK clothing retailer Primark had subcontracted work to homeworkers, among them children. This was despite Primark having a supplier code of conduct that expressly bans the use of child labour in accordance with its status as a member of the Ethical Trading Initiative that monitors and promotes international labour standards.

Regional integration

A key dimension of the international context of HRM is the developing pattern of regional integration. At the end of the twentieth century there were 100 regional

BOX 5.5
GLOBAL INSIGHT

Culture, institutions and HRM in India

Over recent years, India has proved to be one of the fastest growing economies in the world, primarily driven by service sector expansion and associated foreign direct investment, but increasingly by improvements in international competiveness in key strategic industries, such as automobiles and pharmaceuticals (Sharma, 2006). India is a complex multicultural society with many languages, religions and traditions, but with certain characteristics that are viewed as shared by the population as a whole (Tayeb, 1987). Indian culture, both in relation to wider society and work organisations, can be described as collectivist in a 'clannish' sense with individuals displaying strong ties to their immediate community, extended family, friends and their religious group. Social stratification is rigid, not by social class but according to the caste system that dictates a person's position in society, regardless of professional status and qualifications, thus impeding social mobility. Browaeys and Price (2008) suggest that loyalty to the extended family takes priority over loyalty to work organisations resulting in low levels of commitment to organisational interests and objectives, although strong loyalty can develop towards one's professional groups. Drawing on Hofstede's measures of culture difference, Indian culture is characterised as demonstrating relatively low levels of uncertainty avoidance, particularly as risk-taking is viewed from the perspective that failure is 'fated' rather than a result of personal incompetence, reflecting the deep sense of fatalism associated with Hinduism (Browaeys and Price, 2008).

National and plant-based (rather than craft or occupational) trade unions present a strong countervailing challenge to management resulting in confrontational industrial relations. Labour legislation has traditionally been pro-worker aimed both at protecting jobs and employee well-being, although as the Indian economy has become more open there has been some deregulation albeit failing to keep pace with the reforms in industrial and trade policies (Saha, 2006). Part of the effect of the restrictive and complex labour laws that exists in India is to create inflexibility of employment and limit the growth of jobs in the formal economy (Sharma, 2006), leading to rising employment in the informal economy where jobs are insecure and terms and conditions are poor (Saha, 2006).

These social and cultural characteristics are reflected in work organisations in a number of ways. Budhwar and Khatri (2001) suggest that the operation of internal labour markets in Indian firms is based on social and familial relations, political contacts, caste, religion and economic power, and that the strength of these relationships can act as a 'drag' on performance. Although legislation restricts the ability of employers to fire and lay off workers by making redundancy costly for the firm, a lack of enforcement tends to be reflected in poorly developed internal labour markets. Rules regarding practices such as recruitment, training promotions and lay-offs are ad hoc in nature and subject to easy manipulation by employers. Budhwar and Khatri report that the tendency to under-invest in training in Indian firms is mainly due to financial constraints and the non-availability of required courses, but also the fear of losing trained managers and subsequent difficulties in recruiting externally. That said, Stumpf et al. (2010) report on research that suggests significant and rapid modernisation in HRM as a source of competitive advantage, including increasingly widespread use of performance management and professional development.

Organisations often display a clear distinction between white- and blue-collar workers in terms of power, control strategies, remuneration and working conditions and their levels of education and skill. As such, Indian work organisations tend to be hierarchical and decision-making is centralised with little or no authority or job autonomy delegated to lower ranks. However, the authority of those in positions of power, both in companies and society, is open to challenge, reflecting the strength of trade unions. Singh (1990) suggests that Indian managers score low on each of Hofstede's measures of cultural difference, suggesting that the 'typical' Indian manager favours a consultative or participative management style, is at ease with uncertainty, places an emphasis on loyalty and belongingness and underplays the use of power. Managers may behave in an authoritarian fashion but are expected in turn to show care and consideration to employees.

BOX 5.6
UNDERSTAND

International Labour Organisation

The International Labour Organisation is devoted to advancing opportunities for women and men to obtain decent and productive work in conditions of freedom, equity, security and human dignity. Its main aims are to promote rights at work, encourage decent employment opportunities, enhance social protection and strengthen dialogue in handling work-related issues. In promoting social justice and internationally recognised human and labour rights,

the organisation continues to pursue its founding mission that labour peace is essential to prosperity. Today, the ILO helps advance the creation of decent jobs and the kinds of economic and working conditions that give working people and business people a stake in lasting peace, prosperity and progress. (www.ILO.org)

Source: taken from the ILO's Mandate and Goals, www.ilo.org Reprinted by kind permission of the International Labour Organisation (ILO)

trade agreements, up from 45 a decade earlier (Thomas, 2008). The three largest trade groups, the European Union (EU), the North American Free Trade Agreement (NAFTA) and the Asia-Pacific Economic Cooperation, account for approximately half of world trade. It is important, however, to distinguish between different forms of regional cooperation or integration to assess their impact on employment (Box 5.7).

BOX 5.7
UNDERSTAND

Four types of regional agreement

- *Free trade agreement*, such as the NAFTA between the USA, Mexico and Canada. This form is the least integrated and represents an agreement to remove all barriers to the free movement of goods and services across national borders and accounts for the vast majority of regional pacts.
- *Customs union*, which is a free trade area with a common external tariff applied to all goods entering the area, regardless of which country within the union they are entering (for example, the Southern African Customs Union (SACU) comprising South Africa, Botswana, Lesotho, Swaziland and Namibia).

- *Common market*, which goes beyond a customs union by implementing common policies across a region on product regulation and allowing the free movement of labour, capital, goods and services.
- *Economic union*, such as the European Union (EU). This involves the highest form of regional economic integration short of full-scale political union. In an economic union, in addition to the removal of internal trade barriers, a common external tariff and the free movement of all factors of production, broader economic policies are harmonised and subject to supranational control.

Source: Dicken, 2007

THE EUROPEAN UNION

The EU is the most developed example of regional integration and wields a growing influence both on its member states and on global affairs. It is a political and economic union of 27 member states and is the result of a process of European integration that began in 1952 with the establishment of the European Coal and Steel Community. The European Union (previously the European Community) was formed in 1992 with the signing of the Maastricht Treaty, which came into effect in November 1993. As integration has deepened, the economic policy-making of individual member states has been increasingly relocated to the supranational level although there are significant areas where policy remains at national level, for example, that concerned with labour markets and taxation. However, alongside the promotion of economic cooperation, the EU is increasingly developing common social policy, including the regulation of employment (Box 5.8). The Maastricht Treaty included a social protocol setting the agenda for employment policy and paved the way for greater action to improve employment standards across the EU. Social policy is generally enacted through EU directives that must then be integrated into the national legal systems of member states within a particular timeframe. European case law is also binding on member states.

This greater emphasis on social policy is partly due to fears that the asymmetry between economic and social development might contribute to the unequal treatment of workers. The reluctance of some countries, particularly the UK, to endorse European harmonisation beyond the economic aim of creating a free market, has led to a 'variable geometry' of Europeanisation reflected in differing levels of employment protection afforded to workers between countries. Greater common social policy across Europe is seen as essential to enable parallel progress in both economic and social development and it is possible to identify, therefore, a range of social policy measures intended to develop these inter-related objectives.

BOX 5.8
UNDERSTAND

EU Directives

EU Directives relating to HRM include laws on:

- collective redundancies
- transfer of undertakings (TUPE)
- data protection
- discrimination (gender, racial and ethnic origin, disability, age, religion/belief and sexual orientation)
- employee rights in the event of employer insolvency at work
- equal pay
- health and safety
- information and consultation (both national level and European Works Councils as well as consultation in the event of collective redundancies, mergers and takeovers)
- protection of 'atypical' workers (for example, part-time, fixed-term and teleworkers)
- protection of pregnant workers
- protection of young workers
- rights of workers transferred within the EU and to the EU from third countries ('posted workers' directive)
- rights of temporary agency workers
- working time.

Social integration in the EU

In 2000, a declaration of the European Council stated that 'the [European] Union has today set itself a new strategic goal for the next decade: to become the most competitive and dynamic knowledge-based economy in the world, capable of sustainable economic growth with more and better jobs and greater social cohesion' (European Parliament, 2000). This model for social and economic development seeks to combine economic competitiveness with social justice and is often viewed as a 'third way' alternative to neo-liberalism (which is argued to lead to social disintegration) and socially regulated markets (which are viewed as economically inefficient). Under this model, there is an acceptance of the 'state' as both an economic actor working for the interests of organisations and as a guarantor of social cohesion and inclusion. In particular, the state has a role to play in ensuring a set of strong worker rights and welfare provision to promote job security, strong internal labour markets, high wages and investment in training (to promote skills flexibility) and ensuring that organised labour has both the right and ability to participate directly in industrial decision-making.

This 'European Social Model' represents an emphasis on 'negotiated' or 'egalitarian' capitalism where the interests of all stakeholders are recognised and industrial democracy is promoted through social dialogue, voluntaristic practices (legislation is viewed as a last resort) and the resolution of social conflict by democratic means. Much emphasis is therefore placed on the involvement of key social partners in the law-making process, including the European Trade Union Confederation (ETUC) representing national trade unions associations and Business Europe representing leading national employer organisations. In one sense, therefore, this model of Social Europe represents a desire to implement a model of best practice social regulation as embodied by certain member states, such as Sweden or Germany, with those outside of this group, including the UK, being forced to raise employment standards to this level.

ETUC

Problems of integration

The development of European social policy and the move towards a more consistent system of EU employment protection represent a considerable challenge. Some commentators and politicians across Europe have long contended that increased EU intervention in social policy is not desirable and could potentially be damaging to the competitiveness of both individual member states and the union itself. In particular, they argue that increased regulation of employment, particularly enforced from outside the nation state with little consideration for national history, culture and institutions, will actually act to hinder economic growth by discouraging enterprise and entrepreneurialism. The creation of less flexible labour markets through regulation is argued to contribute to unemployment and the status of trade unions as social partners will limit managerial prerogative.

Politicians from the UK have been among the most vocal critics of European social policy, most notably the Conservative party of the 1980s and 1990s (reflected in the negotiated opt-out of the social provisions of the Maastricht Treaty). However, the recent Labour government have also proved resistant to greater convergence along the lines of the model outlined above, despite being more conventionally pro-European. This resistance is manifest in the watering-down of EU directives when passing them into national law (for example, the European Working Time Directive) and the promotion of UK-style neo-liberalism as the path the Union should take.

A significant problem with attempts to promote greater convergence of social policy across the European Union is the fact that, despite their geographic proximity, each nation state or region within Europe tends to represent different institutional models and ideologies which are the result of their historical and cultural development. At a basic level, conflict often arises between 'market' and 'social' economic ideologies: between the UK's more neo-liberal position and that of France and Germany, where the principle of the social market remains strongly entrenched. However, there is considerable diversity of ideology even within continental Europe as the role of the state and organised interests such as trade unions varies considerably. The sheer diversity of the national systems represented by 27 member states renders the creation of consensus on social policy extremely difficult, particularly given the expansion of the Union into Eastern Europe. Therefore, despite claims of a European social model, different models of socio-economic governance are likely to continue to co-exist, representing different approaches to economic growth and social policy. This has resulted in the persistence of diverse management styles and approaches to HRM across the countries that make up the EU (Nikandrou et al., 2005).

The ongoing impact of the Eurozone crisis, which began in 2008 and which has had a differential impact on member states across the EU, also calls into question the desirability of and potential for further social integration. With countries across Europe adopting alternative responses to the crisis, and wider global recession, the question remains of whether economic difficulties fundamentally undermine attempts to create an EU-wide egalitarian capitalism in light of the drive towards weakened worker rights as a means of improving national economic competitiveness (as in the UK) or whether closer social integration might form part of the solution to rebuilding economic prosperity. The crisis faced by the EU in 2015 of the possible exit of Greece from the EU single currency (as a result of a failure to reach agreement with other nations regarding debt repayment to other nations and the IMF) and the potential UK exit from the EU itself (via a national in/out referendum) lay another level of complexity onto a complex situation with both countries arguing for reform of the European project. As such, the future of the EU is highly uncertain, not least in respect of social integration.

NATIONAL BUSINESS SYSTEMS AND MNC ACTIVITY: GOING GLOBAL?

The rapid expansion of MNC activity over the last two decades has inevitably resulted in greater interest in the impact of culture and institutional differences on management practice. In particular, there has been significant debate about the extent to which particular models of best practice HRM can be transplanted from one business system to another, alongside an increased recognition that an understanding of national diversity is vital to the development of international competitive advantage through an organisation's ability to attract, retain, remunerate, develop and motivate staff across borders.

Despite the rhetoric suggesting that MNCs transcend national boundaries, the financial, legal and political framework in which they developed as domestic firms tends to result in a persistent 'country of origin' effect in how they are managed. In addition to this 'home' country influence, MNCs are also subject to regulation and custom in 'host' countries which impact upon company practices in subsidiary operations overseas. These host country characteristics can act either to constrain the preferred home country practices or provide opportunities for profitable deviation from them. It is important therefore to understand the interplay between these two influences on international HRM. A research example of the interaction between host and home country effect is outlined in Box 5.9.

Further online reading The following article explores the challenges of transferring HRM practices from developed to developing countries. It provides a useful account of cultural differences between the nations involved and how these shape the HRM practices and the ability of MNCs to transplant practices from one context to another, particularly where culturally distant.

Mamman, A., Baydoun, N. and Adeoye, B. (2009) Transferability of management innovation to Africa: A study of two multinational companies' performance management systems in Nigeria, *Global Business Review*, 10 (1): 1–31.

BOX 5.9
RESEARCH INSIGHT

The transferability of HRM practices in Nigeria

The extent to which it is possible to transfer HRM policies and practices from the country in which they have developed into another is a key issue of interest in the field of international human resource management (IHRM). For MNCs, the degree to which it is successful in transferring HRM practices into an overseas venture can mean the difference between competitive advantage and inhibition of employee performance. This can be a particular challenge when seeking to transfer practices between two culturally distant contexts.

Mamman et al. (2009) sought to explore the transferability of performance management systems of a Swiss and a Swedish firm into a Nigerian subsidiary. They report that 'Nigeria is a masculine society with high collectivism, high power distance and strong uncertainty avoidance' and that 'these cultural orientations and values impact on performance management practices and employees' attitudes to them' (2009: 6). They also note that other elements of African culture such as mutual obligation and the need for belonging and affiliation also can have direct relevance and influence for the operation of HRM practices, not least through its manifestation in nepotism. The authors contrast this culture with that of the country of origin of the other two firms that will have influenced (rather than entirely determined) HRM policies. Swedish culture is characterised as reflecting concern for equality, weak uncertainty avoidance and low power distance. Swiss culture is again characterised as reflecting low power distance, but as more masculine and demonstrating mid-levels of uncertainty avoidance. The contrast between the cultural characteristics of the home and host countries is, therefore, likely to represent a challenge to the effective transfer of performance management practices between them, not least in respect of how local managers implement practices and how employees respond to them.

The research found that the wholesale transfer of HRM policies in both cases was problematic because subsidiary managers drawn from the local region sought to adapt these practices to reflect practices traditional to that country. This suggests, therefore, that the wholesale transfer of practices is more likely to be achieved in culturally similar countries where local practices are not radically dissimilar from those imposed. However, the authors suggest that MNCs can mitigate the risks associated with the local adaptation of practices (for example, the risk of local managers using performance management to reinforce divisions in the workforce) by recruiting managers on the basis of their ability to work with the imported system or employing managers drawn from the parent country, rather than recruited from the local labour market. The middle ground between local adaptation (polycentrism) and imposition (ethnocentrism) is for firms to maintain control of the process of adaptation so that such risks can be avoided but also to ensure the effectiveness of HRM in the overseas context.

The centralisation of management decision-making

In establishing an overseas subsidiary, MNCs must consider a wide range of factors in determining appropriate HR strategy, practices and management style. At a basic level, a company can either adopt a multi-domestic strategy (decentralisation) or a global strategy (centralisation) (Porter, 1986). In the former, overseas subsidiaries have significant autonomy to respond to local needs and norms and, subsequently, HR policies and practice are differentiated across the firm. In the latter, policies are determined globally and are integrated across the worldwide organisation, regardless of local context. This approach seeks to minimise or override differences in national systems, emphasising the importance of organisational, rather than national, culture. Similarly, Nohria and Ghoshal (1994) distinguish between firms that make a strategic decision to develop 'differentiated fit' with distinctive local conditions and those that promote global 'shared values' across the company.

Kidger and Allen (2006) suggest that the impact of globalisation has been to encourage MNCs to move towards greater global harmonisation or standardisation of management practice. However, the decision to adopt a strategy of centralisation or decentralisation is complex and subject to a range of influences. For example, whilst differences in labour market conditions between a home and host country – such as the strength of local unions, labour law and the composition of the labour force – might encourage the adoption of a multi-domestic approach to employment management, other factors can promote a global strategy. For example, a need for consistency in product quality and service delivery might require coherent management practices and the presence of a unifying corporate culture (Gamble, 2003). The decision may also reflect whether a company moves into a foreign country by acquisition or start-up. In the former, it is more likely that the existing approach to managing employment is retained. In the latter, management are likely to have greater freedom to import management practices.

Furthermore, the preference for standardised or differentiated strategies may reflect the stage of development of the organisation. For example, Bartlett and Ghoshal (1989) suggest there are four approaches to the international marketplace that equate to stages of MNC development: multinational, global, international and transnational. 'Multinational' firms are likely to adopt decentralised approaches to HRM but as firms develop towards 'transnational' status there will be a commensurate movement towards a more centralised approach. Similarly, Perlmutter (1969) suggests a number of approaches that an organisation might adopt to the relationship with subsidiaries. As with Bartlett and Ghoshal's typology, these categories can also be understood as stages in an evolutionary process towards geocentrism:

- Ethnocentric – management policy, practices and values in the home country are regarded as superior and subsequently implemented in all subsidiaries worldwide.
- Polycentric – management accepts that practice in subsidiaries should be based on local norms and, therefore, corporate headquarters devolves autonomy over local matters to each subsidiary.
- Geocentric – management in both corporate headquarters and local subsidiaries collaborate to establish global best practice in the interests of the whole organisation, resulting in a synergistic mix of policy and practice (although these practices are still likely to display some 'country-of-origin' influence).

The extent to which MNC senior management recognise cultural difference informs a number of approaches to designing HRM policy and practices in subsidiary operations. Taylor et al. (1996) identify three generic strategic orientations:

1 An *adaptive* orientation is one in which top management of the MNC attempt to create HRM systems for affiliates that reflect the local environment. The MNC generally copies the HRM systems that are being used locally by hiring competent HR specialists or managers who have knowledge of local practices.

2 An *exportive* orientation is one in which top management of the MNC prefer a wholesale transfer of the parent firm's HRM system to its overseas affiliates.

3 MNCs with an *integrative* orientation attempt to take the 'best' approaches and use them throughout the organisation in the creation of a worldwide system. The focus is on substantial global integration with an allowance for some local differentiation.

Similarly, Farndale and Paauwe (2007) refer to strategies of adaptation, adoption and innovation. These typologies suggest that the decision for MNCs is not simply to either impose home country or adopt host country employment practices. Even with a broadly defined decentralised approach to HRM, this might not necessarily mean there is no corporate coordination or influence. Corporate managers can shape practices in subsidiaries indirectly through vetoing strategic or operational plans or by guiding subsidiary management through the use of internal benchmarking to facilitate convergence of best practice. Furthermore, firms might differentiate their approach according to different employee groups. For example, international managers might be managed according to global policies and practices, whereas lower level employees are more likely to be subject to localised management.

To illustrate the approaches MNCs can adopt when faced with an institutional system that contrasts with that of its country of origin, Box 5.10 assesses the research evidence surrounding MNC activity and the German model.

Further online reading This article reports on research examining whether German multinationals operating in an Anglo-Saxon setting design their employee relations primarily on the basis of the German or the Anglo-Saxon model. It provides a useful insight into the process of adaptation of practice when transferred across borders.

Tuselmann, H., McDonald, F. and Heise, A. (2003) Employee relations in German multinationals in an Anglo-Saxon setting: Towards a Germanic version of the Anglo-Saxon approach, *European Journal of Industrial Relations*, 9 (3): 327–49.

In determining the appropriate approach to HR practice in subsidiaries, headquarters managers must be willing to accept that local methods might be more appropriate and effective. It is also important for firms to identify possible resistance to headquarters policies and to seek to understand the underlying cause (for example, whether resistance is a result of cultural differences or simply a political desire for local autonomy). Whilst centrally imposed policies might have the effect of providing a focus for resistance among subsidiary staff, flexibility towards local practice may enhance local buy-in. MNCs need to consider not only the institutional and cultural context in attempts to diffuse best practice into overseas subsidiaries but also the ability and motivation of managers to implement such practice (Martin and Beaumont, 1998; Edwards et al., 2007). Björkman and Lervik (2007) stress the importance of trust between headquarters and the subsidiary in the likely success of HRM transfer.

Further online reading This article examines the extent to which multinational firms adapt internally consistent human resource strategies across national boundaries and the degree of local adaptation, concluding that whilst some adaptation to local context occurs, the diffusion of home country practices is more significant.

Chew, I. K. H. and Horwitz, F. M. (2004) Human resource management strategies in practice: Case-study findings in multinational firms, *Asia Pacific Journal of Human Resources*, 42 (1): 32–56.

ARE GLOBAL APPROACHES TO HRM POSSIBLE?

Tayeb (1998) makes an important distinction between HRM practices and policies arguing that, whereas organisations 'might find it feasible to have company-wide

BOX 5.10
RESEARCH INSIGHT

MNCs and the German model

To illustrate the diverse approaches that MNCs take to the centralisation–decentralisation question when operating an overseas subsidiary, we can consider the case of Germany. The 'German model' represents a distinctive institutional framework that provides extensive co-determination rights and employment protection for workers and a positive role for trade unions in both negotiating terms and conditions for workers and as a legitimate partner in 'Deutschland Inc'. This contrasts strongly with the Anglo-Saxon model where employment regulation is minimised and trade unions have limited or no legal rights to recognition. For this reason, it is interesting to assess the interaction between these two systems through the activities of MNCs. Some commentators argue that the activities of MNCs are putting increasing pressure on social market economies such as Germany to reform their markets along neo-liberal lines.

Taken together, research in German and Anglo-Saxon MNCs suggests that patterns of HRM transfer are complex. On the one hand, Schmitt (2003) found far-reaching compliance of Anglo-Saxon-owned subsidiaries to the central German institutions of industrial relations, including both works councils and collective bargaining. In contrast, Tempel (2001) reports that British MNCs tend to exert country-of-origin influence in personnel management and Royle (1995) reports that McDonald's in Germany used specific strategies to avoid the obligations placed on employers by German institutions and custom.

Similarly, Williams and Geppert (2006) found that a Finnish MNC sought to depart from the German model and adopt an Anglo-Saxon approach to employee relations by imposing a more unilateral management style that sought to ignore the role of works councils as a source of employee voice. However, they also found that the MNC had been forced to abide by the legal framework of works council rights and to adopt a negotiated, rather than imposed, approach to workplace change (Muller, 1998, 1999).

MNC activity overseas can also bring about changes in the home nation. Ferner and Varul (2000) report on evidence of 'backward diffusion' of practices from UK-based subsidiaries of German-owned MNCs who had rejected some elements of German industrial relations traditions. Ferner et al. (2001) also found that German MNCs in Britain and Spain were adopting Anglo-Saxon style HR practices (such as global performance management systems and increasing proportions of variable pay).

Overall, Tuselmann et al. (2003) suggest that the transfer of practices in German MNCs to an Anglo-Saxon setting reflects a complex interaction between subsidiary characteristics, home country, host country and global best practice. Whilst they report that German MNCs were as likely as UK firms to adopt a 'low road' Anglo-Saxon approach, German firms were more likely to adopt more progressive variants developed within a collectivist, pluralist framework. German MNCs in the UK, therefore, were found to represent a better fit with the partnership approach advocated by some UK unions (see Chapter 10).

policies they might find it unavoidable to be responsive to local conditions when it comes to HRM practices' (Tayeb, 1998: 332). Reporting on the case of a US company operating in Scotland, Tayeb argues that the choice between polycentric, ethnocentric and global strategies is too simplistic. Tayeb suggests that whilst some practices can be transferred from one country to another without change, others must be modified to become workable, whilst still others are deeply culture-specific and may not be transferable. Subsequently, research has found notable evidence of the emergence of hybrid approaches to HRM, reflecting both home and host country influence and the internal culture of the firm (Bae et al., 1998; Myloni et al., 2004).

In certain conditions, MNCs can act as 'pioneers' by influencing host country management practice leading to the diffusion of best practice. For example, Myloni et al. (2004) suggest that HRM in Greece is in a state of development, influenced both by the activities of MNC subsidiaries and the diffusion of ideas emanating from those who have studied or worked abroad. In other environments, MNCs are likely to face significant problems in attempting the wholesale transplantation of HR practices, especially where implemented across cultural clusters (Khan and Ackers, 2004). For example, Ishida (1986) found that 'collectivist' Japanese managers experienced considerable difficulties when they were appointed to lead employees from 'individualist' countries overseas.

Further online reading This article presents three case studies examining change management processes in the work systems at the subsidiary level of MNCs. It examines how these processes are shaped both by globalisation and the national institutional context.

Geppert, M., Matten, D. and Williams, K. (2003) Change management in MNCs: How global convergence intertwines with national diversities, *Human Relations*, 56 (7): 807–38.

Universalism or continued diversity of management practice?

There is significant debate about whether the increasing size and scope of MNCs is leading to the worldwide or regional convergence of management practices or the sharpening of national differences. Lucas and Curtis (2006) suggest that, as a result of globalisation, managers in both the developing and industrialised nations have access to knowledge of how successful firms operate and often seek to mimic associated practices. Furthermore, some commentators suggest that the widespread dominance of neo-liberal capitalism has triggered an unstoppable process of 'Anglo-Saxonisation' manifest through the global diffusion of US institutions (for example, the primacy of shareholder value) and policies, including privatisation, liberalisation and deregulation. Developing patterns of regional integration are also viewed as creating conditions under which organisations can transcend their national origins. For example, Schulten (1996) argues that legislation emanating from the European Union and economies of scale created by the single market have led to the creation of Euro-companies.

However, given the extent of contextual variation, the notion of universal best practice HRM is problematic. Ferner and Quintanilla (1998) suggest that despite globalisation, MNCs continue to be embedded in the national business system of their home country and that whilst institutional arrangements are not immutable, the Anglo-Saxonisation process is occurring in nationally specific ways, through processes of the diffusion and reverse diffusion of HRM, whereby firms cherry-pick and adapt HRM practices from overseas to meet particular local requirements (Björkman et al., 2008). Similarly, Geppert et al. (2003) report that the process of globalisation ultimately reinforces the importance of different national contexts, suggesting that the more global a firm becomes the more it allows national institutions to play a key role in the operation of subsidiaries. In particular, management practice developed in industrialised nations requires significant adjustment to be applicable in the developing countries (Wasti, 1998; Mamman et al., 2009). In the same way that MNCs might develop hybrid approaches to HRM which are transnational, Lucas and Curtis (2006) argue therefore that an alternative to greater convergence of management practice towards Western universalism or continued culturally determined divergence is the creation of a unique value system that represents neither one nor the other.

SUMMARY POINTS

NATIONAL CONTEXT OF HRM

- Understanding the national and international context of HRM is important to appreciate both the diverse approaches that organisations in different national settings take towards management practice and their influence on MNC activity.

- The cultural context of an organisation influences HRM practices informally by providing the set of assumptions that underpin management decision-making. The institutional context has a more direct, formal influence by establishing the political, economic and social parameters within which management acts.

- Cultural and institutional frameworks cannot be understood in isolation. Cultural assumptions influence the formation and development of national institutions which in turn both reflect and reinforce these assumptions.

- For MNCs, the national context of subsidiary activity is of paramount importance both as a source of constraint on managerial decision-making and as an opportunity for innovation and competitive advantage.

- The EU provides an example of the problems involved in attempting to create common social policy across culturally and institutionally diverse nation states.

- The extent to which MNCs acknowledge the importance of cultural diversity shapes the extent to which they adopt centralised or decentralised HR strategies.

- Whilst some degree of global convergence is taking place in approaches to HRM, the contextual differences between nations limit its extent. However, some global 'version' of best practice HRM might well emerge as a result of the international transfer of ideas, knowledge and technologies.

SELF-TEST QUESTIONS

1 Why is it useful to distinguish between the ways in which national culture and institutions shape management practice?

2 How do typologies such as Hofstede's help us to understand variation in management practice?

3 Why might cultural and institutional differences represent a potential source of competitive advantage for a firm operating internationally?

4 How does the institutional framework in a nation constrain management practice?

5 How might the approach an MNC adopts towards HRM reflect their broader internationalisation strategy?

6 Why might managers be compelled to adopt a global approach to HRM?

7 Under what circumstances might it be more advantageous to managers to adopt a differentiated approach to HRM?

8 Outline the tension that often exists between home and host country culture in the management of labour.

9 What are the prospects for the global convergence of HRM practice?

TEST YOURSELF

TEST
YOURSELF

TEST YOURSELF

Want to know more about this chapter? Review what you have been learning by visiting:
https://edge.sagepub.com/wilton3e

- Print out or download the chapter summaries for quick revision
- Test yourself with multiple-choice questions
- Revise key terms with interactive flashcards

CASE STUDY

Tesco and international employee relations

The supermarket chain Tesco is the largest private sector employer in the UK, with over 280,000 staff. Their corporate website sums up their approach to the marketplace by stating that 'our success depends on people: the people who shop with us and the people who work with us ... If our customers like what we offer, they are more likely to come back and shop with us again. If the Tesco team find what we do rewarding, they are more likely to go that extra mile to help our customers.'

In relation to employment, their central value is 'treat people as we like to be treated', a statement reflected in a set of core beliefs:

- Work as a team
- Trust and respect each other
- Listen, support and say thank you
- Share knowledge and experience
- So we can enjoy our work.

Commensurately, Tesco's corporate website claims that they 'offer a market-leading package of pay and benefits' such as childcare vouchers and two share schemes, rewarding staff for their hard work and commitment with free Tesco shares as well as an award-winning pension scheme. Tesco also have numerous mechanisms through which employees can share their views – such as staff question time sessions and employee feedback surveys – and promote strong internal labour markets.

Most significantly, Tesco in the UK reports having a good relationship with its 'union partner' the Union of Shop, Distributive and Allied Workers (Usdaw). The Tesco/Usdaw partnership is the biggest single trade union agreement in the UK private sector and has contributed significantly to the good employment practice in Tesco and serves as recognition among senior management that employee involvement and participation in decision-making can contribute to the achievement of strategic goals.

In 2006 Tesco entered the American marketplace, opening supermarkets under the name Fresh and Easy. Given its reputation in the UK for good employee relations and corporate social responsibility, the United Food and Commercial Workers' Union (UFCW) – the counterpart union to Usdaw in the USA – had expected to enter into a similar partnership agreement to that which existed in the UK. However, in June 2008 the UFCW published a report entitled *The Two Faces of Tesco* to 'tell British investors, politicians, employees and shoppers why we think that the Tesco they know and admire as a business, with a great track record on community and employee relations, can be a very different organisation when it operates away from British shores'. The report details how, in the eyes of the UFCW, Tesco, 'Instead of engaging positively with community partners ... refuses to meet with them. Instead of offering partnership, it accepts conflict. Instead of defending freedom of association, it actively pursues a policy to keep out trades unions.'

The primary concern of the union is that Tesco refuses to extend its principle of partnership to all of its employees outside the UK (UFCW also cite union avoidance activity in Thailand and Turkey) and claim that Tesco's US management refuse to even meet with the UFCW. In 2006 a job advertisement for the employee relations director listed 'maintaining non-union status' and 'union avoidance activities' among the post-holder's responsibilities. Tesco later claimed that this advertisement was a mistake.

In 2013, Tesco took the decision to sell Fresh and Easy to an investment firm, ending a six-year foray into the US market. In total, the exercise is suggested to have cost Tesco almost £1.5 billion. The conditions of the sale mean the closure of 50 stores with the loss of 1,000 jobs (the remaining 150 stores and distribution centre are to remain open, safeguarding 4,000 jobs). Whilst the failed venture has been blamed on the economic downturn, poor store locations, and apathy towards the brand from shoppers (Ruddick, 2013), the negative publicity surrounding its treatment of workers is likely to have played a part in its downfall.

Questions

1 Why has Tesco chosen not to extend its domestic employee relations practice to workers outside of the UK?

2 Given Tesco's guiding strategic principles, what might be the implications for business success in their US ventures?

Sources: **www.tesco.com/talkingtesco/listening**; United Food and Commercial Workers International Union (UFCW) (2008) *The Two Faces of Tesco*, Washington DC, available online at www.ufcw.org/tag/tesco/ (accessed 11 March 2009).

USEFUL READING

Journal articles

Edwards, T., Colling, T. and Ferner, A. (2007) Conceptual approaches to the transfer of employment practices in multinational companies: An integrated approach, *Human Resource Management Journal*, 17 (3): 201–17.

Drawing on data from a multi-level case study of a multinational in the USA and Britain, this article examines the transfer of employment practices across borders and concludes that an integrated approach to understanding HRM transfer is necessary, focusing both on the inter-relationships between markets and institutions and the material interests of actors.

Scullion, H., Collings, D. G. and Gunnigle, P. (2007) International human resource management in the 21st century: Emerging themes and contemporary debates, *Human Resource Management Journal*, 17 (4): 309–19.

This article introduces a special issue of *HRMJ* on international HRM in the twenty-first century. It considers some of the key aspects of the changing landscape of international business and the key emergent issues for international HRM, including an assessment of the changing nature of the global economic landscape, international careers and patterns of global staffing.

Books, book chapters and reports

Dicken, P. (2007) *Global Shift* (5th edn), London: Sage.

This book provides an invaluable multi-disciplinary resource for understanding the globalisation process and the relationship between MNCs, developed and less developed nations and other interest groups. It provides the backdrop by which to assess the influence of globalisation on HRM practices.

House, R. J., Hanges, P. J., Javidan, M., Dorfman, P. W. and Gupta, V. (eds) (2004) *Leadership, Culture and Organizations: The GLOBE Study of 62 Societies*, Thousand Oaks, CA: Sage.

This book presents the findings from a 10-year research programme, including a survey of over 17,000 middle managers in three industries, to explore the relationship between culture and societal, organisational and leadership effectiveness.

FURTHER ONLINE READING

The following articles can be accessed for free on the book's companion website **https://edge.sagepub.com/wilton3e**:

Chew, I. K. H. and Horwitz, F. M. (2004) Human resource management strategies in practice: Case-study findings in multinational firms, *Asia Pacific Journal of Human Resources*, 42 (1): 32–56.

Geppert, M., Matten, D. and Williams, K. (2003) Change management in MNCs: How global convergence intertwines with national diversities, *Human Relations*, 56 (7): 807–38.

Gerhart, B. (2008) Cross-cultural management research: Assumptions, evidence and suggested directions, *International Journal of Cross Cultural Management*, 8 (3): 259–74.

Mamman, A., Baydoun, N. and Adeoye, B. (2009) Transferability of management innovation to Africa: A study of two multinational companies' performance management systems in Nigeria, *Global Business Review*, 10 (1): 1–31.

McSweeney, B. (2002) Hofstede's model of national cultural differences and their consequences: A triumph of faith – a failure of analysis, *Human Relations*, 55 (1): 89–118.

Tuselmann, H., McDonald, F. and Heise, A. (2003) Employee relations in German multinationals in an Anglo-Saxon setting: Towards a Germanic version of the Anglo-Saxon approach, *European Journal of Industrial Relations*, 9 (3): 327–49.

Want to know more about this chapter? Visit the companion website at: **https://edge.sagepub.com/wilton3e** to access practice questions, videos and selected journal articles to further enhance your study.

PART TWO
HRM IN PRACTICE

PART MAP

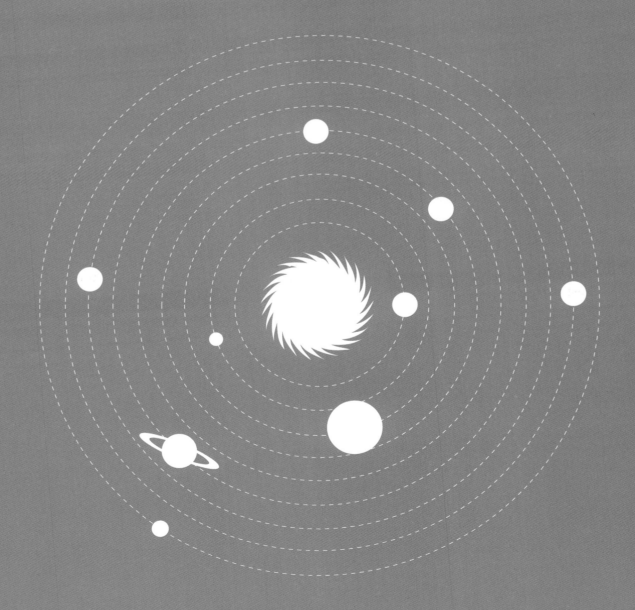

Having provided some theoretical and real-world context, this section sets out contemporary practice and debate in five core sets of organisational activities that come under the broad banner of HRM. Whilst each of these areas of activities represents a discrete set of activities and, in some larger firms, might represent distinct areas of responsibility for individuals or teams of HRM professionals, in many organisations the role of the HR professional would include a concern for all of these areas. Moreover, these activities also constitute key areas of responsibility for managers at all levels of an organisation who hold responsibility for people management. Therefore, each chapter considers each specific area of HRM from an organisational, managerial and individual perspective to fully understand the issues and challenges of HRM for all stakeholders.

The section opens with a discussion of people resourcing. People resourcing is a catch-all term for a wide range of activities that determine the constituency of a firm's workforce from human resource planning, recruitment and selection through to termination of the employment contract. Chapter 7 then discusses how, once employees are within the firm, they might be managed to elicit required levels of performance. Connectedly, Chapter 8 concerns employee reward and the multiple ways in which workers are financially and non-financially compensated for their exertions at work. Chapter 9 discusses the vast area of human resource development,

the aspect of HRM that is concerned with training, education and employee development to meet the needs of both the organisation and the individual involved. Finally, Chapter 10 considers employment relations with a specific focus on how firms manage the collective employment relationship that exists between a firm's workforce and its management. Specific focus in this chapter is on employee communication and how firms might involve employees in organisational decision-making either directly or via trade unions.

Whilst each chapter discusses a discrete area of HRM, a recurring theme throughout this book is the importance of considering their inter-relationship when making decisions about organisational policy and practice. For example, whilst Chapter 6 is concerned with how a firm is 'resourced' with people the nature of a firm's workforce is equally determined by activities to develop their skills and knowledge, as well as how they are motivated to perform to their potential. Therefore, in order to fully understand the role of HRM in contemporary organisations consideration of all these areas of HRM is critical. For this reason, each chapter makes repeated reference to ideas and practices developed in others.

By the end of this section, the reader should have a sound grasp of the key issues and HRM practices and processes in each of these broad areas of managerial activity, as well as the role of different actors in each.

6

PEOPLE RESOURCING

TALENT AND TALENT MANAGEMENT

CHAPTER OBJECTIVES

- To outline the rationale for human resource planning and associated activities

- To discuss the implications of labour turnover and outline mechanisms by which organisations can seek to maximise employee retention

- To outline organisational approaches to succession planning and talent management

- To describe and critique the systematic approach to recruitment and selection

- To identify ethical issues in recruitment and selection

- To identify cross-cultural considerations for conducting recruitment and selection.

INTRODUCTION

This chapter focuses on the broad area of people resourcing that consists of a number of specialist activities that seek to ensure that human resources of the right quantity and quality are available to meet the overall objectives of the company. These activities include human resource planning (HRP), recruitment and selection, talent management, succession planning and employee retention and termination of the employment contract. Figure 6.1 outlines the people resourcing process that is discussed in this chapter. The diagram portrays a rather 'neat' sequence of activities that, if conducted properly, should result in the effective deployment of capable employees. However, as will become clear throughout this chapter, at each stage there are a number of debates about the effectiveness of approaches to management practice in resourcing.

HUMAN RESOURCE PLANNING

Human resource planning (HRP) is the process of assessing current HR capabilities and forecasting future labour supply and demand, to produce HR plans that will enable an organisation to achieve its strategic objectives. In other words, it is concerned with ensuring an organisation has the right people in the right place at the right time. Formal HRP (previously 'manpower' planning) was especially prevalent during the mid-twentieth century, where statistical techniques were used to forecast and plan future employment needs, often based on extrapolations from previous experience. However, since the end of the relatively benign and stable economic climate that characterised the 'golden age of manpower planning' (Marchington and Wilkinson, 2005: 158), it has been often argued that such long-term approaches to predicting future labour requirements are no longer feasible under more unpredictable market conditions. However, despite the important criticism of HRP discussed later, Marchington and Wilkinson (2005) suggest that planning remains vitally important during turbulent times, if only to ensure that employers have workers of the required quality and quantity. They suggest four sets of reasons for the continued importance of HRP:

1 It encourages employers to develop clear and explicit links between their business and HR plans, and so integrate the two more effectively.

2 It allows for better control over staffing costs and numbers employed.

3 It enables employers to make more informed judgements about the skills and attitude mix in the organisation, and prepare integrated HR strategies.

4 It provides a profile of current staff, which is important to any organisation claiming to promote equal opportunities.

A contemporary understanding of HRP suggests a more complex process than simply the collection and analysis of market and labour market data to determine an organisation's quantitative demand for labour. To be effective, HRP requires a wider consideration of how firms can best configure people and processes to achieve sustained competitive advantage and whether required capacity can be sourced internally or externally. Current approaches to HRP are concerned with establishing a firm's future labour requirements both in terms of 'hard' quantitative dimensions (for example, the number of employees and required skills) and 'soft' qualitative labour attributes (desired behaviours, values and attitudes and competencies). Torrington et al. (2008: 51) suggest that the HRP process supports HR strategy by identifying gaps in capabilities that would prevent strategy being implemented successfully, surpluses in capabilities that may provide opportunities for efficiencies and responsiveness and poor utilisation of people in the organisation.

The planning process

In broad terms, there are three components to the HRP process: forecasting future demand for human resources; forecasting the internal and external supply of human resources, including assessing current capabilities; and formulating responses to the forecasts.

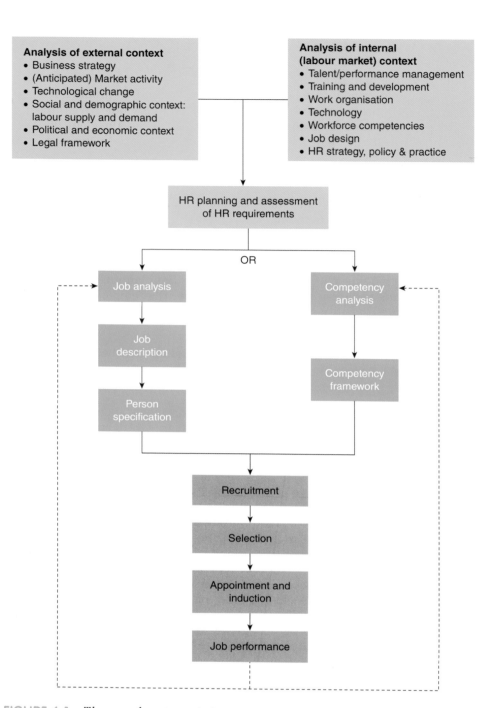

FIGURE 6.1   The people resourcing process

DEMAND FORECASTING   Demand forecasting is concerned with predicting the impact of future developments internal and external to the organisation (for example, changes in market conditions or proposed organisational restructuring) on the firm's requirement for labour. The hard or quantitative element of demand forecasting involves the use of statistical techniques to make an assessment of future labour requirements. For example, trend analysis can be used to assess business patterns to inform judgements about future demand. In the public sector, population projections can be used to predict future demand for nurses, teachers and so on.

However, statistical approaches to demand forecasting are often viewed as being ineffective in unpredictable conditions, particularly where trends and past experience are unlikely to be a sound indicator of future needs. Subsequently, more subjective forms of planning based on managerial judgement are increasingly prevalent (Arnold and Pulich, 2007). For example, scenario planning can be used to predict the possible future direction of key variables such as legislation, new technology and markets to develop a number of possible scenarios and assess their impact on resourcing. McKenna and Beech (2008) suggest that scenario planning represents an 'early warning system' to enable a firm to 'beat the future'. Soft approaches to demand forecasting involve predicting the qualitative characteristics of required labour, such as behavioural capabilities, attitudes and values, required to fulfil particular strategic objectives.

SUPPLY FORECASTING Before seeking to evaluate future labour supply, an assessment needs to be made of current capacity in the form of workforce profiling. To forecast future internal supply, it is important to identify patterns in the movement of labour, both internally and into and out of the organisation. This requires an assessment of patterns of internal promotion, transfer, redundancy, temporary withdrawal (for example, employees going on maternity leave, sabbatical or secondment) and dismissal.

There is a range of quantitative techniques that firms can draw upon to assess future internal labour supply on the basis of prior trends. These include *wastage analysis* (to forecast the proportion of the workforce that is predicted to leave the organisation over a given period), *stability analysis* (the proportion of the workforce that is expected to remain in the firm), *cohort analysis* (turnover among a specific employee year 'group', for example, a particular cohort of graduate recruits) and *internal promotion analysis* (the incidence of posts being filled by internal promotion).

Recruitment trends can also be used to assess the most effective methods and sources of external recruitment and to identify problems, such as apparent inequality of opportunities for minority groups. Increasingly firms are investing in sophisticated Human Resource Information Systems (HRIS) to maintain up-to-date information on internal workforce composition and to monitor turnover, the internal movement of labour and the changing supply of skills and qualifications at management's disposal (Kovach and Cathcart, 1999). Evaluation of the external labour supply focuses on some of the local, regional, national and international labour market dynamics discussed in Chapter 4. For example, the planning process will need to take account of changing demography, rates of economic activity, the skills mix and educational distribution of the available workforce, as well as competition for desired labour.

To address the soft element of current and future HR capability, firms can assess the current organisational culture, performance standards and employee attitudes and behaviours drawing on staff attitude surveys, interviews or focus groups. Such techniques provide management with information on levels of job satisfaction, employee commitment and motivation and the clarity of individual and business objectives. Exit interview data or leavers' questionnaires can be used to assess the reasons why employees leave the organisation. Attitude surveys and performance management data can also be used as a form of risk assessment, providing managers with information regarding the likelihood that workers will leave the firm so as to assess the potential consequences of turnover. In order to evaluate the ability of the external labour supply to meet behavioural and

BOX 6.1
UNDERSTAND

Possible responses to demand and supply forecasting

- Introduce new equipment or technology to replace or augment workforce skills.
- Change the organisation of work processes, for example, by introducing teamworking or altering the demarcation between jobs.
- Increase or change the focus of individual and organisational development to address competency requirements.
- Restructure the organisation, for example, by centralising or decentralising decision-making, implementing new departmental boundaries,

shifting towards flexible project structures or outsourcing certain functions.
- Relocate operations to take advantage of local labour force characteristics, for example, the availability of cheap or highly skilled workers.
- Seek to improve individual and group performance and productivity, for example, by introducing performance management and performance-related reward or promoting greater employee participation in decision-making.
- Attempt to change the culture of the firm to promote some required dimension of behaviour or particular values.

attitudinal requirements, firms need to assess changing societal attitudes partly associated with demography and wider social change.

ORGANISATIONAL RESPONSES TO THE FORECASTS There are a wide variety of organisational responses to demand and supply forecasts, beyond workforce downsizing or the further recruitment of required labour. HR plans that derive from the forecasting process can also be concerned with a wide range of methods to change employee utilisation and performance, not least the reconfiguration of HR policies and processes, whether used in conjunction with or instead of altering workforce numbers and composition (Box 6.1).

One particular response to the labour requirements identified in the HRP process might be the redesign of jobs. Discussion of job design often contrasts the Taylorist and Humanist traditions discussed in Chapter 2. The former focuses on the rationalisation of jobs and work processes as a key source of efficiency and tends to be associated with the dehumanisation of work by removing opportunities for worker discretion and variation. In contrast, the Humanist approach to job design is concerned with achieving high levels of intrinsic job satisfaction, motivation and, therefore, efficiency by creating challenging and varied jobs through job enlargement, job enrichment and job rotation.

Organisational responses to supply and demand forecasts are subject to a number of constraints, not least labour market conditions. Labour markets that have an abundant supply of required labour are often referred to as 'loose' and those where required labour is scarce are described as 'tight'. Windolf (1986) suggests that employee resourcing practices differ according to both labour market conditions and the extent to which the organisation possesses sufficient labour market 'intelligence' to respond to these conditions in a novel or creative manner. For example, firms might seek to proactively maximise workforce diversity in 'loose' conditions, rather than maintain the existing status quo or adopt flexible approaches to resourcing and labour organisation in 'tight' labour markets to reduce a reliance on scarce labour. Box 6.2 outlines one organisation's approach to recruiting in a diverse labour market as an example of the

BOX 6.1
HRM IN PRACTICE

People resourcing and diversity – The UK Civil Service

The UK Civil Service constitutes those employees working in departments of central government such as the Ministry of Defence, the Treasury and Home Office, supporting government in developing and implementing policies. In 2014, it had approximately 447,000 employees and has long been a prestigious graduate recruiter through its 'Fast Stream' graduate development programme. It has been a long established commitment of the Civil Service to work towards a workforce representative of the population it serves and, consequently as its principal source of recruitment, significant efforts have been made to increase the diversity of the graduate recruits, in terms of gender, race, disability, socioeconomic status and age.

In order to address the need to increase workforce diversity, a number of interventions were put in place, including:

- Training in diversity awareness and unconscious bias for Fast Track recruitment assessors.
- Establishment of a diversity internship programme, including a short work placement, coaching programme and a buddy system for providing advice and guidance on applications, to increase the number of applicants from black and minority ethnic and lower socioeconomic backgrounds.
- Greater use of social media, including YouTube, Twitter and Facebook, to engage potential applicants and encourage applications.
- The use of a planning 'game' to demonstrate the work of the Civil Service and available careers.
- The establishment of partnerships with external diversity groups to attract applicants.
- The targeting of a broader range of types of universities to ensure the sufficient 'reach' of recruitment activities.
- Early engagement strategy to connect with students at earlier stages of their education, including schools and further education colleges.

In addition, beyond the 'Fast Stream', the Civil Service has also introduced a positive action pathway (a one-year development programme) to enable disabled, minority ethnic and female employees to build their skills and confidence and a new performance framework and information pack for 'diversity champions' in the organisation.

Such initiatives have contributed towards growth in the proportion of black and minority ethnic employees in the Civil Service from 5.7 per cent of the total workforce in 1992 to 9.6 per cent in 2013. Similarly, the proportion of workers with a disability has risen from 3.1 per cent in 2001 to 8.6 per cent in 2013. Women make up 53 per cent of the workforce across the Civil Service with the proportion of women in senior positions doubling since 1996.

Sources: IDS, 2014; Faragher, 2014

way in which strategic people resourcing helps both to develop a workforce of 'all talents' and to anticipate and respond to social change.

Further online reading This article considers the challenges of staffing in modern organisations, including workforce diversity, skills shortages and competition for applicants, and provides a critical analysis of recent literature on staffing best practices.

Ployhart, R. E. (2006) Staffing in the 21st century: New challenges and strategic opportunities, *Journal of Management*, 32 (6): 868–97.

It is important that the organisational response to the forecasting process is viewed as acceptable by a range of internal and external stakeholders, such as line managers, senior management and trade unions, to remove any possible impediment to the successful implementation of HR plans. Thus, acknowledgement of internal power structures and organisational politics is important and efforts need to be made to ensure that all stakeholders are involved in the planning process. For example, employee attitude surveys and focus groups should be used to engage staff both to facilitate change and also to generate potentially valuable contributions to the process. To ensure the adequate integration of HRP into the wider strategy-making process, planning should be 'owned' and driven by senior managers.

**WORKFORCE
PLANNING NHS**

For a detailed example of HRP in action, please see the NHS London Case Study available on the book's companion website (https://edge.sagepub.com/wilton3e).

Issues in HRP

As noted previously, the value of HRP, particularly in times of uncertainty or in unpredictable markets, has been challenged. Mintzberg (1976, 1994) argues that planning actually impedes the achievement of objectives, for example, by ignoring unpredictable one-off events that might constitute sources of potential advantage. Furthermore, recent trends in organisational restructuring associated with the increased decentralisation of decision-making and the more flexible utilisation of labour are viewed as rendering 'grand' HRP unfeasible and impractical. Taylor (2008) argues, however, that HRP can be an important process in particular circumstances and identifies a number of organisational characteristics in which traditional HRP is likely to prove beneficial:

- large enough to be able to dedicate resources to the establishment and maintenance of an HRP function, such as public sector organisations
- operating in reasonably stable product and labour markets
- having key staff groups who require lengthy or expensive training
- competing in industries in which decisions concerning future investment in plant and equipment are made a number of years ahead and are essential to effective product market competition (i.e. capital-intensive industries).

Nevertheless, even considering the shorter planning horizons of those firms competing in turbulent markets, HRP may be beneficial in developing organisational flexibility and adaptability and reducing the impact of uncertainty. Some changes to organisational environment (for example, the introduction of new legislation, expansion into new markets or demographic change) can be anticipated and, subsequently, proactive micro-planning can be used either to address specific developments or to plan for a limited part of the workforce. In this way, HRP can contribute to the generation of responses to a changing environment that are swifter and more innovative than those of the business's competitors.

EMPLOYEE RETENTION AND TURNOVER

The retention of valued elements of the existing workforce is clearly important to ensuring a firm's future capability. What constitutes acceptable levels of labour turnover varies by occupation, sector and organisation, but in broad terms, excessive labour turnover is generally considered problematic. Most obviously, turnover has financial costs both in filling the vacant posts (i.e. the cost of recruitment, selection, induction and training) and in respect of the 'lost' resource invested in the departed employee. CIPD (2012e) suggest that the average cost of filling a vacancy for a senior manager/director is £8,000 and £2,500 for other employees. Excessive labour turnover can also be of concern where it is symptomatic of organisational problems, such as low employee morale or job dissatisfaction, and where it communicates negative signals to potential recruits about what it is like to work for the firm. Even for low-skilled positions, labour turnover is likely to have a negative impact on performance, at least in the short term, where a less experienced employee replaces an experienced worker.

However, whilst most labour turnover can be considered dysfunctional and to have negative implications for many aspects of organisational performance (Shaw, 2011), labour turnover can sometimes be viewed as positive, albeit within certain parameters. Labour turnover can lead to the recruitment of 'fresh blood' – new employees with innovative ideas or valuable knowledge – which prevent the firm becoming stale or complacent. Turnover can also lead to the exit of poor performers or those employees ill-suited to the organisation or job. In certain sectors, for example the fast food and hospitality sectors, high levels of labour turnover are often viewed as unavoidable where a combination of relatively low pay, deskilled work and extensive use of transient labour result in relatively low levels of employee commitment and high quit rates (Rowley et al., 2000). Many managers therefore do little to address high turnover but simply attempt to minimise its impact on service quality, using this natural wastage as a source of both flexibility and cost reduction. Even in the same sector, however, other firms will proactively seek to maintain workforce stability as a source of competitive advantage (see Box 6.3).

Either way, it is important for firms to monitor employee turnover by conducting exit interviews to investigate the reasons why an employee is leaving the organisation, analysing patterns of attrition to identify problem areas (Heavey et al., 2013) and benchmarking turnover rates with competitors. Firms can be proactive in identifying and addressing potential causes of turnover, for example by conducting employee attitude surveys to assess employee morale.

BOX 6.3
RESEARCH INSIGHT

Labour turnover in the hotel industry

Despite a widespread acceptance of high labour turnover as an unavoidable characteristic of the hospitality industry, some hotels actively attempt to minimise labour turnover. Wilton (2006) reports on a case study of a four-star hotel in the south-west of England where recognition of the positive benefits of workforce stability to service quality led to the implementation of proactive policies to minimise wastage. The hotel's general manager claimed that turnover could often be attributed to mistakes made in recruitment and candidates' misconceptions about the industry, specifically over pay and working hours. This was reflected in the fact that departing staff rarely left to work in other hotels, unless at a higher level, but tended to leave the industry itself. Attempts to address turnover, therefore, focused on training management to interview more effectively and ensuring that candidates were made aware of the idiosyncrasies and demands of the industry.

Explanations for employee exit

Explanations for labour turnover can be categorised as representing either 'push' or 'pull' factors. Pull factors include the attraction and availability of alternative employment, relocation for non-work reasons and an employee's changing personal circumstances. Research also shows the demography is an important variable in understanding patterns of labour turnover (Wocke and Heymann, 2012). To some degree, these might be viewed as outside the control of management, although firms might seek to aid retention, for example, by improving employee terms and conditions or altering working arrangements. The costs of addressing such turnover must, however, be balanced against the cost of losing the employee. Push factors typically reflect employee dissatisfaction with organisational practices or policies (for example, pay or development opportunities) (Do Monte, 2012), the nature of the work and its personal impact on the individual (Bridger et al., 2013; Hwang et al., 2014) and both personal and professional relationships at work. Winterton (2004) distinguishes between 'triggers' that lead to increased intention to leave an employer, such as low job satisfaction and perceived alternative opportunities, and factors associated with actual *voluntary separation*, such as low organisational commitment and ease of movement. He suggests that these four factors represent key pressure points that management can address to minimise labour turnover.

Further online reading This article reviews the literature on turnover rates and organisational performance from a variety of perspectives, concluding that high employee turnover has negative implications for many aspects of organisational performance. It argues, however, that the content of turnover rates is important in determining the degree of impact.

Shaw, J. D. (2011) Turnover rates and organizational performance: Review, critique, and research agenda, *Organizational Psychology Review*, 1: 187–213.

Addressing labour turnover

To address labour turnover, managers might seek to maximise the retention of all staff or alternatively concentrate on retaining high-performing employees or those with scarce skills. Ultimately, all HRM practices have a function in minimising labour turnover. For example, the development of a positive psychological contract through induction, early socialisation and the management of expectation at the outset of employment (realistic job preview) can minimise the chances of early exit.

Dissatisfaction with reward might be a key determinant of employee exit or intention to quit, although pay is often not a primary determinant of turnover. For example, Purcell et al. (2005) reported in a study of the early careers of teachers that the most common reasons for leaving the profession were workload, working hours and unrealistic expectations of the job prior to entering the profession. Whilst pay was not unimportant it was not a pre-eminent cause of teachers leaving the profession. Where pay is a cause for dissatisfaction it is likely to be in respect of internal (comparison with others in the organisation) or external (comparison with the wider labour market) equity. Firms, therefore, must ensure that in order to retain staff they are paying at an appropriate market level, reward structures are internally consistent and the importance of non-financial incentives such as recognition of achievement and opportunities for progression is acknowledged. Family-friendly HR practices, such as enhanced maternity and paternity leave, crêche provision, career breaks and opportunities for flexible working, can also be important in reducing the propensity to quit among particular groups of workers and reducing the relative attractiveness of alternative employment.

A problematic area for management in addressing staff retention is training and development. On one hand, investment in employee development can be viewed as contributing to the development of a positive psychological contract, on the other, such opportunities have the potential to contribute to employee turnover through increasing worker employability. This is particularly the case where employees develop transferable, rather than firm-specific, skills.

SUCCESSION PLANNING AND TALENT MANAGEMENT

One potentially crucial aspect of HRP is formulating contingency plans for the loss of employees holding key positions in the firm. Typically characteristic of large organisations, succession or replacement planning focuses on providing long-term development plans for individuals identified as possible successors to senior managerial posts. This requires the identification of high potential individuals early in their careers and providing opportunities and experience that prepare them for specific 'once in a generation' appointments.

The increasing importance of knowledge to firm performance and the high mobility of talented people have resulted in many firms adopting a broader approach of 'talent management' (IDS, 2008a), reflective of an increased recognition of the importance of internal 'resources', such as its human capital, to competitive advantage (Sheehan, 2012). Whilst talent management can be 'exclusive', that is, narrowly focused on key senior or strategically important positions and individuals within a firm, often it can be more 'inclusive' and concerned with creating a 'pipeline' or pool of talented people at all levels of a firm through ensuring that workforce development is accessible to all those of potential. Talent management requires data collection on current internal labour supply, tracking individual performance and progress and providing opportunities for development. Therefore, talent management connects a number of areas of HRM, including resourcing, performance management, reward and training. Cunningham (2007) suggests that the talent management process can take the approach of aligning people with roles (treating roles as fixed and developing people to fit these jobs) or aligning roles with people (creating and adapting roles to satisfy the aspirations of the most talented). Talent management is further discussed in Chapter 12.

RECRUITMENT AND SELECTION

A key element in enacting an HR plan is addressing any identified imbalances in the workforce and ensuring that the organisation is adequately staffed with people possessing the right mix of attributes to support a particular business strategy. Under strategies for organisational growth, diversification or development, or where organisations seek to replace leavers, this will require firms to recruit new members of staff or reposition existing employees. Recruitment and selection (R&S), taken as a single process, refers to all activities a firm undertakes to fill a staffing vacancy. It is useful, however, to consider recruitment and selection as two separate processes: the first involving the initial activity undertaken to attract a pool of suitable applicants for a vacancy and the second

HIRING TIPS

concerned with selecting the most competent individual from this pool. These two processes are likely to follow sequentially and considerations in one process ultimately shape activity in the other.

The ultimate objective of the R&S process is to get the right people into the right jobs so as to minimise the likelihood of poor performance, turnover or disciplinary issues. The R&S process can be viewed as a two-way flow of communication or negotiation where the employer and applicant make representations to each other about what can be expected of a future employment relationship and constitutes a vital element in the formation of the psychological contract. Recruitment and selection is, therefore, as much about the employee selecting an organisation and the work on offer as the employer selecting an employee.

In broad terms, a 'systematic' approach is often advocated to ensure both effectiveness and fairness in recruitment and selection. This systematic approach is based on the assumption that it is possible to predict future job performance of candidates through the rational assessment and comparison of personal characteristics, prior achievements and experience to meet pre-established criteria based on prior job evaluation and person specification. Such an approach is advocated to ensure procedural fairness by being 'open' to all qualified candidates and 'formal' to ensure it is auditable, transparent and eliminates illegitimate personal bias. However, this systematic approach has been criticised for being overly focused on the nature of static jobs, rather than the people that are best equipped to perform them (Taylor, 2008). Therefore, an alternative approach is advocated using competency frameworks that are people-focused and afford greater flexibility in recruitment. In the following sections we address both these alternative approaches.

The systematic approach to recruitment and selection

JOB ANALYSIS   Once a vacancy has been identified through the HRP process, the next stage is to specify the nature of that job. Job or role analysis is the methodical process of assessing and defining the components of a post, including the nature of the work performed, the associated responsibilities and accountabilities, the equipment used, the skills and knowledge required, the working conditions, the position of the job within the organisation and the outputs or performance standards expected. Such information might be collected through direct observation or interviewing of the incumbent role holder (or group interviews with a number of role holders), 'critical incidents techniques' (focusing on those aspects of the job central to achieving job-related performance outcomes) or role holder questionnaires or work diaries. For some roles, supporting evidence can be provided using performance appraisal data, training manuals or consultation with experts.

As well as providing a basis for recruitment and selection decisions, job analysis is also important for determining pay differentials, identifying training needs, setting performance targets and making and justifying decisions for promotion, redundancy and disciplinary action for poor performance. However, objective job analysis is often perceived as problematic because the methods employed can fail to reflect the whole job or can be affected by subjective bias, particularly of the incumbent, who may wish to 'talk up' their own position and importance.

JOB DESCRIPTION   Resulting from the job analysis process is the formal job description, which contains key information on the post including the specific job title and department to which it is attached, its location, specific duties and responsibilities, relationships with other staff (for example, who the person in the job reports to and which staff, if any, report to the role holder) and associated performance standards. It provides a template for the R&S process by providing a guide for the design of job advertisements and represents the basis of the selection criteria against which applicants are assessed. It also serves as a basis for the employment contract. Taylor (2008) suggests a move away from job descriptions in some companies towards 'accountability' or 'role profiles' that focus on achievement rather than a straightforward description of duties to encourage employees to think of their job, not as a set of discrete activities, but in terms of overall responsibilities.

PERSON SPECIFICATION   Effective job analysis enables managers to identify the profile of the 'ideal' candidate. This profile is represented in the person specification, which details the specific attributes required for the position, including qualifications, knowledge, skills, previous experience, attitudes and behaviours. In other words, the person specification represents the selection criteria.

RISKS OF HIRING
PEOPLE WHO
'FIT'

Attributes can be divided into essential requirements (without which a candidate would not be acceptable) and desirable characteristics that, whilst not essential, are likely to positively impact on job performance and may help to discriminate between many similarly qualified applicants. A person specification might also make reference to disqualifying factors, which constitute a total bar on employment, such as a lack of essential accreditation. The person specification should also contain some means of grading applicant characteristics between acceptable and unacceptable levels.

The person specification serves a number of important purposes. It provides an objective criterion for selection to guard against subjective or impressionistic assessment of a candidate's suitability. It informs what recruitment channels and selection techniques are likely to be most appropriate and makes clear the key aspects of the job that candidates need to know before deciding to apply.

Traditionally, person specification has been based upon attribute classification systems such as those in Rodger's (1952) seven-point criteria (physical make-up; attainments; general intelligence; special aptitudes; interests; disposition; and circumstances) or Munro-Fraser's (1958) five-fold system (impact on others; acquired qualifications; innate attitudes; motivation; and adjustment). Contemporary practice is to make explicit those key performance outcomes or standards according to which the role holder will be assessed, thus shifting the focus from inputs (i.e. personal attributes) to outputs (i.e. achievement). Lewis (1985) suggests that there are three aspects of the selection criteria that are essential to credible decision-making: *individual job criteria*, to assess person–job fit (usually contained in the person specification); *functional/departmental criteria*, to assess the extent of candidate fit with established group norms; and *organisational criteria*, to assess person–organisation fit.

ISSUES WITH THE SYSTEMATIC APPROACH   There are, however, a number of criticisms of the systematic approach to recruitment and selection, not least that it is ineffective in the context of the contemporary organisation. For example, changes in organisational forms in favour of more complex networks of business units, self-managed work teams and greater functional flexibility have led to a decline in clear demarcation between roles and, consequently, the focus on person–job fit is argued to have become outdated. Job analysis tends to create a rather static 'one best way' snapshot of a job at a particular point in time and therefore lacks the dynamic orientation required in a rapidly changing environment (Worren and Koestner, 1996).

In order to address this issue, Taylor (2008) suggests either the regular updating of job descriptions and person specifications to maintain their relevance, or the use of looser, more flexible or 'fuzzy' descriptions that specify broadly defined expectations rather than specific tasks or duties. More generic role definitions can also be used to describe many different types of jobs, such as descriptions of job families. Whilst attribute classification systems such as Munro-Fraser's and Rodger's are still influential in constructing person specifications, such classifications have been challenged as leading to unfair discrimination (for example, on the basis of personal circumstance) and being ineffective in assessing candidate suitability.

In response to these criticisms, Newell and Rice (1999) propose an alternative 'processual' approach to recruitment and selection that takes a more emergent view. In such an approach neither the job nor the individual are viewed as fixed entities and negotiations between the individual and the organisation take place over the nature and content of work informed by the adaptability of the organisation to meet individual needs. The focus is likely to be on the fit between the individual and the team, organisation and environment, keeping the nature and design of the job as flexible as possible. Over time, this process of exchange and negotiation would shape the ultimate nature of the role.

Competency frameworks

The most frequently cited alternative approach to that of the systematic process of job analysis, job description and person specification is the use of competency frameworks. Competency is defined by Boyzatis (1982: 21) as 'the behavioural characteristic of a person which is causally related to effective or superior performance in a job'. Competencies, therefore, represent a broader definition of the determinants of job performance or ability than definitions traditionally associated with the notion of skill, and reflect the range of attributes required for proficiency within a particular organisational context. Such competencies might include customer service orientation, teamwork, communication skills, leadership ability, self-development, adaptability, relationship building or problem-solving.

Pilbeam and Corbridge (2006) suggest that a competency framework is both a list of these competencies and a tool by which they are expressed, assessed and measured. This framework can either emphasise behavioural competencies, technical competencies (required skill and knowledge) or both. A competency framework bears some similarity to a person specification, however, competency frameworks are the result of people analysis (rather than job analysis) to determine the attributes required to achieve desired performance, for example, by identifying the competencies of 'high' performers already in the firm. In this way, competency frameworks are more generic than person specifications and certain competencies can be applied across job roles, departments or even entire organisations. Such broadly defined competencies are particularly relevant in organisations where personality attributes are considered more or equally important as the possession of particular skills or qualifications or where common competencies are identified as being required across the entire organisation. In such cases, competency frameworks provide a means of assessing a candidate's person–organisation fit.

The use of competencies in recruitment can assist in attracting a wider variety of candidates for a post who might have attained desired attributes in unconventional ways (for example, through experiences beyond work and education, such as volunteering). The use of competencies can also help organisations achieve a more objective and reliable assessment of an applicant's suitability for a job and the organisation (Farnham and Stevens, 2000). This is particularly the case where the identification of organisation-wide competencies is used to create and reinforce the behaviours, values and attitudes that underpin organisational culture. They can also be used to inform and support structured approaches to training and development (Wood and Payne, 1998), to managing individual or group performance, and as a benchmark for rewards and promotion decisions. Competencies can, therefore, assist in ensuring horizontal fit between HR activities.

The use of competencies is, however, subject to criticism. The extensive use of competencies in recruitment is perceived by some to result in 'cloning' where recruitment tends towards similar types of people with similar behaviours and approaches to work. This contradicts the importance often placed on workforce diversity as a source of 'creative tension' and competitive advantage. For example, in male-dominated firms competencies based on successful performers may reflect 'male' attributes thus limiting opportunities for women (Griffiths, 2005).

RECRUITMENT

Once an organisation has identified and specified a vacancy and constructed a profile of the ideal candidate – whether in the form of a competency framework or person specification – the next question is whether those attributes can be acquired from inside the organisation, through promotion, work reallocation, internal transfer or the development of existing employees, or whether an external recruit is required. In most cases a firm is likely to consider applications from both external and internal applicants but a predominant focus on one or the other carries with it certain advantages and disadvantages. An internal focus is less expensive and time-consuming and more likely to result in continuity and a good fit between the candidate and organisation. An internal focus can also be a source of motivation for existing employees. However, an internal focus has the obvious disadvantage of limiting the potential field of applicants, restricting the ability of the firm to recruit 'fresh blood' and limiting its potential to yield the advantages of a diverse workforce by perpetuating the existing workforce profile.

Recruitment methods

To raise awareness of the vacant post(s), managers can choose between or combine a range of informal and formal methods of recruitment (Box 6.4). Informal methods include word-of-mouth recommendations from current employees or 'walk-ins'. Formal methods can range from newspaper advertisements to the use of specialist head-hunters for senior managerial posts. Informal methods of recruitment are often used because they are quick, inexpensive and, where recommended, the new recruit can constitute a 'known quantity'. However, these informal methods may be both unfair and inefficient, leaving organisations open to accusations of discrimination against under-represented groups and failing to find the best candidate.

There are a number of key considerations when choosing how best to attract an adequate number of applicants for a vacancy. A first concern is whether the chosen method(s) is cost-effective and appropriately targeted at the intended audience (Matthews and Redman, 1998). A further consideration is the recruitment norms of the sector in which the firm operates. For example, it might be conventional industry practice to advertise in specific trade publications that tend to be read by potential applicants. Of course, eschewing or supplementing these conventions might be a source of recruitment advantage, as innovative approaches might widen the potential talent pool.

Whilst managers might seek to maximise the reach of its recruitment activity, they should also consider that too many applications can make the process of shortlisting extremely time-consuming. In choosing a mix of methods, firms should be careful to ensure consistency in the message they are communicating to potential applicants and that multi-methods are not used where one would have sufficed. Firms must also ensure that the media and channels for recruitment adequately convey the nature of work and the terms and conditions on offer as well as selling the post and organisation to potential applicants.

BOX 6.4
UNDERSTAND

Potential sources and channels of recruitment

- advertising
  - internal message boards/intranet
  - external vacancy lists
  - national/local media – press, television, radio or 'mail shots'
  - technical/professional/trade media
- e-recruitment (Internet/company intranet/social media)
- 'word-of-mouth' recommendation – friends, relatives or associates

- succession planning
- job centres
- employment agencies
- recruitment consultants – 'head-hunting'/executive search agencies
- walk-ins/casual callers/unsolicited approaches/waiting lists
- university 'milk round'
- schools or university careers services
- student placements/internships
- government training schemes and apprenticeships
- open days and recruitment fairs.

BOX 6.5
RESEARCH INSIGHT

Social networking and recruitment

Inevitably, with the explosive growth in the use of social networking sites in recent years, social media have become an increasingly important and widely used channel by which firms raise awareness of opportunities and interact with (potential) applicants. Reflecting developments in web interactivity associated with Web 2.0 technology, 'professional' (such as LinkedIn) and 'social' (such as Facebook) networking sites offer firms means by which to target and attract applicants,

create a dialogue between applicants and recruiters, to create communities and talent pools for future recruitment and to market and promote the company's culture and employer brand (IDS, 2013). Similarly sites can be mechanisms by which jobseekers can approach potential recruiters, market themselves and seek out opportunities (Broughton et al., 2013). This is alongside the benefits of more long-established benefits of e-recruitment discussed elsewhere in this chapter. CIPD (2013a) report that, among respondents to their resourcing and talent planning survey, over half of organisations make use of social media in resourcing, although just 19 per cent have a dedicated social media strategy. Moreover, 59 per cent of those who don't use social media in resourcing believe it would benefit them to do so. Just over two-fifths of respondents who use social media report that someone in their resourcing team has been trained in its use whilst a quarter have a role dedicated to social media.

The most commonly reported purpose for employing social media as part of a resourcing strategy was attracting candidates and brand building, with 84 per cent of respondents reporting that its use had increased the strength of their employer brand and 83 per cent believing it had increased their potential selection pool. Nearly three-quarters report that using social media has reduced their resourcing costs.

Broughton et al. (2013) highlight, however, a number of critical issues that firms need to consider before seeking to use social media for recruitment purposes, including:

- ensuring the accuracy of information available on social media
- ensuring accessibility across a sufficiently wide pool of applicants
- applicant privacy
- implications for equality and diversity.

Give the potential benefits of social media as a recruitment and communications channel it can be expected, therefore, that companies will increasingly make use of social media at different stages of the recruitment process, not least to respond to the changing behaviour of job seekers. For instance, Clements (2012) reports a strong preference among young job seekers for online communication with recruiters.

Alongside choosing the right channel in order to effectively target the appropriate pool of potential job candidates, IDS (2013) suggest ten things for employers to think about when using social media to recruit:

1 Decide on your measure of success upfront – Is the employer concerned with number of applicant visits to the 'apply' page, job views, likes and/or shares?

2 When information isn't relevant, people turn off – Communication should be tailored, relevant, engaging and sufficient to retain interest among the target audience(s).

3 Increasing the number of applications is not always desirable – Is the approach encouraging the right applicants and, equally, discouraging those that are unsuitable?

4 Social media can improve the candidate experience – Social media can improve employer brand even for unsuccessful applicants through, for example, helping applicants self-screen, offering timely feedback and customising the applicant experience.

5 It's about employee not employer branding – Social media can be a means of employing existing employees to act as employer advocates and brand champions, potentially a more powerfully persuasive tool in attracting the right candidates.

6 Timing is everything – Timing, consistency and appropriate frequency to ensure engagement and discourage disengagement. Messages need also be timed to ensure maximum impact.

7 Interaction is the key to engagement – Posts and messages should encourage engagement and dialogue, encouraging potential applicants to ask and respond to questions and to engage in online activities such as quizzes and webinars.

8 Be in it for the long term – In order to maintain and develop interest, social media recruitment strategies need to plan for long-term engagement in order to build a talent pipeline of interested followers that can become an important channel of future recruitment.

9 Make the company stand out – Use innovative ways to make the company stand out, using technology in novel ways and presenting information in a variety of media.

10 Don't underestimate the resources needed – Whilst often presented as a 'cheap' means of attracting candidates, a well-executed social media strategy needs to make judicious choices about resource investment and be prepared to invest both time and money in its success.

CONTEMPORARY TRENDS IN RECRUITMENT PRACTICE CIPD (2008b) report that the most popular methods used to attract applicants for vacancies are recruitment agencies (used by 78 per cent of survey respondents), corporate websites (75 per cent), local newspaper advertisements (74 per cent), trade press advertisements (62 per cent) and speculative applications/word of mouth (47 per cent). To a degree, this preference reflects employers' views on the most effective methods used to attract applicants, with corporate websites and recruitment agencies being deemed most successful (CIPD, 2013a). Recent trends, however, suggest a number of important changes in employer 'recruitment spend'. They report that 40 per cent of respondents had increased their expenditure on social and professional networking sites, whilst a similar proportion (38 per cent) reported a decrease in spending associated with recruitment agencies. Whether this represents a short- or long-term trend in activity, Box 6.5 provides some discussion of how firms might benefit from using social networking sites as part of a resourcing strategy.

Despite this reported reduction on corporate expenditure on agencies, recruitment outsourcing remains a significant aspect of this area of HRM, particularly for firms recruiting specialist fields, for more senior positions or where widespread use is made of temporary labour. Outsourced service providers or agencies can undertake all or some aspects of the recruitment and selection process from creating job descriptions and profiles, sourcing and screening candidates to carrying out assessment and selection. The use of recruitment agencies varies according to sector and size of employer (CIPD, 2008b), but there are a number of broad reasons why firms use agencies to attract applicants, including a desire to source candidates from a specific talent pool, to reduce the time and in-house resources dedicated to recruitment, to draw on a range of specialist skills and to gain flexibility to meet market demands (CIPD, 2008c). Beardwell (2006) distinguishes between three different types of agency activity: *contingency* (ad hoc recruitment of temporary or casual staff); *advertised selection* (agency-run campaigns on firm's behalf); and *search* (head-hunting). The last is typically conducted by specialist 'executive search' agencies to fill senior managerial positions via networks or contacts that may be unavailable to the firm itself. The growth of outsourcing in HRM is further discussed in Chapter 15.

Behind these figures lie a number of important trends in recruitment practice. Whilst it has always been the role of recruitment to 'sell' the organisation to potential applicants, recent years have seen more concerted attempts by organisations to brand themselves as an 'employer of choice' and to differentiate themselves from their competitors. Through 'cues' in recruitment advertising, for example, organisations can publicise corporate culture and values in order to attract the right kind of applicant. Such messages might emphasise challenge, social conscience, innovation and creativity, 'cutting edge', uniqueness, market leadership or even fun. Successful employer branding is also likely to have the impact of soliciting pre-emptive approaches for employment from people who perceive a fit between themselves and the firm that may have the impact of reducing proactive recruitment activity and cost.

As mentioned above, an area of dramatic change in both recruitment and selection is the rapid growth in the use of information and communication technology, particularly the Internet (Singh and Finn, 2003). E-recruitment can take a number of forms and operate at various levels of sophistication. At its most basic level, the Internet is fast becoming the most common source of information on vacancies whether through employers' websites or dedicated cyber-agencies and job search engines. Most firms also encourage the submission of applications online. Increasingly, firms are using new technology to assist in the shortlisting and selection process itself, through the use of online testing and the automatic

BOX 6.6
ETHICAL INSIGHT

Ethical practice in recruitment and selection

A consideration of ethics is particularly critical in recruitment and selection because of the high potential of hiring decisions to be directly or indirectly informed by individual or group prejudice. However, ethics in employee resourcing is more than ensuring fairness in the recruitment process. Pilbeam and Corbridge (2006) suggest that there are a number of ethical principles that an employer should adhere to in recruitment and selection:

- advertising only genuine jobs
- not abusing the power position
- soliciting only information that is necessary
- not asking loaded questions or seeking to entrap candidates
- assessing suitability on the basis of ability
- maintaining confidentiality on the use and storage of candidate information
- informing candidates appropriately of the selection decision.

As in other areas of HRM, ethical behaviour in recruitment can be associated with improved organisational performance. For instance, through the adoption of a thorough, systematic selection process and ensuring that decisions are made without regard to personal bias or self-interest, Alder and Gilbert (2006) suggest that ethical hiring practices enable managers to make better

decisions. A central ethical issue in recruitment is providing equal opportunities for minority groups by ensuring decision-making is based only on necessary job-related criteria and using appropriate recruitment methods to positively encourage and enable applicants from under-represented groups. Ethical issues can also arise from the use of certain selection methods. For example, personality testing is considered ethically problematic given its potential to contribute to social engineering of the firm by promoting 'cloning' in selection decisions and 'weeding out' those applicants with 'deviant' attitudes and values. The rise of e-recruitment also raises ethical questions both for firms and applicants. For example, Philips (2006) notes that more than one in ten students surveyed admitted cheating in online selection tests by consulting friends and family. A contemporary practice of considerable debate is the use by employers of information available on personal profiles on social networking sites to inform judgments about candidate suitability for employment. This practice raises questions about both the validity and reliability of information on such sites to inform selection decisions (Davison et al., 2011) as well as the ethics and legality of this practice (Roberts and Roach, 2009; Brown and Vaughn, 2011), not least given the variability of information on social networking sites across competing applicants and questions over the extent to which the information drawn upon in decision-making is job relevant, with the potential to lead to discrimination.

sifting of applications (Anderson, 2003). The benefits of utilising such technology include the wide reach of the Internet, the speed of communication, relatively low cost (Smith and Rupp, 2004), greater flexibility and ease of use for candidates. However, there are a number of drawbacks. The untargeted nature of much online recruitment activity can result in over-response and non-human processes in short-listing might result in missing key information and thus rejecting appropriate or non-standard applicants where human judgement might have 'taken a gamble' on an unconventional candidate. Therefore, reservations remain about the effectiveness and reliability of e-shortlisting and online testing, as well as security issues. Nevertheless, the use of the Internet in recruitment and selection is likely to increase as familiarity with new technology grows (Bartram, 2000) and innovation continues apace. For instance, a report by the consultancy Tomorrowtoday (2013) details how the telecommunications company, O2, developed an online game to screen candidates for a new role, resulting in both considerable cost savings as 3,800 of the 10,000 applicants were screened out immediately and increased success at face-to-face interview.

The growing importance of e-HR is discussed in more detail in Chapter 15.

Further online reading This article provides a review of literature in the area of recruitment and provides a number of suggestions regarding future research in this area.

Breaugh, J. A. and Starke, M. (2000) Research on employee recruitment: So many studies, so many remaining questions, *Journal of Management*, 26 (3): 405–34.

SELECTION

Matching the right person with the right job, especially in key positions, is critical to organisational performance. The central objective in selection is to provide an employer with sufficient information to predict the future job performance of a candidate by formulating and utilising techniques that are both valid (they accurately measure the dimension of 'suitability' for which they are devised) and reliable (they consistently produce comparable results over successive use). Given that the notion of good performance varies according to job and organisation, then the most effective method or mix of methods to maximise the predictive validity of a selection process will vary. The validity and reliability of selection methods rely both on the appropriateness of these methods to the job role in question and the measures of job performance to which they are 'matched'. For example, if the same person were to repeatedly undertake the same selection test and achieved a different score on each occasion, this method would tell the employer little that is useful about an applicant's potential future job performance. Similarly, if measures of job performance (such as the outcomes of performance appraisals) are inconsistent then it will be difficult to design selection methods that provide a sound basis for choosing the right person for a job.

Assuming an adequate number of appropriately qualified applicants for the vacancy, the firm then needs to shortlist the most suitable candidates to enter the subsequent selection phase, using the selection criteria based upon the person specification. Shortlisting is most often based on the information, particularly the biographical data, presented in the candidate's curriculum vitae (CV) or application form. CVs have the benefit of allowing individual expression, however they may conceal or omit critical information and can be difficult to use as the basis for comparison. Application forms are standardised and easy to compare, but may prevent applicants effectively presenting their 'case' and fail to collect unanticipated information that can be useful in decision-making. Alternative tools for shortlisting prior to final selection include mini-interviews, often conducted over the telephone, which are a quick means of further screening employees but can be costly and time-consuming.

Selection methods

Box 6.7 outlines the range of activities managers can use in selecting from a pool of applicants. Selection techniques can be broadly divided into those that are subjective (those that rely on individual or group judgement, for example, interviewing) and those that are objective or, at least, purport to be (for

BOX 6.7
UNDERSTAND

Selection methods

- Application forms/curriculum vitae (CV) – collection, analysis and comparison of biographical information (biodata)
- Self-assessment
- Interviews
  - individual or panel
  - structured or unstructured format
  - telephone or face-to-face
- Psychometric testing
  - aptitude tests, general intelligence tests, trainability tests, attainment tests, personality tests, literacy/numeracy testing

- Assessment centres
  - combination of techniques, usually involve group element (e.g. simulated teamworking or role-playing)
- Work sampling/portfolios with relevance to job analysis (e.g. typing sample, hypothetical case studies, presentations, in-tray exercise)
- References
  - specific or general/open-ended
  - character or job performance
- Graphology – handwriting analysis

example, psychometric tests). Typically, it is considered good practice to use a range of devices. For example, interviewing, testing and references might be used to give a rounded perspective on a candidate's suitability for a post. CIPD (2013a) report the continued dominance of interviewing as the principal method of employee selection, with the top two most commonly used methods being competency-based interviews (82 per cent) and interviews following contents of CV/application form (used by 71 per cent of respondents). The continued preference for interviewing is followed by significant use of selection testing: testing for specific skills (used by 55 per cent of respondents); literacy/numeracy tests (45 per cent) and general ability tests (45 per cent).

INTERVIEWING   Interviewing remains the main means of assessing applicant suitability for a job, and can be conducted either one-to-one or by a panel of interviewers. In certain circumstances, groups of candidates might be interviewed together. Interviews are useful not only for assessing personal characteristics, especially interpersonal and communication skills, but also for assessing practical intelligence and demeanour. They are an important means by which employers can further explore the information contained in the CV or application form and assess the fit between the person and the organisation. The interview also acts as a forum for negotiating the terms and conditions of employment, contributing to the development of the psychological contract, and answering applicants' questions, as well as providing an opportunity to 'sell' the organisation. Whilst interviews often focus on the biographical information provided in the application form or CV, it is suggested that alternative approaches might enhance predictive validity. For example, *competency-based interviews* (Newell, 2006) focus not on what the candidate has achieved but the competencies displayed in achievement or 'critical incidents' in their past experience relevant to the applied-for role. Alternatively, applicants might be asked to reflect upon hypothetical situations to explore how they might behave. A more recent innovation among some graduate recruiters has been the adoption of *strength-based interviewing*. This approach, whilst bearing some relation to established competency-based approaches by, for

INTERVIEW
QUESTIONS AND
ANSWERS

instance, seeking to assess generic capability to augment an assessment of technical skill, focuses more greatly on rapid fire questions to identify the possession of particular desirable 'authentic' strengths (such as passion, interest and motivation), leading to more natural and less well-rehearsed responses and a greater focus on an individual's capacity for 'excellence' and not merely 'competence'.

Selection interviewing is, however, highly subjective and subsequently subject to criticism. Evidence suggests that interviewers often make rapid judgements based on little information or are not adequately prepared or trained to conduct interviews effectively, compromising their capacity to adequately predict future work performance. There are a number of psychological processes that might serve to compromise an interviewer's ability to focus on job-related factors. First or last impressions of an interviewee may cloud a subjective assessment of a candidate, particularly where accompanied by stereotyping of an applicant's social class, gender, ethnic group, physical appearance or accent. Making a judgement of a 'whole' candidate on a single characteristic is referred to as the 'halo' (positive impression) or 'horns' (negative impression) effect (Anderson and Shackleton, 1993). Prejudice can also arise from a misjudged assessment of the 'type of person' that would be suitable for a post based on organisational traditions or custom. Similarly, a recruiter might unconsciously respond more favourably to candidates who are similar to themselves in some way (for example, educational background). To overcome the potential for individual bias and ensure procedural fairness, interviews are often done by panels, rather than individuals, and often include managers external to the department in which there is a vacancy, especially where internal candidates are involved. McKenna and Beech (2008) advocate structured interviews that assist in standardising questions, recording information and rating applicants. They suggest that unstructured interviews might encourage a genuine two-way conversation but tend to be more casual and haphazard, diminishing their ability to provide a viable basis for selection.

Further online reading The article articulates how the selection interview frequently serves as a political arena for various power networks in the organisation, whose interests may be conflicting, and discusses how this political game can be played out in the selection process.

Bozionelos, N. (2005) When the inferior candidate is offered the job: The selection interview as a political and power game, *Human Relations*, 58 (12): 1605–31.

For highly competitive posts, for example, places on graduate training schemes, firms might use assessment centres. These are intensive selection programmes involving a combination of techniques alongside interviews, often including work simulations, presentations and testing. Box 6.8 discusses how subjective decision-making in selection processes is still influential in such centres despite a veneer of objectivity.

PSYCHOMETRIC TESTING Organisations often choose to supplement interviews with other selection methods in order to assess specific candidate qualities, such as aptitude testing. *Aptitude testing* covers a wide range of practices including tests of physical ability for manual work or tests of mental ability such as numeracy, literacy or general intelligence. *Analogous tests* are those that seek to simulate some aspect of the vacant job. For example, administrative or clerical staff might be asked to complete a word-processing test and teachers are often asked to plan and conduct a short lesson as part of the selection process. For managerial roles,

BOX 6.8
RESEARCH INSIGHT

Decision-making in graduate assessment centres

Brown and Hesketh (2004) suggest that the use of assessment centres to recruit high-potential graduates has improved the quality of decision-making as a result of 'genuine attempts to relate candidates to pre-determined behavioural competences' and a move away from recruiting on the basis of 'old school tie or family contacts' (2004: 186). However, they also note how small differences, such as the way a candidate phrases a response to a question, can make the difference between success and failure, especially because candidates who have reached this late stage in the recruitment process are typically very alike. They also report that because of the similarities between candidates, despite a veneer of scientific

objectivity in decision-making, the recruitment decision often 'boiled down to a subconscious feeling for which candidate one would rather work or socialise with' (2004: 187). Brown and Hesketh suggest, therefore, that those who seek to 'play' the recruitment game will only succeed if they are able to make social connections with those assessing them and that this very often depends on the 'same cultural props of class and ethnic privilege that characterised social elites in the past' (2004: 187). Despite the expansion of higher education, they note that the only major recent change in the graduate labour market has been 'the success of women from mainly privileged backgrounds to give their male counterparts some serious competition' in the race for a highly prized place on graduate development programmes.

group problem-solving exercises, presentations or in-tray exercises (to assess a candidate's ability to prioritise) can be used. Increasingly common in a wide variety of jobs, *personality tests* seek to ascertain the extent to which an individual possesses required traits, often using a questionnaire designed to rate respondents on various personality dimensions (such as persuasiveness, social confidence, decisiveness, introspection, competitiveness and so on) in order to predict behaviour.

Testing is largely seen as advantageous in making recruitment decisions because it is perceived as being objective. Personality tests, for instance, provide quantitative data on 'temperament' and enable the objective comparison of candidates, which can help guard against favouritism or unfair discrimination. Moreover, the predictive power of testing can be assessed and verified by comparing test results at selection with employee performance at a later date. For instance, personality testing, where used appropriately, is generally felt to have good predictive validity.

However, testing has also been criticised for a number of reasons. For example, in personality testing, socially desirable responding (seeking to give the answer that an employer might want to receive rather than reflecting one's true attitude) or 'faking it' (Griffin et al., 2004) might render the exercise inadequate as a predictor of organisational or job fit. Rosenfeld et al. (1995) refer to such activity as 'impression management'. Moreover, testing is criticised as focusing on a relatively narrow range of dimensions of personality and might be unable to adequately capture important nuances or differences between people. Perhaps most significantly, rather than providing objective data, personality testing might actually be intrinsically biased towards, for example, those of a particular socio-economic background or gender. Questions have been raised about the underlying assumption of personality testing that there exists a clear link between personality traits and job performance or outcomes. Consequently, good practice typically advocates that information gathered in testing requires careful interpretation and findings should be treated as tentative and not used as the sole reason for selection.

BOX 6.9
MANAGEMENT SKILLS AND ATTRIBUTES

Line managers and recruitment and selection

As with other aspects of HRM, there has been a trend towards greater line management ownership of R&S processes. This reflects a declining direct role for HR specialists in selection, although evidence suggests a continued role in recruitment (IRS, 2004). HR specialists are increasingly likely to be more focused on coordinating the various elements of the wider R&S process, providing specialist advice to line managers (for example, on the use of selection methods or legislative compliance) and skills training. HR practitioners are also likely to be involved in the evaluation of selection effectiveness. There is a growing tendency towards the centralisation of line manager support for recruitment either in the form of 'HR partners' allied to certain parts of an organisation or shared service centres that provide routine administrative support and advice to all managers. Shared service centres are often staffed by in-house HR advisors but there is an increasing trend for centres to be outsourced to third-party service providers, to provide some if not all of the recruitment and selection functions (McCormack and Scholarios, 2009).

Whilst line managers may play some role in determining appropriate channels of recruitment either directly or indirectly (for example, by providing specialist expertise on how best to communicate with particular constituent groups among which are likely to be suitable candidates), the principal role of line managers will be assisting in selecting among the pool of candidates. For effective interviewing, for instance, alongside a keen understanding of the work context, the labour market and the requirements of the role being recruited to, effective practice requires a critical set of skills including interpersonal skills, such as active listening (a means by which to ensure clarity of understanding) and ability to ask questions in an unambiguous manner, alongside planning skills, self-awareness (for example, of one's own preferences), analytical skills by which to reflect upon and respond to the interviewee and reflexivity and insightfulness to guide probing and follow-up questions. Moreover, line managers are likely to need a range of additional skills in establishing an appropriate context and tone for the interview or assessment centre, as well as skills in managing the interviewing process, such as opening and closing the interview in an appropriate manner.

EVALUATING THE RECRUITMENT AND SELECTION PROCESS

Following the employment decision – most often the offer of the vacant job to one of the candidates but occasionally the decision not to appoint – the final stage in the recruitment and selection process is evaluation. Evaluation is important not least to ensure that mistakes identified are not repeated or to identify and replicate good practice. The R&S process should be assessed according to a number of criteria:

- *Cost* – the extent to which the R&S process represented value for money, taking into account its administrative convenience (Arnold et al., 1994), the cost of recruitment media or third-party fees, the development cost of selection tools and the cost of labour turnover if the selected staff are not retained or the wrong person is recruited.

- *Effectiveness* – evaluation both of the formal process and its execution (Newell, 2006), to assess both the predictive validity of the process (its ability to recruit and select the right person based on a prediction of future performance) and its reliability (its ability to do so over repeated usage and across candidates) (Muller-Camen et al., 2008). Measures for evaluation might include the number of initial enquiries received, the number of applicants, the number of candidates shortlisted, the number of candidates recruited, the number of candidates retained in the organisation after a pre-determined period and the performance of recruits. The selection criteria, and by association the person specification, should be evaluated on whether they enabled fair discrimination between candidates and the extent to which they accurately reflected the quantitative and qualitative elements of the job description and the job itself (criterion-related validity).

- *Fairness* – the extent to which the R&S process provided equality of opportunity for a diverse pool of potential applicants. This can be evaluated by collecting data on the proportion of candidates from minority groups at each stage of the process (awareness, application, shortlist and appointment). The process should also be evaluated in respect of its execution and the use of mechanisms to minimise the possibility of individual prejudice. The criteria for selection should be evaluated on the basis that it was fair and objective and did not contain discriminatory or unfair factors.

INDUCTION

Following the offer of employment to the selected candidate and them joining the organisation, the process of induction will begin. Whilst induction can often be thought of as a short period of information provision at the outset of employment

---

BOX 6.10
GLOBAL INSIGHT

International considerations in recruitment and selection

The national, cultural and institutional context will shape the behavioural norms that surround both good and acceptable practice in recruitment and selection decision-making. For MNCs, an understanding of such differences is essential in making international resourcing decisions or recruiting within an overseas subsidiary. For example, there are culturally based preferences around the acceptance of agency involvement in recruitment, the importance placed on informal networks and the legitimacy of nepotism. Björkman and Lu (1999), for instance, found recruitment and selection to be one of the major concerns for managers in Western–Chinese joint ventures, particularly the extent to which nepotism was used to fill vacancies. Variation also exists across national borders with regard to the practice and acceptance of testing. McKenna and Beech (2008) note that Italy does not permit the use of selection testing, whereas in Sweden and Holland applicants have the right to see test results before the employer sees them, and can destroy the results in the event of a withdrawal of the application. Attitudes also vary in relation to the operation of internal labour markets. For instance, Huang (1999) reports that the adoption of formal succession planning was far lower in Taiwanese firms than in subsidiaries of Taiwan-based Western MNCs because of a reluctance among managers in indigenous firms to implement practices that might weaken paternalistic authority.

MNCs operating overseas should seek to strike a balance between acknowledging local customs and developing alternative approaches, based on an assessment of which norms to respect and which can be ignored, possibly as a source of competitive advantage. MNCs can exploit the recruitment 'blind spots' of national companies by recruiting from talent pools that can be overlooked (for example, female managers in certain male-dominated cultures).

(for example, concerning the workplace rules governing health and safety), it more accurately refers to the whole process during which employees adjust or acclimatise to their new job and working environment, extending well beyond the initial 'orientation' and socialisation period of the first few days or weeks of employment. Pilbeam and Corbridge (2010) suggest that induction represents the protracted period that begins with an offer of employment and continues until both parties are reasonably satisfied with the employment relationship.

The period between an offer of employment and the start of the contract is referred to as the pre-engagement period and is important because it is where the more specific elements of the contract of employment, and the basis of the psychological contract, are made clear or negotiated. It is a period during which the prospective employee might also choose to reject the offer of employment and, therefore, it is the employer's responsibility to ensure they are provided with all necessary information and are as adequately prepared for employment as possible, not least by minimising the likelihood of any dissonance between the anticipated and actual job.

Following the commencement of employment, many employees are engaged on a probationary basis – a pre-determined period of time of anything up to two years, but more likely three to six months – during which the employer will evaluate the individual's competence and performance, determine any need for training or development interventions and also determine the likelihood of long-term employment in the firm. The period of probation will be stipulated in the contract of employment and will vary according to, for example, level of remuneration or job complexity. The contract of employment may also provide for dismissal during the probation period in cases where job performance or capability is deemed to be unacceptable.

Whilst the nature of an effective process of induction will vary according to the nature of the job, the background of the employee and the organisation itself, there are some key elements common to an effective programme, including: orientation to the physical location of work; orientation to the organisation including its strategy, goals, culture, values, history, workplace rules and processes (such as those for performance management) and so on; orientation to the employee's role and key relationships; introduction to key members of staff, including senior organisational members and team/departmental colleagues; introduction to health and safety issues; and clarification of terms and conditions of employment. Providing this information will not only smooth the transition of the employee into the organisation and ensure their more immediate effectiveness in their role, it should also act to reinforce the new recruit's decision to join the organisation and strengthen the psychological contract. The importance of induction and workplace socialisation in reinforcing corporate culture and values is further discussed in Chapter 7.

TERMINATING THE EMPLOYMENT CONTRACT

Whilst recruitment, selection and induction represent the opening acts of the employment relationship, employee resourcing also involves drawing this relationship to a close through termination or, alternatively, an employee disengaging from the organisation. Such termination can arise from dismissal (for whatever reason), resignation or retirement.

In circumstances that require cuts to staffing levels, compulsory or voluntary redundancy might be necessary. Redundancy can occur where an organisation, or part of it, closes down or where it no longer requires the particular kind of work for which an employee is employed. Redundancy is caused by factors external to the individual, whether those in the external environment of an organisation (such as weakened demand for a product or service or economic recession) or those in the organisation itself (such as organisational restructuring or the adoption of new technology which alters the requirement for labour and skill). Of course, redundancies might not necessarily be the outcome of such change (as outlined in Box 6.1). For example, during the recession of 2008–9, the UK saw many firms, including Honda, Jaguar Land Rover and Toyota, adopting innovative employment solutions to a decline in demand, opting to negotiate pay freezes, temporary suspensions of production, limitations on overtime, changes to shift patterns and reduced working hours, rather than resorting to redundancies (BBC, 2009).

The redundancy process requires careful management both to assist those leaving the firm and to ensure the retention of required skills, knowledge and competencies. Firms also need to ensure compliance with the relevant legislation. In the UK, firms have a number of legal obligations in the handling of redundancy. First, there is a requirement for the employer to consult with employees in order to discuss ways of avoiding redundancies, ensuring such consultation takes place sufficiently in advance of the proposed redundancies and that employees are provided with information regarding the number of employees likely to be affected, the criteria for selection and so on. Such consultation can be collective, via trade unions or other employee representatives, or individual. Second, employers are required to compensate employees for redundancy where employees have accrued sufficient length of service with the legislation setting out formula for the calculation of minimum payments based on, for example, age and length of continuous service. In the case of non-compulsory or voluntary redundancy, employers often offer enhanced redundancy payments in order to entice (for example, where individuals are offered early retirement), rather than select or force employees to leave the organisation. Third, the employer must ensure that employees are not unfairly selected for redundancy. Whilst the legislation does not specify what criteria can be considered lawful, it places the onus on employers to follow agreed or customary arrangements and employ criteria that are both objective and reasonable. Whilst, in the UK, redundancy forms one of the potentially 'fair' reasons for dismissing an employee, selection for redundancy can often give rise to claims for unfair dismissal, for example, where employees claim that their dismissal was based on subjective managerial judgement, rather than reasons supported by objective evidence (the legal framework for dismissal is discussed in detail in Chapter 13). Fair and reasonable criteria can be determined through the process of HRP, for example, where the identification of critical skills and competencies and performance standards required to meet specific strategic objectives forms the basis for selection for redundancy. Finally, employers have a legal obligation to make every reasonable attempt to find a comparable post for affected employees and to assist workers in finding alternative employment, for example, by allowing 'reasonable' time off for job interviews or training opportunities.

In many ways these legal requirements reflect what might be considered good practice in handling redundancies, not least in being sympathetic to the emotional impact on the individual of losing their job largely through no fault of their own, and in reducing the negative consequences of 'survivors' syndrome' – the emotional and psychological repercussions for those who remain employed by the firm following a programme of redundancy. Such 'survivors' are likely to fear for their own job security, feel under increased pressure and stress or that the psychological contract has been violated, and therefore, become demotivated or distrustful of management (Chiumento, 2003). In handling redundancy, therefore, firms should be mindful of the need for clear and comprehensive policies on handling redundancy, effective channels of communication (not least to counteract the inevitable hearsay and rumour that characterise periods of organisational change) and ensuring managers are able to sensitively handle the redundancy process and opportunities for affected employees to seek support, for example, through counselling.

SUMMARY POINTS

- Human resource planning is the process of forecasting the future supply and demand for labour and involves an assessment of both 'hard' and 'soft' dimensions of human resource capability and current practices and policies.

- There is a range of HR responses to the HRP process beyond recruitment or workforce downsizing, including job redesign, the adoption of new technology or workforce restructuring.

- The feasibility of HRP in unpredictable environments has been questioned: however, it remains important for organisations operating in more stable conditions and where firms seek to 'beat the future.'

- All aspects of HRM have a role to play in managing employee turnover and addressing both the 'push' and 'pull' factors associated with an employee's decision or intention to quit.

- A systematic approach is typically associated with fairness, validity and reliability in selection decision-making; however, increasing flexibility of organisational form and labour undermines the extent to which rigid job descriptions and person specifications remain appropriate.

- Competency frameworks are increasingly used as the basis for selection decisions to better reflect the importance of person–organisation fit and to ensure the horizontal integration of HRM policies and practices. However, strength-based selection techniques are becoming increasingly prevalent

- The use of social media as part of a recruitment strategy represents a significant trend, driven by an appreciation of its potential to reduce costs, effectively target and engage suitable candidates and to build employer brand.

- Interviewing remains the most common method for selecting among candidates, alongside continued growth in the use of testing, the proliferation of e-recruitment techniques and the use of outside agencies and outsourcing.

- The recruitment and selection process should be evaluated on the basis of three main criteria – cost, effectiveness and fairness – in order to inform future recruitment and selection activity.

SELF-TEST QUESTIONS

1 How can HRP contribute to the achievement of an organisation's strategic objectives?

2 To what extent is HRP both feasible and useful in an organisational climate of uncertainty?

3 What is meant by 'hard' and 'soft' approaches to labour supply and demand forecasting?

4 In what ways can a firm respond to labour supply and demand forecasting beyond recruiting new employees or downsizing their existing workforce?

5 How does the systematic approach to recruitment and selection seek to address the twin aims of effectiveness and fairness?

6 Why is it argued that the use of competencies to inform the recruitment and selection process is more appropriate than more traditional approaches? Why do you think some firms have moved to the use of strength-based, rather than competency-based, interviewing?

7 What are the key considerations firms must account for when developing the use of social media as an element of their recruitment strategy?

8 In what ways do cultural differences shape the conduct of recruitment and selection in different countries?

9 What are the problems associated with the use of (a) interviewing and (b) testing in

selection? How might these problems be overcome?

10 What is the significance of the notions of reliability and validity in choosing an appropriate selection method or mix of methods?

11 Why is it important to evaluate and review the recruitment and selection process and what measures should be used to inform such a review?

TEST YOURSELF

Want to know more about this chapter? Review what you have been learning by visiting:

https://edge.sagepub.com/wilton3e

- Print out or download the chapter summaries for quick revision
- Test yourself with multiple-choice questions
- Revise key terms with interactive flashcards

CASE STUDY

The call centre at Tengo Ltd

Tengo Ltd is a manufacturer of notebook computers. Since first entering the market in 2000 they have enjoyed rapid growth due to the ongoing popularity of their low-cost laptops aimed at the student market and the development of a range of higher-spec 'business' notebooks. Their products sell in 30 countries across Europe and the Far East, although their main manufacturing operations, research and development, and support functions (HR, finance, sales, marketing and IT) continue to be based in the UK where they employ over 500 members of staff. Given that Tengo trade exclusively over the Internet – they do not have retail outlets nor do they sell their products through high street retailers – the company's customer contact centre provides a number of key functions: it is the customer point of contact for spares, accessories and extended product warranties; it provides technical support for existing customers; and it is the channel for customer complaints and fields enquiries about Tengo products. The contact centre was built three years ago on a greenfield site on the outskirts of a large town in the Midlands. There are a number of other customer contact centres situated nearby and, following a number of new employers locating to the region, competition for labour is intense, especially for those with prior call centre experience.

The workforce in the contact centre consists of a customer service director, an HR advisor, a call centre manager, eight team supervisors and 95 contact centre advisors. Out of these 95 advisors, approximately 20 form the technical liaison team who deal with detailed technical questions and ten members of staff working in the complaints department also deal with some low-level technical enquiries. Twenty-five advisors deal with the ordering of spares and accessories and the remainder field enquiries about Tengo products. Tengo's call centre is known locally to offer comparatively high pay, however, a recent benchmarking study of local competitors found that other terms and conditions of employment are less favourable. In particular, advisors are required to work longer shifts than employees in other nearby centres, receive less holiday entitlement and have fewer opportunities for training and development.

Following a periodic HRP exercise six months ago, the HR director (based in London) feels that Tengo's rapid growth over the previous three years has led to overstaffing at the call centre, particularly among the customer service department. As a result, a programme of rationalisation and restructuring has been undertaken resulting in the loss of 30 jobs in the contact centre. As a result, 18 workers have been made redundant, with 12 other posts lost through 'natural wastage'. Significant investment has also been made in providing more effective and interactive online product support for customers, particularly technical advice. A customer satisfaction survey undertaken at the turn of the year rated satisfaction with after-sales customer service as poor and, subsequently, further investment has been made in a new automated computer system which seeks to standardise customer service, speed up response times and improve management's ability to monitor service quality. It is also hoped that this will reduce training and development costs for new employees.

Following the restructuring, employee advisors are graded into three bands. Level 1 advisors, typically those dealing with customer complaints, are entry-level positions. The majority of advisors across most of the departments are Level 2. Advisors at Level 3 are mainly those dealing with detailed technical problems, commonly felt by the advisors to be the more interesting and desirable work, as well as having the best reward package. Among the technical support team, 16 of the advisors have joined the company at a lower level and have previously worked in at least one of the other areas of the contact centre. There is, however, greater 'churn' of employees in all other sections, particularly the complaints department in which 25 per cent of new recruits have left within the first two months. Whilst prior to restructuring there had been a degree of movement between the departments, with workers often trained to undertake a variety of roles, the customer service director has decided to more clearly delineate the responsibilities of each department in the hope that customer service will be improved by encouraging advisors to specialise in particular areas.

Prior to the organisational restructuring, employee turnover was found to reflect both the industry and regional average. Management tends to consider a certain level of turnover to be acceptable and even beneficial to the firm. Since the restructuring, however, labour turnover has increased by 10 per cent and a number of long-serving advisors have left the centre. Employee absence has also risen significantly. Management has taken the decision to seek to tackle recruitment in the technical support and team leader roles outside of the organisation to reduce training and development costs.

Task

Recent customer service feedback highlights growing customer dissatisfaction with after-sales support and complaint handling and the customer service director is under significant pressure to address these problems. He has asked you – the HR advisor – to explore the 'people' issues that might be contributing to poor service quality. In doing so, consider the following questions:

1 What do you think are the main causes of poor customer service quality at Tengo?

2 How can you explain high labour turnover in the call centre?

3 What information do you need to collect in order to understand and remedy turnover? How might this information be collected?

4 Is turnover in the call centre likely to be universally dysfunctional?

5 What changes would you make to HR practices and process within the call centre to address any identified problems?

USEFUL READING

Journal articles

Alder, G. S. and Gilbert, J. (2006) Achieving ethics and fairness in hiring: Going beyond the law, *Journal of Business Ethics*, 68: 449–64.

This article draws on multiple perspectives to explore the ethical meaning of fairness in recruitment practice, and suggests that ethical 'fairness' beyond the requirements of regulation enables managers to make better hiring decisions.

Bartram, D. (2000) Internet recruitment and selection: Kissing frogs to find princes, *International Journal of Selection and Assessment*, 8 (4): 261–74.

This article discusses the development and widespread application of the Internet as a recruitment and selection tool. It outlines a range of issues associated with its use including security, confidentiality, authentication and equality of access and identifies potential areas of abuse.

Davison, H., Maraist, C. and Bing, M. (2011) Friend or foe? The promise and pitfalls of using social networking sites for HR decisions, *Journal of Business Psychology*, 26 (2): 153–9.

This article seeks to address the many questions that remain relatively underexplored about using social networking sites for HR practice, including questions about the validity and usefulness of information obtained on these sites and applicant perceptions of employers' use of these sites. The article describes issues associated with using social networking websites for recruitment, selection and termination of employment and provides recommendations for future research studies in this area.

Vaiman, V. and Collings, D. G. (2013) Talent management: Advancing the field, *International Journal of Human Resource Management*, 24 (9): 1737–43.

This article introduces a special edition of the journal focused on talent management. The edition contains articles exploring talent management from a range of perspectives and in a variety of contexts and provides a well-rounded overview of contemporary research in this area of management.

Books, book chapters and reports

CIPD (2013) *Resourcing and Talent Planning Survey Report*, London: CIPD

This report provides an up-to-date overview of contemporary practice and trends in employee resourcing with a particular focus on the use of social media and the impact of the contemporary labour market context of recruitment practice.

Tomorrowtoday (2013) The future of recruitment, a paper prepared for the AGRG Annual Conference 2013, www.agr.org.uk/CoreCode/Admin/ContentManagement/MediaHub/Assets/FileDownload.ashx?fid=87959&pid=12689&loc=en-GB&fd=False (accessed 20 June 2015).

This brief report provides some interesting insights to the graduate recruitment activity of a range of global firms in light of a range of contemporary developments in technology and social behaviour. In doing so, it provides some insight into ongoing developments in the field.

FURTHER ONLINE READING

The following articles can be accessed for free on the book's companion website **https://edge.sagepub.com/wilton3e**:

Bozionelos, N. (2005) When the inferior candidate is offered the job: The selection interview as a political and power game, *Human Relations*, 58 (2): 1605–31.

Breaugh, J. A. and Starke, M. (2000) Research on employee recruitment: So many studies, so many remaining questions, *Journal of Management*, 26 (3): 405–34.

Ployhart, R. E. (2006) Staffing in the 21st century: New challenges and strategic opportunities, *Journal of Management*, 32 (6): 868–97.

Shaw, J. D. (2011) Turnover rates and organizational performance: Review, critique, and research agenda, *Organizational Psychology Review*, 1: 187–213.

Want to know more about this chapter? Visit the companion website at: **https://edge.sagepub.com/wilton3e** to access practice questions, videos and selected journal articles to further enhance your study.

7

MANAGING PERFORMANCE

DIMENSIONS AND
INFLUENCES ON
PERFORMANCE

CHAPTER OBJECTIVES

- To outline the mechanisms through which management can seek to manage and improve individual, team and organisational performance

- To explain what is meant by the term 'performance management' and how this relates to other areas of HRM

- To outline the component parts of performance management systems

- To discuss the mechanisms by which individual performance is measured

- To explain and critique the rationale for the management of organisational culture in pursuit of improved individual and organisational performance.

INTRODUCTION

The performance equation outlined in Chapter 2 suggests that individual performance at work can be understood as a function of ability, motivation and opportunity (Boxall and Purcell, 2003). From this perspective it is clear that the effective management of individual performance at work requires attention to be paid to a number of elements of HRM, including recruiting people with the right mix of skills and knowledge, ensuring their ongoing training and development and rewarding them in a way that encourages effort. In a broad sense, therefore, managing performance is concerned with how organisations plan, coordinate, utilise, motivate and equip their workers to achieve desired outcomes and objectives. Chapter 3 outlined best practice variants of HRM and suggested that such models are predicated on their universally positive impact on employee motivation and commitment through the provision of career opportunities, job challenge, employee involvement in decision-making, employee development, cooperative line manager relations and the management of organisational culture. It is these multiple mechanisms by which work organisations can seek to improve individual performance, in line with the wider performance requirements of the organisation, that are the concern of this chapter.

The chapter begins by defining performance and then considers the specific notion of performance management (PM) and the components of performance management systems (PMS), including goal-setting, performance-related pay and performance measurement. It then discusses how organisational culture can be managed to improve individual and organisational performance.

DEFINING THE CONCEPT OF 'PERFORMANCE'

In order to fully understand the mechanism by which managers can effectively manage and improve employee performance, it is important to first define what constitutes 'performance' (Armstrong and Baron, 1998). In one sense, performance at work can be understood both as a process and an outcome or, in other words, it is 'about doing the work as well as being about the results achieved' (Armstrong, 2000: 3). Performance, therefore, represents a demonstrative act that is concerned both with the outputs of work *and* the skills knowledge, competencies and behaviours employed to achieve them (Forrester, 2011).

The performance equation provides a useful starting point in considering how organisations might maximise the individual or team contribution to the achievement of organisational objectives. In essence, HR policies and practices can improve performance by addressing each of the three dimensions: ability, motivation and opportunity. HRM represents a broad range of processes and practices by which an organisation can influence the relative 'strength' of each of these elements, including employee resourcing and learning and development (ability), reward management (motivation) and job design and employee involvement and communication (opportunity). A key point here is that a deficit in any of these areas will likely lead to poor performance, irrespective of the value of the other two. Therefore, management must be keenly aware of the need to effectively manage all three components.

However, Purcell et al.'s (2006) model of the people–performance link, introduced in Chapter 2, suggests that ability, motivation and opportunity do not directly determine individual performance, but that their effect is mediated by line management activities, the effective implementation of HR policies and practices, employee commitment and job satisfaction. These factors determine employee engagement (Gruman and Saks, 2011) and the expression of discretionary behaviour which ultimately shapes performance. On this basis, it is imperative to consider all of these elements when seeking to manage performance. Neal and Griffin (1999, citing Borman and Motowidlo, 1993) make the important distinction between *task performance* and *contextual performance*. The former relates to the behaviours, skills and knowledge that relate to the core technical aspects of a given job. The latter is not directly related to a job role, but reflects those behaviours that maintain the broader organisational, social and psychological environment within which that job is carried out. This includes cooperating with and helping colleagues and exerting discretionary effort. Consideration of both in understanding work performance is important because it is the latter that helps to translate improvements in the former into wider improvements in organisational performance (Neal and Griffin, 1999).

Overall, it is important for managers to recognise that there is a wide range of individual and organisational influences on employee performance. On the worker side, job performance can be affected by personal characteristics, such as 'drive' and ambition, experiences in previous job roles, personal relationships, the coherence of values with those of the firm and factors relating to one's personal life. On the organisational side, performance will at least partly reflect job design (Garg and Rastogi, 2005), 'person–job' fit, the appropriateness of reward and the state of the psychological contract. The nature of performance is also determined by the organisational strategy that determines how 'good' performance is defined (for example, a focus on sales or customer service). Management must therefore recognise that a lack of motivation, and therefore performance, is not solely the 'fault' of the individual (Shields, 2007). Given the wide range of influences on performance it can often be difficult to disentangle the impact of HR policies from environmental conditions, both those inside (such as the effect of new technology) and outside the firm (such as favourable or unfavourable market conditions). As a consequence, the management of performance is a complex problem, made more difficult in light of the changing nature and context of work outlined in Chapter 2.

A useful perspective on performance and its determinants is that which considers why workers under-perform. Gillen (2002: 36–8) suggests that there are four main reasons (other than incapability) for under-performance that can be resolved through managerial action. First, the employee may not know what the manager wants them to achieve. Second, the employee knows what is required but does not know how to do it. Third, the employee knows what is required and can deliver to the standard expected but they lack influence over resources or effective work systems that would enable them to achieve higher levels of performance. Fourth, the employee knows what is required and how to do it but they do not want to do it or cannot see the importance of the task. From this perspective, the performance equation remains a useful tool in diagnosing under-performance in that, alongside the effective communication of employee objectives, standards or role requirements, the reasons for poor performance reflect a deficit of skills, motivation or opportunity/resources.

Further online reading This interesting article reviews the literature on 'creative' performance in the knowledge economy and explores how performance management can contribute to the fostering of creativity and innovation in both routine and non-routine jobs.

Waples, E. P. and Friedrich, T. L. (2011) Managing creative performance: Important strategies for leaders of creative efforts, *Advances in Developing Human Resources*, 13 (3): 366–85.

WHAT IS PERFORMANCE MANAGEMENT?

PERFORMANCE
MANAGEMENT

In line with the growth in interest in HRM since the 1980s (outlined in Chapter 1), there has been a commensurate significance attached to 'managing' organisational performance. In the private sector, this has largely been in response to growing global competitive pressures, the need for firms to compete with lower-cost overseas competitors and to consistently deliver shareholder value. In the public sector, the desire to improve the delivery of public services has led to a plethora of initiatives, such as schools and university league tables and UK NHS waiting list targets designed to measure, manage and improve organisational performance. Performance management systems have subsequently become a widely practised organisational activity across the public, private and not-for-profit sectors (Ridder et al., 2012), driven by the need for all organisations to become more efficient, effective and productive through improving the contribution of individuals, teams and departments towards the achievement of explicit organisational objectives.

The process of effective PM begins at the strategic level. Chapter 3 discussed the importance to HR strategy formation of identifying the employee behaviours required to pursue a particular organisational strategy in order to determine the content of HR policies and practices. One understanding of 'good' performance, therefore, is the widespread expression of the employee behaviours required to fulfil specific strategic objectives. An important element of an organisation's HR strategy should, therefore, be to ensure that employees are aware of the part they play in the success of the firm, the particular importance of individual performance and what constitutes good performance. This requires senior managers to identify and clearly communicate a 'shared vision' (Fletcher, 2008) for the firm, the values that underpin required behaviour and the 'critical factors' required for organisational success (Pilbeam and Corbridge, 2006). Some commentators stress the importance of a 'big idea' in creating sustainable advantage, a unifying conception of what the organisation stands for and what it is trying to achieve.

From this perspective, PMS provide an integrative framework of HR policies and practices that enable organisations to explicitly connect the organisation's strategic intentions with the efforts of its employees and to define work activities and individual or team objectives according to these intentions. In other words, PM represents the range of HRM activities that enable, encourage, coordinate and support employees to achieve their objectives, monitor, measure and reward their achievements and, fundamentally, to contribute to the long-term success of the organisation. Understood another way, PM is the HR infrastructure aimed at addressing the four reasons for under-performance outlined previously by ensuring that employees know and understand what is expected of them (Harper and Vilkinas, 2005), and that they have the competencies to deliver on these expectations, as well as providing employees with the opportunity to contribute to objective-setting and motivating them to achieve these objectives through financial and non-financial means (Armstrong and Baron, 2005). Therefore, whilst it is the 'social climate' of the firm that acts to stimulate 'employees' efforts', the techniques associated with performance management act to channel this effort towards strategic priorities (Bourne et al., 2013).

Gruman and Saks (2011) point out that many contemporary developments in both the nature and context of work (as outlined in Chapter 4), such as the multifaceted nature of modern jobs and the importance of emotional intelligence, creativity, adaptability and proactivity (Waples and Friedrich, 2011), require not so much the 'management' of performance, rather its 'facilitation' through creating the conditions for performance to improve. Box 7.1 outlines the wide range of 'levers' that organisations can employ to facilitate such improvements in individual and organisational performance, many of which relate to the fundamental aims of PM. Clearly, virtually all elements of HRM, including learning and development, reward, recruitment and selection, culture management, communication and involvement, constitute mechanisms by which an organisation can manage performance. To do so effectively, however, requires that HR policies and practices are horizontally integrated, mutually supportive and constitute an integrated framework for employee and organisational improvement.

Further online reading This short article summarises some of the persistent criticisms of performance management, and its potential to contribute to improved organisational performance. It argues that if performance management is to be successful it requires a concerted focus on preparing and supporting managers to perform their roles in eliciting high employee performance effectively.

Risher, H. (2011) Getting performance management on track, *Compensation & Benefits Review*, 43 (5): 273–81.

CHAPTER 7 MANAGING PERFORMANCE

BOX 7.1
RESEARCH INSIGHT

'Action levers' that contribute to improved performance

- Top management levers, including:

    Consistent messages that senior managers value the workforce, recognition in decision-making of the importance of employee commitment to organisational success, clear communication of the organisation's mission, guiding principles and core values, regular communication to inform employees of performance results, periodic communication to recognise the importance of employee efforts, publicising past success stories to build pride in the organisation, recognising significant group, team and individual accomplishments, providing the technology and resources needed to meet performance expectations, balancing the importance of organisational performance and employee personal goals.

- Organisational levers, including:

    Self-managed teams, employee empowerment, broadening span of management control, minimising hierarchy and status distinctions, eliminating structural barriers between individuals, teams and groups, knowledge management and employee problem-solving.

- Human resource levers, including:

    Investment in skill-building, salary increase on pay-for-contribution basis, profit-/gain-sharing, results-based PMS, banded salary systems to encourage employee flexibility, competency-based HR systems to focus on employee capabilities and generic job classifications.

- Supervisory levers, including:

    Job rotation and cross-training, flexible work schedules, regular constructive feedback on employee strengths and development needs, encouragement and support for skill development and learning, teamworking, encouragement for employees to broaden the scope of their role, definition of individual and team performance goals and measures, effective coaching, ongoing employee involvement, recognising and celebrating employee accomplishments, providing opportunities for fun at work, consistency in decision-making and discipline.

Source: adapted from Risher, 2005

Importantly, effective PM should be concerned not only with outcomes (the achievement of desired objectives) but also with processes (the mechanisms and behaviours through which to achieve current and future objectives). Its focus is, therefore, on the compatibility and continuous improvement of both people and organisational systems to facilitate individual effectiveness. PM is increasingly associated with the need to identify, nurture and retain talent both in respect of the narrow focus of succession planning and the wider interests of talent management and developing overall organisational capability.

Taking all these elements together, CIPD (2008d) suggest that performance management is about:

- establishing a *culture* in which individuals and groups take responsibility for the continuous improvement of business processes and of their own skills, behaviour and contributions

- creating *shared expectations* by which managers can clarify what they expect individuals and teams to do; likewise individuals and teams can communicate their expectations of how they should be managed and what they need to do their jobs

- identifying *inter-relationships* and improving the quality of relationships between managers and individuals, between managers and teams, between members of teams and so on

- defining performance *expectations* expressed as objectives and in business plans
- *measurement* of performance following the dictum that 'If you can't measure it, you can't manage it'. This should apply to *all employees*, not just managers, and to teams as much as individuals.

Further online reading This discussion piece explores the challenges that MNCs face in conducting performance appraisals in a variety of national contexts and the options available to such firms. Despite its focus on MNCs operating across borders, the article provides useful insight into conducting performance appraisals more generally.

Shen, J. (2005) Effective international performance appraisals: Easily said, hard to do, *Compensation & Benefits Review*, 37: 70–9.

The performance management cycle

On a strategic level, managing performance is concerned with the connection of organisational mission and values, corporate strategy and HR strategy with unit, team and individual objectives and the HRM mechanisms to support and measure performance. This should not be considered a one-off activity, but a continuous process of monitoring and evaluating the continued efficacy of organisational values and objectives in the light of changing internal and external context. In other words, a PMS should be both strategically and contextually congruent (Aguinis et al., 2011). At an operational level, as well as constituting an integrative framework for activities to enhance individual contribution to organisational success, we can also understand PM as a systematic process or continuous cycle involving a number of distinct, but integrated, stages (see Figure 7.1).

Whilst these stages are likely to be common to most effective PMS, it is important to note that there is no 'one right way' of managing performance and the specifics of each component need to be appropriate to the individual organisation. Notions of good performance differ from organisation to organisation and, subsequently, objectives and measures of performance will vary, as will the appropriate support to be provided by managers. Moreover, the PM process should be flexible enough to be amenable to adaptation at each stage in response to changing organisational context.

The first stage of the cycle reflects the fact that vital to the success of individual performance management is a detailed understanding of the job role, associated work processes and the conditions under which work is being performed. This is both to assess current performance and to better understand performance requirements, expectations and possible areas for improvement. Following this observation phase, performance objectives and standards should be agreed between managers and employees alongside the means by which the organisation will support their achievement (for example, whether the individual requires further training). Job performance should then be aided by line management support, such as mentoring and coaching, continuous feedback on performance, and training and development activity. Finally, individual performance is reviewed, appraised and, where appropriate, rated and/or ranked against that of the employee's peers or a pre-agreed criteria. This informs an appropriate managerial response; for example, the allocation of reward for the achievement of objectives or remedial activity if performance is considered unsatisfactory. Given that this cycle is a continuous process it is clear that the initial period of performance observation and planning

BOX 7.2
GLOBAL INSIGHT

Performance management in international context

Inevitably, national culture shapes the extent to which performance management and appraisals are desirable and effective for the management of people. Schneider and Barsoux (2008: 163) indicate that the very notion of managing performance is 'heavily embedded in an instrumental view of organisations which might have little appeal to those cultures that see organisations in terms of social relationships where what counts is managing people, not tasks'. The cultural assumptions that underpin performance management systems include the views that: goals can be set and achieved (representing the view that control over one's environment is possible); that objectives may be given timeframes for their achievement (time can be managed); the attainment of goals and performance can be measured (that reality is objective); and that it is possible to hold a bilateral dialogue and develop manager–subordinate agreement with an acceptance of the employee's right of input and willingness to accept responsibility (reflecting small power distance and individual orientation – Fletcher, 2001). Moreover, PM criteria often reflect cultural assumptions about what constitutes effective performance and which behaviours are desirable (for example, individual ambition, assertiveness and showing initiative) which might have limited acceptability across cultures (Claus and Briscoe, 2008). Clearly, these issues present significant problems for firms operating across a variety of countries seeking to impose standardised approaches to PM (Shen, 2005). However, it is not only cultural differences, but also differences in organisational and managerial capacity across borders that render PM problematic. Ohemeng (2009) reports that the introduction of PM into public organisations in Ghana has been problematic as a result of unwieldy administrative systems and a lack of leadership capacity, allied to a lack of understanding of the roles associated with PM. Equally, institutional differences in context – such as the presence and role of trade unions – also shape practice within MNCs (Bartram et al., 2015).

Significant research, therefore, tends to support the view that PM does not necessarily 'travel well' from its origins in the USA. For example, Elenkov (1998) suggests that direct feedback is perceived as less acceptable in the more collectivist culture of Russia. Huo and Glinow (1995) found that managers in China (a high power distance culture) were reluctant to engage in two-way communication in the appraisal process. Kanter and Corn (1994) report that in a Swedish-owned firm in the USA American managers complained that the Swedes were overly critical and never gave positive feedback. Europeans, in turn, complain about the American 'hamburger' approach to feedback: surrounding the criticism (the meat) with empty praise (the bun). In the typically collectivist cultures of Asia, the emphasis on individual responsibility for performance is particularly problematic. Furthermore, performance appraisals often clash with the importance placed on protecting one's social capital and maintaining group harmony. Criticising an employee is likely to be considered tactless and Western MNCs have had to adapt appraisal processes: for example, by using third parties to conduct appraisals. Similarly, Shipper et al. (2007, cited in Fletcher, 2008), Brutus et al. (2001) and Pollitt (2004) all found that the effectiveness of 360-degree feedback processes varied significantly across countries. In summary, a culturally diverse workforce creates problems for PM where interpersonal communication becomes more complex to manage (Kikoski, 1999). These studies indicate that the effective operation of PM across diverse cultures often requires local interpretation or adaptation. Even where PM is focused on expatriate workers in international firms, evidence suggests that more international firms tend towards a focus on the hard aspects of PM, such as appraisals and goal setting, rather than the soft dimensions, such as training and mentoring (Fee et al., 2011).

Nonetheless, whilst recognising the importance of ensuring performance management systems be 'context congruent' (Aguinis et al., 2011), Aguinis et al. (2012) suggest that there are a number of 'universals' that apply to all organisations, regardless of a particular cultural context:

- congruence between job descriptions and organisational goals
- measurement of performance based on behaviours and results at the individual and collective levels
- training regarding performance management

- delivering performance feedback using a strengths-based approach
- allocating rewards that are meaningful.

However, the application of these principles in practice requires consideration of cultural context. For instance, delivering performance feedback in a context of low individualism (for instance, South Korea, Singapore or China) requires the use of non-confrontational and indirect language, preferably in an informal setting.

is interlinked with the performance review process. It is important to note, however, that whilst this cycle portrays a rather formal process disconnected from the day-to-day work of the organisation, effective PM tends to be that which is part of the way of working within an organisation rather than an adjunct to it (Pulakos and O'Leary, 2011).

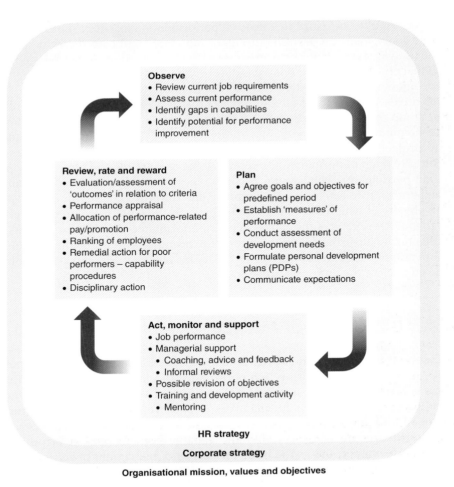

FIGURE 7.1 The performance management cycle in strategic context

SETTING PERFORMANCE OBJECTIVES

Central to managing individual performance is the maxim of 'what gets meas-ured gets done' or, alternatively, the elements of work that are subject to scru-tiny and observation will determine what people take to be important. Chapter 2 introduced the expectancy models of motivation that suggested that the extent to which an individual is motivated to achieve a particular objective is related to the extent to which they believe that its achievement will result in desired out-comes or reward. This theory suggests that the identification and communication of clear goals enhance an individual's ability to accurately define and enact the behaviour required to achieve desired objectives.

Management by objectives (MBO) was an influential antecedent of PM that gained prominence in the 1950s and 1960s. MBO represented an initial attempt to systematically align organisational and individual objectives, involve all levels of management and use appraisals as the focus for interventions in managing perfor-mance (Hall, 2009). MBO has a number of key elements: the setting of objectives and targets through agreement between managers and employees, monitoring and reviewing performance, development mechanisms to improve performance and constructive feedback on individual performance. These components clearly reflect contemporary PM. The planning phase of the PM cycle is concerned with the setting of performance objectives and expectations for individuals and teams, requiring the determination of both *what* to measure to assess performance out-comes and *how* to measure it. Effective performance measures should relate to strategic goals, focus on desired outputs or outcomes, indicate the evidence that is to be used as the basis for measurement and provide a sound basis for feedback. Individual objectives can be related either to the job itself, such as sales targets or improvements, or to the individual, such as developmental objectives.

Objectives are important for a number of reasons. First, they direct the individ-ual or group to behave in a specific, desirable manner or focus their attention on a specific outcome that clearly links to organisational performance. For example, where project teams are put together for long-term assignments, objectives and measures of team performance can reinforce the team ethos and promote coopera-tive and participative behaviours. Second, objectives are the principal means by which performance can be assessed, ranked and rewarded. Third, the use of appro-priate objectives which have been agreed by both the employee and manager can help to prevent several of the causes of poor performance identified at the outset of the chapter by ensuring communication of expectations and providing a stimulus to motivation (Locke and Latham, 1990). Finally, effective goal-setting contributes to the efficacy of the appraisal process.

MEASURING PERFORMANCE

An essential component in setting realistic targets and reviewing prior perfor-mance is the ability to measure job performance in an objective manner (as far as this is possible). Setting appropriate measures of performance is essential for providing useful feedback, allowing areas of positive performance to be further developed and areas of poor performance to be addressed through corrective action. Measures need to be viable and reliable both in respect of promoting desired performance and as the basis for accurate assessment of achievement.

There are two broad approaches to performance measurement. The first is focused on results or outputs where performance can be quantified (for exam-ple, sales targets) and metrics used to determine the achievement of objectives.

BOX 7.3
HRM IN PRACTICE

Performance management at Adidas Group

The Adidas Group 'strives to be the global leader in the sporting goods industry with brands built on a passion for sports and a sporting lifestyle'. To this end, the group places emphasis on 'creating a work environment that stimulates innovation, team spirit, engagement and achievement ... by unlocking the talent of our workforce, we bring to life our company's strategy and drive business results'.

Informing an 'employer of choice' approach to people management is a set of core values: performance, passion, integrity and diversity. This approach reflects recognition that to fulfill the ambition of becoming market leader 'depends on the potential, dedication, knowledge and performance of our employees and the excellence of our leaders'.

The global performance management system in place at Adidas Group, called 'The Score', was rolled out in 2013, and represents 'the cornerstone of our performance culture'

with the aim of facilitating open and honest feedback on performance and growth opportunities. In its first year, over 91 per cent of eligible employees completed their year-end appraisals. Employees receive regular feedback based on individual business targets, job tasks and further expectations in line with the key principles regarding the way employees are expected to work with the company.

Building on defined development goals, they offer and support employees with targeted development activities both on and off the job that 'seek to build on their strengths, grow their skills and help them to overcome individual challenges'. Overall, the firm claims that 'our highest priority is to match individual employee aspirations with our organisational needs'.

Source: Adidas Group (2013); www.careers.adidas-group.com/mission-and-values.aspx; www.adidas-group.com/en/careers/our-offer/ (accessed 29 September 2015)

ADIDAS GROUP

The second approach involves the grading of performance levels where performance cannot be measured in absolute or quantitative terms. This is particularly useful when assessing the attitudinal, behavioural or competency-based aspects of performance. This latter approach is gaining in importance as organisations place greater emphasis on the kind of behaviour or competencies they want their employees to exhibit and the process by which desired objectives are achieved. In some circumstances, qualitative or behavioural performance indicators such as 'excellent' customer service might be measured quantitatively (for example, the number of customer complaints). Where it is not feasible to set time-bounded quantitative targets (such as when a long-standing objective exists that does not change significantly from one review period to the next) performance standards can be set or an assessment made on the demonstration of competency, reflecting the behaviours and capabilities that underpin effective performance.

Arguably, both goals and behaviours should be considered when assessing performance to guard against inappropriate and undesirable employee behaviour in the achievement of objectives. For jobs that do not have a clear quantitative output, it can be difficult to establish adequate measures or performance standards to reflect the wide range of formal and informal elements that constitute effective performance. Such difficulties can result in an over-emphasis on objectives that can be easily measured at the expense of less tangible elements which might be equally, or more, important.

Appropriate measures to assess performance will vary according to both the nature of the job being done and the nature of the organisation. For example, public service organisations are likely to focus on aspects of service delivery and value for money (alongside greater consideration of personal development) whilst private sector firms are likely to focus more on financial returns and the use of metrics to inform decisions on performance-related pay. A contingent approach should therefore be taken to designing systems to suit local circumstances that should be flexible enough to respond to the impact of unforeseen circumstances on achieved performance.

To be effective, it is often suggested that performance objectives should be SMART – *specific, measurable, attainable, realistic* and *time-bounded*. We can also add to this list that objectives should be *agreed* between manager and employee. Agreed rather than imposed objectives are likely to have greater legitimacy for employees working to achieve them. Objectives should also be *flexible* to allow for 'renegotiation' in response to changing circumstances and continually reviewed to maintain relevance. Goals should also be *equitable* in the sense that they can be objectively measured and are applied similarly to all relevant employees. Finally, objectives should be *auditable* in that they allow for the substantiation of decisions relating to rating and reward. Failure to address these dimensions of performance objectives and measures can lead to employee disenchantment with PMS (Stiles et al., 1997).

Key to the success of PM is setting objectives and measures that give an adequate representation of whole job performance. Measure the wrong dimension(s) of the job and it is unlikely that management will learn anything meaningful about employee performance and their contribution to organisational objectives. It is also likely to have a negative impact on individual job satisfaction and morale, as a worker will be working towards goals that do not necessarily contribute to overall performance. However, attempting to measure multiple dimensions of a role can result in a huge amount of complex information that presents a confusing impression of performance both to line managers and workers. Hendry and Perkins (2000: 59) advocate a 'focus on a few key activities which make a difference', thus limiting the amount of measurement. In agreeing objectives, the employee needs to fully understand the evidence required as the basis for measuring their achievement. Where there is a lack of representative data on performance or transparency of decision-making then justifying evaluation and reward decisions can be difficult. Indeed, an overt focus on quantitative performance measurement can often result in a crude distillation of an individual's 'worth' to the organisation to a single performance rating (such as 'satisfactory' or 'average') which is unlikely to be a complete reflection of the rounded contribution an individual has made. Therefore, firms need to guard against the process of performance measurement becoming an exercise in 'elegant bureaucracy' (Armstrong and Ward, 2006: 28) rather than a means by which individuals can be motivated and supported to achieve superior performance. This reflects more fundamental criticisms of objective setting as the basis for performance management based on the view that it can act to inhibit 'beneficial opportunism' among employees and is too inflexible for fast-paced organisational contexts (Brown, 2013: 306). Ordonez et al. (2009: 2) go further and identify 'specific side effects associated with goal setting, including a narrow focus that neglects non-goal areas, a rise in unethical behavior, distorted risk preferences, corrosion of organizational culture, and reduced intrinsic motivation'. Despite such criticisms, goal setting remains central to most PMS.

Many organisations use the core values of the firm to guide, support and assess employee performance, and incorporate these into the appraisal process to promote congruity of behaviour among workers (see Box 7.5). In order

BOX 7.4
HRM IN PRACTICE

Redesigning performance management at Deloitte

In an article in *Harvard Business Review*, published in April 2015, Buckingham and Goodall report on attempts to redesign the performance management system at the consultancy and financial services firm, Deloitte, because of a widespread perception that the existing system was not adequately driving either engagement or high performance. Instead, the authors propose the need for a system that is 'nimbler, real-time, and more individualised – something squarely focused on fueling performance in the future rather than assessing it in the past'. They suggest this new system will surprise many because 'it will have no cascading objectives, no once-a-year reviews, and no 360-degree feedback tools'.

The redesigned system was to reflect three pieces of evidence: the findings an assessment of the number of hours spent on performance management for its 65,000-plus employees (2 million a year), an appreciation of just how much of the differential in employee ratings was down to subjectivity rather than performance and a better understanding of what makes effective teams at Deloitte.

> All this evidence helped bring into focus the problem we were trying to solve with our new design. We wanted to spend more time helping our people use their strengths – in teams characterized by great clarity of purpose and expectations – and we wanted a quick way to collect reliable and differentiated performance data'.

The starting point for this new system were three objectives:

1 To recognise performance, particularly through variable compensation.

2 To be able to clearly see performance.

3 To fuel performance – 'if the performance snapshot was an organizational tool for measuring it, we needed a tool that team leaders could use to strengthen it'.

To be able to clearly 'see performance' Deloitte sought to simplify the process of producing a 'performance snapshot' by asking only immediate team leaders to rate individual performance by asking them 'a different kind of question' which focused not only on the skills of the team member but also their own future actions with respect to that person. The rationale for this was that whilst raters are inconsistent on their rating of others, they are highly consistent when rating their own feelings and intentions. Consequently, team leaders were asked to consider only four statements for each team member:

1 Given what I know of this person's performance, and if it were my money, I would award this person the highest possible compensation increase and bonus (to measure overall performance and unique value to the organisation).

2 Given what I know of this person's performance, I would always want him or her on my team (measures ability to work well with others).

3 This person is at risk for low performance (identifies problems that might harm the customer or the team).

4 This person is ready for promotion today (measures potential).

As to fuelling performance, Deloitte identified that the most effective team leaders met regularly with their teams and, therefore, the focus is on regular and frequent check-ins that are central to the role of team leaders. This aids individual clarity of expectations and acts to focus on coaching individuals through current work, rather than providing feedback on past performance.

In all, to 'recognize, see and fuel' performance, Deloitte sought to implement three interlocking rituals – the annual compensation decision, the quarterly or per-project performance snapshot, and the weekly check-in.

Source: Buckingham and Goodall (2015)

PERFORMANCE MANAGEMENT, DELOITTE

BOX 7.5
HRM IN PRACTICE

Performance management at Marie Stopes International

Marie Stopes International (MSI) is one of the largest family planning organisations in the world, delivering contraception, safe abortion, and mother and baby care in 42 countries, often working with the poorest and most vulnerable people in the world.

MSI describes its culture as 'more commercial than a lot of people would expect – It's driven, it's professional, and it's a faster pace than a normal NGO or charity'. Describing itself as a '"social enterprise" – a commercial business that is driven to address need through its success', MSI stresses a 'progressive and collaborative work environment', and a workforce of 'passionate, focused, intelligent, high-achieving, talented individuals'. MSI's core values are:

- mission driven
- customer focused
- results orientated
- pioneering
- sustainable
- people-centred.

To support the corporate 'vision' encompassed in these values, in 2009, MSI introduced a new PMS to replace a system deemed dysfunctional and which was widely disliked across the organisation. This new system – 'Performance Plus' – was initially rolled out in the UK, where MSI has 350 team members across the country, but has subsequently been adopted across many of its international offices to the extent that the process is now well embedded and has become part of the wider organisation's culture.

'Performance Plus' is based around a compulsory end-of-year review for all employees, as well as a mid-year review designed to provide employees with an opportunity to discuss their development and career. Employees are asked to set no more than six objectives, agreed with their manager, to be assessed at their year-end review

Team member behaviours	Leadership behaviours
Driven	*Leading self*
Motivated	• Develop yourself
Responsive	• Be accountable; take ownership
Working efficiently	• Be resilient
Initiative	• Be a compelling and influential communicator
Commitment	*Leading others*
Accountable	• Insist on excellence
Innovative	• Lead with authenticity, integrity and empathy
Embracing change	• Develop others; strengthen, nourish and nurture future talent
Sharing information	*Leading MSI*
Focusing on learning	• Focus on customers
Effective communications	• Consistently deliver world-class performance and results
Team player	• Be a visionary

as either 'achieved', 'partially achieved' or 'not achieved'. However, in acknowledgement that performance is not always encapsulated within the six agreed objectives, managers are also advised to make a note of any other employee achievements during the year.

Reflecting the importance of both 'how' employees achieve their objectives as well as 'what' they have achieved, employees are also assessed on how they have demonstrated in the course of their work a range of behaviours that underpin the core values of MSI. To this end, MSI introduced a competency framework identifying 13 'team member' behaviours and 11 core 'leadership' behaviours. Employees are expected to identify incidences of how they demonstrated these behaviours but also to be reflective about where they have failed to do so.

The performance review also considers information on performance collected through an automated system of 360-degree feedback collected from a range of colleagues and direct reports (agreed between manager and team member) to help the recipient identify what they are doing well and should continue to do and what they need to do more of or less of. Again, questions are linked to the behaviours set out in the competency framework.

Based on the assessment against both objectives and behaviours, managers are asked to consider what the team member's main achievements have been and what has gone particularly well during the review period. Managers must also consider what could have gone better, what has been particularly challenging or difficult, and the skills and abilities that have been developed in the previous year. Considering all of the evidence collated during the review period, and upon reviewing the rating definitions, managers must identify an appropriate indicator of the individual's overall performance. The ratings are: 'exceptional', 'commendable', 'successful' or 'improvement required'. MSI expects 10 per cent of employees to fall into the 'exceptional' rating; 30 per cent into 'commendable'; 50 per cent into 'successful'; and 10 per cent into 'improvement required'.

Managers are asked to calibrate performance ratings across their team to ensure there is consistency in application of the ratings, both for fairness and equity but also so that reward is commensurate with levels of performance. Any individual who disagrees with the rating can raise the issue using the organisation's formal grievance procedure.

Reflecting the view of performance management as a continuous process, rather than one of periodic review, MSI expects managers to hold regular one-to-ones with their employees. Employees are also encouraged to arrange mid-year reviews with a focus on development and career progression. In 2012, MSI introduced a new talent management framework to be incorporated into its performance management system. The mid-year review provides managers with an opportunity to assess individual potential against the organisation's 'potential model' that measures aspiration, commitment, engagement and performance track record. This assessment informs the employee's development plan and is also collated centrally to inform talent management activities by classifying employees into a range of groups from 'under-performer' (low potential and low performance) to 'exceptional potential' (high on both measures).

Sources: IDS (2013); http://mariestopes.org/careers/ (accessed 17 August 2015)

to assess these dimensions of performance, managers might request that employees provide evidence to demonstrate how particular competencies or behaviours have contributed towards the achievement of objectives (for example, through professional development records) or use the information generated in 360-degree appraisals. As discussed in Chapter 3, the balanced scorecard (Kaplan and Norton, 1992) is increasingly used across the private and public sectors to provide the basis for the achievement of broad organisational strategy or vision. The four perspectives of performance associated with the balanced scorecard can provide a useful framework to aid the establishment of interconnected goals at the level of the organisation, department, team and individual (Nankervis and Compton, 2006).

Further online reading This article reports on a survey of Australian HR professionals to assess the use of and satisfaction with performance management. It suggests that whilst problems persist, the increasing incorporation of the balanced scorecard into PM processes is enabling managers to better connect individual, group and organisational objectives.

Nankervis, A. R. and Compton, R.-L. (2006) Performance management: Theory in practice?, *Asia Pacific Journal of Human Resources*, 44: 83–101.

The assessment of performance in relation to agreed objectives typically leads to either the rating or ranking of individual performance, a process that subsequently determines the level of performance-related pay for each employee. Performance rating refers to the use of a scale by which differing levels of performance are differentiated (for example, a five-point scale where 1 is *exceptional performance*, 3 is *performance at the required standard* and 5 is *performance below the required standard*). Ranking refers to the process of putting staff in rank order on the basis of individual performance. In this case, performance-related pay is based on the relative position of the individual in this ranking (for instance, the top 10 per cent of performers), as are decisions over poor performance and, ultimately, termination of employment (a process referred to as 'rank and yank' – Mulligan and Bull Schaefer, 2011). Whilst this approach clearly seeks to reward those who are deemed to have contributed most to the organisation, this can cause problems where the number or proportion of employees who can be assigned to a range is limited (i.e. a quota is imposed) in order to manage the cost of reward and, therefore, two similarly effective employees can receive different performance ratings and levels of performance-related pay (Armstrong and Ward, 2006).

PERFORMANCE APPRAISALS

PERFORMANCE
APPRAISAL

Performance appraisals or performance and development reviews form a critical operational component of PMS and are increasingly common in firms of all sizes. Whilst formal appraisals have long been used as a means of assessing the performance of managers, recent evidence suggests their prevalence continues to grow among non-managerial staff (the 2011 *Workplace Employment Relations Study* found that 70 per cent of UK workplaces reported using appraisals for at least some non-managerial employees, compared to 43 per cent in 2004 – van Wanrooy et al., 2013). Formal appraisal takes place regularly, usually annually, representing both the start and finish point of the yearly PM cycle. Appraisals also most often involve formal employee interviews, usually carried out by line managers rather than HR professionals. Such 'top-down' appraisals are often favoured because line managers are felt to be best equipped to assess the performance of their subordinates through knowledge of prior performance and the conditions under which the appraisee has worked. The principal role of HRM specialists is the design and implementation of the appraisal process and to support line managers in dealing with any issues resulting from the appraisal process. The key elements of appraisals are outlined in Box 7.6.

In short, appraisals provide a formal opportunity for both parties to review and reflect upon employee progress against agreed objectives and, most importantly, to plan for individual performance improvements. They also provide an opportunity to discuss decisions on merit-based salary increases, training, promotions or necessary remedial action for poor performance. Despite the importance of appraisals to

PM it is wrong to think that performance appraisals *are* performance management (Fletcher, 2008; Aguinis et al., 2011). In the absence of the supporting infrastructure provided by the other components of PM, appraisals are likely to be ineffective or potentially damaging to individual motivation and performance. For example, if the achievement of performance objectives agreed in the appraisal is not supported with appropriate learning and development activity then this may result in a failure to achieve objectives and employee disillusionment.

Whilst appraisals often form a key focal point in the PM cycle, more regular review of employee performance is often required to ensure continuous improvement, to promote personal development, to encourage and reinforce desired standards and to 'head-off' and resolve problems, especially those that happen early in the review period. In order to do this, managers must provide regular and constructive feedback to employees, avoiding excessive criticism that is likely to diminish motivation. The aim of feedback should be to promote individual understanding of the impact of their actions and behaviour both on their own performance and on that of other employees by identifying examples of both good and poor practice. Regular reviews of performance also ensure that formal appraisals do not become overly focused on problems that have occurred during the immediately preceding period and ensure that performance over the entire process cycle is considered rather than only recent events.

Dealing with poor performance in appraisals can be difficult for managers, not least for fear of creating conflict and disrupting working relationships. Again, to address such issues openness and honesty in conducting the appraisal are important, as is the objectivity provided by basing critical feedback on agreed objectives and performance data. If carried out effectively, an appraisal should represent a dialogue, rather than an interrogation or lecture, about the individual's performance and their support and development needs going forward.

360-degree appraisal

An increasingly common form of performance appraisal (Fletcher, 1997), particularly for more senior managerial positions, is the 360-degree or multi-rater appraisal that seeks to provide a more rounded assessment of individual performance by collecting performance 'data' from a number of sources. These sources might include

---

BOX 7.6
UNDERSTAND

Key elements of the performance appraisal (CIPD, 2008b)

Measurement – assessing performance against agreed targets and objectives.

Feedback – providing information to the individual on their performance and progress.

Positive reinforcement – emphasising what has been done well and making only constructive criticism about what might be improved.

Exchange of views – a frank exchange of views about what has happened, how appraisees can improve their performance, the support they need from their managers to achieve this and their aspirations for their future career.

Agreement – jointly coming to an understanding by all parties about what needs to be done to improve performance generally and overcome any issues raised in the course of the discussion.

---

the appraisee's manager, subordinates, peers (for example, team colleagues), internal and external customers and the appraisee themselves, in the form of self-assessment. The aim of 360-degree appraisals is to address some of the accusations of subjectivity associated with purely top-down appraisals and to improve the validity of the appraisal process. Mosley (2013) suggests that new technology now provides means by which to collect individual performance feedback from a much wider range of co-workers, effectively leading to the 'crowdsourcing' of the performance review.

Such appraisals can be useful where line managers might not have sufficient contact with all employees to conduct individual appraisals. The inclusion of external customers in the review process can also act to increase customer focus and the involvement of peers can help to support team initiatives. Peer review can also be useful where performance evaluation is based on qualitative or behavioural outcomes rather than (simply) quantitative measures. Peer appraisal can, however, only be of benefit where peer appraisers possess sufficient knowledge of the appraisee and their objectives to be able to undertake meaningful assessment and where they possess the skills needed to provide open and honest feedback. Of course, 360-degree appraisals are still open to bias and can be problematic where personal agendas, loyalties and conflicting interests distort the reliability of feedback. Increasingly, new technology, such as company intranets, is being used to support 360-degree appraisal to facilitate the collection and analysis of large volumes of performance data (Miller, 2003).

Upward appraisal by subordinates of the appraisee can be a potentially useful form of assessment for management development purposes by providing feedback on managerial style and effectiveness and helping managers to better understand how they might contribute to the performance of their employees. This process is likely only to be appropriate and effective in organisations with a high-trust culture and where the involvement of all staff in decision-making and problem-solving is encouraged.

Self-assessment

Either as part of 360-degree appraisals or incorporated into top-down schemes, it can often be beneficial for appraisees to undertake self-assessment in advance of the formal appraisal to encourage them to critically review their own performance as the basis for discussion. If appraisees have had prior opportunity to assess their own performance against targets and standards and to reflect on individual strengths and weaknesses, they are likely to be more willing to accept feedback. Self-assessment is also more likely to facilitate a two-way dialogue and encourage employees to take responsibility for their performance. The use of self-assessment is likely only to be effective in a climate of trust where appraisees feel comfortable making a critical self-appraisal.

Further online reading This short article makes the case for performance appraisals as critical in managing organsational talent. It sets out a number of critical success factors, in particular, stressing the need for senior managerial leadership and ownership of PMS.

Lawler, E. E., Benson, G. S. and McDermott, M. (2012) What makes performance appraisals effective?, *Compensation & Benefits Review*, 44 (4): 191–200.

BOX 7.7
MANAGEMENT SKILLS AND ATTRIBUTES

Line managers and the pitfalls of performance appraisals

Performance appraisals have been subject to a number of criticisms, often associated with injustice in the way that they are conducted. Perhaps inevitably, line managers can lack impartiality (or at least be perceived as such) and be subject to allegations of bias, favouritism and inconsistency (whether of the single manager or across different managers). Moreover, line managers may respond differently to employees based on personal preferences, lack all the information required to make an accurate assessment of performance, use appraisals simply to justify prior decisions (Grint, 1993) or hold specific intentions in rating employee performance (such as rating to avoid conflict) (Murphy, 2008; Spence and Keeping, 2013). Evidence suggests that managers often play 'organisational games' in appraisals by seeking to punish poor performers, 'scare' appraisees into better performance (Redman, 2006) or view them as an exercise in managerial muscle-flexing. For instance, IRS (2005) report that line managers can store up unfavourable opinions that they then 'spring on' an unsuspecting employee during the appraisal. The negative impact of such poor practice is accentuated, given the research finding that trust and perceived justice among employees act to mediate the relationship between performance management practices and organisational commitment (Farndale et al., 2011).

It is important, therefore, that in order to ensure that appraisals are conducted effectively, managers have the required interpersonal skills, such as asking the right questions, active listening and providing constructive feedback, and know how to handle the political issues that surround decisions of promotion, reward and discipline, particularly how best to deliver 'bad news'. Line managers must also guard against promoting dysfunctional behaviour through appraisals. For example, Brown and Benson (2005) report that even well designed appraisal systems can result in employee work overload.

Many of the problems of increased line management responsibility for HRM activities are crystallised in the appraisal process to the extent that appraisals appear to be 'one human resource activity that everyone loves to hate' (Redman, 2006: 165). Where line managers are not convinced of their importance appraisals can be viewed as an administrative burden, especially where managers are not given adequate time or resources to conduct them. It is important, therefore, that the commitment of these managers to PM and ownership over its operation (Risher, 2012) are gained through consultation in the design and implementation of PM systems to avoid imposing practices that they might not think workable or worthwhile. This 'buy-in' and input into design is likely to result in a more effective PM system.

Whilst decisions on performance-related reward are often a principal outcome of the performance appraisal, there is an argument for separating the two. This argument centres on the tension between the dual aims of most formal appraisal processes. On the one hand, appraisals seek to identify future development needs, encouraging employees to be self-critical and articulate both strengths and weaknesses. On the other, appraisals are concerned with assessing, rewarding and rating prior performance, which encourages employees to 'talk-up' their achievements and de-emphasise their limitations, especially if it is felt that this is likely to negatively impact on received reward. Therefore, it is unlikely that, considering these two demands together, employees will be completely honest in self-appraisal. In such circumstances, line managers are required to fulfil the potentially irreconcilable roles of both 'coach' and 'judge' (Pilbeam and Corbridge, 2006).

Further online reading This article presents research exploring the impact of a firm's recent introduction of a performance management system. In doing so it discusses the challenges of evaluating the impact of such systems on individual and firm performance.

Harper, S. and Vikinas, T. (2005) Determining the impact of an organisation's performance management system, *Asia Pacific Journal of Human Resources*, 43 (1): 76–97.

LEARNING AND DEVELOPMENT AND PERFORMANCE MANAGEMENT

Chapter 9 discusses in detail the broad area of human resource development, but it is important here to highlight the role of learning and development (L&D) in performance management and in fostering a culture of continuous improvement. Alongside the acquisition of high-performing individuals from outside the firm, employee development is clearly a key mechanism through which an organisation can improve organisational performance. In addition to the identification of training requirements through the human resource planning process, individual, team or departmental training needs and learning objectives can often originate in the PM process. L&D provides a key linkage within the cycle by forming part of both the planning phase ('what L&D activities would help improve performance?') and the review or evaluation phase ('how has L&D contributed to improved performance?'). L&D can also play an important role as remedial action to address performance problems.

Training needs are usually identified in the appraisal in the form of personal learning objectives, the achievement of which supports the achievement of performance targets or standards. Development interventions should subsequently be designed to enable the achievement of these learning objectives. These often form personal development plans (PDPs) which outline the actions that the various parties, particularly the individual and their line manager, propose to take to help develop individual capability. These plans should reflect the individual's aspirations, performance and potential within the firm and the fit with the future needs of the organisation. The training needs identified in the appraisal process are likely to inform the key performance indicators (KPIs) that firms can use to assess, compare and rank individual performance. An important part of the review process is, therefore, to assess the achievement of learning objectives and how these have contributed to the achievement of performance standards or developed individual competency. This evaluation can then be used to modify future L&D interventions or as examples of good practice.

A key element of L&D support in managing performance is coaching provided by line managers to develop the skills or knowledge of their subordinates. Reinforcing the cyclical nature of the PM process, whilst the performance appraisals and reviews constitute important forums in which managers can offer advice and guidance to employees, coaching is not limited to these activities and should be carried out on a continuous basis.

REWARD AND PERFORMANCE MANAGEMENT

Chapter 8 discusses employee reward in detail but it is important here to stress the key role that reward plays in performance management. Chapter 2 introduced content and expectancy models of motivation, both of which stressed the importance of anticipated reward as a factor in determining the direction, strength and duration of individual motivation. Performance management often represents an attempt to motivate both by appealing to the 'head' (or indeed, 'wallet') and 'heart', that is by emphasising both financial and non-financial rewards. Typically, financial reward and performance management are linked through the use of performance-related pay. Such pay can be in the form of end-of-period bonuses, incentivised pay for achieving pre-determined targets, competence-related pay (which provides for pay progression to be linked to levels of achieved competence), contribution-related pay (based on both results and competence), merit pay (which combines a bonus for performance plus a reflection of individual competency), or commission (for example, in sales-related jobs commission might reflect a percentage of total sales achieved). Most often PRP forms a limited proportion of total pay (on top of base pay) but in some cases all remuneration can be linked to performance.

The proliferation of PRP in contemporary organisations reflects the view that financial reward plays a considerable part in motivating employees. PRP represents a key mechanism for communicating performance, competency and behavioural expectations to employees by rewarding 'good' performers and, effectively, punishing under-performance. The 'distributive fairness' of PRP is appealing to organisations in that it helps to allocate finite resources to employees who have contributed most greatly to organisational objectives. However, PRP can often be perceived as unfair, particularly where it is determined by subjective assessment of achievement. Contingent pay can also have a demotivating effect on those employees who fail to achieve required standards, rather than compelling improved performance in future. Moreover, the use of the 'wrong' form of PRP or its ineffective operationalisation can act to inhibit the expression of desired behaviours (for example, individual bonuses can inhibit teamworking) and lead to 'short-termism' and limited focus among employees on just those aspects of performance deemed to contribute to higher reward. Performance-related pay can also be viewed as passing on to the employee at least some of the risk of under-performance traditionally borne by the employer. In other words, employees have become more financially accountable for their own performance, often irrespective of factors outside of their control.

Of course, motivation is not solely the result of an economic transaction. An over-emphasis on financial reward can generate undesirable behaviour and fail to motivate those individuals that respond positively to recognition of achievement, positive feedback and the provision of opportunities for personal development, rather than simply financial gain. The provision of non-financial reward is therefore central to PM, particularly in ensuring its success over the long run. Non-financial and contingent forms of reward are discussed further in Chapter 8.

DEALING WITH POOR PERFORMANCE

Ultimately, an effectively designed and implemented PM system should create an organisational environment in which success is encouraged, supported, acknowledged and rewarded. Inevitably, however, PM systems also require mechanisms to address and eradicate poor performance. Given that under-performance can be a consequence of both employer and employee-related factors, effectively dealing with poor performance requires openness and honesty from both parties. For example, appraisals provide an opportunity for managers and employees to jointly diagnose poor performance and to devise means of resolution. Effective diagnosis requires managers to be prepared to acknowledge their role in employee under-performance (Risher, 2005) and avoid making snap judgements about its root cause. It also requires employees to be candid in identifying problems even where they fear the consequences (for example, loss of reward, damage to career progression or relationships with colleagues). If the diagnosis suggests incapability then learning and development interventions or redeployment to another position should be considered. If these solutions are ineffective or unfeasible, or where poor performance is identified as the 'fault' of the individual, disciplinary action may need to be taken which can result in dismissal. Chapter 13 discusses in more detail the legal context and process of handling employee dismissal.

ISSUES WITH PERFORMANCE MANAGEMENT IN PRACTICE

As with much critique of HRM practices it is important to divide the problems associated with PM between those of underlying principles or design and those of operationalisation. In other words, problems arise from both the assumptions that underpin the PM process and the people charged with its enactment (Risher, 2011). The prior discussion identified a number of potential problems or pitfalls in PM including a failure to gain the support of line and senior managers, inadequate training for line managers in conducting appraisals, a failure to invest in L&D initiatives to support performance improvements or a failure to identify and apply appropriate measures of performance. These are clearly problems of implementation. Ineffective or partial implementation may create processes that neither motivate employees in the desired direction nor provide the tools with which to maximise performance.

At a more strategic level, an overly rigid and bureaucratic PMS in which goals are too narrow or inflexible and in which there is too great a focus on short-term achievement can lead to the system becoming an inhibitor of change rather than a force for employee motivation and continuous improvement. This can also be the case where the focus on collecting and reporting performance data takes primacy over those activities that actually contribute added value, such as effective employee communication and better workplace relations (Pulakos and O'Leary, 2011). In such circumstances, rather than facilitating and supporting improved performance, PM processes begin to dictate strategic decision-making by overly focusing on the achievement of quantitative targets and outputs without a commensurate consideration of longer-term organisational development. In short, whilst there can be value attached to the effective measurement and management of performance so that employee contribution is both recognised and rewarded, many performance measurement systems are poorly designed and inappropriately applied (Clegg et al., 2011) so that their ultimate impact is to undermine their original purpose.

More fundamental criticism of PM tends to focus on two central assumptions that underpin practice: first, that performance improvements can arise from measuring and rewarding the performance outcomes of individuals in relation to one another; and, second, that employee interests are fundamentally in line with those of managers and PM processes are mutually beneficial (Winstanley and Stuart-Smith, 1996). An alternative 'radical' perspective suggests that firms are comprised of a plurality of groups with conflicting interests and even within a well-designed PM process the interests of the various parties are not always aligned, so that individuals can seek to meet individual objectives whilst undermining overall achievement. A further critique of PM relates to the inherent subjectivity associated with performance measurement and how managerial discretion in appraisals reflects the exercise of power in the employment relationship (Bach, 2005). Under a radical perspective, PM is viewed as a form of Taylorism based on the specification of objectives and indirect control and regulation of the labour process.

BOX 7.8
ETHICAL INSIGHT

Performance management, control and authority

Performance management can be viewed as an important driver of organisational outputs, partly because it enhances managerial control of individual behaviour. However, this control (for example, through reward allocation) is often placed in the hands of a few individuals, such as line managers, and this raises a number of ethical issues related to subjectivity and bias in the assessment of individual performance. In order to address these concerns, there is a need for organisations to ensure procedural fairness and to provide opportunities for those affected by decisions to scrutinise the basis for decision-making and to make an appeal against those decisions that are believed to be unfair.

Control can also be embedded in the PM system itself. How systems are designed determines whether people are treated as a means to an end (reflecting an overt focus only on objectives) rather than an end in themselves (reflecting the consideration of personal development). For the PMS to effectively serve both the organisation and the individual, employees should be able to participate in the design of the system, rather than simply be subjected to processes over which they have no influence. Winstanley and Stuart-Smith (1996) suggest that for PM to be both effective and meaningful, a number of ethical principles need to be incorporated into the design and operationalisation of the system: *respect for the individual* (all stakeholders in the firm must be given a voice in defining organisational strategy and objectives to ensure mutual gain); *mutual respect* (to ensure the satisfactory reconciliation of inevitable conflicts of interest); *procedural fairness*; and *transparency of decision-making* (so that conflict and 'competing claims' for resources can be viewed collectively against available resources and other claims and decisions are open and clearly represent a balance of those interests).

THE ROLE OF CULTURE IN MANAGING PERFORMANCE

In Chapter 1, Storey's model of HRM suggested that one of the key levers for improving individual performance was the management of organisational culture. In relation to work organisations, Mullins (1993: 649) defines culture as 'the collection of traditions, values, policies, beliefs and attitudes that constitute a pervasive context for everything we do and think in an organisation'. Culture, therefore, reflects the underlying assumptions about the way work is performed, the way in which people interact with one another and what behaviour is encouraged and discouraged. Storey (2007: 9) suggests that managing culture can be 'more important than managing procedures and systems' in establishing the formal and informal context in which employees not only understand required behaviours and performance standards but also internalise these requirements so that they become simply 'the way things are done around here' (Deal and Kennedy, 1982). Whilst often used interchangeably, Cheyne and Loan-Clarke (2006) make the distinction between 'organisational culture' and 'corporate culture'. *Organisational culture* can develop organically in different parts of an organisation (for example, within a department or at various ranks of hierarchy) providing a social group has sufficient shared experience (Schein, 2004). Alternatively, *corporate culture* can be understood as the espoused values and expectations of the dominant management group (Linstead and Grafton-Small, 1992) who seek to propagate and diffuse these values throughout the firm as part of a specific competitive strategy. In this sense, culture is deliberately constructed rather than unconsciously developed.

HRM AND THE MANAGEMENT OF CULTURE

HRM practices can play a key role in determining, shaping and managing a desirable corporate culture that can represent a source of sustained competitive advantage. In basic terms, the objective of culture management is to encourage employees to adopt corporate values and attitudes and strengthen their association with the organisation. Subsequently, the complexity and formality of managing employees can be dramatically reduced as individuals increasingly 'think' and form 'identities' in concert with their employer and feel a greater level of commitment to the firm. In this way, rather than employee control necessitating close supervision and strict application of rules and procedures, control itself is internalised through adherence of the guiding values that underpin corporate culture (Peters and Waterman, 1982). Implicit, therefore, in discussing how organisational culture can shape individual and organisational performance is an assumption of unitarism: that it is possible to engender a collaborative spirit in working towards shared organisational goals. However, the strength of corporate culture in managing performance is not accomplished simply through achieving greater commitment and consistency of outlook among employees. The development of core organisational values and corporate identity can also inform the strategic direction of the business by shaping the manner in which the firm and its employees contend with challenges and opportunities.

There are a variety of HRM mechanisms that can act to shape and reinforce organisational culture. Like the management of employee performance, management of culture is an all-encompassing activity in which all management practice and policy have a role to play. Box 7.9 suggests that there are a number of formal and informal processes, practices and structures in which organisational culture is manifest and which act to communicate this culture to employees. An understanding of these dimensions of culture helps to assess how HRM itself can shape, reinforce and communicate organisational culture.

Employee socialisation and learning

Organisational socialisation is the process by which organisational members 'absorb' company culture and become acquainted with the values and behaviour expected of them, whether formally through training, mentoring and induction programmes or informally through social events and everyday interaction with colleagues. This process of 'acculturation' begins before an individual is even employed in a firm, through employer branding and exposure to recruitment advertisements that make reference to the core values of the firm. Representations made about the company in the recruitment process, for example in job advertisements, act to give prospective employees a preview of what future employment in the firm might be like and to assess the extent to which the espoused values fit with their own. In the selection process, firms with a strong corporate culture might focus on this person–organisation fit rather than focusing purely on an individual's experience, qualifications or skills.

Once in employment, the initial process of formal and informal organisational socialisation takes place. This might take the form of an induction programme where newcomers to the firm learn not only the formal policies and procedures of the organisation but also the norms, values, attitudes and behaviour consistent with the dominant culture. For example, in a study of the organisational socialisation of new graduate recruits, Garavan and Morley (1997) suggest that the objectives of induction programmes were: to challenge the individual orientation of

BOX 7.9
UNDERSTAND

Manifestations of organisational culture

- *Routine behaviours* of organisational members, both inside and outside the firm, are the everyday manifestations of culture. Such behaviours can enable the smooth running of the organisation but can also be a source of resistance to change.
- *Organisational rituals* are particular activities or special events through which the organisation emphasises what is important and which can reinforce the dominant culture. Rituals can be formal, such as induction, training programmes or performance appraisals, or informal, such as social events.
- *Stories* told by organisational members represent devices for communicating what is important in the organisation. Stories might be used to convey the organisation's historic origins and past successes and to flag up important personalities in its history (for example, its founders, heroes and villains). These stories can be told formally (for example, in promotional material) or informally (for example, in the form of hearsay or 'legend').
- *Organisational symbols* are physical representations of culture and include the dominant language and terminology, office layout and job titles. These might reflect organisational structures and hierarchy, for example, by stressing deference and respect for authority or, alternatively, a culture of single status.
- *Power structures* underpin organisational culture, for example, by reflecting the core attitudes and beliefs of the dominant group. Informal and formal power structures might not necessarily correspond and, therefore, several sources of power can co-exist in a work organisation. Power might derive from hierarchy (formal power), influence (informal power), control of strategic resources, possession of knowledge and skills or involvement in strategic implementation (e.g. by exercising discretion).
- *Organisational structures* communicate important roles and relationships within the organisation and, to a degree, reflect formal power structures. For example, formal hierarchical structures might reflect the absolute authority of senior managers and a unitary ideology. More devolved structures might emphasise employee participation and involvement in decision-making.
- *Control and reward systems* dictate what aspects of individual and organisational performance and behaviour are monitored and measured and, therefore, shape what individuals take to be important and desirable.

Source: Johnson, G., Scholes, K. and Whittington, R. (2007) *Exploring Corporate Strategy: Text and Cases*, Harlow: Pearson. Reproduced with permission from Pearson Education Limited.

new graduates; to develop in them a spirit of cooperation and company loyalty; to instil in them the ethos of the company; and to sensitise them to the duties and responsibilities expected of them when they become managers in the future. Part of organisational induction often takes the form of a one-on-one relationship with an 'insider' with responsibility both to train and educate the new recruit (either through mentoring or 'buddy' schemes), with a focus both on acquiring the skills, knowledge and behaviours related to one's job and on learning the formal and informal 'way things work'. Effective socialisation should lead to greater coherence between the values of the individual and those of the organisation. Subsequent learning and development interventions have a key role to play not only in developing employee skills and knowledge but also in shaping individual behaviour (Gibb, 2002) to make it consistent with corporate culture and instil and reinforce core values. This might be particularly important in the process of cultural change.

Employee communication and participation

Employee communication and participation play a central role in aligning worker values, attitudes and behaviours with the prevailing culture. For example, company newsletters, team briefings, staff intranets and notice boards can be used to report organisational success and publicly recognise individual or group achievement, thereby communicating managerial expectations of behaviour and performance. Employee participation in decision-making, for example through employee attitude surveys to gauge collective employee feeling or to sound them out on new practices or policies, can act as a means of sense-making for both management and workers by providing a dialogue between the parties to clarify and assert dominant values.

Culture, performance management and reward

As we have seen above, performance management and reward can represent key factors in shaping employee behaviour and, consequently, reinforcing corporate culture. In particular, PM can be useful in focusing employees on specific strategic objectives that might constitute a central tenet of corporate culture such as 'quality', 'innovation' or 'service delivery' or to instil core values such as openness, cooperation or trust. However, PM can also undermine efforts to instil corporate values and attitudes in staff by prioritising short-term objectives over longer-term association with the behavioural dimensions of organisational culture. As discussed in the following chapter, reward systems can be central in directing required employee behaviour towards the achievement of specific organisational goals. For example, team-based rewards can be used to promote a teamworking ethos over the celebration of individual 'stars', and profit-sharing can be used to develop strong commitment and loyalty to the firm. In organisations undergoing cultural change, HRM can also play a role in identifying and 'removing' those staff that might resist change, particularly senior management who might have a vested interest in the old regime.

BOX 7.10
GLOBAL INSIGHT

Organisational and national culture

As outlined in Box 7.9, implicit within an organisational culture are assumptions regarding, for example, the nature of peer and manager–subordinate relationships. In certain organisations, for example, the dominant culture might emphasise the importance of group cooperation whereas others might promote competition among the workforce. Whilst these values might be acceptable in the national cultural context in which they were developed, when attempts are made to export them overseas this may present problems. However, just as senior managers might find it desirable to export HR practices from home to host country, because, for example, they represent a source of competitive advantage, certain values might be central to the operation of a firm and subsequently need to be upheld even where they run contrary to existing national cultural norms. Sparrow and Hiltrop (1994) caution, however, that national culture is so deeply engrained within individuals that even strong organisational cultures cannot override its influence on behaviour at work. Therefore, where there is no justification for seeking to shape behaviour that contradicts national culture, firms should be cautious about seeking to do so, for fear of alienating and demotivating their workforce.

Issues in culture management

The creation and management of a strong organisational culture can have positive implications for individual and organisational performance. However, the extent to which management practices can act to shape the mindset of employees in line with values of senior management, rather than simply their observable behaviour, is questionable. Moreover, the creation of a universal corporate culture is problematic given that organisations are likely to be made up of numerous social groups and subcultures with their own distinctive culture that has a more direct influence on individual behaviour and may result in internal conflict (Sinclair, 1991). A strong culture requires a consistency of formal and informal cultural cues and organisational practices to reinforce core values. However, this can be

---

BOX 7.11
HRM IN PRACTICE

Corporate culture, leadership and News International

In July 2011, the 168-year-old British newspaper the *News of the World* was closed by its owners, News International (a subsidiary of News Corporation), with the loss of approximately 200 jobs. This closure took place in the context of accusations of widespread illegal activity among journalists and sub-contractors at the paper, principally the hacking of the mobile phones of celebrities and other newsworthy individuals. Much has subsequently been written about the apparent failures of corporate governance among senior executives and successive editors at the paper and its parent company, and a supposed culture of, at best, ignorance of wrongdoing at the paper and, at worst, active encouragement of and complicity in such wrongdoing.

Amid ongoing investigations, this saga has culminated in the UK House of Commons Select Committee on Culture, Media and Sport concluding their investigation into the phone hacking allegations by stating that:

> On the basis of the facts and evidence before the committee, we conclude that if at all relevant times Rupert Murdoch [the News Corporation Chairman and Chief Executive Officer] did not take steps to become fully informed about phone hacking, he turned a blind eye and exhibited wilful blindness to what was going on in his companies and publications ...

This culture, we consider, permeated from the top throughout the organisation and speaks volumes about the lack of effective corporate governance at News Corporation and News International. We conclude, therefore, that Rupert Murdoch is not a fit person to exercise the stewardship of a major international company. (BBC, 2012)

This verdict was, however, far from unanimous among the MPs on the Committee. Subsequently, other commentators, some British MPs and News Corporation itself have refused to place blame on Rupert Murdoch, instead looking to place blame upon those 'closer to the ground' in organisational management. One MP commented that 'we have seen absolutely no evidence to suggest that Rupert Murdoch knew what was going on at News International ... yes, of course, he has made mistakes, of course James Murdoch [Rupert's son, who resigned as chairman of News International in February 2012] has made mistakes, but we all make mistakes, I make mistakes all the time' (*The Guardian*, 2012b).

Questions

1   To what extent can those at the top of large organisations be expected to take responsibility for the actions of all employees?

2   How might the actions of organisational leaders at all levels act to shape corporate culture and the actions of those throughout the firm?

difficult to achieve, for example, where employees might be subject to differing or contradictory messages from managers and peers. It is also important to note that despite the positive impact that strong organisational culture can have on individual performance, as Box 7.11 suggests, the creation of such a culture is not always to the benefit of either employees or the company itself, particularly where it promotes the 'wrong' sorts of behaviour.

CONDUCTING PERFORMANCE APPRAISALS

SUMMARY POINTS

- A combination of worker-side and organisational factors determines individual job performance.

- To be effective, the strategic management of performance should address equally those factors that constitute the performance equation: ability, motivation and opportunity.

- Effective performance management (PM) requires HR strategies, practices and processes that vertically integrate individual and team objectives with the clearly communicated mission, values and aims of the firm.

- Performance management systems (PMS) are more than the sum of their parts. Done well, PM can assist with creating an organisational culture with both an explicit and implicit focus on continuous improvement.

- Individual, team and organisational performance is the concern of all organisational actors, including senior managers, line managers, HR specialists and all employees.

- Whilst an integral part of managing employee development, performance appraisals alone do not constitute effective PM.

- Continuous line manager support for employee performance through constructive feedback, regular formal appraisals and ongoing coaching is critical for the achievement of individual objectives.

- The creation and effective management of a strong organisational culture that reinforces and communicates the core values and objectives of the firm can be a highly effective means both of controlling and motivating employees.

SELF-TEST QUESTIONS

1. What worker-side and organisation-side factors might lead to worker under-performance?

2. Why is effective goal-setting important to performance management?

3. What are the potential problems associated with attempts to measure performance in jobs where there is no clear quantitative output?

4. In what ways can line managers formally and informally support the continuous performance improvement of their team?

5. Explain the tension that arises from line managers having to act as both 'coach' and 'judge' in the appraisal process.

6. Why is non-financial reward important to the success of performance management systems?

7. What options are available to managers if an employee's performance is deemed to be unsatisfactory?

8. Why do some commentators suggest that performance management does not 'travel well' internationally?

9. How does corporate culture manifest itself in both the formal and informal operation of a work organisation?

10. In what ways can HRM support the management of organisational culture?

TEST YOURSELF

Want to know more about this chapter? Review what you have been learning by visiting:
https://edge.sagepub.com/wilton3e

- Print out or download the chapter summaries for quick revision
- Test yourself with multiple-choice questions
- Revise key terms with interactive flashcards

CASE STUDY

Managing performance at Beach House

Beach House Software develops computer software for the entertainment industry, including that used in film animation and to create computer-generated images (CGI). Beach House was one of the early pioneers in the industry and is still highly regarded as both a provider of innovative new products and as an employer. However, as the demands of film and programme makers grow and competition in the market intensifies, Beach House has begun to see its market share and its reputation in the industry diminish. Broadly speaking, new business for Beach House is generated in two ways. First, it provides custom software designed to the specification of customers. This is typically through the modification of existing products. Second, it develops new, improved and, occasionally ground-breaking, products which it seeks to establish as industry standards. The former tend to be the company's 'bread and butter', providing the majority of its revenue. The latter, however, is how the company develops prestige in the industry, but provides much more sporadic return for the company. The last significant 'breakthrough' product it produced was three years ago and as a result the company has seen its competitive edge gradually eroded.

As an employer, Beach House typifies the 'collegiate' approach to people management that is common in the ICT industry. The company employs 35 workers, approximately two-thirds of whom are directly involved in the core activity of software development. There are two vaguely defined work groups: the first producing customised products to customer specification (locally known as the 'tweakers'); the second, developing new products from scratch (who refer to themselves as the 'A Team'). A development manager has oversight of the two work groups but they are largely self-managed. Both groups of workers are highly skilled, possess scarce skills and knowledge and tend to have similar educational backgrounds. Working styles, however, differ between the two departments. New product developers typically work independently on their own ideas, occasionally sharing their work informally or jointly problem-solving. In the past, however, where new ideas have shown potential, much of the team becomes involved in development and share in bonus payments for successfully taking the product to market, although the originator typically takes a greater share of the bonus pot. In the custom product team, knowledge and ideas are shared more widely and workers collaborate extensively, partly out of necessity in order to get the job done. Reflecting this, working patterns are also distinct. Workers in the new product team are very relaxed about timekeeping, often starting late in the morning and working late into the night, although there is no real way of knowing an individual's working hours. They also make extensive use of the company's chill-out rooms, often playing pool or videogames for long stretches of time. In contrast, the custom team keep relatively regular hours and make more limited use of recreation facilities. This reflects the fact that their work is constrained by tight deadlines. At present all developers, regardless of the team to which they belong, are paid on the same salary scale and salary tends to reflect length of service.

Despite the *laissez-faire* management style and the relaxed approach to work at Beach House, rivalry between the two groups has intensified over recent months and the usually collaborative working relationship between the groups, previously characterised by a fluid exchange of ideas, has begun to disappear. The 'tweakers' have become increasingly dissatisfied with the 'A Team', both over their failure to make any substantial breakthroughs in new products over the past few years and with the fact that senior managers appear to treat the

'A Team' with 'kid gloves' and give them preferential treatment despite this failure, particularly the managing director and finance director, neither of whom have any substantial technical expertise in the area of software design. The 'tweakers' feel that their contribution to the business is largely taken for granted, despite them providing 100 per cent of revenue over recent years.

The development manager has some sympathy with the perception of the 'tweakers', yet recognises the potential of the new product team to make a huge impact on company performance through the development of a single innovation. Indeed, without such innovation the demand for custom products would soon begin to decline. He also recognises that successful new products that make it from development to market are difficult and time-consuming to create.

Task

Senior managers have expressed concern about the lack of new product ideas that have come out of the development team and, subsequently, about the long-term viability of the company. They have asked you, as an HR consultant, to design a PMS for workers in this department. In doing so, consider the following questions:

1 What performance 'issues' are there in the company?

2 What would the rationale for a PMS be?

3 How will performance be defined and 'measured'?

4 Is the use of contingent pay suitable in the organisation and department? If so, how could performance be incentivised?

5 What potential problems might be caused by the relationship between the two teams?

6 What do you think is significant about the type of work that these employees do that might influence your approach to performance management?

7 What will be the impact on workers of your PMS? What potential problems might arise from the introduction of a PMS?

8 How will the system impact on the relationship between management and the software developers?

USEFUL READING

Journal articles

Aguinis, H., Joo, H. and Gottfredson, R. K. (2012) Performance management universals: Think globally and act locally, *Business Horizons*, 55: 385–92.

A short article that discusses the broad challenges associated with cultural influences on performance management but which concludes that there are five performance management 'universals', principles that lead to effective PM regardless of cultural context. The article also discusses how dimensions of culture act to influence PM processes and their effectiveness.

Gruman, J. A. and Saks, A. M. (2011) Performance management and employee engagement, *Human Resource Management Review*, 21: 123–36.

This article provides a useful resource for understanding 'where we are' in respect of an understanding of performance and its impact on employee engagement. It outlines how the component elements of performance management systems might impact on engagement as a key mediating factor in improving performance.

Pulakos, E. and O'Leary, R. (2011) Why is performance management broken? *Industrial and Organizational Psychology*, 4: 146–64.

This article discusses what constitutes the 'formula' for effective performance management, suggesting that the secret of success lies not in the development of formal, prescriptive administrative systems but in improvements in workplace communication and in configuring a more productive employment relationship. To reflect this perspective, the authors propose a model of more effective performance management.

Winstanley, D. and Stuart-Smith, K. (1996) Policing performance: The ethics of performance management, *Personnel Review*, 25 (6): 68–84.

This article challenges traditional approaches to performance management that, the authors argue, often demotivate workers and are inappropriately used to 'police' performance. It presents an alternative methodology for developing performance objectives and managing performance based on a number of ethical principles.

Books, book chapters and reports

Cheyne, A. and Loan-Clarke, J. (2006) Organisational and corporate culture, in T. Redman and A. Wilkinson (eds), *Contemporary Human Resource Management* (2nd edn), Harlow: FT Prentice–Hall.

This book chapter provides a useful overview of the concept of organisational culture, how HRM can contribute to the management of culture and key contentions and debates concerning, for example, the feasibility of cultural change.

Shields, J. (2007) *Managing Employee Performance and Reward: Concepts, Practices, Strategies*, Cambridge: Cambridge University Press.

This book provides a comprehensive critical account of theory and practice in the fields of both performance management and reward, covering both the basics and more complex themes.

FURTHER ONLINE READING

The following articles can be accessed for free on the book's companion website **https://edge.sagepub.com/wilton3e**:

Harper, S. and Vikinas, T. (2005) Determining the impact of an organisation's performance management system, *Asia Pacific Journal of Human Resources*, 43 (1): 76–97.

Lawler, E. E., Benson, G. S. and McDermott, M. (2012) What makes performance appraisals effective? *Compensation & Benefits Review*, 44 (4): 191–200.

Nankervis, A. R. and Compton, R.-L. (2006) Performance management: Theory in practice? *Asia Pacific Journal of Human Resources*, 44: 83–101.

Risher, H. (2011) Getting performance management on track, *Compensation & Benefits Review*, 43 (5): 273–81.

Shen, J. (2005) Effective international performance appraisals: Easily said, hard to do, *Compensation & Benefits Review*, 37: 70–9.

Waples, E. P. and Friedrich, T. L. (2011) Managing creative performance: Important strategies for leaders of creative efforts, *Advances in Developing Human Resources*, 13 (3): 366–85.

Want to know more about this chapter? Visit the companion website at: **https://edge.sagepub.com/wilton3e** to access practice questions, videos and selected journal articles to further enhance your study.

8

MANAGING REWARD

CHAPTER OBJECTIVES

- To discuss the various functions of reward in the employment relationship

- To identify different types of employee reward

- To outline key considerations and issues in the management of reward

- To outline key processes in the management of reward

- To discuss current trends in reward, particularly the growth of contingent pay and the increasing complexity of reward packages.

INTRODUCTION

This chapter is concerned with both the function and form of reward in the contemporary employment relationship. In many respects, this and the previous chapter on managing performance should be considered together because both reward and performance management systems are ultimately concerned with motivating and engaging employees and compelling them to express desired behaviours. Ultimately, employee reward is concerned with recruiting, motivating and retaining employees with the required competencies to achieve organisational objectives.

A strategic approach to managing reward emphasises the importance of reflecting the wider organisational strategy, objectives and culture in reward systems and ensuring a fit between reward, other elements of HRM and the organisational context. In Chapter 2 both content and process theories of motivation were discussed. In short, content theories are concerned with the 'needs' that motivate people, whereas process theories are concerned with the decision-making process by which people determine the direction, level and duration of their motivation. Reflecting this distinction, the effective management of reward requires consideration of both these dimensions and of both the extrinsic and intrinsic motivation of workers. Extrinsic motivation is addressed through financial reward, including pay and bonuses, and benefits in kind, such as company cars. Intrinsic motivation is concerned with satisfying employees' psychological needs, for example, through the provision of interesting and challenging work, opportunities for personal and professional development, recognition of achievement, social contact and a voice in decision-making. In this sense, reward management cuts right across multiple other areas of HRM, including performance management, learning and development and employee relations. Overall, the development of a mutually beneficial employment relationship requires the development of reward systems that satisfy both the needs of employer and employee.

Like HRM more widely, new approaches to managing reward tend to be contrasted with the more inflexible, bureaucratic systems which have gone before and which are now deemed inappropriate in a more competitive and unpredictable global economy. More incentivised reward systems, often incorporating pay contingent on individual or organisational performance or development, continue to increase in popularity. Rather than focusing individual efforts on the relatively predictable ascent of hierarchical pay scales – thus promoting loyalty and length of service – new pay systems tend towards satisfying a range of employee needs and expectations to generate increased contribution to organisational objectives. Marchington and Wilkinson (2008) suggest that this strategic approach reflects the contemporary orthodoxy in pay. This orthodoxy is not, however, without challenge.

FORMS OF REWARD

Bratton (2007: 360) defines reward as referring to 'all the monetary, non-monetary and psychological payments that an organisation provides for its employees in exchange for work they perform'. Typically, a distinction is made between three broad categories of reward:

MOTIVATING EMPLOYEES

- *Financial (or monetary) rewards* refer to pay or earnings, and include basic pay (as wages or salary) as well as bonuses, conditional or variable pay (for example, where pay is tied to individual performance), commission and overtime payments.

- *Non-financial (or non-monetary) rewards* encompass the psychological or intrinsic rewards that stem from the work that people do and their working relationships and environment. Non-financial rewards, therefore, include feeling valued, receiving praise and recognition of achievement, job satisfaction and job interest, challenge and variety. Non-financial reward also includes overt expressions of one's value to an organisation, such as promotion, advancement and personal or professional development, which can be associated with commensurate changes in monetary reward.

- *Benefits* (or benefits in kind, perquisites or perks) refer to the non-pay elements that make up the individual reward package such as pensions (or deferred payment systems), healthcare, subsidised meals, membership of fitness or health clubs and company cars. Other benefits associated with working for a particular organisation might include flexible working arrangements and enhanced maternity, paternity or sickness leave.

REWARD AND THE EMPLOYMENT RELATIONSHIP

It is important to consider the meaning and purpose of different elements of the reward offering, not least because it cannot be taken for granted that organisational stakeholders share common views about the value, function and meaning attached to the substantive elements of reward. As discussed in Chapter 2, there are multiple perspectives on the employment relationship and it is important that we consider reward from each viewpoint. In particular, we need to consider the objectives and needs that both parties seek to fulfil through reward.

The legal perspective

From a legal perspective, reward constitutes a contractual 'right' for the employee and 'obligation' or duty for the employer, the exact nature of which is determined by the express terms and conditions of employment. Once agreed upon, the employer is required to pay the employee for the work they perform for the length of the contract or until it is terminated by either party. This pay is likely to include the basic wage or salary, holiday entitlement, pension provision and benefits associated with the specific job role or wider organisation. Whilst many elements of reward are automatic in that they should be immediately forthcoming if the employee meets his or her own contractual obligations, reward can also be either contingent (for example, related to the achievement of pre-specified conditions, often associated with performance) or discretionary (for example, where an employer decides to reward employees with a one-off bonus outside of any formal agreement) (Banfield and Kay, 2009).

The economic perspective

From the perspective of the wage–effort bargain, the principal purpose of reward for the employer is to 'buy' the exertions of the employee for as long as they are needed. For the employee, reward constitutes the 'price' of one's labour and, at least in part, represents an employee's worth to an employer. In rational economic terms, one might expect employers to seek to minimise the financial cost of employed labour whilst employees seek to maximise the price at which they sell their labour and ensure that reward reflects their perceived self-worth. However, employee reward is multifaceted and, therefore, the buying and selling of labour is not a purely economic transaction. Employers need to consider a range of factors before setting the rate at which to buy labour, such as the scarcity of such labour, the reward offering of competitors and the range of other benefits and non-financial incentives provided. Similarly, in assessing their own worth, employees needs to consider a range of issues, such as the prevailing labour market climate and the other elements of reward available from prospective employers. Employees also might seek to balance short-term financial gain with long-term security or the development of employability.

Reward, social exchange and the psychological contract

As discussed in Chapter 2, the employment relationship is a social exchange reflecting a wider range of cost–benefit transactions beyond the wage–effort bargain. Reward is a key determinant of a positive psychological contract, not least because it represents an explicit indicator of an employee's worth to the employer, is implicit in the construction of notions of fairness, equity and trust and will demonstrate any incongruence between the expectations of the two parties. Indeed, it is perhaps the 'delivery' of formal or informal agreements on reward that often results in either the reinforcement or violation of the psychological contract. Non-financial rewards play a considerable role in determining the strength of the psychological contract and in shaping employee attitudes. For example, praise and recognition of achievement are key means by which individuals can be motivated to perform to their potential and managers can reinforce desired behaviour. Public sector workers in the US, for instance, have been found to place greater emphasis on intrinsic versus extrinsic reward (French and Emerson, 2015). However, reward can only act as an inducement to particular behaviours if reward is valued. As discussed in Chapter 2, financial reward constitutes a hygiene factor and unlocking discretionary effort is only possible through non-financial rewards that are intrinsically motivating (Herzberg et al., 1959). Pay and material benefits are only likely to impact negatively on behaviour where received reward is felt to be unfair or unrepresentative of perceived self-worth (reflecting the notion of distributive justice) or where there are concerns over the fairness of reward decision-making (reflecting procedural justice). In short, pay may have less of an impact on employees' day-to-day behaviour than other forms of reward, although monetary reward – particularly in the form of performance-related pay – clearly remains a central component of employer attempts to improve employee performance.

Reward and employee behaviour and attitudes

Individual performance requires motivation to be appropriately directed and sustained and, therefore, reward can be viewed as a lever for controlling or shaping behaviour in a desired direction, for reinforcing organisational values or enabling cultural change through 'buying' employee compliance. Ultimately, the behaviours and actions that are rewarded will tend to be the focus of employees' attention and it is important for managers to direct this focus on those that are consistent with its mission, values and strategic objectives. Bratton (2007) suggests that there are three broad behavioural objectives of reward systems: *membership behaviour*, demonstrated through cooperation with colleagues and managers or, alternatively, competition between workers; *task or goal behaviour*, associated with the exercising of discretionary effort in doing one's job, the pursuit of agreed individual objectives and the expression of desired role behaviours; and *compliance behaviour*, associated with the use of reward as a control mechanism to ensure employees adhere to the formal and informal 'rules' of the workplace and cooperate with management in the achievement of organisational goals.

Reward is a key determinant of employee attitudes towards their job and the organisation. Employee dissatisfaction with the composition of their reward package is likely to manifest itself in lowered productivity, greater intention to quit, lack of employee engagement and dysfunctional behaviour. Employee satisfaction with reward is determined both by the comparative and absolute level of reward and the overall composition of the reward package. As such, the impact of reward on, for instance, engagement will be at least partly locally determined (Brown and Reilly, 2013). External to the organisation, financial reward provides purchasing power and employees will assess reward according to the extent to which it affords them a desired standard of living. Employees might also compare their level of pay with other people doing similar jobs in other organisations or relative to other attainable employment. Within the organisation, employees might assess their satisfaction with pay according to internal relativities (their pay comparative to other people in the firm) and according to whether they perceive themselves as receiving a fair share of the wealth generated by their labour.

The employment relations perspective

From an employment relations perspective, reward has a socio-political function and constitutes perhaps the most prominent battleground in the power relationship between management and labour. As is discussed in more detail in Chapter 10, managing the employment relationship under a pluralist perspective concerns the continuous attempts to reconcile the different interests and expectations of various organisational stakeholders. Reflecting the plurality of interest groups in work organisations there are likely to be inevitable differences in opinion about what constitutes 'fair' reward systems and the equitable distribution of generated wealth. Therefore, disputes over pay constitute a significant source of workplace conflict, reflecting the tension between what employers are able and willing to pay and what employees feel they are worth. Pay disputes represent the key cause of industrial action across the UK and European Union. For instance, ONS (2015b) report that in 2014, 89 per cent of working days lost were due to disputes over pay, accounting for 57 per cent of all stoppages.

THE MANAGEMENT OF REWARD

It is perhaps in the area of reward management that the need for horizontal and vertical integration of business and HR strategy, philosophy, policy and practice is most clearly illustrated. Armstrong and Brown (2001: 5) define reward strategy as 'a business-focused statement of the intentions of the organisation concerning the development of future reward processes and practices, which are aligned to the business and human resource strategies of the organisation, its culture and the environment in which it operates'. Reward strategy therefore acts as a yardstick against which all elements of reward can be evaluated (CIPD, 2006b) to ensure that they are both internally and externally consistent.

Without a coherent and clearly articulated reward strategy, the positive effects of complementarity between different components of reward will be lost and there may be misunderstanding of the aims of the overall system of reward. Despite the apparent importance of a reward strategy to the effective management of employee reward, evidence continues to suggest that the majority of firms do not have a clear reward strategy to support business goals and to recruit, retain and reward high performers (CIPD, 2010).

Vertical integration and reward

Reward is likely to be a highly visible element of HRM in respect of its 'fit' with the competitive strategy of the firm and, in particular, its financial strategy and objectives. Reward also constitutes a principal means by which employers attempt to generate and direct required effort and behaviours to be consistent with organisational objectives. It is important, therefore, that employers are mindful of the signals transmitted by their reward strategy, systems and practices and ensure that the connection between reward and behaviour is effectively communicated.

Total labour costs – which include pay and non-wage costs such as benefits, pensions and national insurance contributions – often constitute a large proportion of a firm's total costs, particularly in the service sector. Therefore, consideration of labour costs, particularly pay, is likely to be a significant element in the financial planning process and in the ability of a firm to enact organisational strategy. A strategic approach to HRM would therefore require reward policies to be designed, not necessarily to minimise costs or to match market rates, but to ensure that reward supports the achievement of strategic objectives. For example, offering above-average pay can be viewed as a sound investment rather than simply an additional cost where it results in a commensurately high level of productivity.

The strategic reward orthodoxy stresses that reward systems should be contingent on both internal and external context. Reward strategy and systems should therefore be flexible enough to respond to changing conditions as well as to ensure they continue to meet the motivational needs of the workforce. Flexibility in reward systems (for example, through the use of pay tied to organisational performance) can be important for organisational viability through the ability to coordinate reward spend with financial and market circumstances. Consequently, a one-size-fits-all set of reward practices suitable for all organisations in all contexts is unfeasible. Whilst it is usual to regard the reward system as responsive to broader HR strategy and, in turn, business strategy, Marchington and Wilkinson (2008) suggest that reward systems can exercise a constraint on corporate strategy, so the relationship is often bilateral.

Reward and horizontal fit

In respect of horizontal fit, reward systems should be complementary to other key functional elements of HRM. For example, both financial and psychological rewards play an essential part in supporting performance management systems and effective PRP can support a high-performance culture and reinforce desired employee behaviours. Similarly, the reward package and level of pay are also key components in enabling organisations to recruit and retain the employees it requires with the skills and competencies to contribute towards the achievement of organisational objectives. For example, offering high wages is likely to attract more and better applicants allowing greater choice in employee selection. The right reward systems and structures and the composition of the reward package are therefore essential to ensure that other aspects of HRM are not undermined. Firms not only need to consider issues of fairness, cost-effectiveness, employee value and performance in reward decisions, but also the implications for wider HRM policies and practices, employee behaviours, organisational culture and the relationship between employees and management. In other words, managers must concern themselves with both strategic and equity considerations in reward determination (Kessler, 2007).

THE CONTEXT OF REWARD

A wide range of environmental factors influence the approach a firm takes towards reward management and the forms of reward offered to employees. McKenna and Beech (2008) suggest that external market and environmental conditions are now of greater importance in determining pay levels and structures, than what are referred to as 'internal relativities' – the relationship between pay grades and levels within the firm – and pay structures. It is therefore important to consider the range of internal and external contextual factors and how they can influence reward strategy and systems (Perkins et al., 2008).

Strategic context

As discussed above, a firm's organisational strategy and ambition are influential in determining the form and content of reward, particularly the level and type of pay. Reflecting the discussion of best fit strategies in Chapter 3, different reward strategies can be seen as complementary to particular competitive strategies. For example, a cost leadership strategic orientation is likely to be reflected in reward strategies that emphasise tight controls over pay levels, the importance of matching pay to market rates and the use of flexible, contingent pay to ensure wage costs vary according to performance. Alternatively, a strategy of market differentiation, particularly where employees are seen as critical to business success, would stress the importance of remuneration above market rates to aid the recruitment and retention of key skills and competencies. The latest evidence (CIPD, 2012b) suggests that more firms appear to be adopting a 'talent management' approach to pay positioning with a greater likelihood of offering pay above the market norm for those groups of employees or individuals likely to bring greater value to the organisation, typically professionals and managerial workers.

The degree to which strategy and decision-making in the firm is centralised is also likely to shape reward strategy and practices. Firms with a centralised strategy will tend to focus on the standardisation of pay across the firm, usually coordinated by a central HR department, to ensure internal equity. In decentralised organisations, greater flexibility allows for more variation to reflect local market conditions. A further key consideration is the profitability and cost structure of the firm which will determine the available resources for reward and the degree of affordability it can sustain. These two factors – strategic choice and affordability – must be balanced against one another. Moreover, evidence suggests that the notion of fairness and justice in reward is also organisationally specific and must be carefully considered by management in designing pay systems (Chen and Fu, 2011).

Market context

At local, national and international level, the market context of the firm has a significant influence on the determination of rewards (Druker and White, 1997). As previously indicated, firms are increasingly looking towards 'external relativities' rather than internal equity to set pay levels. In the same way that firms might determine their competitive and HR strategies relative to those of their competitors, firms often seek to ensure a degree of comparability with competitors operating in their marketplace (known as the 'market rate'). Clearly, reward strategies that differentiate a firm from its competitors can be a source of competitive advantage. For example, a firm can position itself as an 'employer of choice' through adopting a policy of market leadership in remuneration so long as other HRM policies are commensurate. Alternatively, undercutting the pay of competitors might increase profitability through enhanced ability to lower prices for goods and services. Firms also need to take account of customs and traditions in the industry in which they operate. For firms operating overseas, pay comparability is becoming ever more complex and firms will need to take account of the local market conditions as well as broader international comparability. For example, some countries have institutional frameworks that might allow firms to pay lower wages (often where trade unions and labour legislation are not well established).

In turbulent market and constrained economic conditions, wage setting and the development of effective reward strategies become particularly problematic. This challenge accounts for the greater use of flexible strategies for pay setting in recent years and the importance of firms developing scenario-based planning approaches to reward management to anticipate and prepare for future 'shocks' through the development of sustainable reward strategies (Greene, 2012).

Political, economic and legal context

Chapter 5 outlined the range of factors that can influence HRM practices within different nation states or regional blocs, such as the European Union. Clearly, in the area of reward the need to comply with local labour legislation is paramount. In the UK, for example, firms must be aware of and comply with legislation in the areas of minimum pay, equal pay and discrimination, pensions, taxation, working time, maternity and paternity rights, and so on. Firms must also be aware of their obligations in relation to specific groups of workers (e.g. part-time workers). The increasing complexity of labour legislation and the significant repercussions of failing to comply have led increasing numbers of firms to outsource their payroll and pension functions to specialist third parties (CIPD, 2009c).

BOX 8.1
ETHICAL INSIGHT

The distribution of organisational wealth

Employee perceptions of fair treatment are central components both of quality of working life and a positive psychological contract. In particular, notions of fairness and equity are important considerations for effective reward management, partly because remuneration is where evidence of unfair treatment is likely to be manifest. The extent to which employees feel that they are rewarded fairly in relation to other employees inside and outside the organisation (reflecting internal and external equity) is a key determinant of motivation and commitment.

One dimension of internal equity reflects the differential in remuneration between managers and non-managerial employees. In recent years, the UK has experienced increasing polarisation in earnings in line with broader trends in wealth distribution where the poorest in society hold a declining share of national income and the richest hold a rapidly increasing share. For example,

since 1998, whilst the average British employee's income went up by 35 per cent, the average FTSE 350 company boss's income rose by 163 per cent. The longer-term trend is even more striking. For instance, in the US, in 1965, the CEO-to-worker compensation ratio was 20-to-1 rising to 29.9-to-1 in 1978. By 1995, this had grown to 122.6-to-1 in 1995, peaked at 383.4-to-1 in 2000, and was 295.9-to-1 in 2013, far higher than it was in the 1960s, 1970s, 1980s, or 1990s (Mishel and David, 2014). In 2013, the average FTSE 350 CEO compensation package stood at $15.2 million.

These trends raises a number of ethical questions about the extent to which the organisational wealth generated by its entire workforce should be more equally distributed, if only in terms of year-on-year increases. It also raises the question of whether such an attitude to senior managerial pay is sustainable in the long term, not least because of the de-motivating effect it is likely to have on the majority of the workforce.

The political environment influences reward beyond the government's role as legislator. For public sector employees, reward is clearly connected to the wider political context because pay is partly determined by the government and is a highly politicised issue. For example, during an economic downturn, the government might urge wage restraint in the public sector to curb government spending. Public sector pay and investment is also politicised in that it is partly determined by levels of taxation and government investment in public services.

Over the last three decades, the prevailing political environment has had a marked impact on pay systems. In the 1970s, a significant proportion of UK employees' pay was set through a process of collective bargaining: negotiations conducted between employers and trade unions resulting in a collective agreement covering employees' terms and conditions of employment. However, the decline in union membership and recognition alongside the free market philosophy and policies of the incumbent Conservative government during the 1980s and 1990s resulted in increasing decentralisation of collective pay decisions from a national to a local level to allow for greater flexibility in pay determination and the increasing popularity of systems of reward focused on rewarding individual performance (Heery, 1997a, 1997b). The decline of trade union membership and collective bargaining are discussed in more detail in Chapter 10.

The economic context of HRM is influential in that levels of inflation and interest rates determine the cost of living and therefore shape employees' perceptions of their reward package. Moreover, the economic climate shapes attitudes towards pay. For example, in times of high unemployment and/or recession, employees are less likely to agitate for pay increases.

BOX 8.2
HRM IN PRACTICE

Trends in reward in an economic downturn

Research conducted by the Hay Group (2010) in 230 companies in 29 countries identified four, potentially conflicting, challenges in the management of reward: cost containment; talent engagement, motivation and retention; performance improvement; and the management of risk in a climate of uncertainty. The research identified five key themes in how organisations were addressing these challenges:

1 *Making pay for performance a reality* – greater focus on creating a performance culture through aligning reward to performance metrics associated with business growth.

2 *Differentiating and rewarding 'mission critical' roles* – focusing limited resources – both financial and non-financial – more greatly on rewarding employees seen as vital to future success, whether top performers, those with high potential or those with scarce skills.

3 *Increasing variable pay* – greater focus on variable pay associated with achievement of critical goals, reducing the firm's fixed costs in reward, tying reward more closely to actual performance and broadening the notion of performance to include employer reputation and CSR.

4 *Centralisation* – increased centralisation of reward decision-making to ensure greater consistency, whilst maintaining a degree of local flexibility in pay-setting.

5 *Market benchmarking* – a stronger focus on benchmarking reward against that of competitors, both to ensure retention of talent and to avoid over-paying in certain areas of the business.

Source: Hay Group, 2010

Labour market context

As discussed in Chapter 4, firms operate across a range of external labour markets depending on the type of required labour. Therefore, just as employee resourcing strategies are likely to differ between employee groups, reward strategies also need to be differentiated. For example, executive searches are likely

---

BOX 8.3
GLOBAL INSIGHT

Reward, national difference and MNCs

Both attitudes and organisational approaches to reward are underpinned by culturally grounded assumptions. For example, culture shapes the value placed on particular forms of reward, the relative position of particular jobs in organisational structures, the acceptance of risk associated with contingent pay and the extent to which pay should be individually or collectively based. Subsequently, reward is perhaps the most visible demonstration of the overarching approach a firm takes to resolving the host versus home country dilemma, through the extent to which it adopts, adapts or ignores local norms.

Barsoux and Schneider (2008) contrast, for example, the US approach to reward that emphasises equity ('getting what you deserve') and the more European notion of equality ('deserve what you get'). They suggest that the American perspective reflects cultural assumptions of individualism and control over nature. The European view is underpinned by cultural assumptions of egalitarianism and group solidarity that are reflected in a greater tendency to campaign against the unfair distribution of wealth. Cultural differences are particularly pronounced when considering performance-related pay. PRP tends to be individualised and to emphasise short-term objectives and competition between co-workers. Whilst this might be acceptable in a US context, it is likely to be unworkable in Eastern cultures as it undermines group or social harmony and works against a more long-term focus. Therefore, assumptions regarding uncertainty, control and temporal orientation influence the degree of acceptance for variable rather than fixed compensation.

The relative importance of financial and non-financial rewards – and their potential to motivate employees – also varies across cultures. For example, the importance placed on quality of life in Sweden is reflected in the importance attached to leave entitlement and encouragement among employers for workers to take their maximum leave. In contrast, in Japan workers tend to take only a small proportion of their comparatively meagre holiday entitlement, reflecting the view that taking one's full entitlement is selfish and indicates a lack of concern for the group.

For MNCs, reward management is clearly problematic, particularly where there is a desire to ensure strategic consistency and to transfer home country practices across borders. A successful approach to the management of international reward requires a clear understanding of national laws, values, customs and employment practices and of shifting political, economic and social conditions (Dowling and Welch, 2004). Firms that ally this knowledge with the ability to identify potentially advantageous areas of variation and global best practice are likely to be better placed to effectively recruit, retain and motivate an international workforce. However, as labour markets, particularly for senior management and highly skilled or knowledgeable workers, have become more global, approaches to and levels of reward in one country have an increased ability to shape those in another. For instance, Russell (2009) reports that 'the increase in total pay for chief executives and senior directors of the UK's largest companies is "on a curve to infinity" as management fight to catch up with their better paid peers from the US'. This can create significant problems where it undermines the relationship between the pay of those who operate in such global labour markets and those who don't, creating greater perceptions of inequity among those whose pay is constrained by national, rather than international, comparisons.

to be effective only where they are underpinned by a reward package commensurate with the global market in which higher-level management operates. Whilst for lower-level employees local conditions often need only be considered, the potential for offshoring has heightened interest in international pay comparisons for a wider range of occupations. For instance, the acceptability of high pay coupled with an institutional framework that does not act to constrain pay awards in some countries (such as the USA) can have significant repercussions for pay-setting in others (see Box 8.3).

Changes to the structure of labour markets and the supply and demand for workers with particular skills also need to be evaluated in establishing reward structures and systems in that they set the limits within which reward management operates. For example, the growing importance of knowledge workers to competitive advantage in many firms raises issues about how to attract and retain such workers through the design of reward practices to meet their expectations and needs (Horwitz et al., 2003). Consequently, reward systems that are effective for one group of workers might not be so for another occupational group or those involved in different 'types' of work (Howard and Dougherty, 2004). Moreover, changing labour market demography, particularly an ageing workforce and rising female employment, alongside the development of equal opportunities legislation, places greater responsibility on employers to ensure that reward systems are equitable, fair and address the needs of a diverse workforce (Kessler, 2005). As the constitution of the labour market has changed so too have organisational practices in the area of reward (Ledford, 2014).

Further online reading This article presents research to explore employee reactions to different reward strategies, contrasting the attitude of blue- and white-collar workers. It concludes that 'job type' constitutes an important contingency factor influencing the viability of particular reward strategies.

Howard, L. W. and Dougherty, T. W. (2004) Alternative reward strategies and employee reactions, *Compensation & Benefits Review*, 36 (1): 41–51.

REWARD SYSTEMS

REWARD
EMPLOYEES

There are a number of key considerations in designing reward systems to fit both with the wider HR and corporate strategies and with other elements of HRM, including the objectives of the reward strategy, the types or range of rewards to be offered, the composition of the total reward package, the formal processes that are used to manage reward and an underpinning concern for fairness, effectiveness and value-for-money.

First, managers must decide what objectives they hope to achieve through their reward system. For example, managers might choose to prioritise one or more central aims for reward, such as rewarding individual performance, engendering employee commitment and retention, facilitating external recruitment or promoting employee development. These objectives ultimately determine the most appropriate form(s) of reward. For example, reward systems that emphasise length of service and seniority might increase employment commitment. Alternatively, performance-related reward schemes should emphasise the behaviours and standards required for individuals to contribute to organisational objectives. Skills-based pay has its focus on continuous individual development and learning, often in firms relying on innovation and creativity for competitive advantage.

Bratton (2007) suggests that the level at which reward is offered (individual, work group/team or organisational) relates to the types of behaviour that managers wish to promote. Individual rewards, such as basic pay, overtime, bonuses, benefits, commission and forms of PRP, seek to buy employees' *time* (attendance at work), *energy* and *competence* (completing work tasks without errors and to a desirable standard). Team rewards, such as team bonuses, seek to engender *cooperation* with co-workers. Organisational rewards, such as profit-sharing and share ownership, are designed to elicit employee *commitment* to organisational objectives. Firms must then decide on an appropriate mix of rewards to constitute the overall reward package and the levels at which reward is to be offered. For example, if variable pay is to form an element of reward, management must decide the ratio of contingent reward to base pay. Ultimately, the form of rewards offered and the overall package should reinforce desired behaviours and be consistent with dominant organisational values. Below we consider key components of the reward package, such as basic pay, incremental pay, variable or contingent pay, benefits and non-financial reward.

BASIC PAY

For most employees, basic or base pay constitutes the single largest (if not only) component of their financial reward and represents the minimum compensation expected for carrying out a particular job. Overall, it represents the largest element of fixed labour costs for employers and, consequently, how much to pay incumbents in the different roles that populate an organisation and the criteria and mechanisms used to determine base pay are critically important decisions for managers. Most jobs have a fixed or flat rate for undertaking a job role for a fixed period, usually either an hourly wage or annual salary. Some jobs, for example those involved in the assembly of non-complex manufactured goods such as clothing, are paid by 'piece rate' for each item of work completed. However, this has the problem of focusing employees on production quantity rather than quality and is associated with boring and repetitive work. For jobs that are typically paid according to an hourly, daily or weekly wage and where non-standard working hours are not the norm (for example, those working in the hospitality industry are typically expected to work unsocial hours), employers will typically offer enhanced or premium rates for working out of contracted hours (overtime) or for shift work (for example, night or weekend shifts or where the job occasionally requires early starts or finishes). Ledford (2014) notes that, over the last 35 years in the US, basic (or base) pay constitutes a declining proportion of total reward and pay, whilst benefits and perks have made up an increasing proportion, reflecting changes to the manner in which employers construct reward packages. This trend seems set to continue with recent evidence suggesting that employers advocate a continued shift in focus from base pay to variable pay (CIPD, 2013c).

Determining basic pay

As outlined above, establishing the appropriate level of pay for different jobs – and the differentials between them – is likely to be the most important element in developing an effective reward system. Typically, pay differentials are determined either by job characteristics or 'job size' (for example, the degree of decision-making responsibility, level in the organisational hierarchy and complexity) or the individual characteristics of the incumbent such as experience, qualifications, contribution to the organisation or the possession of particular skills. Pay rates need to be affordable and sustainable over the longer term and they must address both internal (job-to-job comparison) and external (market) relativities. There are a number of means by which to determine appropriate pay rates:

- *Collective bargaining* – management and employee representatives, usually trade unions, negotiate wage rates for groups of employees either at a workplace, local or national level (often alongside job evaluation).
- *Market pricing* – setting pay according to the 'going rate' for a job in a particular location and marketplace. Ledford (2014) suggests that market pricing is now the dominant approach to wage setting, partly as a result of more ready access to market data to inform decision-making.

BOX 8.4
UNDERSTAND

Methods of job evaluation

- Analytical methods

Analytical methods of job evaluation represent the most objective means of establishing the worth of a job. One such method is a *points-based* system using job content criteria (including, for example, required knowledge, skills and educational level, responsibilities and accountability, complexity and task difficulty) against which all jobs can be scored, often using job descriptions. Under such an approach, certain criteria can be weighted to reflect their greater relative importance to the organisation. A contemporary approach is *competency-based* job evaluation that focuses on those skills and competencies that are value-adding.

Advocates of analytical methods of job evaluation argue that they represent a fair and objective means of establishing vertical and horizontal pay relativities. However, these claims are challenged by the argument that the establishment of the evaluation criteria and the process of scoring jobs is itself subjective.

- Non-analytical methods

Non-analytical methods of job evaluation are based on the more subjective judgement of a job's relative worth. One such approach is *job ranking*, which involves deciding on the 'order' of jobs in the organisation from the highest to lowest (for example, on the basis of importance or value to the firm).

Pre-determined criteria can be used for this purpose but there is no attempt to quantify job content. This approach might be useful in determining the relative position of a newly created role. An alternative approach is *paired comparison*, where two jobs are considered relative to one another to decide on their respective position in the job structure. Job classification can also be conducted by establishing grades – for example, based on differences in skills, knowledge and responsibility – to which jobs can be allocated.

Clearly, non-analytical methods based on managerial judgement are more prone to bias and procedural unfairness than approaches that produce a paper trail of decision-making. Subjective job evaluation carries with it the greater likelihood of evaluating the incumbent rather than the job itself and, consequently, non-analytical techniques tend to be viewed less favourably by employment tribunals in pay dispute cases.

A number of criticisms of job evaluation analysis were highlighted in Chapter 6. Principal among these was that the assumptions that underpin job evaluation, for example that organisations are constructed of a hierarchy of clearly delineated jobs, tend to be contradicted in reality. Subsequently, as the basis for evaluation decisions, greater flexibility in job structures and flexible job descriptions are often advocated. Such flexible approaches are associated with broad banding in pay structures (discussed below).

- *Job evaluation* – a systematic process to determine the relative value or worth of a job within an organisation, involving an evaluation of job size. Job evaluation assesses and grades the job, rather than the person, to develop hierarchies of jobs and pay structures and to establish internal relativities. Methods of job evaluation can be classified as either analytical (quantitative) or non-analytical (non-quantitative) (Box 8.4).

INCREMENTAL PAY SCHEMES

Job evaluation is associated with the creation of pay structures and incremental pay schemes. In incremental pay schemes length of service drives pay increases (alongside periodic cost-of-living increases). In such schemes, annual progression up the pay scale tends to be automatic until a bar or progression point is reached (for example, progression to a higher salary band) at which point performance is evaluated and, if successful, rewarded with promotion.

Incremental schemes are becoming less common in the private sector because increases in pay under such schemes are generally unrelated to performance or contribution to organisational objectives. However, they remain prevalent in the public sector. Box 8.5 outlines commonly adopted approaches to managing pay structures.

VARIABLE OR CONTINGENT PAY

Variable pay or contingent reward are umbrella terms used for forms of remuneration that are conditional upon the achievement of pre-determined objectives,

---

BOX 8.5
UNDERSTAND

Common approaches to managing pay structures

- *Narrow grades* – narrow-grade structures provide a detailed sequence of job levels in which all jobs at a particular level or grade are of broadly equal value to the organisation and thus are associated with a single salary or limited range of salaries.
- *Broad bands* – broad-banded structures consist of fewer grades or bands, each consisting of a wider range of jobs. In contrast to narrow bands, the range of pay attached to a grade is significantly broader allowing for greater flexibility in pay decisions. This can help to better reflect internal and external relativities in pay decisions, to acknowledge changes in the content of jobs and to better reward those who acquire new competencies.
- *Pay spines* – a series of incremental points stretching from the highest to the lowest paid jobs in an organisation.
- *Individual pay rates* – places each separate job in its own grade, with its own salary or range. Such a structure is useful where the job content for individual positions varies widely, or where flexibility in response to rapid organisational change or market-pressure is vital.
- *Job family pay structure* – separate pay structures for occupational groupings or job families. Job families may be task-based (covering specific group of workers who do similar work) or generic (covering similar types of work across functions, based on required skills, knowledge or competency).

mostly related to individual, group or organisational performance. Common conditions include individual targets or performance standards, organisational profit or the individual acquisition of new skills or qualifications. McKenna and Beech (2008) distinguish between incentives – forms of pay to encourage future performance through the explicit promise of reward in return for the achievement of established targets – and bonuses that recognise past performance and achievement. Similarly, Armstrong (2002) makes the distinction between 'financial incentives' and 'financial rewards'.

The resurgence of incentivised pay – such as PRP – since the 1980s has been driven by changes to the political and economic environment and is commensurate with both the managerial trend towards greater individualism, entrepreneurialism and self-interest. Firms wishing to become leaner and meaner in response to intensified global competition have viewed contingent pay as a means by which wage costs could reflect differing levels of individual contribution and variations in organisational performance. Indeed, such forms of contingent pay can represent a considerable source of financial flexibility for the firm. For example, Russell (2009) reports that bonuses make up an average 72 per cent of chief executive pay in larger companies (see Box 8.6).

Variable pay has now become firmly entrenched within most firms, the CIPD (2012b) reporting that 65 per cent of survey respondents used performance-related reward, incentive and recognition schemes, but that this rose to 77 per cent in the private sector. Most commonly, firms employed individual-based plans, such as individual bonuses (67 per cent of respondents) or merit-based pay increases (57 per cent), however, the use of group or team-based incentive schemes was reported to be on the increase (48 per cent of organisations).

Performance-related pay

PERFORMANCE-RELATED PAY

An increasingly popular form of incentivised pay is performance-related pay, typically applied to individual employees but sometimes covering work groups, teams or entire departments. Put simply, PRP represents an additional payment over and above base pay, the level of which is determined by the achievement of pre-agreed objectives or standards and, in certain circumstances, can constitute a significant element of overall financial reward. As discussed in the previous chapter, PRP often represents an integral part of wider performance management systems.

In one sense, PRP can be seen as an attempt to fairly distribute the finite resources available for rewarding employees by ensuring those that add the most value to the organisation receive the highest proportion. However, as discussed in Chapter 7, the subjective assessment of performance that can often form the basis of PRP has the potential for procedural injustice leading to the unfair distribution of reward. For this reason, effective PRP requires managers to clearly identify and communicate how the achievement of objectives is to be measured and how this translates into reward.

PRP is associated with the goal theory of employee motivation (Locke and Latham, 1990) that emphasises the importance of appropriate and desirable goals – and reward for the attainment of those goals – to enhance motivation and performance. However, when applied in the context of PRP, this assumes that extrinsic motivation represents an adequate stimulus for employees to exert the required effort and express the desired behaviours necessary to meet these objectives.

Skill-, knowledge- and competency-based pay

Where a firm places emphasis on employee and organisational development an alternative to PRP is pay contingent on the development of new skills, knowledge or competencies. In contrast to PRP, which focuses on the achievement of specific business-related goals, skills-based pay emphasises goals related to personal development. This might be particularly appropriate in organisations with High Performance Work Systems and which value skills flexibility among its workforce. The impetus for improved performance is obviously not as direct as in the case of PRP but such pay is partly based on the assumption that more highly skilled employees will be more able and motivated to perform to their potential. Whilst a distinction has been made here between performance-related pay and competency-based pay, some firms employ the broader term 'contribution-based pay' to refer to approaches to reward that seek to recognise both employee achievement and competencies. Such approaches are increasingly apparent in the public sector (Perkins and White, 2010).

Organisation-wide pay schemes

Contingent pay can also be based on the performance of the organisation itself. Forms of organisational PRP include profit-sharing, employee share ownership and gain-sharing (where employees share in productivity gains or savings resulting from improved performance). Such forms of incentivised pay seek to increase employee commitment to the organisation and to promote a longer-term perspective on performance by allowing employees to take a financial stake in the firm (Greene, 2014). An employee profit-sharing scheme was reported in 38 per cent of organisations and gain-sharing (the distribution of 'gains' from increases in productivity) in 22 per cent (CIPD, 2012b). In particular, share ownership schemes form a considerable element of executive remuneration. Organisation-wide reward schemes are further discussed in Chapter 10 in the context of financial participation.

Issues with incentive-based rewards

As discussed in the previous chapter, PRP is not without its critics. Those who doubt the effectiveness of PRP suggest that rather than forming inducements to particular behaviours, incentives constitute 'bribes' that can only achieve temporary compliance and short-term changes in behaviour (Kohn, 1993). Similarly, Decktop et al. (1999) note that where employee commitment is low, performance-related incentives are a disincentive to organisational-citizenship behaviour and it is only where high levels of commitment are pre-existing that PRP can act as a stimulus to such behaviour. This suggests that PRP is itself not a panacea for low levels of employee commitment but can contribute to its development under the appropriate conditions. In Chapter 7, the problems of effective measurement of performance were discussed and the issues outlined there, such as the problems of formulating measurable objectives, the challenges of rating and ranking employees and the risk of real or perceived bias or inconsistency, are clearly amplified when the issue of money is attached to such measurement.

A key strategic issue for PRP is overcoming the tendency towards short-termism generated by particular forms of contingent reward. For example, where rewards are tied closely to short-term performance cycles, employees might not devote time and energy to longer-term objectives, potentially sacrificing the long-term viability of the organisation, or at least key aspects of sustained competitive advantage, for short-term success. In fact, behavioural change generated through reward can sometimes be at odds with the intentions of the firm. By focusing purely on incentivised goals and the behaviours that contribute to their achievement, employees can lose sight of other unrewarded behaviours and activities that can be value-adding. Therefore, not only can PRP fail to alter underlying attitudes that shape

BOX 8.6
HRM IN PRACTICE

Executive pay and the 'shareholder spring'

In May 2010, *The Guardian* reported that the UK Trade Union Congress and the Institute of Directors, typically the best of enemies representing as they do the two sides of the employment relationship, were united in the belief that executive pay in the UK was out of control. This view reflects growing unrest among both politicians and shareholders that executives often appear to reward themselves handsomely despite poor or declining organisational performance. For example, in 2012, Bob Diamond, chief executive of Barclays Bank, was reported to have received a total reward package of £17 million as a result of long-term incentive plans paying out. This was despite Diamond himself describing the bank's recent financial performance as 'unimpressive' (*The Guardian*, 2012c). Across all FTSE100 companies, whilst median chief executive officer remuneration (including salary, cash bonuses, deferred bonuses, pensions, benefits-in-kind and the expected value of share options and other share plans) rose by 32 per cent to £3.5 million between 2009 and 2010, the FTSE100 index only rose 9 per cent over the same period, suggesting little relationship between executive pay, firm performance and shareholder value (Executive Director Total Remuneration Survey, 2011).

In order to curb such pay excesses, the UK government has encouraged shareholders to vote against the annual pay reports which detail the intended rewards for executives if they feel they represent excessive compensation and has sought to strengthen the ability of shareholders to resist such rewards. In the round of shareholder

meetings held in spring 2012, this growing distaste for excessive pay appeared to be coming to a head when a number of companies (including Barclays, the insurance group Aviva and newspaper publishers Trinity Mirror) witnessed a substantial proportion of shareholders taking the rather unprecedented step of voting against the annual remuneration reports. In some cases this revolt was enough to defeat these reports and in others enough to lead to a reconsideration of reward packages or to force the resignation of executives.

However, in many cases, despite a growing appetite among shareholders to voice concerns, these votes have not been substantial enough to reject the pay awards or to lead to a review of arrangements. This begs the question of why shareholders might not vote against large pay awards, particularly where they are not accompanied by a commensurate improvement in performance and, therefore, shareholder dividends (particularly when we consider that, in the case of Barclays, the total bonus pool for the organisation was three times the amount awarded in dividends). Is it that shareholders sincerely believe that executives are worth their pay? Or is there a lack of will among shareholders to exercise their new powers to reject pay awards, leading us to question the government's approach of shareholder empowerment to tackle excess pay? Or, is it simply the fact that many shares held in large companies are not held by individual shareholders who might have both a moral and financial 'bone to pick' with such reward, but by investment funds which are likely to have less of a long-term vested interests in demanding high performance from senior management in return for such huge rewards?

behaviour over the longer-term but also it can promote the 'wrong' type of behaviour. Moreover, there remains a concern that having an element of pay tied to performance represents the passing-on of risk from the employer to employee leading to greater insecurity and unpredictability and potentially leading to dysfunctional behaviours such as overwork (Lewis, 2006).

One of the key issues in decision-making over PRP is the suitability of different forms of contingent reward, in particular occupational, organisational, sectoral and cultural contexts (Chiang and Birtch, 2007). For instance, Box 8.7 provides some insight into the impact of PRP on employee behaviours and attitudes when implemented in organisations in China, suggesting that the effects of PRP can be unpredictable and, therefore, its use may not be appropriate in all circumstances. Individual PRP can act to undermine attempts to develop cooperation among employees (Dowling and Richardson, 1997; French et al., 2000) that can be problematic in work settings and roles where teamworking is critical. An alternative, therefore, is team-based pay based on objectives that are established for work groups to encourage and sustain effective team performance.

A final set of problems with PRP concern its impact on job satisfaction and the psychological contract. Heywood and Wei (2006) report that different types of contingent pay are associated with varying levels of job satisfaction. Whilst commission, tips, stock options and bonuses were associated with greater job satisfaction, piece rates had a negative impact on satisfaction. Managerial discretion over reward levels is most pronounced in individual PRP (Kessler and Purcell, 1992) and the non-payment of expected reward, especially where such 'withholding'

BOX 8.7
RESEARCH INSIGHT

Performance-related pay in China

As outlined above, one of the most important dimensions of reward decision-making is employee response to both the level and form of pay. Therefore, basing reward decisions on an accurate prediction of both employees' psychological and behavioural response to reward systems can be an important means of achieving improved performance and avoiding costly mistakes in implementation. Predicting employee response to HRM is, however, difficult, not least where firms seek to implement practices developed in one country or region in another, particularly where the 'cultural distance' between those two areas is significant. Performance-related pay is one aspect of HRM where the assumptions of unitarism and individualism that underpin much contemporary management practice are brought to the fore. However, this has not stopped many MNCs and domestic firms seeking to implement PRP in countries where the dominant culture does

not necessarily reflect these ideas, with variable results.

Du and Choi (2010) sought to explore the response of engineers working in both domestic and foreign firms in China to the introduction of performance-related pay (or, in their words, pay for performance). They found that whilst PRP was positively associated with conscientiousness and motivation at an individual level (where properly implemented), it was shown to negatively impact on employees' organisational commitment and organisational citizenship behaviour. They suggest, therefore, that the impact of cultural distance is more likely to be manifest at the collective level (i.e. in undermining traditional patterns of collectivism in Chinese organisations) rather than at the individual level through channelling individual attention towards their specific work objectives, and 'making individual identity or individual well-being more salient than group or collective identity' (Du and Choi, 2010), even in contexts where socialistic values in wider society predominate.

is perceived as unfair, can be a significant source of de-motivation and constitute a fundamental breach of the psychological contract. Therefore, the management of expectation is a key element in effective contingent pay arrangements as the use of PRP can often lead to inflated expectations among employees, particularly where managers attempt to motivate by reinforcing the maximum one might achieve for improved performance. If this maximum is not obtained this can to lead to resentment and demotivation among workers. This is particularly problematic where only a limited proportion of employees can achieve maximum reward and most repeatedly receive average levels of PRP, leading to a lack of incentive to improve performance over the longer term.

EMPLOYEE PERKS AND BENEFITS

Aside from financial reward, extrinsic motivational needs can also be addressed through the use of perks and benefits, sometimes referred to as indirect pay. Often the terms are used interchangeably, but the CIPD (2006b) distinguish between 'benefits', which are offered to all employees, and 'perks', which are offered to discrete groups of workers or certain individuals. Employee benefits or perks are payments in kind in addition to financial reward but which hold some financial, and often status, value. The more common forms of indirect pay include paid leave, deferred income plans (occupational retirement or pension plans), occupational sick pay, enhanced maternity and paternity leave, life insurance, company cars (or schemes for organisational contribution to car purchase), health club membership, childcare provision and extra annual leave. Evidently, some benefits are intended to enhance employee commitment and to address employees' well-being at work. CIPD (2013c) report that the most common employer-provided benefits (available to all employees) were paid bereavement leave, 25 or more days' paid leave, life assurance, training and career development opportunities, pension scheme and Christmas lunch/party.

Armstrong (2007) suggests that benefits can account for up to one-third of individual remuneration. The decision to provide benefits, rather than simply pay employees more, partly reflects the different roles that different elements of the reward mix play in recruiting, retaining and motivating employees. For example, high-quality pension schemes can engender long-term employee loyalty. Indeed, the provision of benefits allows employers to provide deferred remuneration alongside immediate financial reward.

Benefits also represent a key area where employers can differentiate themselves in order to attract and retain employees. For example, in the UK public sector employees such as teachers tend to be paid less than equivalently qualified employees of the private sector. However, good pension arrangements and longer-than-average holidays are often viewed as making up for this difference in basic pay. Therefore, employee benefits can be a means by which to match or exceed market practice. There can also be tax advantages associated with certain employee benefits, for example, childcare provision and relocation expenses (Armstrong, 2007).

Expectancy theories of motivation stress that reward can only motivate if it is valued by the recipient. For this reason, firms are increasingly using flexible benefit systems where individuals can create their own reward package to reflect their own individual needs by choosing from a 'menu' of benefits (hence, sometimes referred to as cafeteria benefits) (IDS, 2008b). CIPD (2013c) report that one-fifth of organisations responding to its reward management survey use flexible benefit schemes. As with wider reward strategies,

Baeten and Verwaeren (2012) highlight the importance for firms of ensuring such approaches are embedded in and driven by the firm's internal and external context. Box 8.8 provides an example of the system of flexible benefits employed at the technology firm, Samsung.

Further online reading This short article reports on a survey of reward and HR managers in Belgium and Netherlands regarding the prevalence and perceived outcomes of adopting flexible reward plans. It reinforces the importance of considering both the internal and external environment as part of a strategic alignment of reward management.

Baeten, X. and Verwaeren, B. (2012) Flexible rewards from a strategic perspective, *Compensation & Benefits Review*, 44 (1): 40–9.

NON-FINANCIAL REWARDS

Alongside financial rewards and benefits, non-financial rewards are an important part of the reward mix that can play an essential role in motivating employees, attending to their well-being and increasing employee commitment (Walsh and Taylor, 2007). According to Herzberg (1966), whilst financial rewards are purely hygiene factors, non-financial rewards address the basic psychological needs of

---

BOX 8.8
HRM IN PRACTICE

Samsung and flexible reward

In 2013, the global technology firm, Samsung, launched its flexible benefits scheme, 'Samsung Highlights', using an online portal to provide employees with more opportunity to actively shape their benefits package. The scheme gives employees a 'flex allowance' of £50 a month to spend on a wide range of benefits, including gym membership, dental insurance and private medical insurance. The scheme was introduced following an organisational review of its benefits package which found that whilst the firm was spending considerable money on benefits – not least through a fixed set of core benefits which varied only by grade – employees were not engaging with their benefits package, were unaware of their full package or were receiving benefits that they didn't consider valuable.

> We could have the best benefits in the world but if it is not what employees want, then it doesn't really matter. We have a diverse workforce so wanted to offer something they wanted, something that helps retain [staff] and gets them engaged and using their benefits. (VP of HR at Samsung, cited in Crawford, 2014)

Having sought employees' views about what benefits the company should offer and employed a third-party benefits consultancy to inform the creation of a competitive rewards package, Samsung has developed a more flexible approach to benefits that enables staff to see the value of their core benefits and, drawing on employee feedback, constantly reviews and updates the benefits on offer. For instance, in 2014, the organisation introduced new options including loans to purchase travel season tickets, personal accident insurance and a discount dining card.

Samsung also uses its benefits package to drive home key messages regarding employee well-being and to communicate the value of its employees to organisational success.

Sources: IDS, 2014; Crawford, 2014

employees and can unlock latent effort and engender greater organisational commitment. Armstrong (2007) suggests that non-financial rewards focus on the following factors: achievement, recognition, responsibility, influence and personal growth. Examples of non-financial rewards include:

- opportunities for personal and career development
- flexible working (such as home-working or flexitime)
- employee communication, involvement and participation
- pleasant working environment and well-considered job design
- good performance management practices and appraisals
- practices to recognise the contribution of employees (such as an 'employee of the month' award).

Consideration of non-financial rewards clearly demonstrates that reward in its totality is the concern of all elements of HRM and job design. Those job characteristics that have been linked to increased job satisfaction and motivation include variety, autonomy, positive feedback, as well as the overall meaningfulness and impact of work. In order to achieve such outcomes, managers have a range of options in the design of jobs, including job rotation, enlargement and enrichment, as outlined in Chapter 6. Box 8.9 outlines both the limits of material reward and the importance of recognition and praise in maintaining motivation over the longer run, suggesting that a holistic approach to worker motivation is needed in

---

BOX 8.9
RESEARCH INSIGHT

Irrationality and reward

In his book on irrationality, Sutherland (2007) suggests a number of counter-intuitive ideas about the way in which rewards and punishment tend to be misused. In particular, Sutherland stresses the problems associated with material reward. For example, experiments on both children and adults in a variety of different contexts emphatically show that a large reward has the effect of devaluing a pleasant task. This is explained by the fact that people perceive that tasks cannot be intrinsically interesting or pleasurable – or worth doing in their own right – if a large reward for undertaking that task is deemed necessary.

Sutherland suggests that whilst material rewards might be a useful way of getting people to do something in the short run, where tasks are intrinsically pleasurable people who are rewarded will engage in less of an activity after reward is withdrawn compared to people who have never been rewarded. This runs contrary to the often-held belief that if people are rewarded for some

activity, the desire to engage in it will eventually become automatic and they will be motivated to perform that activity even without reward. This has important implications for managers who might decide to offer one-off bonuses. Material reward can also have the effect of leading people who are pursuing a particular 'prize' (or an end-of-year bonus) to do less imaginative and flexible work compared to those of equal talent who are not.

Sutherland stresses, however, that praise functions in a different way from material rewards and does not have the undesirable effect of devaluing tasks. This is for two fundamental reasons. First, praise can be internalised – people derive satisfaction or 'praise themselves' for doing something well even in the absence of the praise of others. Second, praise is not finite – as is the case with material reward – and subsequently praise can always be offered. This suggests that managers need to create the conditions under which praise is routinely given to others and in which employees can derive intrinsic satisfaction from their work.

---

order to elicit high performance. The greater importance placed on recognition – alongside more sophisticated approaches to the use non-cash rewards – is reported to be increasingly important to staff motivation (Van Dyke and Ryan, 2013). These relatively 'cost-free' forms of employee reward constitute a particularly important dimension of total reward in times when firms are operating in difficult economic conditions where firms have to balance the needs for employee motivation and retention whilst containing costs (Hay Group, 2010).

TOTAL REWARD

In recognition of the importance of non-financial reward and the importance of adopting a more holistic and strategic approach to employee reward, some firms adopt 'total reward strategies'. The notion of 'total reward' acknowledges the value of a wide range of both tangible and intangible rewards to employees and seeks to ensure that the various components of reward on offer are complementary and compatible with the philosophy, values and culture of the firm in order to secure improved performance (Azasu, 2009). Whether addressing top performers (Zingheim and Schuster, 2005) or all employees, firms are increasingly providing workers with regular 'total reward statements' that detail the cash value of the totality of their pay and benefits package. This has the dual purpose of clearly communicating the investment that the firm has made in that individual over a given period and helping management to think about reward in a more strategic and holistic manner. However, total reward in many firms goes beyond the mere consideration of salary and non-salary remuneration to include a wide range of social, psychological and developmental benefits that might accrue from employment and the working environment.

As an example, Box 8.10 shows the model of total reward utilised at KPMG, the global professional services firm, to support their reward statement: 'to attract, develop, motivate and retain the best talent in the market, KPMG Europe is committed to a fair and flexible offering that sees us share our financial success through market-leading reward for market-leading performance'. The model clearly demonstrates how the firm conceptualises and seeks to communicate to employees that pay is only one element of the investment that it makes in its staff in exchange for their labour.

O'Neill (1995) suggests that the development of an effective total reward strategy requires a comprehensive assessment of internal business factors, outside environmental and market issues and an analysis of how the current reward components meet these internal and external demands. The CIPD reward management survey (CIPD, 2013c) reported that only 15 per cent of employers provide employees with total reward statements, but evidence suggests a fluctuating commitment to the principles of total reward in recent years, which the CIPD suggest may be partly explained by the fact that some employers may have abandoned a more strategic approach to reward in the current economic downturn. This is despite the view that even in difficult economic conditions firms have an imperative to shift from a 'extreme cost focus towards policies that more positively engage their employees and develop their talents' (2013c: 131) to drive growth.

The relatively limited take-up of total reward perhaps gives credence to Marchington and Wilkinson's (2005: 322) claim that the notion is 'more myth and hype than reality' and that management often tend to assess parts of the remuneration package in isolation and fail to evaluate their pay schemes in any real depth or against any clear criteria. Similarly, Kessler (2007) argues that the rhetoric suggesting that business strategy represents a primary concern in reward practice is

BOX 8.10
HRM IN PRACTICE

The total reward model at KPMG

Individual **growth**

- Investment in people
- Up-to-date skills
- Development
- Performance management
- Career enhancement

Total **pay**

- Base pay
- Variable pay
- Benefits
- Recognition

Compelling **future**

- Vision and values
- Growth and success
- Stakeholdership
- Image and reputation

Positive **workplace**

- People focus
- Leadership role models
- Challenging work
- Trust/empowerment
- Open communication

Source: Reprinted by kind permission of Incomes Data Research from IDS, 2008d

typically not reflected in reality and managers very often make changes to reward systems on the basis of short-term cost considerations and the need to respond to labour market pressures rather than any longer-term strategic concern.

Chen and Hsieh (2006) provide a useful summary (Table 8.1) of the principal changes in approaches to reward management over the last three decades that incorporates the notion of total reward. In particular, they stress that reward systems need now be considered as *multiplex*, that is, they are conceptualised so as to incorporate 'everything employees perceive to be of value resulting from the employment relationship' (Chen and Hsieh, 2006: 66). They argue that this multiplex approach, along with a great focus on coordination between elements of reward and wider organisational aims, employee contribution (or performance), intrinsic motivation and ongoing and 'personalised' reward mechanisms, constitutes the face of reward management in the twenty-first century. Despite rejecting the notion of total rewards as often implemented in a generic and inflexible manner, Brown (2014) similarly advocates a move towards 'smart rewards' that are clearly focused on core values and principles, that seek to actively engage staff, are transparent and which are subject to greater line management, transparency and open communication.

Further online reading This short discussion piece neatly summarises many of the trends associated with the shift towards more strategic and holistic approaches to reward management and design. It provides a useful piece to sit alongside the KPMG example provided earlier in the chapter.

Chen, H.-M. and Hsieh, Y.-H. (2006) Key trends of the total reward system in the 21st century, *Compensation & Benefits Review*, 38 (6): 64–70.

TABLE 8.1 *Key trends in reward management*

Dimensions of reward	From: 'Traditional' or 'old' pay systems	To: 'New' pay systems
Basis	Seniority	Contribution
Method	Simplex	Multiplex
Function	Extrinsic	Intrinsic
Frequency	Periodic	Instantaneous
Object	Unitary	Differential
Design	Independent	Coordinated

Source: adapted from Chen and Hsieh, 2006

Further online reading This short research article presents some key messages to arise from research exploring the role of line managers in reward management. They suggest that high-performing organisations involve line managers in the planning, design and implementation of reward systems and ensure that HR professional provide them with support to ensure their ongoing success.

Brown, D. and Purcell, J. (2007) Reward management: On the line, *Compensation & Benefits Review*, 39 (3): 28–34.

ISSUES IN REWARD MANAGEMENT

A central criticism of strategic approaches to reward management focuses on the assumption that it is possible to effectively 'match' business, HR and reward strategies. Such a top-down approach to forming reward strategy is deterministic in that it assumes that employee behaviour and performance will be directly and positively affected by the level and composition of reward to align it with that required to achieve organisational objectives. In other words, it assumes organisational unitarism. Indeed, reward is often presumed to direct employees to act in a way that they otherwise would not. As the discussion in Box 8.9 suggests, however, humans do not always respond to stimuli in ways that we might expect. Consequently, investment in complex reward systems can often be misplaced, especially considering the multiplicity of variables that shape the employment relationship and inhibit such a direct cause–effect relationship.

An associated problem is that reward is an area of HRM that is particularly sensitive to individual interpretation. As such, the meaning attached to reward by the employee might be considered more important than the reward itself and its intended meaning. In other words, it is not the perceived worth of the reward from an employer's perspective that is important but rather its extrinsic or intrinsic value to the receiving employee. This understanding sits neatly with the concept of the psychological contract in that it stresses the possibility that the intentions of management in providing a particular reward may be misinterpreted, leading to tension in the employment relationship. Reward systems based on flawed managerial assumptions about what employees value and

BOX 8.11
MANAGEMENT SKILLS AND ATTRIBUTES

Line managers and reward

Line managers play an increasing part in developing and implementing reward systems, particularly in the context of growing emphasis across job roles on variable performance-based pay. Under such systems, line managers are those within the firm who have to 'set and explain the standards of performance and behaviours required, clarify the aims of the scheme, make decisions about assessment, communicate the decision to staff and defend any judgments made between levels of performance' (Purcell and Hutchinson, 2007b: 8). Often, however, as discussed elsewhere, line managers are not well equipped to undertake appraisals effectively, either because of a lack of skills or requisite training or because of the challenges of having difficult conversations and making decisions that result in employee disappointment. Of course, it is also line managers who have to attempt to motivate workers who may have received less than they feel entitled to.

Line managers also have the most significant role to play in the delivery of non-financial reward, notably employee recognition, praise and positive feedback. Just as bad news can be difficult to deliver, some managers also struggle to deliver good news in the form of positive reinforcement. Understood in its widest sense, line managers also have a direct and indirect impact on employee reward through contributing

to the working environment, job design, providing opportunities for learning and development, flexible working practices and so on. Taken together, therefore, line managers have a significant influence on the total reward package available to their subordinates, over and above any formal or informal influence they may have on an employee's base pay at recruitment or subsequently.

It is clear, therefore, that possession of a range of interpersonal and managerial skills is crucial if line managers are to be effective in implementing a suitable reward strategy. These skills include negotiation, conflict resolution, providing feedback and managing expectations. Perhaps more importantly, line managers must demonstrate, and be seen to demonstrate, a commitment to fairness, transparency and equity in both the processes and outcomes of reward management.

Without these capabilities, confusion and contradictions can arise from a failure of line managers to implement reward systems effectively and a lack of effective communication regarding the content and aims of these systems. Brown and Purcell (2007) stress, therefore, the importance of involving line managers in the planning, design and implementation of reward systems and the importance of ongoing support from HR professionals to ensure the continued effectiveness of these systems.

the behavioural impact of particular kinds of rewards are therefore likely to be unsuccessful in supporting business objectives. As with the use of cafeteria benefits, employers are increasingly recognising both the subjectivity and complexity of reward and that, after a certain point, non-financial reward can be more important to people than financial remuneration. A further level of complexity is added when we consider the behavioural requirements of different groups of workers and that to be effective reward systems have to be adequately flexible to respond to a range of employee needs and expectations in order to elicit the full range of required behaviours.

Overall, Marchington and Wilkinson (2008) argue against employers jumping on the reward bandwagon and adopting the latest fad, recognising the continuing debate over the behavioural or performance consequences of different forms of reward and the viewpoint that there is no one-size-fits-all answer to reward management. Reward decisions should be made contingent on the firm's market and labour market conditions, associated technology and the attitudes prevalent among different groups of employees. For example, changes in the wider environment have placed a greater onus on firms to develop reward systems and practices to promote knowledge-sharing among employees (Swart and Kinnie, 2003). Marchington and Wilkinson also stress the importance of a continuous evaluation of pay systems to ensure that they meet business requirements in the face of changing technology, business objectives, organisational structures, work organisation and the supply and demand for labour.

SUMMARY POINTS

- An employee's reward package is typically comprised of three key elements: financial reward, non-financial reward and perks or benefits. The concept of 'total reward' emphasises the importance of all three elements to the reward mix.

- Reward performs a number of functions in the employment relationship. Remuneration expresses the perceived value of a worker to the organisation, constitutes a key factor in the development of the psychological contract, acts to shape employee behaviour and contributes to the development of organisational culture. Remuneration also constitutes a key point of conflict between management and workers.

- An organisation's reward strategy outlines the philosophy, principles and underpinning values that inform its reward system and the types of employee behaviours it wishes to promote. The reward system constitutes its pay structures, processes for job evaluation, the types of

- reward on offer and the schemes for the allocation of reward.

- A strategic approach to reward management requires both the vertical and horizontal integration of reward processes and practices and effective communication of the purpose and aims of reward and how they connect with organisational objectives.

- The design of reward systems needs to consider issues of fairness, effectiveness in promoting desired behaviour and value-for-money.

- A contingent approach to reward management is necessary to reflect the strategic, labour market, political, social, economic and legislative factors that act to shape the viability and acceptability of reward in context.

- Decisions regarding the use of contingent reward need to be made in the light of wider performance management systems and the desired behavioural outcomes to be achieved through the use of variable pay.

SELF-TEST QUESTIONS

1 What forms of non-financial reward might contribute to increased employee commitment and loyalty to the organisation?

2 Provide two examples of how pay can be used to promote specific types of behaviour.

3 What do you understand by the term 'total reward'? How can you explain the recent growth in the adoption of total reward strategies?

4 What are the main contextual factors that influence organisational decision-making about reward?

5 Why have some organisations adopted a 'cafeteria' system of employee benefits, allowing employees to construct their own benefits package?

6 What do you understand by the terms 'internal equity' and 'external equity'?

7 What are the principal methods used for determining base pay? What are the problems associated with each approach?

8 Explain how individual PRP might lead to the development of undesirable employee behaviours or inhibit the expression of desirable behaviours.

9 How do gain-sharing and profit-sharing differ?

10 For non-managerial employees, why might linking an element of remuneration to organisational performance not be effective in engendering greater work effort and organisational commitment?

TEST YOURSELF

TEST YOURSELF

Want to know more about this chapter? Review what you have been learning by visiting:
https://edge.sagepub.com/wilton3e

- Print out or download the chapter summaries for quick revision
- Test yourself with multiple-choice questions
- Revise key terms with interactive flashcards

CASE STUDY

Reward management at Shearwater Ltd

Shearwater Ltd designs and manufactures a range of electronic and electro-mechanical sub-systems for the aerospace and defence industry. It is located in south-west England, an area with a strong defence tradition. Shearwater is a manufacturing division of the Wilco Group, an American conglomerate mainly involved in the manufacturing of automobile components, which acquired the company in 2003. Shearwater employs 120 staff, of which approximately half are skilled and semi-skilled staff directly involved in the manufacturing process, 20 are engineers and the remainder are spread across various business functions including sales, finance and procurement. Since the company was acquired by Wilco it has reduced its workforce by approximately 40 per cent – mainly through voluntary redundancy and the non-renewal of fixed-term contracts – in response to perceived overcapacity and reduced demand for its products due to increasing overseas competition. Shearwater has also responded to these pressures by explicitly pursuing a high-quality business strategy as a means of market positioning, in contrast to many of its competitors that tend to focus on cost, and has rationalised its product range to focus on core technologies and areas of expertise.

Despite the success of these changes and relatively healthy company performance over the last two financial years, Wilco continues to exert pressure on Shearwater for greater cost savings and efficiency. These demands have partly been blamed for high levels of labour turnover among senior management at Shearwater. In particular, in the last six years the company has had three managing directors. The current managing director has been in the post for only three months and was transferred from another Wilco company in the USA. In contrast, many workers, particularly on the manufacturing side of the business, have been with the company for some time. The average length of service is eight years but many employees have been with the company for considerably longer. A recent staff attitude survey found that whilst many employees remain committed to the firm (and, importantly, the work they do and the sector they work in) and are proud to tell people that they work for Shearwater, employee morale is low and intention to quit unusually high. The turnover of senior management, further threat of redundancy and what is seen as 'meddling' from its parent company are all cited as reasons why employees report having limited faith in the long-term viability of the firm.

The new managing director has, however, spent the first few months at Shearwater considering how the firm might make further cost-savings and having reviewed business and production processes has decided that labour costs is an area that requires 'trimming'. He has, however, reassured staff that, given a relatively healthy order book over the short to medium term, redundancies are not on the table. Currently, pay arrangements for all staff are established via periodic management review following brief consultation with the company council that is made up of union and non-union representatives from across the workforce. Ultimately, it is management who decide on pay arrangements. Current arrangements reflect long-existing traditions in the company. Manufacturing staff are paid a basic pay rate, periodically upgraded to reflect inflation (although this is not done by automatic review and tends to be done at the whim of management) alongside shift premiums and modest overtime payments which staff view as a means by which to top-up their basic pay.

Task

The new managing director has decided that a new approach to reward is necessary and has asked you to advise him on developing a new reward strategy for the firm. In particular, he has asked you to provide answers to the following questions:

1 What are the business objectives that need to be reflected in the new reward strategy? What desirable behaviours should the strategy seek to reinforce? Are there any undesirable behaviours that the strategy might seek to eradicate?

2 How might performance-related pay be an effective way of 'trimming' the labour costs in relation to overall company performance?

3 What might be the benefits of consulting staff over ways in which to reduce labour costs?

4 Consider the following forms of performance-related pay and consider their applicability to the different groups of workers at Shearwater: skills-based pay; individual- or team-based performance-related pay; incentive bonuses; and profit-sharing. What are the benefits and weaknesses associated with these forms of contingent pay?

USEFUL READING

Journal articles

Kohn, A. (1993) Why incentive plans cannot work, *Harvard Business Review*, 71 (5): 54–63.

This short, thought-provoking article discusses problems with the use of incentives, particularly in relation to their ability to bring about long-term changes to worker behaviour and motivation.

Ledford, G. E. Jr. (2014) The changing landscape of employee rewards: Observations and prescriptions, *Organizational Dynamics*, 43: 168–79.

This article provides an extremely useful summary of the key trends in employee reward over the past 35 years and considers the drivers for this change both internal and external to the firm. Whilst the article's focus is on the US, it has wider resonance across nations.

Books, book chapters and reports

CIPD (2013) *Reward Management Annual Survey Report 2013*, London: Chartered Institute of Personnel and Development.

This or any subsequent CIPD annual survey on reward management provides a snapshot of contemporary trends in remuneration practice. It provides a useful backdrop by which to assess the extent to which reward is employed in a strategic manner.

Kessler, I. (2007) Reward choices: Strategy and equity, in J. Storey (ed.), *Human Resource Management: A Critical Text* (3rd edn), London: Thomson Learning.

This book chapter presents a discussion of recent changes in remuneration practice in the light of a perceived shift away from a concern for equity in pay systems and structures towards an emphasis on contribution to business strategy.

FURTHER ONLINE READING

The following articles can be accessed for free on the book's companion website **https://edge.sagepub.com/wilton3e**:

Baeten, X. and Verwaeren, B. (2012) Flexible rewards from a strategic perspective, *Compensation & Benefits Review*, 44 (1): 40–9.

Brown, D. and Purcell, J. (2007) Reward management: On the line, *Compensation & Benefits Review*, 39 (3): 28–34.

Chen, H.-M. and Hsieh, Y.-H. (2006) Key trends of the total reward system in the 21st century, *Compensation & Benefits Review*, 38 (6): 64–70.

Howard, L. W. and Dougherty, T. W. (2004) Alternative reward strategies and employee reactions, *Compensation & Benefits Review*, 36 (1): 41–51.

Want to know more about this chapter? Visit the companion website at: **https://edge.sagepub.com/wilton3e** to access practice questions, videos and selected journal articles to further enhance your study.

HUMAN RESOURCE DEVELOPMENT

INTRODUCTION

Human resource development (HRD) is concerned with both individual and collective learning and, as a distinct area of HRM, encompasses the constantly evolving practices and processes that act to develop the skills, knowledge, behaviours and attitudes of an organisation's human resources required for effective job performance both now and in the future. A number of factors have contributed to the increasing attention paid to HRD in contemporary work organisations. This greater focus is partly based on the perception that encouraging workers to continuously enhance their skills and knowledge, and to foster creativity and innovation, are crucial contributors to competitive advantage in a knowledge economy (Thompson, 2004). It also reflects the view that continuous learning represents a key strategy for coping with uncertainty and the importance of employee and organisational adaptability and responsiveness to an evolving business environment (Ruona et al., 2003). In other words, an organisation's ability to learn and adapt faster than its rivals represents a key source of sustained competitive advantage.

The growing emphasis on workplace learning also reflects the changes in the worker experience of work and employment. Gruman and Saks (2011) suggest that many contemporary developments in both the nature and context of work (as outlined in Chapter 4), such as the often multifaceted nature of modern jobs and the importance of emotional intelligence, creativity, adaptability, proactivity and autonomy (van der Veen, 2006; Waples and Friedrich, 2011), require not so much the 'management' of worker performance, rather its 'facilitation' by creating the conditions for individual, and thereby organisational, performance to improve. As such, HRD holds a critical position within many work organisations by seeking to ensure that employees are properly equipped with not only the skill required to do a particular job, but also the attributes and behaviours that are a precursor for individual and organisational success.

The greater job insecurity and flexibility of employment experienced by many workers in the contemporary labour market have also increased pressure on employers to provide the means by which employees can develop their employability as part of an increasingly transactional employment relationship. In addition, the greater focus on continuous or lifelong learning and workforce upskilling in national economic strategies (for example, Confederation of British Industry, 2009) to create more competitive domestic economies and the increased focus on individual self-reliance for career development increasingly stresses the importance of continuing professional development (CPD).

The chapter begins by defining HRD, considers in more detail the specific drivers of HRD in practice and then considers the relationship between organisational strategy, HRD and individual and organisational learning. It then looks at HRD in practice, discussing specific practices and contemporary approaches to individual and organisational learning, including an exploration of the role of new technology in HRD. Finally, the chapter discusses the growth in emphasis on both management development and CPD.

DEFINING HUMAN RESOURCE DEVELOPMENT

Before discussing the substantive content of workplace HRD and its potential contribution to individual and organisational performance, it is important to define a number of key terms. A useful starting point for appreciating the role of HRD in contemporary organisations and its importance to individuals and wider society is the suggestion by Swanson and Holton (2001: 145–6) that HRD reflects 'a strong belief in learning and development as avenues to individual growth; a belief that organisations can be improved through learning and development activities; a commitment to people and human potential; [and] a deep desire to see people grow as individuals and a passion for learning' (2001: 145–6). Gold et al. (2009) suggest that the term HRD emerged in common usage in the US sometime in the 1970s and attribute the first specific formulation to Nadler (1970) who defined HRD as 'organized learning experiences provided by employers, within a specified period of time, to bring about the possibility of performance improvement and/or personal growth' (quoted in Nadler and Nadler, 1989: 4). Since then, alternative definitions have been put forward, whether broadening or narrowing the concerns of HRD or reflecting a specific ideological or practical position. An encompassing definition of HRD is provided by Harrison and Kessels (2004: 89) who suggest that

HRD 'comprises the skillful planning and facilitation of a variety of formal and informal learning and knowledge processes and experiences, primarily but not exclusively in the workplace, in order that organisational progress and individual potential can be enhanced through the competence, adaptability, commitment and knowledge-creating activities of all who work for the organisation' (Harrison and Kessels, 2004: 89). Overall, therefore, HRD represents the contemporary umbrella term used to denote the activities associated with people development, encompassing a wide range of formal and informal activities, both internal and external to work organisations, that is the concern of a wide range of stakeholders, including employers, governments, society and workers themselves.

Training, learning and development

Traditionally, the requirement for employees to learn new skills or acquire new knowledge has been dealt with through workplace training or education. Training is defined by Armstrong (2006: 535) as: 'planned and systematic modification of behaviour through learning events, programmes and instructions that enable individuals to achieve the levels of knowledge, skill and competence needed to carry out their work effectively'. As such, training tends to denote learning by instruction, for example, through demonstration, guided practice or coaching, in a particular skill or practice. Training is intended to result in changed behaviour in the workplace leading to improved individual performance to meet the needs of an organisation at a particular point in time. Given many of the recent changes to organisational context and the changing nature of work and employment, however, an organisational focus on formal training and education tends now to be considered too narrow and reflective of only one of many means by which individuals develop in the workplace and beyond. This perspective has led to a shift in emphasis from training to learning and development and from the inputs of worker improvement (training) to the outputs (learning).

Training has typically been associated with a 'deficit model' where provision is used to fill gaps in capability. Learning, by contrast, is more likely to be associated with the more proactive development of employee capacity and fostering organisational agility in dealing with future challenges. If we consider development as 'the growth or realisation of a person's ability and potential through the provision of learning and educational experiences' (Armstrong, 2006: 535), it is clear that this can occur in many ways other than formal training (Poell et al., 2004). Therefore, to encapsulate all the means through which employee development can occur, including training and education, the use of the terms 'learning' and 'development' reflects an acknowledgement of the wide range of formal and informal mechanisms that contribute to the enhancement of an individual's portfolio of skills, knowledge and competencies and behaviours (Sloman, 2005) and, collectively, that of the employing organisation. This increased recognition of the importance of learning in all its forms to organisational success has led to a contemporary focus on creating contexts that foster learning and self-development – 'learning environments' or 'learning climates' – both through formal and planned activities and informal, accidental or incidental processes and activities. In particular, there is greater recognition of the value of learning through everyday activities and interactions at work through mimetic processes of observation, imitation and action (Billett, 2014). It is also reflective of the recognition of the fact that job performance in the twenty-first century, particularly among knowledge or professional occupations, is a product of more than the possession of specific skills that can be acquired through content-driven training and education, but also a range of competencies critical to performance, whether behaviours, attitudes or a particular mindset, that are often best developed by immersion within jobs, groups and context. In other words, there has been an increased recognition of the role of learning by doing, learning from colleagues and learning from mistakes, as well as acknowledgement of the diversity of individual learning styles that has precipitated a movement away from a 'one-size-fits-all' approach to employee development.

Further online reading This article provides an interesting and comprehensive discussion of the processes of learning through work and interactions and of the concept of mimesis through which learning takes place through a process observation, imitation and action. It concludes with some implications of mimesis for HRD in practice.

Billett, S. (2014) Mimesis: Learning through everyday activities and interactions at work, *Human Resource Development Review*, 13 (4): 462–82.

BOX 9.1
HRM IN PRACTICE

Learning and development at PwC

The business consultancy firm, PwC, employs a range of approaches to developing their staff in order to fulfil the objective of 'helping people be the best they can be'. In response to development plans devised by individuals, their line managers and specialist people managers and that derive from the process of performance review, PwC employs both formal and informal learning:

- *formal learning* including classroom-based programmes, e-learning and technical education to achieve professional qualifications
- *informal learning* incorporating both 'learning from others' through coaching and mentoring and 'learning by doing' in order to help employees gain the 'right experiences at the right time'.

A critical dimension of this broad trend is the evolving notion of responsibility for employee development. Within the context of training, employee development is largely the responsibility of the organisation, for example, in identifying training needs, often those of the organisation itself, and designing, delivering or identifying appropriate training courses or programmes to meet those needs. The shift towards an emphasis on learning has, however, been commensurate with the growing expectation that employees will take more responsibility for their own learning, not only for the benefit of the organisation but also themselves, whether in respect of maximising their employability beyond their current employer or increasing the likelihood of progression and development within it. Hence, the notions of lifelong learning, continuous professional development and career self-management are critical dimensions of developing 'career consciousness' (van den Berg et al., 2006) among employees. However, whilst employees have no doubt been tasked ever more greatly with taking both ownership and responsibility for their own learning and development, managers and HRD specialist still play a critical role, both in helping and encouraging employees to understand how they learn and how they can learn differently and also providing the organisational infrastructure in which employees can manifest their potential.

Further online reading This short editorial places HRD in its broad historical context and outlines its emergence in the 1970s. The article also discusses the future of HRD.

van der Veen, R. (2006) Human resource development: Irreversible trend or temporary fad?, *Human Resource Development Review*, 5 (1): 3–7.

Personal development and the workplace

People Management (2012: 52), in an article on ways to reward staff without giving them a pay rise, report that a London-based digital solutions agency rewards its employees by offering to pay for some 'welcome relief' from work – an opportunity to try something new. Each year staff can claim £1,500 towards the cost of a developmental activity with only two stipulations: it must be nothing to do with work and it must provide them with a skill. *People*

Management reports that this fund has been drawn upon by employees 'to take up photography, try sea kayaking, literature appreciation and even advanced trapeze lessons'.

Discussion question

Firms rarely do things without a consideration for the bottom line and improving both individual and organisational performance. From a developmental perspective, what benefits might accrue to the firm of employing this means of rewarding staff?

WHY INVEST IN HRD?

The benefits of learning and development can be understood at three levels: the individual, organisational and societal. McGuire (2010) suggests that 'HRD has evolved as a field of theory and practice with a distinctive tripartite agenda of human betterment, organisational enhancement and societal development' and, as such, can be understood as concerned with the processes by which people develop the capacities to enable full economic, political and cultural participation in society (see also, Horwitz et al., 1996; McLean and McLean, 2001; Kim, 2012). As an example of this 'tripartite agenda' in practice, the *Financial Times* (2012c) reports how, in a period of high levels of youth unemployment across many Western economies, 'businesses have an important role to play in helping young people acquire the skills that can prevent them becoming a lost generation' through the improved provision of apprenticeships as a means by which to reduce barriers to employment for young workers, develop future workforce capability as well as contribute to the greater social good.

HRD AT HANSEN GROUP

For the individual, the benefits of training and development include the acquisition of new or updated skills and knowledge, enhanced employability, greater value to their current and future employers, improved job security and possible increases in reward. Moreover, learning – whether undertaken for work or non-work reasons – is consistently shown to have a positive impact on employment outcomes, particularly in terms of lowered potential for unemployment and higher earnings.

At the level of society and national economy, despite the complexity of assessing the impact of learning on economic competitiveness, governments consistently stress the importance of education and training for both social and economic well-being. In the UK, for example, the policy of successive governments over the last three decades has stressed the importance of widening participation in higher education, both to eradicate social disadvantage and to ensure national competitiveness in the global economy (Wilton, 2008).

At the level of the organisation, the benefits of learning, training and development might include a range of positive HR outcomes, such as the improved quality of employed labour, reduced labour turnover, the reinforcement of organisational culture (particularly among new recruits), enhanced employee commitment, the facilitation of change, increased skills flexibility and improved standing as an employer to potential employees. Investment in learning and development might also have a wider impact on employee behaviour beyond that directly shaped by the training intervention. Individual L&D will often be viewed by the employee as recognition of their value to the employer and of future potential. L&D can, therefore, contribute to a positive psychological contract, increased job satisfaction and greater levels of 'emotional' employee commitment (Lee and Bruvold, 2003). Conversely, a failure to invest in staff and provide the means for career development is likely to lead to lowered levels of positive employee behaviours and, potentially, employee exit. To understand the value of HRD, it is also important to appreciate how learning can be understood at the level of the organisation as a whole. Work organisations are 'path dependent' in that each organisation develops in its own unique way and in doing so learns from its successes and

---

BOX 9.3
GLOBAL INSIGHT

Learning and development across cultures

Just as alternative perspectives on HRD are evident between that which reflects a US-centric focus on performance and the more European concern for individual development (see Chapter 1 for the background to this distinction in perspectives on HRM), definitions of HRD can vary from one country to another. In the context of these national cultural differences, employee learning and development presents a challenging set of complexities. National culture influences the relative appropriateness of different learning methods, whether the employer or employee should take responsibility for training, what constitutes appropriate sources of wisdom, the relationship between teacher and pupil, and favoured learning styles. For example, some Eastern cultures tend to advocate structured, instructive forms of training and passive learning. This reflects the view of the teacher as a source of unchallenged wisdom. Alternatively, many Western cultures tend to emphasise education and training through facilitative, investigative techniques, teacher and peer interaction, active learning and debate.

National institutional context also influences approaches to training and development adopted in domestic employers, for example, reflecting the level of government intervention in economic and social policy. At a basic level, governments might tend towards a voluntarist approach to ensuring an adequate supply of required skills to the labour market (characterised by a reliance on market forces and work organisations for workforce development) or an interventionist approach (the state seeks to influence workplace training to benefit the economy as a whole, for example, through grants for training investment in a particular area). Home country cultural and institutional influences can also shape management practice in MNC subsidiaries overseas (Collings, 2003) through the transfer of HRD traditions.

Overall, national context shapes individual and organisational attitudes towards employee development and determines the relative degree of adoption and effectiveness of particular forms of training. For example, CIPD (2011c) report that in terms of the adoption of Web 2.0 technology for learning there is variation by country that might be reflective of cultural norms and institutional developments. For instance, the use of webinars and virtual classrooms is reported as significantly higher among US firms and the use of blended learning programmes was more prominent among UK organisations. The greater use of newer learning technologies, such as mobile applications, in India, however, perhaps reflects the 'emergent national hunger for technology' and 'their ability to leap over some of the stages of technology-based learning – and perhaps the embeddedness and commitment to other approaches in the UK and US' (2011c: 4).

failures and through the processes of growth, expansion, development, restructuring and change. It's a well-worn adage that those who do not understand the past are destined to repeat it and, therefore, those organisations that learn faster than their rivals, and use this learning to avoid the mistakes of the past or consolidate or repeat the successes, are likely to gain competitive advantage in doing so.

Reflecting a performance perspective on HRD, the ultimate aim of organisational investment in HRD is to improve productivity, efficiency and profitability through, for example, the enhancement of quality, creativity or innovation. Chapter 3, however, discussed in detail the difficulties in providing evidence that demonstrates the link between HRM and organisational performance. A similar set of problems exists in establishing a measurable link between HRD activity and organisational performance (Machin and Vignoles, 2001) that goes beyond a qualitative connection between, for example, investment in HRD and improved employee commitment. One particular problem relates to establishing the direction of causality between HRD and improved performance. Is it the case that higher-performing organisations spend more on HRD activities, or do high levels of HRD investment result in better performance?

Even where there is an acceptance of the HR and business benefits of investment in HRD, these benefits need to be offset against the cost of this investment. The cost of learning activities varies significantly depending on their form, purpose and scope but might include the cost of training equipment, the payroll costs of internal or external specialists, the costs of developing training materials, travel and accommodation costs, and the cost associated with the hours of work lost by those participating in training. These costs can be assessed either as absolute (for example, on the basis of affordability) or relative to competitors or firms operating in the same labour market through a process of benchmarking. When assessing the costs and benefits of HRD, account also needs to be taken of

---

BOX 9.4
RESEARCH INSIGHT

Investment in training and recession

Felstead et al. (2012) provide an interesting and perhaps counter-intuitive assessment of a range of contextual factors and their collective influence on investment in training among UK firms. Within the context of the 2008–9 recession, the authors report that, despite the severity of the recession and the expected impact on training budgets as firms look to cut costs among 'soft targets', the interplay of both current and anticipated performance demands, such as meeting operational needs, countering skills shortages and satisfying customer demands, and wider contextual considerations (such as the imperative to comply with legal requirements and those of professional bodies) resulted in firms being compelled to sustain training investment during the recession.

In the context of the assessment of training needs, these findings highlight the importance of the consideration of both market and wider organisational context in the assessment of training need and that firms do not, even in a relatively deregulated training market, have a 'free hand' to focus only on an assessment of internal need as the basis for investment in training. However, the research also suggests that firms sought new ways to maintain their training coverage in the context of a desire to reduce costs or, as they put it, 'train smarter' through, for instance, leveraging existing capabilities to enhance learning. Despite this survey, successive surveys by XpertHR find that HRD budgets remain broadly tied to economic conditions, with the 2014 survey reporting an overall increasing in spending per firm as a result of improving economic conditions (Wolff, 2014).

the costs of *not* training (Marchington and Wilkinson, 2008) as well as the costs of providing unnecessary training and the impact on motivation of employees unable to practise newly acquired skills in their jobs. The challenges of evaluating the impact and return on HRD investment provide one explanation for why HRD budgets are often cut where firms experience challenging economic conditions (IRS, 2009) despite widespread acceptance of the importance of employee development for ensuring competiveness. However, as discussed in Box 9.4 such a fall in investment cannot be taken for granted.

Further online reading This article presents research findings that, despite a deregulated training market in the UK, a range of data sources shows that the impact of the recent recession on training participation and budgets was minimal. The authors conclude that employers in the UK do not have a completely free hand in making decisions about investment in training and that a combination of market intervention and business requirements obliged most of them to sustain training despite difficult conditions.

Felstead, A., Green, F. and Jewson, N. (2012) An analysis of the impact of the 2008–9 recession on the provision of training in the UK, *Work, Employment & Society*, 26 (6): 968–86.

DRIVERS OF HRD ACTIVITY

Table 9.1 outlines a range of internal and external drivers that might compel organisational investment in learning and development (although it is by no means exhaustive). In the internal environment, firms might be required to retrain existing employees to fill vacancies or in preparation for succession, for individual or collective performance improvement or as a response to the HRP process. Alternatively, training might be required to facilitate organisational change. In the external environment, technological, legislative or market changes may lead to skills deficiencies. For example, changes to employment legislation, such as that governing equal opportunities, would likely require

TABLE 9.1   *Drivers of investment in HRD*

Internal drivers	External drivers
(Changing) internal labour market context: replacement, succession and requirements derived from HR planning process	(Changing) external labour market context: for example, skills supply, level of employment and education
(Changes to) internal systems, management and roles relating to training	National/international legislation and/or codes of practice
Developing or strengthening core and functional competence	Accreditation criteria: for example, for membership of professional bodies
(Changing) organisational strategy, mission, plan or culture and values	Developments in technology or business processes
Employee career and personal development needs (often derived from performance management process)	Market factors: for example, needs resulting from benchmarking HRD practices against competitors
Capacity for organisational flexibility	Wider economic, political and social factors

those managers involved in employee selection to undergo awareness training. Where firms have a degree of latitude in how to respond to external pressures, whether to and how to do so are dependent on a range of factors. These include the level of integration of HRD with organisational and wider HR strategy, the presence of HRD specialists and the extent of their influence on organisational decision-making, the culture of the firm and the extent to which line managers accept responsibility for learning and development.

Two notable considerations arise in determining organisational responses to an imperative for investment in HRD. First, how to prioritise competing demands for investment from multiple drivers of HRD. Second, ensuring that the organisational response is not based purely on past behaviour and the potential to innovate is considered. For example, HRD is not necessarily the solution to perceived under-performance and alternative responses (for example, the redesign of jobs, internal redeployment, recruitment from the external labour market or the re-evaluation of the wider conditions under which employees work) might yield more effective results.

BUSINESS STRATEGY AND HUMAN RESOURCE DEVELOPMENT

Employee learning, development and training represent central elements in models of high performance or high-commitment HRM. In such models, continuous learning through formal and informal means represents key levers by which to achieve greater employee commitment, flexibility and product or service quality. Best practice models of HRM tend to emphasise a complementary focus on both 'make' and 'buy' approaches to employee resourcing: developing internal capacity through HRD and the creation of a strong internal labour market, alongside effective recruitment and selection strategies and practices. Reflecting this dual emphasis, it is important for firms to recruit employees as much on the basis of acquired skills, knowledge and experience as for their ability to have learnt from those experiences and their potential to develop new competencies.

HRD AND
ORGANISATIONAL
NEEDS

Garavan (2007: 25) defines strategic HRD as 'a coherent, vertically aligned and horizontally integrated set of learning and development activities'. Therefore, as well as being complementary with other aspects of HRM, such as performance management and reward, HRD should have 'vertical fit' with organisational strategy and objectives. More broadly, McCracken and Wallace (2000), developing a model put forward by Garavan (1991), suggest there are a number of features of a strategic approach to HRD:

- top management leadership
- HRD shapes organisational mission and goals
- environmental scanning by senior management in HRD terms
- (development of) HRD strategies, policies and plans
- strategic partnership with line management and wider HRM
- trainers as organisational change consultants
- ability to influence corporate culture
- emphasis on cost-effectiveness evaluation.

These characteristics of strategic human resource development (SHRD) can clearly be read as a checklist for the effective enactment of a strategic approach. For instance, without the buy-in and commitment of both senior management and line managers to such an approach it is destined to be ineffective in meeting its objectives. Similarly, without detailed appreciation and on-going consideration of the internal and external context of the firm then the development of HRD strategy, plans and practices is likely to be lacking in fitness for purpose.

Of course, not all firms conform to these standards of SHRD and, arguably, in some firms the costs of such an approach may not be commensurate with the benefits. SHRD would seem to have particular relevance to organisations in which the production and sharing of new knowledge are central to competitiveness and where learning is critical to organisational renewal. McCracken and Wallace (2000) distinguish between degrees of strategic maturity in organisational approaches to employee development. At one end of the continuum, a low level of strategic maturity – labelled as, simply, 'training' – reflects little or no integration of HRD activity with organisational mission and strategic objectives and no culture of learning. HRD reflects a more systematic approach to employee development but one that is largely determined by corporate strategy. Finally, an SHRD approach reflects a bilateral relationship between employee development and corporate strategy where each influences the other and learning processes are embedded in all organisational activities, both strategic and operational, reflecting a learning-oriented culture. In this latter category, for line managers, activities associated with supporting and enabling learning are not peripheral add-ons to their roles, but central and indistinguishable from other responsibilities.

Organisational learning and emergent strategy

The manner in which an organisation responds to internal and external drivers for investment in HRD partly reflects the strategy-making process discussed in Chapter 3. Under the classical approach to strategy formation, organisational strengths and weaknesses would be evaluated in the light of environmental pressures or opportunities and the resulting HRD strategy would seek to bridge the gap between the perceived current and desired-for position. This clearly places HRD as subservient to organisational strategy formation. In other words, in the context of environmental influences, HRD is responsive to predefined organisational strategy and the skills, knowledge and behaviours identified as necessary for its implementation. As such it is reflective of the best fit model of HRM. Some commentators have argued, however, that organisational learning can and should have a more proactive influence on organisational strategy. Chapter 3 discussed how certain models of strategic HRM reflect a more bi-directional relationship between HR and organisational strategies and how strategy-making can be an emergent, bottom-up phenomena. Reflecting this perspective, Mintzberg (1987) suggests that rather than taking its cue from environmental pressures, strategies can also develop from the emergent learning of organisational members, reflecting insights gained from close interaction with organisational processes, people and customers that lead to the acquisition and development of new and valuable knowledge. The combination of external (environmental) and internal (learning) influences on strategy or practice can lead to the creation of a more effective and sustainable strategy that can respond quickly to change or new challenges and avoid the mistakes of the past. López et al. (2005), for example, found that improved organisational learning was an important mediating factor through which high performance human resource practices can have a positive effect on business performance.

According to the resource-based view of the firm, firms can develop competitive advantage through an ability to learn and adapt faster than their rivals and, therefore, the interaction between individual and organisational learning can be a primary source of organisational agility, particularly in turbulent product markets or where technology develops rapidly. RBV suggests that both organisational processes and human capital have the potential to be a source of competitive edge. Therefore, both the informal and formal means through which employees learn and develop and the outcome of these development processes, such as knowledge, skills, behaviours or competencies, are vital organisational assets. Indeed, it is often the informal mechanisms for individual and organisational development that meet the VRIO criteria for sustained competitive advantage.

One important dimension of a strategic approach to HRD is the creation of a learning climate or culture that both encourages and supports employee development, particularly through informal and self-directed learning, and encourages all employees to commit to continuous learning (Dalton, 2010). Fuller and Unwin (2003) suggest that such an expansive learning environment exists where employees have ready access to learning and opportunities for progression, where skills and knowledge are valued and managers act as facilitators of development. This resonates with the notion of the learning organisation associated with the development of practices and processes to enable individual and group learning to benefit the entire organisation, through their contribution to continuous performance improvement and cultural renewal. In the context of either transformational or incremental organisation change, only where individual learning is shared and drawn upon collectively to do things differently can firms move forward. This notion of the learning organisation, creation of 'learning space' and concern for both social and human capital has particular resonance with the management of organisational knowledge discussed in Chapter 15.

Central to the learning organisation concept is employee empowerment to take responsibility for their own learning, facilitated and supported by HR specialists, line managers and the organisational provision of opportunities for self-development. In other words, a learning organisation is that in which the organisation's learning goals are reconciled with individual learning needs (Nyhan et al., 2004) and one that facilitates the learning of its members as a means of continuous organisational transformation and renewal (Pedler et al., 1991). Garavan (1997) notes, however, that the learning organisation tends to represent an 'ideal type' rather than an organisational reality. Nonetheless, ideas and practices associated with the learning organisation such as a clear connection between learning and competitive advantage, systematising and leveraging informal or accidental learning, knowledge-sharing, creation of a culture or climate of sustained learning (Senge, 2006) and a concern for pan-organisational and cross-disciplinary collaboration tend to be seen as increasingly critical to organisational success.

....

Further online reading This article reviews the literature on strategic human resource development and proposes a model of SHRD focusing on the interactions between internal and external organisational context, HRD processes, stakeholder satisfaction and the characteristics of HRD professionals.

Garavan, T. N. (2007) A strategic perspective on human resource development, *Advances in Developing Human Resources*, 9 (1): 11–30.

....

The importance of collective, informal learning and culture to organisational success lies at the heart of organisational learning and the idea that organisations can be understood as an accumulation of the collective and individual learning – and the patterns and processes that facilitate such learning – that both enables an organisation to develop and can be a source of competitive advantage. The notion that an organisation can learn through the acquisition of the learning of its members is, however, contentious. One way in which this might happen is through formal and informal mechanisms to facilitate and encourage the creation and sharing of knowledge among organisational actors. Organisational learning requires, therefore, employees to become more reflective and to reject 'habits of thought' (Argyris and Schon, 1978), entrenched ways of thinking developed by individuals through organisational socialisation, in order to better recognise and accept change and to increase receptivity to new ideas and ways of working. Therefore, a central focus of organisational learning is on changing the way in which individuals think about the organisation and make sense of their circumstances, including the challenges and problems they are faced with and opportunities that present themselves. Effective learning requires an appreciation both of this context and the established paradigms or theories that have been socially constructed within the organisation through the process of collective sense-making, both to reflect on their ongoing appropriateness and relevance and to allow experimentation with new alternative theories. Consequently, Yanow (2000) suggests that organisational learning should be viewed as a cultural phenomenon, in that the collective learning of a firm is embedded in the values, beliefs, meanings, language, practices and norms of behaviour that are shared among organisational members and develop over time. Again, this stresses the importance of drawing on learning at all levels of the organisation to inform strategic decision-making.

At the level of the workgroup, the notion of 'communities of practice' is important to understanding how organisational learning can function in reality. A community of practice (Brown and Duguid, 1991; Lave and Wenger, 1991) is 'a naturally occurring and evolving collection of people who together engage in particular kinds of activity, and who come to develop and share ways of doing things – ways of talking, beliefs, values, and practices – as a result of their joint involvement in that activity' (Galagan, 1993: 33). This process of collectively making sense of their working environment through collaboration and the sharing of knowledge, understanding, experiences and 'good practice' enables the development among this group of the most effective ways of being, learning and working that become taken-for-granted over time. Therefore, learning arises and is shared spontaneously within a culture in which individuals are empowered to improvise, experiment and take responsibility for learning in ways that challenge the existing norms of behaviour. The conflict that arises within teams or communities of practice can, therefore, become a key source of learning. Overall, a central tenet of organisational learning is that learning becomes a part of work, rather than an adjunct to it.

A key criticism of the learning organisation concept is that it is underpinned by an assumption of organisational unitarism: that individual learning is consistent with that which is of benefit to the wider firm and that the inevitable conflict and power dynamics that form part of all work organisations are not an absolute bar to knowledge-sharing. In particular, in organisations where trust in management is low and an individualised working culture prevails, processes of unconscious knowledge-sharing associated with communities of practice are unlikely to develop.

BOX 9.5
ETHICAL INSIGHT

Corporate social responsibility and human resource development

So far in this book's discussion of ethics in human resource management the focus has primarily been on ethical considerations in how HRM is carried out. However, HRM, and particularly HRD, is clearly well placed to be a driver of ethical behaviour in all areas of a business through creating a culture of social and environmental responsibility (Garavan and McGuire, 2010). This social role might take a variety of different forms, including raising awareness among employees and developing positive attitudes towards sustainability, environmental awareness and corporate citizenship, and contributing to the development of a culture that supports CSR and ethical behaviour both within and outside of the organisation. It might also be concerned with ensuring those with jobs that can have a significant environmental impact have the required skills and knowledge, or with reaching beyond the organisation to provide training opportunities to those in wider society who have specific needs. In all, HRD investment has been found to be associated with a positive impact on the triple bottom line of business, social, and environmental performance (Preuss et al., 2009).

A tension exists, however, in balancing the dual role of HRD as both concerned with advancing the economic interests of the firm and the development needs of its workforce and, by extension, society at large. In order to promote through HRD activity an individual, and thereby corporate, concern for CSR and ethics, firms need to address the ethical issues in HRD itself, principally the need to ensure equity in access to developmental opportunities (Wilcox, 2006). Arguably, therefore, HRD at a strategic and operational level needs to lead by example and before it can play a significant role in promoting ethical behaviour among employees it must demonstrate the virtues of ethical treatment itself by ensuring that all workers have equal access to opportunities for development and advancement.

Further online reading This article introduces a special edition of the journal and examines the role of HRD in addressing important societal issues. It discusses and provides a useful framework by which to understand how HRD at different levels of the organisation can actively contribute to a firm's CSR agenda, whilst also ensuring ongoing business success.

Garavan, T. N. and McGuire, D. (2010) Human resource development and society: Human resource development's role in embedding corporate social responsibility, sustainability, and ethics in organizations, *Advances in Developing Human Resources*, 12 (5): 487–507.

HRD IN PRACTICE

There are a number of key issues to be considered in the design and delivery of effective training interventions to respond to strategic imperatives or internal or external demands. These include how training needs are identified and whose needs take precedence, the stakeholders whose interests should be served by the training (and whether these interests can be reconciled), who should be responsible for delivering HRD (for example, HRD specialists or line managers), what formal or informal learning activities should be used and how should the success of the intervention be assessed.

THE SYSTEMATIC TRAINING MODEL

The systematic training model (Figure 9.1) outlines the decision-making process an organisation might go through in responding to these questions. The systematic training mode represents a structured, logical, approach to identifying training needs and responding through a logical and sequential process of planning and designing, delivery and evaluation of appropriate training or HRD interventions (alternatively, the ADDIE acronym is used to identify the phases of analysis, design, development, implementation, and evaluation – Clayton Allen, 2006). This model consists of four main stages. In short, the process starts with the identification and assessment of learning needs. This might be done, at the individual level, through performance appraisal or as a consequence of workforce audits or HR planning. This is followed by the planning phase in which the overall purpose and objectives of the learning intervention are established, which is clearly linked to the needs identified, and to specific outcomes. From this a detailed plan or framework is devised outlining the type and structure of the 'learning event', required resources, funding, roles, structures and location, bearing in mind the size and profile of the learning population. This is followed by delivery of the learning event and, finally, a review and evaluation of the learning experience and outcomes.

The systematic process presents an apparently rational and efficient approach to managing workplace training. It is, however, subject to a number of criticisms and failings, relating both to underlying assumptions and implementation. Most fundamentally, there is scepticism over whether the sequential completion of each stage is a realistic or feasible representation of workplace practice. For this reason, the systematic model tends to be viewed as an ideal state of affairs. Marchington and Wilkinson (2008) caution that sequential models such as this can lapse into a closed cycle, in which there is little linkage to other aspects of HR, business strategy and objectives and environmental context. This might result in a rather restrictive training culture focused on short-term requirements and on addressing gaps in learning rather than anticipating and responding to future challenges. Indeed, where a disconnected training cycle exists, and which has become divorced from its broader purpose, then it may be difficult to gain the support of either senior management or line managers for HRD investment.

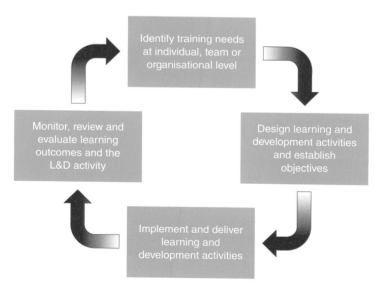

FIGURE 9.1   The systematic training model

Gold (2007) suggests that the systematic approach tends to be associated with formal learning (for example, training courses) that can be easily assessed and their outcomes measured and quantified. Such an approach is, therefore, less appropriate for informal or on-the-job learning with, often intangible, benefits. From this perspective, the systematic model would appear contrary to the more holistic and integrative view of HRD outlined previously.

Despite criticisms of the practical usage of the systematic model of training and development it remains useful for analytical purposes. For this reason, whilst not necessarily advocating a mechanistic approach to learning and development, the following section draws on the systematic model to outline the key options and issues for managers at each stage of this process.

Assessment of L&D needs

The first stage of the L&D process is concerned with identifying training needs often by analysing gaps between current work performance and desired standards of work or performance criteria. Inevitably, all organisations are subject to performance problems, gaps or deficiency in some way or another and at one time or another. The causes of performance deficiencies are as manifold as the inputs that different firms employ to deliver services or produce goods, from technology to work processes to organisational structures. From a human resources perspective, under-performance is often associated with individual deficit in the skills, knowledge or attitudes that are required for acceptable, if not optimal, performance, and that can be addressed via training. This view is seductive because it acts to isolate the performance problem as one of individual competence rather than something more systemic. Such an attitude, however, tends to lead to a rather myopic focus on day-to-day operational issues and 'patching up' workplace performance through reactive training as opposed to taking a more holistic view of performance and orientating training, learning and development activities directly at the strategic objectives of the firm (Gold et al., 2013). This latter approach requires placing the apparent training need in the broader organisational context so as to identify the full range of factors that impact on job performance and the relationship between job effectiveness and business objectives (Gibb, 2011).

L&D AT CHOCCO

With this view in mind, there is a wide range of means by which firms can identify gaps in performance and, therefore, potential areas of HRD intervention (see Table 9.2). These range from direct observation of individual performance to formal training needs assessment or analysis (TNA) that seeks both to identify and formally articulate L&D needs in order to provide data according to which an employer can decide on the purpose, specific objectives, form and scale of the required training intervention and how the impact of this intervention will be assessed. Boydell (1976) identified three possible levels at which training needs can be identified: organisational, job or occupational, and individual. From a top-down strategic perspective, the identification of training needs starts with establishing at the *organisational level* how L&D might contribute to the achievement of strategic objectives, for example, by focusing on skills deficiencies identified in the HR planning process. *Job/occupational level* analysis is conducted in order to identify and outline the purpose of a specific job and to specify what learning needs are associated with effective work performance. Such job analysis can draw on a range of sources of information, including that collected directly from job-holders, line managers, customers and team members. *Individual level* analysis involves assessing the skills and knowledge of role-holders in relation to performance requirements.

From a unitarist perspective, all three levels of training needs can be integrated, and needs identified at an organisational level should influence occupational and

TABLE 9.2 *Sources of information in identifying training needs*

Level of training need assessment	Sources of information
Individual	• Recruitment and selection data • Performance standards or objectives • Comparative analysis (between workers in similar roles) • Direct observation • Individual appraisal • Development centres • Self-assessment • Career or talent management processes
Job or occupation	• Job training (needs) analysis • Problem or critical incidence analysis • Competency analysis • Work diaries • Customer or client satisfaction surveys • Performance standards and targets • Self-assessment • Observation, interviews and questionnaires
Organisational	• HR planning data • Skills audit • Performance management data • Staff attitude survey • Management information systems

individual level needs (Reid et al., 2004). However, taking a pluralist view, it is conceivable that the needs at each level might not necessarily coincide. The job of line managers and HR specialists, therefore, is to reconcile the career and personal development needs of individuals with job and organisational requirements. Where strategy making is reflexive to the experiences and input of employees, identified individual learning requirements, for example those that emanate from the performance management system, can be used to shape organisational training needs.

Training needs are often identified in response to environmental change, for example, changing customer demands, developments in the wider marketplace, implementation or amendment of legislation or the development of new technology. Training needs can also be identified in anticipation of future opportunities or to enable planned organisational change. Reactive identification of training needs often tends to focus on filling a gap or deficiency between current and required performance. Whilst such a gap-led approach can help in establishing clear learning objectives, aids the choice of intervention type and enables more accurate evaluation of outcomes, it is retrospective and by relying on a gap-led approach, firms are unlikely to anticipate future skills needs to which responding might be a source of competitive advantage. Problems might also arise from this approach where the causes of an apparent gap in capability might be hidden or complex.

Designing L&D interventions

Once training needs have been identified, the next stage is to translate these needs into the specific aims and objectives of a learning intervention. This is likely to be in the form of the performance outcomes to result from the intervention, for example, behavioural change, efficiency gains or the specific knowledge or skills to be developed. Setting clear objectives informs the design and content of the learning event or process and assists in providing information by which to evaluate its effectiveness, specifically the extent to which it has resulted in addressing the performance gap or achieved these predefined objectives.

Defining the criteria for training success might involve the establishment of benchmarks or standards and require an evaluation of both qualitative (such as behavioural change) and quantitative (such as improvements in productivity) measures of performance improvement. It is important, however, to ensure a degree of flexibility is built into expectations, especially where performance can be affected by external factors. The design of the learning intervention should also consider the available budget, the specific context in which the learning is to take place and the characteristics of the targeted learner group, including their existing skills, knowledge and experiences, attitudes towards learning, motivation and reasons for participation, expectations and preferred learning styles (Box 9.6). The involvement of employees and line managers in the design of the training event is likely to have the dual benefit of ensuring buy-in and more participatory and willing involvement in the training as well as ensuring that it addresses specific and relevant real-world training needs. Table 9.3 summarises the key considerations or constraints on the design process.

TABLE 9.3 *Factors and constraints to be considered in the HRD design process*

Factors or constraints		Key questions
Design principles	Purpose, objectives and intended outcomes	What specific learning needs are to be addressed?
	Learning principles	What are the principles or values that underpin the approach and methods to be adopted?
	Learning methods and interventions	Through what methods might the identified purpose and objectives best be achieved?
	Learning transfer and application	How is transfer of learning to the work situation to be facilitated and assessed?
	Evaluation	How will achievement of the objectives and learning outcomes be evaluated?
Organisational factors	Stakeholder perspectives	Who are the key internal and external stakeholders and what are their expectations, concerns and desired outcomes?
	Organisational context: structure and culture	Is the existing organisational culture supportive of learning and the use of specific forms of employee development?
	Business and HR strategy	How can the intervention be most effectively aligned with wider corporate, HRD and HRM strategy and associated practices and policies?
	Resources (including timescales)	What facilities, staff and equipment are required and who is to pay for them?
	Organisational capability	Who will design and deliver the intervention and do we have such capability in-house?
	The learner group	What learning skills, preferences, experiences and prejudices do the learners bring with them?

BOX 9.6
RESEARCH INSIGHT

The learning process and learning styles

Recognition of the strategic importance of workplace learning and a desire to harness the potential of informal learning has led to an increased interest in explanations of the learning process as applied to the work context. There is a range of theories that seek to explain how people learn, which can be broadly categorised into psychological and sociological explanations. Among the former, behavioural learning theory – most notably, the work of Ivan Pavlov (1849–1936) and Burrhus Skinner (1904–90) – focuses on learning as the process by which punishment and reward can be used to reinforce desirable learned behaviours (referred to as 'operant conditioning'). However, behavioural theory does not fully explain the way in which people internalise learning. Cognitive learning theories, on the other hand, seek to explain the process by which an individual accesses, processes and transforms information obtained from their environment. One such theory is the experiential **learning cycle** (Kolb, 1984), which suggests that people learn through a process of experience, observation and reflection, theorising (abstract conceptualisation) and testing/experimentation of new understanding.

Both cognitive and behavioural learning theories explain learning in terms of individual psychological changes and, consequently, have been criticised as reflecting learning as a passive, asocial phenomenon. Conversely, situational (Lave and Wenger, 1991) and sociological explanations of learning focus on the notion of learning as embedded in social interaction (Easterby-Smith and Araujo, 1999) and reflecting processes of informal collaboration.

A key premise of more recent theories of learning is that people have preferred learning styles and that effective learning can best be facilitated where the learning intervention is matched to the prevalent learning style. Learning preferences can be shaped by individual characteristics (e.g. age, ability, personality, prior learning experience, gender or familiarity with technology) or wider cultural or social differences. A well-known typology of learning styles that reflects Kolb's learning cycle is Honey and Mumford's (1992) four-fold classification which suggests that there are four broad categories of learner: *activists*, who learn best by active involvement in tasks; *reflectors*, who learn best through observing, listening and reflection; *theorists*, who learn best when new problems or information can be related to theory and divorced from day-to-day situations; and *pragmatists*, who learn best by linking new information to real application. In addition to the process by which they learn, James and Galbraith (1985) suggest that people have perceptual preferences for how they take in and process information including visual, print, aural, interactive, tactile and kinaesthetic (active). Weinstein and Mayer (1986) suggest that people can adopt learning strategies to fit a particular context and 'better performing' learners are those who are more flexible and adaptable in how they learn. Recognition of learning preferences is important in the design of learning interventions in order to account for such preferences in structure, pace and choice of learning methods.

Clearly, a key factor in the planning and design phase is consideration of the most appropriate method or mix of methods for delivering training and development activities. The options available are considered in the following section.

Delivering L&D activities

There are many factors to consider in designing and delivering effective learning interventions, including whether it should be delivered in-house or externally provided, whether it should be conducted on- or off-the-job, the degree of structure required and whether it should be carried out on an individual or collective basis. The choices made in each of these areas will affect the role of line managers, tutors or providers, the cost and, ultimately, the effectiveness of the intervention in addressing specific training needs. Employers are, however, unlikely to have an infinite range of options in designing training activities and will be constrained by financial and time limitations, strategic goals and mission, the availability of in-house expertise, customs and established practices, the learner group profile and organisational culture. Considering the complex interaction of these factors, the suitability of methods will vary according to the specific circumstances in which they are to be used and the characteristics of the participants.

CATEGORISING L&D ACTIVITIES   Gibb (2002) suggests that training delivery methods can be placed on a 'delivery continuum' between methods that focus on 'instruction' and those that focus on 'facilitation'. Under instruction methods, learning is focused on the inculcation of programmable skills, knowledge and behaviour, the transfer and rote learning of information and training in standard or routine ways of working. For example, instruction might be appropriate where the focus is on teaching learners standard operating procedure, such as in driving lessons, or in disseminating factual knowledge. This can involve learning through trial and error and often leads to assessment based on testing to gauge the attainment of competence. Instructional methods are typically trainer-led in respect of the content, pace and structure of the intervention. In contrast, facilitation emphasises learning as a social process involving less tutor control over the learning event and requiring learner participation and interaction (for example, role-playing workshops and group case studies). Facilitative techniques are often characterised as learner-led. Beyond training and learner-led methods, Hackett (2003) suggests a third category of 'coaching' exists which is characterised by a learning partnership between learner and trainer.

Alternatively, Marchington and Wilkinson (2005) place training methods in four distinct categories, differentiated according to whether the activity is *andragogical* (self-directed and participative) or *pedagogical* (trainer-driven, allowing little room for student input into the learning situation) and whether it is individual or group-based. *Pedagogical individual* methods refer to one-to-one instructional techniques and simulations, for example, flight simulators or individual 'tuition' learning of a call centre script. *Pedagogical group-based* methods are appropriate for conveying information to large groups of people with little or no input from learners, for example, lectures and presentations. *Andragogical group-based* methods are group-led, including group case studies, projects and role-playing exercises. Finally, *andragogical individual* methods are self-managed and include learning methods where the individual learner dictates the pace, timing and location of learning, for example, e-learning.

IN-HOUSE OR EXTERNAL PROVISION?   Dependent on the type of learning required and the extent of in-house expertise, firms can employ in-house training and development or external provision. In-house training has the benefit of being embedded in the firm and, therefore, might lead to a better transfer of learning and direct applicability in the workplace. Instructional in-house training might be appropriate for employee induction, updating knowledge of regulation (for example, health and safety) or where new organisation policies need to be communicated. Typically, in-house training of this sort is devised and delivered by HRD specialists. More participatory in-house training is often provided on-the-job, for example, through coaching and mentoring.

External training includes short courses provided by external training consultants, and longer courses, often at educational institutions such as universities. Such courses are often used where in-house expertise does not exist or is inadequate: for example, the introduction of a new IT system supported by training for relevant employees, often provided by the supplier. External courses have the benefit of exposing employees to other ways of thinking or working, drawing on experiences from either the trainer/tutors or from other participants. However, learning transfer back into the workplace can be more limited than with in-house provision, particularly on generic programmes (rather than those specifically designed for the organisation), and the process of transfer needs to be effectively managed so that new ideas can be integrated.

ON-THE-JOB OR OFF-THE-JOB? The shift from training to learning has been embodied in the greater emphasis placed on informal workplace learning. This has implications for the types of training that organisations are offering, leading to a greater focus on on-the-job training. As discussed above there are a number of advantages and disadvantages associated with training that occurs either on- or off-the-job. Formal training typically occurs off-the-job, often in the form of classroom learning, and can be beneficial in providing greater structure to learning and a clearer connection between formal objectives, skills and knowledge development and the evaluation of outcomes. Conversely, on-the-job training (or those that take place 'through work' rather than 'at work' – Stewart and Rigg, 2011) has the advantage of being conducted closer to the work situation (integrated with, rather than distinct from, work-related activities – Gold et al. 2013) and more able to facilitate the effective transfer of learning to the real world. It can, however, lead to the transfer of poor working practices and the perpetuation of mistakes or errors. Nonetheless, it is the most commonly used form of employee development, consistently viewed by employers as among the most effective (CIPD, 2014). The main forms of on-the-job learning include 'sitting by Nellie', which is the name given to the act of learning by watching others carry out their work, and job rotation, secondment and work-shadowing, which can be used to smooth role transition, to multi-skill workers and to promote knowledge-sharing and understanding of the wider organisation and its processes.

COACHING AND MENTORING Whilst the terms are often used interchangeably there are notable differences between coaching and mentoring. Mentoring tends to denote a developmental, often long-term, relationship between a senior and more junior employee (typically, managers) to help the protégé or mentee learn the ropes of a particular job role and prepare them for future advancement. Mentoring is extensively used as part of succession planning and management development, particularly to prepare candidates for senior management roles.

Coaching, however, typically takes place between an employee and their immediate line manager with the more explicit, short-term purpose of contributing to performance improvements and developing individual skills, sometimes with a focus on remedying employee under-performance. Coaching might be conducted on an ad hoc basis, as part of more structured performance management processes or a wider commitment to creating a 'coaching culture' where 'coaching is the predominant style of managing and working together and where commitment to improving the organisation is embedded in a parallel commitment to improving the people' (Clutterbuck and Megginson, 2005: 44). CIPD (2012c) report an increasing focus on coaching, and line manager responsibility for L&D and coaching is consistently viewed by managers as one of the most effective means of employee development (CIPD, 2014). There are, however, a number of problems with coaching, principally the degrees to which managers possess the required skills to act as effective coaches and the problems associated with evaluating its effectiveness. There are also tensions between the role of manager – focused on controlling and managing performance in the short term – and the more developmental focus of 'coach'.

E-LEARNING AND BLENDED LEARNING The CIPD (2009d: 1) use the following inclusive definition of e-learning: 'Learning that is delivered, enabled or mediated using electronic technology for the explicit purpose of training in organisations'. This broad description stresses that e-learning is an approach to learning that encompasses a wide range of forms or techniques, including web-based learning (online courses or information sources that are typically unsupported by training professionals), supported online learning (where course content is delivered using a range of methods including e-learning but where there is greater interaction, support and collaboration between learners and tutors and/or other users) and informal e-learning (for example, the use of company intranets as a source of information and communication). E-learning techniques can be grouped into three categories reflecting their relationship with more traditional face-to-face or classroom-based training:

1 *Alternative* – where new technology allows for the replacement of traditional means of learning, such as remote access to formally delivered training courses or virtual involvement in webinars.

2 *Complementary* – where e-learning interventions operate to supplement traditional forms of training delivery, for example, the use of virtual learning environments to complement face-to-face training or educational delivery. The use of e-learning as complementary is typically referred to as 'blended learning'.

3 *Transformative* – where new technology provides the means by which learning is enabled in new and innovative ways, such as in the virtual realm or via social media.

Despite recent developments in ICT (as discussed later), e-learning does not necessarily offer the opportunity to replace all existing organisational learning processes and it is important to understand e-learning not as a distinct and separate dimension of organisational learning but as an increasingly integral element of it. E-learning is most often used in conjunction with other forms of learning, often those that are face-to-face, for example, educational courses on which the majority of learning content is delivered through face-to-face interaction (for example, through classroom-based instruction, coaching and mentoring) supplemented both by textual material and supporting online materials, and providing for remote collaboration with peers and tutor support online.

There are two contrasting trends in both the use of e-learning and attitudes among managers towards it. On the one hand, more than three-quarters (78 per cent) of respondents to a CIPD survey (CIPD, 2011c) reported the use of e-learning and 53 per cent had increased their use of e-learning over the previous 12 months. The 2014 XpertHR learning and development survey (Wolff, 2014) found that e-learning solutions were the most common way in which firms sought to create efficiency savings in HRD activities. On the other hand, e-learning is widely felt to be among the most ineffective forms of training and development, despite being the third most used form of intervention (CIPD, 2014), particularly when used alone and not as adjacent to more tried and tested forms of learning (CIPD, 2012d). It is clear that e-learning is currently considered a supplementary or, at best, complementary form of learning rather than a stand-alone form of training and development in many organisations. The use of e-learning alongside more traditional forms of interactive content delivery (e.g. classroom-based learning) is often referred to as 'blended learning'.

There are a number of potential benefits of e-learning. These include reductions in cost and time spent on delivery, flexibility in the 'where' and 'when' of access, the ability to reach large numbers of employees, the ability to personalise learning, the possibility of virtual collaboration among trainees and the ability to track learner activity remotely (CIPD, 2009d). E-learning also provides employers with the opportunity to place a greater onus on employees to take responsibility for their own learning, although problems might arise for learners with learning styles that are not commensurate with self-instruction. There are, however, a number of barriers to the effectiveness of e-learning, including the limits of current technology infrastructure, lack of time and space to learn, lack of learner support, lack of required IT skills among employees and employee hostility towards e-learning (CIPD, 2009d).

New technology and HRD

Web 2.0 technologies present a host of opportunities that have already begun to revolutionise the way people learn at and for work. The term 'Web 2.0' was first coined in the late 1990s to describe the evolutionary changes in the way in which users interact with web pages and resources beyond simply the retrieval of information and the one-way creation and publication of online content. It is associated with the more dynamic means by which individuals interact, collaborate and participate via the web, create content and networks and, ultimately, add value to the Internet as a resource. Web 2.0, therefore, denotes openness, decentralisation, participation, collaboration and user-control (Reddington, 2012). Such technologies have a central role to play in shaping both current and future opportunities for the enhancement of workplace learning. The following section considers four significant areas of development in e-learning associated with Web 2.0 technology.

Further online reading This article discusses the notion of 'just-in-time learning' ('anywhere, anytime, anyhow learning that is just enough, just for me and just in time') and how the growing demand for such learning presents a significant challenge for HRD practitioners and the field of HRD.

Brandenburg, D. C. and Ellinger, A. D. (2010) The future: Just-in-time learning expectations and potential implications for human resource development, *Advances in Developing Human Resources*, 5: 308–20.

SOCIAL MEDIA   In the context of the shift in emphasis towards the facilitation of learning from peers and colleagues (Martin et al., 2009), the ability of social and interactive media to enable collaboration, co-creation, real-time and just-in-time access to knowledge and rapid information sharing presents a significant opportunity for the enhancement of individual and organisational learning. Social media can play a critical role in developing a firm's social capital through the enablement of networks for knowledge exchange and creation (CIPD 2012f), addressing many of the most important aspects of effective workplace learning, including relevance, timeliness and effective learning transfer. Social media also help to address the social dimension of learning – often absent from the e-learning experience – whereby the finding, filtering and sharing of information can take place remotely in much the same way it can take place in a proximate team environment.

Social media can be used in a variety of ways to enhance individual and organisational learning and development. For instance, they can be used to deliver training via social channels such as blogs, videos, online 'help', 'wikis' (online applications that allow people to add, modify, or delete content in collaboration with others, to create collective knowledge from the 'wisdom of crowds') and discussion forums (Zielinski, 2012). In addition, social media can allow people to work together across projects and track progress and activity (Semple, 2011), even when geographically dispersed, as well as share knowledge and experience and co-create new knowledge in the form of virtual communities of practice. Corporate blogs and RSS feeds (a means of subscribing to web updates, news items and so on relevant to an individual, group or organisation) can be used to help people learn about important and up-to-date knowledge of matters that are relevant to them and to prompt engagement.

These innovations alter or add another dimension to the role of HRD specialists towards that of 'curators', rather than creators, of training content (Churchard, 2012). HRD professionals will help employees make sense of the information to which they might be exposed (for instance, the knowledge of more experienced colleagues) in relation to their own job role and development needs, finding, filtering and directing employees to the best content on a continuous basis (Bennett and Bierema, 2010).

MOBILE TECHNOLOGIES Alongside developments in online content and its potential to facilitate learning, developments in ICT hardware are also revolutionising the ways in which people interact and share and access information. In particular, developments in mobile technologies have made possible truly flexible learning where individuals hold ever-greater control over the where, how and when of learning. Beyond the potential to remotely connect people in real time, mobile technology has the potential to lead to greater individual investment in personal learning and development, as firms benefit from employee familiarity with mobile technologies. Mobile learning can incorporate social media as a means of knowledge sharing, the ability to remotely access information (for example, that situated on company networks) or downloading of learning modules for playback on portable audio or video players. There is, however, significant debate to be had regarding the implications for work–life balance of the ubiquity of mobile technology and the extent to which individuals can be expected to engage in work-related activities beyond the limits of contracted hours of employment. The effective management of learning via mobile technology requires, therefore, a clear statement of expectations from the employer as well as the provision of necessary hardware and network facilities to allow as-and-when-required access. However, despite the clear potential for mobile learning, recent research suggests limited take-up of these opportunities (CIPD, 2013d). Box 9.7 provides an illustration of how mobile technology aids in the learning of remote and module workers.

VIRTUAL HRD Associated with the ever-increasing ability of technology to simulate real-life connections and collaboration and to enable people to connect through technology, an area of growing interest within e-learning is virtual HRD (VHRD). Bennett (2009: 365) defines VHRD as 'a media-rich and culturally relevant web[bed] environment that strategically improves expertise, performance, innovation, and community building through formal and informal learning'. Whilst the notion of 'virtual' dimensions of HRD – such as virtual communities of

BOX 9.7
HRM IN PRACTICE

Mobile learning in the UK National Health Service

Norman (2011) reports on research conducted for the UK National Health Service which sought to explore the utility of mobile learning for those workers, such as district nurses and midwives, who work remotely in the community and away from hospitals or surgeries, making conventional e-learning difficult. Aside from benefiting from many of the advantages of e-learning more broadly – the flexibility and convenience of any-time access to learning – mobile learning was also found to result in better professional judgments, to

encourage reflection, to enhance content retention (as a result of accessing bite-sized 'nuggets' of directly relevant information), to lead to improved learner confidence and to enhance relevance of learning where it is accessed close to the site of practice. Using already familiar devices such as tablets or smartphones was found to reduce the technological barriers associated with deploying new technologies. However, as with all new methods of learning, particularly those associated with 'always on' technology, resistance to mobile learning was found, stressing the importance of communicating the added value of this channel of learning to ensure buy-in.

practice and virtual mentoring – has been used since the turn of the century, as well as the creation of integrated and media-rich learning environments VHRD is more closely associated with the use of virtual space as the site of collaboration and participation in learning, often in the form of a 3D virtual world where people can interact in real-time using 'avatars' as virtual representations of themselves. These environments have the potential to recreate, in a meaningful manner, face-to-face interaction and collaboration through facilitating social presence and, therefore, are viewed by some as being an important resource for knowledge sharing and management (Bennett, 2010). Therefore, such virtual worlds have the potential to offer more realistic simulations, for example, of scenarios for the purpose of health and safety training, for developing 'soft' skills associated with customer service interaction, negotiation or interviewing.

GAMIFICATION OF LEARNING   The use of learning games to maximise motivation, involvement and performance associated with e-learning has long been a strategy employed by organisations (DeRouin et al., 2005), for instance, the use of quizzes to reinforce learning or games based on scenarios for contingency planning. CIPD (2012d: 12) suggest, however, that 'the use of games in learning is set to accelerate with the proliferation of gaming technology and, more importantly, insights about how people learn in gaming situations'. More than this, Squire (2008: 8) suggests that interest in game-based learning reflects recognition that games can represent 'experiential learning space ... where learners have rich, embodied, collaborative and cooperative interactions where they think with complex tools and resources in the service of complex problem-solving'. The gamification of learning is viewed as one means by which to address the perennial problem of a lack of worker engagement with e-learning, drawing on insights from gaming as a leisure pursuit, and to enhance the ability to tailor learning to preferences and needs. CIPD (2012d) reports that whilst only 9 per cent of respondent practitioners regularly or frequently use 'serious games' as part of their HRD mix, a further 30 per cent reported some use of these methods, indicating some potential for growth in their application. Squire (2008) identifies four broad categories of use for games-based learning: games as a space for experiential learning; games as a context for discussion; games as a tool to think with; and, games as a space for exploring new identities. Such games used both within business education and professional development include business and scenario simulations, and entrepreneurship games designed to develop critical skills within a low-risk, but often competitive environment.

Review and evaluation

The final stage of the systematic HRD model is evaluation. This is not, however, to suggest that evaluation should occur only at the very end of the process and many commentators advocate the continuous assessment of learning effectiveness. In most cases, however, evaluation takes place as a final act to provide feedback to trainers, often with the explicit purpose of improving the learning intervention for its next 'run', to determine whether stated objectives have been achieved and to weigh up overall costs and benefits. In essence, the purpose of evaluation is to assess the extent to which the training intervention has met the needs of all stakeholders (including the organisation, trainees, customers and budget holders) and their specific objectives (for example, improvements in job performance or service quality, career and personal development, return on investment and cost-effectiveness).

Post facto evaluation can be in the form either of informal feedback from line managers and trainees on the extent of learning transfer or the utility of learnt skills and knowledge, or a more formal evaluation of learning outcomes through, for example, testing. As noted previously, the choice of methods and the specific learning objectives outlined in the planning phase will inform the most effective form of evaluation (for example, learner testing tends to be most useful in evaluating instructional training). The presentation of the systematic learning and development process as a cycle in Figure 9.1 stresses that a key part of the evaluation phase should be a reflection – both on the part of the trainees and those providing the training – on future training needs that might have arisen from the prior intervention.

In order to fully assess training effectiveness and to consider the viewpoints of a range of stakeholders, evaluation should take place at a number of levels and there have been a number of models developed which propose the alternative levels at which training evaluation should take place (such as Warr et al., 1970; Bushnell, 1990; Easterby-Smith, 1994; Fitz-Enz, 1994). Of these, the most influential and enduring is that of Kirkpatrick (1987) who proposes the following levels of evaluation:

- *Reaction* – the most commonly used (Wolff, 2014), evaluation at this level seeks to establish the learners' views on the training event post-completion. Such evaluation is useful to trainers as it provides direct feedback to inform improvements but it is limited in that it may not differentiate between the experience (for example, enjoyment of an event) and its actual value to job performance.

- *Learning* – measurement of the achievement of training objectives, particularly in terms of acquired knowledge, skills and attitudes, through, for example, testing or interviews.

- *Behaviour* – assessment of the impact of training on job performance and the extent to which a learning gap has been filled. Such evaluation (typically conducted through the performance management process and interviews or questionnaires with trainees, line managers and customers or clients) is problematic because training is likely to be only one variable affecting job performance and employee behaviour and it might be difficult to isolate and measure the impact of training.

- *Results* – an attempt to provide a holistic assessment of the impact of training on the individual's overall performance (not simply the element of the job addressed in the training) and on departmental or organisational performance on the basis of specific criteria (for example, sales, productivity or labour turnover). This can be used to evaluate the overall cost-effectiveness of the training.

The enduring influence and pervasive use of Kirkpatrick's model are perhaps testimony to its simplicity, however, a range of criticisms have been levelled at the model and the extent of its full use in practice questioned (Holton, 1996; Harrison, 2005; Holton and Naquin, 2005; Guerci et al., 2010; Simmonds, 2010).

ISSUES WITH THE EVALUATION OF L&D INTERVENTIONS As with any form of measurement in HRM, evaluating L&D activity is subject to problems of validity and reliability. Moreover, there is the question of when L&D activities should be assessed, particularly where benefits might be long term rather than immediate. A strategic perspective on HRD is likely to place greater emphasis on long-term employee development and the opportunity for the realisation of potential, rather than the training cost, and to accept that the benefits of learning cannot always be quantified. Anderson (2007) advocates the use of 'return on expectation' measures (as opposed to return on investment) using both 'hard' numerical and 'soft' qualitative information to assess the strategic value of learning.

Clearly, effective evaluation can prove valuable for a range of stakeholders. For individual employees, effective evaluation can provide validation of learning (for instance, towards a qualification) and be used as the basis for continuous professional development. For HRD specialists, effective evaluation can contribute to more effective interventions in future and aid in the process of seeking resources for activities. For line and senior managers, effective evaluation helps to ensure the most effective allocation of resources and also helps in the process of continuous improvement in collective and individual performance.

However, despite this range of reasons for effective evaluation, managers often fail to carry out a systematic assessment or do so in a perfunctory 'bolt on' manner, not adequately integrated into the broader training cycle or wider strategic context. Gold (2007) suggests that the dominant employer perspective remains on the costs rather than the benefits of training, based on quantitative measures and a focus on short-term return on investment or increase in productivity. This perspective partly reflects the complexity of providing a more comprehensive assessment of learning interventions given the different levels of assessment, the variety of stakeholders to be considered, their criteria for acceptability and the potential for conflicts of interest. A narrow focus can have the effect of promoting a cost-minimisation approach to HRD and lead to attempts to redesign jobs to reduce the reliance on skills and the need for investment in learning, contrary to the approach advocated under more strategic perspectives. As such, the benefits to be gained from insightful evaluation to on-going strategic decision-making are foregone.

MANAGEMENT DEVELOPMENT

The growing importance of knowledge work, and the role of management both in making knowledge productive and in facilitating organisational change, has intensified long-held debates about both the nature of managerial work and,

BOX 9.8
MANAGEMENT SKILLS AND ATTRIBUTES

Line manager responsibilities and HRD

Consistent with the wider devolution of responsibility for people management issues to line managers, the contemporary focus on continuous workplace learning and development puts significant onus on line managers to become fully involved in the development of their teams or departments. Line managers increasingly hold responsibility for conducting performance appraisals, help to identify training needs, contribute to personal development plans, design and deliver training interventions, act as 'gatekeepers' to external training opportunities (Hutchinson and Purcell, 2007) and evaluate the impact of training on work performance. Subsequently, line managers play a crucial role in creating a learning climate where employee development becomes a more proactive and continuous process through both informal learning and more formalised processes of coaching, mentoring, job rotation and secondment. Line management involvement can also help in establishing a clear link between individual and organisational needs. Where formal learning is undertaken, for example on external training courses, line managers can prove useful in ensuring the transfer of learning into the workplace and in facilitating knowledge-sharing across employees. Ultimately, greater line manager responsibility for employee development – and embedding such responsibility into managerial competencies and their own performance objectives – has the potential to alter the nature of the relationship between manager and subordinate in a direction that is more cooperative and consensual and to generate greater employee commitment to the organisation and its aims. By virtue of being closer to the work situation, line managers can also be more successful than remote HRD specialists in identifying training needs and applying appropriate solutions.

However, the substantial devolution of HRD responsibility to line managers presents a number of problems. Possible pitfalls include a lack of line manager willingness or ability to effectively encourage and support employee learning, not least where new approaches to organisational development advocate a greater focus on organic processes of organisational renewal and away from bureaucratic modes of control. Line managers might also consider HRD activity as an inconvenient or unimportant part of their role, allowing short-term operational pressures to override considerations of longer-term learning needs. Indeed, evidence suggests that a minority of employers feel that line managers take L&D very seriously (CIPD, 2007c), despite the vast majority of employers believing that line managers were important or very important to the effectiveness of L&D, and many employers reporting that they anticipate the continued devolution of responsibility for L&D to such managers (CIPD, 2012c). As the gatekeepers to learning and development opportunities, line manager discretion can also lead to inequity in the distribution of access to these opportunities. Even with training in, for example, training needs assessment, line managers are unlikely to be as skilled as HRD specialists and, therefore, specialists have continued importance in supporting line managers, identifying organisational training needs and dealing with specific individual needs.

subsequently, the importance of management development. Management development covers a wide range of learning activities designed to improve managerial effectiveness, including formal education and training (such as MBA or undergraduate management degrees), shorter, often skills-specific training courses delivered inside or outside of the organisation, outdoor teambuilding and problem-solving exercises, project-working, secondments, coaching, counselling and mentoring and continuing professional development (see below). The identification of management training needs can emanate from appraisals, talent management or succession planning processes, organisational skills audits or from managers' self-assessment.

A principal problem for management development is the nature of managerial work itself and determining what constitutes managerial effectiveness. Subsequently, there is a long-running debate over what skills are required to effectively 'manage'. The Chartered Management Institute suggest that managers are required to: 'communicate coherently and persuasively, have a built-in sensitivity to what makes the organisation tick, listen to what is being said as opposed to what he or she may prefer to hear, organise and motivate others, respond to and manage change, be able to coach and counsel colleagues, make decisions fast while assessing risk, think strategically with a broader perspective and longer-term' (CMI, 2002: 1).

However, an overarching schema of management skills is difficult to define because core competencies will vary with the level and type of responsibilities and the nature and context of the organisation (Skills Advisory Group, 2004). A principal problem for management development is, therefore, whether it is possible to train someone to be a truly effective manager or whether at least part of what makes a good manager is intuitive (Starkey and Madan, 2001) given that empirical studies suggest a manager's role is essentially responsive and opportunistic and not an analytical activity (for example, Mintzberg, 1973). Nonetheless, the practical implication for management development is that, in order to be effective, it must be tailored to fit the demands of managers working in particular social, economic and organisational contexts and be appropriate to the managerial level at which it is directed.

Despite these on-going debates, there is evidence to suggest that there are positive returns to an investment in management development in the form of improved organisational competitiveness (Sheehan, 2012) and that there is a relationship between higher levels of managerial competency and individual and wider workplace performance (Levenson et al., 2006). Much recent literature tends to identify two central skills sets essential to the modern managerial role that tend to form a broad focus for contemporary management development (Wilton, 2007); the development of interpersonal skills and competencies associated with managing in a context of uncertainty and rapid change, such as innovative and flexible thinking (Winterton et al., 2000).

CONTINUING PROFESSIONAL DEVELOPMENT

Megginson and Whittaker (2007: 3) define continuing professional development as 'a process by which individuals take control of their own learning and development, by engaging in an on-going process of reflection and action'. The growth in emphasis on CPD as a holistic perspective on individual learning reflects a number of strands in thinking about personal development. First, it reflects the view that different people learn in different ways and that learning does not need to take place in the workplace or in work-related activities to be beneficial to work performance. Second, individuals must take greater responsibility for and ownership of their own personal and professional development and the manner in which it connects to the needs of the organisation.

The importance of personal reflection in CPD reflects the importance of taking a holistic view of development, the ongoing integration of the learning acquired in all elements of one's life, the regular self-diagnosis of personal learning needs and the personal identification of opportunities to address these needs. The ultimate aim is that CPD becomes an almost unconscious process whereby learning outcomes from a diverse range of experiences are used to develop better ways of working and generate new knowledge. However, the focus of CPD is not only the process of learning but also the process of becoming a better learner through reflection and evaluation of learning outcomes. Many models of CPD do not focus only on organisational motives, but also on learning for personal benefit and not only for instrumental reasons associated with employability. In this sense, CPD is one aspect of lifelong learning, the notion that all in society must ensure that they continually update their skills and knowledge in order to ensure their ongoing employability, to attain personal and professional fulfilment and to contribute fully to the wider economy and society at large (Green, 2002).

Encouraging CPD and providing support for employees to become better learners might have indirect benefits for employers, such as greater commitment and engagement, a desire among employees to undertake new challenges, lowered employee turnover and a more positive psychological contract. Importantly, Torrington et al. (2008) note that self-development requires time, patience, tenacity and careful planning and that individuals have to be capable of taking on this greater responsibility for personal development. Marchington and Wilkinson (2005) suggest that the sort of activity that can be put forward as part of CPD can be categorised into three groups: that which relates to an ongoing qualification, such as research for coursework and presentations; everyday work-related activities such as new projects or assignments, attending training courses and secondments; and personal development activities such as learning a new language, acting as a school governor or organising sports events.

The concept of CPD has largely been driven by the need for professionals to continually update their skills and knowledge. In the field of HRM, for example, the 'reflective practitioner' model for HRM specialists advocated by the Chartered Institute of Personnel and Development stresses the importance of continual development and embedding learning in everyday activity. Consequently, evidence of CPD is now required for practitioners to achieve and maintain membership of the Institute.

SUMMARY POINTS

DEVELOPING A LEARNING STRATEGY

- Firms are increasingly recognising the value in encouraging workers to continuously enhance their skills and knowledge, and to foster their creativity and initiative as part of a drive for continuous improvement in individual and organisational performance.

- Under a strategic approach to HRD, employee development can be of benefit to the individual – in terms of personal and career development – and to the organisation – in terms of productivity gains, coping with change and increased motivation of its employees.

- Contemporary models of HRD emphasise the importance of informal, alongside formal, learning and greater employee responsibility for their own learning through continuing professional development.

- National cultural and institutional factors influence the approach and design of organisational learning interventions.

- Investment in HRD can be brought about by broad strategic imperatives or from 'drivers' in the internal or external organisational context.

- The systematic model outlines four stages in the learning and development cycle: identifying training needs; designing L&D interventions; delivering L&D activities; and evaluating L&D outcomes.

- E-learning has the potential to transform how training is delivered in organisations but the development of e-learning in practice remains limited. Web 2.0 technology presents a number of areas of significant potential for work-related learning.

- Perceived deficiencies in managerial skill and the importance of managers in responding to the challenges of the knowledge economy have focused attention on the importance of management development.

- It is an ever-greater requirement for managerial and professional workers to ensure the relevance of their skills and knowledge, as well as their employability, through continuous professional development and lifelong learning.

SELF-TEST QUESTIONS

1 Why has there been a recent shift from training to learning in both organisational theory and practice?

2 How might individual and organisational learning shape organisational strategy?

3 What are the three levels at which Boydell (1976) suggests training needs can be identified?

4 What are the principal benefits and potential drawbacks of e-learning? How might contemporary developments help to address some of these difficulties?

5 What are the four levels at which Kirkpatrick (1987) suggests that learning interventions should be assessed?

6 Why is evaluating the effectiveness of learning and development activity problematic?

7 What are the key factors that should be considered in designing appropriate learning interventions?

8 What principal roles do line managers undertake in HRD?

9 Why are generic approaches to management development problematic?

10 What possibilities do Web 2.0 technologies present for the future of human resource development?

TEST YOURSELF

TEST YOURSELF

Want to know more about this chapter? Review what you have been learning by visiting: https://edge.sagepub.com/wilton3e

- Print out or download the chapter summaries for quick revision
- Test yourself with multiple-choice questions
- Revise key terms with interactive flashcards

CASE STUDY

Facilities management and distributed knowledge

The British Institute of Facilities Management (BIFM) defines facilities management as 'the integration of processes within an organisation to maintain and develop the agreed services which support and improve the effectiveness of its primary activities'. Facilities management encompasses multi-disciplinary activities within the built environment and the management of their impact upon people and the workplace.

As a result of organisational cost cutting, many firms seek to outsource their facilities management to specialist service provides. Stevenson Aukerman (SA) are one such firm, providing a range of facilities management services – contract management, property strategy development, space management, health and safety, building maintenance and management of communications infrastructure. Having a presence in 18 countries across Europe and the Middle East, SA employ approximately 250 facilities managers who are responsible for the buildings and associated services which support clients' businesses. Either working solely for a specific client – usually large multinational firms who operate large buildings – or working across a number of smaller clients, these facilities managers are required to have a wide body of knowledge across multiple areas of facilities management – such as ICT, mechanical and electrical engineering and the principles of building design and ergonomics, as well as that pertaining to the specific context in which they operate, such as local contract and health and safety law, cultural traditions and wider business infrastructure. In addition, they require a detailed understanding of the organisations in which they work, including other related aspects of their operation, particularly HR and operations.

In response to a recent growth in business and the possibility of entering a number of new national markets arising from more firms seeking to outsource their facilities management as part of cost-cutting strategies, the HR director has sought the views of the company's workforce to identify specific HRD concerns or issues. Among the facilities managers, there was a significant consensus that the most pressing need was to facilitate the sharing of expertise across the geographically dispersed managers. Whilst many gained great value from using social media, such as LinkedIn, to help one another solve specific problems or issues or to gain additional perspectives, this was piecemeal and tended to exist only where managers knew each other before their current assignments. Indeed, it was most prevalent among managers in the UK who met informally from time to time. More recent recruits overseas often worked in isolation from the wider group, sharing information only sporadically with those working out of the same national office. That the facilities managers typically spend their time on clients' sites increased the problems of isolation.

Although the firm is headquartered in the UK, and much technical expertise tended to be centred there, the HR director recognised that as the firm grew, more and more valuable knowledge – for example, over good practice and business solutions – would develop and exist in subsidiary offices. Moreover, as the firm recruited more facilities managers to cope with its growth, it needed to develop ways to leverage the existing knowledge of all staff.

In response, the firm set out to create a virtual community of practice to capture and share this distributed knowledge, in order to enable facilities managers in different locations to contact one another and share expertise and experiences, without necessarily having to go through headquarters to facilitate contact with the 'right person' with the 'right knowledge'. The hope was that this greater connectivity and visibility of knowledgeable individuals would support informal learning and distribute knowledge.

To support this initiative, the firm engaged an e-learning consultancy – Sundfor Solutions – to create a common portal that contained information regarding the location and contact details for all other facilities managers, and a detailed expertise inventory. Given the value of this knowledge the firm made the decision to make this information available only via secure desktops. On Sundfor's advice, they also embedded within this portal a platform for employee collaboration, internal social networking and corporate communication. In order to democratise access to the discussions that had previously taken place via public social networking sites, the firm insisted that all work-related discussions needed to take place via this channel and sought to discourage use of public sites.

In implementation, however, the firm encountered a number of problems. Many engineers reportedly were reluctant to enter information into the inventory either because it represented an additional demand on their time or because they had already provided such information to headquarters. Others had difficulties accessing the site because of software incompatibilities and because it was difficult to navigate in areas of low broadband speeds. There was also some resistance among more senior engineers to share their expertise owing to a lack of trust regarding the motives for the rather sudden introduction of this system and a lack of guidance on the use of social networking. That many of the facilities managers had not met one another only appeared to add to the reluctance to engage with the new system.

Questions

1 Prior to the introduction of the new portal, what were the specific knowledge management imperatives at SA and what barriers to the effective sharing of knowledge existed in the firm?

2 In your opinion, what were the problems associated with the introduction of the new portal that led to a failure of the firm to address many of the knowledge-sharing problems it identified?

3 In your view are the problems encountered at SA, social, managerial or technological in nature? Why?

4 What might you do in order to address the problems identified in the case?

USEFUL READING

Journal articles

Poell, R. F., van Dam, K. and van der Berg, P. T. (2004) Organising learning in work contexts, *Applied Psychology: An International Review*, 53 (4): 529–40.

This article discusses the broad shift in emphasis from training to learning in the workplace. The article reviews the literature in three related areas: the learning potential of work. learning in the workplace and learning environments.

Books, book chapters and reports

CIPD (2012) *Research Insight: From e-Learning to 'Gameful' Employment*, London: CIPD.

This report explores the possibilities in the development of e-learning covering the use of social media, smartphone technology and artificial intelligence and their current and potential role in supporting learning in the workplace.

CIPD (2014) *Learning and Talent Development Survey Report 2014*, London: CIPD.

A useful starting point in the study of HRD is to explore what's happening NOW in respect of organisational practice in the area of learning and development. The annual CIPD learning and development survey report is a valuable resource that identifies key trends that are explored in later chapters, including the impact of prevailing economic conditions on HRD, the use of e-learning and the balance in employer focus between formal and informal, and on-the-job and off-the-job, learning interventions.

FURTHER ONLINE READING

The following articles can be accessed for free on the book's companion website **https://edge.sagepub. com/wilton3e**:

Billett, S. (2014) Mimesis: Learning through everyday activities and interactions at work, *Human Resource Development Review*, 13 (4): 462–82.

Brandenburg, D. C. and Ellinger, A. D. (2010) The future: Just-in-time learning expectations and potential implications for human resource development, *Advances in Developing Human Resources*, 5: 308–20.

Felstead, A., Green, F. and Jewson, N. (2012) An analysis of the impact of the 2008–9 recession on the provision of training in the UK, *Work, Employment & Society*, 26 (6): 968–86.

Garavan, T. N. (2007) A strategic perspective on human resource development, *Advances in Developing Human Resources*, 9 (1): 11–30.

Garavan, T. N. and McGuire, D. (2010) Human resource development and society: Human resource development's role in embedding corporate social responsibility, sustainability, and ethics in organizations, *Advances in Developing Human Resources*, 12 (5): 487–507.

van der Veen, R. (2006) Human resource development: Irreversible trend or temporary fad?, *Human Resource Development Review*, 5 (1): 3–7.

Want to know more about this chapter? Visit the companion website at: **https://edge.sagepub.com/wilton3e** to access practice questions, videos and selected journal articles to further enhance your study.

10

EMPLOYMENT RELATIONS

CHAPTER OBJECTIVES

THE EMPLOYMENT
RELATIONSIP

- To outline alternative perspectives on power and authority in the employment relationship

- To outline the relationship between HRM and employment relations

- To discuss key trends in employment relations, particularly trade union decline and the rise of non-unionism

- To outline the notions of employee voice, employee involvement and participation

- To identify the various means by which employees can be given a voice in organisational decision-making and the rationale for doing so

- To introduce 'partnership' approaches to employment relations.

INTRODUCTION

In broad terms, employment relations (ER) is concerned with the theory and practice associated with the management and regulation of the employment relationship. In particular, it is concerned with the socio-political dimension of the employment relationship and the distribution of power between management and employees, the incidence and expression of conflict and the social and legislative regulatory framework within which the employment relationship exists.

Employment relations is the contemporary term used to refer to what has traditionally been called 'industrial relations'. As both an academic area of study and a set of organisational activities, industrial relations has traditionally referred to the management of the relationship between trade unions and management, and associated processes including collective bargaining, negotiation and consultation, and industrial conflict. The use of the term 'employment relations' rather than industrial relations reflects a range of developments in the political, economic, social and legal context of the employment relationship that have taken place over the last three decades. The advent of new forms of employee management, such as HRM, alongside shifting industrial structures to a service-dominated economy, declining trade union power and influence, political antipathy towards the union movement, greater individualisation and flexibility in the management of labour and changing social attitudes have created a more diverse employment landscape. Subsequently, employment relations is concerned with the management of the employment relationship at both the individual and collective level (Latornell, 2007), both in union and non-union workplaces and in all industry sectors. In short, Kaufman (2004: 45) defines employment relations as 'the study of the employment relationship and all the behaviours, outcomes, practices, and institutions that emanate from or impinge upon the employment relationship'. CIPD (2009e) suggest that employment relations in practice is best understood as a skill-set or a philosophy for employers, rather than as a specific management function or well-defined area of activity. Boxall (2014) notes that, whilst much HRM research has tended to focus on the organisational agenda – how managers hire, motivate and develop people – research in employment relations has been more greatly focused on analysing employer behaviour in its wider societal context. As such, HRM can learn much from the understanding of the employment relationship generated within the field and how it might lead to more sustainable and mutually beneficial organisations.

Further online reading The discussion presented in this article provides an interesting backdrop against which this chapter can be understood, not least in respect of the relationship between HRM and employment relations. In particular, Boxall discusses the different focuses of research in these fields in order to suggest a greater focus on the nature of the employment relationship, both individually and collective, to shape HR practice that is both sustainable and mutually beneficial.

Boxall, P. (2014), The future of employment relations from the perspective of human resource management, *Journal of Industrial Relations*, 56 (4): 578–93.

This chapter begins by considering a number of theoretical perspectives of the employment relationship and how particular viewpoints can inform approaches to managing people. It then considers developments in ER associated with the decline in workplace trade unionism. The chapter then outlines the range of means by which employees can have a voice in organisational decision-making on both operational and strategic issues. The chapter ends by discussing partnership approaches to employee relations.

CONTROL, POWER AND AUTHORITY IN THE EMPLOYMENT RELATIONSHIP

In Chapter 2, the socio-political dimension of the employment relationship was briefly introduced. This dimension is concerned with control, power and authority in the collective employment relationship and represents the predominant concern for employment relations analysis and study. Power in the employment relationship reflects the ability of one party – whether management or employees as individuals or a collective group with shared interests – to shape or control the conduct or behaviour of the other in a desired manner, as well as the extent to which this influence can be exerted without the need to modify their own conduct or position (for example, through bargaining or negotiation). In short, it is the extent to which one party can compel the other to act pursuant to their own agenda and interests. With this in mind, the employment relationship can be argued to be based on a fundamental imbalance of power, with the party who has most to lose by its termination tending to be the weaker party. Typically, this will be the employee, reflecting, for instance, the emotional, financial and social impact of job loss.

Managerial power has a number of different sources that represent levers by which individuals or the managerial ranks as a whole might seek to exert control over workers and in some cases vice versa. French and Raven (1959) refer to five distinct forms of power in the employment relationship that management can employ to advance their own agenda:

1 *Reward power*, reflecting the ability of managers to give and withhold reward in accordance with the compliance of workers.

2 *Legitimate power*, conferred by hierarchical authority and status and reflecting the 'right' to make decisions according to office.

3 *Expert power*, reflecting possessed expertise and knowledge and the ability to make decisions on the basis of this expertise (such power can also be exerted by employees).

4 *Referent power*, based on the identification of employees with the personality ('charisma'), values or beliefs of managers or management as a whole, and an association with these collective values and/or respect for the individual and their reputation.

5 *Coercive power*, reflecting control by fear and ability to punish non-conformity or non-compliance with the will of management.

Most employees accept the social convention of some level of managerial or organisational power and control in the employment relationship, even if only in respect of conforming to the overall purpose of the organisation. However, given that the interests of workers and management do not necessarily always coincide, it is perhaps inevitable that the exertion of power can create conflict, for example, where it is perceived to have been used unfairly or contrary to the interests of the other party.

The extent of the imbalance of power depends, therefore, on the relative strength of employees to resist the will of management, typically through the collectivisation of the workforce and the subsequent willingness and ability of management to cede to this collective power. The relative strength of each party determines the degree of authority that management possesses to make decisions unilaterally or the extent to which it must seek the consent of workers through processes of consultation, negotiation and bargaining. It is these 'political' processes, and the way in which they are enacted and perceived in individual firms, that reflect the institutionalisation of power, conflict and authority in the employment relationship. Through such processes of discussion and negotiation, workers can seek to resist managerial authority depending on their collective strength or importance to the organisation (their centrality to the firm's activities) or their individual value to the firm (their degree of substitutability in the labour market).

On a theoretical level, there are a number of competing perspectives or conceptualisations of the relationship between capital (employers) and labour (employees) that reflect different views of the relative balance of power and the legitimacy of worker dissent and resistance to managerial action. (Table 10.1 provides details

TABLE 10.1 *Perspectives on the employment relationship*

	Ideology	Power	Conflict	Processes	Trade unions
Unitarism	Organisations are viewed as unified entities All parties have common objectives	Primacy of 'managerial prerogative' Management as single source of authority Employment relationship is essentially consensual, reflecting common interests	Conflict is unnatural/irrational Where conflict exists, it is the result of trouble-makers or agitators, misunderstanding or mis-communication	Unilateral decision-making by management Employer actions and legal initiatives to contain or suppress conflict are legitimate	Trade unions are viewed as either unnecessary or illegitimate Management must have the freedom to operate in accordance with the dictates of the market
Pluralist	An organisation comprises a coalition of different sectional interests and groups Parties have both shared and diverse interests and objectives	Management leads but its authority can be legitimately contested and questioned Power relations are fluid and the relative dominance of parties can change over time	Conflict is inherent, unavoidable and, within limits, legitimate and healthy Industrial action is a legitimate expression of conflict	Range of processes needed to maintain 'dynamic equilibrium' Conflict of interests should be contained and resolved through rules, negotiation and collective bargaining	Trade unions and other collective bodies are legitimate representatives of separate interests
Radical/Marxist	Relationship between capital and labour based on class conflict – 'them' and 'us' The employment relationship is marked by deep conflicts of interest (class conflict rather than group conflict)	Fundamental imbalance of power Power lies with owner of means of production (employers) – reflecting an exploitative relationship	Constant, inevitable and irreconcilable conflict of interests Disputes may be settled but underlying conflict remains until the structure of society changes	Social unrest required to break the status quo Employee relations processes do not fundamentally alter the status quo	Unions are collaborators in the maintenance of the status quo True workplace democracy impossible without worker control of means of production

of three key theoretical standpoints.) These perspectives can inform and underpin particular approaches to the management of people and are useful in considering the underlying assumptions that inform particular managerial practices, as well as raising fundamental questions around the nature of the employment relationship (Budd and Bhave, 2008).

HRM AND EMPLOYMENT RELATIONS

As briefly discussed in Chapter 2, in addition to representing perspectives on the employment relationship, unitarism and pluralism can also be understood as 'ideal types' (Fox, 1974) associated with particular managerial ideology and representing a set of assumptions that can underpin HRM practices. For example, the unitarist view is reflected in an authoritarian and autocratic management style where managerial prerogative in decision-making is maintained through strict control and discipline (reflecting hard HRM) and hostility towards unions (union suppression). Alternatively, unitarism can underpin more paternalist approaches to management, where employees are encouraged to think of the organisation as akin to a 'family' or 'team' where the employer will take care of the workforce and make decisions that reflect the common interests of all organisational members (soft HRM). Under this approach, managers 'substitute' for unions by concerning themselves with employee welfare and removing the need for union presence. Best practice models of HRM that have emerged since the 1980s are often referred to a neo-unitary, reflecting the adoption of cooperative employee relations in pursuit of organisational goals. Pluralism underpins management styles that accept or are forced to accept the presence of conflicting interest groups within the firm and the legitimacy of trade unions to represent workers' interests.

To develop this distinction, Purcell and Sisson (1983) suggest a typology of five 'management styles' based on the degree to which unitarism and pluralism are emphasised (Box 10.1). Notably, *sophisticated human relations* firms display the neo-unitarism, individualism and union substitution associated with high-commitment approaches to HRM. A pluralist approach to people management based upon a combination of individualism and collectivism is present in *consultative sophisticated moderns*, reflecting a cooperative partnership between management and trade unions. On this basis, 'high-commitment' HRM practices and trade unions are not necessarily mutually exclusive and, in some circumstances, union presence can contribute to the achievement of the goals of HRM, such as employee commitment, flexibility and quality. Nonetheless, HRM practices often tend to represent, either implicitly or explicitly, a strategy of union substitution or are used to disguise anti-union sentiment among management.

The interaction between HRM and employee relations is also explored in Guest and Conway's (1999) framework for analysing the relationship between, on the one hand, unitarist, individualised HRM practices and, on the other, employee relations, denoting pluralism and trade union recognition. Firms placing emphasis on both employee relations and HRM are characterised as *partnerships* combining individual and collective mechanisms for the management of employees. Such an approach is common in the public sector and a few high-profile large private sector firms. *Traditional pluralist* firms emphasise negotiation, consultation and information-sharing across a wide range of issues solely via recognised trade union representatives. Firms that prioritise the individual management of labour and soft HRM are referred to as *individualist*. Finally, Guest and Conway identify firms that have neither mechanisms for the collective management of labour nor sophisticated HRM practices, referring to these organisations as *black holes*, characterised by an absence of formal people management practices.

BOX 10.1
UNDERSTAND

A typology of management style

- Traditional

  Authoritarian unitarism: Workers are excluded from decision-making, and power is concentrated in the hands of management whilst a policy of union suppression or avoidance is adopted. Workers are treated as factors of production and a cost-minimisation approach is taken to the management of labour.

- Sophisticated human relations

  Paternalist unitarism: Workers are regarded as organisational assets and management seeks to maximise employee identification with the aims of the company. Sophisticated HRM policies are believed to remove any need or justification for opposition by workers and, therefore, trade union recognition is unlikely.

- Sophisticated moderns

  Pluralism: Workers, normally via unions, are seen as legitimately involved in specific areas of decision-making. There are two types of sophisticated moderns:

  ○ constitutional – the emphasis is on formal agreements to regulate relationships, particularly the adoption of a legalistic approach to establish clearly the demarcation between areas of power-sharing and managerial prerogative

  ○ consultative – reflects a less formal, more flexible approach to employee relations where union participation in decision-making is encouraged through recognition, problem-solving mechanisms and two-way communication.

- Standard moderns

  Management's approach to employee relations swings between unitarism and pluralism: Contingent or opportunistic management where the adopted approach reflects the prevailing employee relations climate. When union power is perceived as low, management makes decisions; when power is high, a negotiating or consulting approach may be adopted. This can be characteristic of large companies where responsibility for employee relations is devolved to subsidiaries resulting in a lack of standardisation.

  Source: Purcell, J. and Sisson, K. (1983) Strategies and practice in the management of industrial relations, in G. S. Bain (ed.), *Industrial Relations in Britain*, Oxford: Blackwell, pp. 95–120. Reprinted with permission.

KEY TRENDS IN BRITISH EMPLOYMENT RELATIONS

The range of factors that have acted to shape the role and trade union influence over management and wider society vary from nation to nation. As an example of how a range of economic, political and social phenomena over the last 30 to 40 years have influenced trade union activity and power the following section explores key trends in the UK. The experience of the UK has, however, resonance with that of other nations.

Over much of the twentieth century, trade unions in the UK have been viewed as legitimate vehicles for the representation of employee interests, and collective bargaining the main mechanism for wage setting. During the course of the 1980s and 1990s, however, successive Conservative governments sought to deregulate the economy and labour market to give greater freedom and flexibility to managers to respond to changes in organisational context. This process of deregulation was achieved through the limiting of employment protection for workers and restricting the ability of trade unions to undermine the 'right to manage'.

BOX 10.2
GLOBAL INSIGHT

International employment relations

Chapter 5 discussed Hofstede's (2001) model of cultural difference, which suggests that national cultures differ along a continuum between individualism and collectivism. To a certain degree, the position of a nation state along this continuum reflects attitudes towards trade unionism and the extent to which employees are given a voice in organisational decision-making.

The power distance dimension in Hofstede's typology is reflected in the extent to which managers tend to hold the prerogative in decision-making, the coverage and preferred level of collective bargaining and the extent to which industrial conflict is viewed as legitimate. For example, in the USA, a highly individualised culture, trade unions are typically marginalised and management tends to hold the right to make decisions unilaterally. In Japan, however, a more collectivist culture is reflected in greater employee involvement in decision-making, although trade unions are rarely independent from the organisation whose employees they represent (enterprise or company unions). However, as noted in Chapter 5, patterns of cultural difference are complex and nation states often display characteristics and institutional practice that might appear contradictory in another context,

reflecting the different roots of similar practices. For example, whilst employee involvement is promoted in both Germany and Japan, in the former it is reflective of processes of industrial democracy that exemplify a pluralistic perspective on organisations and a need to institutionalise naturally conflicting interests. In the latter, however, it reflects a more unitarist perspective and the pursuit of workplace harmony and joint decision-making to achieve shared objectives.

The institutional context of employee relations also differs from nation to nation. For example, in the UK, the state tends to seek to avoid direct intervention in the employment relationship. This lack of state intervention and deeply embedded class structures are reflected in an adversarial relationship between capital and labour. In countries characterised by 'social partnership' the state tends to intervene more directly by laying the foundations for more peaceable relationships and cooperative dialogue between unions and management. A key tension between the UK and the European Union is the contrast in employee relations traditions, where the UK tends to reject attempts at intervening in employment regulation, reflecting the dominant voluntaristic approach, which contrasts with the 'continental' system favouring greater social and legal regulation of employment.

Among other factors, this government policy has significantly altered the conditions under which workers are engaged by their employers.

Trade union decline

Trade unions have traditionally played a significant role in regulating the employment relationship in the UK through collective bargaining with employers over pay, working practices and terms and conditions of employment. The union movement reached its peak of political and economic power, membership and density (the proportion of the working population who are members of a trade union) in the late 1970s. In 1979, there were 13.2 million members of trade unions in the UK equating to 58 per cent of all those in employment. By 2008, however, unions had only 7.2 million members representing 24.9 per cent of those in employment. Across all sectors, just under half of UK employees

TRADE UNIONS STRIKES

(46.7 per cent) were in a workplace where a trade union was present (Barratt, 2009). However, whilst figures on overall union density are useful in assessing the relative state of unionism in a given context they tend to mask significant variation in union membership within sections of the labour market. Bryson and Forth (2010) note, for instance, that the downward trend in union membership is most pronounced among manual workers, male workers, younger workers and those in the private sector. In contrast, union membership has remained relatively stable among non-manual workers, female workers, older workers and those in the public sector.

This means that, despite unions having traditionally been dominated by male employees, union density among female workers exceeds that of men (28 per cent compared to 23 per cent in 2013). The most marked contrast is among workers in the public sector compared to those in the private sector, with 55 per cent of workers in the former being union members compared to 14 per cent in the latter (BIS, 2014). Connectedly, union density is also notably lower in smaller workplaces: 35 per cent of those in workplaces with more than 50 employees being union members compared to 17 per cent of those in workplaces with less than 50 employees. Professional unions – such as those representing teachers and health workers, and those representing workers in construction and retail – have seen growth in membership in recent years (Wright, 2011). Employees in professional occupations constitute 37 per cent of all union members (BIS, 2014).

Table 10.2 shows that union decline is not just a UK phenomenon with unions in many other advanced industrial economies having experienced a significant decline in both membership and influence in recent years. The table also shows, however, that national trends in union coverage and importance are divergent. For instance, in India, despite low density (Datt, 2008), trade unions continue to exert strong pressure on HRM practices (Budhwar and Khatri, 2001).

There are several factors that have combined to contribute to the decline in both union strength and influence, many of which are pervasive across nations. The shift in many countries from a manufacturing to a service-based economy has meant that much of the traditional 'heartland' of trade union activity and membership has been eroded. Trade unions have traditionally been less well established in the service sector and the smaller workplace size in this sector has provided significant challenges to union organisation and recruitment compared to the larger workplaces associated with manufacturing which are more conducive to worker solidarity. A key contributor to union decline is therefore a reduction in the number of large employers (associated with a shift towards service sector employment), where unions have traditionally been more successful in organising and recruiting members. Unions continue to be a strong presence in the public sector but the extensive privatisation of state-owned organisations, notable in the UK during the 1980s and 1990s, and introduction of market pressures in the remaining public sector (Brown and Marsden, 2010) mean that union strength is further weakened.

The political climate during this period also contributed to the decline in union influence. In the UK, the Conservative government elected to power in 1979 considered union power at the time to be a significant impediment to UK competitiveness in the emerging global economy. Subsequently, successive governments have sought to weaken the ability of unions to challenge managerial prerogative. A wide range of statutory provisions were introduced to restrict trade union activity, for example, through the introduction of stringent rules governing lawful industrial action and banning 'closed shops' (workplaces where all employees were required to join a particular union). Therefore, whilst echoing the traditions of voluntarism in their actions towards management and the protection of workers, Conservative governments used increased legalism to significantly shift the balance of power

TABLE 10.2 *Trade union density, 1997 and 2012, selected OECD countries*

	Trade union density	
	1999	**2012**
Australia	25.4	18.2
Austria	37.4	27.4
Belgium	54.3	55
Canada	28	27.5
Chile	13.5	15.3
Czech Republic	29	13.4
Denmark	74	67.2
Estonia	16.3	6.4
Finland	76.3	68.6
France	8.1	7.7
Germany	25.3	17.9
Greece	26.8	21.3
Hungary	24.5	10.6
Iceland	87.4	82.6
Ireland	38.7	31.2
Italy	35.4	36.3
Japan	22.2	18
Luxembourg	43.3	32.8
Mexico	15.8	13.6
Netherlands	24.7	17.7
New Zealand	21.7	20.5
Norway	54.8	53.3
Poland	20.5	12.5
Portugal	22.5	20.5
Slovak Republic	34.2	16.8
Spain	16.8	17.5
Sweden	80.6	67.5
Switzerland	20.9	16.2
Turkey	10.6	4.5
United Kingdom	30.1	25.8
United States	13.4	11.1

Source: OECD (2015)

in the employment relationship in favour of management. Despite the coming to power of a Labour government in 1997 and some greater rights for union recognition, the most meaningful curbs on union activity imposed by the Conservative governments remain in place.

For management, the weakening of union power allowed the reassertion of the 'right to manage' and concerted efforts to derecognise or marginalise unions. The 1980s also saw growing diversity of managerial practice with the influence of HRM, the activities of foreign MNCs and greater scope for innovation afforded by weak unions contributing to a 'mosaic' of workplace arrangements for the management of people. On the worker side, the 1980s are often associated with growing individualism and self-interest, which undermined worker solidarity. A failure of unions to adequately respond to labour market change (for example, the growth of female participation and the increased use of non-standard forms of employment) is also argued to have contributed to a decline in union membership.

These explanations for union decline are not exclusive to the UK. For instance, Suzuki (2010) reports that a decline in union membership in Japan over the three decades from the mid-1970s was caused by a combination of a shift towards service sector employment, improvements in standards of living and a rise in atypical employment.

Further online reading This article reviews the recent developments in employment relations in Japan and discusses how traditional Japanese employment relations systems with long-term employment still apply to core workers in large firms, but their share has been diminishing in favour of the continued growth of atypical employment or non-regular employees.

Suzuki, H. (2010) Employment relations in Japan: Recent changes under global competition and recession, *Journal of Industrial Relations*, 52 (3): 387–401.

Decline in strike activity

One effect of union decline is to contribute to a perception of industrial 'peace'. A catalyst for desire among the Conservative government to restrict union activity was the 'Winter of Discontent' in 1978–79 which brought to a head a prolonged period of industrial unrest during difficult economic conditions from the mid-1970s onwards. The 1970s constituted a peak of strike activity. For example, in the period 1970–74, 14.1 million working days were lost to strike action compared to only 924,000 working days in 2000–2. The effect of union restrictions on the ability to take strike action has meant that the UK has now fallen below the average strike rate of other OECD and EU countries in every year bar one since 1992. The question remains, however, whether this decline in strike activity – typically used as a measure of the degree of industrial discontent among the workforce – truly represents growing satisfaction with employee relations or whether declining strike activity masks continued discontent and the greater use of alternative forms of expression. This question is considered in more detail in Chapter 14.

Union renewal?

A key question in UK employment relations is the extent to which union decline since the 1970s is fundamental and irreversible. Historically, unions have experienced peaks and troughs in membership numbers and periodic restrictions on union activity through legislation and government action. For some, therefore, recent union decline is merely part of a longitudinal cycle and reflects a period of readjustment to changing economic conditions and structures. Others argue, however, that the combination of factors that has contributed to union decline is such that unions are likely to struggle to recover any significant presence, particularly in the private sector.

Unions have adopted a number of strategies for renewal and to increase both membership and political strength. For example, the last decade has seen greater union consolidation through mergers and the creation of a number of super-unions – general unions representing a wide range of worker groups, created through the amalgamation of several smaller, occupationally specific unions. Currently, approximately three-quarters of UK union members are concentrated in 11 trade unions (for example, AMICUS, T&G, GMB, Unison).

Other strategies for renewal include the adoption of an 'organising model' with a greater focus on grassroots recruitment among workers traditionally under-represented by unions such as women, young workers and those from minority ethnic groups. Similarly, some unions have also seen renewal stem from the development of new structures and means of sharing information to support union members in negotiating at local levels, whilst maintaining a collective union identity at a national level (Cumbers et al., 2010). Alternatively, a 'servicing model' is based on expanding membership through the provision of a wider range of benefits to members, such as credit cards, loans and insurance services. Wright (2011) suggests that an increased union focus on 'learning and skills' appears to present a promising boost for union relevance. Such a focus holds the benefits of appealing to both employers and workers as well as enabling unions to connect with a more diverse labour market through supporting employees to develop valuable skills. As such, learning has become an increasingly significant dimension of the dialogue between employer and unions and evidence suggests this can lead to improved union–management relations (Stuart et al., 2010). Finally, in order to boost recognition among employers, some unions have also been promoting themselves as partners, rather than adversaries to management, and seeking to develop more a conciliatory and trusting employment relationship from which positive gains for both parties can develop (Saundry et al., 2011). Partnership is discussed in more detail later in the chapter.

The rise of non-unionism

Clearly, the decline in union coverage and influence has coincided with a commensurate rise in non-unionism. A non-union workplace is identified by the absence of union membership, recognition and representation, but such workplaces can fall into a number of distinct categories. First, union presence can be limited through the use of paternalistic or sophisticated HRM practices which substitute for the need for trade union protection (rather than replacing or seeking to replicate the activities of trade unions themselves) through welfare policies, informal or formal channels of communication and (often) good terms and conditions of employment. Paternalism is typical of smaller family firms whereas sophisticated HRM substitutes are more common in larger 'excellent' employers who are better able to offer superior terms and conditions of employment. In both cases the effect is that unions are viewed as unnecessary because positive employer practices lessen the causes of unionism, such as worker dissatisfaction (Fiorito, 2001). However, whilst the introduction of particular HRM practices can be an attempt to marginalise unions (Markey, 2007), union substitution is not necessarily always part of a purposefully anti-union strategy.

BOX 10.3
RESEARCH INSIGHT

Airlines, country of origin and employment relations

As outlined in Chapter 5, the institutional and cultural context in which firms develop and operate tends to exert influence over their approaches to people management. To explore the extent of this influence in the airline industry, Bamber et al. (2009) look at the extent to which a number of airlines, both new entrants to the market and well-established 'legacy' airlines that were previously under state control as national carriers (such as British Airways, SAS and Lufthansa), were influenced by their country of origin in the adoption of ER strategies. In order to establish the nature of this relationship in each case, the authors classified each airline according to how they sought to reduce cost (whether by minimising wages or seeking high productivity), their ER strategies (whether through *controlling* employee behaviour or seeking their *commitment* to the goals of the airline) and whether the airline sought to *avoid*, *accommodate* or *partner* with unions.

The authors suggest that new entrants to the marketplace have greater scope to determine their approach to ER irrespective of the traditions of their country of origin. For example, on the one hand, Ryanair, the Irish low-cost airline, have adopted an aggressive anti-union approach to employment relations (as part of a wider strategy of cost minimisation and 'command and control' of employees) that runs counter to recent trends in Ireland to develop partnership approaches to ER.

On the other hand, easyJet, the low-cost British airline, has gradually shifted its approach to ER from employee control and union avoidance towards a commitment approach and an accommodation of union presence, reflecting a greater focus on developing a 'strong people culture' that had been successful in the US airline, Southwest.

Of the legacy airlines, British Airways is characterised as having adopted a strategy of union accommodation, despite its use of the language of 'partnership' and stressing the importance of its employees to success. This reflects the antagonistic union–management relations that have long characterised BA and in spite of the neo-liberal economic context in the UK in the period since the company was privatised. Similarly, albeit under the conditions of the German coordinated-market economy, Lufthansa has largely been compelled to adopt a partnership approach to employment relationship, negotiating change with employees rather than imposing it, because of the embeddedness of such relations between employers and unions within the German institutional context. They have, for instance, largely sought to avoid significant redundancies in the face of intense competition and other adverse conditions (for example, the impact of air travel after 9/11) in contrast to the job losses seen in the UK and USA.

In short, whilst national institutional context can clearly shape the approach to employment relations adopted in a particular airline, its effect is mediated by the origins and development of the individual firm and can change over time.

Further online reading

Bamber, G. J., Hoffer Gittell, J., Kochan, T. A. and von Nordenflycht, A. (2009) Contrasting management and employment-relations strategies in European airlines, *Journal of Industrial Relations*, 51 (5): 635–52.

Non-unionism can also be found in anti-union firms where 'suppression' tends to be the main mechanism for avoidance (McLoughlin and Gourlay, 1994). This approach tends to be characteristic of firms who compete on (lowest) cost, and where poor employee relations are reflected in high staff turnover and de-skilled or low-skill employment. Dundon and Gollan (2007) note, however, that substitution and suppression are not mutually exclusive approaches and can overlap and co-exist, even within the same firm. A case study of anti-union activity is provided at the end of this chapter.

As discussed above, non-unionism is more prevalent in some sectors of the economy than others. Unions continue to be a powerful presence in the public sector and parts of the manufacturing sector (for example, the aerospace and automotive industries). Nonetheless, the Workplace Employment Relations Study 2011 (van Wanrooy et al., 2013) indicates that only 14 per cent of private service sector firms, and only 12 per cent of private manufacturing firms reported any union members among their workforce, compared to 89 per cent of public sector organisations. Commensurately, only 9 per cent of private manufacturing firms and 12 per cent of private service sector firms reported recognising a trade union, compared to 92 per cent in the public sector. There is evidence to suggest, however, that non-unionism is not necessarily a wholly beneficial position for employers. Wright (2011) reports that, as unions appear to be becoming more conciliatory (Ruhemann, 2010), perceptions among employees and managers of the value of trade unions appear to be improving.

EMPLOYEE VOICE

As discussed above, employment relations is concerned with power and control in the employment relationship and the degree to which management is free to make decisions unimpeded. Subsequently, a key dimension of employee relations

---

BOX 10.4
HRM IN PRACTICE

When does union avoidance become union-busting?

In February 2012 the defence technology company QinetiQ announced plans to end recognition of trade unions for collective bargaining purposes, claiming that because only around 30 per cent of its workforce of 5,500 employees were union members it was not 'logical' to 'bargain with a minority when their decisions affect the majority'. Management claimed this view was reinforced through feedback from employees who felt that such bargaining did not represent majority opinion and, therefore, sought to replace the process of collective bargaining with a new elected consultative body – the QinetiQ Employee Engagement Group – representing the entire workforce (*Financial Times*, 2012b).

However, those unions with members in QinetiQ saw this move by management rather differently, with one union leader referring to the decision to terminate union recognition as nothing more than crude union-busting in response to union members voting against a controversial pay offer in 2011 and despite a previously constructive relationship. A representative of the GMB union suggested that 'it is clear … the chief executive wishes to neutralise any challenges to employment conditions allowing the company to drive through changes to established terms and conditions of employment without any union moderation or consultation'.

A QinetiQ spokesman said:

We are looking forward to working with all of our employees to set up the new Employee Engagement Group, which will have real powers and budget to act as a representative body for providing recommendations and consultation in the future. This change is another step forward in our on-going plans to evolve the company to meet the changing market and is responding to employee feedback to provide everyone in the company with an equal voice. It helps set the company up with a modern employee engagement strategy appropriate for a commercial, private sector business that will still see the unions continuing to represent employees on an individual basis.

is the means by which employees are able to influence managerial decisions. Employee voice is used to refer to 'a whole variety of processes and structures which enable, and at times empower, employees, directly and indirectly, to contribute to decision-making in the firm' (Boxall and Purcell, 2003: 162). In other words, there are a number of mechanisms through which employees can contribute to or share in decision-making with management although, despite the suggestion of influence, giving employees a voice is not necessarily giving them any influence over decisions that affect them (Markey and Townsend, 2014).

Traditionally, the pressure for employees to be allowed a say at work has stemmed from notions of industrial democracy or 'industrial citizenship' (Gollan and Wilkinson, 2007). This pressure is typically exerted by employees themselves as a reflection of the extent to which they feel empowered and entitled to articulate concerns to management (Wilkinson et al., 2004), although this is increasingly being supplemented by the employer view that allowing and utilising employee voice can make good business sense. In the 1970s, employee voice in decision-making tended to be through 'indirect' worker participation via trade union representation. In the 1980s, reflecting declining trade union membership and recognition, 'direct' voice was afforded through employee involvement via managerially established forums or communication channels. In the 1990s, the focus shifted to 'partnership' between management and workers and joint decision-making (Rollinson and Dundon, 2007).

Mechanisms or channels for employee voice can be both formal and informal and can have a range of intentions, ranging from simply imparting information to a means through which employers and employees share responsibility for decisions. In order to connect together the form, purpose, mechanisms and outcomes of employee voice, Table 10.3 provides a fourfold classification of employee voice.

TABLE 10.3 *Employee 'voice'*

Voice represents:	Purpose of voice	Possible mechanisms or channels for voice	Potential positive/negative outcomes
Articulation of individual dissatisfaction	To remedy a problem and/or prevent deterioration in relations	Informal complaint to line manager; formal grievance procedure	(Reinforced) loyalty to organisation/employee exit, withdrawal of beneficial discretionary behaviour or informal expressions of dissatisfaction
Expression of collective organisation	To provide a countervailing source of power to management	Recognition of trade union by employer; collective bargaining; industrial action	Partnership between management and employees/non- or de-recognition of union; anti-union management 'tactics'
Employee contribution to management decision-making	To seek improvements in work organisation, quality and productivity	Employee involvement and participation (e.g. upward problem-solving initiatives; suggestion schemes; attitude surveys; self-managed teams)	Employee commitment and identification with aims of organisation; improved performance/disillusionment and apathy
Mutuality and cooperative workplace relations	To achieve long-term viability for the organisation and greater 'people added-value'	Partnership agreements; joint consultative committees; works councils	Significant employee influence in decision-making/management lip-service to employee contribution; 'sweetheart deals'

Source: Dundon et al. (2004) The meanings and purpose of employee voice, *International Journal of Human Resource Management*, 15 (6): 1149–70. Reprinted by permission of the publisher Taylor & Francis Group

Some forms of employee voice are clearly bottom-up, resulting not from managerial forums but a desire among employees to be heard, whether collectively or individually, formally or informally, directly or through representatives. Mechanisms for employee voice are, however, often introduced by management, whether as a response to pressure from employees, or as part of a strategy to be more inclusive in decision-making. As it is often management that dictates the extent of employee voice, Dundon and Rollinson (2007) use the term representation gap to refer to the difference between how much influence employees report having over management decisions and how much influence they would like to have. Mechanisms for employee voice can be analysed using the following framework (Marchington et al., 1992):

- *depth* – the extent to which employees (or their representatives) share in decision-making outcomes with management
- *scope* – the range of issues or matters on which employees (or their representatives) have a say
- *level* – the hierarchical level in an organisation at which voice mechanisms operate
- *form* – the type of voice mechanism used, which can be direct (individuals or small groups of workers) and/or indirect in nature (via worker representatives).

Using two of these measures – scope and depth – Figure 10.1 outlines the extent of employee voice, suggesting there are five degrees of influence that employees can have over organisational decision-making. Geary (1994) suggests that employee involvement and participation can be viewed as either consultative, whereby employees are encouraged to contribute their view, but management retains the right to make the final decision, or delegative, with employees taking on decisions that traditionally fell within the remit of management (also shown in Figure 10.1).

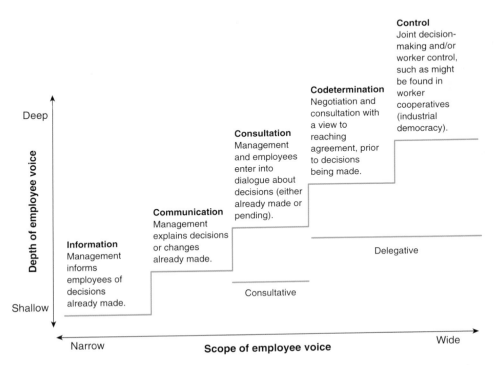

FIGURE 10.1 The extent of employee 'voice' (adapted from 'Voice mechanisms', in Marchington et al. (1992), reproduced under the terms of the Click-Use Open Government Licence

Even where management purports to consult with employees over decisions, the intentions of doing so can vary significantly (Butler and Glover, 2007). Low-level consultation exists where managers give workers (or their representatives) prior notice of certain decisions in order to afford workers a chance to voice their views but these rarely impact upon the final decision made by management. At the mid-level, workers' views may stimulate managerial reconsideration of their decision. Finally, at a high level, workers initiate criticism and suggestions and whilst management retain sole decision-making power, worker proposals are given serious consideration and are likely to influence the final decision.

Further online reading This article presents case study research findings and considers different managerial definitions and approaches – in terms of scope, level, form and depth – to employee voice. It also considers the problem of demonstrating a link between voice and organisational performance.

Wilkinson, A., Dundon, T., Marchington, M. and Ackers, P. (2004) Changing patterns of employee voice: Case studies from the UK and Republic of Ireland, *Journal of Industrial Relations*, 46 (3): 298–322.

BOX 10.5
HRM IN PRACTICE

Worker cooperatives

In January 2012, the British Prime Minister David Cameron announced plans to encourage the formation of worker cooperatives to promote 'socially responsible capitalism' and a 'fairer economy', promoting both economic efficiency and greater 'morality' in the operation of organisations by forming 'a direct link between contribution and reward; between effort and outcome' (*Personnel Management*, 2012b). The plans to promote such organisations involve streamlining existing legislation governing the establishment of cooperatives and the ability of workers to share in the benefits of such organisations.

Cooperative organisations are those that are owned by their members, whether customers, employees or local residents, and exist to serve those members (rather than shareholders) through sharing profits and allowing them to actively shape the decisions that the organisation makes. In the UK in 2010, there were 571 worker cooperatives or worker-owned businesses with 78,400 people as owners (Co-operatives UK, 2011). Worker cooperatives are notably more prevalent in continental Europe, particularly, France, Spain and Italy.

The largest worker cooperative in the UK (as opposed to worker-owned businesses such as the retail chain John Lewis) is Suma Wholefoods, which employs approximately 150 people and in 2010 had a turnover of more than £25 million. Their website (www.suma.coop) states that:

> Unlike most UK companies, Suma operates a thoroughly democratic system of management that isn't bound by the conventional notions of hierarchy. As a workers' cooperative the business is jointly owned and managed by all of us. Everyone is paid the same and we collectively do all the jobs that need doing, whatever they happen to be.

Evidence appears to bear out the view that cooperatives are an effective means of organising economic activity. Co-operatives UK (2011) report that the cooperative sector (which includes all forms of cooperative businesses) has grown by 21 per cent since 2008 whilst the UK economy as a whole has grown by only 1.3 per cent over the same period.

SUMA
WHOLEFOODS

The form, scope, level and depth of voice mechanisms present in an organisation will depend on a range of organisational factors, including organisational performance, union presence, market sector and management style (Lloyd and Newell, 2001), which, in turn, also shape employees' attitudes to these initiatives (Marchington et al., 1994). Ackers et al. (1992) suggest that the extent to which a firm emphasises high-quality service delivery or products or operates in tight labour market conditions determines the extent to which they would benefit from the employee commitment and adherence to organisational values that can stem from positive employee involvement in the decisions that affect the workforce. For example, Hoque (1999) suggests that under tight labour market conditions, managers in the hospitality industry attempt to incorporate the workforce by allowing them to participate in management decision-making, partly to engender greater commitment to the organisation from valued staff.

EMPLOYEE INVOLVEMENT AND PARTICIPATION

The terms 'involvement' and 'participation' are often used interchangeably in reference to the extent of decision-making influence afforded by employee voice mechanisms. Lewis et al. (2003: 248) suggest, however, that 'important differences exist between the concepts in relation to the exercise in power, the locus of control, the nature of employee influence, and the driving force behind each approach in practice'. For this reason, the following sections outline the distinction between the two terms.

Involvement

Employee involvement (EI) is defined as having the dual aim of engaging 'the support, understanding and contribution of all employees in an organisation' and 'seeking to ensure their commitment and cooperation in the achievement of its objectives' (CIPD, 2009e). EI seeks to harness the talents of employees through the soliciting of their views, opinions and ideas to identify and address organisational problems. Importantly, however, EI stops short of any degree of power-sharing between managers and employees in eventual decision-making and, as such, is regarded as a relatively weak form of voice in that whilst it seeks to engage employees and provide a channel for employee expression it preserves management's right to make decisions and generally provides for limited employee influence. Clearly, therefore, EI is underpinned by the unitarist assumption that managers and employees share common interests, and that management should retain fundamental control of decision-making. Therefore, whilst often associated with employee empowerment, EI does not represent a true redistribution of power in the employment relationship as management can retract this empowerment if it no longer serves their purpose.

In practice, EI is often focused on the engagement of small groups and individuals in addressing local, operational issues by facilitating information-sharing within work groups and between line managers and employees. Generally, EI does not extend to providing the opportunity for workers to have any input into higher-level, strategic decision-making, such as pay, working conditions or wider organisational policy. Mechanisms for employee involvement are invariably 'direct' in that they do not involve employee representatives. Examples of involvement mechanisms include suggestion schemes, quality circles, teamworking and self-managed workgroups. The decline of trade union representation in UK workplaces outlined above has coincided with some positive trends for employee involvement and participation. For example, The Workplace Employment Relations Study 2011 (van Wanrooy et al., 2013) found that, compared to the previous survey in 2004, employees were more likely to view positively management's attempts at consultation, responses to suggestions from employees and allowing employees and their representatives to influence decisions.

Participation

Employee participation (EP) is generally regarded as a more substantial form of voice than EI, because it tends to incorporate a greater degree of joint decision-making between management and employees. EP is grounded in pluralism in that it implicitly acknowledges the existence of a range of organisational stakeholders whose interests do not always coincide. EP implies some degree of power-sharing and dilution of the absolute 'right to manage' among employers and therefore associated practices are often resisted by managers, particularly where it involves trade union representation and where it is perceived to slow down the decision-making process. Participation can be contrasted with involvement in that the mechanisms for participation often derive from employees themselves rather than being managerially imposed and controlled. EP results, therefore, not from managerial desire to improve individual and organisational performance but rather from a desire among employees to have greater influence over decisions that directly or indirectly affect them (Strauss, 2006). Finally, whereas involvement is typically direct, participation is often indirect, involving the use of (elected) employee representatives to represent the interests of all employees. It, therefore, has more collective connotations than many forms of involvement.

Further online reading This extremely useful article explores the evolution of employee involvement and participation and presents a detailed discussion of definitional ambiguity surrounding 'employee voice'. It provides a more detailed supplement to the discussion presented in this chapter.

Markey, R. and Townsend, K. (2013) Contemporary trends in employee involvement and participation, *Journal of Industrial Relations*, 55 (4): 475–87.

Because participation is often concerned with negotiation, conflict may occur between employees and management, particularly where employees participate in higher-level decisions and differing interests are most likely to be visible. However, employee participation can also help to channel conflict to more effective resolution (Gollan and Wilkinson, 2007). Despite the greater level, scope and depth of employee participation, CIPD (2009e: 9) suggest that the 'informal climate of involvement and consultation appears to be more strongly associated with employee satisfaction and commitment than the collective machinery for negotiation and consultation'.

BOX 10.6
ETHICAL INSIGHT

The ethical dimension of employee empowerment

Claydon and Doyle (1996) suggest that much of the appeal of employee empowerment is that it can lead to both business benefits, through improving individual and collective performance, and the satisfaction of employees' need for self-expression and autonomy at work. In other words, the win–win rhetoric of empowerment is seductive because it is underpinned by assumptions that it is both economically and morally the 'right thing to do'.

Research suggests, however, that involvement and participation initiatives can serve as a tool for employee manipulation, particularly where channels of communication are controlled by management. Therefore, the extent to which empowerment has a 'control motive' is important in assessing the ethics of associated practices. Ramsay (1980) suggests that management are more likely to introduce the means for employee involvement to head-off a perceived challenge to their authority from employees by presenting involvement as a concession to employees but with the underlying purpose of marginalising trade unions. Therefore, involvement becomes a means by which to suppress conflict, pacify employees and resist more extensive forms of power-sharing. Where unions are established, employers might implement mechanisms for direct employee involvement in order to marginalise or weaken the position of trade unions within the firm by effectively 'cutting out' the union from communication channels. Practices such as teamworking and quality circles have also been criticised for utilising peer surveillance as a means of supervisory control.

There are also ethical questions over the extent to which the use of quality initiatives and self-managed workgroups is driven by a desire for management to pass on the responsibility and accountability for mistakes and divest itself of some of the risk for poor work organisation and management practice, particularly where worker reward is tied to particular performance measures.

EMPLOYEE VOICE IN PRACTICE

Marchington et al. (1992) identify four broad categories of employee involvement and participation initiatives that provide employees with differing degrees of influence over workplace decisions:

1 downward communication
2 upward problem-solving
3 representative participation
4 financial participation.

Downward communication

Downward communication refers to top-down communication from management to employees. Typical practices include company magazines and newsletters, team briefings, communication meetings, video briefings, employee reports, noticeboards, memoranda, presentations and staff intranets. In recent years there has been a substantial increase in the use of ICT in employee communication, for example the use of email and e-bulletins. As Figure 10.1 suggests, communication is limited to methods that are shallow in depth and narrow in scope, affording employees limited or no influence over managerial decisions. The size of the organisation will influence the style and formality of appropriate communication.

Communication practices tend to refer to processes by which management inform staff about decisions they have made and explain the rationale for these decisions, particularly when communication is from senior management with the purpose of communicating organisational strategy, mission and objectives. Alternatively, downward communication between line managers and employees might be used to communicate performance expectations and the impact on staff of wider business decisions.

Effective communication with employees is an essential means by which to develop a positive psychological contract, enhance the individual's identification with the organisation's strategic objectives (de Ridder, 2004) and develop and sustain organisational culture. However, despite being often cited as an important element in effective employee management, problems in the employment relationship frequently result from misunderstanding or inadequate communication where the intentions of either party are not made clear, are misrepresented or kept hidden. In such cases, employees and managers are prone to 'filling in the blanks' as regards the other's position, and informal channels of communication – 'the 'grapevine' – gain prominence and contribute to further misunderstanding.

Upward problem-solving

Upward problem-solving is concerned with empowering workers to improve work processes by encouraging them (either individually or in small groups) to suggest improvements and solutions to specific 'local' problems and to take greater responsibility for decisions over, for example, work organisation and allocation. This is often as part of a broader focus on high performance and/or high quality. In particular, the rationale for such initiatives is to give employees greater 'ownership' over decisions in order to develop increased association with the strategic objectives of the firm and to improve motivation and job satisfaction.

Workers can represent an untapped source of knowledge and understanding of job roles and work processes and, therefore, such involvement can reap benefits for the organisation by drawing on the expertise of those closest to the work situation. Examples of upward problem-solving mechanisms include quality circles or problem-solving groups, attitude surveys, employee focus groups, suggestion schemes and autonomous teamworking or self-managed teams where employees working in groups take responsibility for their job tasks, decide how their tasks are to be accomplished and appoint their own team leader from among members of the group.

The scope of upward problem-solving schemes can vary from small groups or individuals charged with solving specific problems or broader measures designed to seek the opinion of employees on a broad range of issues, allowing differences between employees and managers to surface and be resolved helping employees and managers to better understand each other's concerns, expectations, needs and wants. The level at which such involvement can operate can also vary, depending on the matter at hand. Drawing on Marchington et al.'s (1992) 'escalator', upward problem-solving often represents a form of consultation, with employees views being sought but not necessarily influencing managerial action or decisions. Indeed, direct participation may often be at the expense of representative forms where such systems are unilaterally imposed by management (Markey and Townsend, 2014).

Involving employees in decision-making, particularly where their views have a discernible influence, can improve the efficacy of the process and facilitate the effective implementation of decisions. Such involvement can also be a key means by which to reinforce company culture and ethos and, in particular, promote the unitarist notion that employees and managers share common interests and goals. However, whilst employee empowerment might contribute to a more positive psychological contract it might also have the opposite effect. Paul et al. (2000) suggest that employee empowerment will eventually lead to the unfulfilled expectations of influence, because management cannot always meet the 'ever-increasing entitlement beliefs' of employees.

Representative participation

Representative participation refers to mechanisms for indirect and collective employee participation in decision-making through management consultation and negotiation, either with trade unions or elected workers' representatives.

Such participation typically provides employees with a degree of influence over a range of issues as part of decision-making bodies, such as joint consultative committees, advisory councils and works councils. In the case of participation via trade union recognition by the employer, clearly the terms and form of participation are not entirely controlled by management. Trade union representation tends to yield greater power and influence over decisions, particularly because a failure to account for employees' views or to come to agreement can result in industrial action. This threat tends to ensure that management take the views of the workforce seriously. However, it would be amiss to assume that a positive effect on the employment relationship is inevitable simply because such mechanisms are in place (Danford et al., 2005).

The ultimate outcome of representative participation is some degree of industrial democracy. This is most apparent in the election of worker directors who advocate for employees' interests in strategic decision-making at boardroom level. Worker directors are more common in continental Europe than in Anglo-Saxon economies. Two of the most common forms of representative participation are collective bargaining and works councils/joint consultative committees.

COLLECTIVE BARGAINING   The most powerful form of representative participation is collective bargaining, which refers to the joint regulation of certain aspects of the employment relationship (most commonly, pay) by employers and recognised trade union representatives.

The worker solidarity that lies at the heart of collective bargaining results in a stronger employee bargaining position *vis-à-vis* management. Recognition agreements between trade unions and management specify both the issues covered by collective bargaining (and which can only be determined through agreement between the parties) and the bargaining level at which it takes place, whether workplace, organisational/employer or sectoral/national (covering all employees within a particular industry sector, sometimes referred to as multi-employer bargaining). Within the single organisation, therefore, there may be a number of collective agreements, reflecting the range of unions recognised for bargaining purposes, which cover different groups of workers.

Collective agreements typically cover a wider range of issues than other forms of involvement and participation, but are generally focused only on substantive issues such as pay and conditions (such as leave entitlements, pensions and working hours), staffing arrangements, the content of work and the demarcation between jobs. Negotiation over strategic matters is rarely covered by collective bargaining. Overall, the bargaining scope is both wide and deep.

As well as an economic function, collective bargaining also represents a governmental process through which the power politics of the employment are played out, with both sides often attempting both to maximise their own positional power and to diminish that of the other. Evidence suggests that where managers are concerned with the minimisation of labour costs, collective bargaining can be a significant problem with union members earning higher salaries on average than non-members. In 2013, for instance, the wage premium associated with union membership in the UK was 16.4 per cent per cent (19.8 per cent in the public sector and 7 per cent in the private sector) (BIS, 2014).

The coverage of collective bargaining in the UK has declined in the last three decades alongside the decrease in union membership and union recognition. In 1970, 80 per cent of the UK workforce was covered by collective bargaining for the purposes of pay setting but by 2013 that had declined to 30 per cent (BIS, 2014). In particular, there has been a significant decline in national (industry-level) collective bargaining, which is now rare outside the public sector. In 1960, 60 per cent of the UK workforce was covered by such bargaining but this had declined to 14 per cent in 1998, following a move among employers to decentralise bargaining to an organisational or workplace level in order to increase degrees of flexibility in negotiations. However, in certain sectors where collective bargaining has traditionally been extensive, such as transport and education, the collective bargaining process remains a principal source of employee voice. Whilst in the private sector collective agreements now cover only 17 per cent of employees, in the public sector collective agreement coverage is almost four times greater, at 64 per cent (BIS, 2014).

However, the UK example, where the decline in collective bargaining has partly been driven by widespread reform of employment regulation and the privatisation of state assets, is not necessarily instructive of global trends. Table 10.2 shows that in many countries trade union density has been in decline; in contrast, however, there has been relative stability over recent years in the numbers of workers covered by collective agreements in many countries, which often far outstrip the proportion of the workforce who are union members (Hayter et al., 2011).

Further online reading This article reviews recent national trends and developments in respect of the scope and coverage of collective bargaining, examining the evolution of collective bargaining institutions in different regions of the world and how these structures have adapted to competitive pressures. The article also considers challenges facing collective bargaining, including the prospects for increased coordination of bargaining practices both within and across borders.

Hayter, S., Fashoyin, T. and Kochan, T. A. (2011) Collective bargaining for the 21st century, *Journal of Industrial Relations*, 53 (2): 225–47.

WORKS COUNCILS AND JOINT CONSULTATIVE COMMITTEES   In the UK, the collective bargaining process is often supplemented by workplace joint consultative committees, where employee representatives are consulted over a range of issues but which fall short of joint decision-making. Similarly, but with greater influence over managerial decision-making, works councils are forums usually made up of representatives of workers (typically union officials) and management, and are used extensively in a number of European countries. Works councils typically operate at the organisational level and meet to discuss issues such as employee relations and business matters and to engage in joint decision-making.

BOX 10.7
HRM IN PRACTICE

Industrial democracy at John Lewis Partnership (JLP)

The John Lewis Partnership is one of Europe's largest models of employee ownership and has been operating a form of employee involvement and participation since its formation in 1929 when the business was legally put in trust for the workers 'present and prospective' (Cathcart, 2013: 605). Today the company defines itself as representing:

a visionary and successful way of doing business, boldly putting the happiness of Partners at the centre of everything it does. It's the embodiment of an ideal, the outcome of nearly a century of endeavour to create a different sort of company, owned by Partners dedicated to serving customers with flair and fairness.

Today, JLP constitutes 43 John Lewis stores and 338 Waitrose Supermarkets, as well as an online business, employing 93,800 'partners'.

The JLP Constitution sets out a vision of a co-owned business based on the principle of 'sharing knowledge, gain and power' (Cathcart, 2013: 605). The principle of power sharing at JLP is achieved by dividing it between several bodies including the Chairman, the Board and the Partnership Council, made of elected representatives from each store, that act to hold management accountable and to make key governance decisions. Each store also has a Branch Forum where elected representatives from each department discuss key issues.

Gain sharing is achieved by establishing both a minimum (based on living costs) and maximum wage and annual profit-sharing for all employees ('Partnership Bonus') averaging 15 per cent of pay over recent years.

Finally, knowledge sharing is achieved through a number of mechanisms including in-house magazines (to which partners can write anonymously to senior managers, letters and their replies having to be published) and the publication of detailed business information.

Despite the constitutional and legal framework that governs industrial democracy at JLP, Cathcart (2013) reports that it 'remains vulnerable to challenges from people who seek to constrain and direct it in ways that meet instrumental ends' (2013: 615). Cathcart reports, for instance, on the 'democracy project' that in 2005/6, as a response to high levels of employee dissatisfaction on a range of employment issues, sought to reinterpret the guiding principles of governance enshrined in the constitution in such a way that they acted to undermine democratic practices, for example, through managerial attempts to reform the 'Branch Councils' that had decision-making powers, into 'Branch Forums' that would have merely the ability to influence. As such, these forums would shift in focus from indirect participation, through voting rights on branch decisions, to mere involvement through consultation.

Therefore, Cathcart argues that JLP, despite being held up as an exemplar of partnership and industrial democracy, provides a case study of how 'management and employees contest the meaning and practice of employee involvement and participation'.

See Cathcart (2013) for a full discussion of the changes to industrial democracy at JLP.

Further online reading This article explores the John Lewis model of employee involvement and participation and how these practices have changed over time as a result of competing employee and managerial interests. It provides an interesting backdrop against which to consider the 'contested terrain' that is industrial democracy and how it can be undermined by management challenge.

Cathcart, A. (2013) Direct democracy: Competing interests and contested terrain in the John Lewis Partnership, *Journal of Industrial Relations*, 55 (4): 601–20.

Works councils are common in countries where they have strong statutory under-pinnings and are embedded in wider employee relations systems that recognise the interests of labour. For example, under German labour law, employers with more than five employees have a statutory duty to establish works councils at the request of employees, which then have a range of information rights (covering financial matters), consultation rights (covering, for example, workforce planning, working environment, job content and the adoption of new technology) and co-determination (joint decision-making) rights (covering 'social' matters including the principles of remuneration, PRP, work schedules, overtime, holidays, recruitment and dismissal).

2011
WERS

The 2011 Workplace Employment Relations Study (van Wanrooy et al., 2013) found that the incidence of joint consultative committees has declined since the previous survey in 2004. Overall, 25 per cent of all employees covered by the survey worked in a workplace with either a workplace or higher level JCC compared to 33 per cent seven years earlier.

IPA

PARTNERSHIP   Earlier in this chapter, reference was made to shifting patterns of employee voice over the past 30 years in the UK. Since the 1990s, much emphasis has been placed by UK government, employers and trade unions on the notion of 'partnership' (or 'mutual gains' as it is referred to in the USA). Politically, partnership represents a changed relationship between employers and employees, to one 'based not simply on power and rights but on the satisfaction of mutual as well as separate interests' (Acas, 2005: 2). Therefore, whilst it has pluralist underpinnings, it emphasises the mutual understanding and accommodation of these interests through cooperation rather than opposition and conflict. As Ackers and Payne (1998: 530) suggest, partnership represents 'the institutional process of applying the spirit of business ethics and the theory of stakeholding to the employment relationship'. Whilst partnership often refers to cooperative management–union relations, non-union partnership arrangements exist (Dietz et al., 2005; Johnstone et al., 2010).

Guest and Peccei (2001) note three approaches to partnership: the *pluralist* approach is based on a recognition of differences of interest between managers and workers and seeks to institutionalise these differences through democratic processes: the *unitarist* approach explicitly seeks to integrate employer and employee interests and maximise employee (direct) involvement and commitment to the organisation; the *hybrid* approach combines

TABLE 10.4   *Partnership principles*

Involvement and Participation Association (IPA, 1997)	Trade Union Congress (TUC, 1999)
Four key building blocks of the partnership principle: • Recognition of employees' desire for security and the company's need to maximise flexibility • Sharing success within the company • Informing and consulting staff about issues at workplace and company level • Effective representation of people's views within the organisation	• A shared commitment to the success of the organisation • Recognition of the legitimate roles of employer and trade union • A commitment by the employer to employment security for all workers and a commitment by the union to engage positively in the process of change • A focus on the quality of working life • Openness on both sides and a willingness by the employer to discuss plans and thoughts about the future when they are at the 'glint in the eye' stage • A shared understanding that the partnership is delivering measurable improvements for all parties

unitarist and pluralist perspectives, recognising the importance both of representative systems and direct involvement in delivering mutual gains. Such a model where direct and representative forms of employee voice are viewed as complementary – rather than mutually exclusive – is more common in Germany and Scandinavia (Knudsen et al., 2013)

Partnership is viewed as representing a 'positive-sum game' where both parties win. Underlying the notion of partnership is the idea of social partnership. Social partnership reflects the stakeholder ethos that underpins certain models of European employee relations where employer and employee groups and government are considered social partners charged with considering the needs of all parties in determining social and economic policy. In the UK the New Labour government (1997–2010) was pivotal in promoting partnership approaches to employee relations as a 'third way' between managerial autonomy and adversarial industrial relations.

The proposed mutual gains of partnership are clear if we consider the principles of partnership in Table 10.4. At its heart, partnership focuses on the idea that both parties to the employment relationship have an underlying interest in the success of the organisation and that, ultimately, the continued success of the organisation is reliant on mutual satisfaction of each party's needs. On the one hand, employers need to understand that employees require security and dignity at work, a right to be involved in decision-making that affects them and to be rewarded for their contribution to success. On the other hand, employees have to understand the needs of the business and that to manage effectively managers require a degree of flexibility, recognising that difficult decisions sometimes have to be made for the overall success of the firm.

Partnership is linked to current notions of high-performance or high-commitment organisation (Kochan and Osterman, 1994). Guest and Peccei (1998) note a number of partnership practices that both reflect the mutual gains ethos and suggest that partnership is a combination of worker participation and progressive HRM practices. These practices include direct participation by employees in decisions about their own work, direct participation by employees in decisions about personal employment issues, participation by employee representatives in decisions about employment issues, participation by employee representatives in decisions about broader organisational policy issues, flexible job design and focus on quality, performance management, employee share ownership, communication, harmonisation and employment security.

The IPA (1997) suggests that at the heart of the partnership proposition is the importance of resolving the traditional areas of disagreement between management and workers, such as pay and working hours, because without such resolution underlying tensions will lessen the likelihood of agreement over key dimensions of the partnership such as the 'security/flexibility trade-off'. They also suggest that harmonisation of terms and conditions of employment between managers and workers is important in sending out the right signals about the organisation's commitment to 'true' partnership.

Further online reading Situated in an ongoing debate regarding the meaning, rationale for and effectiveness of non-union partnership arrangements, this article presents the findings of research undertaken to explore the operation of non-union partnership in practice and to evaluate its effectiveness.

Johnstone, S., Ackers, P. and Wilkinson, A. (2010) Better than nothing? Is non-union partnership a contradiction in terms?, *Journal of Industrial Relations*, 52 (2): 151–68.

IMPLICATIONS AND ISSUES WITH PARTNERSHIP Some research evidence supports the positive rhetoric of mutual gains (Guest and Peccei, 2001). Partnership can provide a framework within which a more positive psychological contract can develop, with the improved communication channels and cooperative relationship between employer and employees enhancing mutual trust and perceptions of fairness. For trade unions, evidence has suggested that partnership can lead to increased trade union membership and influence and, as such, during the 1990s and 2000s was one of a number of revitalisation strategies employed by trade unions. However, Ackers and Payne (1998: 530) suggest that 'partnership combines seductive rhetoric with ambiguous and shifting meaning'. In particular, questions arise over partnership as a viable long-term model for the relationship for employer and employees, particularly in an employee relations climate of historic distrust and antagonism. Therefore, whilst partnerships have not necessarily been found to be 'mechanisms for employer dominance' as many had predicted, they have fallen out of favour among many UK trade unionists (Wright, 2011).

Some of the disquiet over partnership agreements lies in the extent to which they truly represent a redistribution of power as implied by the use of the word 'partnership'. Given the imbalance of power in the employment relationship, management are likely to define the terms of a partnership agreement and retain a greater degree of power, even where trade unions are strongly entrenched. In the UK, where partnership agreements are not legally underpinned, the continuation of the agreement relies on managerial adherence and commitment to its terms, a position that might be challenged in hard times or where management feels it is not in its interests to continue with the partnership agreement. Moreover, management may be inclined to continue to prioritise its 'needs' over those of employees (Martinez-Lucio and Stuart, 2002). In respect of non-union partnerships, there is contradictory evidence to suggest whether such arrangements simply reinforce managerial prerogative or truly offer significant voice to employees (Johnstone et al., 2010).

A challenge to partnership has also come from within the union movement itself. Some unionists feel that unions that enter into partnership agreements compromise their position as 'adversaries' of management, surrendering the independence necessary to effectively defend the rights of their members. There is also concern that union officials may lose touch with their members and become the agents of management, making greater efforts to rationalise and explain the managerial position rather than representing members' interests. Despite some high profile examples (for example, British Aerospace) and political advocacy for such an approach, partnership is not widely used in the UK, partly reflecting adversarial employment relations traditions. However, the involvement and participation regulations emanating from the EU encourage partnership arrangements and may have the effect of increasing their popularity and effectiveness by underpinning their principles in legislation.

Financial participation

Finally, Marchington et al. (1992) include financial participation in their schema of the mechanism for employee involvement and participation. Financial participation represents a range of mechanisms that allow employees a financial stake in the firm. Whilst clearly not a form of voice and affording little opportunity to exert influence over management (Strauss, 2006), financial participation represents a form of participation complementary to voice initiatives that seek to develop the long-term relationship between employees and employer by connecting the overall success of the firm with individual reward. Typical mechanisms include employee share ownership schemes, profit-related pay or profit-sharing and bonus payments.

SUMMARY POINTS

- Employment relations is concerned with the management and regulation of the employment relationship in its political, economic, social and legal context.
- Key trends in UK employee relations (in common with many other nations) include a decline in trade union membership, recognition and influence, a decline in collective bargaining and the increasing individualisation of the employment relationship.
- The range of explanations for union decline over the last three decades includes shifting industrial structures, political antipathy towards the union movement, greater individualisation and flexibility in the management of labour, changing social attitudes and an increasingly diverse labour market.
- Traditions in the management of the employment relationship differ between nation states influenced by dominant cultural values and institutional structures, such as the level of state intervention in economic activity.
- 'Employee voice' is the catch-all term used for a multitude of practices and processes by which employees can, either directly or indirectly,

contribute to organisational decision-making.

- The extent to which different forms of employee voice empower employees to influence management decisions varies according to their depth, scope, form and level.
- Often used interchangeably, employee participation tends to refer to practices that offer the opportunity for joint decision-making, whilst employee involvement is associated with practices that seek to engender employee contribution and commitment to organisational objectives.
- Marchington et al. (1992) discern four broad categories of employee involvement and participation initiatives that offer differing degrees of influence over decision-making: downward communication, upward problem-solving, representative participation and financial participation.
- Partnership agreements are based on the rhetoric of mutual gains for employer and employees, but some commentators question the extent to which such outcomes are possible.

EMPLOYEE VOICE, TENGO LTD.

SELF-TEST QUESTIONS

1 Outline the characteristics of the unitarist, pluralist and radical perspectives in each of the following areas: ideology, conflict, power, processes and legitimacy of third-party involvement in the employment relationship.

2 What are the key explanations put forward for the decline of UK trade unionism since the late 1970s?

3 What do you understand by the terms 'union substitution' and 'union suppression'? What managerial practices might be employed in adopting either of these strategies?

4 Outline the concepts of depth, scope, level and form in relation to mechanisms for employee voice?

5 What examples of mechanisms and processes can you give that relate to each of the following

categories: downward communication, upward problem-solving, representative participation and financial participation (Marchington et al., 1992)?

6 What might be management's motives for entering into a partnership agreement with a trade union? What might be the union's rationale for doing so?

7 At what levels can collective bargaining take place? Why have we seen a decentralisation trend in collective bargaining over the last two or three decades?

8 To what extent do you consider there is the potential for 'mutual gain' outcomes from a partnership agreement?

TEST YOURSELF

Want to know more about this chapter? Review what you have been learning by visiting:
https://edge.sagepub.com/wilton3e

- Print out or download the chapter summaries for quick revision
- Test yourself with multiple-choice questions
- Revise key terms with interactive flashcards

CASE STUDY

Wal-Mart and union suppression

Wal-Mart is the largest retailer in the world, employing more than 2.1 million 'associates' at more than 8,000 retail units in 15 countries. In the UK it is the owner of Asda, who employ over 170,000 people. Wal-Mart has long been the target of persistent allegations of aggressive anti-unionism. For example, Wal-Mart fought a two-year legal battle to prevent the world's largest labour union (the All China Federation of Trade Unions) organising in its 60 stores in China (although the company ultimately lost the battle) (Watts, 2006).

The company clearly states that it does not feel that union presence is needed in the firm, stating on its corporate website that: 'We are not against unions. They may be right for some companies, but there is simply no need for a third party to come between our associates and their managers'. Wal-Mart suggests that the reason for this is that employee welfare is the concern of the employer. In particular, it suggests that direct communication – an 'Open Door' policy that allows grievances to be addressed anywhere up the corporate ladder – negates the need for third-party intervention in disputes between employees and the employer.

Many claim, however, that Wal-Mart goes far beyond 'substituting' for the presence of unions with alternative forms of direct communication. Many unions have accused Wal-Mart of actively suppressing union presence and of 'union-busting', a range of practices designed to hinder union activity and dissuade membership among workers. For example, the United Food and Commercial Workers union (UFCW) in Canada has accused Wal-Mart of harassing union members and closing only unionised stores as a reprisal against union members. In response, Wal-Mart claimed that meeting union demands in these stores would be against its business model and the stores were struggling (Ceausu, 2006).

In the UK, Asda has also been accused of union-busting activity. In 2006 an employment tribunal ruled that Asda had breached the Trade Union and Labour Relations Consolidation Act (1992) by offering staff at its Washington (UK) depot a 10 per cent pay rise if they gave up membership of the GMB union. Hencke (2006a) reports that the tribunal blamed Asda's PR agents for producing material that was 'very hostile to trade unions and highly disparaging of the process of collective bargaining'. Despite this ruling, however, GMB shop stewards accused Asda of subsequently employing fresh bullying tactics, including putting CDs in drivers' cabs urging them to vote against a strike to gain national negotiating rights, making lorry drivers go for interviews with senior management to persuade them not to strike and writing to their families warning them against strike action. Despite these tactics, GMB members voted in favour of industrial action. However, Asda and the GMB struck a deal that saw the strike called off at the last minute (Hencke, 2006b).

Task

Conduct some online research on Wal-Mart/Asda, their employment practices and attitudes and approach to dealing with trade unions and answer the following questions.

1 On the basis of your research, would you categorise Wal-Mart's and Asda's approach to resisting trade union organisation as union substitution or suppression? What examples can you give of the strategy they appear to have adopted?

2 Why do Wal-Mart and Asda appear to pursue aggressive policies of union avoidance?

3 Why do you think that Asda employees chose to reject a 10 per cent pay rise, opting instead to maintain union recognition at the depot?

4 Wal-Mart's strategy of union avoidance is partly a product of the US institutional and cultural context in which the organisation originated. What are the characteristics of the employee relations system in the UK that might make such an approach less appropriate and less likely to succeed?

USEFUL READING

Journal articles

Dundon, T. and Gollan, P.J. (2007) Reconceptualising voice in the non-union workplace, *International Journal of Human Resource Management*, 18 (7): 1182–98.

This article discusses the notion of non-unionism and examines approaches to employee voice in non-union firms. In particular, it considers the internal and external factors that shape approaches to voice in such firms.

Strauss, G. (2006) Worker participation – some under-considered issues, *Industrial Relations*, 45 (4): 778–803.

This wide-ranging article provides a useful account of the historical development of approaches to employee participation and reviews the literature on forms of participation.

Books, book chapters and reports

Dundon, T. and Rollinson, D. (2007) *Understanding Employment Relations*, Maidenhead: McGraw Hill.

This book offers a comprehensive introduction to employment relations, expanding on many of the themes introduced in this chapter.

FURTHER ONLINE READING

The following articles can be accessed for free on the book's companion website **http://edge/sagepub.com/wilton3e**:

Boxall, P. (2014), The future of employment relations from the perspective of human resource management, *Journal of Industrial Relations*, 56 (4): 578–93.

Cathcart, A. (2013) Direct democracy: Competing interests and contested terrain in the John Lewis Partnership, *Journal of Industrial Relations*, 55 (4): 601–20.

Hayter, S., Fashoyin, T. and Kochan, T. A. (2011) Collective bargaining for the 21st century, *Journal of Industrial Relations*, 53 (2): 225–47.

Johnstone, S., Ackers, P. and Wilkinson, A. (2010) Better than nothing? Is non-union partnership a contradiction in terms? *Journal of Industrial Relations*, 52 (2): 151–68.

Markey, R. and Townsend, K. (2014) Contemporary trends in employee involvement and participation, *Journal of Industrial Relations*, 55 (4): 475–87.

Suzuki, H. (2010) Employment relations in Japan: Recent changes under global competition and recession, *Journal of Industrial Relations*, 52 (3): 387–401.

Wilkinson, A., Dundon, T., Marchington, M. and Ackers, P. (2004) Changing patterns of employee voice: Case studies from the UK and Republic of Ireland, *Journal of Industrial Relations*, 46 (3): 298–322.

Want to know more about this chapter? Visit the companion website at: **https://edge.sagepub.com/wilton3e** to access practice questions, videos and selected journal articles to further enhance your study.

PART THREE
CONTEMPORARY ISSUES IN HRM

PART MAP

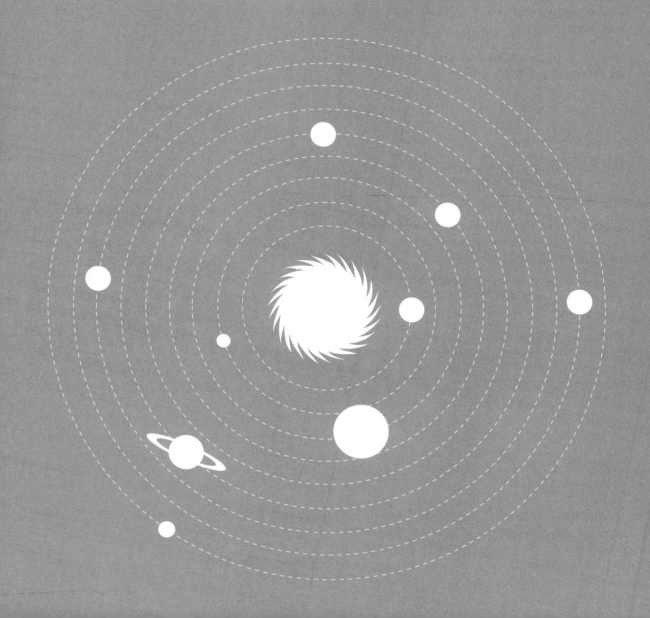

As with the first section of this book, this final section on contemporary issues in HRM has two purposes: first, to set out some key practical issues regarding management of particular dimensions of people management, such as workplace conflict and the management of diversity; second, to discuss how these areas of HRM are being shaped by contemporary trends to make them increasingly important. Whilst the issues discussed here – equality and diversity; workplace conflict; employee well-being and career development – are by no means new concerns for people managers, they represent areas where contemporary trends in practice or context have 'moved the goalposts' for management or represent areas of both innovative and poor practice.

Chapter 11 sets out the social, legal and organisational context that acts to stress the importance of providing equal opportunities for all workers and the benefits to be had from creating a workforce of diverse characteristics and talents. It also sets out two competing approaches to addressing the challenges of ensuring equality of opportunity and benefiting from workforce diversity. The focus of Chapter 12 is to discuss contemporary changes in both the nature of careers and the way in which organisations manage the careers of its employees. Perhaps more than any other chapter, it takes both the perspective of the individual employee, alongside that of managers, in discussing how the interests of both parties can be reconciled through career management practices. Conflict is certainly not a new phenomenon in the employment relationship, yet it is one area of people management that is often handled poorly. The purpose of Chapter 13, therefore, is to discuss the reasons why conflict arises in the employment relationship, both individually and collectively, and how it can be managed. In doing so, it sets out a number of trends in how conflict is expressed by both employees and managers and the specific challenges of handling both workplace grievances and discipline. Chapter 14 focuses on an issue of ever-more importance in HRM, that of employee well-being and the role of management in ensuring both the physical and mental health of employees, alongside a consideration for their dignity in the workplace. The final chapter revisits a number of important issues in contemporary HRM that have been introduced elsewhere in the book, such as the use of new technology, knowledge management and HR outsourcing, but which warrant further discussion because they represent both important challenges and opportunities for management and provide an indication of the future direction of HRM.

By the end of this section, readers should have a sound understanding of some critical contemporary challenges for all managers in the area of people management as well as an appreciation of the means by which firms might address such challenges.

HRM, EQUALITY AND DIVERSITY

EQUAL
OPPORTUNITIES
AND MANAGING
DIVERSITY

CHAPTER OBJECTIVES

● To discuss the increasing diversity of the contemporary labour market

● To explore the persistence of labour market inequality and to outline explanations for its continuance

● To discuss the implications of increasing labour market diversity, its positive benefits for organisations and the pitfalls associated with a failure to address inequality

● To outline how organisations might manage diversity and its implications for the various functions of HRM

● To outline the legal and political context of managing diversity.

INTRODUCTION

The increasing labour market diversity outlined in Chapter 4 presents a number of opportunities and challenges for managers. The purpose of this chapter is to further examine workplace diversity, the nature of these opportunities and challenges and how managers can seek to reconcile a number of competing pressures in the management of a diverse workforce. This chapter explores the continued incidence of employment inequality in various contexts in order to provide a backdrop against which to consider possible explanations and consequences, how inequality manifests itself within organisations and the current UK legislation aimed at eliminating discrimination. In particular, the chapter outlines the debate surrounding how managers can best address discrimination and inequality, contrasting two major approaches: equal opportunities (EO) and managing diversity.

THE INCIDENCE OF INEQUALITY IN THE LABOUR MARKET

LABOUR MARKET
AND INEQUALITY

The UK labour market, like that in virtually all capitalist economies, is increasingly diverse. The estimated 31 million people in work or actively seeking employment (of a total population of almost 61 million) include 14.1 million women, 7 million people with disabilities and 4.6 million people of minority ethnic backgrounds (CBI, 2008a). Furthermore, approximately 7 per cent of the UK population hold non-Christian religious beliefs, an estimated 6 per cent are gay or bisexual and, as reported in Chapter 4, the UK population is ageing. This growing diversity of the UK (working) population is accompanied by historic patterns of labour market inequality.

Since the 1970s, inequality has become an ever-greater focus of social policy and successive UK governments have introduced anti-discrimination legislation to eradicate disadvantage on the basis of age, gender, race and ethnicity, sexual orientation, religious beliefs and disability. However, despite the wide-ranging nature of the legislation, research continues to reveal evidence of significant labour market inequality. There is a range of measures that can be used to assess and compare labour market outcomes for different sections of the workforce. This section focuses on evaluating the evidence for inequality in four main areas: pay inequality, unemployment, and horizontal and vertical segregation. Horizontal segregation refers to the extent to which different groups are represented in different industry sectors and occupations. Vertical segregation refers to the extent to which different groups are represented at different levels of the organisational and occupational hierarchy.

Gender

In the UK, women make up over half the workforce in 52 per cent of workplaces (van Wanrooy et al., 2013). In the four decades since the first introduction of legislation to protect against employment discrimination on the basis of gender there has been a gradual, albeit 'painfully slow' (Centre for Women and Democracy, 2013: 5), diminution in employment inequality between men and women, although the UK is still some way from full equality. For example, women are still paid, on average, 18 per cent less than men. In OECD countries, the gender pay gap is 16 per cent (OECD, 2012). Table 11.1 shows that, whilst divergent, the gender pay gap remains high across nations.

Furthermore, despite the UK having one of the highest rates of female employment in Europe (ONS, 2008), the labour market for men and women is highly segregated with a tendency for high-paying and high-skilled roles to be filled by men. For example, ONS (2013b) report that 82 per cent of employees in the caring and leisure sector and 77 per cent of those in administration and secretarial occupations were women. In contrast, only 33 per cent of those working in managerial occupations were women. This pattern is reflected across Europe where men typically dominate senior managerial roles. Moreover, in 2013, 42 per cent of women worked part-time compared to just 12 per cent of men (ONS, 2013b).

Alternatively, however, there are professional occupational groups in which women make up a significant, if not a majority, proportion of total UK employment, such as teachers (EHRC, 2011), solicitors (Cole et al., 2010) and doctors (Elston, 2009). Nonetheless, there remains significant under-representation of women at senior positions across a variety of organisations. The *Sex and Power*

2013 report (Centre for Woman and Democracy, 2013) found that, although there had been some positive improvement in recent years, only 16.7 per cent of directorships of FTSE 100 companies were held by women (significantly behind some other European countries) and even among public sector employers (who have a statutory duty to promote equal opportunities and where the greatest strides have been taken towards gender equality) there is still evidence of a 'glass ceiling' in operation. For example, women made up only 31 per cent of top managers in the civil service, 14 per cent of the senior judiciary, 18 per cent of senior police officers, 23 per cent of MPs, and 14 per cent of university vice-chancellors. Table 11.1 provides an international comparison of the proportion of seats in national parliaments held by women in 2013, ranging from 8.1 per cent in Japan to 45 per cent in Sweden, and demonstrates the significant divergence of gender equality across nations.

Internationally, the picture for gender equality more widely is diverse. Table 11.1 compares the distribution of men and women in selected countries according to a range of measures of equality. What is most evident from the table is that, whilst there is some association between patterns of labour market participation and outcomes such as employment in managerial jobs and the gender pay gap, inequality between the genders is significant, particularly with respect to pay, across nations. Even in countries that rank highly according to the United Nations Gender Inequality Index (of those countries in Table 11.1, Australia, Netherlands, Germany, the US and UK are all in the top ten nations), gender inequality remains, therefore, stubbornly persistent.

Disability

There are also patterns of significant inequality for those with disabilities in the UK. In 2012, 46.3 per cent of working-age disabled people were in employment compared to 76.4 per cent of working-age non-disabled people. Whilst this gap has reduced by 10 percentage points since 1998, it remains significant, representing over 2 million people. The Disability Rights Commission (2007) reports that, on average, disabled people are 40 per cent less likely to get a job compared to those without a disability and even when in work earn 10 per cent less on average. The overall employment rate of disabled people has grown by about 1 per cent per year from 43 per cent in 1998 to 50 per cent in 2006, whilst the employment rate of people with mental health problems rose from 15 per cent in 1998 to just 20 per cent in 2005, despite evidence that with support 60 per cent of people with more serious mental health problems could work. The employment rate for people with learning disabilities is approximately only 10 per cent.

Ethnicity

Patterns of inequality according to ethnicity are more complex, reflecting the different experiences of diverse ethnic groups, but suggest that certain groups display significantly unequal employment outcomes. For example, at the end of 2011, 21 per cent of white 16–24-year-olds were unemployed, compared to 47.4 per cent of the black population in the same age range (ONS, 2012d). Inevitably, members of certain minority ethnic groups appear to face 'double jeopardy' in the labour market, experiencing inequality on a number of fronts. For example, the unemployment rate in late 2011 among 16–24-year-old black females was 56 per cent compared to 17 per cent for white females in the same age group (ONS, 2012d). However, not all minority ethnic groups experience similar degrees of

TABLE 11.1 *Gender inequality in international perspective*

	Labour force participation rates (2012)		Unemployment rate (quarter 4, 2013)		Proportion of employed persons with managerial responsibilities (2013)		Proportion in service sector employment (2013)		Proportion of seats in national parliament held by women (2013)	Gender pay gap (2013)
	Men	Women	Men	Women	Men	Women	Men	Women	–	–
Australia	71.9	58.8	5.9	5.6	12.7	8.5	65.9	90	26	–
Brazil	80.9	59.5	No data	No data	5.5 (2007)	4.2 (2007)	51.8	77.9	8.6	18
Finland	64.3	56	8.8	8.2	3.8	1.7	58.1	88.6	42.5	No data
France	61.8	56	9.8	9.8	8.5	5.2	63.1	83.7	26.9	18.7 (2012)
Germany	66.4	53.5	5.6	4.9	5.8	2.7	58.2	84.9	36.5	14.1 (2010)
India	80.9	28.8	No data	No data	No data	No data	29.8 (2010)	17 (2010)	11	16.6 (2011)
Italy	59.4	52.7	11.6	13.4	4.7	2.4	57.9	83.7	31.4	No data
Japan	70.4	48.1	4.1	3.6	3.5	0.6	61.8	82.2	8.1	11.1 (2012)
Mexico	80	45	4.7	5	3.6	3.2	51.8	80.2	36.8	26.6
Netherlands	87.3	79.9	7.5	6.6	9.6	3.6	74.1	93.3	38.7	15.5
Russia	71.4	57	5.7	5.3	8.6 (2008)	5.3 (2008)	53.4	77.7	13.6	20.5 (2010)
Spain	66.5	52.6	25.2	26.6	6	3.2	64.5	89.2	36	No data
Sweden	68.1	60.2	8.2	7.8	7.1	4.3	67.6	91.3	45	8.6 (2012)
Turkey	70.8	29.4	8	10.9	6.2	2.4	51	47.7	14.4	15.1 (2012)
United Kingdom	68.8	55.7	7.5	6.7	13.3	7.8	69.9	92	22.5	20.1 (2010)
United States	69.3	56.8	7.2	6.6	16.3 (2008)	13.9 (2008)	70.6	91.1	17.8	17.5
										17.9

Source: http://stats.oecd.org/index.aspx?queryid=54751 (accessed 24 July 2015)

inequality. For example, the earnings of Chinese males in the UK are on a par with those of white males.

Therefore, despite legislation and an increasing number of employers claiming to be equal opportunities employers or to promote workforce diversity, there remains significant evidence of labour market inequality for groups of workers who are making up an increasing proportion of the labour supply. Dickens (2005) observes that despite some evidence of progress towards greater workplace equality, it is both slow and often difficult to identify. Whilst these figures do not represent *prima facie* evidence of discrimination and it is important to recognise that they reflect the historic interaction of a wide range of social, educational, economic and political factors, they do demonstrate that certain groups of workers appear to be disadvantaged in accessing employment, obtaining particular types of work and achieving earnings comparable to the majority. These patterns of interaction vary from country to country.

EMPLOYMENT TRIBUNAL

Perhaps a better indication of the extent of discrimination in the UK labour market is provided by the incidence of claims made to employment tribunals on the basis of discrimination or unfair treatment. In 2010–11, UK employment tribunals accepted 218,100 separate claims (Tribunals Service, 2011), equating to 382,400 separate cases to be heard across different areas of jurisdiction (as some of these claims covered two or more areas of 'jurisdiction', for example, both unfair dismissal and sex discrimination). Approximately 73,420 of these claims accepted were in the area of discrimination or unfair treatment, including 34,600 equal pay claims, 18,300 claims of sex discrimination, 7,200 claims of disability discrimination, 5,000 claims of race discrimination and 6,800 claims of age discrimination. Whilst more recent evidence suggests a significant decline in employment tribunal claims, including those for discrimination, Smith (2014) attributes this to the introduction of large fees for claimants wishing to take their employer to tribunal.

FORMS OF DISCRIMINATION

Before discussing explanations for discrimination and, subsequently, how firms can manage employee diversity, it is important to consider how discrimination can manifest itself in the workplace. Pincus (1996: 186) identifies three levels of discrimination:

1 *Individual discrimination* refers to the behaviour of individual members of one race/ethnic/gender group that is intended to have a differential and/or harmful effect on the members of another race/ethnic/gender group.

2 *Institutional discrimination* refers to the policies of the dominant race/ethnic/gender institutions and the behaviour of individuals who control these institutions and implement policies that are intended to have a differential and/or harmful effect on a minority race/ethnic/gender group.

3 *Structural discrimination* refers to the policies of dominant race/ethnic/gender institutions and the behaviour of the individuals who implement these policies and control these institutions, which are race/ethnic/gender neutral in intent but which have a differential and/or harmful effect on a minority race/ethnic/gender group.

Importantly, Pincus argues that both individual and institutional discrimination constitute intentional discrimination. Examples of individual discrimination might include a male manager who discriminates against women in selection decision-making or in performance appraisals. Institutional discrimination

BOX 11.1
RESEARCH INSIGHT

Social class inequality, social mobility and HRM

Research conducted by the Debrett's Foundation and published in March 2015 (Crush, 2015) suggests that social mobility (the individual and collective movement of people within or between social strata in a society) in the UK has 'changed little since the 18th century'. That is, the strata of society to which people are born still largely determine their subsequent experience of life and work.

For young people, a lack of social mobility is at least partly a product of the interaction between the resources and social networks to which they have access in their early career. This interaction is particularly manifest in access to work experience, particularly where a period of low paid or unpaid work is required for a career in particular organisations or sectors of employment. The Debrett's research – a survey of 5,000 people – found that 72 per cent of children from privileged backgrounds admitted to using family connections to secure work placements and 47 per cent of children from lower socio-economic backgrounds said they didn't apply for work experience in London because of the cost. The research found 25 per cent of all young people felt the system for getting work placements and internships in Britain was 'unfair'. The research concludes that: 'While nepotism isn't any more widespread than it was in the past, it has a greater impact today. When there are so many candidates for the top graduate jobs it follows that those with the best experience have a better chance of securing them'.

Even where paid, internships are often poorly remunerated (ONS, 2014), making work experience increasingly unavailable to all but those with family support to supplement earnings. The Sutton Trust (2014) cite UK government figures that there are up to 70,000 interns in the UK at any one time and, drawing on data for recent graduates, estimate that approximately one-third of these are likely to be unpaid, reflecting CIPD figures showing that 21 per cent of businesses employing interns reported that interns were not paid (despite this contravening minimum wage legislation). The Sutton Trust concludes, therefore, that poorer graduates are missing out on many of the better jobs in Britain because they can't afford to take unpaid internships.

Social mobility is clearly predicated on more than simply the recruitment patterns of some employers and also reflects the direct and indirect influence of wider government social and economic policy. However, in the context of many firms' claims that they value workforce diversity as crucial to improving organisational performance, then the use of low paid or unpaid internships, particularly for long periods of time, or where such work is essential for access to particular professions, would appear to contradict these claims. As such, HR practitioners need to consider carefully how approaches to recruiting students or recent graduates, and the use of internships, really do reflect a desire to recruit talent from across the widest possible social spectrum.

---

reflects the open expression and tolerance of discrimination within a group or entire organisation so that it forms part of the culture, language and norms of behaviour of that group and is embedded within both formal and informal policies and practices. Noon (2007a) identifies a number of processes that could represent evidence of institutional discrimination and which are prejudicial to workplace equality. These include:

- word of mouth methods for recruitment
- dress codes that prevent people practising their religious beliefs
- promotions based on informal recommendations, rather than open competition

- informal assessments rather than formal appraisals
- assumptions about training capabilities
- assumptions about language difficulties and attitudes.

Like institutional discrimination, structural discrimination represents the differential and/or harmful effects of institutional policies and practices on a minority but is distinguished by a lack of intent to harm. It therefore represents the unwittingly discriminatory practices employed by an organisation or its members.

The combined effects of these forms of discrimination are implicated in a number of organisational phenomena associated with the employment experiences of disadvantaged groups. For example, the 'glass ceiling' refers to the invisible barrier that prevents certain groups reaching higher-level positions. The term has typically been used to describe the under-representation of women at senior managerial and director level. The term 'sticky floor' refers to the phenomenon where certain groups are more likely to have difficulties in moving out of lower-level jobs.

Stereotypical assumptions about the type of work that particular groups are best suited to also contribute to the creation of employment 'ghettos' where these groups are over-concentrated, and group closure in other areas that exclude those that are 'different'. By factoring in the evidence that minority groups (including women) tend to be subjected to poorer terms and conditions of employment we can understand the labour market as segmented into primary and secondary labour markets. Those in the primary labour market have access to better terms and conditions, greater job security and improved opportunities for career progression than those in the secondary market, where minority groups are more likely to be concentrated.

CONSEQUENCES OF DISCRIMINATION

Clearly, the patterns of inequality outlined at the start of this chapter have significant financial and emotional implications for individual workers. Furthermore, to limit the employment prospects and, therefore, the 'life chances' for some members of society leads inevitably to social exclusion, unrest and an economy in which the talents and potential of all members are far from realised. Similarly for work organisations, as well as the financial implications associated with failure to comply with legislation, discriminatory practices and behaviours, whether institutional, structural or individual, can be damaging to business competitiveness; for example through a failure to select or promote the best candidate, a failure to create a balanced workforce reflecting social diversity and the creation of resentment, poor morale and workforce divisions. There is, therefore, a strong business case for ensuring equal access to jobs, training, promotion and pay. The question remains, however, to what extent do firms have a moral obligation to ensure equality of opportunities and is the pursuit of organisational objectives compatible with social responsibility?

THE POLITICAL AND LEGAL CONTEXT OF INEQUALITY

In one sense, discrimination on the grounds of factors not associated with competence represents a distortion in the proper working of the labour market. Social problems like discrimination and inequality are, however, shaped by a range of historical, political, legal, economic and social processes. For example, sex discrimination is rooted in historical patterns of the division of labour between men and women as well as in the political and legal means through which it is addressed. For work organisations, the political and legal context of discrimination and inequality in any given country shapes the obligations under which they operate.

In the UK, a minimalist, liberal legislative approach to tackling discrimination has been adopted (Jewson and Mason, 1986). The rationale for legal intervention in the area of equality is that without it groups of workers that have been traditionally disadvantaged in the labour market will continue to be vulnerable to intentional and unintentional discriminatory behaviours and practices. Lupton and Woodhams (2006: 339) suggest, therefore, that UK anti-discrimination legislation is primarily a 'moral response to historic patterns of vertical and horizontal segregation in the labour market which is designed to produce a "level playing field"'. In other words, the legislation seeks to provide equal opportunities for all by removing both the individual and group-based barriers to allow individuals to compete equally in the labour market. This approach is essentially punitive in that the legislation provides mechanisms for individuals to seek redress and financial compensation through employment tribunals in cases of proven discrimination. However, the legislation provides little positive imperative for organisations to promote equality, ensure they recruit from across the social spectrum in all positions or to ensure equal pay. Foster and Harris (2009) observe that UK legislation, in common with the broader EU regulatory framework, has been based on the provision of negative rights (i.e. individuals should not be discriminated against) rather than a legal requirement to promote the positive rights of staff to achieve equality in the workforce. There are, however, specific statutory duties placed on public sector employers in the UK to eliminate discrimination on the grounds of sex, race and disability and to promote equality of opportunity.

As outlined in Table 11.2, there are a number of pieces of legislation that have been enacted in the UK over the previous four decades that have outlawed discriminatory behaviour, processes and practices on the basis of age, gender (including marital status), race, disability, sexual orientation and religious beliefs. The individual rights enshrined in these acts sought to promote equal treatment in employment, irrespective of social group, by ensuring fair and unbiased processes and procedures, for example in recruitment, selection, redundancy, dismissal and promotion. This framework of statutory regulation developed to ensure that workplace decisions, for example over whom to recruit or promote, are made on the basis of job-related criteria (for example, qualifications or relevant experience) and to avoid intentional discrimination and unwitting prejudice against certain groups on grounds that are irrelevant to the job. It therefore emphasises the notion of equal treatment, consistency and neutrality in respect of the social group characteristics covered under the legislation.

Table 11.2 highlights, however, the way in which UK discrimination legislation developed in a piecemeal fashion over a protracted period of time which, along with the impact of four decades of case law reflecting the judicial interpretation of this legislation, resulted in a number of inconsistencies and a growing need to update and harmonise the protection against unfair treatment enshrined in these acts. Subsequently, with the aim of streamlining and simplifying this provision into one piece of legislation and to address certain shortfalls in protection (for example, in the case of disability discrimination), the Equality Act 2010 was introduced. The development of this act was also a reaction against the perceived lack of progress on equality in the UK despite the existing legal provision (CIPD, 2011b).

In total, the Equality Act brought together nine separate pieces of legislation, including those in Table 11.2. In consolidating these acts, the Equality Act offers protection to people from discrimination on the basis of specific 'protected characteristics'. These protected characteristics are: age; disability; gender reassignment;

TABLE 11.2 *The development of UK anti-discrimination legislation*

Legislation	Basic principles and aims
Equal Pay Act 1970	The Equal Pay Act outlaws unjustifiable differences in the treatment of men and women in respect of pay and other conditions of employment. There are three types of claim that can be made under the legislation where a member of one sex claims unequal treatment in respect of a comparator job done by a member of the opposite sex: • *Like work* – where two jobs are compared that are the same or similar • *Work rated as equivalent* – where two jobs are compared that, whilst of a different nature, have been assessed as equivalent under a job evaluation scheme • *Work of equal value* – where two jobs are compared which, though different, are equal in nature on the basis of, for example, required skills.
Sex Discrimination Act 1975	The focus of this act is on anti-discriminatory practices and behaviour in broader employment matters (covers discrimination on basis of the sex, marital status and gender reassignment)
Race Relations Act 1976	The act covers discrimination on grounds of race, nationality and ethnic or national origin. Race Relations (Amendment) Act 2000 extends the 1976 Act by protecting against racial discrimination by public authorities and places an enforceable positive duty on public authorities to promote equality
Disability Discrimination Act (1995, amended 2005)	This act makes it unlawful to treat a person less favourably for a reason related to their disability, and places a duty on employers and service providers to make 'reasonable adjustment' to accommodate disability in the provision of employment, goods and services, education and transport
Employment Rights Act 1996	This act sets out a number of reasons for dismissal that are 'automatically unfair', including membership of a trade union, pregnancy, refusal of retail employees to work on Sunday and spent convictions (for ex-offenders)
Employment Equality (Sexual Orientation and Religion or Belief) Regulations 2003	Prohibits employers from unreasonably discriminating against employees on the grounds of sexual orientation and religious beliefs. The regulations were introduced to comply with the EU Framework Directive 2000/78/ EC on religion or belief, age, sexuality and disability
Employment Equality (Age) Regulations 2006	Prohibits employers from unreasonably discriminating against employees on the grounds of age. The regulations were introduced to comply with the EU Framework Directive 2000/78/EC on religion or belief, age, sexuality and disability

marriage and civil partnership; pregnancy and maternity; race; religion or belief; sex; and sexual orientation. Under the new Equality Act, the provisions outlined in Table 11.2 have largely remained the same; however, a number of new provisions have been introduced. For instance, the Equality Act now protects against dual discrimination, whereby it is discriminatory to treat someone less favourably because of a combination of two of the protected characteristics, imposes an obligation on public sector employers to promote equality in the workplace and to improve transparency on pay (for example, by outlawing 'pay secrecy' clauses in contracts of employment) to help address continued gender pay inequality. Table 11.3 outlines the types of discrimination covered by the Equality Act.

Under UK law, there are some areas of work where discrimination in favour of a particular social group is permitted in the recruitment, transfer, training, dismissal or promotion of certain roles. The Equality Act sets out the test for employers as to whether to discriminate represents a 'proportionate means of achieving a legitimate aim' (what, under previous legislation was referred to as either a 'genuine occupational requirement' or 'qualification'). Under the pre-Equality Act legislation, Torrington et al. (2008: 551) suggest there are three main headings under which exceptions from the legislation have been made and where, for example, a woman can be recruited over a man explicitly on the basis of gender: authenticity (for example, for an acting or modelling job); decency (for example, changing room attendant); and personal services (for example, counsellor working in a rape crisis centre).

TABLE 11.3 *Types of discrimination covered by the Equality Act (2010)*

Types of discrimination	Description
Direct discrimination	Someone is treated less favourably than another person because of a protected characteristic
Discrimination by association	Direct discrimination against someone because they associate with another person who possesses a protected characteristic (for example, discrimination against a person because of actions needed to take care of a disabled relative or because they are perceived to have a particular religious belief)
Discrimination by perception	Direct discrimination against someone because others think they possess a protected characteristic, even if they do not in fact do so
Indirect discrimination	Can occur when an employer enforces a provision, criterion or practice (PCP) that applies to everyone but disproportionately disadvantages people or a person with a particular protected characteristic (e.g. shift patterns that disproportionately disadvantage women because of their greater likelihood to have caring responsibilities)
Harassment	Defined in the Act as: 'Unwanted conduct related to a relevant protected characteristic, which has the purpose or effect of violating an individual's dignity or creating an intimidating, hostile, degrading, humiliating or offensive environment for that individual'. Employees can complain of harassment even if they don't possess the protected characteristic or the harassment is not directed at them
Third-party harassment	Employers are potentially liable for repeated (at least two previous occasions) harassment of their staff by non-employees (for example, customers) where they have known of it and failed to take reasonable steps to prevent it happening again
Victimisation	Someone is treated less favourably because they have made or supported a complaint or grievance under the act.

Source: adapted from Acas (2010) © Acas, Euston Tower, 286 Euston Road, London NW1 3JJ - Crown copyright Open government license.

UK legislation allows for voluntary positive action by employers to remove inequality by equipping individuals in disadvantaged groups with the means to compete equally (through, for example, encouraging job applications from under-represented groups or by providing targeted training). Historically, this has not extended as far as positive discrimination, where disadvantaged groups can be favoured in decision-making on the basis of their visible social group characteristics, however, the Equality Act does now allow employers to favour candidates for a job from an under-represented minority in cases where two candidates for a job or promotion are equally well qualified (although this must be considered on a case-by-case basis). More far-reaching positive discrimination (alternatively known as affirmative action) is lawful in, for example, the USA, South Africa and India, reflecting the desire to eradicate historical divisions in society.

EHRC

The UK anti-discrimination legislation is supported by the Equality and Human Rights Commission (EHRC), which was formed in 2007 with the merger of the three bodies that previously supported the legislation on gender, race and disability discrimination: the Equal Opportunities Commission; the Commission for Racial Equality; and the Disability Discrimination Commission. The EHRC has a remit to promote equal opportunities and assist organisations in eliminating unfair treatment of workers, for example, through the publication of codes of practice to support legal compliance by employers. Equality legislation is often criticised by business interest groups, especially those representing the interests of small businesses, as presenting a significant constraint on business operations (for example, in relation to flexible working). However, legislation can also act as the catalyst for the creation of 'better' working practices and employment policies that can positively contribute to individual and organisational performance.

As well as national legislation, the UK is also subject to European law. Discrimination is an area in which the European Union has been particularly influential on national legislation, for example, in respect of gender, age, ethnicity and sexual orientation. Alongside the European Union, two other international bodies contribute to the framework of anti-discrimination regulation, albeit with little direct influence on member states: the International Labour Organisation and the United Nations. The ILO, as part of its wider remit for improvements in the treatment of workers, campaigns for equal worker rights and the eradication of discrimination against workers of different minority ethnic backgrounds, lesbian and gay workers, those who are HIV-positive and older workers. As discussed in Chapter 5, however, the ILO tends to be viewed as lacking sufficient enforcement mechanisms and, as such, these campaigns have limited impact. The UN states in the Universal Declaration of Human Rights (1948) that 'everyone is entitled to all rights and freedoms set forth in this declaration without discrimination of any kind, such as race, colour, sex, language, religion, political opinion, national or social origin, property, birth or other status' (www.un.org/en/documents/udhr/). This declaration is, however, not legally binding on member states and tends to be viewed as an aspiration.

Issues with the UK's legislative approach

The liberal approach to addressing discrimination adopted in the UK is often criticised as inadequate and the persistence of labour market inequality suggests that more than three decades after the introduction of the first pieces of equality legislation it has been far from entirely successful. In particular, this approach has been criticised as failing to challenge the embedded nature of discrimination. By promoting a focus on ensuring procedural fairness in organisational decision-making, the entrenched structures and culture that tend to underpin discriminatory practice remain unchallenged.

Foster and Harris (2009) observe that claims of discrimination under UK legislation can only be pursued on the basis of an individual demonstrating less favourable treatment compared to the norm, often with reference to a comparator (for example, someone of the opposite sex). They suggest that this can lead to reinforcement of existing discrimination as it fails to challenge this norm and reflects the need for under-represented groups to mirror or mimic the behaviour of the dominant group to succeed. Furthermore, Fredman (2001: 155) notes that whilst the legal framework is based on ensuring consistency of treatment across social groups, 'there is no difference in principle between treating two people equally badly, and treating them equally well'.

Subsequently, there have been calls for a more radical approach to better challenge workplace inequality. Rather than focusing on equal opportunities, such an approach would seek to generate equal outcomes particularly through positive discrimination and preferential treatment of disadvantaged groups. In other words, it would seek to tip the playing field in favour of disadvantaged groups in order to redress historical disadvantage, through influencing the outcomes of organisational decision-making rather than just processes.

HRM, EQUALITY AND DIVERSITY

DIVERSITY AT
APPLE

There are many areas of people management where intentional and unintentional discrimination can occur. As discussed in Chapter 6, at the core of the systematic approach to recruitment and selection is the importance placed on fairness and objectivity to ensure that the best person is selected for a post. Unfair discrimination can occur at any one of a number of phases in this process, including advertising, job description, person specification, short-listing, interviewing, personality or competency testing and selection. Clearly, at any of these points, for any suitably qualified candidate to choose not to apply, discontinue their application or be rejected on the basis of non-work-related characteristics is problematic for any firm wishing to maximise its ability to recruit from the widest pool of available labour. Unfair discrimination can also occur in the terms and conditions offered to employees, in the performance management process (for example, in employee appraisals), in treatment over disciplinary or grievance matters, in promotion, redundancy and dismissal decisions, and in opportunities provided for learning and development.

Despite the business case for providing equal opportunities, the social justice argument and the legal imperative to eradicate discrimination, the organisational adoption of a coherent approach to ensuring equality and actively managing diversity is patchy. The CIPD *Resourcing and Talent Planning Survey* (2013a) found that 58 per cent of employers have a formal diversity strategy, rising to 79 per cent of public sector employers and 82 per cent of employers with more than 5,000 employees, although this does not necessarily indicate the presence of a strategic approach to diversity (Foster and Harris, 2009). CIPD (2013a) report that the most common practices adopted by employers to encourage workforce diversity were recruitment/workforce monitoring (78 per cent of respondents), interviewer training (62 per cent) and an active approach to attract talent of all ages (60 per cent). These figures represent an increase of attention in some areas, when compared to figures for previous years, but a decline in others, including workforce monitoring and recruiter training. Importantly, only 48 per cent of employers report 'operating policies that go beyond basic legislative requirements' suggest that a positive attitude to diversity, as opposed to a concern for legal compliance, remains a minority concern among UK employers. Indeed, only 14 per cent of employers set recruitment targets to correct a workforce imbalance. Other initiatives that firms might adopt to address inequality include equality audits and benchmarking, for example, by comparing workforce diversity with that of competitors. Employers can also use exit interviews and staff attitude surveys to assess the impact of policies and the extent to which inequality contributes to employee dissatisfaction.

The Workplace Employment Relations Study 2011 (van Wanrooy et al., 2013) found that 77 per cent of surveyed UK workplaces had a formal written equal opportunities or diversity policy compared to 66 per cent in 2004. Such policies

BOX 11.2
HRM IN PRACTICE

Gender diversity at Lego Group

The Lego Group, the Danish firm 'engaged in the development of children's creativity through play and learning', remains a family-owned company, more than eight decades since its creation in 1932. As part of its desire to leave 'a positive impact', both for its stakeholders and the wider community, the group states a commitment to diversity as one of four main organisational focus areas for its management and 'as a great opportunity when it comes to adapting to and solving global challenges ahead … employees with diverse backgrounds bring with them individual talents and expertise that contribute to an attractive and dynamic workplace environment that fosters innovation and creativity'.

The company 'provides equal opportunities for all employees and no employee may be discriminated because of background, race, religion, age, disabilities, sexual orientation or gender'. Within this broad focus Lego has chosen to focus its efforts on improving gender diversity, as it suggests this is the most difficult form of diversity to achieve and that 'if an organization is able to leverage gender diversity it improves its general ability to leverage diversity in all kinds and shapes, including cultural, professional, religious, and national'. In addressing gender equality, the company suggests it will benefit from 'a positive ripple effect on other diversity dimensions' and move 'towards being a more capable global organisation'.

In 2014, the company introduced a new gender diversity policy that focuses on the company's commitment to hiring and promoting women at management level, particularly director level or above, with the ultimate goal of having a truly diverse organisation by 2020. The long-term aspiration is to have a management team made up of an equal number of women and men. For the LEGO Group's board of directors, the target for 2017 is to have one to two members of the underrepresented gender among the four independent members of the full seven-person board. At present, one of the independent members is female. At the end of the 2014, the proportion of females appointed and recruited to management level was 43 per cent, up from 37 per cent in 2013.

The policy reinforces Lego's position to always hire the most suitable and competent person for any job and details the practical steps taken to this end, including paying attention to the design and wording of job advertisements, questioning techniques and gender-balanced interview situations, as well as integrating gender considerations in internal talent pipeline management. Some specific examples of how Lego Group is pursuing its diversity agenda are:

- seeking to ensure that both genders are represented in job interview panels for managerial positions
- training of recruiters on the diversity agenda within Lego and on means by which to ensure job advertisements attract both females and males
- recruitment and selection partners are required to provide the group with a diverse slate of candidates
- redesign of the job webpage with focus on women in leadership in the LEGO Group
- plans for including gender diversity into the employer branding
- development of succession candidates for the corporate management team with one of the success criteria being to achieve a balanced gender split of successor candidates
- leadership development programme to enable and support leaders in leveraging diversity and becoming better at developing diverse talents
- continuous tracking and analysing of performance-related pay and salary for gender differences
- tracking managerial/director-level promotions to monitor for potential gender imbalances
- incorporation of gender diversity metrics into the standard HR reporting across the LEGO Group to allow for detailed follow-up within each part of the company to create transparency on potential challenged areas
- continuous evaluation of the progress and effect of these efforts to ensure that 'the focus areas are impactful and effective and to allow for corrective actions in the event that this is not the case'.

Source: www.lego.com/en-gb/aboutus/responsibility/employees (17 September 2015) were almost universally found in larger workplaces, in workplaces where trade unions were recognised and in the public sector, although much of the growth in recent years was found among smaller employers. EO policies most often cover gender, race and disability, but increasingly are likely to cover religion, sexual orientation and age. Despite increased coverage of formal policies for equal opportunities and diversity, the survey also found that there was limited substance behind these policies with comparatively few respondents reporting that they actively monitored recruitment, selection and promotion for different employee groups or reviewed relative pay rates or procedures for recruitment, selection and promotion to identify indirect discrimination.

Further online reading This article draws on WERS data to explore the nature and incidence of EO policies in the UK. In particular, it assesses the extent to which such policies are 'substantive' or simply 'empty shells'.

Hoque, K. and Noon, M. (2004) Equal opportunities policy and practice in Britain: Evaluating the 'empty shell' hypothesis, *Work, Employment and Society,* 18: 481–506.

Box 11.3 outlines a number of practices and policies that Purcell et al. (2002) suggest underpin a strategic approach to recruiting from the graduate labour market.

THE EQUAL OPPORTUNITIES APPROACH

Reflecting the dominant legal and political perspective adopted in the UK, the most pervasive approach to ensuring workplace equality is a liberal, equal opportunities approach. Again, the emphasis under such an approach is on creating a level playing field by emphasising 'sameness' between diverse social groups. In other words, EO advocates treating people as if the differences between them do not exist. Reflecting the focus on social justice that underpins the statutory provision, EO tends to be informed by a moral or ethical argument for ensuring equality of access to jobs and earnings. Therefore, whilst economic benefits to the organisation may stem from the tackling of discrimination, ensuring equal opportunities represents primarily an employer's social duty (Goss, 1994).

EO emphasises the importance of formal or procedural arrangements focused on the examination and continual monitoring of processes and practices to ensure they are free from discrimination and to ensure, as far as is possible, fair, objective, transparent and meritocratic decision-making and treatment. This represents one aspect of 'mainstreaming' equality by building concern for equal opportunities into all organisational processes and involving all organisational members in the design and implementation of policy, rather than equality being an add-on or remote activity.

Box 11.4 outlines a number of recommendations to ensure that employers treat all employees equitably, regardless of age.

EO allows some special treatment for disadvantaged groups in the form of positive action to redress the effects of previous unequal treatment, for example by targeting under-represented groups in recruitment. Whilst not strictly adhering to the principle of 'sameness', positive action recognises the potential for continued disadvantage of particular groups and informs the development of policies which seek to ensure that all employees or potential employees have the opportunity to compete on an equal basis. For example, employers have been encouraged to create policies to enable women to compete freely with men by developing policies relating to career breaks, childcare provision, flexible working and single sex training.

BOX 11.3
RESEARCH INSIGHT

Policies and practice that support recruitment from a diverse graduate labour market: evidence from best practice employers

In all their information about their organisations, they explicitly state that they are an equal opportunities employer and are proud of the diversity of their workforce.

In all their job vacancy information and job specifications, they include explicit statements about their EO/diversity approach and state that they welcome applications from suitably qualified people, regardless of age or social or cultural background.

Their job specifications are very clear about the requirements for the job, including details such as whether they involve extensive travel or the requirement to work flexible hours.

They do not make assumptions that some job characteristics will be more attractive to young candidates or preclude older ones, but provide people with sufficient information to rule themselves in or out.

They avoid expressions or visual images that might discourage 'non-traditional' candidates, but depict the diversity of their intake.

Where they provide information about vacancies to higher education institutions careers offices or academic departments, they do so to all HEIs or target a diverse range of them in the specialist or regional areas where they seek to recruit.

They run workshops which help potential candidates to assess their suitability for vacancies and to develop the skills required in the application process.

They recognise and take account of non-traditional routes into higher education and value the enterprise and initiative which achievement of these indicates.

In the selection processes, they ask only for information and evidence that is of direct relevance to the skills and knowledge required for the post.

They invest time and resources in the selection procedure, using a variety of approaches to enable candidates to demonstrate their suitability for appointment.

They monitor their recruitment and selection processes and outcomes to ensure effective and non-discriminatory practices.

They train all staff involved in recruitment and selection to take account of diversity issues and promote equal opportunities.

They treat job applicants with courtesy, acknowledging applications, informing them of outcomes, providing constructive feedback, and routinely paying expenses incurred in the interview process.

They have a flexible approach to appointing staff which allows them to take account of particular circumstances. For example, older candidates with relevant prior work experience can have this reflected in their salary and progression opportunities.

Those with constraints can, where it does not interfere with their capacity to fulfil their role, work flexibly and/or concentrate periods of training or travel to fit in with their other commitments.

They work with HEIs to develop, sponsor or support courses that provide career development opportunities for their staff.

Source: Purcell et al., 2002. Reproduced with permission of the National Centre for Universities and Business (NCUB) which has now taken over from the CIHE.

BOX 11.4
UNDERSTAND

Top tips for being 'Age Positive'

Learn from the good practice of Age Positive champions by removing age limits from recruitment advertisements. Avoid using words like 'young' or 'mature'.

Use a mixed-age interview panel in the selection process wherever possible.

Promote on the basis of measurable performance and demonstrated potential rather than age.

Offer employees of all ages the opportunity to train and develop themselves – encourage reluctant older and younger workers by

using, as role models, employees who have benefited from training.

Base redundancy decisions on objective, job-related criteria. Automatically making workers over a certain age redundant, or operating a last-in-first-out system will lead to a loss of key knowledge, skills and corporate memory.

Agree a fair and consistent retirement policy with employees. Offer pre-retirement support and, where possible, consider flexible or extended retirement options.

Source: www.gov.uk/government/collections/age-positive Reused under the Open Government Licence v3.0 © Crown copyright

AGE POSITIVE

Criticism of the EO/liberal approach

The liberal approach to equal opportunities has been criticised for a number of reasons. Most importantly, due to the emphasis on neutrality and consistency of treatment, EO tends to lead to a managerial focus on procedural justice and ensuring that evidence of fair treatment can be provided if an employer is accused of unfair discrimination. EO is, therefore, felt to be inadequate in changing underlying attitudes (Liff, 1999) and eradicating the continued effects of historical disadvantage. Under EO, tackling workplace equality can be partially viewed as an administrative exercise. Therefore, whilst EO policies based on compliance have gone some way to eradicating overt discrimination, embedded prejudice and stereotyping within organisations can often remain. The associated failure to secure a managerial commitment to ensuring equal opportunities as a strategic issue can result in 'empty shell' EO policies that are devoid of adequate supporting EO practices and where only a minority of employees have access to these or are aware that they exist (Hoque and Noon, 2004). Within this context, employees' perceptions of EO policies are often of poor implementation and a lack of senior manager commitment to the principle of equality (Creegan et al., 2003).

EO has also been criticised as failing to identify, and even potentially nullifying, those dimensions of individual difference that can positively contribute to organisational performance. Subsequently, the focus on procedural fairness doesn't necessarily benefit either the employer or under-represented groups. Employers can also shy away from positive action for fear of being seen to favour under-represented groups and therefore fail to adequately challenge the status quo. This might satisfy the majority by demonstrating that justice in decision-making is being served but does not promote the progressive policies and practices from which the firm might benefit from greater workforce diversity. Foster and Harris (2009) suggest that a long-standing criticism of the EO approach is that because of the underlying assumption that individual characteristics (such as gender) can and should be discounted in HR decision-making, it reinforces a negative view of difference. This leads us to consider an alternative approach based on the belief that difference should be valued and recognised.

MANAGING DIVERSITY

The notion of managing diversity emerged in the 1990s partly as a response to the perceived failings of the EO approach. As opposed to focusing on sameness, managing diversity (MD) is focused on 'creating a working culture that seeks, respects, values and harnesses difference' (Schneider, 2001: 27). It is therefore underpinned by the view that the differences between people should be valued and can represent a source of competitive advantage (Kirton and Greene, 2004).

Liff (1997) notes two distinct approaches to MD on the basis of whether an employer focuses on individual difference or differences between social groups. The former perspective de-emphasises social group difference as a factor in inequality, focusing instead on equality achieved through 'the opportunity to be acknowledged for the person one is and to be helped to make the most of one's talents and reach one's own goals' (Liff, 1997: 15). The second approach partially reflects the EO approach in recognising inequality as at least partly determined by social group membership, but is distinctive in that it argues that such differences should be acknowledged rather than ignored. Here equality is sought through the adaptation of management practices so that under-represented groups can succeed (Maxwell, 2004). Similarly, recognition of workforce difference can reflect both or either visible and non-visible differences (Kandola and Fullerton, 1994). The former includes social group characteristics such as gender, age, ethnicity or disability. The latter refers to individual differences in personality, attitudes to working and favoured management style. Whether the focus is on responding to individual or group needs, MD does not lead to a uniform approach to employee treatment as under EO.

Liff (1997) suggests there are four approaches to managing diversity based on the degree to which social group equality represents an organisational objective and on the perceived relevance of social group differences to organisational decision-making. In Liff's model, *dissolving differences* is to stress individualism, rather than social group differences, so that a firm responds to the needs of individual employees rather than their social group. Noon (2007b) suggests that this approach to managing diversity is problematic because it diminishes the significance of the impact of social group on employment opportunities. In contrast, *valuing differences* recognises socially based disadvantage and advocates action to address inequality focused on under-represented groups, such as targeted training. *Accommodating differences* reflects policies to address social group disadvantage through providing standardised policies to ensure equal opportunities and fairness and neutrality of treatment (i.e. social group differences are de-emphasised). Finally, *utilising differences* reflects recognition of socially based difference and the development of policies to ensure the best use of staff mindful of this diversity. The aim, therefore, is not equality per se, but rather social group characteristics are used as the basis for devising a variety of policies to best serve organisational interests.

The business benefits of diversity management

MD tends to be framed within a managerialist discourse and presented as, or alongside, a business case for tackling inequality (Ross and Schneider, 1992).

Rather than focusing on the notion of social justice that informs the legislation and the EO approach, the rationale for adopting a more strategic MD approach often focuses on its benefits to organisational performance. In broad terms, this business case stresses that if opportunities to develop and progress are artificially blocked for any group this will result in sub-optimal use of human resources. MD is, therefore, internally driven through the imperative to make best use of available resources as opposed to the external (legislative or social) focus of EO (Wilson and Iles, 1999).

There are two sets of specific benefits associated with diversity management. The first relates to HRM outcomes, including the ability to recruit, retain and motivate the best available talent. Ng and Burke (2005: 1206) present evidence to indicate a link between diversity management practices and the attraction of high achievers, suggesting that 'individuals with high levels of ability prefer to work for more progressive organizations'. As employees' individual needs are recognised and valued, employees will be more committed to the organisation and, consequently, the incidence and cost of negative employee relations outcomes such as turnover, skills shortages or gaps, low staff morale and absenteeism will be reduced. Recruiting from a diverse labour market can also help to reduce recruitment costs and the costs incurred through an inability to manage minority groups effectively (Cox and Blake, 1991). Diversity is increasingly seen as a key means by which firms can reinforce the employer's brand and position themselves as 'employers of choice', enabling them to recruit from the widest possible pool of talent through encouraging the greatest diversity of applicants by creating a 'culture of inclusion' (CBI, 2008a). Responding to the individual needs of workers in a diverse internal labour market can also be a source of employment flexibility through the need to create policies and practices that are innovative and adaptable.

MANAGING ACROSS GENERATIONS

The second set of benefits associated with MD is the wider business benefits from employing a diverse workforce. These include enhanced creativity and innovation, responsive to the needs of a wider and more diverse range of clients and customers, and improved public image. In other words, given the imperative of responding to an increasingly diverse customer base, diversity can be a useful source of long-term organisational viability and competitive advantage through an ability to respond to changing market demography and to identify and take advantage of new opportunities. In summary, Mulholland et al. (2005) suggest that the business benefits of managing diversity can be classified into the four dimensions of the balanced scorecard: customer focus; innovation, creativity and learning; business process improvement; and the financial bottom line.

A number of commentators observe, however, that there is a lack of empirical evidence demonstrating a direct link between diversity management and performance outcomes (Anderson and Metcalfe, 2003; Curtis and Dreachslin, 2008). Indeed, much of the evidence claiming such a link tends to be anecdotal, based on a limited number of cases and lacking rigour, especially in the evaluation of outcomes (Curtis and Dreachslin, 2008). More broadly, Kochan et al. (2003) suggest there is a lack of evidence to support the claim that demographic diversity is good or bad for business. This is partly a product of the fact that the impact of diversity management is often difficult to measure. Wentling (2000) identifies a number of areas of 'impact' that are difficult to evaluate, including the impact on profitability and productivity, return on investment, behaviour changes, employee attitudes and internal readiness to respond to change. The difficulty of evaluating diversity initiatives might present a problem for ensuring long-term investment in MD policies if the business benefits cannot be readily identified and quantified.

Ortlieb and Sieben (2013) suggest that firms adopt alternative strategies for the employment of minority ethnic employees based on the resource value they bring to the firm. From this perspective, they suggest that firms adopt one of five strategies:

1 *Exclusion* (ethnic minorities are not employed)

2 *Adding value through mere labour* (a strategy based on the mere working capacity attributed to ethnic minorities)

3 *Anti-discrimination* (a strategy devised to gain access and legitimacy with regard to different markets)

4 *Adding value through ethnic background* (where ethnic background, or perceived associated competencies, are viewed as highly critical)

5 *Learning* (where ethnic minorities are viewed as possessing new perspectives and approaches to work that are essential for innovation).

Whilst referring specifically to minority ethnic workers, this typology is useful in helping us understand alternative approaches to diversity management more widely and why some firms may prioritise particular aspects of the diversity agenda or ignore it entirely, whether on legitimate grounds or not.

Further online reading This article presents a typology of diversity strategies adopted by firms depending on the kind of critical resources that minority ethnic employees provide to an organisation. These strategies range from exclusion to learning, under which strategy ethnic minority groups are viewed as bringing new perspectives and approaches to work that are essential to innovation.

Ortlieb, R. and Sieben, B. (2013) Diversity strategies and business logic: Why do companies employ ethnic minorities? *Group & Organization Management,* 38 (4): 48–511.

Managing diversity in practice

Rather than focusing on the avoidance of discrimination and legislative compliance, the emphasis of MD is to create greater inclusion of all individuals into both the formal and informal activities of the organisation through cultural change and the challenging of the attitudes and assumptions that are embedded in everyday behaviour. In this sense, learning and development is likely to be a key element of diversity management, particularly in challenging existing cultures, communicating the aims of MD policy, persuading workers to re-examine stereotypes, influencing conscious and unconscious behaviours, and breaking down workforce division.

Diversity management requires senior management buy-in, recognition at a strategic level of its importance to business success and the ability of those tasked with overseeing diversity initiatives to actively shape decisions that create a more diverse workforce (Rivera, 2012). To be effective it also needs to become the responsibility of all organisational members and not just the HR function (Ross and Schneider, 1992). Importantly, the devolution of greater HR responsibility to line managers has increased their importance in tackling inequality and developing innovative practices to manage diversity (Hutchinson and Purcell, 2007). In order to respond to both the visible and non-visible differences within their teams or departments, line managers are likely to need greater knowledge of their employees to ensure they are managed appropriately (for example, by adapting management styles to respond to individual preference). In terms of monitoring, in addition to broad-brush assessments that are typical under an EO approach (for example, assessing the proportion of new recruits who come from minority backgrounds), diversity management advocates the gathering of data on individuals and monitoring their progress.

Further online reading This article reviews the managing diversity literature published between January 2000 and December 2005. It provides a useful overview of diversity literature and the range of approaches adopted and themes addressed.

Curtis, E. F. and Dreachslin, J. L. (2008) Diversity management interventions and organizational performance: A synthesis of current literature, *Human Resource Development Review*, 7 (1): 107–34.

Issues with diversity management

The central criticism of the MD approach is that, because it is not underpinned with a social duty to address discrimination and inequality, managerial commitment to diversity can fluctuate. MD effectively depoliticises inequality, reducing it to being simply an impediment to profit-making. As social justice is a secondary concern to business improvement, if it is a concern at all, then if workforce diversity is viewed as not delivering performance benefits, management might seek to reduce investment and remove it from the strategic agenda. This is a particular problem where firms might expect a short-term return from investment in diversity policies where a longer-term perspective is required (Mulholland et al., 2005).

Further online reading This article provides an excellent critique of diversity management, particularly the associated business case, and challenges its logic and the dangers of adopting such an approach in practice.

Noon, M. (2007) The fatal flaws of diversity and the business case for ethnic minorities, *Work, Employment and Society*, 21 (4): 773–84.

Similarly, investment in diversity policies might be contingent on particular labour market conditions or competitive strategy and when these contextual factors change so might the organisation's commitment to a diverse workforce (Dickens, 1999). This raises the issue of whether discriminatory practices might be tolerated if they are seen as delivering business benefits and whether MD might actually erode progress towards equal opportunities by de-emphasising social group disadvantage (Overell, 1998). Mavin and Girling (2000) warn, therefore, that the increased adoption of MD might lead to a dilution of the social justice argument for equal opportunities. For example, Zanoni and Janssens (2004) found that managers tend not to be interested in the diversity of their workforce, rather in how difference can be used to achieve organisational goals. They found that where social group differences can help in the attainment of goals then it is perceived in positive terms, but where difference has no economic utility, or is viewed as potentially harmful to business (Ashley, 2010), it is perceived as a 'lack'. They suggest that such a conceptualisation tends to reinforce existing power relations between management and employees where it is the more compliant social groups who tend to be viewed as the norm. Following from this, Noon (2007b) argues against the adoption of the language of diversity and the acceptance of the business case rationale, claiming that the diversity discourse fails to confront structural problems in organisations that might lie at the root of inequality.

Further online reading This article presents a discussion of the research findings from interviews conducted with HR managers on the subject of diversity. In particular, it discusses how HR managers define diversity, how their diversity discourses reflect existing managerial practices and underlying power relations, and how they reaffirm or challenge those managerial practices and power relations.

Zanoni, P. and Janssens, M. (2004) Deconstructing difference: The rhetoric of human resource managers' diversity discourses, *Organization Studies,* 24 (1): 55–74.

Managing diversity can also present problems for both HRM specialists and line managers. In responding to individual needs, rather than treating all employees alike as under the EO approach, diversity management increases the complexity of HRM decision-making. In adopting an MD approach, line managers need to be more aware of how their actions towards one individual or group are perceived by others and how in making allowances for one employee or group they may create feelings of unfairness among others. Overell (1998) notes that the dual demands of treating everyone the same and celebrating difference lead to pressure on managers to adopt 'schizophrenic' attitudes. This complexity might be used as an argument for the adoption and application of the standardised procedures and practices associated with equal opportunities as being a safer bet in defending individual decisions and as a guard against litigation (Harris, 2000; Foster and Harris, 2005). In this sense, EO becomes no more than an exercise in risk avoidance with a focus on demonstrating fairness, reasonableness and similarity of treatment that can inhibit the freedom of line managers to make effective decisions and respond to individual need.

BOX 11.5
RESEARCH INSIGHT

Diversity management at elite law firms

Ashley (2010) reports on the reality behind diversity management initiatives adopted in five elite law firms in the City of London. The research reports that all firms investigated had incorporated elements of a diversity approach into their recruitment and other practices, including diversity training for all staff, and had actively engaged with organisations and programmes that aimed to encourage a more diverse range of applicants to consider entering the legal profession.

Ashley found, however, that despite involvement with such programmes tending to form a central element of the firm's approach to increasing workforce diversity, a significant proportion of those responsible for recruitment in these firms were unaware of their firm's diversity agenda or policy. Moreover, the author found that alongside this agenda there existed a number of competing policies that acted 'to perpetuate existing forms

of discrimination against non-traditional and less privileged candidates' (2010: 718), particularly a continuing tendency to recruit only from a very select group of old universities, graduates of which are typically less diverse than those from newer universities. The exclusivity of access created by this formal recruitment policy was reinforced by informal selection criteria reflective of deeply entrenched attitudes towards issues such correct dress, speech and manner, which acted as barriers to recruitment for those from lower socio-economic groups.

Therefore, Ashley reports that whilst many employees at these firms saw the diversity agenda as the 'right thing to do', they also viewed its enactment as representing a risk to their professional reputation and firm brand. In particular, many expressed concern about the potential for poor person–organisation fit arising, not necessarily on the basis of visible differences of age and ethnicity, but on the basis of the 'wrong' upbringing and social class.

Importantly, there is a long-running debate over the extent to which MD constitutes a new or alternative approach to addressing workplace equality. Some commentators suggest that a focus on 'difference' rather than 'sameness' constitutes a rejection of the EO approach. Mulholland et al. (2005) suggest, however, that diversity management complements equal opportunities initiatives because the arguments for ethical and fair treatment can be combined with the recognition and valuing of difference for competitive advantage. Liff and Wajcman (1996) argue that, in reality, both the 'sameness' and 'difference' approaches are relevant in addressing inequality, depending on the particular circumstances and the problem to be tackled. For example, sameness might be the most appropriate perspective to adopt in ensuring that selection procedures are free of bias but differences should be acknowledged in order to redress prior disadvantage through positive action. Dickens (1999) subsequently argues that, rather than seeing them as alternatives, a three-pronged approach to equality is required, with social regulation (for example, through trade unions and employee voice) and legal regulation addressing the limitations of the business case approach.

Further online reading

Ashley, L. (2010) Making a difference? The use (and abuse) of diversity management at the UK's elite law firms, *Work, Employment and Society*, 24 (4): 711–27.

The impact of context

The extent to which an organisation is faced with an imperative to manage diversity derives from a range of contextual factors and, therefore, employers must ensure they adopt an approach to equality and diversity that is reflective of organisational needs and capabilities (Mulholland et al., 2005). These needs might include long- and short-term strategic objectives, the changing demands of its customers or clients, its obligations under the regulatory framework and its approach to corporate social responsibility.

The ability of a firm to respond adequately to the need to manage workforce diversity and tackle inequality reflects its managerial capabilities (the extent and effectiveness of training), the sophistication of HR policies and procedures and the presence of trade unions to police procedural fairness. Employer responses to the strategic or legal imperative to manage diversity and ensure equal opportunities are likely to be partly a function of the size of the organisation. Whilst larger and more bureaucratic organisations might have more well-developed procedures for ensuring equality of opportunities, smaller, more adaptive firms might be better placed to offer more diverse working arrangements and conditions reflective of individual need.

The extent to which an organisation must consider anti-discrimination legislation in decision-making is also related to the diversity in the labour markets in which it operates, reflecting both the local demography as well as the extent to which the organisation employs or attracts applicants from a diverse population. Even in a labour market seemingly lacking in diversity, a firm can take steps to develop its practices *vis-à-vis* its labour market and ensure it actively takes advantage of the full spectrum of available labour. The diversity of a firm's workforce and its potential labour supply is also partly determined by outsiders' perceptions of the employer (shaped, for example, by the visible profile of the company's existing workforce) and the industry sector in which it operates.

BOX 11.6
GLOBAL INSIGHT

Diversity and management practice in MNCs

Jonsen et al. (2011) report that the very nature and meaning of 'diversity' and what constitutes effective diversity management vary across cultural contexts. These differences ultimately shape the importance placed upon the diversity agenda within organisations themselves and what workforce diversity might look like. For instance, Simons (2002) finds that European companies have a tendency to try to embrace a greater range of diversity 'dimensions' than US-owned companies and Singh and Point (2004) found significant differences in the main diversity types mentioned on company websites (for example, 73 per cent of UK companies mentioned gender compared to only 29 per cent of Swiss firms). These tendencies are reflective of national cultural, political and social

history, not least the legislation and policy measures put in place to create greater social equality which vary across nations, and might help explain, therefore, why global diversity initiatives in MNCs have been seen to fail. Nonetheless, Wentling (2000) notes how changing workforce composition, both within national and international labour markets, presents a challenge both to MNCs and institutions throughout the world and how business forces, such as global competition and the need to remain competitive, are driving diversity into organisations regardless of their geographical location. She also notes that, theoretically, international business has been one of the pioneer fields of valuing diversity, partly because embracing differences emerged as a need for survival and success, reflecting the need to recruit and retain a diverse workforce that mirrors the diverse markets of MNCs.

Further online reading This extensive literature review covers many of the issues raised in the discussion of diversity management earlier in this chapter but with a specific focus on identifying the limitations of both research and practice in the field that fail to reflect cross-cultural differences.

Jonsen, K., Maznevski, M. and Schneider, S. (2011) Diversity and its not so diverse literature: An international perspective, *International Journal of Cross Cultural Management,* 11 (1): 35–62.

SUMMARY POINTS

EQUAL
OPPORTUNITIES
AND MANAGING
DIVERSITY

- Only by understanding inequality in its social and historical context can managers adequately address the problems created by inequity of employment outcomes and benefit from creating a more diverse workforce reflective of the markets they serve.

- Continued labour market equality is evident according to four main measures: horizontal and vertical segregation, earnings and unemployment.

- Pincus (1996) identifies three levels of discrimination: individual, institutional and structural.

- UK and EU equal opportunities legislation is characterised as both minimalist and liberal, focusing on procedural fairness and the promotion of sameness.

- Equal opportunities and managing diversity represent two responses, both theoretically and practically, to the same question of how to remedy labour market inequality (Liff, 1997).

- At the heart of dealing with inequality is the fundamental challenge for managers of how to recognise individual differences, comply with anti-discrimination legislation and promote a general feeling of fair treatment among the workforce.

- Managing diversity developed as an approach to tackling inequality alongside the more strategic focus of HRM and its emphasis on developing people and processes to better contribute to the productivity and profitability of the enterprise.

- The extent to which diversity management, without an underpinning ethical dimension is sustainable in a turbulent organisational context is questionable.

- There are inherent tensions between market forces, employment regulation and the ethical and social responsibilities of the firm that need to be balanced for a firm to arrive at a sustainable, flexible and effective means of tackling inequality and benefiting from a diverse workforce.

SELF-TEST QUESTIONS

1 What are the key measures according to which it is possible to assess labour market inequality?

2 What is meant by the concepts of individual, structural and institutional discrimination?

3 What is the difference between positive action and positive discrimination?

4 What are the fundamental characteristics of the approach to equality legislation adopted in the UK and much of the EU?

5 What are the business benefits associated with organisations ensuring they recruit from the widest possible talent pool?

6 What are key criticisms of an equal opportunities approach to tackling discrimination and disadvantage in the workplace?

7 What are the fundamental points of contrast between an equal opportunities (EO) and managing diversity (MD) approach to addressing inequality at work?

8 What are the potential problems associated with approaches to tackling equality that are based solely on the business benefits that might accrue from doing so?

TEST YOURSELF

Want to know more about this chapter? Review what you have been learning by visiting:
https://edge.sagepub.com/wilton3e

TEST YOURSELF

- Print out or download the chapter summaries for quick revision
- Test yourself with multiple-choice questions
- Revise key terms with interactive flashcards

CASE STUDY

Workforce diversity at Roygbiv Solutions

Roygbiv is a leading IT and business services consultancy employing 10,000 people worldwide, delivering consultancy and outsourcing services and technological business solutions. Established in 1974 by three recent university graduates, it has risen to be one of Europe's most innovative consultancies. It currently has activities in over 40 countries and places great stress on its ability to understand and respond

to the needs of its clients or partners in any market in any country.

Despite its size and origins in the UK, where its headquarters remains, Roygbiv has sought to position itself as 'global in capability, local in application', combining the best talent from around the world to deliver tailored solutions to clients' problems. The company is still headed up by Noah Lennox, one of the original founders of the company (the two other founders have long since left the company, one having had a falling out with Lennox, the other to pursue alternative business opportunities). A key focus of Lennox's leadership – and arguably an integral part of the company's success – has been to create a strong corporate culture centred around Roygbiv's core values: innovation, integrity, respect, quality, value. The company stresses the importance of these corporate values when recruiting new members of staff. Europe and North America have been the main markets for Roygbiv in the past but Lennox has recently unveiled ambitious plans for a stronger presence in both South America and the Far East. Integral to these expansion plans is the recruitment of a significantly increased number of graduate recruits on its graduate development programme.

Typically, Roygbiv has focused its graduate recruitment on redbrick universities, reflecting the long-held view that they are the best source of technical graduates. Most of their graduate intake typically comes from 20 universities, although, occasionally, outstanding candidates from newer universities are accepted on the graduate development programme. In line with the emphasis on the importance placed on person–organisation fit and the focus in induction of inculcating core values, Roygbiv has tended to prefer to recruit 'blank canvases' who can be moulded into 'Roygbiv people'.

Following feedback from clients that Roygbiv's systems developers and designers can often lack the ability to convey complex ideas to non-experts, the company has begun to stress the importance of recruiting new employees on the basis of possessing both technical expertise (which has tended to be the pre-eminent concern) and inter-personal/communication skills. Drawing on this emphasis, Roygbiv has developed a competency framework to reflect the 'ideal employee' that provides the basis for HR decisions in the areas of recruitment, learning and development and performance management, which has been rolled out throughout the company. This framework had been based on assessing the characteristics and behaviours of corporate high-flyers.

At a recent meeting, however, one senior manager at a US client joked to Lennox that Roygbiv must have a corporate 'cookie cutter' which they use to produce duplicate employees. This has concerned Lennox and he instructed HR to explore the issue. Initial findings suggest a notable lack of diversity – particularly with regard to age and gender – among the grades of workers that are the visible face of Roygbiv, that spend considerable amounts of time at clients' premises, often undertaking international assignments, and are responsible for designing technological solutions to client problems.

Questions

1 How might the lack of diversity at Roygbiv be explained?

2 Why should Noah Lennox consider this lack of diversity to be a problem for the organisation?

3 How would you advise Lennox to help resolve this lack of diversity?

USEFUL READING

Journal articles

Liff, S. (1999) Diversity and equal opportunities: Room for a constructive compromise? *Human Resource Management Journal*, 9 (1): 65–75.

This article provides an excellent overview of the contrasts between equal opportunities and managing diversity approaches, assesses the criticism of each approach and discusses how they might be used together in practice.

Ng, E. S. W. and Burke, R. J. (2005) Person–organisation fit and the war for talent: Does diversity management make a difference? *International Journal of Human Resource Management*, 16 (7): 1195–210.

This article reports on a study that highlights the importance of diversity management in female and ethnic minority applicants' job choice decisions. It also suggests that high achievers and new immigrants rated organisations with diversity management as more attractive as potential employers.

Books, book chapters and reports

CBI (2008) *Talent Not Tokenism: The Business Benefits of Workforce Diversity*, London: CBI/TUC/EHRC.

This guide to managing diversity presents the business rationale for managing diversity and provides a number of case studies of leading-edge employers and tips for creating and managing a more diverse workforce.

Gatrell, C. and Swan, E. (2008) *Gender and Diversity in Management: A Concise Introduction*, London: Sage.

As the name suggests, this short book packs in a concise, yet accessible and detailed discussion of key terms, concepts and debates in the field of equality and diversity, and provides a useful supplement to much of the discussion in this chapter.

Kirton, G. and Greene, A. M. (2004) *The Dynamics of Managing Diversity: A Critical Approach* (2nd edn), Oxford: Elsevier Butterworth-Heinemann.

This well-regarded text supplied a comprehensive and critical discussion of equality and diversity in the workplace. It provides an excellent resource to explore in more depth many of the issues discussed in this chapter.

Mor Barak, M. E. (2011) *Managing Diversity – Towards a Globally Inclusive Workforce* (2nd edn), London: Sage.

A readable book that provides important evidence of the dangers of organisational exclusion and how firms might yield the benefits of a more diverse workforce. It provides some useful international comparisons on, for example, discrimination legislation.

FURTHER ONLINE READING

The following articles can be accessed for free on the book's companion website **https://edge.sagepub.com/wilton3e**:

Ashley, L. (2010) Making a difference? The use (and abuse) of diversity management at the UK's elite law firms, *Work, Employment and Society*, 24 (4): 711–27.

This excellent article, summarised in Box 11.5, outlines research findings from a study of the impact of diversity management practices in five elite UK law firms and how competing policies and entrenched attitudes among hiring managers tend to act to maintain traditional barriers to entry to such firms for under-represented groups, notably on the basis of social class background.

Curtis, E. F. and Dreachslin, J. L. (2008) Integrative literature review: Diversity management interventions and organizational performance: A synthesis of current literature, *Human Resource Development Review*, 7 (1): 107–34.

Hoque, K. and Noon, M. (2004) Equal opportunities policy and practice in Britain: Evaluating the 'empty shell' hypothesis, *Work, Employment and Society*, 18: 481–506.

Jonsen, K., Maznevski, M. and Schneider, S. (2011) Diversity and its not so diverse literature: An international perspective, *International Journal of Cross Cultural Management*, 11 (1): 35–62.

Noon, M. (2007) The fatal flaws of diversity and the business case for ethnic minorities, *Work, Employment and Society*, 21 (4): 773–84.

Ortlieb, R. and Sieben, B. (2013) Diversity strategies and business logic: Why do companies employ ethnic minorities?, *Group & Organization Management*, 38 (4): 48–511.

Zanoni, P. and Janssens, M. (2004) Deconstructing difference: The rhetoric of human resource managers' diversity discourses, *Organization Studies*, 24 (1): 55–74.

Want to know more about this chapter? Visit the companion website at: **https://edge.sagepub.com/wilton3e** to access practice questions, videos and selected journal articles to further enhance your study.

12

CAREERS AND CAREER MANAGEMENT

OLD VS. NEW CAREERS

CHAPTER OBJECTIVES

- To outline the different meanings of career and career development

- To discuss how careers are changing and the potential implications for organisations and workers

- To outline common career management interventions and outcomes

- To outline how individuals are increasingly being asked to take greater responsibility for career development.

INTRODUCTION

Chapter 4 outlined a number of developments in the economic, social and technological spheres that have impacted upon the ways in which work organisations engage labour. In particular, the chapter outlined the perceived need for organisational and labour flexibility and how this had led to changes both to organisational form and increasing diversity in contractual arrangements with workers. The impact of these developments is manifold but one of the most profoundly affected areas of HRM is career management. Jackson et al. (1996: 1) state that 'careers as lifetime experiences of individuals and as pathways through occupations and organisations are in a profound state of change ... [as a result of] a wide range of revolutionary forces affecting labour markets, employment structures, organisational practice and educational provision'. In particular, organisational restructuring and the pursuit of increased labour flexibility have led to widespread changes to how individuals develop careers and the extent to which firms provide both the infrastructure and support for career development. In addition, many of the changes to the labour supply discussed in Chapter 4 are altering what organisations can assume employees demand from employment and, subsequently, their expectations in respect of careers. Social trends, such as the rise in dual career couples, increased worker demand for work–life balance and demographic changes are redefining an appropriate career proposition from employers.

This chapter begins by outlining contrasting notions of careers and explores how the traditional notion of career progression is changing. It then explores what the developing context of employment implies for the way in which workers develop careers within and outside of organisations, the implications of these changes for the individual and how HRM can provide support for career development. Finally, the chapter outlines the rationale for career management interventions and outcomes.

THE 'TRADITIONAL' CAREER

The traditional notion of a career is exemplified by the definition put forward by Sparrow and Hiltrop (1994; cited in Counsell, 1997: 34) as 'advancement within a profession or occupation, made possible within an organisation by the provision of a cradle-to-grave employment philosophy'. Similarly, Wilensky (1960: 554) suggested that a 'career is a succession of related jobs arranged in a hierarchy of prestige, through which persons move in an ordered (more or less predictable) sequence'. More broadly, Arnold (1997a: 16) suggests that 'a career is the sequence of employment-related positions, roles, activities and experiences encountered by a person'.

Implicit in these definitions are a number of attributes that tend to denote the traditional perspective on careers. In particular, these definitions firmly focus on (paid) work. They also embody the notion of a 'job for life' or, at least, the idea that careers are longitudinal phenomena that take place within a single or limited number of organisations. The emphasis is, therefore, on careers taking place within a bureaucratic context and on continuous vertical advancement through the organisational hierarchy. In this sense, careers tend to be structured around well-trodden paths or ladders that link a sequence of jobs resulting in the achievement of some pre-determined goal or 'career capstone experience' (Leach and Chakiris, 1988: 51). Careers, therefore, display a coherence that can be objectively defined. Importantly, it is the goal orientation that distinguishes a career from a sequence of jobs: 'jobs need not lead anywhere, it is just something a person gets paid for' (Leach and Chakiris, 1988: 50). In other words, jobs are simply the building blocks of careers. The traditional perspective is associated with models of stable, predictable career and life development, such as those presented in Table 12.1 that suggest a largely universal developmental experience which can be broken down into distinct phases.

REDEFINING THE CAREER

In contrast to the traditional viewpoint, alternative definitions suggest that the notion of career has different meanings for different groups of workers operating in different contexts. Whilst careers might universally denote a relationship between an individual and an organisation or the labour market in some sense, some perspectives on career suggest that rather than being objectively defined (i.e. a specific and pre-determined occupational pathway or a

TABLE 12.1 *Models of career/life development*

Career stages (Super, 1957)	Phases of adult life development (Levinson, 1978)
Growth: expansion of capabilities and interests (ages 0–14)	–
Exploration: clarify self-identity (ages 15–24)	Early adult world (ages 17–22) Entering adult world (22–28)
Establishment: finding a suitable career (ages 25–44)	Settling down (ages 33–40) Mid-life transition (ages 40–45)
Maintenance: hold position, compete against younger people (ages 45–64)	Entering middle age (age 45–50) Speculatively discuss late adulthood (age 50+)
Decline: decreasing capabilities (age 65+)	

sequence of identifiable job roles) careers are subjectively constructed and shaped by the significance and meaning that the individual attaches to their career experiences.

Schein (1996) refers to a shift from external careers, where the formal stages and roles are defined by organisations and society, to internal careers which involve 'a subjective sense of where one is going in one's work life' (1996: 80). In this sense, many people do not simply act out a prescribed career path but instead construct their career in dynamic negotiation with their social, economic and cultural context. Bird (1994: 326) conceptualises careers not as a sequence of jobs but as 'accumulations of information and knowledge embodied in skills, expertise and relationship networks acquired through an evolving sequence of work experience'. In this sense, careers can therefore be understood as both the connective tissue between jobs and the outputs of these jobs in respect of personal development. This perspective can be developed by acknowledging that careers can also be defined to encompass all aspects of personal and social development inside and outside of paid employment. Consequently, career success and individual self-worth can be thought of in wider terms than simply employment-based achievement – such as the attainment of power, status and remuneration – with non-paid work as a student, parent or community member seen as important, reflecting the importance of 'social good' (Leach and Chakiris, 1988).

VARIATION IN CAREER FORM

Careers for many have never universally conformed to the 'ideal type' of an organisationally bounded, linear progression through a hierarchy of positions. This is partly because career form is determined not only by the individual and the employing organisation but also by the nature of the work itself, the orientation of different occupational groups and the employment sector in which it takes place. Kanter (1989) suggests three broad career forms:

1 *Bureaucratic careers* conform to traditional definitions of career and are characterised by 'the logic of advancement' and involve 'a sequence of positions in a formally defined hierarchy of other positions' (Kanter, 1989: 509). Such careers typically take place within the confines of a single large organisation, although increasingly, organisational careers are not just about

upward progression, but about being able to meet both the individuals' needs for job variety and interest and the organisation's resourcing requirements.

2 *Professional careers* reflect a more complex relationship between the individual and the organisation where status is not conferred by hierarchical position but by reputation or standing in a particular field or profession, based on the accumulation of scarce, socially valued knowledge or skill.

3 *Entrepreneurial careers* are defined as those 'in which growth occurs through the creation of new value or new organisational capacity ... the key resource is the capacity to create valued outputs' (Kanter, 1989: 515). Career development is, therefore, associated with project working, transient employment relationships and status conferred not by hierarchical progression but by alternative recognition of achievement (such as the ability to contribute to the strategic aims and objectives of the firm). This reflects the 'new' career forms outlined later (Parker and Inkson, 1999).

Whilst this typology is limited and there are likely multiple forms of career (Cohen and El-Sawad, 2006), it is useful in identifying the 'pressure points' where career forms can vary. Specifically, they differ in respect of what constitutes development, how status is conferred or achieved and the nature of the relationship between the individual and the organisation.

THE 'DEATH' OF THE CAREER?

As a consequence of organisational and economic restructuring, the traditional notion of career is argued to have become outdated (even if such bureaucratic careers are argued only ever to have existed for a minority) (Arnold, 1997a). For an increasing proportion of the workforce, it is suggested, linear conceptions of the career need either to be revised or discarded as the mutual investment by employer and employee in long-term, stable relationships is no longer appropriate in the context of the broader demands for organisational and labour flexibility. The Association of Graduate Recruiters sum up this perspective:

IS THE CAREER DEAD?

In the new world of work, careers are very different. Gone is the job for life with its planned career structure and company training scheme. Gone is the clear functional identity and progressive rise in income and security. Instead there is a world of customers and clients, adding value, lifelong learning, portfolio careers, self-development and an overwhelming need to stay employable. (1995: 4)

Adamson et al. (1998: 251) go as far as to signal the 'death' of the career and the emergence of 'new deals' in employment, suggesting that: 'pervasive definitions of organisational or managerial careers have long encompassed notions of hierarchical progression ... [but] the flattening of organisational hierarchies has reduced or eliminated entire levels of management and, as such, career paths have become increasingly blurred'. They suggest three fundamental changes in organisational career philosophy:

1 The employer–employee relationship is not now conceived as long-term, and thus the future-time orientation of careers now seems less appropriate.

2 Whilst career progression may indeed still mean moving between positions over time, it no longer necessarily means hierarchical movement.

BOX 12.1
UNDERSTAND

The shape of careers to come?

The following case is based on an interview conducted as part of a study of early graduate careers. The case highlights a number of characteristics of 'new' careers, including intensive periods of learning and development, the requirement for geographic mobility, the potential for high earnings, the importance of professional networks for career development, periods of both direct and self-employment and the development of a more subjective and values-driven interpretation of career success. In talking of her career-to-date, Rebecca summed up the new career dynamic:

> My idea of what a successful career might look like has changed significantly. Previously I thought you just stick your head down and keep working and you'll work your way to the top and now I think, is that a measure of success if it doesn't make you happy? I think success would be having control of my own life and being sufficiently successful and financially independent to do that.

Over her early career, Rebecca had shown considerable willingness to be geographically mobile for career success. Within two years of graduation, she was working as a quality control manager for a food manufacturer in north-east England before moving to another part of the UK to take on a more senior position. When interviewed seven years after graduation, Rebecca was working as a technical manager for another food processing company in the south-west,

earning approximately £60,000 per annum. Shortly after this interview, however, Rebecca left this employer to embark on an MBA to facilitate a career change (which required further relocation) after having become dissatisfied with her current job. Upon completion of her studies, Rebecca started working as a consultant project manager for a utilities company on a fixed-term basis, a job for which Rebecca and her partner moved to South Wales. Her partner, who works as a product manager for an international pharmaceutical company, worked from home when not travelling and had kept the same job despite the couple's mobility. After ten years, however, Rebecca expressed a desire to begin to put down roots. Having set herself up as self-employed to pursue consultancy work, often doing work resulting from networking within her MBA cohort, she was earning the equivalent of £85,000 a year. Asked about how she envisaged her career progressing, Rebecca said:

> With this job I've taken the view that I'll work for six months and if I want to go travelling for three months I can ... then I'll come back and do another contract. It's a completely different way of life for me. The MBA has opened my eyes to the possibilities. The other point is in order to do the contracts I've set up my own company, which enables me to potentially do other things as well other than whatever specific contract I'm doing. I feel quite liberated, when you work for yourself you don't do things you don't want to do.

Source: Purcell et al., 2006

3 From both the organisational and individual perspectives it is no longer apparent how a logical, ordered and sequential career may actually evolve.

As a result in these changes, 'new' careers are marked by 'numerous transitions between jobs, organizations, or fields of professional activity, as well as a lack of institutionalised and ordered career paths and/or career rules' (Strunk et al., 2004: 1), with greater focus on the external labour market as a means for advancement (Herriot et al., 1994). Under this perspective, careers and career development are better understood as chaotic systems, characterised by complexity and unpredictability, cyclical rather than linear progression, lateral rather than upward movement and periods of re-skilling. Vaughan and Wilson (1994: 45) suggest, therefore, that for some 'the [career] ladder has unexpectedly turned into a hamster wheel'. The key contrasts between the 'old' and 'new' career are outlined in Table 12.2.

NEW CAREERS AND THE PSYCHOLOGICAL CONTRACT

This less stable, less predictable career is variously labelled as 'boundaryless' (M. B. Arthur, 1994), 'protean' (Hall, 1996), 'free-form' (Leach and Chakiris, 1988), 'entrepreneurial' (Kanter, 1989), 'multi-directional' (Baruch, 2004) or 'post-corporate' (Peiperl and Baruch, 1997) (see Box 12.2 for an overview of these conceptions). Whilst each of these labels refers to subtly different models of the new career, they are underpinned by the assumption that the links between organisations and individuals have become weakened, less structured and more temporary (Brousseau et al., 1996).

TABLE 12.2 *The 'old' and 'new' career compared*

	'Old' career	'New' career
Form	Structured, linear, continuous, predictable	Unstructured, discontinuity, cyclical, unpredictable
Career success	Objective and externally defined	Subjective
Function	Organisational need	Individual need
Principal concern	Career progression	Personal development, growth and lifelong learning
Measure of Achievement	Hierarchical progression and accumulation of status, power and authority	'Psychological success' (Mirvis and Hall, 1994), 'Self-fulfilment' (Hall, 1996)
Objective	Job security through loyalty	Employment security through employability
Context	Bureaucracy, organisationally-bound	Network, boundaryless
Focus	Work	Work–life balance
Constituencies	Jobs and job titles	Competencies, skills, assignments and projects
Nature of psychological contract	Relational 'Service rewarded with salary increments, security both in employment and retirement and career opportunities' (McGovern et al., 1996: 81)	Transactional 'Exchange [of] performance for continuous learning and marketability' (Sullivan, 1999: 458)
Timeframe	Long-term	Short-term
Control	Organisational	Individual
Orientation	Future	Present

BOX 12.2
RESEARCH INSIGHT

Conceptions of the 'new' career

- Boundaryless careers (M. B. Arthur, 1994)

Characterised by three themes that can be contrasted with traditional careers: complex mobility patterns; required strategies and competencies of 'knowing-why' (identity), 'knowing-how' (marketability) and 'know-whom' (networks of influence and information); and a high degree of self-responsibility and self-reliance, including the pursuit of personally 'meaningful values.

- Protean career (Hall, 1996)

Focused on careers as managed by the individual rather than the organisation, and guided by the search for self-fulfillment. As such careers are proactively self-directed, requiring individuals to be flexible, adaptable and versatile (Hall, 2002). The protean career can be understood as a set of attitudes, orientation or approaches to career that is values-driven, in relation to 'whole life space', rather than about the 'structure' of the career and the degree of mobility required for achievement.

- Multi-directional careers (Baruch, 2004)

Careers that are driven by individual choice and self-determination where career decisions are taken on the basis of personal development and the achievement of subjectively defined 'success'. Such careers 'take into account the full scale of [career] landscapes. You can choose. You can climb the mountain, you can opt for another mountain, take some hills instead, wander along the plains – a variety of options is accepted. You navigate your own career, creating a new path when and where you feel it is right, you select whichever direction you wish to pursue and feel capable in reaching personal development. Moreover, you define your success' (Baruch, 2004: 61).

- Freeform careers (Leach and Chakiris, 1988)

Free-form careers include work for pay (such as permanent or temporary part-time jobs, consulting, entrepreneurial activity) or unpaid work.

- Post-corporate careers (Peiperl and Baruch, 1997)

Model of career that reflects the multiple options and direction of career moves that people can opt for, as opposed to options offered to an employee by their employer. This model stresses the importance of individual career navigation and the demise of clear and stable career systems.

Under this analysis, rather than provide long-term employment, organisations provide opportunities to develop transferable skills to help people become more employable rather than relying on the organisations to provide development and advancement opportunities. Subsequently, McGovern et al. (1996: 81) suggest that a shift towards new deals in employment has meant the abandonment of the 'traditional' psychological contract of a 'long-term moral commitment to serve in organisational interests in exchange for rewards of a prospective kind', at the core of which is the 'understanding that service will be rewarded with salary increments, security both in employment and retirement and career opportunities'. This has been replaced by a new contract where workers 'exchange performance for continuous learning and marketability' (Sullivan, 1999: 458) and, rather than *career* development, the focus of the employment relationship is on *personal* development (Ball and Jordan, 1997).

 Further online reading This article provides a comprehensive dissection of the boundaryless career concept, both conceptually and operationally, and suggests that it fails to provide a comprehensive account of the complexity of contemporary careers. The article also addresses the lack of empirical evidence in support of the boundaryless career in reality, suggesting that data on job stability do not support the assumption of the collapse of the traditional career.

Rodrigues, R. A. and Guest, D. (2010) Have careers become boundaryless? *Human Relations*, 63 (8): 1157–75.

ARE TRADITIONAL CAREERS REALLY DEAD?

The extent of the demise of the 'old' and the proliferation of the 'new' career concept is strongly contested. Whilst careers are becoming less predictable and their boundaries more permeable, the dramatic changes described by some commentators are likely to have been overstated (Kidd, 2002) and Baruch (2006) argues against portraying the current state of careers as 'all change'. Strunk et al. (2004) suggest that although most of these 'new' career concepts appear valid and sound, empirical support for the 'complexity hypothesis' is still rather scarce, with most research based on case studies, interviews and anecdotes which are limited in the extent to which they can support greater incidence of these new careers. Similarly, Inkson et al. (2012: 329) suggest that whilst the 'boundaryless career' is best understood as an 'ideal-type' it is often treated as an 'empirical phenomenon' despite limited evidence to support claims of its increasing pervasiveness. For instance, Pringle and Mallon (2003) suggest that boundaryless career theory is applicable only to a minority of workers, particularly professionals, and both Zaleska and de Menezes (2007) and Donnelly (2008) report continued access to traditional careers across a diverse sample of employers. Inkson et al. (2012) and Lazarova and Taylor (2009) argue that there exists relatively little empirical evidence to support assertions that boundaryless careers now predominate. Rodrigues and Guest (2010) suggest that far from being boundaryless, contemporary careers remain bounded albeit in potentially more complex ways, for example, by occupation, geography, employment contract and family, if not organisation.

Further online reading This article takes as a starting point the assumption that notions of boundaryless careers now represent the 'status quo' in analysis of modern careers. The authors then evaluate the contribution of the concept to the study of careers and critique, including the lack of empirical support for the claimed dominance of boundaryless careers, and offer new directions for theory and research.

Inkson, K., Gunz, H., Ganesh, S. and Roper, J. (2012) Boundaryless careers: Bringing back boundaries, *Organization Studies*, 33 (3): 323–40.

Moreover, there is evidence to suggest that traditional career attitudes among workers still prevail, despite the positive rhetoric of the new career of self-determination and freedom. Guest and Conway (2002) found that most employees expect to stay with their employer for the next five years and to be promoted during that time. King (2003: 17) reports in a study of attitudes to careers that recent graduates appear to 'pay lip service to the idea of the new career but nonetheless expect to progress in a more conventional manner' and concerns about their employability have as much to do with progression within their current firm as beyond it. King also reports, however, that the evidence indicates that only a minority of graduates now have access to a traditional career (either in the professions or in a large blue-chip employer), and most will be expected to take responsibility for planning and managing their careers and focusing on employability as a source of security. King (2004: 9) suggests, therefore, that workers (typically younger and higher-skilled workers) have 'internalised messages about the decline of traditional careers by favouring jobs that offer "employability" rather than career progression'.

Some studies do, however, give credence to certain aspects of the new career dynamic. In a study of US MBA students and graduates, Anakwe et al. (2000) found that the acquisition and utilisation of skills that foster self-management, interpersonal management and environmental learning were likely to enhance career management. Strunk et al. (2004) found that, compared to a graduating cohort from 1970, the careers of a small sample of business studies graduates who started their professional careers in the 1990s were notably more complex. Heckscher (1995) found some change in personal orientation towards careers, reporting that managers increasingly viewed their loyalty as task-focused and temporary, based on professional challenge rather than a long-term commitment to organisations. Similarly, Wilson and Davies (1999) report that managers are adjusting to the changing psychological contract by adopting career strategies that have the purpose of maintaining a particular lifestyle, rather than ensuring the survival of a specific form of career.

Further online reading This article outlines a number of strands in career research and in doing so highlights many of the changes and drivers of change associated with contemporary careers.

Arthur, M. B. (2008) Examining contemporary careers: A call for interdisciplinary inquiry, *Human Relations, 61 (2): 163–86*.

THE INDIVIDUAL AND CAREER DEVELOPMENT

Drawing upon the perspectives outlined above, career development can be understood as the proactive choices made by people both about the kind of work they do and how they develop skills, knowledge and attributes through a sequence of work and work-related experiences to ensure continued employability.

Individual approaches to and expectations of career development are highly diverse. For example, career priorities and goals are determined by a range of influences including gender, age, family circumstances, previous employment experience, financial commitments and lifestyle choices. Some people may prioritise job security and stability whilst others might focus on achieving high financial reward and status. Some might prioritise doing socially useful work (for example, working in health or social care or for an 'ethical' company). In a survey of graduate careers, Purcell et al. (2006) found that whilst over half of both male and female respondents claimed that interesting and challenging work were the most important characteristics of their jobs, a greater proportion of men reported high financial reward and opportunities to reach managerial level as being the most important aspect. In contrast, women were more likely to value job security, continual skills development and doing socially useful work. Career priorities and goals are shaped by a range of internal and external factors and are likely to be subject to change according to both current circumstance and future life plans. For example, the influence of changing family situation on career is profound for both men and women (Wilton and Purcell, 2010). Employers therefore need to understand that the increasing diversity found in the labour supply is accompanied by greater diversity of career expectations and aspirations.

The importance of career self-management

Regardless of the extent to which the new career concept is accepted, the implication of labour market change is that careers are becoming more complex and uncertain. As a consequence, workers are required to become more self-reliant in managing their careers, self-reflective about motives and capacities (Kuijpers and Scheerens, 2006), to assume ownership of career development and to acquire and develop a demonstrable set of portable skills and knowledge which fosters adaptability in any environment (Hall, 1996; Harvey et al., 1997; Nabi and Bagley, 1998; Sullivan, 1999; Anakwe et al., 2000; O'Connell et al., 2008). The promotion of lifelong learning and continuing professional development has become of central importance both for organisations to ensure sustained competitive advantage and for individuals to develop the capability to gain and maintain employment and obtain new employment if required. This requires that employees accept individual responsibility for determining their own learning needs and for articulating and satisfying those needs in concert with the performance requirements of the firm. Arnold (1997b: 457) suggests that effective career self-management requires the individual to 'be able to adopt many different perspectives, to deal with contradiction, to accumulate diverse experience, to distinguish between knowing about and knowing how to do something, to tolerate uncertainty and to process information heuristically'. In respect of the boundaryless career, the required strategies and competencies for 'success' are summarised as *knowing-why* (one's sense of personal identity and motives), *knowing-how* (one's human capital and, therefore, marketability) and, *knowing-whom* (one's networks of influence and information) (M. B. Arthur, 1994).

Similarly, for effective career self-management, Stewart and Knowles (1999) emphasise 'the continuous construction and maintenance of a healthy self-concept, congruent with individuals' changing strengths and weaknesses, shifting beliefs and attitudes and future aspirations' (Adamson et al., 1998: 257). This self-concept reflects a person's career anchor: the stabilising and driving force of a person's career which is manifest in the values, motives and needs that a person prioritises above all others. Schein (1990) identifies eight career anchors: security/stability; autonomy/independence; (specific) technical-functional competence; general managerial competence; entrepreneurial creativity; service or dedication to a cause; pure challenge; and lifestyle. Of course, some of these anchors are 'threatened' as a result of career change. For example, careers focused on the possession of technical-functional competence (specific ability or skill) are potentially problematic given the rapid obsolescence of skills and knowledge in the changing world of work, requiring the continual updating of such competence. Schein (1996) argues that those who favour security and stability are facing the most severe problems, whilst those anchored in autonomy are likely to find this new world easier to navigate and cope with.

The implications of 'new deals' in employment

It is perhaps easy to see how the notion of new careers fits with the grand narrative of the growth of more chaotic economic conditions that require of workers a more dynamic entrepreneurial spirit and a commitment to lifelong learning and self-development. An optimistic perspective suggests that 'organisationally bounded' careers promote an unhealthy reliance on firms and that the new career form has the potential to liberate the individual from such dependency. For example, Mallon and Cohen (2001) found in a study of women's transitions from organisational careers to self-employment that the majority had made this shift as a result

BOX 12.3
UNDERSTAND

Competencies required for effective
career self-management

- Optimising the situation

  - creating the circumstances to support
    career advancement
  - setting broad career objectives
  - anticipating future changes in labour
    markets, organisations and one's life
  - ensuring the ability to respond to change
  - identifying and utilising opportunities for
    development
  - developing networks of contacts to
    provide assistance and guidance when
    needed.

- Career planning

  - learning how to continually review one's skills
    and assess future learning requirements.

- Personal development

  - recognising the needs for lifelong learning
  - taking opportunities for development as
    they arise
  - identifying learning needs and making
    plans to meet them
  - being self-aware about one's skills and
    competencies.

- Striking a balance between work and non-work

Source: adapted from B. Ball (1997) Career management competencies: The individual perspective, *Career
Development International*, 2: 74–9 © Emerald Group
Publishing Limited all rights reserved. Reprinted with
permission

of dissatisfaction and disillusionment with their employer. As such, optimists suggest that the ultimate upshot of the economic transformation associated with a knowledge economy will create a win–win situation for employers and employees and an economy increasingly made up of 'free workers' who are 'demanding, mobile and self-reliant, high on human capital and low on loyalty' (Thompson, 2004: 9). As such, the new career currency of adaptability, employability and marketability can be seen to trump traditional labour market disadvantage (such as gender, ethnicity or disability) and lead to the achievement of employment (rather than job) security, the acquisition of satisfying and well-rewarded work and, overall, an equalisation of life chances (Wilton, 2012).

However, as discussed in Chapter 4, a more realistic perspective on the impact of economic and organisational restructuring suggests that whilst it can have positive implications for some workers, for others it is likely to undermine job security and stability through a weakening of employers' commitment to their employees. In contrast to those assessments that stress the unequivocally positive impact of new career forms, the movement to new modes of working can often reflect a trade-off between the benefits of the old and the new. In a study of professionals and managerial workers who had moved from organisational to portfolio working, Cohen and Mallon (1999: 347) reported that this transition was accompanied by a series of 'tangible losses', like salary, pension and access to training opportunities, but also a number of 'abstract gains' such as (work–life) balance, autonomy and integrity. Overall, however, reduced employer responsibility for career management can be seen as part of the transference of the risk (Grote and Raeder, 2009), rather than the real empowerment of workers to take control of their own careers.

Child and McGrath (2001) suggest that one of the great unknowns of changes in organisational form is their effect on the employment relationship and that whilst the possibility for personal empowerment may be enhanced among some talented (and fortunate) individuals the impact is likely to be negative for others who have to live with perpetual insecurity. Indeed, the employer side of the 'new deal' in employment is likely to vary according to different sections of the workforce reflecting the relative worth of the employee to the firm. Torrington et al. (2008) suggest that three groups of workers are discernible according to the level of support for career development they are likely to receive from employers:

1 *Senior managers and 'high potential' staff* – careers at this level are managed by the organisation, not always for life, but with succession planning to fill senior positions.

2 *Highly-skilled workers* – attempts are made to attract and retain key workers by offering career development paths.

3 *The wider workforce* – more limited development opportunities are evident, often caused by and resulting in uncertainty over career paths; there is an expectation that these workers should look after themselves.

A number of studies have reported considerable rhetoric from employers promoting individual employability and career self-management. However, this is often shown to take place alongside the erosion of job security, substantially altered career structures and little or no practical measures to support and facilitate self-development (McGovern et al., 1998; Wilson and Davies, 1999; Atkinson, 2002; Grimshaw et al., 2002). On this evidence, reduced employer responsibility for career management can be seen as part of the transference onto the employee of the risk associated with restructuring, downsizing and the need for flexibility (Grote and Raeder, 2009), rather than the real empowerment of workers to take control of their own careers. Prevalent short-termism among senior managers in many firms has also led to career management often being viewed as a cost rather than an investment. CIPD (2003b) found that whilst the majority of HR professionals surveyed showed a desire to improve career management for all employees, very few reported a career strategy for these employees (most effort was focused on elite groups) and only a third felt that senior managers were firmly committed to career management activities. Similarly, Baruch and Peiperl (2000) found little recognition of the post-corporate career in a study of UK career management practices or a need to develop practices to manage such careers, despite the trend towards the declining relevance of organisational careers for many workers.

Paradoxically, recent labour market change and economic and organisational restructuring have arguably made career management even more important for employers (Hite and MacDonald, 2008). For example, effective career management represents an important means by which to minimise the loss of valuable skills and knowledge and as an effective means by which to cope with both expected and unexpected change.

ORGANISATIONS AND CAREER MANAGEMENT

'Career management' is the umbrella term used to refer to management practices, policies and initiatives that are employed either to intervene directly in the career development of employees or support individuals in progressing their own careers. The distinction between direct intervention in the management of careers and the provision of support for self-development is important as, commensurate with the supposed shift from old to new careers, there is also an argument that firms are changing their career proposition away from one of career management to one of career facilitation.

BOX 12.4
HRM IN PRACTICE

Career management at Michelin plc

In April 2012 *People Management* magazine (Stevens, 2012) reported on Michelin's 'paternalistic' approach to career management that actively manages the long-term career paths of employees – an approach at odds with much of the rhetoric of the 'new' career and pervasive career self-reliance.

Michelin is a global corporation employing approximately 115,000 employees across a number of business areas, most famously, the manufacturing of tyres. The people management philosophy at Michelin is outlined in the following statement by Jean Michel-Guillon, corporate vice president for personnel:

> The personal qualities of every individual interest us because we take a long-term view. We are looking for people with personality and human potential, and rarely for a particular skill to fill a particular post. All employees, regardless of position, know they can count on their career manager to help them to develop themselves and advance in their careers.

This approach to career management is pervasive across its multinational operations. For instance, the North American Michelin website states that:

> 'At Michelin you'll have the opportunity to let your talents and interests guide your career. Opportunities are not limited by formal education. There are plenty of opportunities to receive professional enrichment, education and training at Michelin.'

Supported by a range of technical and professional training programmes, the company promote a range of HR initiatives to enable employee career development and progression, including a focus on open and transparent internal promotion through middle management, the appointment of dedicated 'career managers' for those in middle and senior management positions and the active support of line managers for long-term career planning. Career management activities are also clearly embedded within performance management processes. All employees are encouraged to establish clear career objectives, to have regular and ongoing dialogue with their manager about career interests and receive regular feedback on their performance mindful of these interests.

In all, career management at Michelin appears to reflect the 'career partnership' approach advocated by Hirsh and Jackson (2004) with responsibility for personal and career development being shared between the employee, their line manager and corporate career managers. The responsibilities of each which were set out by Michel-Guillon have been quoted in brief below:

- **The employee:** *'...we like to represent career management as a triangle to underline the complementary roles of the employee, the immediate superior and the career manager.'*

- **Line manager:** *'...to assist team members in performing their current mission by setting targets, providing support in attaining them, assessing performance, designing training itineraries and promoting career development.'*

- **Career manager:** *'The career manager takes a broader, more long-term view and looks at both company needs and the prospects for people development.'*

This approach to career results in low levels of labour turnover and with employees often remaining at the firm for the duration of their careers (Stevens 2012). These practices accord with the principles of a strong internal labour market discussed in Chapter Four. That is, Michelin actively encourages internal promotion, seeks to balance individual and organisational priorities and interests and enables advancement through the provision of training and development opportunities. Moreover, low levels of labour turnover at the firm would suggest that the Michelin limits new employee entry to particular points in the organisational structure. Overall, Michelin clearly places itself in a strong position to yield the employee relations benefits of such a labour market: high levels of employee commitment, engagement and performance.

Source: Stevens (2012); **www.michelin.com**/cor porate/EN/careers/work-at-michelin; http://careers. michelin-us.com/you/career-dev/

MICHELIN

Traditionally, career management has fulfilled a number of important functions in work organisations. It has an economic utility as a means of ensuring the optimal deployment of appropriately skilled and motivated labour, ensuring that the most able employees are positioned where they are needed. Career management can promote organisational knowledge-sharing, create greater organisational adaptability and contribute to employee engagement and commitment. Effective career management can also help to reconcile individual and organisational objectives and aspirations, for example by promoting the development of transferable skills and abilities and by supporting employees' fulfilment of their non-work obligations, so ensuring they are productive whilst at work. It also has a socio-cultural utility as a means of transmitting corporate culture through socialisation and promoting shared norms. However, whilst organisations view careers and career management in terms of such organisational advantage, employees view careers through 'the lens of personal advantage, and consider how those careers may provide opportunities to optimize earnings, status, personal development and family life, both immediately and in the long term' (Inkson and King, 2010: 38). Therefore careers, and who takes responsibility for their development, represent one dimension of the 'contested terrain' of the employment relationship (Edwards, 1979, in Inkson and King, 2010).

Further online reading This article explores the differing interests in careers and career management held by workers and organisations and how the 'new career studies' provides a fresh perspective where both individual and organisational perspectives are valid. The authors propose that a model based on the psychological contract provides an opportunity to further bring together different perspectives on careers.

Inkson, K. and King, Z. (2010) Contested terrain in careers: A psychological contract model, *Human Relations*, 64 (1): 37–57.

Models of career management

Hirsh and Jackson (2004) distinguish between three models of organisational career management. The first is *supported self-development*, where employees take primary responsibility for their own career but there is extensive support provided by the employer, mostly in the form of information and advice. Second is *corporate career management*, which reflects a career 'deal' that is more greatly driven by the organisation. Such an approach is characteristic of development programmes for senior managers, high-flyers or high-potential employees whose career development is more actively planned by the organisation through planned job moves and succession planning (for example, graduate training schemes). Finally, Hirsh and Jackson identify the best practice notion of *career partnership*, where the individual and organisation take equal responsibility for careers in order to meet the needs of both parties. This approach differs from supported self-development in that rather than simply providing employees with guidance, the intentions of both parties are explicitly discussed and agreed. Moreover, the career 'deal' is formally coordinated by some 'agent' of the organisation (one person or group of people) and the organisation shares responsibility for the implementation of the career plan by, for example, supporting access to work experience and job moves.

As suggested previously, however, the approach of many large organisations is likely to be segmented, with only key groups having access to corporately managed careers whilst most employees are expected to manage their own careers with or without organisational support. Subsequently, career interventions need to take greater account of the *processes* involved in career decision-making, rather than just the *outcomes* (Arnold, 1997b). In other words, for career self-development to be effective it must be enabled by the firm. King (2004) suggests that there are a number of underlying principles that characterise effective career management (Box 12.5).

HRM AND CAREER MANAGEMENT INTERVENTIONS

King (2004: 45) stresses that career management is 'a critical challenge for HR professionals in the twenty-first century ... it is essential for developing and sustaining organisations in the long-term and for giving each individual within the organisation a meaningful focus for the future'. King (2004) suggests that effective career management represents a confluence of the needs of the individual and the organisation, drawing on the past experiences, present priorities and future intentions and projections of both parties.

Career management itself is not necessarily a distinct HRM activity, rather a range of activities involving several core HR processes, which ideally should be integrated with both one another and the wider corporate strategy (Baruch, 2003). However, CIPD (2003b) report that career management activities are seldom integrated into a coherent strategy or clearly linked to business strategy or organisational objectives. They found a tendency to focus on particular aspects of career management rather than provide coverage of all areas, which may detract from the inclusivity and flexibility of career management provision and fail to meet the needs of all employees. Just as the notion of career management can refer to either active corporate involvement in the careers of employees or more 'hands-off' support for self-development, so career management interventions range from simply employee notification of internal job opportunities to highly-structured, prolonged programmes of employee development to facilitate or leading to promotion (such as graduate training schemes).

In the first instance, effective career management should be concerned with defining, and communicating to all employees, career development strategies and processes that satisfy organisational requirements. The main roles of HRM in career management include management of the internal labour market, providing the organisational infrastructure by which the best equipped individuals are matched with the most appropriate roles, the provision of careers advice and counselling and active involvement in facilitating the provision of development assignments to appropriate employees (such as providing secondments and job shadowing).

Career management is clearly related to a number of other HR processes and practices such as performance management and appraisals – as a principal means by which career intentions and ambitions are discussed between line managers and employees – and training and development – as the means by which individual employability is developed. It is important therefore that career management is not conceived as a stand-alone issue and is integrated with these processes. Moreover, HRM should provide a support function for line managers charged with carrying out performance appraisals and individual goal setting.

As above, career development initiatives can be divided into a number of categories. For instance, CIPD (2003b) divide career management activities into five distinct 'clusters': those concerned with basic career planning and support; those that provide career information and advice; those that create and support a strong internal job market; development assignments and secondments; and, initiatives aimed at specific organisational populations. Figure 12.1 divides career management activities into four broad categories based, firstly, on the extent to which they are aimed at specific groups within an organisation (for instance, managers, graduate recruits or employees of high potential – see Box 12.6) or available to all employees and, secondly, whether they perform a supportive role or are more interventionist and directive (for instance, they aim to prepare individuals for specific roles rather than broad advancement or develop among them specific skills). The notions of inclusive and exclusive talent management also sit within this framework of career management activities understood both in terms of intended recipients and degree of intervention. As outlined in more detail below, 'inclusive' talent management refers to approaches to identifying and developing talent throughout the organisation through a range of formal and informal means. Exclusive talent management focuses development activity very directly on specific individuals and/or groups that are deemed to present core talent (often senior managers or those in possession of valuable skills).

BOX 12.5
UNDERSTAND

Principles of effective career management

- *Consistency* – where all those involved in employee career management (including HR professionals and line managers) present a coherent and consistent picture of the organisation's career strategy.
- *Pro-activity* – career management should be concerned both with maintaining current capabilities and ensuring future flexibility

by anticipating the future direction of the organisation.
- *Collaboration* – effective career management is based on partnership between the employer and the employee.
- *Dynamism* – career management should be flexible enough to respond to changing organisational and individual circumstances and needs.

Source: King, 2004

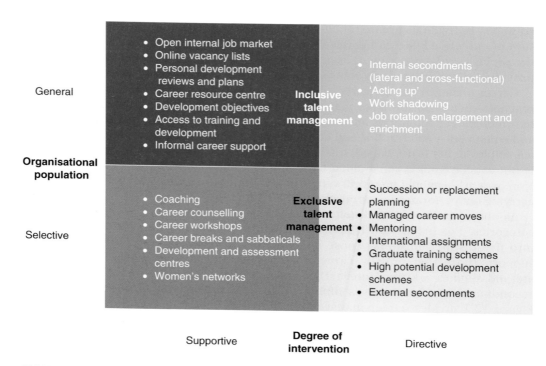

FIGURE 12.1   Career management interventions

Supportive mechanisms often available to all employees in larger organisations typically focus on those that form part of wider performance management processes, such as personal development plans and objectives, those that seek to create strong internal labour markets through, for instance, the promotion of job opportunities to encourage internal applicants and those that provide the infrastructure to support employee self-development, such as guidance, advice and resources to aid career planning and decision-making. The creation of a strong internal labour market through raising awareness among current employees of vacancies and development and promotion opportunities, and encouraging internal applicants, supported by performance management practices which seek to align individuals' development goals with the future business needs of the organisation, both stresses individual self-reliance and encourages proactivity in seeking out opportunities, but also has the effect of widening the talent pool, fostering a culture of openness and overcoming potentially unfair, informal practices for internal promotion. Both King (2004) and Hirsh and Jackson (2004) stress that for internal job markets to operate effectively, especially in flatter organisational structures where the 'learning gap' between hierarchical levels is likely to be significant, firms must ensure that developmental opportunities exist for employees with potential. Of course, these types of mechanism also apply and may be specifically tailored to specific organisational groups, but may be supplemented by those interventions that are more labour- or cost-intensive, such as one-to-one coaching or career counselling. These supportive initiatives for specific groups also include those that seek to correct historic patterns of unequal opportunities for career progression within the firm, such as women-only networks and training interventions.

More directive initiatives that may be widely available to all employees might include internal secondments or developments in job design that either seek to prepare individuals for advancement or lateral job moves or simply offer opportunities to develop and exercise a wider set of skills. Secondments, development

BOX 12.6
HRM IN PRACTICE

Career management for specific groups

As firms increasingly look to ensure cost efficiency of organisational investment in career management practice and to ensure the effective targeting of resources, it is likely to be of benefit to modify practice according to distinct employee groups. These groups might include:

- *Employees of specific value or talent* – with a focus on employee retention and motivation, firms are likely to feel compelled to offer formal, structured career management 'with purpose' for employees who already represent a significant source of value to the firm. This purpose is likely to be to demonstrate on-going development and preparation for future advancement.

- *High potential staff* – for employees of high potential who the employer wishes to 'lock in' to the firm (for example, graduate recruits), the focus is likely to be on ensuring the demonstration of organisational commitment to their development by offering a long-term stake in the firm through continuous development.

- *Highly skilled workers* – as above, a critical concern for career management of high-skilled workers is retention and, in following research in the area of knowledge workers, this is likely to be best achieved by responding to individual need in job design, career development and personal fulfilment. An additional concern is managing the 'career value proposition' to ensure the firm is attractive to potential recruits.

- *Under-represented groups* – for groups of employees who are felt to be under-represented, for example, in more senior posts, and where firms wish to increase the diversity of their workforce, organisations can adopt either individual or collective career management initiatives to promote career development among such groups (for instance, women, those from minority ethnic backgrounds or those with disabilities). Collective mechanisms involve developing both formal (such as women-only training courses) and informal (such as the cultivation of organisational networks) to remedy perceived disadvantage. Individual initiatives might include specific targeted mentoring or coaching schemes. Where such initiatives are not in place and an emphasis is placed on career self-management minority groups can be disadvantaged because of their exclusion from existing networks (Hirsh and Jackson, 2004).

- *Non-core/contingent workers* – as internal labour markets become more atomised, firms might seek to develop means by which they might intervene with employees who are consider non-standard in respect of employment contract. For instance, firms might seek means by which to identify temporary or indirectly employed staff with value-adding potential and offer means by which to bring these 'peripheral' workers into the organisational 'core'. Again, this might be done on an individual or a collective basis and might involve incorporating such workers into the internal labour market or offering specific advice and support.

assignments and work-shadowing can expose workers to new challenges, prepare them for promotion, increase job satisfaction through greater job variety, help employees to develop valuable skills and promote knowledge-sharing and greater understanding of the work of others in the organisation. More interventionist and directive initiatives for specific organisational populations are those that seek to prepare these groups or individuals within them for specific roles or particular types of work (such as overseas assignments). Graduate development programmes are one such example of career management interventions that seek to develop recruits of high potential and prepare them for future progression in the firm (see Box 12.7). Often characteristic of large organisations, succession or replacement planning focuses on providing long-term development plans for individuals identified as possible successors for senior managerial posts. This requires the identification of high potential individuals early in their careers and providing opportunities and experience that prepare them for specific 'once in a generation' appointments and to mitigate the impact of the loss of employees holding key positions in the firm.

TALENT MANAGEMENT

The increasing importance of knowledge to firm performance and the high mobility of talented people have resulted in many firms adopting initiatives for 'talent management' (IDS, 2008a). Talent management represents 'a comprehensive and integrated set of activities to ensure that the organisation attracts, retains, motivates and develops the talented people it needs now and in the future' (Baron and Armstrong, 2007: 101). Influenced by the resource-based view of the firm outlined in Chapter 3 and the importance of internal resources,

---

BOX 12.7
HRM IN PRACTICE

Graduate training programmes

- Jaguar Land Rover

The Jaguar Land Rover two-year graduate programme offers a 'personal development plan that will be specifically tailored to you, your role and the things you want to achieve' and 'give you the right blend of technical expertise and carefully planned personal development from the start'. In all graduate pathways – from engineering and design to finance, IT or purchasing – employees are supported to achieve professional qualifications with the relevant professional body (where appropriate). (http://www.jaguarlandrovercareers.com/jlr-roles/future-talent/graduate/, accessed on 5 October 2015.)

- Deloitte

Whatever business area graduate recruits work in (from audit, consulting, corporate finance to risk consulting), they 'will spend around 3 years working towards a professional qualification, and will gain a mixture of client exposure, challenging projects, and extensive training that will develop you into a fully qualified professional'. Deloitte stress the importance of both ongoing support for employee development ('using

everything from coaching and mentoring through to e-learning and performance management') and on-going learning (through 'regular feedback, structured mentoring and a whole host of courses, e-learning and workshops that will enable you to accelerate your all-round performance'). (http://www2.deloitte.com/uk/en/misc/litetopicpage.MF-UK-Tags.graduate-scheme.html, accessed on 5 October 2015.)

- HP

HP stress that their graduate schemes 'put you in control of your career' where the recruit is 'the driving force of your development', as well as a focus on both 'soft' and technical skills, with 'a heavy emphasis on "on the job" learning, as well as formal instruction'. As such the firm encourages recruits to make the most of the 'hands-on experience you'll get on job rotations and cross-functional team project' supported by the provision of 'coaching, mentoring and face-to-face, virtual and interactive training programmes' and 'attendance at conferences, seminars, and training at accredited institutions that would be beneficial for [the] role'. (http://www8.hp.com/uk/en/campaign/graduate/graduate-programmes.html, accessed on 5 October 2015.)

---

such as its human capital, to competitive advantage (Sheehan, 2012), the term 'talent management' is used to describe a combination of succession planning and high potential development activities, whilst the term 'talent pipeline' is used to convey the need for talented people at different career stages, often starting with graduate recruitment (Hirsh and Jackson, 2004). The terms on which an individual is granted access to a 'talent pool' or 'pipeline' can differ from organisation to organisation (see Box 12.8). Therefore, whilst, talent management can be 'exclusive', that is, narrowly focused on key senior or strategically important positions and individuals within a firm (to create a single pool of talent), often talent management can be more 'inclusive' and concerned with creating a pipeline or pool of talented people at all levels of a firm through ensuring that workforce development is accessible to all those of potential, regardless of level or role, creating multiple talent pools. Table 12.3 outlines the advantages and disadvantages of each approach.

King (2004) suggests that the existence of highly managed 'fast-track' or 'high-flier' programmes alongside an explicit organisational message to all other employees of self-development might have de-motivating and alienating effects on the majority of the workforce. Subsequently, many organisations adopt hybrid approaches to talent management that bring together aspects of both inclusive and exclusive forms (Tansley et al., 2007).

GRADUATES
IN CHANGING
LABOUR MARKET

TABLE 12.3 *Inclusive and exclusive approaches to talent management*

Inclusive approach

Pros	*Cons*
Wider employee engagement if entire organisation has access to a talent pool	Learning and development and other resources are spread too thinly
Supports succession planning for all key roles, not just senior management	Increases competition for progression which requires managing
Encourages the development of a more diverse workforce	Individuals with skills core to the business may receive less investment, to the detriment of organisational performance
More opportunity to benefit from all talent in the workforce	

Exclusive approach

Pros	*Cons*
Provides an identifiable, strategic resource for succession planning if aimed at future leaders	High potential for reduced engagement and increased turnover among excluded staff
Targets financial and non-financial resources	Less scope to increase diversity
More opportunity to offer individualised development programmes	Reduced development opportunities and resources for those not on talent programme
Easier to track and evaluate benefits and return on investment	If focused on one occupational group or grade, other types of talent may be overlooked

BOX 12.8
RESEARCH INSIGHT

Who gets to be 'talent'?

Central to developing and implementing effective talent management practices is adequately defining what constitutes 'talent' in order that it be identified and nurtured. The CIPD (2006d) define talent as 'those individuals who can make a difference to organisational performance, either through their immediate contribution or in the longer term by demonstrating the highest level of potential'. It is important to recognise, however, that, to be effective, a working definition of 'talent' needs to be operational at an organisational level and be able to clearly and objectively identify a specific group of workers so as to target investment on individuals within that group. Tansley (2011) suggests that within organisations talent can be individually specific, refer to behaviours, skills or knowledge and/or be focused on high performance or high potential. Consequently, the CIPD suggest that talent has been variously defined within organisations as:

- the top-performing 1 per cent of executives
- the top 10 per cent of high performers, whatever their role or level
- executives with potential for board-level appointments together with high-potential individuals who are identified as future leaders
- graduate trainees with potential for top leadership
- each and every employee – a 'total talent pool'.

Features of effective talent management

Hay Group (2007) stress the importance of adopting a demand perspective on the issue of talent management by stressing the importance of understanding the dynamic internal and external context in which talent is to be deployed in order to ensure a ready supply of individuals with the right skills and attributes to meet these needs now and in the future. As such, the 'management of talent is the fulfilment process to close the gap between demand and supply – ensuring the right number of people of the right quality are ready when the organisation needs them now and in the future' (Hay Group, 2007: 4). As such, a critical aspect of talent management is the reflection of corporate strategy in a firm's talent strategy, albeit in such a way as to be reflexive to changes in strategic objectives and the firm's strategic direction. This process of talent planning then requires firms to define the qualitative and quantitative demand for and supply of talent in order to forecast talent requirements based on the collection of qualitative and quantitative HR information, including the firm's current internal labour supply, anticipated demand and if necessary how and from where required talent can be attracted. Effective talent management inevitably involves a long-term perspective on individual and workforce development and, consequently, needs to be dynamic, flexible and sustainable.

At an operational level, effective talent management requires the communication of a common, organisational understanding of talent, the multiple routes by which talent is identified and selected and transparent processes for doing so. However, in line with this long-term approach, a critical aspect of talent management is the management of expectations regarding the implications of being identified as having potential and the tracking of individual performance and progress alongside the provision of opportunities for development. Therefore, talent management connects a number of areas of HRM, including resourcing, performance management, reward and training, all of which need to be horizontally integrated in order to ensure they are mutually supportive. Cunningham (2007) suggests that the talent management process can take the approach of aligning people with roles (treating roles as fixed and developing people to fit these jobs) or aligning roles with people (creating and adapting roles to satisfy the aspirations of the most talented).

Attracting, developing and rewarding talent

Given that even in 'loose' labour market conditions, required talent is likely to be in short supply, firms need to consider how required labour can be sourced externally. As in the discussion of career management, positioning oneself as an employer of choice and presenting to potential employees both a strong brand and employee value proposition (EVP) that is clearly communicated are critical. Once within the firm, critical to the management of talent is ensuring that promises made in the recruitment process are delivered upon and expectations of employment and the talent management process – both for new and existing employees – are fulfilled in order to create a strong psychological contract based on trust and fairness and a coherence between brand identity and employee perception.

TALENT MANAGEMENT

Consistent with much of the discussion of HRD interventions thus far in this book, the development of talent requires a clear focus and intent and the careful selection of appropriate mechanisms for learning. The appropriateness of interventions is clearly related to the specific nature of the talent pool and may require a mix of interventions. For instance, structured, individualised and formal development processes, involving some form of external input, might be appropriate for select groups of managers, but are likely to be inappropriate and not cost-effective for the wider workforce in inclusive approaches to talent management. The creation of a coaching culture and forms of on-the-job development are more likely to be appropriate for this wider group.

A critical element in retaining talent is reward and ensuring that organisational reward strategy is both connected to business objectives and enables individual reward packages to meets needs and elicit desired employee behaviours. For instance, for those employees that are high performers *now* and who are making a significant current contribution to organisational performance, offering high pay and clear future opportunities for progression is likely to be unavoidable in order to avoid their loss through clearly communicating their value to the firm. For those employees of future high potential, intrinsic reward – such as job satisfaction – and interesting and challenging work, alongside longer-term incentives and bonuses, might well encourage their on-going contribution and retention over the long term.

Further online reading This short article, written from a practical perspective, explores the imperatives for firms to actively develop systems of talent management and the contextual conditions that are driving this 'new significance'. In doing so, it sets out some general principles and dimensions of talent management that firms must consider.

Leisy, B. and Pyron, D. (2009) Talent management takes on new urgency, *Compensation & Benefits Review*, 41 (4): 58–63.

TALENT MANAGEMENT IN PRACTICE

The CIPD (2012e) suggest that, of those UK employers surveyed, three-fifths of organisations report undertaking talent management activities, most often focused on high-potential employees and senior managers.

BOX 12.9
RESEARCH INSIGHT

Creating a 'talent wave'

As discussed elsewhere in this chapter, the notions of talent 'pipelines' and 'pools' are common terms used in reference to organisational approaches to talent management. Clutterbuck (2012: 26) suggests, however, that the former are associated with 'narrow, inflexible paths that can easily get blocked' and the latter suggest 'shallowness and stagnation'. He argues, therefore, that the notion of a 'talent wave' might be a more appropriate concept to adopt for talent management to be successful, given the dynamic relationship between an organisation and its employees. Clutterbuck argues that often talent management adopts a linear, mechanistic approach to filling key roles and that such an approach often fails to recognise some of the best talent and replicates the past, promoting the wrong people based on box-ticking criteria and a backwards-looking perspective on what talent looks like: 'The more HR tries to make talented people fit into standardised talent management and succession planning processes, the more likely it is to fail' (2012: 28).

He argues, therefore, that that an approach to talent management based on organisations as complex, adaptive – and, therefore, unpredictable – systems is required, reflecting three 'rules' of how such systems work:

1   *Emergent* – the aim of talent management should not be to 'fit employees into a grand plan' but to 'channel their energies and ambitions' and encourage the development of deep capabilities. In creating such an environment organisations should trust it to 'deliver the right person at the right time, most of the time'.

2   *Co-evolutionary* – 'When talented people adjust their ambitions and develop new skills in line with their observations of opportunities, they stimulate change, for the business as well as themselves (if they are allowed to!)' (2012: 28–9).

3   *Self-organising* – genuinely talented people find their own ways to respond to opportunities, requiring only information and support to do so. Talent is often invested in networks, not individuals.

Ultimately, Clutterbuck argues that an organisation creates an environment that produces a sufficiently wide and varied talent wave and 'enough motivated, competent and creative people to move into roles when needed' (2012: 29) to fulfil its talent needs now and in the future. He argues that to create such a wave requires alternative ways of creating an alignment between organisation and employee aspirations, allowing employees greater latitude in transforming roles, emphasising opportunities for a much wider range of people, having more honest conversations about career intentions and using social networks to encourage employees to take the initiative and stimulate change. In short, organisations should place less emphasis on simplistic models and frameworks that aim to select and predict leadership talent and a greater focus on the planning of developmental resources and opportunities.

- Only half of organisations with talent management activities rate them as effective and only a very small minority (3 per cent) rate them as very effective.

- Coaching is most commonly rated as one of the most effective talent management activities (49 per cent).

- In-house development programmes, high-potential development schemes, 360-degree feedback and internal secondments are among the most effective methods for a quarter of organisations.

CIPD (2009h) suggest that the war for talent focuses on periods of growth during which required talent is in shorter supply. However, periods of economic downturn present an alternative set of challenges for firms that render talent management no less important, not least in making it critical that firms retain their focus on required talent in order to ensure they remain well placed in the eventual upturn in market conditions. CIPD (2009h), however, report a variety of responses from employers in the current period of limited economic growth. Among what they characterize as 'negative' responses, firms reported cutting learning and development budgets, a re-examination of systems amid pressure to get more 'value' from budgets by 'doing things differently' and less use of external providers and recruiters. More 'positive' responses include a shift in focus to retention, maintenance of investment in view of a longer-term perspective and more creativity in targeting and developing talent.

As discussed in Chapter 7, the evaluation of HRD activities is an important, yet often neglected, aspect of HRD in practice. The effectiveness of both career and talent management rests on a number of key 'success criteria': they are appropriate to the organisational, and workforce, context; they are dynamic and responsive to change; they are sufficiently flexible to accommodate workforce diversity; there exists a mutuality and consensus on their operation and rationale; and there exists a clear connection between individual and organisational need, available resources and wider internal and external context. The CIPD (2012e) report that the most common ways to evaluate talent management activities are through: feedback from employees involved in talent management initiatives (41 per cent of organisations) or from line managers (40 per cent); retention of those identified as 'high potential' (35 per cent); and anecdotal observation of change (35 per cent). Only just over a quarter of organisations (28 per cent) employed a formal annual evaluation process for talent management at an organisational level.

Further online reading Stressing the increasing importance of global talent management, this article outlines the challenges of managing talent in MNCs and presents a series of key roles for HRD to play in overcoming these challenges as well as a framework for global TM, from an HRD perspective.

Kim, S. and McLean, G. (2012) Global talent management: Necessity, challenges and the roles of HRD, *Advances in Developing Human Resources*, 14 (4): 566–85.

Evaluating career management interventions

One specific problem in promoting the benefits of long-term strategic career management is in evaluating and demonstrating its effectiveness, partly because different stakeholders are likely to have different perspectives on its relative 'success'. For example, the individual employee might measure career success according to a subjective assessment of their achievements based on relative reward, hierarchical position or afforded lifestyle. Senior managers are likely to draw on a range of indicators, such as the retention of key staff, strong flow of internal candidates for vacancies or the perceived impact on firm performance. HR professionals might evaluate effectiveness according to the internal consistency with wider HR systems and practices.

Moreover, the evaluation of career management interventions is difficult because of problems in isolating the impact of specific activities on both individual progression and on the achievement of organisational objectives. Regardless of these problems, however, the monitoring and evaluation of career management activities is important to ensure that they are meeting the needs of all groups who could potentially benefit, whilst bearing in mind the need to develop provision to meet changes in organisational context.

BOX 12.10
GLOBAL INSIGHT

The challenges of global talent management

Continued economic globalisation requires managers to adopt a global outlook and to utilise appropriate frameworks and methodologies to effectively manage and develop globally dispersed talent (Collings et al., 2009). Scullion et al. (2010) suggest that global talent management includes organisational activities to acquire, develop and retain talent for organisational strategies on a global scale, taking account of cultural contexts.

Kim and Mclean (2012) argue that global talent management is necessary for three principal reasons: firms are increasingly either operating across borders, or intend to do so; there exists a global deficiency of talent as a result of demographic changes; and, connectedly, their remains intense competition for talent on a global scale. They also note three specific challenges that can occur in developing global talent: overcoming ethnocentrism and a desire for the standardisation of talent management practice; difficulties associated with the impact on workers of global mobility and the management of expatriates; and barriers and a lack of integration between headquarters and subsidiaries.

In order to overcome these challenges, Kim and McLean offer a number of roles for HRM, not least to ensure that employee development is given as much focus within talent management as attraction and retention. They suggest four key roles:

1 *Balancing centralised and decentralised strategies* – ensuring the firm benefits both from the positive impact of shared values, systems and resources across the organisation and the benefits to be gained from localised approaches to recruitment, development and retention.

2 *Developing global competencies* – the identification and development of a global mindset among global talent, including, for example, cultural self-awareness, a global perspective and tolerance for ambiguity and difference.

3 *Creating structured global talent development* – connected to organisational strategies and objectives, and mindful of external and internal factors and resources, the development of global approaches to leadership development, succession planning and expatriate and cross-cultural training.

4 *Conducting global teambuilding* – the provision of organisational activities, as well as systems and cultures, to enhance the effectiveness of geographically dispersed work teams to minimise interpersonal conflict and misunderstanding. Such activities might include diversity training, coaching and mentoring programmes and means by which work goals, roles and responsibilities are clarified.

ORGANISATIONAL CHANGE AND CAREER MANAGEMENT

There are significant implications of the 'new' career, not least the impact of the shifting psychological contract on employee motivation, commitment and cynicism in the context of increased job insecurity (Thite, 2001). Whilst employees are being asked to expend ever-greater effort in their work, organisations are often in no position to offer the opportunities that have been available in the past as reward for their exertion (Whymark and Ellis, 1999). Subsequently, the revised career 'offer' of some employers would appear to constitute a significant breach of the psychological contract, made worse by a widespread failure to develop an adequate career management strategy (Atkinson, 2002).

BOX 12.11
ETHICAL INSIGHT

Employer responsibility, careers and career management

King (2004) stresses that, in the context of increased organisational flexibility, businesses need to consider career management not only for their core employees but also for non-core workers. Among the reasons for doing so is an ethical imperative: 'Many people, and especially the lower skilled, are forced into contingent work through circumstance. Often they can't upgrade their skills because they can only find work on the basis of their existing, proven skills. The employer, perhaps, has as much responsibility for these stakeholders as it does to its core employees' (King, 2004: 39). Subsequently, ensuring equity of access to development opportunities and, therefore, enabling individuals to develop their employability should represent a key dimension of an ethical approach to HRM. For low-skilled workers, such opportunities represent their means both to improve their employment prospects and, subsequently, the opportunity for full participation in society (Lowry, 2009). However, segmented strategies for career management whereby individuals have variable access to organisationally managed careers, and exclusive approaches to talent management can significantly curtail the ability of some workers to progress their careers, both within and beyond an individual employer. Therefore, the ethical question for managers is how best to balance the financial and competitive needs of the firm to deploy scarce resources effectively in the development of staff, and the potentially competing needs of individuals for opportunities for personal and career development. Adopting a stakeholder approach to business ethics, it is clear that career development, insofar as it can contribute to a fairer society by ensuring equality of access to all levels of an organisation, is an important dimension of a firm's responsibilities to both its workforce and the wider community in which it operates.

An additional ethical aspect of career management is the role that it can play in encouraging ethical behaviour among employees. Boo and Koh (2001) suggest that a key determinant of the effectiveness of a firm's code of ethics in promoting acceptable behaviour is the association between such behaviour and career success in the organisation (alongside senior manager support for ethical behaviour and code enforcement). Therefore, if firms make it explicit that ethical behaviour (or simply an avoidance of unethical behaviour) is a consideration in promotion decisions this is likely to have a wider impact on the behaviour of the organisation at large.

The restructuring of internal labour markets can also result in unforeseen problems. For example, organisational 'delayering' can result in a 'promotion gap' and skills shortages that affect a firm's ability to fill positions internally. For example, by removing a layer of middle management the gulf between junior and senior management might be too significant to breach without extensive training.

Despite much of the rhetoric of widespread change to careers, however, evidence indicates that many organisations have not reduced their career management solely to an 'employability' proposition or 'unsupported career development' (Hirsh and Jackson, 2004), nor have they completely disposed of the traditional tools of career management, such as succession planning or internal promotion (King, 2004). Traditional approaches to career management are likely still to be viewed as important because employees continue to value managed career development initiatives and employment security. It follows then that organisations are unlikely to have divested themselves of all responsibility for training and development, especially for new employees. CIPD (2003b) report a clear consensus among employers that whilst individual employees are expected to take responsibility for their own career development, this should be within a supporting framework of advice, guidance and information provided by the employer. This recognises that even if employees are expected to take predominant responsibility for their own careers, employers must provide them with necessary information and access to development opportunities.

IMPLICATIONS FOR RECRUITMENT AND RETENTION

In the current career climate, one particular issue for HRM is to develop new approaches and strategies for recruitment and retention, bearing in mind that opportunities for career development represent a major tool for attracting, motivating and retaining good quality employees. Herriot et al. (1994) suggest that if organisations are to attract and retain employees they will have to (re-)establish a positive psychological contract, which may prove difficult if they are perceived to have broken such contracts in the past through restructuring and rationalisation.

As planning horizons have shortened as a result of economic uncertainty and the future needs of organisations have become less clear, employers are finding it more difficult to articulate an appropriate definition of an organisational career because traditional definitions, emphasising hierarchical progression, no longer provide 'the explanatory vocabulary to understand the apparently changing reality of managerial careers in the post-bureaucratic organisation' (Adamson et al., 1998: 252). They suggest that recruitment literature increasingly refers not to 'world class careers' for graduates but, 'a world class start to a career; talking not of opportunities for advancement and/or progression but of opportunities to improve marketability and employability' (1998: 255). Hirsh and Jackson (2004) suggest that organisations are very nervous of raising expectations around promotion because they also feel uncertain about what the future holds. The result is that many large organisations give their staff no clear or positive message about careers. Purcell et al. (2002: 2) suggest, therefore, that leading practice organisations 'manage the expectations of candidates and recruits, external and internal, so that there is a very clear understanding of the nature of the work, the culture of the organisation and the career development opportunities available'.

Subsequently, organisations must be clear both as to what is expected of their recruits and what entrants can expect of a career, however short-lived, within that organisation. For example, if they are no longer able to guarantee long-term careers, they should offer conditions under which individuals may develop their human capital. Employers must clearly articulate what types of career are available in the organisation, what support the employer can offer in helping employees achieve career ambitions and the specific roles of line managers, HR professionals, senior managers and the employees themselves. Garavan and Morley (1997), in a study of the socialisation of new graduate recruits, found that employee frustration and dissatisfaction arose when there was misunderstanding about the psychological contract and a misconception of their role or prospects in the organisation. It is therefore critical that employers take account of the individual perspective in forming and delivering career management activities and ensure that they adhere to the values of fairness, objectivity and transparency.

CAREER MANAGEMENT AND DIVERSITY

Earlier in this chapter it was suggested that the increasing heterogeneity of the labour force was likely to be reflected in increased diversity of career expectations and aspirations and employers should be wary of making assumptions or generalisations about worker needs and attitudes. 'One-size-fits-all' approaches to career management are unlikely to be appropriate in most organisations as, regardless of their position or the social group to which they belong, individuals have diverse orientations to work and careers. Flexible practices are therefore needed to ensure that both employee and employer needs are met. For example, the labour force is increasingly made up of older workers and those with dependent children or caring responsibilities and it is important that employers acknowledge both their specific (individual) and general (group) needs and aspirations in career management practices. Such acknowledgement might be reflected in employers offering flexible working patterns and better work–life balance alongside more flexible career options and the abandonment of assumptions about ambition and the speed at which progression should be achieved.

Career management interventions should also be made accessible to all groups, especially those who are under-represented in the organisation. An emphasis on individual self-determination in career development is problematic in that it fails to adequately acknowledge the historical and structural disadvantage experienced by particular social groups (for example, women and minority ethnic

BOX 12.12
GLOBAL INSIGHT

Career development across borders

National culture affects careers and career development in a number of ways. Schneider and Barsoux (2008) suggest that both preferred paths for advancement and the traits and behaviour required for promotion are culturally determined. In particular, what it takes to get ahead varies according to assumptions regarding 'being versus doing' (who you are versus what you do).

For example, Derr and Laurent (1989) suggest that American managers perceive drive and ability to be the most important determinants of career success, reflecting a pragmatic, individualistic, achievement-oriented and instrumental worldview. However, this is not universally the case. It is accepted in many countries that personal connections and the school attended are important. In France, for instance, educational background is perceived as enough to be labelled 'high potential'. Similarly, the competencies perceived as most important in developing managerial careers vary. In Germany, technical competence and expertise or achievement are paramount. In contrast, in the UK, interpersonal and communication skills are considered most important to the managerial role.

Favoured career paths also differ across cultures; for example, the preference for developing careers within a single function, company or industry. In different countries, the possibility and

potential leverage of switching in and out of companies or industries varies as this is tied to cultural assumptions of individual versus group loyalty, doing versus being, and the extent to which uncertainty is tolerated. For example, in Japan, where there is a greater emphasis on job security, career development often consists of job rotation to develop company-specific knowledge. As such, mid-career moves are less common than in the West. Similarly, career mobility is not particularly valued within German companies, although this reflects the importance placed on developing company-specific know-how rather than loyalty. In Britain, France and the USA career mobility across industries and companies is acceptable and often considered desirable. These different patterns of career development reflect the strength of internal labour markets within firms, whether managers are likely to be developed internally or recruited externally and the stage at which those with high potential are identified (at entry or later). Furthermore, they reflect the value placed on different types of work experiences acquired within or outside the company or industry (specialist versus generalist) and the criteria for selection and promotion (Evans et al., 1989, in Barsoux and Schneider, 2008). In cross-cultural management, MNCs need to ensure that the perceptions of what it takes to reach the top, and the patterns of career development, do not exclude people with different skills, abilities and perspectives.

workers). In the absence of proactive employer policies to support under-represented groups in career development, particularly those who have typically followed non-standard careers, it is likely that this disadvantage will be sustained. Brousseau et al. (1996) advocate the adoption of a pluralistic approach to career management – a combination of structured approaches to career development and opportunities for diverse career types and experiences – that embraces different definitions of career success to better support the diverse needs of employees and to reward the development of a wide range of competencies and skills.

SUMMARY POINTS

MANAGEMENT OF GRADUATE CAREERS

- Much contemporary discussion of careers focuses on the extent to which the 'traditional' career, based on loyalty and relative security, has been replaced by 'new deals' in employment, based on short-term commitment and the development of employability.

- Most empirical studies indicate that careers in the traditional sense are not 'dead' but that the context in which they are experienced and their stability have undergone considerable change over recent years. Consequently, workers increasingly experience careers in a fragmented, insecure and uncertain manner.

- Even for employees of large organisations where corporately managed careers have traditionally been most prevalent, greater onus is being placed on career self-management, whether supported by the organisation or otherwise.

- The changing nature of careers has led to a shift from a 'relational' to a 'transactional' psychological contract for many workers.

- Three broad approaches to career management are identified – supported self-development, corporate career management and career partnership – representing differences in the balance of responsibility between employer and employee for career development.

- Organisations typically differentiate between employee 'groups' in the extent and type of career management provision, but research suggests that most employers have not reduced their career management solely to an 'employability' proposition or unsupported career development.

- The growing diversity of the labour supply presents a set of challenges for employers in managing a more diverse set of employee expectations, needs and desires. This also presents an opportunity for employers to develop more innovative career management initiatives.

SELF-TEST QUESTIONS

1 How have changes to the external environment of work organisations, and their subsequent impact on organisational structure, acted to shape the notion of careers?

2 What are the key dimensions along which we can contrast traditional and new careers?

3 To what extent can it be argued that the move towards 'boundaryless' careers is positive for employees? What are the associated negative implications of such change?

4 What are implications of the changing career 'offering' for the psychological contract?

5 What does the empirical research evidence suggest about the proliferation of the new career concept in work organisations?

6 What are the organisational benefits associated with a strategic approach to career management?

7 What are the key mechanisms through which work organisations can assist in the career self-management of its employees?

8 What are the implications of increased labour market diversity on the way in which organisations support career management?

9 How do national cultural differences shape attitudes and approaches to career development?

TEST YOURSELF

Want to know more about this chapter? Review what you have been learning by visiting:
https://edge.sagepub.com/wilton3e

- Print out or download the chapter summaries for quick revision
- Test yourself with multiple-choice questions
- Revise key terms with interactive flashcards

TEST
YOURSELF

CASE STUDY

Building a talent strategy at Matsson Finance

Matsson Finance is a market-leading company providing wealth management and financial protection services, operating in more than 40 countries but with major operations across Europe, North America and Asia-Pacific. Worldwide, it has over 50 million customers, both individuals and businesses, and approximately 95,000 employees worldwide working across three of its operating divisions: MF Life and Insurance, MF Investment and MF Healthcare.

In the UK, Matsson is involved in insurance, investment, pensions, healthcare, protection and life cover, employing approximately 8,000 staff in five locations across the country. Its website makes the claim that: 'As the trusted provider of financial services to two million customers in the UK, we seek to employ the best people to ensure both outstanding service and excellent value'. However, whilst Matsson is typically viewed as an 'employer of choice', senior management has in the past two years become concerned that in certain aspects of its HRM practice, particularly employee development and talent management, the company has lost ground to its competitors.

In particular, the firm identified a significant problem in retaining its highest potential staff across its six operating sites. In order to support the firm's aim of achieving more sustainable competitive advantage

through the quality and capability of its people, the firm recognises the need to attract, develop and retain talent throughout the organisation. Subsequently, the firm has recently begun to develop and implement a more strategic approach to talent management that brings together a number of disparate policies and practices already in existence to produce a coherent approach to developing promotable talent and to ensure a pipeline to service most senior positions. To achieve this more strategic approach, Matsson has established a Talent Development Team to support the achievement of competitive advantage through the 'creation and deployment of a continuous pipeline of exceptional business and technical leaders'.

Among the first tasks of this team and central to the firm's talent strategy is the organisation's ability to successfully identify both immediately promotable talent and future leaders, stressing, therefore, the importance of appropriately defining its 'talent pools' to recognise both realised ability and potential. To this end, the company decided to categorise talent in the company in three ways:

1 *Talent* – defined as those throughout the firm who have performance ratings of effective, excellent or outstanding and representing 90 per cent of employees at Matsson UK. These ratings are determined by line managers during annual performance appraisals based on the achievement of individual objectives and the extent to which they display the behaviours

informed by the firm's core values. The company has yet to put in place structures and practices to further develop such staff but their potential is noted and filed for future reference.

2 *Promotable talent* – those employees with the potential to progress to the next career level in the relatively near future, representing approximately 40 per cent of all employees. Individuals are assigned to this group at the request of their line managers based on three key criteria: ability, drive and engagement. The highest-flyers from this group are identified as 'being of future leadership potential'. The company has been surprised at how relatively few staff have been put forward by their managers and take this to be a sign of an absence of such talent. As a result, the company has begun a headhunting exercise to recruit high-potential staff from outside the firm at more senior levels.

3 *Future leaders* – 1–3 per cent of employees with the potential to be a business or technical leader or technical specialist. Such candidates are simply put forward by their line manager as someone of significant potential.

Despite recognition of the importance of talent at all levels in the company, priority has been given to nurturing and developing those staff who fall within the 'future leader' group. Senior management have diverted significant investment to the HR department to develop a bespoke, stand-alone and intensive programme of leadership development for the 'chosen few' (as they have become known in the firm), including paid tuition and time off to study for an MBA at a top UK business school, regular off-site teambuilding activities and fact-finding missions to Matsson sites all over the world. This investment constitutes the major part of the fund available for talent development but senior management take the view that 'if you get the top right, the rest will fall into place'. In other words, if the workforce sees the internal promotion of a select few staff into very senior positions then others will be motivated to pursue such opportunities.

The aim of the future leadership programme is to assess each individual against the leadership behaviours and competencies identified at the most senior level of the firm, in order to map them against future roles. Before the end of the programme, individuals have to produce a portfolio that includes what they have learned about themselves, what they have done as a result of this learning and why they should be considered for specific roles in the organisation. The information then leads into succession planning activities where individuals are earmarked for particular posts in the future and are intensively schooled in the technical aspects of those posts.

Questions

1 How would you characterise the approach that Matsson Finance has adopted towards its talent management?

2 What examples of potentially good practice can you identify in Matsson's approach to talent management?

3 What are the potential pitfalls associated with the policies and practices that Matsson has currently adopted?

4 What are the potential problems of adopting a very structured off-the-job programme of leadership development as the means by which to develop the leadership capabilities of a more junior member of staff?

USEFUL READING

Journal articles

Baruch, Y. (2006) Career development in organizations and beyond: Balancing traditional and contemporary viewpoints, *Human Resource Management Review*, 16: 125–38.

This article presents a balanced perspective on career management, suggesting that whilst much has changed in the context of careers, both within and outside of organisations, the basics in career development theory and practice continue to be valid.

Tansley, C. (2011) What do we mean by the term 'talent' in talent management? *Industrial and Commercial Training*, 43 (5): 266–74.

Drawing on a review of the literature and interviews with professionals associated with talent management, this short article provides a useful summary of the multiple ways in which talent has been defined for the purposes of talent management.

FURTHER ONLINE READING

The following articles can be accessed for free on the book's companion website **https://edge.sagepub.com/wilton3e**:

Arthur, M. B. (2008) Examining contemporary careers: A call for interdisciplinary inquiry, *Human Relations*, 61 (2): 163–86.

Inkson, K. and King, Z. (2010) Contested terrain in careers: A psychological contract model, *Human Relations*, 64 (1): 37–57.

Inkson, K., Gunz, H., Ganesh, S. and Roper, J. (2012) Boundaryless careers: Bringing back boundaries, *Organization Studies*, 33 (3): 323–40.

Kim, S. and McLean, G. (2012) Global talent management: Necessity, challenges and the roles of HRD, *Advances in Developing Human Resources*, 14 (4): 566–85.

Leisy, B. and Pyron, D. (2009) Talent management takes on new urgency, *Compensation & Benefits Review*, 41 (4): 58–6.

Rodrigues, R. A. and Guest, D. (2010) Have careers become boundaryless? *Human Relations*, 63 (8): 1157–75.

Want to know more about this chapter? Visit the companion website at: **https://edge.sagepub.com/wilton3e** to access practice questions, videos and selected journal articles to further enhance your study.

13

THE MANAGEMENT OF WORKPLACE CONFLICT

WORKPLACE CONFLICT

CHAPTER OBJECTIVES

- To discuss the meaning of conflict and how it is expressed in the workplace

- To outline differing perspectives on conflict in work organisations

- To explore the issues associated with rules and procedures in work organisations

- To outline the meaning of discipline in the workplace

- To identify best practice and issues associated with the handling of employee discipline and grievance

- To discuss how collective disputes are managed

- To outline the roles of parties associated with handling grievance and discipline.

INTRODUCTION

Chapter 2 briefly outlined how the employment relationship can be understood as a latticework of formal and informal, explicit and implicit rules that govern the conduct of employer and employee. It also briefly outlined how these rules emanate from a wide variety of sources including the law, the contract of employment, implicit agreements between the parties, negotiations between management and trade unions and organisational custom and practice. This chapter is concerned with what happens when one party or the other is deemed to have breached one of these rules and the procedures that exist to resolve the subsequent conflict.

Considering the wide range of often contradictory rules governing the employment relationship, it is perhaps unsurprising that the relationship between employer and employee can be rather fragile. In Chapter 10, a number of perspectives on the employment relationship were discussed. Under the unitarist view, organisations are viewed as unified entities in which all stakeholders share common interests and objectives. Consequently, conflict is seen as unnatural, illegitimate and, where it does occur, tends to be blamed on troublemakers or poor communication. Alternatively, the pluralist perspective suggests that organisations are made up of competing interest groups who do not always share common objectives and, as such, conflict is inevitable as each party clashes in pursuit of its own agenda.

Each of these perspectives inform particular management styles. For example, unitarism influences authoritarian approaches to management that focus on rooting out troublemakers and asserting the right of managers to make decisions unchallenged. It also informs neo-unitarist approaches that seek to remove the potential for conflict by securing the commitment of employees to the managerialist agenda and promoting mutuality of interests. Management informed by pluralism tends to seek to institutionalise conflict by establishing rules and procedures to contain and manage disagreement, to reconcile the interests of stakeholders and minimise the impact of conflict on performance.

Given all the potential causes of friction in the employment relationship it is perhaps unrealistic to expect that conflict will not occur from time to time, either between individuals or between workers and management as collective groups. The focus of this chapter is on how conflict or discontent arises and how employers can seek to manage this conflict within the context of both the law and organisational procedures.

AN OVERVIEW OF CONFLICT IN THE EMPLOYMENT RELATIONSHIP

Causes of workplace conflict

Chapter 2 outlined a number of dimensions to the employment relationship: socio-political, legal, economic and psychological. In each of these areas, one party or the other can be perceived to have breached the explicit or implicit agreement between the employer and employee and create friction, dissatisfaction, or, at worst, open conflict. Collective disputes can arise simply as a result of the imbalance of power in the employment relationship and attempts by employees to resist the managerial prerogative or managers resisting employees' attempts to collectively exert influence over working arrangements. These underlying tensions can be exacerbated where trade unions exist to provide a counterweight to the power of management. Conflict can also arise as a result of a failure of organisational procedures. For example, a breakdown in negotiation machinery can be a source of collective conflict whether through the intransigence of either party or a failure of the procedures themselves.

CONFLICTION IN THE WORKPLACE

On a purely individual level, employee dissatisfaction in the employment relationship might arise from perceptions of unfair, inconsistent or arbitrary treatment by management. Examples include an unanticipated failure to be promoted or obtain a pay increase, disputed outcomes of performance appraisals or simply as a result of personality clashes with colleagues or line managers. These examples are likely to represent breaches of the psychological contract. Importantly, however, the causes of conflict are not always so explicit. CIPD (2008e) report that workplace conflict can often result from subtle behaviours such as taking credit for other people's work or ideas, talking over people in meetings or not inviting a member to team social events, or from personal issues such as poor hygiene. From an employer perspective, dissatisfaction with employees is most likely to be as a result of poor or unsatisfactory performance or an unwillingness or inability to adhere to expected standards of conduct or behaviour.

Expressions of workplace conflict

Just as conflict can arise from breaches of explicit agreements or of an implied and unspoken understanding, the expression of dissatisfaction can be either formal or informal. Expressions of workplace discord can also be either individual or collective. Figure 13.1 outlines the range of means through which employees can express dissatisfaction. Formal, collective expressions include the withdrawing of labour through strike action (often viewed as a last resort following a failure of dispute resolution) or 'action short of a strike' such as working-to-rule (workers do only what is required under their contract of employment, partly to prove the point that workplace performance relies on workers exercising discretion and initiative and working outside of contracted hours), sit-ins (occupying the workplace), go-slows and overtime bans. Formal channels for individual expression include grievance procedures or a claim to an employment tribunal. Dissatisfied individuals might also resort to informal, anti-social means by which to make their feelings known such as sabotage or theft. Excessive and unwarranted absenteeism can also be both an expression of dissatisfaction and an indicator that all is not well with the employment relationship, as is the withdrawal of individual discretionary behaviour. Clearly, the ultimate action where one is dissatisfied with their employer is to leave the organisation.

Further online reading Discusses research exploring how management that encourages 'fun', 'play' and displays of individuality at work do not necessarily represent freedom from workplace control but managerially prescribed freedom within, and distraction from, more conventional means of worker control.

Fleming, P. and Sturdy, A. (2011) 'Being yourself' in the electronic sweatshop: New forms of normative control, *Human Relations*, 64(2), 177-200.

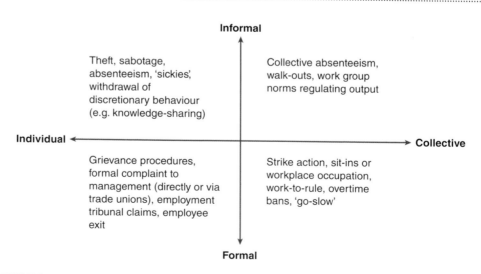

FIGURE 13.1   Expressions of employee dissatisfaction

Employers also have recourse to a variety of actions aimed at expressing dissatisfaction with the collective workforce or individual employees. In collective industrial disputes, management can impose a lockout (closing the workplace to staff and preventing them working) or resort to mass sackings. Firms might also respond to industrial dispute by choosing to close the operation permanently. For individual employees, managers can instigate incapability (for poor performance problems) or disciplinary procedures (for misconduct), which can result in demotion, suspension or dismissal.

Contemporary patterns of workplace conflict and resolution

Van Wanrooy et al. (2013) report some disparity in how positively managers and employees rate their relationship between managers and workers; 96 per cent of managers rate this relationship as 'very good' or 'good', compared to only 64 per cent of employees.

Chapter 10 outlined the broad shift from collectivism to individualism in the contemporary employment relationship and the long-run decline in the incidence of collective industrial unrest in UK workplaces (Dix et al., 2009). Recent evidence (van Wanrooy et al., 2013) suggests that this pattern persists in the private sector with 98 per cent of private sector workplaces reporting no incidence of strike action, action short of a strike or threatened industrial action in the previous 12 months. In the public sector, however, only 64 per cent of workplaces reported such peaceful conditions, significantly up from the previous survey in 2004. Across all workplaces, however, there was relative stability with 94 per cent of employers reporting an absence of strikes, other industrial action or threats of industrial action. Similarly, individualised expressions of conflict were constant between 2004 and 2011, with 41 per cent of managers reporting that at least one employee had been subject to disciplinary sanction, 29 per cent reporting the raising of grievance, 18 per cent having dismissed at least one employee and 4 per cent that an employment tribunal application had been made by an employee.

These figures raise the question of whether the long-term decline in strike activity and collective disputes reflects improving industrial relations or whether, in the absence of union organisation, individual employees are using alternative channels to express dissatisfaction. Indeed, van Wanrooy et al. (2013) point out that the number of working days lost through absence – potentially as an informal expression of dissatisfaction – remains broadly consistent at 3.4 per cent. An important point in considering the impact of the increasing individualisation of the employment relationship is the extent to which individual workers continue to be afforded protection from poor or unfair treatment by employers. Pollert and Charlwood (2009) suggest that the asymmetry in the employment relationship between an employer and individual employee in non-unionised workplaces creates vulnerable workers who are more likely to experience multiple workplace problems, particularly where they possess low labour market power. In the absence of unions, such workers tend to be afforded little scope to assert their individual rights through procedural means and, therefore, have little chance of resolving workplace problems. This asymmetry is likely to be exaggerated at times of high unemployment.

Further online reading This article explores the issue of vulnerable employment. In particular, it explores how low-paid workers without union representation experience multiple problems at work and often fail to achieve resolution of these problems, suggesting that workplace procedures are often inadequate in resolving individual concerns and protecting individual rights.

Pollert, A. and Charlwood, A. (2009) The vulnerable worker in Britain and problems at work, *Work, Employment and Society,* 23 (2): 343–62.

An interesting recent development in the area of workplace conflict is the range of opportunities for workers' expressions of dissatisfaction presented by Web 2.0 technology (see Box 13.1).

BOX 13.1
HRM IN PRACTICE

A virtual axe to grind

In May 2008, *The Guardian* (Paton, 2008) reported on industrial action taken by IBM workers in Italy in a dispute over pay in which they 'marched and waved banners, gate-crashed a staff meeting and forced the company to close its business centre to visitors'. The novel thing about these exploits was that they took place at the IBM corporate campus in the virtual world, Second Life, involving more than 9,000 workers and 1,850 supporting 'avatars' from 30 different countries.

It is perhaps inevitable that workers are now more likely to display individualistic tendencies as workforces have become less cohesive and solidaristic due to declining long-term job tenure and trade union membership, flexible working patterns and international dispersion. However, the potential to 'virtually' mobilise large groups in a collective cause is becoming more apparent as IT-literate workforces have begun to draw on social networking to organise worker resistance. For example, trade unions are increasingly using social networking as a tool for action, protest, mobilisation and support, gathering on a national or global scale alongside more traditional means. A number of trade union organisations from around the world have come together to set up a home for unionists and union issues in *Second Life* to host virtual events, exhibitions and to coordinate campaigns, international networking and online organising (www.unionisland.org).

As traditional forms of industrial action have become more tightly regulated, partly to enable employers to make arrangements to minimise their impact, the Internet and online communication provide a means by which workers can express dissatisfaction on a national or global scale that employers can find difficult to quell. Forms of action can be as simple as 'email attacks', where the inboxes of senior executives are swamped by thousands of messages. More sophisticated and constructive action might involve engendering support for 'real' or virtual disputes through online petitions, blogging networks or online boycotts.

The Internet can also be a medium for the expression of individual dissatisfaction. Harvey (2009) reports that redundancies arising from the recession of 2008–9 increased the risk to US firms of disgruntled or departing employees leaking information about the company. A US survey showed that 31 per cent of companies had dismissed workers for violating email policies by sending confidential information. They also reported growing concern about data leaks caused by employee misuse of blogs, social networks and Twitter, suggesting that 17 per cent of US companies had information exposed through these channels and that 8 per cent had dismissed employees because of such actions. We might even consider simply personal use of the Internet at work as an expression of discontent or, at least, a lack of engagement. If so, the implications for employers are rather bleak. For instance, Newcombe (2013) reports on research showing that, on average, 64 per cent of workers in the UK waste one hour a day at work on the Internet for personal use, whilst 14 per cent waste three hours a day (of which time 48 per cent is spent surfing the Internet for personal use).

ORGANISATIONAL RULES AND PROCEDURES

Chapter 2 briefly outlined the importance of formal workplace rules, but it is worth revisiting their purpose because effective rules and procedures often lie at the heart of good HR practice, particularly in managing and resolving workplace discord.

Organisational rules are determined, enacted and enforced by a wide range of formal and informal processes and procedures. These include procedures to:

- establish the rights of unions to recruit, organise and represent specific groups of workers
- manage collective disputes and individual employee grievance
- discipline employees who are deemed to have breached established rules or failed to meet expected standards of conduct or performance
- guide the handling of redundancies
- promote and monitor equal opportunities.

Procedures are also likely to cover the management of promotion, reward and recruitment and selection. Both workplace rules and procedures can be the result of negotiations between management and employee representatives, or they can be imposed unilaterally by management, prescribed by the prevailing legal framework, evolve via workplace custom and practice or arise out of implicit arrangements and understanding between the parties. Therefore, workplace rules and procedures are not always explicit (for example, stated in company handbooks or in written policies), neither are they always mutually agreed upon by the parties. Where arrangements are informal, unspoken or the result of the evolution of workplace custom, they tend to be open to interpretation and misunderstanding and, subsequently, constitute a greater risk to workplace harmony. Moreover, the tacit understanding of workers and management can contrast with formal rules and policy that can create tension in the employment relationship.

The importance of rules and workplace procedures

Rules and the procedures needed to enforce them and to punish contravention are viewed as being beneficial for a range of reasons, including:

- to clarify the relationship between employer and employee by outlining mutual rights and responsibilities
- to establish appropriate and acceptable standards of employee conduct and performance (and the repercussions for failing to meet these standards)
- to reinforce the strategic aims of the organisation, whether relating to the promotion of the specific behaviour required of a particular competitive strategy or to reinforce aspects of HR policy and practice (for example, an employer's equal opportunities policy)
- where concerned with workplace conflict, rules and procedures help to 'institutionalise' discontent to facilitate resolution and act as a 'safety valve' to ensure conflict does not escalate (Marchington and Wilkinson, 2008)
- to reinforce managerial control and improve administration of the workforce
- to guard against arbitrary managerial treatment of employees, promote greater fairness and consistency in managerial decision-making and provide a counterweight to the generally superior bargaining power of management

- to provide a framework for the actions of line managers in managing employees and help them to comply with legal obligations (for example, procedures to ensure equal opportunities in recruitment and selection help to guard against decision-making processes which might be deemed discriminatory)
- where they are both fair and consistently applied and particularly where employees have a hand in their design, rules and procedures can be important means of establishing a strong psychological contract and promoting employee commitment and motivation. This can have a positive impact on job satisfaction and employee retention.

Rules might not, however, be perceived as beneficial in all circumstances by all parties. For example, whilst employees might think of extensive procedures as useful in curtailing the ability of managers to act in an arbitrary manner, line managers might feel that the bureaucracy created inhibits effective and timely decision-making and undermines the managerial prerogative. Such criticism tends to reflect a hard HRM stance, whilst a soft HRM viewpoint might stress the importance of 'due process' (in dealing with, for example, employee grievance) as a central tenet of the fair treatment of employees. To be truly effective, therefore, rules and procedures should be broadly acceptable to both parties and normative agreement reached that both parties will abide by them. The benefits of rules and procedures are likely to be contingent on the specific circumstances in which they operate. For example, extensive rules governing employee behaviour are unlikely to be appropriate in firms that purport to have a cooperative managerial style. Furthermore, it is important to acknowledge that whilst effective procedures can help to contain and manage workplace conflict they cannot resolve its underlying cause if it is the result of deep-rooted antagonism between the parties.

BOX 13.2
RESEARCH INSIGHT

Workplace procedures and SMEs

As noted in Chapter 1, it is often important to differentiate between HRM practices in larger firms and those in SMEs. A notable characteristic of HRM in SMEs is the greater informality and lower likelihood of employees being subject to extensive procedures and policies. This is partly due to the fact that the proximity of managers or owners and employees is such that informality represents the most appropriate management style. It might also be due to a lack of specialist knowledge or resources to enable the design of more formal policies.

Procedures, however, represent a 'arm's length' reinforcement of managerial authority and, therefore, in their absence such authority must be reinforced 'in person', which can have the impact of disrupting the cooperative spirit that can be of such benefit to the performance of SMEs.

Moreover, procedures formally and explicitly set out acceptable employee behaviours and without such guidelines, ambiguity and misunderstanding might arise. Indeed, Earnshaw et al. (2000) report that smaller firms can find it more difficult to meet the standard of 'reasonable' behaviour necessary to defend claims of the unfair treatment of workers because of the informality that tends to predominate. Similarly, Saridakis et al. (2008) report that small firms are more likely to have employment tribunal cases brought against them than larger firms, at least partly because of the deficiencies in their procedural arrangements. Overall, it can be argued that the informality that exists in SMEs requires careful management rather than the hands-off approach that it tends to suggest, in the absence of the safeguard of procedures that institutionalise conflict, enshrine rules and guard against claims of unfair treatment.

DISCIPLINE AT WORK

Managerial discipline results from the formalised authority of managers to take corrective action against an employee for conduct or performance that is inconsistent with the standards laid out in organisational rules, including those contained in the contract of employment. The most common reasons for managers to take disciplinary action against an employee include absenteeism, unsatisfactory performance, poor time-keeping, theft or fraud, refusal to follow instructions, aggressive behaviour and verbal abuse, health and safety, inappropriate use of company facilities (for example, the Internet or telephone), alcohol and drug abuse, and sexual or racial harassment.

Managerial discipline can have a number of alternative or parallel objectives. Discipline can be punitive and seek to punish employees for indiscretions or poor performance, or it can seek to deter employees from certain activity or behaviour and compel them to comply with specific rules for fear of the repercussions of failing to do so. More positive approaches, however, view employee discipline as correctional and the use of procedures as the means by which to rehabilitate employees, improve performance or resolve unsatisfactory behaviour. Where punishment or compliance/deterrence are the objectives of managerial discipline, sanctions and penalties are likely to be employed. Correctional discipline is more likely to be associated with remedial practices such as employee counselling, training interventions and the clarification of employer expectations. Of course, this does not mean that having taken a constructive approach to employee discipline, sanctions cannot be used, rather that they should be a last resort (Acas, 2004). Such an approach can have the advantage of signalling to employees that discipline is approached in a fair, equitable and ethical manner.

Despite a rehabilitative approach to employee discipline being consistent with more progressive approaches to people management, evidence suggests that a punitive approach to discipline continues to be used in many workplaces (Earnshaw et al., 2004; Cooke, 2006).

....

Further online reading This article discusses the growth in interest in mediation as a preferred mechanism for dealing with workplace conflict. It reports on empirical evidence to support the view that mediation can help to develop more positive workplace relations and allow unions to re-establish influence.

Saundry, R., McArdle, L. and Thomas, P. (2013) Reframing workplace relations? Conflict resolution and mediation in a primary care trust, *Work, Employment and Society,* 27 (2): 213–31.

....

It is important to note that other forms of workplace discipline exist beyond managerial discipline. *Self-discipline* is important in circumstances where workers are empowered and given greater autonomy and discretion in how and when they work, particularly for professionals and knowledge workers. *Peer discipline* can be vital where teamworking is emphasised and working relationships are structured according to project work that requires and promotes peer pressure as an effective means of addressing poor performance or unsatisfactory conduct.

DISCIPLINARY AND GRIEVANCE PROCEDURES

The effectiveness of rules governing conduct in the employment relationship is partly dependent on the presence of formal procedures that provide a means by which to resolve disputes arising from their contravention. Disciplinary and grievance procedures can be understood as two sides of the same coin as both are concerned with resolving individual conflict at work, the former where an employer has a complaint against an employee, the latter where an employee has a complaint against the employer. Disciplinary procedures are used to handle employees who contravene the explicit rules that govern the workplace (for example, persistent unauthorised absenteeism) or who do not meet expected levels of performance. Formal grievance procedures are used to channel and resolve employee dissatisfaction with their treatment at work (for example, bullying or harassment).

Williams and Rumbles (2009) note that grievance and discipline represent unfashionable aspects of HRM because they imply that the employment relationship is characterised by conflict, which runs counter to the unitarist ideology of HRM. Pilbeam and Corbridge (2006: 464) suggest, however, that a positive approach to resolving workplace conflict, consistent with the developmental dimension of soft HRM, is possible if 'discipline is viewed as an opportunity for corrective action and a grievance is viewed as an opportunity for the resolution of employee concern'. Addressed in this manner, effective grievance and discipline procedures represent important levers in improving individual and organisational performance. Regardless of the approach taken, disciplinary and grievance matters make up a significant part of the work of HR professionals and managers (van Wanrooy et al., 2013).

CIPD (2009f) suggest that disciplinary and grievance procedures should provide a clear and transparent framework for resolving conflict in the employment relationship and are necessary for the following reasons: to ensure that everybody is treated in the same way in similar circumstances; to ensure issues are dealt with fairly and reasonably; and to ensure that employers are compliant with current legislation and the associated guidance for handling disciplinary and grievance issues.

The incidence of formal discipline and grievance procedures in UK organisations has grown exponentially over recent years. Van Wanrooy et al. (2013) state that managers in 89 per cent of workplaces reported that they had a formal procedure for handling grievances and 89 per cent reported a formal procedure for dealing with disciplinary and dismissal issues (both reflecting an increase in coverage). In total, 97 per cent of employees were covered by such procedures. Over the long term, part of this growth in coverage reflects the expansion of employment protection legislation (for example, guarding against unfair dismissal and discrimination) and the need for employers to protect themselves against possible employment tribunal claims by implementing and following procedures that meet the statutory standards. This legal impetus has more recently been supplemented by greater managerial acceptance of the positive benefits that such procedures can yield, through positive action to correct unacceptable performance or conduct and to resolve employee concerns. This acceptance also reflects recognition of the implications of poor handling of employee complaints or misconduct, such as the financial cost (for example, of compensating unfairly treated employees) (Edwards, 2000), bad publicity, an escalation of conflict, and lowered employee motivation, commitment and performance. Moreover, disciplinary and grievance procedures are also proposed to act as a mechanism for employee voice and as a way of correcting employee behaviour (Saundry et al. 2013). However, whilst such discourse frames such procedures positively, an alternative perspective suggests that where they are managerially controlled processes, with little input and influence from employees, they simply act to institutionalise management's prerogative (Walker and Hamilton, 2011).

In the UK, the important statutory provisions governing discipline and grievances at work are found in the Employment Act 2008 and the Employment Tribunals (Constitution and Rules of Procedure) (Amendment) Regulations 2008. Whilst the legislation does not prescribe the specific form that employee grievance and discipline handling should take, the Advisory, Conciliation and Arbitration Service (Acas) have issued a Code of Practice (2015) that provides guidance for employers on handling discipline and grievances at work and sets out the 'standard of reasonable behaviour'. The Code of Practice emphasises that employers and employees should always seek to resolve disciplinary and grievance issues internally and as soon as practicable to avoid damaging working relationships and to minimise the time and resources spent on resolution. Where informal resolution of issues is not possible the Code of Practice sets out principles for formal handling informed by the 'basic requirements of fairness', including:

EMPLOYMENT
ACT **2008**

- Employers and employees should raise and deal with issues *promptly* and should not unreasonably delay meetings, decisions or confirmation of those decisions.
- Employers and employees should act *consistently*.
- Employers should carry out any necessary *investigations*, to establish the facts of the case.
- Employers should *inform* employees of the basis of the problem and give them an opportunity to *put their case* in response before any decisions are made.
- Employers should allow employees to be *accompanied* at any formal disciplinary or grievance meeting.
- Employers should allow an employee to *appeal* against any formal decision made.

Whilst a failure to follow the Code does not necessarily make an employer liable where a complaint is made against them, employment tribunals are legally required to take the Code into account when considering relevant cases and may adjust compensation awards for unreasonable failure to comply with any provisions of the Code.

Good practice in handling workplace discipline

As above, most firms have recourse to a formal disciplinary procedure by which managers can take action against an employee who fails to meet reasonable and justifiable expectations of performance or conduct. CIPD (2009f) suggest that disciplinary procedures are needed in work organisations:

- so employees know what is expected of them in terms of standards of performance or conduct (and the likely consequences of continued failure to meet these standards)
- to identify obstacles to individuals achieving the required standards (for example training needs, lack of clarity of job requirements and necessary additional support) and take appropriate action to address these
- as an opportunity to agree suitable goals and timescales for improvement in an individual's performance or conduct
- to try to resolve matters without recourse to an employment tribunal
- as a point of reference for an employment tribunal should someone make a complaint about the way they have been dismissed.

EMPLOYMENT
TRIBUNALS **2013**

A key consideration for an employer in designing and applying disciplinary procedures is the principles of natural justice. Natural justice reflects the accepted norms of behaviour in society regarding the fair treatment of others. Procedures that reflect these norms are more likely to be viewed as reasonable both by employees, resulting in greater compliance with these rules, and employment tribunals.

The key stages in handling workplace discipline as set out in the Acas Code of Practice (2015) are outlined in Box 13.3. In short, there are five key stages: investigation, letter, meeting, action and appeal. It is important that the employer keeps detailed records of the procedures followed in handling disciplinary matters (for example, minutes of meetings and copies of correspondence), in order to demonstrate reasonableness if the matter should result in a case at an employment tribunal. In order to ensure that the formal procedures are followed, it is important that line managers are adequately knowledgeable and skilled in order to conduct investigations and meetings with their subordinates. In particular, line manager training should address the importance of drawing on the evidence available to them to ensure they do not rely on personal prejudices, skills in gathering evidence and statements from associated parties, ensuring meetings constitute a dialogue and that the employee is given ample opportunity to put forward their 'side of the story'. The HR department should play a supporting role, providing advice and guidance on both good practice and the relevant legislation.

BOX 13.3
UNDERSTAND

Keys to handling disciplinary issues in the workplace

- Establish the facts of each case

  - Verify the facts, plan the meeting or interview and decide whether further action is necessary.

- Inform the employee of the problem

  - Notice of the allegation should be provided formally in writing setting out the exact reasons for the meeting, the supporting evidence and informing the employee of their right to be accompanied by an appropriate representative.

- Hold a meeting with the employee to discuss the problem

  - Reasonable notice of the meeting should be given to the employee (although matters should be dealt with as soon as practicable).
  - The manager should be accompanied by another manager to take notes and help conduct the interview.

- Allow the employee to be accompanied at the meeting

  - An employee is entitled to be accompanied by a work colleague or trade union official of their own choice to help present their case (but not to answer questions on their behalf).

- Decide on appropriate action

  - Decisions should take account of mitigating circumstances.
  - Decisions should be confirmed in writing and a full explanation given of the reasons for the decision.

- Provide employees with an opportunity to appeal

  - Employees should be made aware of their right to appeal when informed of the decision.
  - Appeals are often made to more senior managers.

Source: adapted from Acas Code of Practice, 2015 (Acas, 2015a) © Acas, Euston Tower, 286 Euston Road, London NW1 3JJ - Crown copyright Open government license

ACAS CODE OF
PRACTICE 2015

The informal handling of discipline

A key component of good practice approaches to handling discipline which is in keeping with the tenets of soft HRM and which echoes the recommendations of Acas, is that before formal disciplinary procedures are invoked, informal means are used to address minor misconduct. Much of the onus for dealing with employee discipline falls on line managers and supervisors (reflecting the Acas recommendation that disciplinary action takes place at the lowest possible level) and it is likely to be desirable – both for speed of resolution and to minimise the impact on the relationship between line manager and subordinate – if the first stage in handling discipline is an informal chat or counselling to make the employee aware of the problem, discuss the reasons for improper conduct or poor performance and to prompt informal corrective resolution, for example, training interventions or counselling. Such remedial action might be considered more effective, particularly where managers are dealing with performance problems, as recourse to formal disciplinary procedures could be considered too heavy-handed in the first instance.

A problem with the informal handling of employee discipline is consistency. Formal procedures seek to ensure consistency and equity of treatment by establishing a systematic process for line managers to follow. Informal handling requires managers to use their discretion, potentially creating discrepancies in both approach and outcome between managers and across employees. Consistency can also be compromised when managers take into account the track record of the employee under scrutiny and the circumstances of the infringement, leading to different disciplinary outcomes for the same offence. This highlights the dilemma for employers in seeking to combine consistency of treatment with the flexibility to take into account legitimate circumstantial factors. For example, a manager may wish to treat differently an employee with persistently poor time-keeping because of temporary childcare problems and an employee who offers no mitigating explanations for lateness. This might lead to accusations of unfair treatment that can give rise to resentment.

Misconduct, gross misconduct and potential outcomes

Effective and reasonable disciplinary procedures should outline the type of behaviours that would lead to disciplinary procedures being invoked and the possible sanctions that might result from indiscretions. A distinction tends to be made between misconduct and gross misconduct. The former is unacceptable behaviour that has the potential to be remedied through managerial and/or employee action; for example, persistent lateness or absence from work without valid reason, notification or authorisation. Gross misconduct is 'misconduct serious enough to overturn the contract between the employer and the employee thus justifying summary dismissal [dismissal without notice] … acts which constitute gross misconduct must be very serious and are best determined by organisations in the light of their own particular circumstances' (Acas, 2009b: 31). However, despite recommending local determination, Acas provides the following examples of gross misconduct:

- theft or fraud
- physical violence or bullying
- deliberate and serious damage to property
- serious misuse of an organisation's property or name
- deliberately accessing Internet sites containing pornographic, offensive or obscene material

- serious insubordination
- unlawful discrimination or harassment
- bringing the organisation into serious disrepute
- serious incapability at work brought on by alcohol or illegal drugs
- causing loss, damage or injury through serious negligence
- a serious breach of health and safety rules
- a serious breach of confidence.

As noted above, summary dismissal often results from gross misconduct. Alternatively, an employer might choose to demote or suspend an employee. In cases of misconduct, standard practice is for an employer to issue the employee with a warning.

In keeping with the emphasis on the informal resolution of disciplinary issues, the Acas Code of Practice recommends a verbal warning prior to the instigation of formal procedures for cases of minor misconduct or unsatisfactory performance. Formal disciplinary procedures will often result in a first written warning or improvement notice (where a transgression is a first offence), which might be followed by a final written warning for subsequent misconduct and, ultimately, dismissal. In certain circumstances, the manager might decide that no action is necessary following the disciplinary procedure. This might be because the facts cannot be verified and further action justified or it might be determined that misconduct was a result of misunderstanding and can be resolved through additional guidance or support. Acas recommend that the 'life' of warnings should be specified in the formal disciplinary policy, suggesting that first written warnings remain on record for six months and final written warnings for one year.

Fair and unfair dismissal

As the ultimate sanction that can result from the disciplinary process, it is worth considering the law relating to dismissal in more depth, particularly that relating to unfair dismissal. Reflecting the handling of employee discipline more broadly, it is important for employers to have a sound basis for dismissing an employee and to follow fair and reasonable procedures in doing so. Managers should be convinced of the need for dismissal based on demonstrable evidence and consider whether alternative action might be more appropriate or effective (for example formal training or informal advice and coaching to resolve poor performance). Under UK law (the Employment Rights Act 1996 as amended), an employer should ensure that dismissal is for one of six 'fair' reasons:

1 *Lack of capability* – covers 'skill, aptitude, health or any other physical or mental quality'.
2 *Conduct* – where the employee is in contravention of a clearly communicated standard of behaviour or conduct.
3 *Redundancy* – even where genuine redundancy is evident, employers must ensure that the selection process is fair, employees are consulted, prior warning and notice are given and there is an attempt to find alternative employment.
4 *Retirement* – where an employee is dismissed if the employer chooses to end employment when an employee reaches the statutory retirement age, having provided the required notice to do so.

BOX 13.4
HRM IN PRACTICE

Internet and email policies at IBM

IDS (2010) reports that employees at IBM are *'expected to follow a general set of ethical principles, rather than detailed rules and regulations, when using the company's computing facilities'*. Guidance for ICT usage is embodied in the Business Conduct Guidelines that stress that IBM's systems should be used only for *'appropriate purposes'*. Inappropriate uses listed include visiting Internet sites that feature sexual content and gambling, as well as those advocating intolerance of others.

Reflecting the corporate value of *'trust and responsibility'*, IBM stress that it is responsibility of individual employees to ensure their use of company systems is appropriate and the company does not monitor employees' online activities, unless employee behaviour suggests a need to do so, or block access to inappropriate sites. The Business Conduct Guidelines covers personal use of the Internet and email that is permissible so long as *'within reason'*, because of the increased blurring between work and personal time, but not to the detriment of productivity. The guidelines also cover email etiquette again stressing personal responsibility of employees to exercise good judgment in their decisions and action in order to protect the company's reputation, in both the language and content of their messages.

To reflect the growth of social networking, IBM introduced a specific set of Social Computing Guidelines. These guidelines cover both online behaviour and as well as what constitutes appropriate content for posting on social media, blogs or other forums. IBM's guidelines strongly focus on individual responsibility for the content they post online and reminds employees that such content is likely to be publically visible for a long time. In terms of online behavior, the guidelines indicate both the importance of *'respecting the audience'*, acknowledging mistakes where they might occur in online debates or discussion and specifically cite examples of unacceptable language and conduct, stressing the avoidance of *'ethnic slurs, discriminatory remarks, personal insults, obscenity, or engage in any similar conduct that would not be appropriate or acceptable in IBM's workplace'*. The guidelines also stress individual awareness of their association with IBM online and, where individuals identify themselves as an IBM employee, ensure online presentation and content are consistent with how that individual wishes to present themselves to colleagues and clients. In short, the guidelines seek to align appropriate online behavior with that which would be considered acceptable in the physical workplace.

Of course, one aspect of any firm's guidelines on online activity reflect a desire to protect both the reputation of the firm and confidential information relating to the company, clients or and their business. The IBM guidelines for instance, state that *'IBM's brand is best represented by its people and what you publish may reflect on IBM'*. So, for example, IBM promote users identifying themselves where discussing IBM products or services, making clear that comments are personal rather than on behalf of the company, and avoiding the use of IBM trademarks and logos unless authorised to do so. The guidelines also stress the importance of individuals to be mindful of legislation, such as copyright, and to avoid disclosure of confidential or proprietorial information such as that referring to IBM business performance or that belonging or referring to a client.

Finally, the guidelines also suggest the potential value to the firm of IBM employees engaging in online fora through providing 'worthwhile information and perspective' that might contribute to the positive reputation of the firm.

Depending on their nature and seriousness, breaches of these guidelines are dealt with in a range of ways from training or coaching through to stronger measures, including dismissal.

IBM SOCIAL COMPUTING GUIDELINES

Source: IDS, 2010

5 *Statutory restriction* – where an employer would be breaking the law in continuing to employ a worker; for example, a driver who has been banned from driving or a foreign national who does not have the necessary work permit.

6 *Some other substantial reason* – this 'catch-all' covers other grounds for dismissal not covered in the other categories and might include persistent absenteeism, expiry of a temporary contract or reorganisation of the business.

If a worker feels that they have been unfairly dismissed, and they have at least one year's continuous service (or two years' for employees starting work after April 2012) for the employer from which they have been dismissed (known as the 'qualifying period'), they can refer their case to an employment tribunal. The onus then falls on the employer to prove that the reason for dismissal was fair and dismissal procedures were reasonable in the specific circumstances.

As with the wider disciplinary procedures, employers are well advised to follow the Acas Code of Practice or be mindful of the code in designing their own procedures for dismissal. Even where organisational procedures exist, evidence suggests that managers often fail to follow these procedures and bypass stages of the process; for example, by failing to allow employees to state their case prior to dismissal. This may result from an assumption of guilt, leading managers to dismiss employees without due process. Under UK law, dismissal is deemed 'automatically unfair' for a number of reasons, even where an employee has less than one year's continuous service. These include:

- reasons relating to pregnancy, maternity or for a reason connected with pregnancy
- an employee exercising his/her rights to parental, paternity or adoption leave
- trade union membership or taking part in union activities
- participation in lawfully organised industrial action
- an employee alerting their employer to health and safety risks
- an employee exercising rights under the regulations on part-time workers or fixed-term employees
- whistle-blowing
- an employee trying to enforce various statutory rights, for example, rights under the Working Time Regulations, a right to minimum notice or right to the National Minimum Wage.

As discussed in Chapter 11, it is also automatically unfair to dismiss someone on the grounds of sex, marital status, gender reassignment, race, colour, nationality, national or ethnic origin, disability, sexual orientation or religion. The legislation can provide for employees who have been unfairly dismissed to be reinstated or re-engaged but this is exceptionally rare (Mander, 2013). In the majority of cases, compensation is awarded. In the UK, unfair dismissal should not be confused with wrongful dismissal. Whilst unfair dismissal is based on the content of the legislation as above and on the notion of fair or unfair reasons for dismissal, a claim by an employee for wrongful dismissal is based upon whether the employer has reneged on the terms and conditions set out in the contract of employment. For example, a claim for wrongful dismissal might reflect a failure of the employer to give the employee the correct length of contractual or statutory notice when terminating employment or without providing adequate payment in lieu of notice. A claim for constructive unfair dismissal can exist where an employee terminates their contract of employment in direct response to a significant or fundamental breach of contract by the employer (for example, failing to pay agreed wages, forcing an employee to accept unreasonable changes to conditions of employment without agreement or bullying or harassment). Therefore, even if it is the employee who terminates the contract, a claim for unfair constructive dismissal can still be made.

UNDER-PERFORMANCE: A DISCIPLINARY ISSUE?

DISCIPLINE IN THE WORKPLACE

Chapter 7 considered the nature of performance and suggested that poor performance was not merely the product of incapability on the part of the individual employee but needed to be understood as often a product of both employee- or employer-side factors. This raises the question of whether poor performance always constitutes a disciplinary matter.

In keeping with the positive approach to performance management outlined in Chapter 7, and in line with the design of PM systems to create an organisational environment in which success is encouraged, supported and rewarded, addressing poor performance should be concerned with improving future performance rather than punishing prior under-achievement. This requires an openness and honesty from both employees and managers to properly understand the reasons for under-performance and to devise means of resolution. For this reason, some firms have capability procedures that are separate from disciplinary procedures, so as to distance the process of understanding poor performance from one designed to, ultimately, punish employee misbehaviour. Capability procedures have the explicit function of supporting performance improvement and developing employee capability. This approach is clearly consistent with the added-value role of HRM which focuses on improving human capital in order to better achieve organisational objectives, but equally to remove those who are not adequately contributing to the accomplishment of these goals. However, despite the best intentions of these procedures, evidence exists to suggest that the use of capability procedures often tends towards the disciplinary despite these procedures being designed to remedy, rather than punish, under-performance (for example, Earnshaw et al., 2004).

EMPLOYEE DISCIPLINE AND BEHAVIOUR OUTSIDE OF WORK

A contentious issue in employee discipline is the extent to which employers should impose standards of conduct on employees that apply outside of the workplace and, consequently, discipline them for breaching these standards.

Where behaviour outside of work compromises someone's ability to do their job, then firms are likely to feel entitled to take action. For example, certain criminal convictions can be grounds for fair dismissal. However, where personal behaviour does not necessarily impinge on capability the issue becomes more vexed. For example, an employer might feel justified in taking disciplinary action where employee behaviour outside of the workplace brings the organisation into disrepute.

The proliferation of social networking sites (see Box 13.5) and the increasing popularity of personal blogs have added another dimension to this issue. ICT and Internet activity has long been subject to organisational policies outlining their acceptable use *within* the workplace (such as detailing what constitutes acceptable online content to be viewed at work). For example, Harvey (2009) reports that almost a third of US companies had dismissed workers for violating email policies. However, social networking and blogs provide employees with an opportunity to comment on their jobs and employer, often to criticise or disparage, and for these comments to be widely read by other users. Regardless of whether this activity takes place within the work context, it is of increasing concern to employers and an area that managers might seek to control. Clearly, this raises fundamental questions about an employer's right and ability to seek to control the behaviour of employees in their personal activity.

For employees working in occupations where professional reputation is important, the issue of employer jurisdiction over employee behaviour outside of the workplace arguably becomes even more acute. Many occupations have codes of conduct attached to them which inform the acceptable behaviour of employees, including that in their personal lives. This applies to many public sector workers, such as healthcare professionals. However, this is not without controversy, particularly where such codes are seen as impinging on employees' liberty. Shepherd (2009) reports that teachers in England campaigned against a new code of conduct that requires teachers to 'maintain reasonable standards in

---

BOX 13.5
UNDERSTAND

Social networking and managerial discipline

Box 13.1 outlined how new technology was acting to revolutionise how groups of workers are able to mobilise to express dissatisfaction with their employer. An alternative consequence of new technology is that it represents a range of new ways to get fired.

Particularly dangerous to job prospects seems to be social networking, with many examples of how Facebook, Twitter or personal blogs have compromised people's careers. For example, in February 2009, a UK teenager was dismissed after describing her job as boring on Facebook. Her employer dismissed her with immediate effect, equating her actions to putting up a poster on the staff notice-board making the same comments. They argued that 'her display of disrespect and dissatisfaction undermined the relationship and made [her job] untenable'. In November 2008, Virgin Atlantic airline sacked 13 cabin crew staff after discovering they posted disparaging comments about the company's customers. A spokesperson for the airline said: 'It is impossible for these cabin crew members to uphold the high standards of customer service that Virgin Atlantic is renowned for if they hold these views'. Perhaps the most noteworthy

example is of the woman who posted derogatory remarks about her manager and job whilst forgetting that she had added him as a 'friend'. She was dismissed, having been reminded that she was still in her probationary period.

Whilst such examples can appear rather frivolous (albeit not for those involved), they do raise the important question of whether someone's personal online activity should be subject to the same rules that apply in the workplace. Can we draw a parallel between disparaging comments made on Facebook about one's job with letting off steam and 'moaning about the boss' over a drink after work? If so, then do employers have the right to police all work-related comments even when they are made outside of working hours and outside of the workplace?

Questions

1 To what extent do you feel that employers have a right to police the online activity of their employees?

2 What arguments would you use to justify the action that the employers took in the three cases described here?

3 How would you argue that their actions were unjustified?

---

their own behaviour that enable them to uphold public trust and confidence in the profession' and which union leaders claim intrudes into the private lives of teachers and strips them of basic human rights. Even though the code states that it 'sets out expectations of reasonable standards of behaviour, but does not limit a teacher's right to a private life', those opposing the code argue that it implies that teachers cannot be trusted and need to be told how to behave, and that the code is so vague as to be open to interpretation as to what is acceptable conduct.

HANDLING EMPLOYEE GRIEVANCE

RAISING A GRIEVANCE AT WORK

In a specific sense, a worker grievance represents the formal expression of dissatisfaction by an employee with respect to their employer regarding their work, working conditions or working relationships. Grievance procedures are the formal process by which to investigate and resolve this dissatisfaction. Even where an employee grievance is the result of treatment by a co-worker (for example, bullying or harassment) the complaint is still made against the employer for failing to provide protection and it is the employer's duty to investigate and deal with the complaint. Similarly, even where employees raise a complaint about matters not entirely within the control of the organisation (such as treatment by a client or customer), these should be treated in the same way as internal grievances. There are a wide variety of issues that might lead to employee dissatisfaction. Employees might raise grievances over contested managerial decisions (for example, over pay or grading), unilateral changes to terms and conditions of employment, managerial application or interpretation of policies and procedures, changes to working practices, the allocation of work, health and safety, relationships with line managers or colleagues, equal opportunities, bullying and harassment, the work environment, organisational restructuring, access to flexible working, the handling of discipline, and so on.

Employee dissatisfaction with their employer, a colleague or with some aspect of their employment situation only results in a grievance where it is formally presented to management, usually in writing. Therefore, raising a formal grievance can often represent the escalation of an informal employee complaint and might be viewed as a last resort, either where informal resolution has failed or where the dissatisfaction has become serious enough to warrant official action. Individual dissatisfaction or complaint has the potential to escalate into a collective dispute with a group of workers, or the workforce as a whole, in solidarity with the initial complainant or where the grievance is shared. Marchington and Wilkinson (2005) note that the line between grievance and dispute can sometimes be blurred but that, in general, grievance procedures are used for handling individual complaints, whilst collective issues are usually dealt with through dispute procedures (discussed later).

The organisational impact of employee dissatisfaction is manifold. It is likely to negatively affect employee motivation, commitment and work performance. Moreover, failure to adequately resolve an employee grievance can result in a range of employee relations outcomes, including poor attendance and, ultimately, employee exit. Employee grievances may not necessarily represent isolated problems, but an endemic issue within the workplace that has or will have a detrimental impact on wider organisational performance. For example, a complaint of bullying by a single employee might indicate the actions of one employee towards another or it might represent a bullying culture. Conversely, an absence of employee grievances does not necessarily mean that there are no problems in the workplace. It may reflect the view of employees that managers will not be willing or able to adequately resolve the issue or fear of the repercussions of making a complaint. Appropriate handling of individual grievances has, therefore, a wider employee relations function.

Grievance procedures

The advice regarding good practice in grievance handling is similar to that for dealing with employee discipline. Grievances should be dealt with promptly and at the lowest level possible, ideally informally between an employee and their line manager. An indication of a healthy working relationship between a line manager and their team is the extent to which employees feel able to discuss day-to-day issues and concerns informally with their manager. This is likely to be beneficial both to individual and team performance and to the speedy resolution of employee grievance, minimising the potential for protracted conflict. This is also likely to reflect a positive employee relations climate more widely. Where employees do not feel able to raise concerns informally or where concerns cannot or should not be resolved through such channels (for example, because of their seriousness), employers should provide formal, written grievance procedures. As with disciplinary procedures, employers are advised either to conform to the Acas Code of Practice in handling employee grievance or be mindful of its provisions in designing their own procedures. The Acas Code of Practice (2015) sets out a number of key principles in the effective and reasonable formal handling of employee grievances (see Box 13.6).

Acas also suggest that firms might benefit from writing a mediation stage into individual grievance procedures. Mediation is a voluntary form of dispute resolution involving an independent, impartial person acting to help the parties to a dispute reach a solution to a disagreement that is acceptable to all parties. The role of the mediator is not to determine outcomes or make judgements but to enable the parties to arrive at a resolution and restore a functioning working relationship through asking questions, assisting the parties in understanding specific issues and helping to clarify options going forward. Such mediation has been promoted by government (BIS, 2011) as helping to resolve disputes as a way of minimising the potential damage to employee relations that can be caused when more formal procedures are invoked. Provision for mediation is included in 62 per cent of grievance and disciplinary procedures in the UK, albeit not well used (van Wanrooy et al., 2013).

An organisation's policy for dealing with employee grievances should state with whom a complaint should be made, appropriate sources of support for those raising a grievance (for example, counselling), the timescales within which the organisation will seek to deal with the complaint and details of the stages of the grievance procedure. In common with disciplinary procedures, to be effective grievance procedures should be perceived by employees as fair, transparent and consistently applied. Consequently, all managers must be fully conversant with the organisation's procedures.

BULLYING AND HARASSMENT AT WORK

A significant source of workplace grievance, whether reported or otherwise, is bullying and harassment, and evidence suggests that the incidence of bullying in UK workplaces is rising, partly driven by an increasingly competitive and high-pressured working environment (UNISON, 2011). Acas suggest that the terms bullying and harassment are often used interchangeably (as, for example, the

BOX 13.6
UNDERSTAND

Keys to handling grievances in the workplace

- Let the employer know the nature of the grievance

  - Procedures should set out with whom grievances should be raised (particularly where a grievance concerns an employee's immediate line manager).
  - Grievances should be made formally, in writing and setting out the nature of the grievance, sticking to the facts.
  - Assistance can be sought from trade union or other employee representatives or from colleagues when attempting to articulate a grievance.

- Hold a meeting with the employee to discuss the grievance

  - Meetings should be held without unreasonable delay after a grievance is received.
  - Meetings should represent a dialogue and discussion.
  - Employees should be allowed to explain their grievance and how they think it should be resolved.

- Allow the employee to be accompanied at the meeting

  - A colleague or a trade union official or workplace representative is allowed to accompany an aggrieved worker.
  - The companion has the right to put forward and sum up the worker's case, respond on the worker's behalf and confer with the worker during the meeting.

- Decide on appropriate action

  - Decisions should usually be arrived at after adjournment of the meeting to allow for proper consideration and 'fact-checking'.
  - The action to be taken should be set out clearly in writing, the decision explained and the employee's right to appeal made clear.
  - Any action taken should be monitored and reviewed, as appropriate, so that it deals effectively with the issues.

- Allow the employee to take the grievance further if not resolved

  - Employees should have the right to appeal against a decision following a grievance meeting.
  - An appeal meeting should preferably be with a more senior manager.

Source: based on Acas Code of Practice, 2015 (Acas, 2015a) © Acas, Euston Tower, 286 Euston Road, London NW1 3JJ - Crown copyright Open government license.

CIPD do) but that bullying can be subsumed in definitions of harassment. They define harassment as: 'unwanted conduct related to a relevant protected characteristic, which has the purpose or effect of violating an individual's dignity or creating an intimidating, hostile, degrading, humiliating or offensive environment for that individual'. Acas (2013: 1) add that bullying is characterised as 'offensive, intimidating, malicious or insulting behaviour, an abuse or misuse of power through means that undermine, humiliate, denigrate or injure the recipient'. Such anti-social behaviour can be perpetrated by an individual against an individual or involve the actions of groups of individuals, and can be either deliberate or unconscious (Einarsen, 1999). Additionally, bullying is defined as persistent and repetitive in nature (Harvey et al., 2006; Bartlett and Bartlett, 2011) and involves a 'victim–perpetrator' dimension (Salin, 2003) reflecting a perceived power imbalance. Workplace behaviours that can be understood as harassment or bullying can be overt or subtle, but always unwelcome, and can range from physical violence, unwanted physical contact or verbal abuse to excessive criticism of work performance, 'silent treatment' or exclusion from social events. In short, bullying and harassment can be physical, verbal or psychological. As Bartlett and Bartlett (2011) note, however, there is an element of subjectivity on the part of the victim whether certain behaviours constitute bullying in terms of how they perceive behaviour and its effects, and the perception of what constitutes bullying will vary according to, for instance, organisational, occupational and cultural context (Parzefall and Salin, 2010).

Bullying and harassment may be carried out by managers and aimed at subordinates, it may occur between colleagues or a combination of both, whether by collusion or otherwise. Beale and Hoel (2011) note that dominant patterns of bullying vary by country (for instance, co-worker bullying predominates in some Nordic countries, whilst in Britain, managers are usually the perpetrators and subordinates the recipients). For managers, bullying of subordinates can take a variety of forms, including: giving an individual an unfairly heavy workload, menial tasks not commensurate with their role or unrealistic goals; the removal of responsibilities and privileges; withholding information; sharing confidential information with colleagues; or blocking individuals' opportunities for advancement (for example, by giving unfair performance reviews).

The consequences of workplace harassment and bullying for the recipient can be severe and multi-dimensional. Bartlett and Bartlett (2011) identify four categories of impact: *work* (including absenteeism, lowered commitment, impact on career progression, income loss and heightened intention to quit); *physical* (deterioration in physical health through, for example, loss of sleep and drug or alcohol misuse); *emotional* (such as depression and adverse impact on psychological health); and *affective domain* (impact on feelings, attitudes and emotions, such as anxiety, fear, sadness, anger and loss of confidence). The impact of bullying behaviour on the organisation is also wide-ranging and inter-related. This impact includes the loss of productivity through reduced performance, absenteeism and a lack of employee engagement, legal costs, high labour turnover and the associated costs of replacing leavers (both the targets of bullying and those otherwise affected) and reputational damage.

Further online reading This thought-provoking article discusses how organisational approaches to handling workplace bullying are undermined by the nature of the capitalist employment relationship and, despite potential costs, managers can benefits in certain contexts by employing bullying behaviour as one aspect of managerial control.

Beale, D. and Hoel, H. (2011) Workplace bullying and the employment relationship: Exploring questions of prevention, control and context, *Work, Employment and Society*, 25 (1): 5–18.

Salin (2003) suggests that the incidence of bullying in the workplace can be understood as the result of an interaction between organisational structures and processes that are enabling, motivating and precipitating. *Enabling structures are those that provide* 'fertile soil' (2003: 1226) for bullying, such as a perceived power imbalance in the workplace or pervasive frustration or dissatisfaction. *Motivating* structures are those under which it might be considered rational for an individual to bully someone, including, for example, reward systems that are viewed as privileging those deemed to have manipulated or harmed others to achieve advancement. Finally, *precipitating* processes are those 'triggers', typically related to change to the workplace status quo, such as organisational restructuring or downsizing, which both increase pressure on individuals (for example, to retain their jobs) and the benefits of eliminating 'threats' through

BOX 13.7
UNDERSTAND

Workplace bullying and the nature of the employment relationship

In a thought-provoking article, Beale and Hoel (2011) question two common and widely held assumptions in academic and policy-oriented literature (for instance, that regarding the management of workplace bullying): first, that it is within employers' ability to eradicate bullying; second, that it is within employers' interests to do so. They argue that workplace bullying, particularly that perpetrated by managers, is 'an endemic feature of the capitalist employment relationship' and that whilst there are undoubtedly costs to workplace bullying, they may be outweighed by the benefits, depending on the organisational context.

Understood in this way, the authors suggest several reasons why the nature of the employment relationship places significant limits on the 'zero-tolerance' approach to workplace bullying, as advocated by many unions, employers' organisations and the government. First, managers are often those found to be perpetrators of bullying and, therefore, as a group, management are unlikely to have a strong vested interest in tackling such incidences for fear of undermining managerial authority in a wider sense or bringing to light their own bullying behaviours. In other words, managerial loyalty poses problems for the effective implementation of anti-bullying policies. Second, because there appears to be an overriding concern for avoidance of litigation in dealing with bullying, employees are likely to view efforts by managers to tackle such bullying as reflective of self-interest and protection rather than a real commitment to its workforce (Lewis and Rayner, 2003, cited in Beale and Hoel, 2011). Finally, reflecting wider trends of the individualisation of the employment relationship, workplace policies on the handling of bullying can be viewed as an attempt to discourage collective challenges to bullying by unions and workers, reflecting a managerial preference to treat bullying as individual or isolated incidences rather than a wider relational problem.

Subsequently, Beale and Hoel suggest that bullying may be seen as a tool of managerial control, whether it is rational and calculated, spontaneous or a response to an 'unmanageable' situation, and as one of a range of methods and styles of management employed to achieve managerial objectives and implement change through the creation of a 'climate of fear'. As such, the authors propose that all managers who have a vested interest in the achievement of these objectives have an equal interest in ignoring or seeking to mitigate a victim's claim in support of the bullying manager. However, the 'acceptability' of bullying as a means of managerial control depends on both national (for instance, the extent of legal regulation of behaviour associated with bullying) and organisational context (Beale and Hoel, 2010). For example, in firms that adopt practices associated with High Performance Work Systems, even isolated incidences of managerial bullying are likely to be viewed as undermining attempts to develop employee commitment. Similarly, for firms in product or labour markets that require the retention of skilled employees, bullying is likely to be less acceptable and tolerated, compared to those in which labour turnover is viewed as less problematic.

aggression, as well as creating 'chaotic' conditions in which bullying as a means of managerial control can take hold (Harvey et al., 2006; Roscigno et al., 2009). Hutchinson (2012) suggests that there is an empirical link between workplace bullying and changes to organisational and employment policies, such as precarious employment, increased workloads and restructuring. As such, it is questionable the extent to which policies to prevent bullying will be successful in the face of such policies.

As in tackling workplace discipline and grievance more widely, whilst formal procedures exist for both complaint and remedy, informal routes to resolve such complaints are typically favoured and line managers are expected to play a significant role in both seeking to avoid and managing incidences of bullying and/or harassment. Whilst the focus of policy to tackle bullying is often on the eradication of undesirable behaviours from the workplace, an alternative perspective is proposed by the CIPD (2005), who place an emphasis on a broader management strategy based on the promotion of dignity and mutual respect at work (Beale and Hoel, 2011). The notion of dignity at work goes beyond a concern only for the avoidance of bullying and harassment to the 'whole range of circumstances which support or tend to undermine employees' dignity' (Sayer, 2007: 565).

Further online reading Based on a review of the extant literature and interviews with policy-makers, Hutchinson argues that much discussion of workplace bullying as an individual problem overlooks the significance of organisational, employment and cultural factors.

Hutchinson, J. (2012) Rethinking workplace bullying as an employment relations problem, *Journal of Industrial Relations,* 55 (5): 637–52.

COLLECTIVE DISPUTE PROCEDURES

Whilst grievance procedures are used to deal with individual concerns, disputes procedures outline how collective disagreements should be handled. In some workplaces, however, grievance procedures deal with both individual and collective issues. Similar to individual procedures, they detail a number of stages that facilitate fair treatment in the handling of disagreements, for example where collective bargaining has broken down, and assist the parties towards resolution (Rose, 2008). Van Wanrooy et al. (2013) report that only 35 per cent of UK workplaces have dispute procedures in place (down from 40 per cent in 2004) and that only 54 per cent of employees are in workplaces with such procedures. The incidence of disputes procedures is greater in larger workplaces and those with a recognised union, 75 per cent of which have such procedures compared to 24 per cent of workplaces without recognised unions.

Disputes procedures typically provide for third-party intervention from outside the workplace or establishment affected by the dispute, particularly in the form of a referral to Acas or to another independent mediator or arbitrator (Rose, 2008). Acas is a non-departmental UK government organisation whose purpose is 'to improve organisations and working life through better employment relations … by supplying up-to-date information, independent advice and high quality training, and working with employers and employees to solve problems and improve performance' (www. acas.org.uk). Therefore, whilst its principal role remains collective disputes resolution, Acas's remit also includes working to improve workplace relationships and conflict prevention. Although dealing primarily with collective disputes, incidents where individual employees claim their employer has denied them a legal right can also be referred to Acas. Third-party intervention in collective disputes can take three forms:

1 *Conciliation* – the third-party provision of assistance to facilitate discussion between employer and employee representatives to resolve disputes and avoid future conflict.

2 *Mediation* – having heard the evidence of both parties, the third party makes formal but non-binding recommendations to prompt a settlement between the employer and employees

3 *Arbitration* – the parties to the dispute appoint an arbitrator to evaluate the evidence and make a decision that is used to resolve the issue.

Clearly, it is important that referral to a third party is seen as a last resort and it is only when negotiations are at an absolute impasse that the dispute is referred. A premature referral to a third party might be construed as evidence of an unwillingness to actively seek a quick resolution to the dispute and of significant underlying differences between the parties.

BOX 13.8
MANAGEMENT SKILLS AND ATTRIBUTES

Line managers and the management of conflict

The most important person in handling both employee grievance and discipline is the immediate line manager. There is, however, conflicting research evidence regarding the proportion of their time that line managers spend on disciplinary issues. Some studies suggest a trend towards greater line manager responsibility for dealing with employee misconduct, yet CIPD (2008e) report that organisations are increasingly relying on their HR departments to manage conflict as line managers become more fearful of acting in a way that might be held against them during formal proceedings. Table 13.1 outlines the key competencies required by managers to manage conflict effectively within their team or department.

As discussed elsewhere, there is often a tension between the operational concerns of line managers and their growing people management responsibilities. Consequently, rules and procedures regarding the handling of grievance and disciplinary matters are often viewed as unnecessary bureaucracy that detracts from their 'real job'. Procedures can, however, help line managers by providing clarity regarding the approach a firm takes to managing the employment relationship, clarifying the line manager's relationship with employees and identifying legitimate grounds for employee discipline or complaint. The formal handling of grievances and discipline can also reduce the potential for future conflict if matters are left unresolved and allowed to escalate.

HR specialists need to ensure that line managers possess the required skills, know how to use procedures and can explain their purpose and value, both in HR terms and in terms of individual and organisational performance. Line managers might also require training to enable them to reconcile the need for consistency in the application of procedures with the flexibility to deal effectively with individual cases. Despite the importance of consistency of treatment in ensuring procedural justice and in developing a trusting employment relationship, evidence continues to suggest considerable inconsistency among supervisors in decisions regarding disciplinary measures (Cole, 2008) and the use of informal strategies, rather than formal procedures, to address employee discipline (Franklin and Pagan, 2006).

Further online reading This article explores the influence of organisational culture on the tendency for line managers to use informal strategies, rather than formal procedures, to address employee discipline and how tangible and intangible 'cues' for management practice interact to shape the approach adopted to discipline.

Franklin, A. L. and Pagan, J. F. (2006) Organization culture as an explanation for employee discipline practices, *Review of Public Personnel Administration*, 26 (1): 52–73.

TABLE 13.1 *A competency framework for line managers in managing conflict*

Competency	Examples of good practice	Examples of poor practice
Dealing with issues	Intervene quickly Follow up on conflict following resolution	Leaving team members to sort out conflict Intervening without understanding issues
Use of official processes	Communicate policies and procedures Escalate issues to senior managers where appropriate	Make a complaint official against complainant's wishes Not following correct procedures Use 'red tape' to put complainant off raising issues
Participative approach	Acting as mediator Supporting both sides and bringing them together to discuss issues	Taking sides Not listening to employee complaint
Monitoring team relationships	Being aware of tension and keeping it at a low level	Ignoring or not acknowledging when a team member is creating tension/stress among co-workers
Acting as a role model	Maintaining professionalism Communicating expectations of conduct	Losing temper Deliberately creating or engaging in conflict
Integrity	Keep employee issues private Treating employees fairly and consistently	Bullying Using disciplinary action to threaten employees unfairly

Source: Adapted from CIPD (Chartered Institute of Personnel and Development) (2008e) *Managing Conflict at Work: A Guide for Line Managers*, London: CIPD, reproduced with the permission of the publisher, the Chartered Institute of Personnel and Development, London, www.cipd.co.uk

THE ROLE OF HR SPECIALISTS

HR specialists are likely to be responsible for the drafting, implementation and revision of grievance and disciplinary procedures, ensuring that they meet the requirements of the legislation and fit with the specific organisational context and dominant management style. As advocates of the procedures, HR specialists are likely to have a role in promoting their use. HR specialists should provide advice and guidance to managers and help to ensure fairness and consistency in the organisation-wide application of the procedures. In some firms, HR specialists might carry out disciplinary and grievance hearings and decide on sanctions. In other organisations, HR practitioners might be required to act as impartial mediators in such meetings.

As with other aspects of HRM, there may well be conflict between line managers and HR specialists regarding the adherence to procedures. Given that part of their role is concerned with legislative compliance, HR specialists are likely to strongly advocate that line managers address disciplinary and grievance matters through formal means, whereas line managers might prefer to exhaust informal approaches and be reluctant to refer issues to the formal process. Similarly, whilst line managers might desire flexibility in how to handle individual complaints or misconduct – informed by their knowledge of the employee and their circumstances – HR practitioners are likely to stress consistency. HR specialists might experience tension between seeking to ensure procedural justice – both to protect the organisation against litigation and for the benefit of the employee – and a desire to minimise the impact employee discipline has on individual and departmental performance by dealing with a problem as quickly as possible, which might lead to circumvention of due process.

EMPLOYMENT TRIBUNALS

Where individual grievances are not resolved to the satisfaction of the employee or where an employee challenges the outcome of a disciplinary procedure (for example, an individual feels they have been unfairly dismissed), employees have the option of taking their (ex-)employer to an employment tribunal. Employment tribunals are part of the UK civil law system which is concerned with settling disputes between private parties, such as a worker and an employer. Employment tribunals are where most employment issues are dealt with, although as Marchington and Wilkinson (2005) note, some issues may be routed through the County Court or High Court system and, less commonly, dealt with in the criminal courts. Employment tribunals hear cases involving a wide range of issues including unfair dismissal, discrimination, redundancy and transfer of undertakings, equal pay, maternity and time off, health and safety at work, redundancy, terms and conditions of employment, pay and union membership.

The remit and use of employment tribunals have developed significantly since they were first introduced in the 1960s and the rulings of tribunals now form a considerable body of case law that strongly influences managerial practice, not least in endorsing the formalisation of workplace procedures. In 2011–12, UK employment tribunals accepted 186,300 claims, up from 110,000 a decade earlier (albeit down from 218,100 in 2010–11) (Tribunals Service, 2012). This longitudinal increase tends to reflect an increasingly litigious society and a growing tendency of workers to bring claims against their employers. The growth both of legislation and case law governing employment has also meant that tribunals are often far from the speedy and cheap means of resolving disputes that they were originally intended to be. The complexity of labour law has led to a greater likelihood of legal representation for both parties and the involvement of employers' organisations and trade unions.

Appeals against tribunal decisions, on a question of law, for example, where the evidence is in question or the tribunal is thought to have misunderstood the relevant legislation, are made to the Employment Appeals Tribunal (EAT). Appeals against EAT decisions can be made in certain circumstances to the Court of Appeal, then to the House of Lords and ultimately to the European Court of Justice.

SUMMARY POINTS

- Dissatisfaction in the employment relationship can be expressed individually or collectively, and formally or informally.
- Recent developments in the expression and institutionalisation of conflict conform to wider patterns of growing individualism in the employment relationship.
- Rules governing the employment relationship can be explicit and implicit, emanating from a wide variety of sources, including legislation, workplace custom and collective bargaining, to establish the expected standards of conduct, rights, responsibilities and behavioural and performance expectations of the parties.
- Managerial discipline in the workplace can have a range of intentions, including punishment, compliance, deterrence, correction and rehabilitation.

- Effective, fair and reasonable discipline and grievance procedures are essential to good employment relations in providing effective channels for the containment and resolution of conflict.

BRITISH AIRWAYS
AND UNITE

- The informal handling of employee discipline and grievance is desirable in order to remedy workplace problems as quickly as possible. Formal procedures should be used when informal resolution

has failed or where a matter is particularly serious or complex.

- The key stages of fair and reasonable procedures for dealing with discipline and grievance are: investigation, notification, formal meeting, action and appeal.

- Line managers play a crucial role in the handling of employee grievance and discipline, particularly in identifying and resolving potential conflict and dealing with employee transgressions in a speedy and consistent manner.

SELF-TEST QUESTIONS

1 How is workplace conflict viewed under the unitarist and pluralist perspectives on the employment relationship?

2 How can employees express dissatisfaction in the employment relationship:

- Individually?
- Collectively?
- Formally?
- Informally?

3 How might an employer express dissatisfaction either with an individual employee or the workforce more generally?

4 What purposes do workplace rules and procedures fulfil in the employment relationship?

What examples of formal and informal workplace rules can you give?

5 How has new technology created new methods for the collective and individual expression of employee dissatisfaction? What challenges does this pose for employers?

6 Why does the Acas Code of Practice stress the importance of the informal resolution of conflict prior to instigating formal procedures?

7 What are the six 'fair' reasons for dismissal under UK law? What examples can you give of 'automatically unfair' reasons for dismissal?

8 What roles do line managers fulfil in managing employee discipline and grievance?

9 Why are employers increasingly concerned with the behaviour of employees outside of the workplace?

TEST YOURSELF

TEST
YOURSELF

Want to know more about this chapter? Review what you have been learning by visiting:
https://edge.sagepub.com/wilton3e

- Print out or download the chapter summaries for quick revision
- Test yourself with multiple-choice questions
- Revise key terms with interactive flashcards

ACTIVITY

Employee discipline and grievance at Pavement Field Marketing

You are the managing director of Pavement, a field marketing company based in south-east England

who design and enact field marketing campaigns for a growing number of clients. Pavement provides a full range of field marketing activities, including point of purchase auditing, merchandising, mystery shopping, sampling and demonstrations.

The company has grown considerably over recent months and you are in the process of appointing an HR manager. Currently all HR decisions are made by you and the office manager, Olivia. You are also in the process of interviewing for two new account executives and an administrator. Owing to your workload you have allowed a number of HR problems to accumulate, including the following issues:

- Steven has recently been promoted to account manager, having worked in his previous role of account executive for only four months. The previous account manager left abruptly and Steven has had little guidance in carrying out his new role. Among his responsibilities is managing a team of dedicated field staff who carry out road shows for clients' products, setting up in-store samplings and ensuring the visibility and promotion of clients' products at point of purchase. Steven was recently charged with setting up a demonstration at a large food trade show for a key client. However, a senior manager at the client company has phoned to complain about the staff at the trade show lacking product knowledge and the product presentation being 'shambolic'. This follows poor feedback from another client about the poor in-store presentation of a recent promotion organised by Steven.

- Two members of another team have made separate complaints about the excessive use of profanity by an account executive, Jamie. This follows an earlier complaint about Jamie's swearing made three months ago by an administrator who has since left the company. At that time you spoke informally to Jamie, who denied the accusations and claimed that the administrator was just 'stirring up trouble' because he had reprimanded her for the poor standard of her work. You had taken Jamie at his word, partly because he has always been one of your most successful account executives.

- Your personal assistant, Shelley, has worked for the company for a year and a half and has proved invaluable in helping you grow the company, often staying late at the office at critical times. In the last six weeks, however, the standard of her work has dropped. She has failed to give you a number of important messages, arrived late and phoned in sick on a number of occasions and failed to complete important tasks on time, such as compiling a much-needed report. A client also mentioned to you that she had been 'off-hand' on the phone. From overhearing private phone calls that Shelley has been making at work, you understand that she has been having marital problems.

- Your office manager, Olivia, has recently learnt on the office grapevine that Beth, the company finance manager, is a regular user of recreational drugs. Olivia believes that this might account for a spate of payroll errors over recent months. As her line manager, Olivia has decided that Beth should be summarily dismissed on the basis that her drug use is having a detrimental effect on her work. She has asked you for your approval for the dismissal.

- Steven has informed you that he has dismissed one of the temporary workers, David, who had been working on a major in-store promotion. David and a permanent member of the promotions team, Elaine, had previously been given an informal warning about drinking alcohol on their lunch break. Subsequently, Steven had suspected that the entire promotions team had gone to the pub yesterday lunchtime to celebrate a colleague's birthday. Steven dismissed David, justifying his decision on the basis that he was a troublemaker and only had four weeks left on his six-month contract anyway. Steven assumes that having 'made an example' of David then the other team members will have learnt their lesson.

Task

Your task is to determine how best to deal with these scenarios and to identify the key issues in each case.

Olivia has informed you that the company has an employee discipline and grievance policy that complies with the latest Code of Practice. You should draw on this Code to assess how best to deal with each of the cases outlined above. She also reports that the company has a rudimentary capability procedure as advised by the company lawyer.

USEFUL READING

Journal articles

Cole, N. (2008) Consistency in employee discipline: An empirical exploration, *Personnel Review*, 37 (1): 109–17.

This article reports on research that indicates significant inconsistency in the way in which supervisors deal with employee discipline. It highlights the problem faced by line managers of achieving consistency whilst taking account of individual circumstances in handling disciplinary cases.

Earnshaw, J., Marchington, M. and Goodman, J. (2000) Unfair to whom? Discipline and dismissal in small establishments, *Industrial Relations Journal*, 31 (1): 62–73.

This article explores the role of workplace disciplinary and grievance procedures in small firms and their influence on employment tribunal claims for unfair dismissal. It provides an insight into managerial treatment of workers in matters of discipline and whether small firms tend to be disadvantaged when defending tribunal claims.

Books, book chapters and reports

Advisory, Conciliation and Arbitration Service (Acas) (2015) *Code of Practice on Disciplinary and Grievance Procedures*, London: Acas.

Advisory, Conciliation and Arbitration Service (Acas) (2015) *Discipline and Grievances at Work: The Acas Guide*, London: Acas.

To fully understand good practice in handling employee discipline and grievance in the UK, the Acas Code of Practice and accompanying guide are essential reading. They provide the basis for the vast majority of organisational practice in this area and represent the benchmark for fair and reasonable procedures.

FURTHER ONLINE READING

 The following articles can be accessed for free on the book's companion website **https://edge.sagepub.com/wilton3e**:

Beale, D. and Hoel, H. (2011) Workplace bullying and the employment relationship: Exploring questions of prevention, control and context, *Work, Employment and Society*, 25 (1): 5–18.

Fleming, P. and Sturdy, A. (2011) `Being yourself' in the electronic sweatshop: New forms of normative control, *Human Relations*, 64(2), 177–200.

Franklin, A. L. and Pagan, J. F. (2006) Organization culture as an explanation for employee discipline practices, *Review of Public Personnel Administration*, 26 (1): 52–73.

Hutchinson, J. (2012) Rethinking workplace bullying as an employment relations problem, *Journal of Industrial Relations*, 55 (5): 637–52.

Pollert, A. and Charlwood, A. (2009) The vulnerable worker in Britain and problems at work, *Work, Employment and Society*, 23 (2): 343–62.

Saundry, R., McArdle, L. and Thomas, P. (2013) Reframing workplace relations? Conflict resolution and mediation in a primary care trust, *Work, Employment and Society*, 27 (2): 213–31.

Want to know more about this chapter? Visit the companion website at: **https://edge.sagepub.com/wilton3e** to access practice questions, videos and selected journal articles to further enhance your study.

14

HRM, WORK AND WELL-BEING

CHAPTER OBJECTIVES

- To define the concept of employee well-being

- To discuss contemporary workplace health and safety issues, including mental health and stress

- To present the business case for the effective management of employee well-being

- To outline the UK legal framework concerning health and safety (H&S) at work

- To detail the mechanisms by which organisations can actively manage employee well-being, including dealing with stress at work

- To discuss the importance of work–life balance to individual well-being and effectiveness at work.

INTRODUCTION

Employer concern for employee health, safety and well-being would appear to lie at the heart of a positive employment relationship. It would be very hard for employers to argue that they value their employees whilst disregarding their welfare in the workplace. Subsequently, the claim of many employers that people represent a valued organisational asset is perhaps nowhere better examined than in the light of their approach to health and safety at work. Alongside the growing emphasis on people-added value in contemporary firms, the CIPD (2007d) note that the concept of 'employee well-being' has grown in significance over the past few years. This concern is partly associated with the high cost to businesses of ill health and associated absence, the development of legislation covering workplace health and safety, demographic change (associated with, for example, an ageing workforce) and the shift to a service-dominated industry – developments that have contributed to the creation of a wider set of health, safety and welfare concerns for both employers and employees. Moreover, trends in the management and experience of work – including the greater use of contingent reward, flexible working, work intensification, increased job insecurity and work-related stress – are placing greater pressures on employees and have contributed to a rise in the experience of work-related mental ill health.

This chapter is primarily concerned with this multi-dimensional notion of employee well-being and the rationale for the effective management of well-being. It discusses contemporary trends in workplace health and safety, outlines the UK legal framework governing H&S at work and the means by which well-being can be managed.

DEFINING WELL-BEING

CIPD (2007d) define the management of well-being at work as being concerned with:

> creating an environment to promote a state of contentment which allows an employee to flourish and achieve their full potential for the benefit of themselves and their organization ... well-being is more than an avoidance of becoming physically sick. It represents a broader bio-psycho-social construct that includes physical, mental and social health. (2007d: 4)

This very broad definition reflects the wide range of dimensions to employee well-being (see Table 14.1) and the view that the effective management of well-being involves consideration both of the way in which work itself can affect people and the more specific hazards to physical and mental health in the individual workplace. Therefore, employee well-being represents a wider concern for employees than simply the minimisation of risks to health and the prevention of accidents, injuries and disease that have traditionally been the H&S concerns of employers. The notion of employee well-being stresses both a preventative/proactive approach through the provision of rewarding work, a nurturing work environment, correct fit between worker and job/organisation, the prevention

TABLE 14.1   *Five domains of well-being*

Domain	Indicative elements
Physical	Physical health, mental health, working environment, physical safety and accommodation
Values	Ethical standards, diversity, psychological contract and 'spiritual expression'
Personal development	Autonomy, career development, lifelong learning and creativity
Emotional	Positive relationships, emotional intelligence and social responsibility
Work/organisation	Change management, work demands, autonomy and job security

Source: adapted from CIPD, 2007d

of accidents, injuries and stress and the promotion of healthy lifestyles, as well as a curative/reactive approach to assist employees in remedying the causes and consequences of accidents or injuries and dealing with mental health issues.

Understood in a broad sense, the notion of well-being at work is constructed both of subjective and objective elements: subjective in that individual physical and mental well-being differs between people, depending on their underlying health, their values, attitudes, expectations, priorities and personal circumstance, and objective in that there are certain 'baseline' features of employee wellness. This perspective stresses that the effective management of employee well-being requires an individual, as well as collective, focus. Moreover, effective management of employee well-being requires consideration of a wide range of organisational characteristics: prevailing culture, management style, line manager behaviour, work allocation, job design and the use of technology. In summary, employee well-being is concerned with:

- maintaining a safe and stable working environment
- managing effectively risks to physical and mental health
- promoting supportive, trusting, nurturing and respectful relationships and a positive psychological contract
- enabling individual employees to achieve their potential through sympathetic job design and supportive HR policies and practices
- providing intrinsically rewarding, challenging and satisfying work
- encouraging and supporting good physical and mental health both inside and outside of the workplace.

The CIPD (2007d) suggest that there has never been a greater imperative for organisations to address employee well-being, citing three principal sources of pressure to do so:

1 The costs of long-term sickness and absence and the damage to organisational productivity, growth, employee retention and brand.

2 Increasing demand from employees that their employers help them achieve individual well-being.

3 The growing body of legislation and government policy driving employers to recognise their impact on employee health and to assist in getting more of the working population back and active in the workplace.

Nonetheless, the CIPD question whether the apparently greater focus on employee well-being in management discourse constitutes a new phenomenon or just a 'clever re-labelling of traditional absence management, occupational health and good management practice' (CIPD, 2007d: 1).

DIGNITY AT WORK

The notion of 'dignity at work' is often used in conjunction with bullying and harassment, as outlined in Chapter 13. A number of organisations, including trade unions (for example, UNITE and AMICUS in the UK), employer organisations and government departments, use the term to refer to the objective of creating a positive working environment which is free from bullying and harassment and which promotes mutual respect between colleagues and between managers and their subordinates.

Sayer (2007) argues, however, that the prominent focus on bullying and harassment tends to frame the idea of dignity at work rather narrowly and that greater attention needs to be paid to 'the whole range of circumstances which support or tend to undermine employees' dignity' (2007: 565). In broadening the dignity at work agenda, Sayer argues for the association between dignity and autonomy, recognition, being taken seriously by others, respect and self-respect and trust. To a degree, therefore, dignity at work is closely associated with employee well-being, as outlined in Table 14.1. Sayer argues, however, that the nature of work undertaken by a worker, and whether they are viewed in an instrumental manner, is also a key determinant of one's dignity (Hodson, 2001). Therefore, whilst bullying and harassment represent severe instances in which someone's dignity is undermined, involvement in 'decent work' (Bolton, 2007) and management that treats employees in a respectful manner are also critical elements in ensuring the avoidance of indignity.

Further online reading This article argues that the focus on bullying and harassment in the discussion around dignity at work fails to recognise the importance of a range of factors associated with social relationships in the workplace including trust, recognition, respect and autonomy.

Sayer, A. (2007) Dignity at work: Broadening the agenda, *Organization*, 14 (4): 565–81.

HEALTH AND SAFETY AT WORK

A key component of employee well-being is health and safety at work. The Health and Safety Executive (HSE), the body responsible for enforcing and promoting UK H&S legislation, report that in 2010–11, 1.2 million people in the UK who worked during the previous year were suffering from an illness they believed was caused or exacerbated by their current or previous work (of which approximately 500,000 were new cases) (HSE, 2011a). There were 171 fatal injuries to workers in 2010–11, up from 149 in 2009–10 but consistent with a longer-term downward trend, and 115,379 other reported injuries to employees (under the Reporting of Injuries, Diseases and Dangerous Occurrences Regulations), a rate of 462.1 per 100,000 employees. In terms of fatalities, the most dangerous industries in 2010–11 were *construction* (50 fatal injuries, 2.3 deaths per 100,000 workers), *agriculture* (34 fatal injuries with a corresponding rate of 9.9 deaths per 100,000 workers) and *manufacturing* (27 fatalities, 1.0 deaths per 100,000 workers). In the entire *service* sector there were 37 fatalities (0.2 deaths per 100,000 workers).

Whilst these figures clearly indicate that workplace H&S should be a significant concern for the employer, they represent a significant improvement in workplace H&S over recent decades. For instance, since 1974 the reported incidence of fatal injuries at work has fallen by 76 per cent and reported non-fatal injuries by 70 per cent. There is a complex pattern of reasons for this improvement in workplace safety, including improved legislation in this area (the Health and Safety at Work Act 1974), the shift to more 'benign' work and improved managerial practice beyond legal compliance (see Box 14.1).

Further online reading This article examines the impact of current work and employment practices, and workforce characteristics, on the incidence of workplace accidents and ill health. It suggests that worker health is poorly served by existing management practice and that work-related injury and illness have a wide range of causes associated with contemporary work.

Robinson, A. and Smallman, C. (2006) The contemporary British workplace: A safer and healthier place?, *Work, Employment and Society*, 20 (1): 87–107.

In the UK, the traditional emphasis of H&S at work has been on the physical working environment. This partly reflects the historic focus of H&S legislation on guarding against the ill effects of manual labour and the dangers associated with manufacturing and agricultural work, both in terms of the risk of physical injury or illness and the potential to exacerbate existing health problems.

BOX 14.1
GLOBAL INSIGHT

An international perspective on workplace H&S

The UK Health and Safety Executive report that the most recent comparative data (2008) show that Great Britain has a considerably lower fatal injury rate (0.99 per 100,000 workers) than many other EU member states, such as France (1.68 per 100,000), Germany (1.87 per 100,000) and Spain (2.63 per 100,000). The highest rate was found in Romania (8.38 per 100,000) (HSE, 2011b). In total, there were 4,416 work-related fatalities in the European Union (http://appsso.eurostat.ec.europa.eu), of which 1,363 were work-related road traffic and transport accidents. These figures are reflective of a broadly downward trend in work-related fatalities (and serious injury) in most industrialised nations, yet the global picture on H&S at work makes for more worrying reading. The International Labour Organisation (2009) report the following:

- 'An estimated 2.3 million men and women die from work-related accidents and diseases annually, including close to 360,000 fatal accidents and an estimated 1.95 million fatal work-related diseases'.

- 'Every day nearly 1 million workers will suffer a workplace accident, and around 5500 workers will die due to an accident or disease from their work'.

- 'In economic terms it is estimated that roughly 4 per cent of the annual global gross domestic product, or US$1.25 trillion, is siphoned off by the direct and indirect costs of occupational accidents and diseases, in lost working time, workers' compensation, the interruption of production and medical expenses'.

- 'Hazardous substances cause an estimated 651,000 deaths, mostly in the developing world. These numbers may be greatly underestimated due to inadequate reporting and notification systems in many countries'.

- 'Data from a number of industrialised countries show that construction workers are three to four times more likely than other workers to die from accidents at work'.

- 'Occupational lung disease in mining and related industries arising from asbestos, coal and silica exposure is still a concern in developed and developing countries. Asbestos alone claims about 100,000 deaths every year and the figure is rising annually'.

The disparity between the EU and the global picture likely indicates significant differences in the dangers of work in the developed and developing world. Given the complex patterns in the international division of labour that have developed in the era of rapid globalisation this raises the question of whether the traditional dangers of certain types of work have also been 'exported' to these less developed nations.

Source: Adapted from International Labour Organisation (ILO) (2009) World Day for Safety and Health at Work 2009: Facts on Safety and Health at Work, Geneva: ILO. Reprinted with kind permission from the International Labour Organisation (ILO)

Recent changes in the emphasis of the management of workplace H&S, and a decline in the incidence of serious injury and deaths at work, have coincided with the continued movement towards a service-dominated economy and associated changes in the nature and demands of work. For example, in the contemporary workplace, particular offices are associated with 'sick building syndrome' (Baldry et al., 1997) referring to the health problems caused by poor air quality

WORKPLACE
HEALTH AND
SAFETY

and inadequate ventilation. Perhaps most significantly, the increasingly wide-spread use of ICT across various working environments has led to a significant increase in the number of cases of repetitive strain injury (RSI) caused by the intensive use of computer keyboards, alongside other forms of musculoskeletal disorders. An estimated 7.6 million working days were lost in 2010–11 through musculoskeletal disorders caused or made worse by work, with, on average, each sufferer taking an average estimated 15 days off during that 12-month period (HSE, 2011b). Bevan et al. (2009) report that almost a quarter of European workers claim that they have experienced muscular pain in their neck, shoulders and upper limbs consistent with RSI.

Further online reading This article provides a detailed assessment of H&S issues in call centres. It concludes that management appears more likely to address the environmental causes of ill health rather than those relating to work organisation and job design.

Taylor, P., Baldry, C., Bain, P. and Ellis, V. (2003) A unique working environment: Health, sickness and absence management in UK call centres, *Work, Employment and Society,* 17 (3): 435–58.

Boyd (2002) notes the growing incidence of violence at work across all sectors of employment, but particularly for customer-facing employees in the hospitality, transport and retail sectors. This includes the prevalence of verbal abuse experienced by people in the workplace which places significant emotional demands on employees and can lead to physical ill health. Cookson and Buckley (2011) report that estimates from the 2010/11 British Crime Survey (BCS) indicated that there were approximately 313,000 threats of violence and 341,000 physical assaults by members of the public on British workers during the preceding 12-month period.

MENTAL HEALTH AND STRESS AT WORK

Perhaps the most significant trend in the area of workplace H&S over recent years has been the increasing prevalence of mental health conditions. Lelliott et al. (2006) report that the proportion of UK incapacity benefit claimants who are claiming due to a mental health condition has increased to nearly 40 per cent in 2006 compared to 25 per cent in the mid-1990s, overtaking musculoskeletal disorders as the most common reason for claiming such benefit. Most frequently, mental health problems associated with work reflect the consequences of work-related stress, but also include anxiety, depression and burn-out. For the period 2008–11, an estimated 416,000 UK employees who had worked in the last year believed that they were experiencing work-related stress, depression or anxiety at a level that was making them ill, a rate of 1,380 in every 100,000 workers (HSE, 2011a). Similarly, Webster et al. (2007) indicate that around 13.6 per cent of all working individuals thought their job was very or extremely stressful and the most recent UK Workplace Employment Relations Survey (WERS) in 2004 found that almost one-fifth of employees surveyed (19 per cent) reported feeling job-related tension all or most of the time, 12 per cent reported job-related worry all or most of the time and 10 per cent reported uneasiness all or most of the time. In contrast, however, 39 per cent said that they felt job-related tension only occasionally or never (Kersley et al., 2006).

The HSE define work-related stress as 'the adverse reaction people have to excessive pressures or other types of demand placed on them' (HSE, 2012b). A more involved definition is provided by Ganster and Perrewé (2011): 'stress can be thought of as (a) a feature of the external environment that acts on an individual, (b) the individual's responses (psychological, physiological, and behavioural) to environmental demands, threats, and challenges, or (c) the interaction of the two'. Both definitions emphasise that stress is subjectively experienced and the fact that different people have different 'tipping points', varying perceptions of potential sources of stress and ability to cope. In other words, the strains that constitute an individual response to stressors (environmental events that act on an individual) (Griffin and Clarke, 2011; Ganster and Rosen, 2013) will differ from person to person.

As the HSE highlight, however, work is not inherently stressful:

> Well-designed, organised and managed work is generally good for us but when insufficient attention to job design, work organisation and management has taken place, it can result in work related stress ... Pressure can be positive and a motivating factor, and is often essential in a job. It can help us achieve our goals and perform better. Stress occurs when this pressure becomes excessive. Stress is a natural reaction to too much pressure. (www.hse.gov.uk/stress/furtheradvice/whatisstress.htm, accessed 30 September 2015)

Therefore, whilst many of the potential sources of stress – for example, working to tight deadlines – are present in many jobs, they might represent a source of challenge and motivation to some employees yet a significant source of stress to others, with the potential to cause physical ill health. This is not to say that stress is purely an individual problem (for example, an inability to cope), rather it can be a reflection of a range of workplace and job-related characteristics. The costs to business of work-related stress can be significant, including prolonged sickness absence, staff turnover, lowered staff morale and productivity and human error, not to say personal injury claims. An estimated 10.8 million working days are lost due to stress and associated psychological disorders (HSE, 2011a) and the HSE estimate that stress costs UK society approximately £4 billion a year (HSE, 2009). Whilst the HSE note that work-related stress is widespread throughout the UK working population and not confined to particular sectors or high-risk jobs or industries, both stress and other mental health conditions are high among certain professions including teachers, nurses, housing and welfare officers, medical practitioners, police officers, prison officers and armed forces personnel.

DEFINING STRESS

There are a wide variety of factors that can contribute to the experience of work-related stress, many of which were discussed in relation to quality of work life in Chapter 4. These include inappropriate work organisation and job design, role ambiguity, the nature of working relationships, a lack of discretion and control, work intensification, the form and degree of managerial surveillance, poor communication, harassment and bullying and excessive workload and pressure. In addition, management style, uncertainty and job insecurity and poor work–life balance or 'spillover' can be significant contributory factors. Of course, in many cases, stress is likely to be a consequence of a range of these stressors (Smith and Elliott (2012) provide an interesting first person account of the interaction between a range of job and organisational factors that contribute to workplace stress).

Using data for 15 European countries, Cottini and Lucifora (2013) found that adverse working conditions, in terms of job demands (i.e. shift work, performing complex and intensive tasks, and having restricted job autonomy) and job hazards are strongly associated with a higher probability of workers reporting mental health problems at the workplace but that job demands, as opposed to job hazards, have a more sizable impact on mental health problems.

Further online reading Alongside some detailed analysis of evidence regarding the incidence of workplace mental health, this article provides an useful overview of the incidence of mental ill health across Europe, its determinants and the broader regulatory contexts within which it manifests.

Cottini, E. and Lucifora, C. (2013) Mental health and working conditions in Europe, *ILR Review,* 66 (4): 958–88.

In all, the HSE (2012a) identify six key areas of work design that, if not properly managed, are associated with poor health and well-being at work, particularly stress. These are:

1 *Demands* – including issues such as workload, work patterns and the work environment.

2 *Control* – how much say the person has in the way they do their work.

3 *Support* – including the encouragement, sponsorship and resources provided by the organisation, line management and colleagues.

4 *Relationships* – including workplace conflict and unacceptable behaviour.

5 *Role* – whether people understand their role within the organisation and whether the organisation ensures that they do not have conflicting roles.

6 *Change* – how organisational change is managed and communicated in the organisation.

THE IMPACT OF ILL HEALTH

WORKPLACE
INJURIES AND ILL
HEALTH

The net impact of work-related injury and illness on the UK economy in 2010–11 equated to 26.4 million working days lost (0.94 days per worker), 22.1 million due to work-related ill health and 4.4 million due to workplace injury (HSE, 2012c). However, if we consider the impact of ill health in general (not necessarily caused or made worse by work) on the UK economy the figures are even more stark. The Black Review (Black, 2008) estimates that the cost of working-age ill health to the British economy is over £100 billion each year in terms of working days lost and worklessness. The CBI estimate that there were 172 million working days lost in 2007 due to sickness absence, and absences that last over four weeks made up around 40 per cent of days lost to absence (CBI, 2008b). CIPD (2007e) report that sickness absence (not necessarily work-related) accounts for 8.4 per cent of working time, equivalent to eight working days for each employee each year at an average cost of £659 per employee per year.

These figures reinforce the importance of organisations adopting a two-pronged approach to addressing H&S at work: first, to prevent injuries and illnesses caused or exacerbated by work and which lead to often-prolonged absence; and, second, to promote healthy lifestyles in order to minimise the risk of employees having to take time off for non-work-related illness. Ill health also has a significant impact on public finances, in particular the costs of providing welfare benefits to those unable to work, whether in the short or long term as a result of injury or illness

BOX 14.2
RESEARCH INSIGHT

The incidence of mental ill health and organisational response

People Management (2015a) refer to mental ill health as the 'secret workplace epidemic', reporting on extensive research evidence that mental health problems associated with work were increasing, including the stark estimation of Stanford Graduate School and Harvard Business School that the negative health outcomes associated with work stresses were killing 12,000 people annually in the US.

Research conducted by *People Management* asked HR professionals to explore the incidence of mental ill health in their organisations and the interventions in place to help those suffering from such conditions. The research found that the most common conditions were stress (88 per cent of organisations), depression (85 per cent), anxiety (83 per cent) and stress-related illnesses (63 per cent). In addition, the research identified the incidence of a range of broader issues associated with mental health including panic attacks (42 per cent), substance abuse or addiction (28 per cent), eating disorders (12 per cent) and self-harm (11 per cent).

In response, those surveyed suggested that the most common interventions were phased return to work (95 per cent), reduced workloads (88 per cent), occupational health support (87 per cent), employee assistance programmes (84 per cent) and counselling (83 per cent). Learning interventions included manager support (56 per cent) and 'resilience and mindfulness training' (43 per cent).

Overall, the research accorded with the prior studies that indicate a worsening situation. Over half of respondents reported that the number of working days lost to mental health issues was increasing (compared to only 10 per cent who thought they were reducing) and 43 per cent of respondents thought the level of mental well-being among employees was getting worse. On the positive side, 45 per cent identified a growing willingness of staff to talk about mental health issues, suggesting that the stigma of mental health is gradually being reduced. However, this positive development must be set against the finding that 61 per cent of respondents suggested that an employee known to suffer from a mental health condition would see their career negatively affected to some extent.

related to work. There is therefore a public policy and economic rationale for addressing ill health among the working population.

THE BUSINESS CASE FOR THE EFFECTIVE MANAGEMENT OF EMPLOYEE WELL-BEING

There are two broad rationales for managing employee well-being. The first reflects the ethical principle that it is a social duty for employers to give due consideration to employee health, safety and welfare. The alternative rationale is that protecting employees from ill health and positively promoting well-being make good business sense. Whilst employers increasingly make claims for greater social responsibility this tends to be underpinned with the hard-nosed business rationale of improving individual and organisational performance rather than any underlying altruism. In other words, it is the business case for employee well-being that tends to be most compelling for employers.

First and foremost, the business benefits of effective H&S management are associated with the direct costs of employee ill health and workplace accidents, such as the costs of employee absence or increased employer insurance premiums. Moreover, an increasingly complex legal framework places considerable obligations on employers that heighten the potential for employee litigation for employer negligence or ineffective H&S policies and practices. However, the business case for a more strategic approach to managing employee well-being that goes beyond legal compliance focuses on its contribution to organisational performance. Put simply, healthy and fit employees are essential to ensuring that a company remains efficient and profitable (Institute of Directors, 2007) and they are more likely to be more engaged, less likely to be absent from work for spurious reasons or to leave the organisation (CIPD, 2007d). For instance, a study by the Harvard Medical School and the Institute for Health and Productivity Management suggests that the healthiest 25 per cent of the workforce is 18 per cent more productive than the least healthy quarter (Jackson and Cox, 2006). Fundamentally, promoting employee well-being and providing a safe working environment would appear to be key attributes of a 'good' employer (Acas, 2009c) and improve the ability to attract, motivate and retain staff through a demonstration that employees are valued. The effective management of employee well-being is, therefore, connected to the wider claim that HRM can positively impact on both individual and organisational performance through the development of a positive psychological contract and increasing employee identification with organisational objectives. Many of the factors associated with high levels of employee engagement (and subsequently improved performance and lowered intention to quit) such as satisfaction with working conditions, task discretion and employee involvement (CIPD, 2006c) fall within the broad concerns of employee well-being. As more employers recognise such benefits, health and well-being in the workplace are steadily 'rising up the business agenda' (CIPD, 2007d).

Nonetheless, whilst the business case for effective management of the health, safety and well-being of the workforce appears clear, there are pressures on management practice which might preclude such a strategic approach. As noted elsewhere in this book, many of the competitive pressures on organisations act both to stress the importance of investment in human resources and, conversely, place greater pressure on managers to maintain tight control over costs, reflecting the tension between long-term strategic and short-term operational demands. Where immediate operational demands are prioritised over H&S considerations, the management of H&S can be reduced to reluctant compliance with the law or a disregard for even the basics of good practice. A failure to recognise the importance of employee well-being in organisational decision-making can, however, have a number of negative consequences. For example, Boyd (2002) observes that customer abuse of staff is exacerbated by organisational policies focused on cost-cutting which place strain both on employees and business processes. This tension is likely to be particularly difficult for line managers with both performance and HR responsibilities to reconcile, even where corporate policy is sound and emphasises their responsibility in protecting worker well-being. Robinson and Smallman (2006) report that a weak H&S culture prevails in most firms with little evidence of employee consultation over health and safety, a problem exacerbated by declining trade union reach and power and a widespread failure among employers to implement the legal requirements for employee representation (Walters et al., 2005).

A clear problem in presenting the business case for employee well-being is that whilst in an ideal world there would be evidence of the clear quantifiable positive outcomes of well-being initiatives, firms are likely to have to take it on faith, or at least partly on the basis of anecdotal evidence, that the health of their workforce is good for business. The impact of well-being initiatives can, however, be measured in a number of ways that might prove persuasive of their positive benefit to the firm. Absence statistics can be used to identify both absolute levels of absenteeism and 'hotspots' of particular injury or illness risks resulting in absence or those parts of the business worst affected. To reflect the wider concern of well-being beyond health problems, employee attitude surveys can be used to assess the health of the employment relationship, for example, by gauging levels of job satisfaction.

Further online reading This article explores attitudes towards workplace health and safety among the owner–managers of Danish SMEs and identifies a range of attitudes towards responsibility for workplace H&S, interpretation of risk and the role of regulation.

Hasle, P., Limborg, H. J., Kallehave, T., Klitgaard, C. and Andersen, T. R. (2012) The working environment in small firms: Responses from owner–managers, *International Small Business Journal*, 30: 622–39.

BOX 14.3
HRM IN PRACTICE

Managing stress at Enterprise Rent-A-Car

Enterprise Rent-A-Car is the largest car rental company in the world with an annual turnover of more than $16.4 billion and a rental and leasing fleet of over 1 million vehicles spread across some 8,100 locations worldwide. Globally, the firm employs 82,000 employees including over 3,000 in the UK across 360 locations.

As a well-regarded employer of both graduate and school-leavers, Enterprise Rent-A-Car UK has a young workforce and takes seriously its responsibility to support individuals at the outset of their careers, including helping manage the stress of transition from education to employment. This proactive support includes extensive employee training to ensure preparedness for their roles, provision of information and resources on 'coping' and the creation of a supportive and open workplace culture where discussing stress, anxiety and depression is not taboo.

The approach taken to stress management at Enterprise is informed by a stress policy statement that opens with the statement that:

> We are committed to protecting the health, safety and welfare of our employees and recognise that workplace stress is a health and safety issue and acknowledge the importance of identifying and reducing workplace stressors.

In seeking to create an culture where employees felt able to discuss mental ill health, Enterprise UK established a series of 'lunch and learn' events for employees and managers which looked to reduce the stigma associated with mental health concerns through highlighting its prevalence in the UK and discussed definitions, common symptoms and the character traits of those more prone to suffering from a stress-related illness.

In supporting staff who experience stress and who take a leave of absence, the organisation identifies a number of practices that constitute good practice:

- *responding quickly* where mental health is reported, by referring individuals to occupational health

- *involving the employee's support network* to support the process of recovery

- *considering each case separately* and being flexible when re-integrating affected employees back into the workplace and regularly checking on progress

- *thinking creatively* in supporting the transition back to work after leave through seeking alternative opportunities where return to their previous job is not appropriate

- *regular progress checks* to ensure that, even after the phased return is complete, ongoing dialogue and support are provided.

Source: IDS, 2011c; www.enterprisealive.co.uk/about-us/ (accessed 18 August 2015)

THE UK LEGAL FRAMEWORK

Organisational practice in respect of employee health, safety and welfare is at least partially influenced by the legal framework within which the firm operates. In the UK, H&S is a complex legal area and it is not the purpose of this section to give a comprehensive account of all legislative provision, rather an outline of the broad approach adopted and the key statutory provisions.

Lewis and Sargeant (2009: 155) suggest that the primary purpose of UK H&S law is to 'make work safe so that it does not cause personal injury ... but provision also has to be made for the compensation of people who nevertheless suffer injury'. In other words, it has a primarily preventative intent, but also a punitive dimension through criminal sanctions and the provision for victims to seek compensation through the civil courts by suing their employer for negligent conduct or breach of a statutory duty. Injury covered by the law refers to both physical and mental impairment caused either by accident or illness.

Health and Safety at Work Act 1974

The principal act governing workplace H&S in the UK is the Health and Safety at Work Act 1974 (HASAWA 1974). It is a framework or enabling act that facilitates the creation of associated regulations and it is the vehicle through which EU Directives in this area are normally implemented (Lewis and Sargeant, 2009). HASAWA 1974 promotes a self-regulatory approach where the onus is placed on employers and employees to identify and minimise workplace risks to injury and illness, in all workplaces and in relation to all forms of work activity. The underlying rationale for the act was to encourage good practice rather than stipulating rules to be applied in all situations, although in certain operational areas, legislation does exist to give unambiguous guidance to employers regarding acceptable practice. Overall, the provisions of HASAWA 1974, and associated regulations, establish a range of rights and responsibilities for different actors in the workplace – employers, employees and other parties such as sub-contractors and manufacturers/suppliers of articles or substances used in the workplace – replacing the prior emphasis on prescribed employer actions in respect of specified buildings, machinery and equipment.

The self-regulatory approach allows for a degree of managerial discretion and judgement in how or whether to deal with potential risks to H&S and is operationalised in the act through repeated reference to the phrase 'as far as is reasonably practicable' in respect of specific employer duties. For instance, Section 2(1) provides that 'It shall be the duty of every employer to ensure, so far as is reasonably practicable, the health, safety and welfare at work of all his employees'. Therefore, the duties under HASAWA 1974 do not require the employer to do 'everything that is physically possible to achieve safety, only that the risks be weighted against the trouble and expense of eliminating or reducing them' (Lewis and Sargeant, 2009: 157). In certain circumstances, what is reasonably practicable might reflect contemporary good practice or existing industry standards and, therefore, employers must ensure they ascertain what constitutes appropriate efforts to minimise risk to reflect these standards. However, employers are not expected to predict unforeseen circumstances that might result in injury or illness. Part of the underlying rationale for adopting a self-regulatory approach is to better engage employers in taking responsibility for H&S and to develop approaches to managing H&S appropriate to the specific workplace. However, the effectiveness of this approach has been questioned, in particular the extent to which it actively promotes employee well-being as an organisational priority, particularly where worker representation is weak (James and Walters, 2002).

Statutory duties under HASAWA 1974

As noted in Chapter 2, employers and employees have a number of common law duties of care relating to H&S. HASAWA 1974 reiterates, supports and extends these obligations and provides for criminal sanctions for non-compliance, such as fines and imprisonment.

DUTIES ON THE EMPLOYER Employers have a duty of care towards their employees to maintain a safe working environment and to take steps to safeguard employees against hazards that are reasonably foreseeable. This obligation is underpinned by a number of more specific duties. These include ensuring the provision and maintenance of machinery and systems of work that are safe and without risk to health, ensuring the safety of employees and absence of risk to health in connection with the use, handling, storage and transport of articles and substances and the maintenance of work premises that are not prejudicial to the health, safety and welfare of employees. The legislation also requires employers to ensure employees are able to work safely through appropriate means of selecting competent employees and providing them with training, information and adequate supervision. Employers are also obliged to establish appropriate procedures to be followed in the event of 'serious and imminent danger' to workers. The employers' statutory duty of care extends to non-employees who are legitimately on work premises (for example, visitors, contractors or customers).

In addition to these general duties, employers are required to prepare, and revise as appropriate, a written statement of their general H&S policy, including the arrangements for enacting that policy, and to communicate this statement to all employees. Whilst the legislation does not provide any specific guidance regarding the content of this policy – reflecting the view that employers should find 'home-grown' solutions to H&S concerns – Lewis and Sargeant (2009) note that as an absolute minimum the safety policy should deal with the various responsibilities of all employees, from the board of directors down to shopfloor workers, general safety precautions, mechanisms for dealing with special hazards, provision for routine inspections, training, emergency procedures and arrangements for consulting the workforce. Employers are obliged to appoint one or more 'competent persons' (preferably an employee but this can also be an external advisor or consultant) to assist them in implementing the measures needed to comply with the legislation.

Complementary to the self-regulatory approach, the H&S legislation also encourages and provides for employee involvement in addressing workplace H&S matters, enabling recognised trade unions to appoint H&S representatives and requiring employers to set up a safety committee (if requested by two or more appointed representatives) to keep workplace H&S measures under review. Where unions are not recognised, employees have a similar right to elect representatives for the purposes of consultation or insist that employers consult directly with staff. As well as a right to be consulted over the full range of H&S issues, union representatives have a right to carry out workplace investigations and inspections, to make recommendations to employers and to consider employee complaints. Non-union representatives have a weaker set of powers (for example, they have no right to inspection). All safety representatives are entitled to the necessary information and training, reasonable paid time off work during normal working hours and appropriate facilities to enable them to fulfil their duties.

DUTIES ON THE EMPLOYEE   In order to promote individual employee responsibility for H&S at work, HASAWA 1974 imposes two general duties on employees in the workplace. First, employees have a duty to 'take reasonable care of the health and safety of themselves and of others who may be affected by their acts or omissions' (for example, by avoiding reckless behaviour, complying with safety rules and procedures and ensuring the correct use of equipment and substances). A failure to comply with this duty can result in disciplinary procedures being invoked and the possibility of prosecution. Second, employees have a duty to cooperate with their employer to enable compliance with the employer's statutory duties, for example, by reporting any work situation that they consider might present serious and immediate danger and notifying their employer of any shortcomings in the H&S arrangements, even where no immediate danger exists.

HASAWA 1974

Further discussion of the UK's legal framework covering workplace health and safety, including those regulations which enact the HASAWA 1974 and how the law is developed and enforced, can be found on the book's companion website: https://edge.sagepub.com/wilton3e.

BOX 14.4
UNDERSTAND

H&S and the European Union

H&S has been a central concern of social policy in the European Union, partly driven by a desire to harmonise H&S standards across member states. Consequently, under qualified majority voting (QMV) H&S proposals cannot be vetoed by any one member state and therefore workplace H&S in member states has been significantly shaped by EU directives. One such directive is the Working Time Directive adopted in 1993 and subsequently implemented in the UK through the Working Time Regulations 1998. The main provisions of the Regulations include:

- a maximum 48-hour working week (averaged over a 17-week period)
- protection for workers against suffering a detriment for a refusal to work more than 48 hours

- limit of an average 8 hours work every 24 hours for night workers
- free health assessments for night workers
- a minimum of 28 days' paid annual leave (including time off for public holidays)
- a minimum of 24 consecutive hours off per week
- a minimum of 11 consecutive hours' rest in every 24 hours
- in-work rest breaks of 20 minutes when working time is more than six hours.

Importantly, however, in the UK an employer and employee can enter into an individual written agreement to opt out of the 48-hour limit. There was considerable debate at the time the Directive was established over the extent to which such regulation should be considered under the heading of 'H&S', particularly from the UK government.

MANAGING HEALTH, SAFETY AND WELL-BEING AT WORK

The legal framework governing H&S at work provides the backdrop against which the management of employee well-being is set. A primary concern for the management of employee well-being is, therefore, ensuring that workplace policies, practices, activities and the working environment comply with legal requirements, including codes of practice and HSE guidelines, and ensuring that statutory responsibilities are clearly communicated and understood.

Reflecting the employer's obligation, the starting point for the effective management of H&S is the development of an organisation's H&S policy. This policy should reflect the specific hazards of the workplace and set out the organisation's general approach to H&S, key responsibilities, the policy objectives and the arrangements in place to achieve these objectives. A second concern for the management of employee well-being is the wider organisational approach adopted towards people management and ensuring 'horizontal fit' between policies to address employee well-being and other elements of the HR mix.

Initiatives that might emanate from a concern for employee well-being can have a positive impact on broader HR aims and vice versa. For example, employee involvement in job or process redesign can help to minimise the possibility of work-related stress as well as improving productivity or quality. It is important that a contingent or flexible approach is adopted in the management of employee well-being to ensure that policies and practices are relevant to all employees and the benefits are clearly communicated. Flexible approaches to workplace H&S are likely to be more effective and aid in the development of a positive H&S culture that promotes joint responsibility. As discussed in Chapter 1, contemporary models of HRM stress that the role of 'employee champion' is seen as a parallel responsibility to that of 'strategic partner', balancing the needs of the employee with those of the organisation. This requires HR specialists to connect the operational concerns of everyday employee H&S and legal compliance with that of promoting employee well-being as a contributor to the achievement of organisational objectives, which can prove challenging at an operational level (Brown et al., 2009). Indeed, some HR practitioners may consider concern for employee welfare to be a retrograde distraction from more strategic considerations.

Further online reading This article examines the relationship between the employee-centred and management-centred roles of HR professionals and the extent to which the two are compatible in the area of employee well-being.

Brown, M., Metz, I., Cregan, C. and Kulik, C. T. (2009) Irreconcilable differences? Strategic human resource management and employee well-being, *Asia Pacific Journal of Human Resources*, 47 (3): 270–94.

The 2013e CIPD absence management survey found that in 2010, 46 per cent of UK organisations surveyed had an employer well-being strategy or similar initiative to help improve the physical and mental health of their workforce, up from 33 per cent in 2009 (CIPD, 2013e). The most common initiatives used to support employee well-being (available to all employees regardless of grade or seniority) were access to counselling services (73 per cent of employers surveyed), employee assistance programmes (69 per cent), support to stop smoking (51 per cent) and advice on healthy eating (49 per cent).

ABSENCE MANAGEMENT SURVEY **2013**

BOX 14.5
RESEARCH INSIGHT

SMEs and workplace health and safety

Throughout this book, a dominant theme in the discussion of employment practices and the experience of work in SMEs has been of heterogeneity and difference. Commensurately, in the area of workplace health and safety, Hasle et al. (2012) found notable variety in the attitudes of owner-managers of SMEs in Danish construction and metal industries on risk, responsibility for the working environment and attitudes towards regulation.

Research among this group of owner-managers found that whilst most take a positive approach to protecting the health and safety of their employees, they also 'talk risk down', typically taking the view that normal work routines and the knowledge and experience of their staff are sufficient to prevent accidents. Where accidents occur, owner-managers tend to blame human error, thus stressing that such risk is unforeseeable. In all, the research found that concern for workplace health and safety was typically viewed in a reactive manner, for example, in making workplace adjustments in response to ill health rather than to avoid it, and did not consider the management of the working environment beyond a concern for isolated activities and their attendant risk and adherence to tiresome bureaucracy. Moreover, the authors also report that a number of managers tended to neglect the working environment, partly as a result of a preoccupation with other aspects of the short-term demands of running a small business and a lack of management resources.

The research found a widespread tendency for owner-managers to push at least a part of the employer responsibility for the working environment on to employees, despite regulation in Denmark

making it clear that business owners carry the main responsibility. The authors suggest that both the downgrading of risk and attempt to distribute responsibility for health and safety relate to the close social relationships that exist in SMEs and a desire to avoid blame, and personal guilt, if a worker was to be injured. Subsequently, owner-managers in SMEs can be seen as being required to balance the requirements to demonstrate acceptance of a degree of responsibility for workplace H&S (and, thus, avoid looking careless and cynical in the eyes of employees) and to leave a considerable share of the responsibility to employees.

Taking the views of owner-managers together, the authors suggest four categories of attitude towards the working environment:

1 *Avoidance* – the owner-manager tries to ignore the working environment.

2 *A necessary evil* – the owner-manager accepts that a basic control of the working environment is necessary in order to avoid trouble with the authorities, but at the lowest possible level. He or she considers the control activities as a waste of time and money.

3 *Standards must be met* – the owner-manager accepts the need to comply with working environment regulations to ensure a reasonable standard that is acceptable for both employees, customers, authorities, and other stakeholders.

4 *Business strategy* – the owner-manager considers the working environment to be a natural part of a successful business strategy, believing that it is important to maintain a high standard and be proactive in control measures.

**HEALTH AND
SAFETY AT WORK**

Employee assistance programmes

A growth area in the management of employee well-being at work is the use of employee assistance programmes (EAPs) (IDS, 2008c). EAPs are a service provided to employees of an organisation, offering support, advice and information in areas related to employee well-being. This support and advice can be legal (for example, regarding employment issues), emotional (for example, relating to stress, anxiety or depression), domestic (such as divorce, separation or relating to care of children or the elderly), or financial (for example, dealing with debt), or relating to work and careers (for example, work–life balance or workplace harassment or bullying) or health (for instance, relating to drugs or alcohol misuse). These services are often available not only to employees but also to their immediate families. They also often offer management support services to advise managers on dealing with HR issues, for example, employee discipline, equal opportunities or employee welfare. EAPs might also provide support for 'critical incidents' (such as workplace fires) and provide benchmarking data to employers to help them identify problem areas of the business or company-wide concerns. Whilst the particular services offered by EAPs differ depending on the specific requirements of the contracting organisation, there are typically a number of core methods of delivery, including a confidential round-the-clock telephone support and information helpline, a dedicated website to provide information and advice, and access to face-to-face counselling to deal with certain personal issues.

Whilst EAPs clearly provide a support function to aid employee well-being, this is not provided for altruistic purposes but rather to address issues that might otherwise affect individual work performance or lead to absence, lowered morale or exit from the organisation. In one sense, focusing on counselling as the means by which to resolve issues depoliticises workplace problems, making them the responsibility of the individual employee rather than a collective concern. However, introducing EAPs for reasons of cost-saving or increased productivity alone, with little concern for wider policies and practices providing employee support, is likely to be ineffective (Arthur, 2000).

The rise in popularity of EAPS is consistent with a number of the trends in HRM discussed in Chapter 1. First, it reflects a trend of greater outsourcing of HRM activities. EAPs are typically provided by dedicated service providers who will supply a tailored service to clients' employees. Second, it reflects the HR function's move away from direct responsibility for employee welfare towards more strategic concerns. Third, the line manager support aspect of EAPs reflects both the increased devolution of responsibility for people management issues and increased use of self-service approaches to HR support. Finally, it reflects the further individualisation of the employment relationship and a continued desire to move away from the collective resolution of workplace problems.

Occupational health

During the twentieth century, occupational health developed as a discipline of medicine aimed at helping in the care of workers. Occupational health (OH) services assist in the rehabilitation of sick workers, seek to prevent accidents through risk assessment, support those responsible for H&S and contribute to the design of jobs (for example, by advising on ergonomics – the 'fit' between people and their work and working environment). Reflecting the wider concerns of employee well-being, OH services increasingly seek to support the health and well-being of employees rather than only those who are sick by providing advice, guidance, training, counselling and education, providing health assessments and monitoring and promoting healthy lifestyles. OH services have tended to be more prevalent in larger organisations either in the form of an internal occupational health specialist or department or through an external service provider. CIPD (2013e) report that 53 per cent of employers use occupational health services to deal with short-term absence, 74 per cent for managing long-term absence and 44 per cent to identify and reduce stress at work.

WHOSE RESPONSIBILITY IS WORKPLACE WELL-BEING?

Ultimately, workplace well-being is the responsibility of both employers and employees. Comprehensive organisational H&S policies and employer compliance with the law will be largely ineffective if employees fail to meet their legal duties. Similarly, investment in well-being initiatives is likely to be wasted if employees make little use of provision. Not surprisingly, worker consultation over well-being initiatives is associated with better H&S outcomes than unilateral management action (Walters et al., 2005), not least in reducing the risk of injury or illness, improving working conditions or avoiding poorly designed work systems. However, whilst employee cooperation with employers in H&S in the workplace is implied in the contract of employment, well-being initiatives tend to widen the concern of employers to encompass activities undertaken outside

---

BOX 14.6
UNDERSTAND

Drug and alcohol misuse and employment

In the previous chapter the question was asked: to what extent should employers seek to control the behaviour of employees outside of the workplace? A similar ethical question can be raised regarding employee well-being. Employee well-being initiatives often seek to promote healthy living, for example by offering support for employees to give up smoking or the provision of workplace gyms and healthy eating canteen choices. The well-being agenda has also renewed a focus on the organisational effects of drug and alcohol misuse and how it can be managed effectively. This raises a number of ethical concerns regarding the boundaries between personal and working lives and employer intervention in employees' personal choices, for example, through drug testing. Nonetheless, greater employer recognition of the link between employee well-being and performance has meant greater scrutiny of, and attempts to influence, employee lifestyle.

Whilst alcohol misuse has long been a concern of employers, the workplace consequences of drug use and its after-effects are an issue of growing significance. The Institute of Alcohol Studies (IAS, 2009) estimate that the combined effect of increased sickness absence, the inability to work (unemployment and early retirement)

and premature deaths among economically active people account for a total alcohol-related output loss to the UK economy of up to £6.4 billion a year. Alcohol-related sickness absence alone is estimated to cost the UK economy between £1.2 billion and £1.8 billion. CIPD (2007f) report that employee drug use costs British industry £800 million a year. In a survey of approximately 8,000 workers, a report by the drug-testing firm Concateno (2012) suggested that more than 1 million workers (1 in 30 of the workforce) in Britain go to work with illegal drugs in their system, most commonly, cannabis, opiates and cocaine, with the most prevalent usage among 25–34 year olds (see also Smith et al., 2004). Concerns regarding employee alcohol and drug misuse focus on a number of areas, including the impact on individual health (and its subsequent effect on work attendance and employee turnover), the H&S implications for the user and their colleagues, and the deterioration in performance, discipline and work quality.

Despite the considerable costs to business, CIPD (2007b) report that only 60 per cent of employers have a combined policy for drug and alcohol problems and rules about alcohol consumption during work time and the possession of drugs and alcohol on the premises, and only 22 per cent report carrying out any testing of employees for drugs or alcohol misuse.

---

of the workplace. This raises significant ethical issues over the extent to which employers should seek to influence and improve employees' lifestyle choices (see Box 14.6).

CIPD (2007d) note that the biggest obstacles to the development of workplace well-being initiatives are a lack of resources and failure to gain senior manager buy-in. Employee well-being initiatives are likely to be most successful where they are implemented within an inclusive and respectful organisational culture in which a concern for well-being is embedded and where joint responsibility for health, safety and welfare is promoted. Without senior management support, the creation of such a culture is likely to be difficult. The success of well-being initiatives also lies with the line managers who are charged with their implementation. Line managers are best placed to understand the impact of job design, processes or workload on the individual employee and help to prevent damage to health or counsel on the impact of personal matters on performance. However, the tension between operational concerns and employee well-being is likely to be most keenly felt by line managers and, consequently, employee health, safety and welfare may not receive adequate attention. To ensure that managers prioritise employee well-being, it might usefully form the basis of performance indicators in managerial appraisals.

TACKLING WORK-RELATED STRESS

TACKLING WORK-
RELATED STRESS

As discussed previously, the causes of work-related stress are complex. They include the nature of the work being undertaken, the working environment and workplace relationships, as well as an individual's capacity to cope with particular situations or activities. It follows that tackling stress can be problematic.

Stress management interventions can be preventative – focused on ensuring that systems and the working environment do not negatively impact on employees' mental health – or curative/therapeutic – concerning the diagnosis of an individual and helping them to recover from stress incidents or to better cope with the demands placed upon them in future. The former is likely to be beneficial to the entire workforce, whereas remedial action tends to focus on dealing with individuals. Clarke and Cooper (2000) suggest that tertiary interventions (individually focused practices, such as encouraging healthy lifestyles through exercise, meditation or relaxation techniques) and secondary interventions (those focused on the organisation–individual interface, such as training in coping strategies and stress management) tend to be more common than primary interventions (those focused on the organisational causes of stress, such as poor employee selection processes, job design or work environment). However, tackling the root causes of work-related stress through primary interventions is likely to be more effective in the longer term by reducing the risk of future mental health problems.

WORK–LIFE BALANCE

WORK LIFE
BALANCE

If employee well-being is understood as both a product of work and non-work activities then it is clear that an imbalance between an employee's work and personal life is likely to be a source of stress and, potentially, ill health. The concept of work–life balance has gained in currency over recent years and refers to the satisfactory reconciliation of the often-competing demands of work and non-work responsibilities and leisure activities (Ackers and El-Sawad, 2006), 'without undue pressures from one undermining the satisfactory experience of the other' (Noon and Blyton, 2007: 356). As Hyman and Summers (2003) note, however, each of these terms presents definitional difficulties, not least the problems associated with clearly delineating between work and the other elements of one's life and the increasing blurring of these boundaries caused by, for example, the ubiquity of electronic communications.

Nonetheless, just as there has been growing employer recognition of the importance of employee well-being to individual performance, there has been a commensurate acknowledgement that where work impinges upon non-work activities and creates conflict between the two then this can be detrimental to both employee health and work performance.

The importance of work–life balance as an employee and employer concern has been driven by a number of changes in the context of employment. These include increasing female participation in the workforce (and the associated growth in the number of working mothers and dual-career couples with dependent children), an ageing workforce, increasing responsibility for care of elderly relatives among the working population and significant activity by trade unions on work–life and family-friendly policies. Moreover, many workers are under pressure to adopt more flexible work patterns, often in response to consumer demands for longer opening or operating hours. A further driver of the need for greater work–life balance is the legal framework surrounding working hours and flexible working. The legislation around working time flexibility – often emanating from the European Union – in particular has grown in significance, in recognition of employee desire for work–life balance and the need for greater protection of workers who work non-standard hours, often due to non-work commitments. Examples in the UK include the Maternity and Parental Leave Regulations (1999) and the Working Time Regulations (1998).

The management of work–life balance encompasses policies and practices that permit some flexibility with respect to hours of work, allow people to work from home, provide leave arrangements that allow people to either meet their non-work commitments or realise non-work goals and provide workplace facilities to assist employees to attend work (for example, crèches).

At a basic level, work–life balance is about working time and the impact of long working hours on employees' personal lives. However, White et al. (2003) found that whilst long working hours were the most significant influence on 'job-to-home spillover', a range of workplace practices also had an impact on negative spillover (for example, appraisal systems, group-based forms of work organisation and individual incentives all contribute to the imposition of the public sphere on the private), suggesting that employees do not always benefit from high performance work practices (Ramsay et al., 2000).

Similarly, Robinson and Smallman (2006) report that many characteristics of modern workplaces and work are associated with a significant risk to health, particularly flexible working practices and the interaction between work and non-work. Concerns for work–life balance, therefore, go beyond simply the length of one's working hours and include patterns of work (for example, working nights, shifts or unsociable hours) and the level of 'energy' employers expect to be expended in the work sphere. Certain work patterns can contribute to poor physical and mental ill health, for example, night-shift working can be both a source of fatigue and mental health problems, and represent an increased risk of cardiovascular mortality (Harrington, 2001).

The potential impact of long working hours and flexible or non-standard working patterns is partly dependent on whether such patterns of work are imposed or chosen. If imposed they are more likely to create tension and stress, whereas if they are chosen they can constitute an enabler of work–life balance. Work–life balance, therefore, is partly a question of control.

The business case for the effective management of employee work–life balance reflects better individual performance at work, reduced absenteeism through ill health or conflicting demands, positioning an organisation as an 'employer of choice', lower levels of labour turnover, and greater employee commitment and motivation through feeling valued by the employer. Hogarth et al. (2001) report significant agreement among employers about the benefits of providing for greater work–life balance through the provision of flexible working practices: 91 per cent agreed people work best when they can balance work and life; 59 per cent agreed that the employer has responsibility to help people find this balance; 52 per cent believed that staff absenteeism and turnover were lower as a result.

Further online reading This article examines work to home 'spillover' in two new sectors of the economy – call centres and software development. The article examines how workers in these sectors attempt to delineate between home and work lives and the factors that shape workers' ability to do so.

Hyman, J., Scholarios, D. and Baldry, C. (2005) Getting on or getting by? Employee flexibility and coping strategies for home and work, *Work, Employment and Society*, 19 (4): 705–25.

Whilst there is evidence to support the positive benefits that accrue from offering flexible working arrangements, and extensive legislation to both promote and enforce a better work–life balance, problems associated with its provision remain. Some employers might resist more flexible arrangements because of the costs involved. For example, providing the means so that employees can work from home can require investment in ICT hardware and support. Managing workers who might be on different working patterns can also create problems for supervision and the effective integration of remote or flexible workers with those working on-site or standard hours. Such problems can create difficulties in securing line manager support for flexible work patterns, regardless of organisational support for work–life balance. Indeed, Kersley et al. (2006) reported that the majority of managers believed it was individuals' responsibility to balance work and life. This can lead to the inconsistent application of organisational policy, for example, regarding employees' entitlement to flexible working arrangements or the modification of workload to reflect alternative arrangements.

For employees, there is evidence that access to flexible working for some groups of workers, particularly men or those without dependent children, can be limited (Kersley et al., 2006). This can cause resentment among employees, who feel treated less favourably. There is also notable variation in access to arrangements to better balance work and personal life between the private and public sectors (Hyman and Summers, 2003), between unionised and non-unionised workplaces (Kersley et al., 2006) and between workers of differential labour market strength (Hyman et al., 2005). The legislation covering work–life balance and family-friendly working arrangements has also been criticised. For example, despite the previous Labour government's stated commitment to supporting families, McColgan (2000) notes the minimalist approach taken to the enactment of EU social policy from which much legislation in this area derives, a situation that compares unfavourably with much of the EU.

SUMMARY POINTS

PROMOTING EMPLOYEE WELL-BEING

- Employee well-being is concerned with maintaining a safe working environment, promoting supportive, nurturing and respectful workplace relationships, enabling individual employees to achieve their potential through sympathetic job design, and HR policies and practices that encourage and support good physical and mental health both inside and outside of the workplace.

- Discussions around the notion of 'dignity at work' have tended to focus on the absence of bullying and harassment, but can also incorporate a concern for wider aspects of the organisation of work, working environment and social relationships.

- The economic and social impact of work-related ill health provides a compelling business case for the effective and proactive management of employee well-being.

- H&S problems continue to proliferate, often as a direct result of, or exacerbated by, organisational practices. This is particularly the case with regard to the increasing incidence of mental health problems.

- An integrative and strategic approach to the management of employee well-being represents a natural extension of other aspects of good practice HRM where attempts to evoke employee commitment and engagement are integrated with mechanisms to manage employee health.

- The UK legal framework advocates a self-regulatory approach to workplace H&S which is the joint responsibility of employers and employees.

- Employer interventions in employee well-being – particularly in the area of alcohol and drug use – raise a number of ethical questions regarding the extent to which employers can and should seek to influence lifestyle choices.

- Employee assistance programmes represent an increasingly popular means of managing employee well-being and seeking to ensure that employee problems do not impede individual performance, through counselling and advice. However, EAPs are criticised for individualising and externalising workplace problems.

- Both legislation and employer practices to support work–life balance have proliferated in recent years, reflecting changing labour market demography and in recognition of the importance of the effective management of the work–life boundary. However, access to working patterns associated with work–life balance is unevenly distributed.

SELF-TEST QUESTIONS

1 What are the key dimensions that need addressing when taking a holistic approach to employee well-being?

2 What are the main trends in workplace H&S associated with the modern workplace and contemporary industrial structures?

3 Outline the business case for the proactive management of employee health, safety and well-being.

4 Why does the UK legal framework advocate a self-regulatory approach to workplace H&S?

5 What duties do UK legislation place on employees in respect of workplace H&S?

6 What role do HR specialists play in workplace H&S and in the management of employee well-being?

TEST YOURSELF

TEST YOURSELF

Want to know more about this chapter? Review what you have been learning by visiting:
https://edge.sagepub.com/wilton3e

- Print out or download the chapter summaries for quick revision
- Test yourself with multiple-choice questions
- Revise key terms with interactive flashcards

CASE STUDY

Promoting employee well-being at Callahan Packaging

In 2008, the findings of the Black Review into workplace health and well-being were published, advocating a shift in attitudes to ensure that employers and employees recognise both the importance of preventing ill health and the key role the workplace can play in promoting health and well-being. The report reiterated the evidence that work is largely good for health and sought to promote among employers a greater understanding of the business case for investment in health and well-being initiatives and the message that good health is good business. Importantly, the review advocated greater consideration of management attitudes, working relationships, wider HR policies and practices and jobs themselves in thinking about workplace health and well-being.

The review made interesting reading for the senior management team at Callahan Packaging who had introduced a number of the initiatives that were advocated in the previous year. Callahan is a consumer packaging manufacturer based in South Wales which employs approximately 450 staff in a manufacturing plant producing rigid plaster containers for the food manufacturing industry. The majority of its workforce are employed on its 24-hour, seven-days-a-week production line working 12-hour shifts in four shift teams. In the first half of 2007, Callahan had undertaken a workplace health audit, funded by a partnership between the local authority and a local university, to assess both the reported and actual health of its workforce and its link to workplace productivity. The local authority was keen for Callahan to be involved because they represent a sizeable employer in the area. Callahan was similarly keen to become involved in the project because senior management felt it might provide some solutions to a range of employment problems it was experiencing at the time, including unacceptable

levels of employee sickness absence and turnover which were impacting on productivity, product quality and the company finances. Whilst the work that much of the workforce does is largely repetitive and routine, training employees to work a particular piece of machinery can be time-consuming and costly. Subsequently, absence and turnover have sizeable financial implications. Moreover, the hiring of inexperienced temps at short notice to work on the production line often had a negative impact on both productivity and quality. Senior management at Callahan also saw their involvement in the initiative as an opportunity to develop its focus on corporate social responsibility, as part of a wider marketing strategy, and to improve relations with the local community and position Callahan as an employer of choice in the area.

Callahan draws many of its semi-skilled and unskilled workers from an area of relative deprivation with high levels of unemployment and poor health. The workplace health audit found that most of the workforce displayed low levels of physical health, even among younger workers: 45 per cent were smokers and over 60 per cent reported drinking to excess at least once a week. The audit also found low levels of physical activity (aside from their work) and poor dietary choices. Alongside its health audit, Callahan conducted its first-ever employee attitude survey. Of most concern, the survey found that only 48 per cent of employees were satisfied with their jobs, 28 per cent were actively looking to leave the company and 56 per cent would consider alternative employment.

Following analysis of the audit and staff survey findings, Callahan decided to fund a series of staff seminars, presented by healthcare experts and academics from the university, on health issues ranging from smoking to heart disease. Surprised by the level of staff interest in the seminars, senior management, with the assistance of local authority occupational health practitioners, decided to introduce a wider range of workplace initiatives with the following objectives:

- To improve employee quality of life both inside and outside of the workplace.
- To raise staff awareness of health and well-being issues.
- To improve the health and physical fitness of its employees.
- To reduce the incidence of work-related injury and illness.
- To improve productivity, employee attendance and staff morale.

These broad objectives continue to inform Callahan's approach to workplace well-being. Since 2007, the company has invested heavily in its programme not least in building an on-site gymnasium for use by both staff and their families. A number of long-term sickness absentees have successfully used the facility, with the guidance of a workplace well-being advisor, to rehabilitate themselves and returned to work. The company now employs a full-time well-being advisor with whom workers can discuss health problems and who undertakes risk assessments, supports workers in stopping smoking and ensures early intervention in alleviating workplace injury and illness. For example, a number of workers had been to see the advisor suffering from repetitive strain injuries and she was able to offer advice on how to minimise pain and reduce strain in carrying out their work. The advisor also carries out routine health checks, offers counselling to deal with workplace stress or other mental health concerns and runs a slimming club and regular seminars advising on healthy eating. The staff canteen now offers only healthy options and all employees are entitled to two free meals per shift. Outside of the workplace, the company has developed a relationship with a nearby leisure centre who provide a range of regular activities and classes which staff can undertake at reduced prices including tennis, badminton, tai chi, yoga and climbing. The company advisor runs a number of staff sports leagues, for example five-a-side football and badminton, to promote health competition among employees. The company has also set up a 'cycle to work' scheme to allow employees to take advantage of tax and national insurance savings on bike purchases in order to commute to work

Importantly, the well-being initiatives have been put in place as part of a wider set of HR policies and practices designed to engage staff, for example, the establishment of a company council, an employee suggestion scheme and more formal performance management practices.

In order to monitor the impact of the well-being initiatives, Callahan conducts an annual health audit and employee attitude survey. The senior management have been very pleased with the results of the well-being programme and cite the following outcomes as an indication of its continued success:

- employee absenteeism well below the sector average
- reduced cost of hiring temporary workers
- increase in reported employee satisfaction
- increased productivity
- reduced employee turnover and intention to quit.

Questions

1 Identify the well-being initiatives discussed in this case study and whether they represent proactive and reactive interventions and whether they focus on the individual, the organisation or the interface between the two?

2 Based on your analysis, are there any notable areas of employee well-being which Callahan appears to have failed to address?

3 What are the potential long-term implications of the approach to employee well-being that Callahan has adopted?

USEFUL READING

Journal articles

Baldry, C., Bain, P. and Taylor, P. (1997) Sick and tired? Working in the modern office, *Work, Employment and Society*, 11 (3): 519–39.

Drawing on case study research, this article outlines the concept of 'sick building syndrome' and argues the importance of considering the built working environment in an analysis of the causes of occupational ill health.

Hyman, J. and Summers, J. (2003) Lacking balance? Work–life employment practices in the modern economy, *Personnel Review*, 33 (4): 418–29.

This article provides a concise summary of many of the debates around work–life balance and the lightly regulated approach to the issue adopted in the UK. In particular, it identifies seven major problems associated with current UK practice over work–life balance.

Books, book chapters and reports

CIPD (2007) What's Happening with Well-Being at Work? Change Agenda, London: CIPD.

This report outlines the meaning of employee well-being, the business case for its effective management and what such management can involve. It also provides a number of organisational case studies as examples of good practice in the management of well-being.

Lelliott, P., Tulloch, S., Boardman, J., Harvey, S., Henderson, M. and Knapp, M. (2006) Mental Health and Work, London: Royal College of Psychiatrists (available at **www.dwp.gov.uk/docs/hwwb-mental-health-and-work.pdf**).

This report provides a detailed discussion of the incidence and cost of mental health problems in the UK and their causes and impact in the workplace. It also outlines the broader social policy context of mental health.

FURTHER ONLINE READING

The following articles can be accessed for free on the book's companion website **https://edge.sagepub.com/wilton3e**:

Brown, M., Metz, I., Cregan, C. and Kulik, C. T. (2009) Irreconcilable differences? Strategic human resource management and employee well-being, *Asia Pacific Journal of Human Resources*, 47 (3): 270–94.

Cottini, E. and Lucifora, C. (2013) Mental health and working conditions in Europe, *ILR Review*, 66 (4): 958–88.

Hasle, P., Limborg, H. J., Kallehave, T., Klitgaard, C. and Andersen, T. R. (2012) The working environment in small firms: Responses from owner–managers, *International Small Business Journal*, 30: 622–39.

Hyman, J., Scholarios, D. and Baldry, C. (2005) Getting on or getting by? Employee flexibility and coping strategies for home and work, *Work, Employment and Society*, 19 (4): 705–25.

Robinson, A. and Smallman, C. (2006) The contemporary British workplace: A safer and healthier place? *Work, Employment and Society*, 20 (1): 87–107.

Sayer, A. (2007) Dignity at work: Broadening the agenda, *Organization*, 14 (4): 565–81.

Taylor, P., Baldry, C., Bain, P. and Ellis, V. (2003) A unique working environment: Health, sickness and absence management in UK call centres, *Work, Employment and Society*, 17 (3): 435–58.

Want to know more about this chapter? Visit the companion website at: **https://edge.sagepub.com/wilton3e** to access practice questions, videos and selected journal articles to further enhance your study.

CURRENT TRENDS AND FUTURE CHALLENGES IN HRM

CHAPTER OBJECTIVES

- To consider the HRM implications of projected labour market change

- To briefly outline the role of HRM in managing change and in an environment of complexity

- To outline how HRM can contribute to the growing need in work organisations for effective knowledge management

- To consider the management implications of the increasing proportion of the labour market comprised of knowledge workers

- To consider the reasons for the growth of HR outsourcing and shared service centres and the problems associated with outsourcing

- To consider how e-HR can contribute to the effective management of people and the issues surrounding their use.

INTRODUCTION

Chapter 1 introduced a number of broad trends in contemporary HRM. These included the devolution of HR responsibility to line managers, the growth in HR outsourcing to specialist third-party sub-contractors and the increasing importance of e-HR. These trends lie at the heart of attempts to focus the efforts of the HR function more greatly on contributing to the strategic objectives of the organisation. They also reflect organisational attempts to reduce the costs of its HR operations and, therefore, reflect the tension between the desire to strategically manage a firm's workforce and the competing pressure to reduce the cost of doing so. The issues associated with greater devolution of HR responsibility to line managers have been discussed in other chapters in relation to specific functional areas of HRM. Part of the purpose of this chapter is to revisit e-HR and outsourcing and to discuss in more detail how they are acting to shape the HR function now and into the future. It also serves to stress the contemporary importance of HRM in managing organisational change and in ensuring firms cope and thrive in an environment of complexity and unpredictability. The chapter begins, however, by revisiting two key developments in organisational context – workforce ageing and the strategic importance of organisational knowledge – which are acting to shape HRM practice and are likely to continue to be pre-eminent concerns for both HR specialists and line managers in the future.

THE DEVELOPING CONTEXT OF HRM

A chief concern of this book has been to place HRM within its wider strategic, economic and social context and show how a wide range of environmental factors act both to constrain organisational practices and provide opportunities to generate competitive advantage. One of the most important constraints on HRM activity in a given organisation is the relative supply and demand of labour, and Chapter 4 outlined the demographic changes that are shaping the contemporary labour market and to which many organisations have responded through HR policies and practices. These changes included increasing female labour market participation, with the commensurate rise in the number of dual-career couples, and the increasing ethnic diversity of the UK labour supply. Perhaps most pertinently, the chapter discussed how most advanced capitalist economies are experiencing an ageing of the labour force and how, in the future, workers in the 'third age of employment' (Weiss and Bass, 2002) will make up an increasing proportion of available labour (Box 15.1). Therefore, a key challenge for HRM is acknowledging and responding to the requirements of older workers, in order to ensure the retention of critical skills and knowledge, maintain continued engagement and to more actively recruit among this group. Consequently, a critical dimension of HRM, both now and in the immediate future, is devising and enacting policies surrounding flexible working, phased retirement, training and career development to meet the needs of these workers, and providing mentoring and coaching opportunities for them to pass on skills and knowledge to younger employees.

Another theme of Chapter 4 was the changing demand for skills, qualifications and competencies commensurate with long-run economic and technological change. The chapter suggested that there was some consensus that work and employment in a knowledge-driven economy required not only the development and use of new skills for employees but also a fundamental restructuring of the management and organisation of knowledge workers. Subsequently a pre-eminent concern for employers is to facilitate the development and sharing of employee knowledge across organisations for their firm's commercial utility (Thompson and Warhurst, 2003). This has placed ever-greater focus within HRM on its contribution to knowledge creation and sharing for competitive advantage (as discussed later in the chapter). However, the impact of new technology on work and employment is not entirely positive and, whilst there is debate about the nature and extent of its differential impact across the workforce, innovation in technology will inevitably have significant implications for all workers and how these are managed.

Change in the UK labour force

The labour force in the UK is projected to grow continuously until 2037, as the national population grows from 63.7 million in 2012 to 73.3 million. However, the most notable long-term demographic trend reflects an ageing of the labour force over this period, extending recent trends over the next three decades. Whilst the number of people of working age in the population is predicted to grow from 39.4 million in 2012 to 44.2 million in 2037, this reflects a decline in the proportion of the total population that this age group constitutes, from 63 per cent in 2012 to 58 per cent in 2037. At the same time, the number of people in the population who are over the age of 60 will increase from 14 million in 2012 (23 per cent of the population) to 22 million (29 per cent of the population). This reflects the transition beyond the age of 70 of those born in the 'baby boom' of the 1960s.

These projected trends mean that the old-age support ratio – the number of people of working age (from 16 to state pension age) to every person over state pension age – is predicted to rise from 3.21 in mid-2012 to 3.39 in 2037.

Questions

1 What challenges do these labour force projections present for HRM over the next decade?
2 How might firms respond to these anticipated labour market changes?

Source: ONS, 2013a

UK LABOUR MARKET 2015

MANAGING CHANGE AND COMPLEXITY

Two interconnected themes are dominant in assessing the current and future challenges faced by organisations, managers, employees and, therefore, the HRM function: increasing complexity and rapid change. Throughout this book it has been repeated often that firms and managers function in an increasingly unpredictable economic, political and social environment, and that they require organisational structures and processes, and commensurate worker attitudes and aptitudes, which allow them to respond rapidly to continuous shifts and 'shocks', or to act in anticipation of them, both to ensure organisational survival and to gain competitive advantage. All in all, the complexity of operating in an increasingly interconnected, yet unstable, context makes the effective management of change and processes of organisational development critical to business success.

Despite attempts to build flexibility and adaptability into firms in an integral manner (for example, by adopting the flexible organisational structures and work organisation as outlined in Chapter 4) firms will inevitably find themselves increasingly faced with the challenge of having to manage processes of change in a more explicit sense, for instance, in the form of organisational restructuring, business process re-engineering, relocation or downsizing (Datta et al., 2010). Table 15.1 provides an insight into the extent of change in UK workplaces that directly impacts on workers. Perhaps, most notably, it shows that only one-fifth of UK workplaces surveyed experienced no significant changes to work practices, technology or HRM practices, over a 12-month period.

Aside from operational changes such as those in Table 15.1, organisational change might also take the form of expansion into new markets, strategic alliances with other firms or organisational mergers and acquisitions. In each of these scenarios, HRM has a role to play, both on a one-off and continuous basis. For instance, in a merger scenario, HR specialists hold the role of bringing together

TABLE 15.1 *Incidence of workplace change (in 12 months prior to survey in 2011)*

	Overall incidence (% of respondents)	Most important change (% of respondents)
Introduction/upgrading of new technology	48	19
Changes in work techniques	44	16
Changes in work organisation	39	17
Product or service innovation	33	10
New employee involvement initiatives	28	7
Changes in working time arrangements	22	8
Introduction of performance-related pay	8	3
None of the above	21	–

Source: van Wanrooy et al., 2013

two workforces and two sets of HR policies and procedures, as well as facilitating the ongoing creation of a unified corporate culture in the newly created firm. HRM has, therefore, a fundamental role to play in ensuring a firm's ability both to cope with change and to actively alter itself in response to external or internal pressures and events. At a strategic level, this might be concerned with the ongoing aligning of HR strategy to shifting corporate goals. At an operational level, HRM will contribute to the management of change, for example, through managing redundancy or redeployment during organisational restructuring, and lay the foundations for ongoing organisational adaptability (for instance, through construction of a flexible workforce and facilitating continuous learning and development).

Further online reading This article reviews the available literature on employee downsizing and develops an integrative framework that incorporates environmental and organisational drivers of downsizing as well as the implications for individuals and organisations.

Datta, D. K., Guthrie, J. P., Basuil, D. and Pandey, A. (2010) Causes and effects of employee downsizing: A review and synthesis, *Journal of Management*, 36 (1): 281–348.

However, it is important to recognise that whilst many of the developments that precipitate organisational change have their roots in macro-economic or political change, organisational adaptation is ultimately experienced by individuals and, regardless of the reasons for change, it is often a painful and fraught process for those affected. Subsequently, change is often resisted at multiple levels. For individuals, change can be associated with a perceived threat to their job roles, expertise, influence or power within the organisation, as well as a challenge to entrenched values and beliefs, and with disruption to established routines and relationships. The management of the anxiety around disruption to the status quo is, therefore, of pre-eminent concern for HRM. At a group or organisational level, resistance might emanate from a lack of trust in senior management over their ability to manage proposed change, or the motives behind it, and about the need both for change in general and the specific measures proposed.

The likelihood of resistance to change re-emphasises that effective HRM requires the management of politicised processes and relationships whereby change or organisational transformation needs to be understood in terms of its impact on existing power structures, organisational culture(s) and the dominant norms of behaviour and values. Understood in this way, the management of people in organisational change is much more than the alteration, reduction or relocation of physical working arrangements.

There are a number of means by which individual and organisational resistance to change can be overcome, from coercion and manipulation to more positive measures, such as the effective communication of the rationale for change and its likely impact. Poor communication is often cited as a principal cause of resistance to change, as well as contributing to the failure of change processes to yield desired outcomes. Therefore, it makes managerial sense not only to communicate in an open and honest manner regarding change (even where the outcomes of changes might be unpalatable for some) but also to solicit the views of staff in how change can best be managed. To secure employee buy-in to the process, it may even be advantageous to consult staff on necessary changes to yield a particular outcome (for instance, cost-savings) and the best approach for enacting this change.

HR specialists, as well as line managers with people management responsibilities, are clearly critical actors in the effective management of change. Alongside external consultants who might be brought in to manage change processes, these managers and specialists have a key role to play as change 'agents' or 'drivers' managing the many activities connected with bringing about desired change. It stands to reason, therefore, that these agents need the requisite degree of enthusiasm and political, interpersonal and technical skill to be able to implement change, alongside supporting affected employees. Senior management, as often the instigators of wide-scale change, have an equally important role to play in communicating the rationale for and benefits of change (acting as 'champions' for change), providing a vision and strategy for change, anticipating barriers to change and removing or nullifying them, and providing the conditions where a new culture can emerge after the change process (Kotter, 1995).

So far this discussion of management of change has characterised organisational transformation as a planned and foreseeable event amenable to top-down management. However, as has been discussed in relation to organisational strategy formation (Chapter 3) and in respect of organisational development (Chapter 9), change should also be viewed as an emergent process that is not always responsive to top-down control; rather it can emerge from the bottom up and inevitably involves informal, as well as formal, processes (Buchanan, 2003). This emergent view of organisational renewal places greater emphasis on those closer to the ground to instigate change and on senior managers to learn from line managers, to facilitate the sharing of knowledge and to manage the political dimension of working relationships.

The sum of this short discussion on the nature of change management – and its importance in an organisational climate of uncertainty and unpredictability – is that there are a number of perspectives on organisational change and a wide range of important actors in its effective implementation. Change management needs to be viewed as contingent according to the specific change process being planned and undertaken, the external organisational context, the goals, structure and culture of the organisation affected, the nature of its workforce and employment relations traditions, as well as the capabilities of its senior and line managers to manage complicated, political processes. Processual–contextual perspectives on organisational change stress, therefore, that to understand organisational change it is important to consider how the context, substance and process of change interact and to recognise change as complex, repetitive, fragmented and politicised (Pettigrew and Whipp, 1991; Dawson, 1994).

NEW TECHNOLOGY, WORK AND HRM

There is little doubt that developments in information and communication technology over the past two decades have yielded a social transformation that has shaped how we live and work in complex, far-reaching and often unanticipated ways. The following series of questions posed by McWhorter (2010) provides a succinct summary of the impact of new and emerging technology on the professional and personal lives of many workers:

> How often do you communicate with colleagues through information and communication technologies (ICT) such as email, texting, chat, video, and audio conference calls? Do you engage in meetings or 'meetups' that occur through social networking platforms such as Facebook, LinkedIn, or possibly through a meeting of avatars in a 3D virtual world such as Second Life? Do you search online or through your organization's intranet for your calendar appointments? Do you use Google to search for terms, to seek expert advice, or access MapQuest or Yahoo to obtain directions, documents, or travel itineraries? What ways have you engaged to connect with colleagues that are in a different location, country, or time zone from you? Are you blogging, wikiing, twittering, or following web discussion forums? How much are modern technologies permeating your personal and professional life?

A key focus of this book is the implications of developments in the context of work and employment that act to influence how people are required to behave and what they need to know and be able to do in the course of their work and that consequently have an impact on how people are best directed and managed. Unlike the influence of some aspects of context that is indirect, such as political and economic change, the development and diffusion of new technology have a very real and immediate impact on work and labour market conditions. Perhaps most notably, in shaping the jobs available in the labour market, the content of those jobs and the required skills and knowledge, technological developments act to provide opportunities for learning and critical imperatives to learn both at an individual and organisational level.

Some of the impact of new technology has already been discussed. For instance, with developments in information and communication technology have come changes to the way in which organisations are structured and managed and the job requirements of many workers. For instance, Sung and Ashton (2006) highlighted various successful cases where ICT adoption has been central to new working practices by, for instance, enabling communication, stimulating innovation and supporting new product and service development. Similarly, Benson et al. (2002) highlight that the impact of technology on the workplace since the 1980s has been to require workers to 'know how to learn', be able to apply problem-solving skills to overcome barriers that arise in new situations, and think creatively as they cope with new challenges. Perhaps the group most affected – and potentially empowered – by new technology are those referred to as 'knowledge workers': those workers whose organisational value resides in their ability to draw upon and manipulate scarce knowledge and create new knowledge, thus producing new and innovative products, services or ways of doing things. In relation to the impact of ICT, Malhotra (1998) suggests 'knowledge workers need to be facile in the applications of new technologies to their business contexts. Such understanding is necessary so that they can delegate "programmable" tasks to technologies to concentrate their time and efforts on value-adding activities that demand creativity and innovation' (Malhotra, 1998: 19, cited in Benson et al., 2002). Therefore, alongside job-related knowledge and skill, such workers will be required to become expert in the efficient use of IT including technical proficiency in using evolving hardware and software, cognitive skills for interrogating this technology, being discerning about the quality of information and at ease with individual, self-directed and self-monitored learning. Such capabilities require particular approaches to the management and development of such workers. This is further discussed in the following section.

Martin (2005) suggests, however, that whilst new technology has the ability to liberate and empower workers, through reskilling and upskilling jobs and potentially making work more enjoyable and satisfying, it also has the potential to control and dominate employees, as well as to deskill work. In other words, technology has the potential to create both 'empowered knowledge workers' and 'disempowered drudges'. These two scenarios have obvious ramifications for the management of people. In the 'positive' scenario, workers are likely to be placed more greatly in control of their working lives with commensurate implications for the nature of their management. In the 'negative' scenario, technology itself becomes more greatly a tool of managerial control, and jobs are at risk from 'digital Taylorism' (reflecting the ideas of Taylorism discussed in Chapter 2): the process of 'extraction, codification and digitalization of knowledge into software prescripts that can be transmitted and manipulated by others regardless of location' (Brown et al., 2011). As such, the requirements for people management practices and policies are modified by alternative means of controlling performance, shape the purpose and nature of recruitment and largely negate the need for training through deskilling of previously skilled work.

KNOWLEDGE MANAGEMENT AND HRM

As noted previously, a critical dimension of organisational success in the twenty-first century is argued to be the effective management of organisational knowledge. Put simply, knowledge management (KM) is 'the attempt by an organisation to explicitly manage and control the knowledge of its workforce' (Hislop, 2009: 426) and which represents attempts to identify and leverage the collective knowledge in an organisation to contribute to its performance. Therefore, in pursuit of these objectives, KM is the range of tools, processes, systems, structures, and cultures designed and implemented for the purpose of effectively creating, capturing, retaining and utilising individual and collective knowledge (Spicer and Sadler-Smith, 2006; Zhang et al., 2006), and of improving organisational learning and performance (Scarborough, 1999). Central to this end is the need for firms to 'facilitate, encourage and develop employee learning and experimentation, communication and trust in order to generate and enable the sharing and capture by firms of ideas and knowledge' (Thompson and Warhurst, 2003: 1). Making knowledge productive requires employees to transform information into valuable knowledge, to share this knowledge with others in the organisation and in the wider organisational network, and to apply it in novel situations to create value, for example in the form of saleable commodities such as computer software and patented technology. In other words, effective knowledge management requires organisations to create, capture and capitalise on knowledge (Ichijo et al., 1998). In this sense, the term 'knowledge worker' refers to those who work *with* knowledge (including their own, that which is shared with colleagues and that which exists within the wider organisation) as opposed to *from* knowledge (which is characteristic of professional occupations, such as lawyers or doctors) (Scarbrough, 1999: 7). In other words, knowledge workers are those who manipulate knowledge to create new technologies and innovation, rather than simply apply an existing body of knowledge.

To understand how HRM practices might facilitate knowledge management it is first important to understand the nature of 'knowledge'. Two types of knowledge are identified in much of the literature on knowledge management. *Explicit knowledge* refers to procedural knowledge that is 'out there' and which can be codified and systematised and is communicable, for example in the form of data, procedures and processes that are written in books, journals, company intranets and organisational manuals. Once codified, this knowledge becomes collectively held and open to distribution to those who might benefit from such knowledge. In contrast, *tacit knowledge* is that which resides within the individual and is often more difficult to articulate and communicate. It is related to an individual's intuitive and taken-for-granted 'know-how' (Polanyi, 1962) and the ability to apply this knowledge, for example, in the conduct of skilled work. Whilst procedural or explicit knowledge might underpin an individual's ability to perform a task in the workplace, tacit knowledge is required when performing in new or unexpected situations (Eraut, 2000) and, therefore, underpins innovation, creativity, problem-solving, coping with ambiguity (Gourlay, 2006) and the development of new ideas and products. However, because such knowledge has yet to be or cannot be codified it is potentially inaccessible to management because those in possession of such knowledge cannot necessarily be compelled to share it.

There are, therefore, two important dimensions to knowledge management (Tsoukas and Vladimirou, 2001). The first element is the dynamic process of turning an unreflective practice (carrying out activities according to predefined rules but without articulating these rules) into a reflective one, whereby the guiding principles of an activity are made explicit so as to enable collective understanding. The second element is developing the tacit knowledge of the individual through managing social relations and encouraging employees to improvise and use their initiative. Nonaka and Takeuchi (1995) suggest that the creation of new organisational knowledge originates in an individual's tacit knowledge which, once expressed to others (through its conversion into words or diagrams), becomes combined with that of others and, ultimately, becomes new tacit knowledge, but of the group rather than an individual. It therefore becomes part of the accepted way of doing things.

Mylonopoulos and Tsoukas (2003) suggest, however, that a tension lies at the heart of knowledge management which needs resolution in order to promote knowledge-sharing. On one hand, organisational knowledge is deeply embedded in the intangible resources of an organisation (particularly its human resources), on the other hand, to be effectively managed this knowledge must be disembedded and objectified. In other words, management needs to make tacit knowledge explicit in order to be able to manage it effectively and exploit it for commercial purposes. Nonaka et al. (2001) identify four modes of knowledge conversion:

1 *Socialisation* (from tacit to tacit) – the acquisition of tacit knowledge directly from others, for example, through shared experience, joint activities, dialogue and demonstration.

2 *Externalisation* (from tacit to explicit) – the creation of concepts from tacit knowledge.

3 *Combination* (from explicit to explicit) – the organisation of concepts drawing on different bodies of explicit knowledge to create, for example, manuals, documents and databases.

4 *Internalisation* (from explicit to tacit) – the process of 'learning by doing' and the internalisation of values and ideas through communication and direct experience.

CHAPTER 15   CURRENT TRENDS AND FUTURE CHALLENGES IN HRM

In broad terms, the approach an organisation takes to the management of knowledge might reflect one of two views on the nature of organisations, or a combination of the two (Newell et al., 2002: 107–9). A *cognitive* perspective adopts an information-processing view of the firm where knowledge management is concerned with the identification, capture and processing of the knowledge embedded either within people or processes (inputs) so that it can be applied in novel situations (outputs). It therefore focuses on the elicitation and codification of knowledge to make it productive. Alternatively, the *community* view stresses the socially constructed nature of knowledge and how it is embedded in formal and informal organisational networks and structures, and reproduced and shared through organisational socialisation. The cognitive view stresses the importance of ICT systems to better enable the processing, storage and dissemination of knowledge, whereas the community perspective stresses the importance of developing a shared culture and values and a relationship of trust between organisational stakeholders (Blankenship and Ruona, 2009).

In order to manage knowledge effectively, both the cognitive and community perspectives need to be combined in an overarching approach to knowledge management that focuses both on processes and people. This reflects the resource-based view of the firm discussed in Chapter 3, which stresses both human capital and organisation process advantage and Boxall and Purcell's (2003) assertion that HR advantage is gained through a combination of an organisation's human resources and the formal and informal processes developed to manage these resources in a given context. Swart and Kinnie (2003) suggest that successful knowledge-intensive firms gain competitive advantage from *both* their human capital (the tacit and explicit knowledge of their workers) and their social capital (the knowledge that is embedded within organisational relationships and routines), thus reflecting a 'knowledge-based view of the firm' as the basis for the enhancement of capability and competitive differentiation (Kang and Snell, 2009). HRM practices can, therefore, be understood both as *antecedents* of organisational knowledge (for example, recruitment activity that brings knowledge into the firm) and as *mediating factors* in linking knowledge to performance (through, for example, effective job design and reward systems that motivate workers to apply their knowledge productively) (Minbaeva et al., 2009).

Storey and Quintas (2001) note, however, that despite acknowledgement among managers of the importance of the people dimension, knowledge management is often approached with a 'technological bias' (Scarbrough, 1999, in Storey and Quintas, 2001: 344), despite evidence to suggest that social enablers, such as trust, are more important to knowledge-sharing than technical support (Choi et al., 2008). The community view clearly stresses the importance of informal and formal channels for knowledge-sharing between individuals, within project teams or departments, throughout an organisation or even within organisational networks. This is becoming a growing concern for managers in a wide variety of work contexts. For example, Felstead et al. (2007) report that the proportion of workers strongly agreeing with the statement that 'my job requires that I help my colleagues to learn new things' rose from 27 per cent in 2001 to 32 per cent five years later.

 Further online reading This article reviews and synthesises literature on social structures within organisations and the types of knowledge shared within different forms of social groups. It usefully develops the discussion in this chapter regarding the importance of human process advantage and the different means by which knowledge is produced and shared within organisations.

Blankenship, S. S. and Ruona, W. E. A. (2009) Exploring knowledge sharing in social structures: Potential contributions to an overall knowledge management strategy, *Advances in Developing Human Resources*, 11 (3): 290–306.

BOX 15.2
HRM IN PRACTICE

Knowledge management at NASA

For NASA, knowledge management is simply 'delivering the systems and services that will help our employees and partners get the information they need to make better decisions'. The organisation identifies three priority areas where KM systems and processes support NASA's ability to deliver its missions:

1 'To sustain NASA's knowledge across missions and generations, KM activities identify and capture the information that exists across the Agency'.

2 'To help people find, organise, and share the knowledge we already have, KM processes help to efficiently manage the Agency's knowledge resources'.

3 'To increase collaboration and to facilitate knowledge creation and sharing, the KM team will develop techniques and tools to enable teams and communities to collaborate across the barriers of time and space'.

The model of KM employed at NASA reflects many of the aspects of good practice identified in this chapter, not least a balance between technological and people-focused solutions and the critical role of HRD. KM is viewed as being made up of four elements: culture; knowledge architecture; IT infrastructure; and supporting services.

The culture dimension concerns achieving a balance between corporate and local/individual goals, facilitating the creation and sustainment of communities of practice, creating appropriate mechanisms for reward and recognition, acknowledgement of knowledge 'ownership' and enabling the sharing and reuse of knowledge. The knowledge architecture refers to the organisation's ability to capture content and provide context for that knowledge, ensure the ability of diverse systems to work together, maintain directories of expertise and knowledge repositories and to categorise and codify knowledge resources.

To support workers and line managers in management of knowledge, NASA created a Knowledge Management Team consisting of 115 members with representation from across the organisation and from a range of disciplinary backgrounds, from system architects to anthropologists, which works in close partnership with the organisation's human resources organisations. The work of the team is based on the following principles:

- 'Find good solutions, fill the gaps, and build a federation of resources to support NASA missions and research communities'.

- 'Support and enable NASA initiatives by advocating best practices, promote re-usable solutions, and build infrastructure and applications to bridge distributed systems'.

- 'Infuse new ideas or needed technology'.

Key people-focused areas for NASA's KM strategy include:

- 'Sustain NASA's knowledge across missions and generations by identifying and capturing the information that exists across the Agency'.

- 'Help people find, organise and share the knowledge we already have by efficiently managing NASA's knowledge resources'.

- 'Increase collaboration and facilitate knowledge creation and sharing by developing techniques and tools to enable teams and communities to collaborate across the barriers of time and space'.

Source: http://km.nasa.gov/what-is-km/ and km.nasa.gov/people/ (accessed 30 September 2015)

KNOWLEDGE MANAGEMENT, NASA

Managing knowledge workers

Swart et al. (2003) report that the growth of the knowledge economy has seen the proliferation of knowledge-intensive firms that are typically small, fast-growing service providers who often work in collaborative ways with partner organisations. Knowledge-intensive firms are argued to have distinctive characteristics that challenge traditional ways of managing and organising and, whilst knowledge workers are employed in a variety of organisations across different industry sectors, it is in these firms that research suggests new models of employee management are developing. Indeed, much of the literature on the effective management of knowledge workers stresses the requirement to do more than simply adapt the policies and practices employed in larger, more traditional firms (Horwitz et al., 2003), but to develop new ways of managing that are more suited to the particular characteristics of knowledge workers themselves and to address the imperative to create and share distributed knowledge (Starbuck, 1992; Robertson and O'Malley Hammersley, 2000; Yahya and Goh, 2002; Swart and Kinnie, 2003; Benson and Brown, 2007). In short, organisations need to consider how best to organise structures, working relationships, technology and physical space to create a platform upon which new knowledge can be created and shared (Nonaka et al., 2001). Such processes of knowledge management have been identified as important drivers of innovation performance among high-tech SMEs (Allegre et al., 2011).

BOX 15.3
RESEARCH INSIGHT

Knowledge management, the resource-based view and sustainable competitive advantage

In an investigation of how knowledge management affects innovative performance among biotechnology firms, Allegre et al. (2011) find convincing evidence that KM enhances sustained competitive advantages in innovation performance. In particular, the authors find that it is the creation of KM dynamic capability – an organisation's ability to reconfigure its KM practices through 'integrating them in novel, specific and flexible ways to develop new KM systems when required' (2011: 5) – that act as the mediating factor between KM practices, such as the formal and informal processes that enhance the spread of explicit and tacit knowledge across the organisation, and knowledge storage systems, and innovative performance. Therefore, the authors conclude, sustained competitive advantage in

the biotechnology industry does indeed require firm strategies that capitalise on KM practice. These dynamic capabilities are created through the implementation and daily use of KM practices that create a repertoire of KM dynamic capabilities through their routinisation and the learning inherent in operational problem-solving. As such, these dynamic capabilities enable KM practices themselves to be more effective through their adaptation to changing contexts and the creation of new practices as required.

They suggest, therefore, support for the RBV by providing evidence that a firm's innovation performance and competitive advantage are functions of complex inimitable resources embedded within the organisation (Barney, 1991). Indeed, it is the KM dynamic capabilities that constitute a particular valuable resource because they are both firm specific and difficult to imitate, because they are based on complex organisational routines.

Further online reading This article covers some of the key issues outlined in this chapter in discussing how KM affects innovation within SMEs. In particular, it sets out how a firm's dynamic capabilities mediate between KM practices and innovation performance and acts to explain differences in performance between firms.

Alegre, J., Sengupta, K. and Lapiedra, R. (2011) Knowledge management and innovation performance in a high-tech SME sector, *International Small Business Journal*, 1–17.

Employees who possess potentially value-adding knowledge are a crucial organisational resource. However, such knowledge workers can be difficult to manage, not least because much knowledge work is intangible and difficult to evaluate and measure (Alvesson, 2001; Burke and Ng, 2006). HRM can play a central role in knowledge management, particularly in the effective recruitment and retention of knowledge workers and the management of their performance. As noted previously, one component of knowledge-sharing is the technological infrastructure through which knowledge can be collected and disseminated as widely as possible. Perhaps more fundamental, however, is encouraging and facilitating staff to share knowledge between themselves. Therefore, it is the role of HRM to create the cultural and structural conditions to encourage worker cooperation, positive interaction and knowledge-sharing rather than rivalry and competition that might inhibit such behaviour. This requires the development of a strong psychological contract and the development of relationships based on trust, equity, mutual respect and honesty between an employee, their peers, line managers and, ultimately, senior managers. Developing such a relationship can, however, be difficult where workers (for example, those in the IT service sector) work across multiple clients (Grimshaw and Miozzo, 2009).

The creation of an organisation conducive to knowledge-sharing requires organisational leaders (Ribiere and Sitar, 2003) to establish the tone and culture within which such behaviour becomes second nature. A strong organisational culture in knowledge-intensive firms can help in addressing the 'managerial dilemma' of how to balance worker autonomy and control, and flexibility and uncertainty, with efficiency (Robertson and Swan, 2003: 831). Creating such a culture can, however, be challenging where senior managers are unwilling to overturn or challenge existing cultures and working practices and knowledge management is simply 'bolted on' to the organisation rather than an integral activity (Storey and Barnett, 2000). Swart and Kinnie (2003) suggest that successfully promoting knowledge-sharing requires paying attention to the needs of individual employees so that they see it as in their own interests to do so, by implementing HR processes that create *complementarity* between the needs of the employee for development and growth and the needs of the organisation to distribute knowledge. MacNeil (2003) stresses the importance of line managers in facilitating knowledge-sharing in teams and the capturing of tacit knowledge. This requires organisational support and the development of line manager skills to enable them to create and communicate a *positive learning climate* conducive to knowledge creation and distribution. Horwitz et al. (2003) suggest that firms should adopt a contingent approach to devising HR policies and practices to manage knowledge workers, taking account of mediating variables such as organisational strategy, industry type, ownership structure and cross-cultural factors. Indeed, management practices in knowledge-intensive firms are likely to be more effective when they have been allowed to develop organically, rather than imposed from the top down

(Alvesson and Karreman, 2001; Swart et al., 2003) so as to reflect diversity in the needs of knowledge workers (Minbaeva et al., 2009).

One of the central issues in the effective management of knowledge workers is the importance that such workers have been shown to place on discretion, autonomy and challenging work, particularly that which involves complex problem-solving and the application of their intellectual capital to unique tasks in order to develop new knowledge. Knowledge development is, therefore, central not only to organisational success, but also to job satisfaction among knowledge workers themselves and, ultimately, to ensure their retention and motivation. Horwitz et al. (2003) stress, therefore, the importance of recognising and responding to the specific career- and work-related needs, interests and aspirations of knowledge workers. Practices associated both with responding to these needs and promoting and facilitating knowledge-sharing include: challenging job design to create the conditions under which workers develop and apply new skills and knowledge; worker involvement in 'crafting' their own jobs; selecting from potential employees on the basis of 'cultural fit' with the firm (stressing an identification with the firm's values); work-based learning within and across project teams and across organisational communities; high levels of reward contingent on performance (particularly in the development and sharing of knowledge); employee mentoring; a strong internal labour market; regular communication; and high degrees of employee participation and employee voice. Informal and formal mechanisms for knowledge-sharing include the induction process, social events and the use of the Internet, as well as forums that emphasise the bringing together of disparate workers and groups, for example project teams, formal and informal networks, cross-functional meetings and organisational committees (Swart and Kinnie, 2003) as well as harnessing the potential benefits to the organisation of 'communities of practice' (as discussed in Chapter 9).

Turnover of knowledge workers is higher than among the rest of the workforce, partly due to their attractiveness in the labour market (Horwitz et al., 2003). Clearly, therefore, employee retention is important to such firms, as the loss of employees might mean the loss of an important, potentially unique, organisational asset. Consequently, engendering employee loyalty represents a crucial dimension of managing knowledge workers (Alvesson, 2000), particularly through developing positive working relationships with co-workers and supervisors (Benson and Brown, 2007). However, firms have to manage turnover to strike a balance between retaining key employees and facilitating the recruitment of 'fresh blood' that has the potential to bring in new ideas and knowledge.

Further online reading This article explores the determinants of organisational commitment for knowledge workers, suggesting that they differ in important respects from those that apply to routine-task workers, creating challenges for organisational decision-makers.

Benson, J. and Brown, M. (2007) Knowledge workers: What keeps them committed; what turns them away, *Work, Employment and Society*, 21: 121–41.

Taken together, the type of work organisation and job design found to be favoured among knowledge workers reflects the CIPD's (2008f) notion of 'smart working' that reflects a number of connected working practices:

- high levels of freedom, autonomy and empowerment
- the use of virtual work groups and teams

- a managerial focus on outcomes, not processes
- ICT-enabled employee flexibility, for example of location and working hours
- high-trust employment relationship
- alignment of job design and work organisation and business objectives.

The implicit assumption in much of the positive literature on the knowledge economy is that knowledge work is associated with better forms of both inter- and intra-organisation relations (Grugulis et al., 2004). Part of this assumption is based on the shifting power balance that underpins the relationship between knowledge worker and employer. Management's traditional authority and control have been partly achieved through a Taylorist separation of task conception from execution, whereby workers are systematically divested of discretion, autonomy and control over the labour process. Theoretically, in more cooperative knowledge-intensive firms this authority is partially ceded to the producers and possessors of knowledge, fundamentally altering the managerial role from one of control to coordination.

According to Nonaka and Takeuchi (1995), the best management style to facilitate knowledge creation is 'middle-up-down' where middle managers provide a 'bridge' between the ideals of senior management and the realities of frontline activities. The CIPD (2008f) note areas of exemplary management practice in organisations where Taylorist division of labour in job design has been replaced by collaboration between manager and worker, resulting in a 'triple win' for an organisation, its employees and customers. However, not all commentators share such optimism about the unfolding changes to the employment relationship associated with the growing incidence of knowledge workers. For example, Sewell (2005) argues that whilst the employment relationship for knowledge workers might be changing it doesn't necessarily follow that this new relationship will be any less exploitative and that power will shift substantially from employer to employee.

Further online reading This article discusses many of the issues surrounding the management of knowledge workers, including the problems of making tacit knowledge explicit and issues of power and control in the employment relationship. The discussion also provides an important context to debates around knowledge management by situating it within wider managerial and labour process theory.

Sewell, G. (2005) Nice work? Rethinking managerial control in an era of knowledge work, *Organization*, 12 (5): 685–704.

Issues in knowledge management

The rise in interest and prescription regarding knowledge management tends to assume that knowledge is amenable to managerial control and direction. However, Scarbrough suggests that in seeking to manage knowledge:

 management becomes the focal agent in attempting to integrate two divergent sets of social practices: on the one hand, the human actions involved in producing and applying knowledge and on the other the exploitation of such actions for economic ends. Management roles thus involve the constant 'quasi-resolution of conflict' and managers' ability to develop and sustain this fragile unity of practices becomes a major determinant of competitive performance. (1999: 6)

An interesting question that this raises is whether employees can be *required* to share knowledge. Once tacit knowledge has been codified in organisational documents or processes it then becomes the intellectual capital of the organisation rather than that of the individual. The adage goes that 'knowledge is power' and if knowledge translates into leverage or currency in the employment relationship then it becomes a potential source of conflict in respect of its ownership and usage (Blackler, 1995). Indeed, the refusal to share knowledge can be considered a form of employee resistance (Hislop, 2005). Drawing on social exchange theory, then it may make more sense to refer to 'knowledge exchange' rather than knowledge-sharing to emphasise the importance of reciprocity and one's expectation of some sort of return for passing on valued knowledge (Konstantiou and Fincham, 2011).

Chapter 2 referred to the notion of organisational citizenship behaviour and discretionary behaviour, for example, collaboration between co-workers or a willingness to go the extra distance to help a customer or colleague. These behaviours can be of significant benefit to the organisation; they cannot, however, be required by the contract of employment, rather they are generated through a positive psychological contract and a fit between the values of the individual and that of the dominant organisational culture. In other words, employees have to be motivated through such relationships to generate these behaviours. Knowledge-sharing between employees clearly represents behaviour that is desirable for the organisation but employees cannot be compelled to share any or all of their tacit knowledge. They might, however, be encouraged to do so as a result of their commitment to the firm and the strength of the relationship with their managers and colleagues (Obembe, 2012).

The factors that may inhibit knowledge-sharing and create difficulties in making tacit knowledge both explicit and productive include the physical and technological infrastructure of the organisation (Ichijo et al., 1998), HR policies (such as reward systems that inhibit the expression of knowledge-sharing by failing to acknowledge individual contribution to organisational knowledge) and the relationships within groups or 'communities of practice'. Becker (2001) raises the problems associated with the dispersed nature of organisational knowledge across its workforce, including the creation of uncertainty in decision-making and the resource requirements of sharing knowledge across large numbers of employees or across national borders (Tregaskis et al., 2010). This creates difficulties in knowledge management because such distributed knowledge can be contradictory and individuals or groups are likely to have access to only part of the knowledge base of an organisation. Becker argues, however, that the centralisation of knowledge (i.e. its codification and redistribution) is limited in its ability to address these problems. Nonetheless, the unevenly distributed nature of knowledge, particularly in larger firms, might act as an explanation as to why technological solutions to promoting and facilitating knowledge-sharing tend to be prioritised.

Further online reading This article investigates the challenges of managing core HR practices within global IT firms given the outsourcing and staff transfer that are central to the IT services sector. It concludes that the internal and external conditions of these firms create tension in the design and implementation of HR practices.

Grimshaw, D. and Miozzo, M. (2009) New human resource management practices in knowledge-intensive business services firms: The case of outsourcing with staff transfer, *Human Relations*, 62 (10): 1521–50.

BOX 15.4
RESEARCH INSIGHT

Knowledge workers, the labour process and organisational change

Danford et al. (2009) provide an insight into the impact of organisational change associated with increased efforts to commercialise the knowledge held by an organisation's workforce. Drawing on a case study undertaken in a UK government-owned research institution responsible for work on meteorology and global climate change, they report that the introduction of a more market-oriented business model resulted in a cultural shift whereby the institution became viewed as 'a business supplying cost-effective services to government, and seeking profit-making commercial opportunities'. Among the workforce, whilst the authors found evidence of a 'deep intrinsic motivation associated with scientific work, a motivation that was based on highly challenging and skilled work located in a field of endeavour with high moral value' (Danford et al., 2009: 227), they also report patterns of worker dissatisfaction associated with recent changes to the way in which scientific staff were managed and expected to work. In particular, employee dissatisfaction was associated with: a loss of autonomy over work 'tempo', task allocation and other issues relating to work organisation; work intensification and excessive work-related stress; a lack of management consultation and weak individual and collective influence over management policy; and pay and conditions. For many of these science workers these causes of dissatisfaction were a direct result of the commodification of knowledge and commercialisation of organisational culture which had seen project lead-times reduced and more routine commercial work prioritised over 'pure' research.

The causes of worker dissatisfaction identified in this case clearly resonate with the defining characteristics of knowledge work and the work requirements of knowledge workers. This case highlights the problems associated with managing such workers in the context of the commercial imperative and the requirement to make knowledge productive. It also raises the question of how organisations can best manage groups of highly qualified workers who are intrinsically motivated by the work they do in such a way as to ensure the mutual satisfaction of both worker and organisational needs.

OUTSOURCING, SHARED SERVICES AND THIRD-PARTY SERVICE PROVISION

OPPORTUNITIES
FOR KNOWLEDGE
WORKERS

One of the most significant trends in HRM in recent years, and one with far-reaching implications for the profession, is the outsourcing of administrative or transactional HR functions (Conklin, 2005). Outsourcing in HRM occurs when an organisation contracts with another organisation to provide specific HR services or activities and, consequently, all or some of the HR functions traditionally done internally are shifted to an external provider. IDS (2011a) report, for example, that 80 per cent of firms that responded to a survey conducted in 2010 outsourced at least one aspect of HR. Belcourt (2006) reports the functions most likely to be outsourced are temporary staffing, payroll, training, recruitment, and benefits administration, whilst IDS suggest that well-being and occupational health provision are most likely. There is, however, the potential to outsource any number of areas of HRM, including induction, internal transfers and relocation, performance management and appraisals, employee exit, management of employee contracts and employee assistance and all aspects of well-being support. Even within a functional area of HRM (such as reward), the decision of what aspects of the function to outsource remains. For instance, a firm might hand over responsibility for all recruitment and selection activity to an outsource partner or choose only to out-source, for example, employee testing, applicant screening, shortlisting, advertising and reference checking.

The key enabler of HR outsourcing is the development of new technology to facilitate the delivery of HRM. In particular, outsourcing is often commensurate with the greater use of e-HR and associated forms of HR service delivery (IDS, 2011a), in particular that which facilitates employee and line manager 'self-service' in conducting local HR transactions (for example, arranging training or booking annual leave).

An associated trend is the increasing use of 'shared service centres' to provide centralised and standardised delivery of routine HR administration across an entire organisation (Ulrich et al., 2008; Coleman Selden and Wooters, 2011). Whilst shared services are typically provided in-house through a reorganisation of a firm's HR provision, such centres often form a key channel of delivery for outsourced HR functions (IDS, 2011a) and because they are 'location neutral' (Caldwell and Storey, 2007: 25) can even be offshored. Where outsourced, the third-party service provider might provide a dedicated centre for a single organisation or a centre providing services to multiple clients. The purpose of shared service centres is to provide greater (internal) customer focus in the delivery of HRM, improve service quality, ensure consistency in the application of policy and practice by providing a single source of HR support and reduce costs by removing the duplication of activities at local levels. Shared service centres often have a hierarchy of specialisation whereby routine HR enquiries, whether from line managers or employees, are dealt with by customer service representatives, but where more specialist advice is required it is escalated to someone with an appropriate level of HR knowledge. Shared service centres are associated with a shift towards HR 'self-service' where employees and line managers, enabled by ICT, can conduct HR transactions without recourse to HR specialists (Farndale et al., 2009). Box 15.5 provides an example of this in practice. A similar concept to shared service centres but which goes beyond basic HR transactions is that of 'centres of expertise' which provide a centralised source of specialist HR knowledge or capabilities.

The move towards greater centralisation of HR services can often reflect a wider process of organisational restructuring (IDS, 2009) which might lead to an evolution in HR provision towards, first, an in-house shared service centre and then a move towards outsourcing this function. In other cases, outsourcing might reflect a step-change in how HR transactions are conducted. Lepak and Snell (1998) suggest that a consequence of greater external provision of HR services is that, for those HR specialists who remain within a firm, their role shifts from the implementation of appropriate HR practices to establishing, supporting and enhancing relationships with service providers.

The drivers of the trend towards greater outsourcing were outlined briefly in Chapter 1. To a degree, outsourcing is a consequence of the greater organisational focus on value-adding capabilities or core competencies and the desire for each business function, including HRM, to maximise their contribution to the profitability of the firm. Therefore, the twin pressures on the HR function – to be more strategic and produce a measurable contribution to the bottom line but to do this whilst reducing overall costs – have increased the pressure on the HR department to divest itself of its administrative role in order to concentrate more fully on being a strategic partner and change agent. Added-value can also be realised through performance improvements associated with the outsourcing arrangement itself. Gilley et al. (2004) report that in a study of almost 100 manufacturing firms, outsourced training and payroll had a positive impact on firm performance, particularly its innovativeness. Overall, Belcourt (2006) identifies six significant, and inter-connected, reasons why firms outsource some or all of their HR activities.

1 *Financial* – firms often outsource to reduce HR costs, for example, by using a specialist recruitment agency rather than directly employing the required specialist skills and knowledge in-house. The use of agencies can therefore reduce overall headcount in HR personnel. Such agencies work across a number of clients and can achieve economies of scale that would not be possible for the HR department of a single company to achieve. Cost savings might also be the driver of the growing use of employee assistance programmes discussed in Chapter 14. Clearly, the costs of running such programmes in-house can be prohibitive, given the level of capital investment in technology and employee training needed to provide adequate levels of service (especially where required levels of service are either unknown or unpredictable). Cost saving might also relate to greater cost control on the basis that HR decisions are likely to be subject to greater scrutiny because the actual cost of an HR activity (for example, a training course) is 'charged-for' rather than being available for 'free' in-house. HR costs are more explicit in an outsourcing arrangement and therefore managers are likely to be more cautious when spending the company's money and have to more precisely justify the measurable benefits that might arise from HR expenditure.

2 *Strategic focus* – as noted above, part of the drive towards greater HR outsourcing is a desire to focus the firm's HR specialists on more strategic concerns and on value-creating HR activities, and this tends to lead to the outsourcing of administrative functions, such as payroll. Belcourt (2006) suggests that core HR functions that should not be outsourced include leadership development, employee relations, final selection decisions, performance management and succession management. This is because they depend on an understanding of organisational culture, a long-term orientation, consistency, trust and access to confidential information. In other words, they are of strategic value and represent a unique or idiosyncratic resource (Klaas et al., 2001). Again, this view links to the resource-based view of the organisation which stresses the importance of core capabilities or competencies that provide competitive advantage on account of their scarcity or inimitability.

3 *Improved service* – firms might also seek to improve levels of service quality through outsourcing. This can result from the choice of a particular service provider with specific capabilities or through an ability to demand more strict performance standards from an outsourcing partner than might be possible with in-house provision. The reputation of service providers is obviously important in gaining new business and, therefore, they might well place a greater emphasis on quality of service provision to their clients. This focus might be reinforced through the quantification of service quality through performance indicators and standards in the outsourcing agreement.

4 *Technical* – outsourcing may reflect a desire to improve technical service and have access to, but not directly invest in, new technologies. It might also reflect a shortage of specific technical skills, either in the internal or external labour market, or it might reflect a desire to improve HR service provision through reducing the time taken to respond to queries through the (semi-) automisation of processes.

5 *Specialised expertise* – for small firms in particular, the decision to outsource might be driven by a desire to access specialised expertise that would be expensive to employ in-house. For example, as made evident in previous chapters, employment legislation is increasingly complex and to ensure compliance and reduce the potential for litigation, firms need to have access to specialist legal expertise. Expert knowledge can also be valuable

when firms require access to leading practice. For example, firms that use 'headhunters' to recruit senior executives do so to draw on specialised industry knowledge and access to professional networks. Specialist expertise might be particularly important for firms operating internationally, where effective HRM requires an understanding of local laws, practices and customs.

6 *Organisational politics* – finally, outsourcing might reflect a desire for organisations to rid themselves of some of the internal politics that can hinder a firm's ability to focus on core competencies. HR decisions are likely to be viewed as less 'politically charged' if made by a 'partner' outside of the firm rather than internally, and regarded more dispassionately by those affected, leading to more effective decision-making.

Conklin (2005) suggests that organisational characteristics influence the extent to which a firm engages in HR outsourcing and the areas likely to be sub-contracted. Belcourt (2006) notes that full outsourcing of the HR function is more likely among smaller employers for the principal reason that it is probably more cost-effective to create a 'virtual HR department' provided by a third party (IDS, 2003). Larger organisations rarely engage in complete outsourcing, partly because the HR function is likely to be seen as critical to the culture and strategic objectives of an organisation and thus should be kept in-house. It might also reflect the view that responding to unpredictability can be better done by an in-house function. Furthermore, Belcourt (2006) suggests there are few service providers that can provide a full range of unified HRM services and, therefore, outsourcing tends to be partial. There can also be differences in the outsourcing activity of firms in different industry sectors. For example, Sheehan (2009) found that private sector firms are more likely to outsource recruitment and selection and performance-related pay initiatives than public sector organisations.

Finally, Conklin (2005) raises the issue of contract clarity in explaining the concentration of outsourcing activity in certain areas of HRM. HR activities differ in respect of the 'clarity of specification' that they allow in the contract of service (i.e. the terms of reference for the contract) and therefore, whilst certain areas of HR are extensively outsourced (e.g. payroll, attendance and workforce administration, where these terms are relatively easy to define), other areas are less often outsourced because their conduct is difficult to specify and performance standards difficult to quantify.

Further online reading This article explores HRM outsourcing activity in Australian firms. It investigates the areas of HRM that are most likely to be initiated using external consultants, whether organisational size or sector impacts on the outsourcing decision, and the type of skills that HRM consultants bring into organisations.

Sheehan, C. (2009) Outsourcing HRM activities in Australian organisations, *Asia Pacific Journal of Human Resources,* 47 (2): 236–53.

Issues in outsourcing

Despite the apparent appeal of outsourcing, the decision to entrust HR activities to a third-party provider carries both risks and limitations. Outsourcing arrangements can be more expensive to operate than anticipated, for example, as a result of unexpected changes in requirements outside of the original outsourcing agreement. Service quality can also suffer from the inflexibility of a specific outsourcing arrangement or from apparent gaps in service provision

(Reilly et al., 2007). Key to addressing this issue is achieving an appropriate fit between an organisation and the outsource partner, particularly the extent to which the client requires ongoing innovation in HR process and technologies and the ability of the provider to deliver on this expectation (Conklin, 2005). Service quality can also suffer through a lack of provider understanding of the specific requirements of workers or the nature or culture of the firm.

A principal risk of outsourcing is the impact on staff, both those in the HR department and those in the rest of the firm. HR professionals are likely to be highly resistant to change (Lepak and Snell, 1998), whether outsourcing means redundancies, worker displacement through transfer into the provider firm, changes to the allocation of roles and responsibilities (particularly if they are transferred to the outsource partner) or the greater use of ICT. Therefore, the decision to outsource can affect employee morale and performance, both for survivors and displaced employees, not least because it is likely to be perceived as an expression of dissatisfaction by senior managers with the HR department itself. Moreover, the decision to outsource HR might be perceived by others in the organisation as indicative of wider policy and induce fear or suspicion about the future of their roles. This can undermine attempts to develop employee commitment and association with the values and culture of the organisation.

Outsourcing may also lead to an unanticipated loss of valuable knowledge and skills, particularly that which is organisationally specific and which cannot be readily accessed through the service provider or in the wider labour market. By outsourcing HR activities, organisations can also run the risk of transferring valuable expertise and insider knowledge to service providers that ultimately might find their way into the hands of competitors. Consequently, the decision for managers is not simply whether to outsource HRM or not, but rather to identify areas of HR where efficiencies might be made by outsourcing or insourcing and to choose an appropriate model to realise these efficiencies in the context of the attendant risks and benefits (Kosnik et al., 2006).

It should be noted, however, that whilst many firms engage in outsourcing or use third-party providers of HR solutions (for example, recruitment agencies), and it continues to hold an attraction as an expedient way to cut costs, there are many incidences of firms taking HR activities back in-house. For example, McCormack and Scholarios (2009) report that in 2007 there was a 10 per cent decrease in the proportion of organisations using recruitment agencies from the previous year.

HRM THROUGH NEW TECHNOLOGY

As discussed earlier in this chapter, new technology has played and will continue to play a central role in transforming economies, organisations and the way people work. The ability of firms to compete effectively in a knowledge economy is at least partly predicated on an ability to manage the relationship between people and technology (Martin, 2005) and to maximise their combined contribution to organisational success. As a result, HRM has a significant role to play in ensuring that the adoption and use of new technology are both effective and productive. More than this, however, the development and diffusion of new technology have the potential to transform the nature of the HR function itself. As Hempel (2004: 163) suggests: 'HR professionals must be able to adopt technologies that allow the re-engineering of the HR function, be prepared to support the organisational and work-design changes enabled by technology and be able to support the managerial climate for innovative and knowledge-based organisations'. In short, Martin (2005) suggests there are five interconnected areas in which new technology can have a transformative effect on the HR function and on the way people work:

1 The creating and sharing of distributed knowledge, leading to greater levels of intellectual integration.

2 Reducing the costs of HR services and enabling HR practitioners to focus more on strategic and change management concerns.

3 Supporting individual and organisational learning.

4 Supporting innovative business models and participative organisational cultures.

5 Creating new forms of community at work and new forms of organisations.

e-HR and HRMS

Recent years have seen a rapid proliferation in the use of new technology in HRM (Parry and Tyson, 2007). The term 'e-HR' (or e-HRM) was first used in the 1990s and referred initially to conducting HRM transactions using the Internet or company intranet, but it now encompasses the use of ICT in a wide range of HR activities (Lengnick-Hall and Moritz, 2003).

Such technology is being used with increasing frequency in organisations (Stone et al., 2006). Whilst initially concerned primarily with workforce administration, e-HR now encompasses a variety of applications in recruitment and selection, reward, performance management, employee communication and involvement, development and e-learning. Reflecting the wide range of possible applications of new technology in HRM and its ultimate purpose in delivering efficiencies and added-value for organisations, Bondarouk and Ruel (2009: 507) define e-HRM as: 'An umbrella term covering all possible integration mechanisms and contents between HRM and Information Technologies aiming at creating value within and across organizations for targeted employees and management'. This definition stresses a number of key points in current thinking on e-HR: first, that IT can support a wide range of HR practices; second, that a wide range of stakeholders can benefit from such technology, including HR specialists, line managers and employees themselves; third, the importance of understanding the consequences of e-HR implementation, particularly its potential to create value for these stakeholders.

Lengnick-Hall and Moritz (2003: 367) identify three major forms through which e-HR has developed that also equate to overarching approaches a firm might adopt in its application:

1 *Publishing information* – this involves one-way communication from the employer to employee/managers using intranets as a delivery medium for information such as company policies and procedures, benefits, job opportunities and directories of HR services.

2 *Automation of transactions* – this involves using intranets and the Internet to replace paperwork and face-to-face administrative support by enabling managers and employees to access databases, update information and to make and record decisions online. For example, employees can access personal records detailing holiday allocation, benefits coverage and performance data.

3 *Transformation of the HR function* – the highest-level form of e-HR, it involves liberating the HR function from its operational focus and redirecting it towards a more strategic one.

In respect of this last category of use, an e-enabled HR function has the potential to develop its strategic role and become a more effective business partner. For example, information technology can facilitate the rapid gathering of strategic data which can be analysed in ways that contribute to the formation and implementation of business strategy (Roehling et al., 2005). The shift towards a greater strategic role is also facilitated by the automation of much of the administrative work usually performed by the HR function. However, the implementation of e-HR alone is unlikely to make the HR function more strategic. It is only where the HR function already has a strategic role that e-HR is likely to enhance the contribution of HRM to competitive advantage (Marler, 2009).

Regardless of the degree of sophistication in a firm's use of new technology in HRM, organisations are increasingly employing Human Resource Information Systems (HRIS) or Human Resource Management Systems (HRMS) to support the HR function. These are systems used to acquire, store, manipulate, analyse, retrieve and distribute data about an organisation's human resources. These systems can provide detailed information about the deployment of people within organisations that can support organisational decision-making in resourcing (for example, regarding the diversity of their workforce) as well as learning and development. New technology can also enable a self-service intranet facility accessible to employees through their desktop PCs which enables them to conduct routine transactions, update personal records and email enquiries to an HR service centre without the direct involvement of an HR specialist.

BOX 15.5
HRM IN PRACTICE

Virgin Media, e-HR and shared services

The following organisational example provides a practical insight into two trends in contemporary HRM that are discussed in this chapter: the centralisation of HRM activities to provide a single focus for employee-facing activities and the increasing use of self-service IT solutions for dealing with day-to-day transactional HR issues.

Virgin Media is a UK provider of broadband, TV, mobile phone and home phone services, employing approximately 13,000 staff. In June 2010, the company reorganised its 'people team' to improve the HR service to its staff by creating a first point of contact for employees with people- or employment-related queries. The customer-facing aspect of the people team consisted of a central employee services department to handle routine transactional HR tasks, supported by Touchpoint, an intranet system, accessible either from desktop PCs or remotely, providing both a self-service portal for employees and managers and a searchable database of frequently asked questions.

The employee services department is structured into six teams. The customer contact team represent a first point of contact for all staff and aim to deal with the majority of employee queries. Where a query is complex and requires specialist advice or support, it is passed on to the relevant specialist team: recruitment, pay and reward administration, pay services, case management (for example, for assistance with grievance and disciplinary procedures), and reporting and systems (which provides specialist HR information for managers).

For employees, the self-service portal allows them to update their personal details, view information regarding pay and bonuses and select among their flexible benefits. For managers, the portal provides access to the company's HRMS in order to view a wide range of employee information, including that on salary and absence, and update information regarding discipline and grievance procedures.

Source: IDS, 2011b

The move towards greater automation and self-service has also changed the nature of line manager involvement in HR activities by enabling them to perform a wide range of activities online, for example, reviewing employee data on skills, turnover or absenteeism, submitting training requests and conducting performance appraisals.

It is not the case, however, that new technology inevitably leads to a more strategic contribution from the HR function. Following Schuler and Jackson's (1987) typology discussed in Chapter 3, Broderick and Boudreau (1992) suggest that the type of approach adopted towards the use of ICT in HRM should reflect the organisation's overarching HR objectives: a cost-reduction approach to HR can be facilitated by systems to streamline processing of administrative transactions; an objective of quality or customer satisfaction can be served by e-HR systems that are responsive to the needs of end-user clients and contribute to the collaborative design of effective HR processes; and an organisational focus on innovation can be served by systems designed to enable better design-making and provide information where creativity and risk-taking might be rewarded.

Considerations in the adoption of e-HR

Despite the growth and potential of e-HR, Stone et al. (2006) note that there is relatively little research on factors that influence the degree to which it leads to positive and negative consequences for both individuals and organisations. The positive effects of e-HR might include improved organisational efficiency and ease of individual access to job opportunities and benefits. Negative consequences include individual perception of intrusions into privacy through data collection and distribution (Ulrich et al., 2008). To combat such a negative perception, IDS (2002) stress the importance of involving both HR specialists and managers in the design and implementation of new systems and of considering the consequences for the individual to overcome the risk of alienating end-users. For example, the design of HR systems and attendant processes should take account of the fact that the greater availability of data and self-service approaches to HRM can lead to increased workload, resentment and resistance, both for line managers and employees.

New technology can also have both positive and negative implications for the HR function itself. For example, whilst the increasing use of technology might have an enriching effect on the work of HR professionals (for example, by providing greater opportunity for challenging and strategically important work) it might also result in fewer meaningful personal interactions of the kind valued by many HR professionals, thereby leading to lower job satisfaction and/or career commitment (Roehling et al., 2005).

Therefore, the effective design, implementation and use of e-HR or HRMS require a consideration of both the technology itself (the hardware and software applications) and the end-users, including HR professionals, line managers and employees, and their requirements (Hendrickson, 2003). In particular, the design of e-HR systems should take into account the specific needs of end-users and their access to and familiarity with new technology (Kettley and Reilly, 2003). Where HR processes and policies are not present to support its introduction and use, such as training and workload considerations, new technology can have a negative effect on employee morale and productivity. As in all areas of work, the development and diffusion of new technology have led to the need for e-HR users to develop further a range of skills that are critical to ensuring its positive contribution to business processes. These include more advanced IT skills and the ability to manipulate, analyse and interpret data and communicate outputs. Research suggests that the training and education of HR professionals currently place limited emphasis on ensuring an understanding of new technologies and their influence (Hempel, 2004).

The utility of outputs from e-HR systems is closely associated with the quality of information that is collected and collated. Therefore, whilst e-HR systems have the potential to supply managers with high-quality management information (Kettley and Reilly, 2003), this information needs to be timely, relevant, accurate and up-to-date if it is to be valuable. In short, it needs to be fit for purpose as the basis for operational and strategic decision-making by a variety of stakeholders.

A further problem in data capture and evaluation is that not all desired information can be codified and collated by e-HR systems. For example, in using new technology to collate and assess workforce capabilities, tacit knowledge, such as intuition and experience that is important to organisational success, can be difficult to capture and therefore may be overlooked. Thus, the technology drives *expedient* decision-making rather than enabling *effective* decision-making. Management should acknowledge, therefore, that there are limits to the extent to which the HR professionals can be supplanted by information systems, particularly in relation to the soft functions of HR specialists such as coaching, which require an understanding of social dynamics to be effective (Stanton and Coovert, 2004: 122).

SUMMARY POINTS

- The continued ageing of the working population in many advanced capitalist economies presents a challenge for HRM, not least in the management of those reaching or exceeding pensionable age.

- Explicit knowledge is that which is communicable, exists in the form of data, procedures and processes and underpins an individual's ability to perform a particular task or function. Tacit knowledge is the taken-for-granted know-how and deeper understanding that reside within the individual and underpin innovation, creativity and problem-solving in novel situations.

- Effective knowledge management requires a consideration of the formal processes, structures and ICT systems designed to enable the effective collection, codification and distribution of knowledge and the informal social relationships and networks through which individuals pass on information and know-how.

- Knowledge workers are most usefully defined as those who work *with* knowledge to innovate and create new knowledge and technologies as opposed to those who work *from* a body of knowledge.

- Managing knowledge workers requires the development of new ways of recruiting, retaining and motivating employees that are more suited to the particular characteristics of knowledge workers themselves and that address the imperative to create and share distributed knowledge.

- Outsourcing of operational HRM functions to a third-party provider has become an increasingly common phenomenon. The reasons why firms might choose to outsource include reducing costs, a desire for a more strategic HR focus, improving service quality, accessing technology and gaining specialised expertise.

- One increasingly common model for the delivery of HR services is through shared service centres to provide a central point of access to HR expertise and guidance.

- HRM has a significant role to play in ensuring that new technology is effective and productive by managing the relationship between people and technology.

- ICT also has the potential to transform the HR function through e-HR and HRM systems, particularly through the self-service delivery of HR operations to managers and employees, and liberating HR professionals to focus on more strategic concerns.

SELF-TEST QUESTIONS

1 What is likely to be the key demographic change affecting the UK labour market – in common with many advanced capitalist economies – over the next two decades? What implications does this have for employers?

2 What role will new technology likely play in the ongoing construction of labour markets?

3 What is 'explicit' and 'tacit' knowledge? What problems does 'tacit' knowledge present for managers seeking to facilitate knowledge-sharing within an organisation?

4 What do you understand by the term 'knowledge worker'? What examples of knowledge 'jobs' can you give?

5 Why is knowledge said to have become the principal value-adding commodity that an organisation possesses? What challenges does this present for managers?

6 In what ways do organisations 'possess' knowledge?

7 What are the main reasons why a firm might wish to outsource some or all of its HRM activities?

8 What problems have been associated with the outsourcing of HR activities that might explain why some firms have brought such activity back in-house?

9 What are the characteristics of a shared service centre? What are the advantages of using such a centre in the delivery of HRM?

10 What are the three broad evolutionary stages through which e-HR has developed which reflect differing degrees to which employers use new technology to fulfil HR functions?

11 What do you understand by the term 'self-service' when applied to the delivery of HRM? What HR transactions are amenable to a self-service model?

TEST YOURSELF

TEST YOURSELF

Want to know more about this chapter? Review what you have been learning by visiting: https://edge.sagepub.com/wilton3e

- Print out or download the chapter summaries for quick revision
- Test yourself with multiple-choice questions
- Revise key terms with interactive flashcards

CASE STUDY

A crisis at Pulsewidth Solutions

The organisation

Pulsewidth Solutions is a UK-based technology firm primarily concerned with the development of computer software and technological solutions and provider of associated consultancy and technical support services. Formed in the mid-1980s, Pulsewidth currently employs approximately 1,000 people in the UK and Western Europe and is held up as a Great British success story.

Its mission statement is:

At Pulsewidth, we do things differently. From the way we treat our staff to the solutions we offer to our clients, we aim to provide the best experience possible and enable all our stakeholders to be the best they can be. Our mission is:

- To enable our clients to compete
- To be the number one business solutions provider in the UK and beyond
- To be renowned for our innovation, service quality and effectiveness
- To be an employer of choice for the brightest and most innovative ICT and consultancy specialists.

In support of this mission, Pulsewidth publicises widely a set of core corporate vales that shape the firm's culture and define employee behaviours, through their embedding in the organisational competency framework that informs recruitment, selection, employee development and performance management. These values are:

- integrity
- client priority
- superior performance
- value creation
- teamwork.

The company's headquarters are in London, with other offices in Glasgow and Birmingham. The main functions of the London headquarters are service, support and sales and marketing for its customers and partner organisations in the UK, as well as leading on its core client activities in the South East. Operations in Scotland, Northern Ireland and the North of England are run from the Glasgow office. Birmingham covers the Midlands, South Wales and the South West. Pulsewidth collaborates with a small sister firm operating in Belgium, as well as a subsidiary operation on the outskirts of Paris that supports its clients where they have operations in Northern Europe. The company also has a research laboratory which specialises in developing bespoke software for clients and 'blue sky' innovation. This lab is located in Bath and works in close collaboration with a local university. The structure of the company is best understood as a loose coalition. Whilst all parts of the firm form part of Pulsewidth, each office operates, to some degree, autonomously from the rest of the organisation.

Much of the firm's headline work (i.e. contracts with prestigious multinational firms) is run from its London headquarters and this is where the majority of the workforce are based. Whilst the firm tries to ensure it recognises the value of the work done in the regional offices – not least because SME clients account for a large proportion of their revenue – the focus in publicity on naming its 'big clients' and the tendency of high fliers in the firm to gravitate towards London cause some resentment 'out in the provinces'.

Market context

Even for an organisation that has been at the cutting edge of new technology for a quarter of century, the pace of technological change presents a significant challenge, not least to develop new and more innovative solutions for its clients and to compete more effectively for new business. Moreover, new competitors from the Far East as well as more aggressive overseas expansion among North American tech firms mean that Pulsewidth has experienced increasing pressure on its cost base. Like many firms it has gradually sought to reduce its operating costs so as to provide a more competitive service to its clients. It has also scoped out the possibilities of developing its European business in order to head-off some contraction in the UK market and the impact of overcrowding. Despite these challenges the firm continues to enjoy a solid international reputation in its field. The company is publically listed and its stock price is currently relatively high amid rumours of an imminent takeover bid from an American firm with a reputation for acquisitiveness and, subsequently, for heavy cost cutting on the firms its buys. Whilst potentially good news for investors, this speculation is inevitably concerning for the employees at Pulsewidth.

Both technological and market pressures have meant a gradual process of rationalisation at the firm, of processes, working practices, estate and investment. In recent months, for instance, Pulsewidth has been able to reduce the office space it uses by one-third by employing hot-desking and getting rid of its staff canteen. The firm reasons that for such a 'technology-forward' firm, a reliance on physical space to get work done is an anachronism.

Despite the somewhat artificial bump to its share price caused by the takeover speculation, the firm has experienced some difficulties in recent months. Six months ago, for instance, the firm lost a key long-standing client – Hercules Finance – which was damaging to Pulsewidth in financial terms and in respect of its reputation. Upon being summoned to London to explain the loss of the client, senior managers informed the board that the client felt a need to 'freshen things up' and engage with consultants that were offering new ideas. When pushed, the Glasgow technical director reported that the client felt that Pulsewidth tended to offer the 'same old solution' for every new problem.

The workforce at Pulsewidth

Pulsewidth is widely recognised as an excellent employer and regularly features in lists of 'best places to work' (although its position in these lists has fallen year on year) and prides itself both on the diversity of its workforce and its employee-friendly flexible working practices to encourage a healthy work–life balance. Pulsewidth prides itself on an open, honest culture in which people can realise their potential.

This workforce is mainly comprised of consultants, business managers, technical account managers and systems engineers, as well as the administrative functions that support the activities of these employees. All these employee groups are typically involved in the process of securing and servicing client contracts, most of which run over several years. Business managers are not technical experts and are concerned with client relations, typically at a senior management level. They pitch for new business and, once a client is interested in the products or services that Pulsewidth offer, hand over to the technical account managers. Business managers do, however, maintain broad oversight of the projects. Typically, they are based in the office for approximately 50 per cent of their time. Technical project managers are typically drawn from the ranks of consultants and have a broad technological expertise. They tend to be promoted on the basis of their proven ability to apply technical solutions to meet the needs of clients and to communicate these requirements to software engineers. Consultants have day-to-day oversight of the projects, typically working between several clients at any one time and primarily working 'on the road'. Finally, the work of software engineers falls into two camps: first, working exclusively on a client site to install systems or software which can often take several months; second, providing technical support for clients post-installation. The software engineers are typically assigned to a particular client so that once initial installation is completed they provide subsequent technical support for that client. Senior management at Pulsewidth feel that this provides consistency of service. They are allocated work on the basis of prior assignments which means they tend to become specialised in particular areas of software development and installation.

Software engineers are graduates in a related discipline typically recruited straight from universities with leading IT departments. The unofficial list of universities from which the company recruits has changed little in the last ten years. During the graduate training programme, engineers are based partly in the office for formal training and also on client sites where they typically work with a mentor, a senior software engineer, to learn both the technology and informal processes of working on-site. New recruits

often report that this is the most important aspect of their training. Once they have completed the graduate programme, they are then able to take work on client sites, typically working alone or in pairs. Where the project is particularly large, a small group of software engineers might be employed. Senior management has identified that it is typically on these projects that new innovations tend to emerge. Consistent with the ideas of continuous professional development, software engineers are encouraged to continually update their skills and knowledge by using the e-learning portal on the company intranet. This portal provided engineers with various learning modules – developed by a third-party e-learning provider – to develop their expertise and that they could 'dip in and out of' whenever they have the time. The HRIS automatically updates once software engineers complete a module.

Working practices

The consultants, technical project managers and software engineers working on a particular project or for a particular client are notionally referred to as a 'project team' and, despite rarely meeting physically, given the varying commitments of each, communicate virtually using the latest in mobile technology (as you might expect for a world leading technological solutions provider). Pulsewidth ensures that all staff have access to such up-to-the-minute technology to help them do their jobs and whilst on client sites all staff have access to the Pulsewidth intranet. In order to aid innovation and new ideas, the intranet has a chat room for software engineers to swap ideas and to contribute to the solving of complex problems, although this tends not to be used a great deal. The HR director has recently brought in a bespoke HR information system to aid managerial decision-making based on more and better information concerning the distribution of skills and knowledge in the firm, the allocation of roles, responsibilities and projects among the workforce and employee and team performance.

Questions

1   Identify the knowledge transfer processes in place at Pulsewidth Glasgow. What is the principal focus of knowledge-sharing activity in the organisation?

2 What aspects of the organisation of work might have contributed to the problems that the client identified in choosing to no longer work with Pulsewidth?

3 What recommendations would you make to the HR director at Pulsewidth to improve the sharing

of knowledge within the company and with its clients?

4 What factors might be considered problematic to knowledge-sharing in the wider organisation (Pulsewidth UK)?

USEFUL READING

Journal articles

Alvesson, M. and Karreman, D. (2001) Odd couple: Making sense of the curious concept of knowledge management, *Journal of Management Studies*, 38 (7): 995–1018.

This article draws on theory and empirical research to discuss the conceptual problems associated with the term knowledge management, not least the apparent contradiction between knowledge and management.

Lengnick-Hall, M. and Moritz, S. (2003) The impact of e-HR on the human resource management function, *Journal of Labour Research*, 24 (3): 365–79.

This article provides a very useful overview of e-HR and its potential to reshape HRM. It discusses the evolution of e-HR over recent years, the costs and benefits associated with its implementation, examples of firms that have introduced e-HR and insight into future developments.

Scarbrough, H. (1999) Knowledge as work: Conflicts in the management of knowledge workers, *Technology Analysis and Strategic Management*, 11 (1): 5–16.

This article provides an overview of many of the debates around knowledge work and workers and the inherent problems of managing such an organisational 'resource'. In particular, it raises the

issue of conflict between an individual's know-how and the exploitation of this knowledge as a saleable commodity, and how management might seek to resolve this conflict.

Ulrich, D., Younger, J. and Brockbank, W. (2008) The twenty-first-century HR organisation, *Human Resource Management*, 47 (4): 829–50.

This article provides an assessment of many of the contemporary trends in HRM discussed in this chapter, including the increasing use of service centres, outsourcing and the use of e-HR, but also considers how HR departments can be structured to meet the challenges of the twenty-first century.

Books, book chapters and reports

Newell, S., Robertson, M., Scarbrough, H. and Swan, J. (2009) *Managing Knowledge Work and Innovation* (2nd edn), London: Palgrave.

This comprehensive book draws on empirical research and explores the management of knowledge and knowledge work from the perspective of both people and ICT. It stresses that the value of knowledge work depends primarily on the behaviours, attitudes and motivations of those who undertake and manage it.

FURTHER ONLINE READING

The following articles can be accessed for free on the book's companion website **https://edge.sagepub.com/wilton3e**:

Alegre, J., Sengupta, K. and Lapiedra, R. (2011) Knowledge management and innovation performance in a high-tech SME sector, *International Small Business Journal*, 1–17.

Benson, J. and Brown, M. (2007) Knowledge workers: What keeps them committed; what turns them away, *Work, Employment and Society*, 21: 121–41.

Blankenship, S. S. and Ruona, W. E. A. (2009) Exploring knowledge sharing in social structures: Potential contributions to an overall knowledge management strategy, *Advances in Developing Human Resources*, 11 (3): 290–306.

Datta, D. K., Guthrie, J. P., Basuil, D. and Pandey, A. (2010) Causes and effects of employee downsizing: A review and synthesis, *Journal of Management*, 36 (1): 281–348.

Grimshaw, D. and Miozzo, M. (2009) New human resource management practices in knowledge-intensive business services firms: The case of outsourcing with staff transfer, *Human Relations*, 62 (10): 1521–50.

Sewell, G. (2005) Nice work? Rethinking managerial control in an era of knowledge work, *Organization*, 12 (5): 685–704.

Sheehan, C. (2009) Outsourcing HRM activities in Australian organisations, *Asia Pacific Journal of Human Resources*, 47 (2): 236–53.

Want to know more about this chapter? Visit the companion website at: **https://edge.sagepub.com/wilton3e** to access practice questions, videos and selected journal articles to further enhance your study.

GLOSSARY

360-degree appraisal/feedback A form of performance appraisal which collects feedback from a variety of sources, typically superiors, subordinates, peers and internal/external customers, to provide a holistic view of whole job performance.

Appraisal See **Performance appraisal**.

Arbitration Intervention in an industrial dispute where the parties to the dispute appoint a third party to evaluate the evidence and make a decision to resolve the dispute.

Assessment centre Often used for highly competitive posts (such as places on graduate training schemes); these are extended selection procedures, which involve a combination of selection methods alongside interviews, such as work simulations, presentations and testing.

Autonomy The extent of employee freedom and discretion to determine how their work is conducted and the process by which agreed outcomes are achieved without significant direction or intervention from management.

Balanced scorecard A framework to plan and assess organisational performance which incorporates consideration of four key perspectives: financial; customer; internal business process; and learning and growth.

Bargaining level The level at which collective bargaining takes place within the organisation (for example, workplace or company-wide) or industry sector (multi-employer or national bargaining).

Bargaining scope The range of issues that are the subject of collective bargaining between employees and managers.

Benefits Payments in kind which are in addition to financial reward but which hold some financial, and often status, value. Sometimes referred to as indirect pay.

Best fit Models of strategic HRM which advocate different approaches to people management to match organisational conditions and strategies. To achieve competitive advantage, HR strategy should fit with wider business strategy, environment, labour market, organisational structure, size and stage of development.

Best practice Universalistic models of HRM which suggest that particular 'bundles' of HR practices can lead to improved individual and organisational performance, regardless of organisational characteristics and environmental factors. Alternatively, referred to as high-commitment HRM or High Performance Work Systems.

Broad banding The grouping of pay grades into a limited number of bands, each consisting of a wide range of jobs, to increase flexibility in pay decisions and to better reflect internal and external pay relativities.

Bundles Groups of HR practices which are complementary and mutually supportive in contributing to increased employee commitment and performance. Associated with best practice HRM.

Bureaucracy An approach to structuring and coordinating organisational activities which emphasises strict demarcation between job roles, formal rules and procedures and rigid hierarchies of control.

Bureaucratic control Employee control via the demarcation of responsibility, detailed formal rules and procedures and the operation of internal labour markets.

Business partner According to Ulrich's typology, one of the main roles of the HR specialist involving supporting senior management towards the achievement of the aims and objectives of the organisation.

Cafeteria benefits See Flexible benefits

Capability procedure Organisational procedures that are distinct from those for handling employee discipline and which have the explicit function of tackling poor employee performance through the development of employee capability.

Career management A range of practices and activities that seek to meet both individual and organisational needs for employee development and progression and that shape the operation of the internal labour market.

Civil law Distinct from criminal law, civil law mostly deals with disputes between people, companies or other organisations (for example, regarding contracts) and is dealt with through civil courts.

Classical approach Approach to strategy formation that stresses the importance of a formal planning process, including a comprehensive assessment of both the external environment and internal resources to inform strategic choice.

Coaching Developmental relationship between an employee and their immediate line manager with the explicit, often short-term purpose of contributing to performance improvements and developing individual capability through the transfer of knowledge and skills.

Co-determination Joint decision-making between management and workers concerning workplace issues.

Collective agreement The agreement on terms and conditions of employment that results from the process of collective bargaining.

Collective bargaining Process by which terms and conditions of employment, particularly pay, are negotiated by an employer, or employer's association, and one or more trade unions.

Collectivism Approach to people management that focuses on managing workers as a group rather than as individuals.

Commitment-based HR strategy Approach to managing people based on the view of human resources as an organisational asset, rather than cost, which can contribute to organisational success if positively nurtured and developed.

Common law That part of the law not embodied in legislation and which consists of rules of law based on common custom and judicial decisions.

Competence The ability to perform a specific task or fulfil a function to a desired standard.

Competencies The underlying characteristics of a person required for effective performance in a particular job in a particular organisational context.

Conciliation Third-party intervention in an industrial dispute to facilitate discussion between employer and employee representatives to assist in resolving the dispute and avoiding future conflict.

Constructive (unfair) dismissal Circumstance where an employee terminates their contract of employment in direct response to a significant or fundamental breach of contract by the employer, thus entitling them to claim unfair dismissal.

Contingent reward See Variable pay

Continuing professional development (CPD) The ongoing process of self-directed and reflective learning and development through which an individual updates their skills and knowledge and maintains competence in their field.

Control-based HR strategy An approach to managing people based on the view that labour is a variable cost that should be minimised through the close monitoring and tight control of employee performance through direct supervision and bureaucratic means.

Convergence The coming together or movement towards similarity of, for example, approaches to HRM adopted in different countries.

Core competencies Specific organisational factors or characteristics (for example, specific knowledge,

processes or relationships) that are viewed as being central to the way the organisation operates and competes in the marketplace.

Core values The guiding principles of a company that can be used to guide, support and assess employee performance.

Core workers Workers who possess valuable, scarce or firm-specific skills and who are typically subject to high levels of job security, good terms and conditions of employment and high levels of task discretion.

Corporate culture A consciously developed organisational culture that reflects the values and expectations of senior management and has the purpose of promoting particular attitudes and behaviours among employees.

Corporate social responsibility (CSR) Corporate self-regulation regarding adherence to the law, ethical standards and social norms, reflecting a recognition of the potential impact of organisational activity on a range of stakeholders.

CPD Continuing professional development

CSR Corporate social responsibility

Custom and practice Workplace arrangements that have evolved informally over time to become the established 'way of doing things'.

Cyclical unemployment Unemployment that reflects business or economic cycles and the varying demand for labour at any one time, rather than a lack of employability of those workers affected.

Delayering Organisational restructuring with the intention of reducing the number of managerial levels in the organisational hierarchy.

Depth (of employee voice) The extent of employee influence afforded by a particular mechanism for employee involvement or participation.

Deskilling The redesign of jobs to reduce organisational reliance on particular skills, either through the greater use of technology or job fragmentation and simplification.

Development The process of individual or organisational change, enrichment and improvement with the objective of realising potential, often via learning experiences.

Dignity at work Narrowly concerned with ensuring freedom from bullying and harassment, but can be understood more widely as concerned with the creation of a positive working environment, involvement in good-quality work and respectful working relationships.

Direct control Worker control through strict and close monitoring and supervision and the subordination of workers to management.

Direct discrimination Where an individual or group is treated less favourably than others on account of social group characteristics such as age, gender or ethnicity.

Disciplinary procedures Formal organisational arrangements by which managers can deal with alleged employee misconduct and poor performance.

Discretionary behaviour Employee behaviour that is of positive benefit to the employing organisation but which cannot be required by contract only encouraged through a positive psychological contract.

Diversity management Approach to workforce management which emphasises the importance of recognising and valuing social group and/or individual differences to maximise the contribution of all employees.

Downsizing Euphemism for employee redundancies, often associated with organisational restructuring and reducing labour costs.

EAP Employee assistance programmes

e-HR (electronic HR) The adoption and use of ICT and new media to perform a range of human resources activities, such as recruitment, training and assessment.

EI Employee involvement

e-Learning (electronic learning) The use of ICT and new media to facilitate or deliver employee training, for example, through the Internet or company intranets.

Emotional labour Work that involves the presentation and/or suppression of particular emotions in the conduct of one's work. Typically associated with service employment but increasingly incorporated into a wider variety of roles.

Employability The ability of a worker to obtain and retain continuous employment through the development of their human capital.

Employee assistance programmes (EAP) EAPs provide support, advice and information for employees through telephone helplines, the Internet and counselling to help deal with, for example, legal, emotional, domestic, financial, health and work-related issues.

Employee attitude survey Management research tool to assess employee morale and attitudes to, for example, organisational issues or decisions.

Employee champion Following Ulrich's (1997) typology, one of the main roles of the HR specialist, involving acting as advocate on behalf of workers and seeking to ensure that worker needs are met.

Employee communication The process by which information is communicated between management and employees and which can be either unidirectional or bidirectional.

Employee consultation A decision-making process by which employee views on managerial proposals are sought (usually via employee representatives) but where management retains the right to make the final decision.

Employee involvement (EI) The opportunity for employees to contribute to managerial decision-making over workplace issues through formal organisational channels designed to elicit greater employee understanding and commitment to the objectives of the organisation.

Employee participation (EP) The opportunity for employees to participate directly in organisational decision-making over pre-designated issues in order to provide a counterweight to managerial prerogative.

Employee turnover The rate of employee exit from an employer, often expressed as a ratio of leavers to overall workforce.

Employee voice Mechanisms through which employee attitudes, opinions and contributions are sought, either with (direct) or without (indirect) the intervention of representatives.

Employment relations (ER) The theory and practice associated with the management and regulation of the employment relationship.

Employment relationship The dynamic economic, socio-political, psychological and legal relationship that exists between a worker and an employer.

Employment tribunal A panel that adjudicates upon legal cases involving employment disputes, usually consisting of a qualified official (akin to a judge) and two lay members.

Empowerment A partial redistribution of decision-making powers and responsibilities to enable employees to make decisions about particular work- and job-related issues without significant managerial intervention and to make them more accountable for their own performance.

EO Equal opportunities

EP Employee participation

Equal opportunities (EO) Approach to addressing labour market inequality informed by the belief that all employees and prospective employees should be treated the same regardless of social group characteristics, enacted by the removal of formal and informal barriers to employment opportunities to create a 'level playing field'.

Equal pay The provision of equal levels of pay for men and women doing the same, similar or equivalent jobs.

ER Employment relations

E-recruitment The use of ICT to conduct aspects of employee recruitment and selection including advertising jobs, facilitating application, online testing and shortlisting.

Ethics A set of moral principles that govern the behaviour of an individual or group.

Ethnocentric Approach to management in MNCs which stresses the superiority of 'home' country practices and seeks to disseminate these throughout the company.

Evolutionary approach Approach to strategy formation that stresses unpredictability and a predominant focus on responding to an organisation's immediate market context.

Exit interview Interviews conducted with departing employees to discuss the reasons for their departure and to better understand drivers of employee turnover and potential organisational problems.

Expectancy theory Theory that suggests employee motivation to perform effectively depends on the individual's specific needs and the expectation of fulfilling those needs through productive behaviour.

Explicit knowledge Collectively held and communicable knowledge that is 'out there' and is codified in the form of, for example, data, procedures and processes that are written down in books, company manuals etc.

External equity Employees' perception of the comparability of their employment 'situation', particularly received rewards, with that of employees in other organisations.

External labour market The external supply or stock of labour available to an organisation, the nature of which is shaped both by the types of labour required and the pool of such workers in the wider economy.

Extrinsic motivation Motivation by factors external to the individual, such as financial reward, as opposed to the internal or intrinsic motivation of, for example, job satisfaction or enjoyment.

Feedback Evaluative information provided to an individual employee or group in response to a particular suggestion, activity or process.

Financial flexibility Flexible approaches to employee reward which seek to link individual performance with received reward and/or ensure that wage costs closely match business performance.

Financial participation Schemes such as employee share ownership or profit-sharing designed to increase employee association with organisational goals and to encourage employee loyalty to the organisation.

Flexible benefits Approach to employee reward provision where individuals can create their own reward package to reflect personal preference by choosing among a 'menu' of benefits.

Flexible firm Theoretical model of how firms use different groups of workers to achieve various forms of workforce flexibility and the associated implications for workers (Atkinson, 1984).

Flexible working Working arrangements that provide employers with scope for workforce adaptability and workers with the opportunity to better balance work and other responsibilities, under certain circumstances.

Fordism Approach to job design and labour processes associated with mass production based on allying scientific management principles such as job fragmentation, deskilling and close worker control to specialised machinery and automated production lines. Associated with repetitive and unsatisfying work.

Form (of employee voice) Mechanisms by which employees are communicated with, consulted or negotiated with over workplace decisions.

Free market Economy with limited state intervention in the activities of business, employees or consumers and where the state does not significantly attempt to plan the economy in a strategic manner.

Frictional unemployment Unemployment that reflects a temporary mismatch in the demand and supply of labour which is always present in the labour market.

Functional flexibility Contributor to organisational adaptability through the ability of employees to undertake a range of tasks, either horizontally (at the same organisational level) or vertically (increased managerial or supervisory responsibility).

Gain-sharing Employee incentive scheme whereby a company shares with employees the savings or 'gains' from improved organisational performance (for example, greater productivity).

Geocentric Approach to management in MNCs focused on the dissemination of global best practice throughout the company.

Global strategy The preference within a multinational corporation for policies and practices to be determined globally and integrated across the organisation, regardless of local context.

Globalisation Phenomena associated with a range of ongoing economic, social and political processes through which nation states are becoming more integrated and interrelated.

Go-slow Working deliberately slowly; used as an employee tactic in an industrial dispute to put pressure on management.

Grievance procedures A formal process used to channel and resolve employee dissatisfaction with their treatment at work.

Gross misconduct Unacceptable employee behaviour serious enough to constitute a breach of the employment contract and to justify summary dismissal.

Harassment Persistent and unwanted conduct towards an individual or group, sometimes but not always with the intention of causing upset or distress, that is intimidating, disturbing, hostile, degrading and/or offensive.

Hard HRM Approach to people management under which workers are used in an instrumental manner to achieve business objectives. Often associated with the exploitation of workers and disregard for worker interests.

High Performance Work System (HPWS) Form of best practice HRM which stresses the importance of specific bundles of HR practices – such as continual skills development, employee participation in decision-making and high pay – to generate an improved employment relationship and mutual gains for both employer and employee.

High-commitment HRM See Best practice

Horizontal integration The holistic implementation of diverse aspects of the HR mix to ensure they are mutually supportive and integrated.

HPWS High Performance Work System

HRD Human resource development

HRIS Human Resource Information Systems

HRM Human resource management

HRM–performance link The contested casual connection between particular configurations of HR practices and policies and improvements in individual, group and organisational performance.

HRP Human resource planning

H&S Health and safety

Human capital The accumulation of competencies, skills, knowledge and attributes acquired through experience, qualifications and learning and possessed by an individual or group.

Human relations Perspective on managing people at work which stresses the importance of recognising the social needs of workers and the informal organisation of work activities.

Human resource development (HRD) The contemporary term used to encapsulate the wide range of informal and formal, on-the-job and off-the-job means by which a firm's human resources learn, develop and increase their contribution to the achievement of organisational objectives.

Human Resource Information Systems (HRIS) ICT systems used to acquire, store, manipulate, analyse, retrieve and distribute information about an organisation's human resources to inform and support organisational decision-making.

Human resource management (HRM) The umbrella term used to refer to all the managerial activities associated with managing the employment relationship. It also denotes a specific approach towards people management which stresses its importance in contributing to the achievement of strategic objectives and promotes particular configurations of HR practices.

Human resource planning (HRP) The formal and systematic process of forecasting labour supply and demand to anticipate and plan for future requirements for human resources.

Human resource strategy The unified set of ideas, policies and practices which management adopts in order to achieve HRM objectives.

ICT Information and communication technology

Indirect discrimination The practice of applying a requirement or condition to organisational decision-making (for example, regarding recruitment or promotion) which, whilst applying to all individuals, disadvantages members of certain social groups.

Indirect pay Employee perks and benefits that supplement direct pay and are associated with employment by a particular organisation or with a particular role or post.

Individualism Approach to people management where the individual worker is the fundamental unit of concern rather than groups of workers.

Industrial relations A term traditionally used to refer to relations between the three main parties to the collective employment relationship: trade unions, management and government. The term has connotations of joint regulation and the institutionalisation of industrial conflict in rules and procedures. Typically now referred to as employee or employment relations to reflect recent changes to the employment relationship.

Institutional framework The inter-related political, legal, social and economic systems that exist in a particular country or set of countries.

Intellectual capital The knowledge possessed by an individual or organisation (the collective knowledge of its employees) that is value-adding and can be a source of competitive advantage.

Internal equity (Employee perception of) the rewards attached to a particular job compared to others in the same organisation.

Internal labour market The labour market that exists within a single organisation and represents its internal supply or stock of labour. It is the mechanism by which existing employees are attributed particular roles within a firm to create a formal structure of job roles.

Intrinsic motivation Motivation that is driven by personal interest or enjoyment in carrying out a task or job role and that exists within the individual rather than deriving from an external stimulus, such as financial reward.

Job analysis The systematic process of collecting and recording information about a specific job, often resulting in a job description.

Job description Formal statement of the duties, responsibilities, accountabilities, requirements, context and outcomes of a particular job, usually derived from job analysis.

Job design The process of allocating, arranging and combining organisational tasks and responsibilities to create whole jobs.

Job enlargement The expansion of a job horizontally to include a wider range of tasks at a similar level to those already undertaken.

Job enrichment The expansion of a job vertically to increase the range of challenge and worker autonomy and to give employees greater ownership of the labour process by which a product is produced or service delivered.

Job evaluation A systematic process by which to determine the relative value or worth of a job within an organisation to develop hierarchies of jobs and pay structures and to establish internal relativities.

Job rotation The periodic movement of a worker from one task to another as a means to improve job variety, alleviate monotony and develop a wider range of skills.

Joint regulation The process by which terms and conditions of employment are determined jointly by employers and employees through collective bargaining.

KM Knowledge management

Knowledge economy An economic system in which knowledge is the pre-eminent national and organisational asset.

Knowledge management (**KM**) Formal and informal organisational attempts to develop, elicit, distribute and make productive the knowledge possessed by its employees.

Knowledge worker Those who work *with* knowledge in creative and innovative ways to develop new knowledge as opposed to *from* a body of pre-existing knowledge (Scarbrough, 1999).

Knowledge-intensive firms Typically small, fast-growing service providers in which knowledge is the central commodity and new models of people management are developing.

Labour market The mechanism through which human labour is bought and sold as a commodity and the means by which labour demand is matched with labour supply.

Labour market segmentation A means of dividing the labour market according to a variety of worker attributes such as social group characteristics, geography, skills or qualifications.

Labour process The means by which human labour is harnessed in the creation of products and delivery of service.

Learning The acquisition of new knowledge, expertise, behaviours, competencies or skills as a result of formal and informal developmental activities and experience.

Learning cycle Model that holds that people learn through a process of experience, observation and reflection, theorising and experimentation (Kolb, 1984).

L&D Learning and development

Learning environment Physical and cultural conditions that exist within an organisation and are conducive to and supportive of formal and informal employee learning.

Learning organisation An organisation in which practices and processes are designed to enable individual and group learning to benefit the entire organisation, through its contribution to continuous performance improvement and cultural renewal.

Learning style Individual preferences for different aspects and ways of learning.

Level (of employee voice) The hierarchical level in an organisation or industry at which mechanisms for employee voice operate.

Line manager Managers who are responsible for a group of employees (for example, a team or department) to a higher level of management.

Locational flexibility Flexibility in the 'location' of employment through, for example, home-working, hot-desking or desk-sharing and teleworking.

Managerial discipline Formalised authority of managers to take corrective action against an employee for conduct or performance that is inconsistent with the standards laid out in organisational rules, including those contained in the contract of employment.

Managerial prerogative The right for managers to make decisions unimpeded by worker or third-party intervention.

Market pricing The setting of pay according to the 'going rate' for a job in a particular location and marketplace.

Matching model See Best fit

MBO Management by objectives

McDonaldization The idea (first posited by George Ritzer) that Western societies are increasingly taking on the characteristics – efficiency, predictability, calculability and control – of a fast-food restaurant.

MD Managing diversity

Mediation Third-party intervention in an industrial dispute where the mediator makes formal but non-binding recommendations to prompt a settlement between the parties based on an evaluation of the evidence.

Mentoring A long-term relationship in which a more experienced colleague supports the development of a more junior member of staff by passing on knowledge and providing guidance and advice.

MNC Multinational corporation

Multi-domestic strategy The preference within a multinational corporation for overseas subsidiaries to respond to local needs and norms in managerial decision-making leading to differentiated practices across the firm.

Multi-employer bargaining Collective bargaining that takes place between an association of employers and one or more trade unions.

Multinational corporation (**MNC**) An organisation that has activities in two or more countries.

Multi-skilling Form of functional flexibility enacted by employees with a range of transferable skills and associated with vertical functional flexibility, empowerment, enhanced employability and job satisfaction. Contrasted with multi-tasking.

National culture A unifying set of learnt, shared and organised values, attitudes, beliefs, assumptions and norms of behaviour that shape how members of the majority group in a given society relate to each other and to outsiders.

Natural wastage The inevitable loss of employees from an organisation that takes place over time and which can be used as a deliberate means by which to reduce workforce numbers.

Negotiation Process by which parties to the employment relationship resolve matters of dispute through discussion and mutual agreement.

Neo-human relations A perspective on people at work which emphasises the idea of employee 'self-actualisation' and the achievement of one's full potential through work as the most important factor in employee motivation.

Non-financial reward Intangible and intrinsic rewards, such as praise, challenging work and recognition, that motivate through contributing to a sense of satisfaction, pride and achievement in workers.

Numerical flexibility The organisational ability to alter the number of employees it directly employs through the use of casual, short-term, temporary, agency and self-employed workers and the outsourcing and sub-contracting of certain activities.

Occupational health (OH) A branch of medicine concerned with employee health and which includes activities such as employee rehabilitation, accident and injury prevention, advising on sympathetic job design and providing advice, guidance, training, counselling and health education.

Offshoring A form of outsourcing where the outsourced activity is done by a third party in another country.

Off-the-job learning Employee development activities that take place outside of the normal place of work, for example training or education courses or teambuilding activities.

OH Occupational health

On-the-job learning Employee development activities that take place in the normal course of work, for example, by undertaking aspects of a role for which an employee is being trained or secondment to a different post.

Organisational citizenship behaviour Individual workplace behaviours (such as altruism or conscientiousness) that are beneficial to the organisation, but that are at least partially discretionary and do not constitute an explicit element of required performance.

Organisational culture Shared values, attitudes and norms of behaviour that develop organically among a social group within an organisation through shared experience.

Organisational learning The notion that organisations can learn through the individuals that populate the firm and which represents a key characteristic of adaptive and adaptable organisations.

Organisational structure The formal arrangement of organisational activities and functions, levels of responsibility and accountability, and job roles.

Outsourcing The process of sub-contracting particular aspects of organisational activity to an external third-party provider.

Partnership Formal agreement between an employer and a trade union that stresses the mutual gains to be achieved through a cooperative relationship, recognition of each parties' needs and expectations, and the identification and pursuit of common goals.

Peer appraisal Feedback on individual job performance provided by one's colleagues, typically used in conjunction with other forms of appraisal in providing multi-source feedback.

Performance A function of individual ability, motivation and opportunity to perform (Boxall and Purcell, 2003).

Performance appraisal Formal, periodic opportunity for managers to assess prior employee performance and to plan for future performance through goal-setting and determining development needs.

Performance management (PM) An area of HRM concerned with connecting and improving individual, group and organisational performance.

Performance management system (PMS) An integrative framework encompassing a number of HR practices, such as performance appraisals, coaching and performance-related pay, designed to create greater association between organisational and individual objectives and to improve individual, group or organisational performance.

Performance-related pay (PRP) Flexible method of employee remuneration where received pay (typically an element of the total reward package) is contingent on an assessment of individual or group performance.

Peripheral workers Workers outside of the core workforce, including those temporarily or casually employed, and who are not central to the core activities of a firm. Often associated with job insecurity and poorer terms and conditions of employment than those offered to core employees.

Perks Employee benefits or indirect pay provided to those holding particular posts or positions rather than to the whole workforce.

Person specification A formal statement regarding the 'ideal candidate' for a post in terms of the skills, competencies and aptitude, experience and qualifications needed to perform effectively. Typically, derived from the job description.

Personnel management The traditional term used to refer to the organisational function or department concerned with managing the employment relationship. Used often to describe an operational approach to managing people which is contrasted with the more strategic approach of HRM.

Pluralism A perspective on the employment relationship that views organisations as comprising a number of competing interest groups with both shared and diverse interests and in which conflict is inevitable and best managed through formal procedures.

PM Performance management

PMS Performance management system

Polycentric An approach to HRM in MNCs where subsidiaries adapt their practices in accordance with local conditions and custom.

Positive action Measures designed to remedy the effects of historic labour market disadvantage for particular social groups and allow members of these groups to compete on equal terms for employment opportunities.

Positive discrimination Preferential treatment afforded to members of historically disadvantaged social groups in relation to recruitment, selection, promotion, etc.

Post-Fordism Flexible approach to manufacturing focused on producing smaller numbers of customised products for niche markets. Associated with flexible working arrangements, high skill, job variety, autonomy, empowerment and the promotion of a team ethos.

Post-industrialism Advanced stage of development for capitalist economies where manual work and manufacturing activity are limited, more flexible forms of work organisations and working predominate and the experience of work and employee relations is improved. Associated with Post-Fordism and a knowledge economy.

Privatisation The transfer of state-owned enterprises into private ownership.

Procedural fairness The use of formal and auditable procedures, for example in recruitment and selection, to eliminate subjectivity and illegitimate bias.

Processual approach Approach to strategy formation that views strategy as emerging patterns of action that enable the achievement of business objectives and which are shaped by the internal politics of the firm.

Profit-sharing Scheme through which employees are given a share of company profits, often with the aim of improving employee loyalty and association with organisational objectives.

PRP Performance-related pay

Psychological contract The set of unwritten expectations and perceived obligations held by each party to the employment relationship.

Psychometric tests A method of employee selection which seeks to 'measure' for the purposes of comparability some psychological aspect of a potential employee, such as personality or intelligence.

Quality circle Small group of employees, often in a specific area of organisational activity, who regularly meet to ensure that work quality is maintained and improved.

Quality of working life (QWL) A holistic construct used to assess the individual's experience of employment based upon the wide range of factors that influence job-related well-being and the extent to which work experiences are rewarding, fulfilling and devoid of negative personal consequences.

QWL Quality of working life

Radical A perspective on the employment relationship which argues that the relationship between capital and labour is marked by deep and irreconcilable conflicts of interest based on class conflict.

This conflict is inevitable and can only be resolved when workers, not capital, own the means of production.

RBV Resource-based view

Realistic job preview Providing prospective employees with a realistic picture of what a job actually entails, either through true-to-life description or some form of job sampling.

Recruitment Process of attracting a pool of suitably qualified applicants for a given position in order to select the best-suited among them.

Redeployment The movement of staff from one part of an organisation to another, often in order to reduce employment in a particular area.

Redundancy The means by which an employer dismisses employees in posts that are no longer required, for example due to a decline in business activity or the adoption of new technology.

Relational psychological contract An informal agreement between an employer and employee where long-term secure and stable employment is exchanged for loyalty, commitment and effort.

Representation gap The difference between how much influence employees report having over management decisions and how much influence they would like to have.

Representative participation Mechanisms for indirect and collective employee participation in decision-making through management consultation and negotiation, either with trade unions or elected workers' representatives.

Resource-based view (RBV) View that competitive advantage can best be achieved through identifying and exploiting a firm's unique and inimitable value-adding assets and that these assets should be used as the basis for strategic decision-making.

Responsible autonomy A mode of employee control based on the assumption that workers will respond positively in respect of motivation and performance to being provided with high degrees of discretion, autonomy and accountability for their work.

Reward Contemporary HR term which covers all financial remuneration and non-financial incentives provided to employees as part of the employment relationship. Emphasises the importance of recognising and responding to employees' psychological, social and economic needs.

Reward strategy Framework within which an organisation determines, communicates and measures the effectiveness of reward processes and practices and ensures they are aligned with wider business and HR strategy.

R&S Recruitment and selection

Sabotage Informal expression of employee dissatisfaction or conflict involving damaging or appropriating employer property and/or disrupting organisational activities.

Scientific management Approach to managing and organising work which seeks to maximise efficiency and productivity through job fragmentation, task specialisation, strict managerial control and an emphasis on financial reward as the primary source of motivation. Often used synonymously with Taylorism.

Scope (of employee voice) The range of workplace issues or matters on which employees (or their representatives) have a say through mechanisms for negotiation or consultation.

Selection The process of choosing from a pool of candidates the most appropriate person to fill a particular post using a range of methods and techniques.

Self-appraisal Employee's own assessment regarding their past performance and future development needs. Typically used in conjunction with top-down appraisals or as part of 360-degree appraisals.

Self-managed team Group of employees, often possessing a range of skills, who assume managerial responsibility and accountability for the organisation of work, scheduling and quality in the completion of a project or set of tasks.

Shareholder approach Approach to business activities which holds that commercial organisations have as their primary or main function maximising the return on investment of shareholders.

Shareholder economy National economic systems which are characterised by organisational ownership by privately owned small and large investors and, therefore, managerial focus on delivering short-term return on investment.

SHRD Strategic human resource development

Social control Informal mechanisms that regulate individual behaviour within a social group to ensure compliance with a set of explicit or implied rules, such as the internalisation of cultural norms or the use of positive or negative sanctions by colleagues.

Social dialogue Negotiation and discussion that take place between the social partners at an industry, national or international level.

Social market Economic system in which the regulation of business and employment activity both through direct state intervention and trade unions is accepted in order to ensure that the needs and interests of all stakeholders are addressed.

Social partners Often associated with the industrial relations in many continental European countries, social partners are the representatives of employees (trade unions) and employers (employers' associations) and government.

Social policy Government policy and interventions concerning social issues including healthcare, education, housing, welfare and social care, crime and justice, and labour markets and employment regulation.

Soft HRM Approach to managing people which emphasises investing in worker development, nurturing employee loyalty, providing

well-rewarded and satisfying work and developing a positive and trusting employment relationship.

Spatial flexibility See Locational flexibility.

Stakeholder approach Approach to commercial business activities which acknowledges and attempts to balance the interests of groups that might be affected by the company, such as employees, customers, the general public and government, alongside those of shareholders.

Stakeholder economy National economic system where substantial organisational investment is provided through long-term relationships between firms and banks rather than simply private shareholders.

Stakeholders All groups and individuals that have an interest in and are affected by the actions of an organisation, including shareholders, employees, governments and the general public.

Statutory provision A stipulation or condition contained in a legislative act (statute) or any document issued under such an act.

Strategic human resource development (SHRD) A holistic approach to workplace learning and development which is consistent with and can exert influence over wider organisational strategy.

Strategy The overarching 'plan of action' regarding how an organisation as a whole engages with its market and how it seeks to achieve competitive advantage, and which informs decisions about the allocation and utilisation of resources.

Strike action The temporary withdrawal of labour by a group of workers undertaken to express a collective grievance or to seek to put pressure on management in collective bargaining.

Structural unemployment Unemployment resulting from a fundamental mismatch between the supply and demand for labour (for example, resulting from an over-supply of particular skills).

Suggestion scheme Method for employee involvement which encourages employees to make suggestions and put forward ideas to management for which employees are rewarded if adopted.

Summary dismissal Dismissal of an employee without notice, typically as a result of gross misconduct.

Systematic approach Approach to recruitment and selection that seeks to achieve both fairness and effectiveness through the formal sequencing of particular activities (such as job analysis, job description and person specification).

Systematic training model A cyclical model of training and development activities structured around a sequence of four key areas of activity: needs analysis and identification, design, delivery and evaluation.

Systems approach Approach to strategy formation which emphasises that long-term planning must take account of the cultural and institutional context in which it is to be enacted.

Tacit knowledge The intuitive know-how which is developed by an individual through experience and which is difficult to articulate and share but is important in developing new knowledge or confronting new challenges.

Taylorism See **Scientific management**.

Team briefing Regularly convened meetings of groups of workers to allow management to communicate organisation decisions and policy.

Teamworking An approach to work organisation which seeks to yield the productive potential associated with allocating work to cooperative groups of workers rather than individuals.

Technical control Approach to worker control where control is 'built in' to machinery and technology to dictate the intensity of work and the sequence and manner in which people carry out tasks.

Temporal flexibility Organisational and individual ability to vary the number and timing of hours worked, particularly through the use of non-standard patterns of working.

Theory X The view that people generally have an inherent dislike of work, that coercion is necessary for compliance and that people have limited ambitions beyond meeting financial need.

Theory Y The view that people often perform better when provided with autonomy and discretion at work and seek to meet psychological needs through work.

Thinking performer Conceptualisation of the role of the contemporary HR specialist at the core of which is the need for practitioners to critically reflect on the contribution of HR activities to overall business success and on developing new and better mechanisms to provide people-added value.

Third party An individual, group or organisation other than the two principal parties to the employment relationship.

Total reward A holistic approach to reward management which recognises the importance of balancing financial and non-financial rewards in a way that is complementary and consistent with the objectives and values of the organisation.

Trade union A membership-based organisation comprised mainly of workers whose main aim is to protect and advance the interests of its members in the workplace.

Trade union density A measure of the membership of trade unions, calculated by the number currently enrolled as union members as a proportion of all those employees potentially eligible to be members.

Trade union recognition Employer agreement (either willingly or forced by legislation) that employees' interests are to be represented by a trade union through collective bargaining.

Transactional psychological contract An informal agreement between an employer and employee where the opportunity to develop one's employability through skills development and experience is exchanged for a short-term provision of service.

Transferable skills Skills that can be applied in a range of jobs and organisational contexts.

Underemployment Either employment in a job that does not require the incumbent's possessed skills and knowledge; or employment in a job that provides fewer hours than are wanted by the incumbent.

Unfair dismissal Dismissal from employment without 'fair' reason (for example, gross misconduct or redundancy), without following the correct procedures or for a reason that is automatically unfair (for example, pregnancy).

Union substitution The implementation of HRM practices that have the effect (deliberate or not) of negating the need for trade union 'protection' or representation.

Union suppression Managerial activity that actively seeks to minimise trade union presence within an organisation, often through hostile means.

Unitarism A perspective on the employment relationship which views organisations as unified entities where both parties have common objectives and interests and, therefore, conflict is irrational and third-party presence is illegitimate.

Universalism See Best practice

Upskilling Term used to describe the trend for the greater demand for skills and qualifications in a particular context, such as a labour market or wider economy. Also used to describe the job requirement for the greater possession of skills and qualifications by workers themselves.

Upward appraisal Often used as part of 360-degree appraisals, upward appraisals allow subordinates to contribute to an assessment of the performance of their immediate manager.

Upward problem-solving Employee involvement initiatives that place greater responsibility on workers to make decisions or suggestions concerning work organisation, allocation and process improvements.

Variable pay Umbrella term used for forms of remuneration that are conditional upon the achievement of pre-determined objectives, mostly related to individual, group or organisational performance.

Vertical integration The extent to which HR practices are aligned with HR strategy, business strategy and organisational objectives. Typically, associated with best fit models of HRM.

Victimisation Unfavourable treatment of an employee by an employer as a result of having made a complaint at work, for example regarding discrimination.

Virtual HRD Formal and informal learning and development that use and take place within a virtual online environment.

Voluntarism The reliance on or encouragement of voluntary action, rather than compulsion, to achieve a particular objective or to follow a particular course of action.

VRIO Value, rarity, inimitability and organisation.

Vulnerable employment Insecure work in which workers are more likely to experience injustice resulting from an imbalance of power in the employer–worker relationship, partly due to an absence of trade unions.

Well-being at work Holistic term used to describe an individual state of persistently good physical and mental health and safety in the workplace alongside feelings of security, satisfaction and challenge in one's work.

Work–life balance An organisational and social policy agenda which stresses the importance of individuals achieving a satisfactory distribution of time and energy between work and non-work.

Working-to-rule Action short of a strike whereby workers do only what is required under their contract of employment

Works council Workplace forum normally consisting of management, employees and union representatives to enable communication, consultation and negotiation between the parties over workplace issues.

Wrongful dismissal Dismissal that is in breach of the terms of the employment contract, for example, where agreed notice is not given or proper procedures are not followed.

BIBLIOGRAPHY

Abbott, K. (2015) The totalitarian dynamic behind HRM's democratic façade, *Asia Pacific Journal of Human Resources*, 53 (2), 204–20.

Abercrombie, N. and Warde, A. (2000) *Contemporary British Society* (3rd edn), Cambridge: Polity Press.

Acas (Advisory, Conciliation and Arbitration Service) (2003) *Appraisal Related Pay*, London: Acas.

Acas (Advisory, Conciliation and Arbitration Service) (2004) *Code of Practice on Disciplinary and Grievance Procedures*, London: Acas.

Acas (Advisory, Conciliation and Arbitration Service) (2005) An enduring partnership, *Employment Relations Matters*, 5 (Winter).

Acas (Advisory, Conciliation and Arbitration Service) (2009c) *Health, Work and Wellbeing*, London: Acas.

Acas (Advisory, Conciliation and Arbitration Service) (2009d) *Varying a Contract of Employment*, London: Acas.

Acas (Advisory, Conciliation and Arbitration Service) (2010) *The Equality Act – What's New for Employers?* London: Acas.

Acas (Advisory, Conciliation and Arbitration Service) (2015a) *Code of Practice on Disciplinary and Grievance Procedures*, London: Acas.

Acas (Advisory, Conciliation and Arbitration Service) (2015b) *Discipline and Grievances at Work: The Acas Guide*, London: Acas.

Accenture (2006) *The High-Performance Workforce Study 2006*, London: Accenture.

Ackers, P. (2006) Employment ethics, in T. Redman and A. Wilkinson (eds), *Contemporary Human Resource Management* (2nd edn), Harlow: FT Prentice Hall.

Ackers, P. and El-Sawad, A. (2006) Family-friendly policies and work–life balance, in T. Redman and A. Wilkinson (eds), *Contemporary Human Resource Management* (2nd edn), Harlow: FT Prentice Hall.

Ackers, P. and Payne, J. (1998) British trade unions and social partnership: Rhetoric, reality and strategy, *International Journal of Human Resource Management*, 9 (3): 529–50.

Ackers, P., Marchington, M., Wilkinson, A. and Goodman, J. (1992) The use of cycles: Explaining employee involvement in the 1990s, *Industrial Relations Journal*, 23 (4): 268–83.

Adams, S., Quagrainie, F. A., Klobodu, E. K. M. (2014) Psychological contract formation: The influence of demographic factors, *International Area Studies Review*, 17 (3): 279–94

Adamson, S., Doherty, N. and Viney, C. (1998) The meanings of career revisited: Implications for theory and practice, *British Journal of Management*, 9: 251–9.

Adidas Group (2013) *Sustainability Progress Report*, www.adidas-group.com/en/sustainability/reporting-policies-and-data/sustainability-reports/ (accessed 24 March 2015).

Aguilera, R. V. and Dencker, J. C. (2004) The role of human resource management in cross-border mergers and acquisitions, *International Journal of Human Resource Management*, 15 (8): 1355–70

Aguinis, H., Joo, H. and Gottfredson, R. K. (2011) Why we hate performance management – and why we should love it, *Business Horizons*, 54: 503–7.

Aguinis, H., Joo, H. and Gottfredson, R. K. (2012) Performance management universals: Think globally and act locally, *Business Horizons*, 55: 385–39

Ahmad, S. and Schroeder, R. G. (2003) The impact of human resource management practices on operational performance: Recognizing country and industry differences, *Journal of Operations Management*, 21: 19–43.

Ait Razouk, A. (2011) High-performance work systems and performance of French small- and medium-sized enterprises: Examining causal order, *International Journal of Human Resource Management*, 22 (2): 311–30.

Albert, S. and Bradley, K. (1997) *Managing Knowledge*, Cambridge: Cambridge University Press.

Alder, G. S. and Gilbert, J. (2006) Achieving ethics and fairness in hiring: Going beyond the law, *Journal of Business Ethics*, 68: 449–64.

Allegre, J., Sengupta, K. and Lapiedra, R. (2011) Knowledge management and innovation performance in a high-tech SME sector, *International Small Business Journal*, 1–17.

Alonzo, A. A. and Simon, A. B (2008) Have stethoscope, will travel: Contingent employment among physician health care providers in the United States, *Work, Employment and Society*, 22 (4): 635–54.

Alvesson, M. (2000) Social identity and the problem of loyalty in knowledge-intensive companies, *Journal of Management Studies*, 37 (8): 1101–23.

Alvesson, M. (2001) Knowledge work: Ambiguity, image and identity, *Human Relations*, 54 (7): 863–86.

Alvesson, M. and Karreman, D. (2001) Odd couple: Making sense of the curious concept of knowledge management, *Journal of Management Studies*, 38 (7): 995–1018.

Anakwe, U. P., Hall, J. C. and Schor, S. M. (2000) Knowledge-related skills and effective career management, *International Journal of Manpower*, 21 (7): 566–79.

Anderson, N. and Shackleton, V. (1993) *Successful Selection Interviewing*, Oxford: Blackwell.

Anderson, N. (2003) Applicant and recruiter reactions to new technology in selection: A critical review and agenda for future research, *International Journal of Selection and Assessment*, 11 (2): 121–37.

Anderson, T. and Metcalfe, H. (2003) *Diversity: Stacking Up the Evidence: A Review of Knowledge*, Executive Briefing, London: CIPD.

Anderson, V. (2007) *The Value of Learning: From Return on Investment to Return on Expectation*, London: CIPD.

Appelbaum, E., Bailey, T., Berg, P. and Kalleberg, A. (2000) *Manufacturing Advantage: Why High Performance Work Systems Pay Off*, Ithaca, NY: Cornell University Press.

Argyris, C. and Schon, D. (1978) *Organizational Learning: A Theory of Action Perspective*, Reading, MA: Addison-Wesley.

Armstrong, K. and Ward, A. (2006) *What Makes for Effective Performance Management?* London: The Work Foundation.

Armstrong, M. (2000) *Performance Management: Key Strategies and Practical Guidelines* (2nd edn), London: Kogan Page.

Armstrong, M. (2002) *Employee Reward* (3rd edn), London: CIPD.

Armstrong, M. (2006) *Handbook of Human Resource Management Practice* (10th edn), London: Kogan Page.

Armstrong, M. (2007) *A Handbook of Employee Reward Management and Practice* (2nd edn), London: Kogan Page.

Armstrong, M. and Baron, A. (1998) *Performance Management: The New Realities*, London: CIPD.

Armstrong, M. and Baron, A. (2005) *Managing Performance: Performance Management in Action*, London: CIPD.

Armstrong, M. and Brown, D. (2001) *New Dimensions in Pay Management*, London: CIPD.

Arnold, E. and Pulich, M. (2007) The department manager and effective human resource planning: An overview, *The Health Care Manager*, 26: 43–52.

Arnold, J. (1997a) *Managing Careers in the 21st Century*. London: Paul Chapman.

Arnold, J. (1997b) Nineteen propositions concerning the nature of effective thinking for career management in a turbulent world, *British Journal of Guidance and Counselling*, 25 (4): 447–62.

Arnold, J., Silvester, J., Patterson, F., Robertson, I., Cooper, C. and Burnes, B. (1994) *Work Psychology: Understanding Human Behaviour in the Workplace* (4th edn), London: Pitman.

Arthur, A. R. (2000) Employee assistance programmes: The emperor's new clothes of stress management, *British Journal of Guidance and Counselling*, 28 (4): 549–59.

Arthur, J. B. (1994) Effects of human resource systems on manufacturing performance and turnover, *Academy of Management Journal*, 37 (3): 670–87.

Arthur, M. B. (1994) The boundaryless career: A new perspective for organizational enquiry, *Journal of Organisational Behaviour*, 15: 295–306.

Arthur, M. B. (2008) Examining contemporary careers: A call for interdisciplinary inquiry, *Human Relations*, 61 (2): 163–86.

Ashley, L. (2010) Making a difference? The use (and abuse) of diversity management at the UK's elite law firms, *Work, Employment and Society*, 24 (4): 711–27.

Ashton, D. and Sung, J. (2002) *Supporting Workplace Learning for High Performance Working*, Geneva: International Labour Office.

Association of Graduate Recruiters (AGR) (1995) *Skills for Graduates in the 21st Century*, Cambridge: Association of Graduate Recruiters.

Atkinson, C. (2002) Career management and the changing psychological contract, *Career Development International*, 7 (1): 14–23.

Atkinson, J. (1984) Manpower strategies for the flexible organisation, *Personnel Management*, 16 (8): 28–31.

Atkinson, C., Mallett, O. and Wapshott, R. (2014) 'You try to be a fair employer': Regulation and employment relationships in medium-sized firms, *International Small Business Journal*, 1–18.

Azasu, S. (2009) Rewards and performance of Swedish real estate firms, *Compensation & Benefits Review*, 41 (4): 19–28.

Bach, S. (2005) New directions in performance management, in S. Bach (ed.), *Managing Human Resources: Personnel Management in Transition* (4th edn), Oxford: Blackwell.

Bacon, N. (2003) Human resource management and industrial relations, in P. Ackers and A. Wilkinson (eds), *Understanding Work and Employment: Industrial Relations in Transition*, Oxford: Oxford University Press.

Bae, J., Chen, S.-J. and Lawler, J. J. (1998) Variations in human resource management in Asian countries: MNC home-country and host-country effect, *International Journal of Human Resource Management*, 9 (4): 653–70.

Baeten, X. and Verwaeren, B. (2012) Flexible rewards from a strategic perspective, *Compensation & Benefits Review*, 44 (1): 40–9.

Bain, P. and Taylor, P. (2000) Entrapped by the electronic panopticon? Worker resistance in the call centre, *New Technology, Work and Employment*, 15 (1): 2–18.

Baldry, C., Bain, P. and Taylor, P. (1997) Sick and tired? Working in the modern office, *Work, Employment and Society*, 11 (3): 519–39.

Ball, B. (1997) Career management competencies: The individual perspective, *Career Development International*, 2: 74–9.

Ball, B. and Jordan, M. (1997) An open-learning approach to career management and guidance, *British Journal of Guidance and Counselling*, 25 (4): 507–16.

Bamber, G. J., Hoffer Gittell, J., Kochan, T. A. and von Nordenflycht, A. (2009) Contrasting management and employment-relations strategies in European airlines, *Journal of Industrial Relations*, 51 (5): 635–52.

Bamberger, P. and Meshoulam, L. (2000) *Human Resource Strategy*, Thousand Oaks, CA: Sage.

Bamberger, P. and Philips, B. (1991) Organizational environment and business strategy: Parallel versus conflicting influences on human resource strategy in the pharmaceutical industry, *Human Resource Management*, 30: 153–82.

Banfield, P. and Kay, R. (2009) *An Introduction to Human Resource Management*, Oxford: Oxford University Press.

Barney, J. B. (1991) Firm resources and sustained competitive advantage, *Journal of Management*, 17 (1): 99–120.

Barney, J. B. (1995) Looking inside for competitive advantage, *Academy of Management Executive*, 9 (4): 49–61.

Barney, J. B. and Wright, P. M. (1998) On becoming a strategic partner: The role of human resources in gaining competitive advantage, *Human Resource Management*, 37 (1): 31–46.

Baron, A. and Armstrong, M. (2007) *Human Capital Management*, London: Kogan Page.

Barratt, C. (2009) *Trade Union Membership 2008*, London: Department for Business, Enterprise and Regulatory Reform.

Barsoux, J.-L. and Schneider, S. C. (2008) *Managing Across Cultures* (2nd edn), Harlow: FT Prentice Hall.

Bartlett, C. A. and Ghoshal, S. (1989) *Managing Across Borders: The Transnational Solution*, Boston, MA: Harvard Business School Press.

Bartlett, J. E. and Bartlett, M. E. (2011) Workplace bullying: An integrative literature review, *Advances in Developing Human Resources*, 13 (1): 69–84.

Bartram, D. (2000) Internet recruitment and selection: Kissing frogs to find princes, *International Journal of Selection and Assessment*, 8 (4): 261–74.

Bartram, T., Boyle, B., Stanton, P., Sablok, G. and Burgess, J. (2015) Performance and reward practices of multinational corporations operating in Australia, *Journal of Industrial Relations*, 57 (2): 210–31.

Baruch, Y. (2003) Career systems in transition, *Personnel Review*, 32 (2): 231–51.

Baruch, Y. (2004) Transforming careers: From linear to multidirectional career paths: Organizational and individual perspectives, *Career Development International*, 9 (1): 58–73.

Baruch, Y. (2006) Career development in organizations and beyond: Balancing traditional and contemporary viewpoints, *Human Resource Management Review*, 16: 125–38.

Baruch, Y. and Peiperl, M. A. (2000) Career management practices: An empirical survey and implications, *Human Resource Management*, 39 (4): 347–66.

Batt, R. (2002) Managing customer services: Human resource practices, quit rates and sales growth, *Academy of Management Journal*, 45: 587–97.

Batt, R. and Banerjee, M. (2012) The scope and trajectory of strategic HR research: Evidence from American and British journals, *International Journal of Human Resource Management*, 23 (9): 1739–62.

BBC (2008) Offshoring 'bad for IT pay in UK', http://news.bbc.co.uk/1/hi/business/7419916.stm (accessed 26 May 2008).

BBC (2009) Pay freezes at '10% of firms', http://news.bbc.co.uk/1/hi/business/7941691.stm (accessed 22 March 2012).

BBC (2012) Phone hacking: Culture Committee's verdict on Murdochs and other key players, http://m.bbc.co.uk/news/uk-politics-17905775 (accessed 10 May 2012).

Beale, D. and Hoel, H. (2010) Workplace bullying, industrial relations and the challenge for management in Britain and Sweden, *European Journal of Industrial Relations*, 16 (2): 101–18.

Beale, D. and Hoel, H. (2011) Workplace bullying and the employment relationship: Exploring questions of prevention, control and context, *Work, Employment and Society*, 25 (1): 5–18.

Beardwell, J. (2006) Recruitment and selection, in J. Beardwell and T. Claydon, *Human Resource Management: A Contemporary Approach*, Harlow: FT Prentice Hall.

Beck, V. (2012) Employers' views of learning and training for an ageing workforce, *Management Learning*, 45 (2): 200–15

Becker, B. and Gerhart, B. (1996) The impact of human resource management on organisational performance: Progress and prospects, *Academy of Management Journal*, 39 (4): 779–801.

Becker, B. E. and Huselid, M. A. (1998) High performance work systems and firm performance: A synthesis of research and managerial implications, *Research in Personnel and Human Resource Management*, 16: 53–101.

Becker, B. E. and Huselid, M. A. (2006) Strategic human resource management: Where do we go from here? *Journal of Management*, 32 (6): 898–925.

Becker, M. C. (2001) Managing dispersed knowledge: Organizational problems, management strategies and their effectiveness, *Journal of Management Studies*, 38 (7): 1037–51.

Beer, M., Spector, B., Lawrence, P., Quinn Mills, D. and Walton, R. (1984) *Managing Human Assets*, New York: Free Press.

Bélanger, J. and Edwards, E. (2013) The nature of front-line service work: Distinctive features and continuity in the employment relationship, *Work, Employment and Society*, 27 (3): 433–50.

Belcourt, M. (2006) Outsourcing: The benefits and the risks, *Human Resource Management Review*, 16: 269–79.

Bell, D. (1973) *The Coming of Post-industrial Society: A Venture in Social Forecasting*, New York: Basic Books.

Beltrán-Martín, I., Roca-Puig, V., Escrig-Tena, A. and Bou-Llusar, J. C. (2008) Human resource flexibility as a mediating variable between high performance work systems and performance, *Journal of Management*, 34: 1009–44.

Bennett, E. E. (2009) Virtual HRD: The intersection of knowledge management, culture and intranets, *Advances in Developing Human Resources*, 11 (3): 362–74.

Bennett, E. E. (2010) The coming paradigm shift: Synthesis and future directions for virtual HRD, *Advances in Developing Human Resources*, 12 (6): 728–41.

Bennett, E. E. and Bierema, L. L. (2010) The ecology of virtual human resource development, *Advances in Developing Human Resources*, 12: 632–47.

Benson, J. and Brown, M. (2007) Knowledge workers: What keeps them committed; what turns them away, *Work, Employment and Society*, 21: 121–41.

Benson, A. D., Johnson, S. D. and Kuchinke, K. P. (2002) The use of technology in the digital workplace: A framework for human resource development, *Advances in Developing Human Resources*, 4: 392–404

Berkley, R. A. and Watson, G. (2009) The employer–employee relationship as a building block for ethics and corporate social responsibility, *Employee Responsibilities and Rights Journal*, 21 (4): 275–7.

Bevan, S., Quadrello, T., McGee, R., Mahdon, M., Vavrosky, A. and Barham, L. (2009) *Fit For Work? Musculoskeletal Disorders in the European Workforce*, London: The Work Foundation.

Bewley, H. (2006) Voice recognition, *People Management*, 12: 40–3.

Billett, S. (2014) Mimesis: Learning through everyday activities and interactions at work, *Human Resource Development Review*, 13 (4): 462–82.

Bird, A. (1994) Careers as repositories of knowledge: A new perspective on boundaryless careers, *Journal of Organisational Behaviour*, 15: 325–44.

BIS (Department for Business, Innovation and Skills) (2011) *Resolving Workplace Disputes: Government Response to the Consultation*, London: BIS.

BIS (Department for Business, Innovation and Skills) (2014) *Trade Union Membership 2013*, Statistical Bulletin, May, London: Department for Business, Innovation and Skills

Björkman, I. and Lervik, J. E. (2007) Transferring HR practices within multinational corporations, *Human Resource Management Journal*, 17 (4): 320–35.

Björkman, I. and Lu, Y. (1999) The management of human resources in Chinese–Western joint ventures, *Journal of World Business*, 34 (3): 306–24.

Björkman, I., Smale, A., Sumelius, J., Suutari, V. and Lu, Y. (2008) Changes in institutional context and MNC operations in China: Subsidiary HRM practices in 1996 versus 2006, *International Business Review*, 17 (2): 146–58.

Black, C. (2008) *Working for a Healthier Tomorrow – Review of the Health of Britain's Working Age Population*, Norwich: The Stationery Office.

Black, S. and Lynch, L. (2001) How to compete: The impact of workplace practices and information technology on productivity, *Review of Economics and Statistics*, 83 (3): 434–45.

Blackler, F. (1995) Knowledge, knowledge work and organisations: An overview and interpretation, *Organisation Studies*, 16 (6): 1021–46.

Blair, M. and Kochan, T. (eds) (2000) *The New Relationship: Human Capital in the American Corporation*, Washington, DC: Brookings Institution Press.

Blankenship, S. S. and Ruona, W. E. A. (2009) Exploring knowledge sharing in social structures: Potential contributions to an overall knowledge management strategy, *Advances in Developing Human Resources*, 11 (3): 290–306.

Blau, P. M. (1964) *Exchange and Power in Social Life*, New York: John Wiley & Sons.

Boisot, M. and Xing, G. L. (1992) The nature of managerial work in the Chinese enterprise reforms: A study of six directors, *Organization Studies*, 13 (2): 161–84.

Bolton, S. C. (2007) *Dimensions of Dignity at Work*, London: Butterworth–Heineman.

Bondarouk, T. V. and Ruel, H. J. M. (2009) Electronic human resource management: Challenges in the digital era, *International Journal of Human Resource Management*, 20 (3): 505–14.

Boo, E. H. Y. and Koh, H. C. (2001) The influence of organizational and code-supporting variables on the effectiveness of a code of ethics, *Teaching Business Ethics*, 5 (4): 357–73.

Borman, W. C. and Motowidlo, S. J. (1993) 'Expanding the criterion domain to include elements of contextual performance', in N. Schmitt and

W. Borman (eds), *Personnel Selection in Organizations*, New York: Jossey-Bass.

Boselie, P., Brewster, C. and Paauwe, J. (2009) In search of balance – managing the dualities of HRM: An overview of the issues, *Personnel Review*, 38 (5): 461–71.

Boselie, P., Dietz, G. and Boon, C. (2005) Commonalities and contradictions in HRM and performance research, *Human Resource Management Journal*, 15 (3): 67–94.

Boselie, P., Paauwe, J. and Jansen, P. (2001) Human resource management and performance: Lessons from The Netherlands, *International Journal of Human Resource Management*, 12: 1107–25

Boswell, W. R. (2006) Aligning employees with the organization's strategic objectives: Out of 'line of sight', out of mind, *International Journal of Human Resource Management*, 17 (9): 1489–511.

Bourne, M., Pavlov, A., Franco-Santos, M., Lucianetti, L. and Mura, M. (2013) Generating organisational performance, *International Journal of Operations and Production Management*, 33 (11/12): 1599–622

Boury, D. and Sinclair, A. (2012) *The Management Agenda 2012*, Horsham: Roffey Park Institute.

Boxall, P. (2014), The future of employment relations from the perspective of human resource management, *Journal of Industrial Relations*, 56 (4): 578–93.

Boxall, P. and Macky, K. (2007) High-performance work systems and organisational performance: Bridging theory and practice, *Asia Pacific Journal of Human Resources*, 45: 261–70.

Boxall, P. and Purcell, J. (2003) *Strategy and Human Resource Management*, Basingstoke: Palgrave Macmillan.

Boyd, C. (2002) Customer violence and employee health and safety, *Work Employment and Society*, 16 (1): 151–69.

Boydell, T. H. (1976) *Guide to the Identification of Training Needs* (2nd edn), London: BACIE.

Boyzatis, R. E. (1982) *The Competent Manager*, New York: Riley.

Bozionelos, N. (2005) When the inferior candidate is offered the job: The selection interview as a political and power game, *Human Relations*, 58 (12): 1605–31.

Brandenburg, D. C. and Ellinger, A. D. (2010) The future: Just-in-time learning expectations and potential implications for human resource development, *Advances in Developing Human Resources*, 5: 308–20.

Bratton, J. (2007) Reward management, in J. Bratton and J. Gold (eds), *Human Resource Management: Theory and Practice* (4th edn), Basingstoke: Palgrave.

Braverman, H. (1974) *Labour and Monopoly Capital: The Degradation of Work in the Twentieth Century*, London: Monthly Review Press.

Breaugh, J. A. and Starke, M. (2000) Research on employee recruitment: So many studies, so many remaining questions, *Journal of Management*, 26 (3): 405–34.

Brewster, C. (1995) Towards a European model of human resource management, *Journal of International Business Studies*, 26: 1–22.

Bridger, R. S., Day, A. J. and Morton, K. (2013) Occupational stress and employee turnover, *Ergonomics* 56 (11): 1629–39.

Broderick, R. and Boudreau, J. W. (1992) Human resource management, information technology and the competitive edge, *Academy of Management Executive*, 6 (2): 7–17.

Broughton, A., Foley, B., Ledermaier, S. and Cox, A. (2013) The use of social media in the recruitment process, Acas Research Paper 03/13, London: Acas.

Brousseau, K. R., Driver, M. J., Eneroth, K. and Larsson, R. (1996) Career pandemonium: Realigning organizations and individuals, *Academy of Management Executive*, 10 (4): 52–66.

Browaeys, M.-J. and Price, R. (2008) *Understanding Cross-cultural Management*, Harlow: FT Prentice Hall.

Brown, D. (2013) Personal objective for 2013? Not to have SMART objectives, *Compensation & Benefits Review*, 44 (6): 305–7.

Brown, D. (2014) The future of reward management: From total reward strategies to smart rewards, *Compensation & Benefits Review*, 46 (3): 147–51.

Brown, D. and Purcell, J. (2007) Reward management: On the line, *Compensation & Benefits Review*, 39 (3): 28–34.

Brown, D. and Reilly, P. (2013) Reward and engagement: The new realities, *Compensation & Benefits Review*, 45 (3): 145–57.

Brown, J. S. and Duguid, P. (1991) Organizational learning and communities-of-practice: Toward a unified view of working, learning, and innovation, *Organization Science*, 2 (1): 40–57.

Brown, M. and Benson, J. (2005) Managing to overload? Work overload and performance appraisal processes, *Group & Organization Management*, 30: 99–124.

Brown, M., Metz, I., Cregan, C. and Kulik, C. T. (2009) Irreconcilable differences? Strategic human resource management and employee well-being, *Asia Pacific Journal of Human Resources*, 47(3): 270–94.

Brown, P. and Hesketh, A. (2004) *The Mismanagement of Talent: Employability and Jobs in the Knowledge Economy*, Oxford: Oxford University Press.

Brown, P. and Scase, R. (1994) *Higher Education and Corporate Realities: Class, Culture and Decline of Careers*, London, UCL Press.

Brown, P., Lauder, H. and Ashton, D. (2011) *The Global Auction for High Skilled Work:*

Implications for Economic Policy, policy brief, Institute for Policy Research, University of Bath.

Brown, V. and Vaughn, D. (2011) The writing on the (Facebook) wall: The use of social networking sites in hiring decisions, *Journal of Business Psychology*, 26 (2): 219–25.

Brown, W. and David M. (2010) *Individualisation and Growing Diversity of Employment Relationships*, CEP Discussion Paper No. 1037, Centre for Economic Performance, London School of Economics and Political Science.

Brown, W. and Marsden, D. (2010) *Individualisation and growing diversity of employment relationships*, CEP Discussion Paper No. 1037, Centre for Economic Performance, London School of Economics and Political Science.

Brutus, S., Leslie, J. and McDonald, D. (2001) Cross-cultural issues in multi-source feedback, in A. Bryson and J. Forth (2010) *Trade Union Membership and Influence 1999–2009*, CEP Discussion Paper No. 1003, Centre for Economic Performance, London School of Economics and Political Science.

Bryson, A. and Forth, J. (2010) *Trade Union Membership and Influence 1999–2009*, CEP Discussion Paper No. 1003, Centre for Economic Performance, London School of Economics and Political Science.

Buchanan, D. A. (2003) Demands, instabilities, manipulations, careers: The lived experience of driving change, *Human Relations*, 56 (6): 663–84.

Buchanan, D. and Huczynski, A. (1997) *Organisational Behaviour* (3rd edn), Hemel Hempstead: Prentice Hall.

Buckingham, M. and Goodall, A. (2015) Reinventing performance management, *Harvard Business Review*, April.

Budd, J. W. and Bhave, D. (2008) Values, ideologies, and frames of reference in industrial relations, in P. Blyton, N. Bacon, J. Fiorito and E. Heery (eds), *Sage Handbook of Industrial Relations*, London: Sage.

Budhwar, P. S. and Debrah, Y. (2001) Rethinking comparative and cross-national human resource management, *International Journal of Human Resource Management*, 12 (3): 497–515.

Budhwar, P. S. and Khatri, N. (2001) A comparative study of HR practices in Britain and India, *International Journal of Human Resource Management*, 12 (5): 800–26.

Buller, P. F. and McEvoy, G. M. (2012) Strategy, human resource management and performance: Sharpening line of sight, *Human Resource Management Review*, 22: 43–56.

Burke, R. J. and Ng, E. (2006) The changing nature of work and organizations: Implications for human resource management, *Human Resource Management Review*, 16: 86–94.

Bushnell, D. (1990) Input, process, output: A model for evaluating training, *Training and Development Journal*, 44 (3): 41–3.

Butler, P. and Glover, L. (2007) Employee participation and involvement, in J. Beardwell and T. Claydon (eds), *Human Resource Management: A Contemporary Approach* (5th edn), Harlow: FT Prentice Hall.

Caldwell, R. (2002) A change of name or a change of identity? Do job titles influence people management professionals' perceptions of their role in managing change? *Personnel Review*, 31 (6): 693–709.

Caldwell, R. (2003) The changing roles of personnel managers: Old ambiguities, new uncertainties, *Journal of Management Studies*, 40 (4): 983–1004.

Caldwell, R. and Storey, J. (2007) The HR function: Integration or fragmentation? in J. Storey (ed.), *Human Resource Management: A Critical Text* (3rd edn), London: Thomson.

Callea, A., Urbini, F., Ingusci, E. and Chirumbolo, A. (2014) The relationship between contract type and job satisfaction in a mediated moderation model: The role of job insecurity and psychological contract violation, *Economic and Industrial Democracy*, 1–22.

Cardon, M. S. and Stevens, C. E. (2004) Managing human resources in small organizations: What do we know? *Human Resource Management Review*, 14: 295–323.

Carey, M. (2011) Here today, gone tomorrow? The ambivalent ethics of contingency social work, *Critical Social Policy*, 31 (4): 540–61.

Cartwright, S. and Holmes, N. (2006) The meaning of work: The challenge of regaining employee engagement and reducing cynicism, *Human Resource Management Review*, 16: 199–208.

Cassell, C., Nadin, S., Gray, M. and Clegg, C. (2002) Exploring human resource management practices in small and medium sized enterprises, *Personnel Review*, 31 (6): 671–92.

Castells, M. (2000) *The Rise of the Network Society* (2nd edn), Oxford: Blackwell.

Cathcart, A. (2013) Direct democracy: Competing interests and contested terrain in the John Lewis Partnership, *Journal of Industrial Relations*, 55 (4): 601–20.

CBI (Confederation of British Industry) (2008a) *Talent Not Tokenism, The Business Benefits of Workforce Diversity*, London: CBI/TUC/EHRC.

CBI (Confederation of British Industry) (2008b) *CBI/AXA Absence Survey*, London: CBI.

Ceausu, J. (2006) Can Wal-Mart keep unions out? *Personnel Today*, 14 March.

Centre for Women and Democracy (2013) *Sex and Power 2013: Who Runs Britain?* London: Centre for Women and Democracy.

Chambel, M. J. and Alcover, C. M. (2011) The psychological contract of call-centre workers: Employment conditions, satisfaction and civic virtue behaviours, *Economic and Industrial Democracy*, 32 (1): 115–34.

Chand, M. (2010) The impact of HRM practices on service quality, customer satisfaction and performance in the Indian hotel industry,

International Journal of Human Resource Management, 21 (4): 551–66.

Che Rose, R., Beh, L., Uli, J. and Idris, K. (2006) Quality of work life: Implications of career dimensions, *Journal of Social Sciences*, 2 (2): 61–7.

Chen, H. M. and Fu, P. C. (2011) Perceptions of justice in extrinsic reward patterns, *Compensation & Benefits Review*, 43 (6): 361–70.

Chen, H.-M. and Hsieh, Y.-H. (2006) Key trends of the total reward system in the 21st century, *Compensation & Benefits Review*, 38 (6): 64–7.

Chew, I. K. H. and Horwitz, F. M. (2004) Human resource management strategies in practice: Case-study findings in multinational firms, *Asia Pacific Journal of Human Resources*, 42 (1): 32–56.

Cheyne, A. and Loan-Clarke, J. (2006) Organisational and corporate culture, in T. Redman and A. Wilkinson (eds) *Contemporary Human Resource Management* (2nd edn), Harlow: FT Prentice Hall.

Chiang, F. and Birtch, T. (2007) The transferability of management practices: Examining cross-national differences in reward preferences, *Human Relations*, 60 (9): 1293–330.

Child, J. and McGrath, R. G. (2001) Organisations unfettered: Organisational form in an information-intensive economy, *Academy of Management Journal*, 44 (6): 1135–45.

Chiumento, R. (2003) How to support survivors of redundancy, *People Management*, 9 (3): 48–9.

Choi, S. Y., Kang, Y. S. and Lee, H. (2008) The effects of socio-technical enablers on knowledge sharing: an exploratory examination, *Journal of Information Science*, 34 (5): 742–54.

Chow, I. H.-S. (2012) The roles of implementation and organizational culture in the HRM-performance link, *International Journal of Human Resource Management*, 23 (15): 3114–32.

Churchard, C. (2012) Social media 'replacing e-learning' for L&D professionals, *People Management*, 27 April.

CIPD (Chartered Institute of Personnel and Development) (2003a) *Where We Are, Where We're Heading*, London: CIPD.

CIPD (Chartered Institute of Personnel and Development) (2003b) *Managing Employee Careers Survey*, London: CIPD.

CIPD (Chartered Institute of Personnel and Development) (2004) *Business Partnering: A New Direction for HR*, London: CIPD.

CIPD (Chartered Institute of Personnel and Development) (2005) *Bullying at Work: Beyond Policies to a Culture of Respect*, London: CIPD.

CIPD (Chartered Institute of Personnel and Development) (2006a) *Smart Work*, London: CIPD.

CIPD (Chartered Institute of Personnel and Development) (2006b) *Pay and Reward: An Overview*, London: CIPD.

CIPD (Chartered Institute of Personnel and Development) (2006c) *How Engaged Are British Employees? Survey Report*, London: CIPD.

CIPD (Chartered Institute of Personnel and Development) (2006d) *Talent Management: Strategy, Policy, Practice*, London: CIPD.

CIPD (Chartered Institute of Personnel and Development) (2007a) *People and Performance, Factsheet*, London: CIPD.

CIPD (Chartered Institute of Personnel and Development) (2007b) *Working hours in the UK*, www.cipd.co.uk/ subjects/hrpract/hoursandholidays/ ukworkhrs.htm (accessed 22 July 2008).

CIPD (Chartered Institute of Personnel and Development) (2007c) *Learning and Development Annual Survey Report*, London: CIPD.

CIPD (Chartered Institute of Personnel and Development) (2007d) *What's Happening with Well-being at Work? Change Agenda*, London: CIPD.

CIPD (Chartered Institute of Personnel and Development) (2007e) *Absence Management Survey Report 2007*, London: CIPD.

CIPD (Chartered Institute of Personnel and Development) (2007f) *Managing Drug and Alcohol Misuse at Work*, London: CIPD.

CIPD (Chartered Institute of Personnel and Development) (2008a) *The Thinking Performer Concept*, www.cipd.co.uk/about/profstands/ thinkingperformer (accessed 13 August 2008).

CIPD (Chartered Institute of Personnel and Development) (2008b) *Resourcing and Talent Planning Survey 2008*, London: CIPD.

CIPD (Chartered Institute of Personnel and Development) (2008c) *The Relationship between HR and Recruitment Agencies: A Guide to Productive Partnerships*, London: CIPD.

CIPD (Chartered Institute of Personnel and Development) (2008d) *Performance Management: An Overview, Factsheet*, London: CIPD.

CIPD (Chartered Institute of Personnel and Development) (2008e) *Managing Conflict at Work: A Guide for Line Managers*, London: CIPD.

CIPD (Chartered Institute of Personnel and Development) (2008f) *Smart Working: The Impact of Work Organisation and Job Design*, London: CIPD.

CIPD (Chartered Institute of Personnel and Development) (2009a) *Employee Engagement, Factsheet*, London: CIPD.

CIPD (Chartered Institute of Personnel and Development) (2009b) *The Psychological Contract, Factsheet*, London: CIPD.

CIPD (Chartered Institute of Personnel and Development) (2009c) *HR Outsourcing and the HR Function: Threat or Opportunity?* London: CIPD.

CIPD (Chartered Institute of Personnel and Development) (2009d) *E-learning: Progress and Prospects*, London: CIPD.

CIPD (Chartered Institute of Personnel and Development) (2009e) *Employee Relations: An Overview*, London: CIPD.

CIPD (Chartered Institute of Personnel and Development) (2009f) *Discipline and Grievances at Work, Factsheet*, London: CIPD.

CIPD (Chartered Institute of Personnel and Development) (2009g) *The Role of Front Line Managers in HR, Factsheet*, London: CIPD.

CIPD (2009h) *The War on Talent? Talent Management under Threat in Uncertain Times*, London: CIPD.

CIPD (Chartered Institute of Personnel and Development) (2010) *Reward Management Annual Survey Report 2009*, London: CIPD.

CIPD (Chartered Institute of Personnel and Development) (2011a) *Resourcing and Talent Planning Survey 2011*, London: CIPD.

CIPD (Chartered Institute of Personnel and Development) (2011b) *Equality Act 2010 Factsheet*, London: CIPD.

CIPD (Chartered Institute of Personnel and Development) (2011c) *Survey Report: Focus on e-learning*, London: CIPD.

CIPD (Chartered Institute of Personnel and Development) (2011d) *Next Generation HR: Insight Driven*, London: CIPD.

CIPD (Chartered Institute of Personnel and Development) (2012a) *Flexible Working Provision and Uptake: Survey Report*, London: CIPD.

CIPD (Chartered Institute of Personnel and Development) (2012b) *Reward Management Annual Survey Report 2012*, London: CIPD.

CIPD (Chartered Institute of Personnel and Development) (2012c) *2012 Learning and Talent Development Annual Survey Report*, London: CIPD.

CIPD (Chartered Institute of Personnel and Development) (2012d) *Research Insight: From e-Learning to 'Gameful' Employment*, London: CIPD.

CIPD (Chartered Institute of Personnel and Development) (2012e) *Resourcing and Talent Planning Annual Survey Report 2012*, London: CIPD.

CIPD (Chartered Institute of Personnel and Development) (2012f) *Harnessing Social Media for Organisational Effectiveness*, London: CIPD.

CIPD (Chartered Institute of Personnel and Development) (2012g) *From e-learning to 'Gameful' Employment*, London: CIPD.

CIPD (Chartered Institute of Personnel and Development) (2013a) *Resourcing and Talent Planning Survey Report*, London: CIPD.

CIPD (Chartered Institute of Personnel and Development) (2013b) *Has Job Turnover Slowed Down?* London: CIPD.

CIPD (Chartered Institute of Personnel and Development) (2013c) *Reward Management Annual Survey Report 2013*, London: CIPD.

CIPD (Chartered Institute of Personnel and Development) (2013d) *Social Technology, Social Business?* London: CIPD.

CIPD (Chartered Institute of Personnel and Development) (2013e) *The CIPD Annual Survey Report 2013: Absence Management*, London: CIPD.

CIPD (Chartered Institute of Personnel and Development) (2014) *2014 Learning and Development Survey Report*, London: CIPD.

CIPD (Chartered Institute of Personnel and Development) (2015a) *Productivity: Getting the Best out of People*, London: CIPD.

CIPD (Chartered Institute of Personnel and Development) (2015b) *Making Maximum Impact as an HR Professional in an SME*, London: CIPD.

CIPD (Chartered Institute of Personnel and Development) (2015c) *Factsheet: Business Partnering*, London: CIPD.

Clark, A. E. (2005) Your money or your life: Changing job quality in OECD countries, *British Journal of Industrial Relations*, 43 (3): 377–400.

Clarke, S. G. and Cooper, C. L. (2000) The risk management of occupational stress, *Health, Risk and Society*, 2 (2): 173–87.

Claus, L. and Briscoe, D. (2008) Employee performance management across borders: A review of relevant academic literature, *International Journal of Management Reviews*, 11 (2): 175–96.

Claydon, T. and Doyle, M. (1996) Trusting me, trusting you? The ethics of employee empowerment, *Personnel Review*, 25 (6): 13–25.

Clayton Allen, W. (2006) Overview and evolution of the ADDIE Training System, *Advances in Developing Human Resources*, 8 (4): 430–41.

Clegg, S., Kornberger, M. and Pitsis, T. (2011) *Managing and Organizations* (3rd edn), London: Sage.

Clements, A. (2012) Social media and recruitment: time for a coherent HR strategy? *HR Magazine*, 16 February.

Clutterbuck, D. (2012) How to harness the energy of the talent wave, *People Management,* October.

Clutterbuck, D. and Megginson, D. (2005) *Making Coaching Work*, London: CIPD.

CMI (Chartered Management Institute) (2002) *Manage Your Career*, www.managers.org.uk/institute/content_3.asp (accessed 11 March 2004).

Cohen, L. and El-Sawad, A. (2006) Careers, in T. Redman and A. Wilkinson (eds), *Contemporary Human Resource Management: Text and Cases*. Harlow: Pearson.

Cohen, L. and Mallon, M. (1999) The transition from organisational employment to portfolio working: Perceptions of 'boundarylessness', *Work, Employment and Society*, 13 (2): 329–52.

Cole, B., Fletcher, N., Chittenden, T. and Cox, J. (2010) *Trends in the Solicitor's Profession: Annual Statistical Report 2009*, London: The Law Society.

Cole, N. (2008) Consistency in employee discipline: An empirical exploration, *Personnel Review*, 37 (1): 109–17.

Coleman Selden, S. and Wooters, R. (2011) Structures in public human resource management: Shared services in state governments, *Review of Public Personnel Administration*, 31 (4): 349–68.

Colling, T. (1995) Experiencing turbulence: Competition, strategic choice and the management of human resources in British Airways, *Human Resource Management Journal*, 5 (5): 18–33.

Collings, D. G. (2003) HRD and labour market practices in a US multinational subsidiary: The impact of global and local influences, *Journal of European Industrial Training*, 27 (2): 188–200.

Collings, D. G., McDonnell, A. and Scullion, H. (2009) Global talent management: The law of the few, *Poznan University of Economics Review*, 9 (2): 5–18.

Concateno (2012) *High Society: Drug Prevalence in the UK Workplace*, Abingdon: Concateno.

Confederation of British Industry (2009) *Future Fit: Preparing Graduates for the World of Work*, CBI Higher Education Taskforce, CBI: London.

Conklin, D. W. (2005) Risks and rewards in HR business process outsourcing, *Long Range Planning*, 38: 579–98.

Conley, H. (2006) Modernisation or casualisation? Numerical flexibility in public services, *Capital and Class*, 89: 31–58.

Constable, S., Coats, D., Bevan, S. and Mahdon, M. (2009) *Good Jobs*, London: The Work Foundation.

Conway, N. and Coyle-Shapiro, J. (2012) The reciprocal relationship between psychological contract fulfilment and employee performance and the moderating role of perceived organizational support and tenure, *Journal of Occupational and Organizational Psychology*, 85 (2): 277–99.

Cooke, H. (2006) Examining the disciplinary process in nursing: A case study approach, *Work, Employment and Society*, 20 (4): 687–707.

Cookson, H. and Buckley, P. (2011) *Violence at Work: Findings from the 2010/11 British Crime Survey*, Bootle: HSE.

Co-operatives UK (2011) *The UK Co-operative Economy 2011*, Manchester: Co-operatives UK.

Cottini, E. and Lucifora, C. (2013) Mental health and working conditions in Europe, *ILR Review*, 66 (4): 958–88.

Counsell, D. (1997) Graduate careers in the UK: An examination of undergraduates' perceptions. *Career Development International*, 1 (7): 34–41.

Cox, P. and Parkinson, A. (2003) Values and their impact on the changing employment relationship, in G. Hollinshead, P. Nicholls and S. Tailby (eds), *Employee Relations* (2nd edn), London: FT Prentice Hall.

Cox, T. and Blake, S. (1991) Managing cultural diversity: Implications for organizational competitiveness, *Academy of Management Executive*, 5 (3): 45–56.

Crane, A. and Matten, D. (2006) *Business Ethics: Managing Corporate Citizenship and Sustainability in the Age of Globalization* (2nd edn), Oxford: Oxford University Press.

Crawford, R. (2014) Samsung evolves benefits strategy, *Employee Benefits*, 5 November.

Creegan, C., Colgan, F., Charlesworth, R. and Robinson, G. (2003) Race equality policies at work: Employee perceptions of the 'Implementation Gap' in a UK local authority, *Work, Employment and Society*, 17 (4): 617–40.

Crush, P. (2015) Nepotism 'alive and well' in the workplace, research shows, *People Management*, 30 March

Cullinane, N. and Dundon, T. (2006) The psychological contract: A critical review, *International Journal of Management Reviews*, 8 (2): 113–29.

Cumbers, A., MacKinnon, D. and Shaw, J. (2010) Labour, organisational rescaling and the politics of production: Union renewal in the privatised rail industry, *Work, Employment and Society*, 24 (1): 127–44.

Cunningham, I. (2007) Talent management: Making it real, *Development and Learning in Organizations*, 21: 4–8.

Curtis, E. F. and Dreachslin, J. L. (2008) Diversity management interventions and organizational performance: A synthesis of current literature, *Human Resource Development Review*, 7 (1): 107–34.

Dalton, K. (2010) *Leadership and Management Development: Developing Tomorrow's Managers*, Harlow: FT Prentice Hall.

Danford, A., Durbin, S. and Richardson, M. (2009) 'You don't need a weatherman to know which way the wind blows': Public sector reform and its impact upon climatology scientists in the UK, *New Technology, Work and Employment*, 24 (3): 215–29.

Danford, A., Richardson, M., Stewart, P., Tailby, S. and Upchurch, M. (2005) *Partnership and the High Performance Workplace: Work and Employment Relations in the Aerospace Industry*, Basingstoke: Palgrave Macmillan.

Datt, R. (2008) Regional and industrial spread of trade unions in India, *Indian Journal of Labour Economics*, 51 (4): 993–9.

Datta, D. K., Guthrie, J. P., Basuil, D. and Pandey, A. (2010) Causes and effects of employee downsizing: A review and synthesis, *Journal of Management*, 36 (1): 281–348.

Davenport, T. H., Jarvenpaa, S. L. and Beers, M. C. (1996) Improving knowledge work process, *Sloan Management Review*, Summer: 53–65.

Davenport, T. H., Liebold, M. and Voelpel, S. (2006) *Strategic Management in the Innovation Economy*, Chichester: Wiley.

Davidson, M. C. G., McPhail, R. and Barry, S. (2011) Hospitality HRM: Past, present and the future, *International Journal of Contemporary Hospitality Management*, 23 (4): 498–516.

Davison, H., Maraist, C. and Bing, M. (2011) Friend or foe? The promise and pitfalls of using social networking sites for HR decisions, *Journal of Business Psychology*, 26 (2): 153–9.

Dawson, P. (1994) *Organizational Change: A Processual Approach*, London: Chapman.

Deal, T. and Kennedy, A. (1982) *Corporate Cultures: The Rites and Rituals of Corporate Life*, Reading, MA: Addison-Wesley.

Decktop, J. R., Mangel, R. and Cirka, C. C. (1999) Getting more than you pay for: Organisational citizenship behavior and pay-for-performance plans, *Academy of Management Journal*, 42 (4): 420–8.

de Grip, A. and Sieben, I. (2009) The effectiveness of more advanced human resource systems in small firms, *International Journal of Human Resource Management*, 20 (9): 1914–28.

Delaney, J. T. and Huselid, M. A. (1996) The impact of human resource management practices on perceptions of organisational performance, *Academy of Management Journal*, 39 (4): 949–69.

Delbridge, R., Hauptmeier, M. and Sengupta, S. (2011) Beyond the enterprise: Broadening the horizons of International HRM, *Human Relations*, 64 (4): 483–505.

Delery, J. E. and Doty, D. H. (1996) Modes of theorizing in strategic human resource management: Tests of universalistic, contingency and configurational predictions, *Academy of Management Journal*, 39 (4): 802–35.

Deloitte (2014) *Global Outsourcing and Insourcing Survey 2014*, http://www2.deloitte.com/us/en/pages/strategy/articles/2014-global-outsourcing-and-insourcing-survey.html (accessed 5 June 2015).

de Ridder, J. A. (2004) Organisational communication and supportive employees, *Human Resource Management Journal*, 14 (3): 20–30.

Derouin, R. E., Fritzsche, B. A. and Salas, E. (2005) E-learning in organizations, *Journal of Management*, 31 (6): 920–40.

Derr, C. B. and Laurent, A. (1989) Internal and external careers: A theoretical and cross-cultural perspective, in M. B. Arthur, D. T. Hall and B. S. Lawrence (eds), *Handbook of Career Theory*, Cambridge: Cambridge University Press.

Dibben, P. and Williams, C.C. (2012) Varieties of capitalism and employment relations: Informally dominated market economies. *Industrial Relations: A Review of Economy and Society*, 51 (S1): 563–82.

Dicken, P. (2007) *Global Shift* (5th edn), London: Sage.

Dickens, L. (1999) Beyond the business case: A three-pronged approach to equality action, *Human Resource Management Journal*, 9 (1): 9–19.

Dickens, L. (2005) Walking the talk? Equality and diversity in employment, in S. Bach (ed.), *Managing Human Resources*, Oxford: Blackwell.

Dietz, G., Cullen, J. and Coad, A. (2005) Can there be non-union forms of workplace partnership? *Employee Relations*, 27 (3): 289–306.

Dietz, G., van der Wiele, T., van Iwaarden, J. and Brosseau, J. (2006) HRM inside UK e-commerce firms: Innovations in the 'new' economy and continuities with the 'old', *International Small Business Journal*, 24 (5): 443–70.

Disability Rights Commission (2007) *The Disability Agenda: Ending Poverty and Widening Employment Opportunity*, Manchester: Disability Rights Commission.

Dix, G., Forth, J. and Sisson, K. (2009) Conflict at work: The changing pattern of disputes, in W. Brown, A. Bryson, J. Forth and K. Whitfield (eds), *The Evolution of the Modern Workplace*, Cambridge: Cambridge University Press.

Do Monte, P. A. (2012) Job dissatisfaction and labour turnover: Evidence from Brazil, *International Journal of Human Resource Management*, 23 (8): 1717–35.

Donnelly, R. (2008) Careers and temporal flexibility in the new economy: An Anglo-Dutch comparison of the organization of consultancy work, *Human Resource Management Journal*, 18: 197–215.

Dowling, B. and Richardson, R. (1997) Evaluating performance-related pay for managers in the National Health Service, *International Journal of Human Resource Management*, 8 (3): 348–66.

Dowling, P. J. and Welch, D. E. (2004) *International Human Resource Management*, London: Thomson Learning.

Druker, J. and White, G. (1997) Constructing a new reward strategy, *Employee Relations*, 19 (2): 128–46.

Drummond, I. and Stone, I. (2007) Exploring the potential of high performance work systems in SMEs, *Employee Relations*, 29 (2): 192–207.

DTI (Department for Trade and Industry) (2005) *High Performance Work Practices: Linking Strategy and Skills to Performance Outcomes*, London: DTI.

Du, J. and Choi, J-N. (2010) Pay for performance in emerging markets: Insights from China, *Journal of International Business Studies*, 41: 671–89.

Dundon, T. and Gollan, P. J. (2007) Reconceptualising voice in the non-union workplace, *International Journal of Human Resource Management*, 18 (7): 1182–98.

Dundon, T. and Rollinson, D. (2007) *Understanding Employment Relations*, Maidenhead: McGraw Hill.

Dundon, T., Grugulis, I. and Wilkinson, A. (1999) Looking out of the black hole: Non-union relations in an SME, *Employee Relations*, 21 (3): 251–66.

Dundon, T., Wilkinson, A., Marchington, M. and Ackers, P. (2004) The meanings and purpose of employee voice, *International Journal of Human Resource Management*, 15 (6): 1149–70.

Earnshaw, J., Marchington, M. and Goodman, J. (2000) Unfair to whom? Discipline and dismissal in small establishments, *Industrial Relations Journal*, 31 (1): 62–73.

Earnshaw, J., Marchington, M., Ritchie, E. and Torrington, D. (2004) Neither fish nor fowl? An assessment of teacher capability procedures, *Industrial Relations Journal*, 35 (2): 139–52.

Easterby-Smith, M. (1994) *Evaluation of Management Education, Training and Development* (2nd edn), Aldershot: Gower.

Easterby-Smith, M. and Araujo, L. (1999) Organizational learning: Current debates and opportunities, in M. Easterby-Smith, J. Burgoyne and L. Araujo (eds), *Organizational Learning and the Learning Organization: Developments in Theory and Practice*, London: Sage.

Eckerd, S., Hill, J., Boyer, K. K., Donohue, K. and Ward, P. T. (2013) The relative impact of attribute, severity, and timing of psychological contract breach on behavioral and attitudinal outcomes, *Journal of Operations Management*, 31 (7–8): 567–78.

The Economist (2012) Amazons at work, 30 June: 53.

Edwards, P. (2000) Discipline: towards trust and self-discipline? In S. Bach and K. Sisson (eds), *Personnel Management: A Comprehensive Guide to Theory and Practice in Britain* (3rd edn), Oxford: Blackwell.

Edwards, R. (1979) *Contested Terrain*, New York: Basic Books.

Edwards, T. and Rees, C. (2006) *International Human Resource Management: Globalization, National Systems and Multinational Companies*, Harlow: FT Prentice Hall.

Edwards, T., Colling, T. and Ferner, A. (2007) Conceptual approaches to the transfer of employment practices in multinational companies: An integrated approach, *Human Resource Management Journal*, 17 (3): 201–17.

EHRC (Equality and Human Rights Commission) (2011) *Sex and Power 2011*, Manchester: Equality and Human Rights Commission.

Einarsen, S. (1999) The nature and causes of bullying at work, *International Journal of Manpower*, 10: 16–27.

Eironline (2007) *Developments in Industrial Action 2003–2007*, www.eurofound.europa.eu/eiro/studies/tn0804039s/#a2 (accessed 12 January 2009).

Elenkov, S. E. (1998) Can American management concepts work in Russia? A cross-cultural comparative study, *California Management Review*, 40: 133–56.

Elorza, U., Aritzeta, A. and Ayestaran, S. (2011) Exploring the black box in Spanish firms: The effect of the actual and perceived system on employees' commitment and organisational performance, *International Journal of Human Resource Management*, 22 (7): 1401–22.

Elston, M. (2009) *Women and Medicine: The Future*, London: Royal College of Physicians.

Eraut, M. (2000) Non-formal learning and tacit knowledge in professional work, *British Journal of Educational Psychology*, 70 (1): 113–35.

Eurofound (2012) *Trends in Job Quality in Europe*, Publications Office of the European Union, Luxembourg.

European Parliament (2000) *Presidency Conclusions*, Lisbon European Council, March.

Evans, P., Doz, Y. and Laurent, A. (1989) *Human Resource Management in International Firms: Change, Globalization, Innovation*, Houndmills: Macmillan.

Executive Director Total Remuneration Survey (2011) *Executive Director Total Remuneration Survey May 2011 Edition*, London: Manifest.

Faragher, J. (2014) Personnel Today Awards 2014 winners, *Personnel Today*, 10 December.

Farndale, E. and Paauwe, J. (2007) Uncovering competitive and institutional drivers of HRM practices in multinational corporations, *Human Resource Management Journal*, 17 (4): 355–75.

Farndale, E., Hope-Hailey, V. and Kelliher, C. (2011) High commitment performance management: The roles of justice and trust, *Personnel Review*, 40 (1): 5–23.

Farndale, E., Paauwe, J. and Hoeksema, L. (2009) In-sourcing HR: Shared service centres in The Netherlands, *International Journal of Human Resource Management*, 20 (3): 544–61.

Farnham, D. and Stevens, A. (2000) Developing and implementing competence-based recruitment and selection in a social services department, *International Journal of Public Sector Management*, 13 (4): 369–82.

Fee, A., McGrath-Champ, S. and Yang, X. (2011) Expatriate performance management and firm internationalization: Australian management in China, *Asia Pacific Journal of Human Resources*, 49 (3): 365–84.

Felstead, A., Gallie, D., Green, F. and Zhou, Y. (2007) *Skills at Work 1986 to 2006*, Oxford: SKOPE (ESRC Centre on Skills, Knowledge and Organisational Performance).

Felstead, A., Green, F. and Jewson, N. (2012) An analysis of the impact of the 2008 -9 recession on the provision of training in the UK, *Work, Employment & Society*, 26 (6): 968–86.

Fernandez, D., Carlson, D., Stepina, L. and Nicholson, J. (1997) Hofstede's country classification 25 years later, *Journal of Social Psychology*, 137: 43–54.

Ferner, A. and Quintanilla, J. (1998) Multinationals, national business systems and HRM: The enduring influence of national identity or a process of 'Anglo-Saxonisation', *International Journal of Human Resource Management*, 9 (4): 710–31.

Ferner, A. and Varul, M. (2000) Vanguard subsidiaries and the diffusion of new practices: A case study of German multinationals, *British Journal of Industrial Relations*, 38 (1): 115–40.

Ferner, A., Quintanilla, J. and Varul, M. (2001) Country of origin effects, host-country effects and the management of HR in multinationals: German companies in Britain and Spain, *Journal of World Business*, 36 (2): 107–27.

Financial Times (2012a) Unions hit back at call for cut in workplace rights, 22 February.

Financial Times (2012b) QinetiQ to derecognise unions, 21 February.

Financial Times (2012c) Youth unemployment: Shrinking skill base fires up apprenticeship programmes, 29 May.

Fiorito, J. (2001) Human resource management practices and worker desires for union representation, *Journal of Labor Research*, 22 (2): 335–54.

Fitz-Enz, J. (1994) Yes ... you can weigh training's value, *Training*, 31 (7): 54–8.

Fleetwood, S. (2007) *Labour Market Flexibility*, UWE (University of the West of England) Working Paper.

Fleetwood, S. and Hesketh, A. (2006) HRM-performance research: Under-theorised and lacking explanatory power, *International Journal of Human Resource Management*, 17 (12): 1977–93.

Fletcher, C. (1997) *Appraisal: Routes to Improved Performance* (2nd edn), London: CIPD.

Fletcher, C. (2001) Performance appraisal and management: The developing research agenda, *Journal of Occupational and Organizational Psychology*, 74: 473–87.

Fletcher, C. (2008) *Appraisal, Feedback and Development* (4th edn), Abingdon: Routledge.

Forbrun, C., Tichy, N. and Devanna, M. (eds) (1984) *Strategic Human Resource Management*, New York: Wiley.

Forrester, G. (2011) Performance management in education: Milestone or millstone? *Management in Education*, 25 (1): 5–9.

Foster, C. and Harris, L. (2005) Easy to say, difficult to do: Diversity management in retail. *Human Resource Management Journal*, 15 (3): 4–17.

Foster, C. and Harris, L. (2009) From equal opportunities to diversity management, in J. Leopold and L. Harris (eds), *The Strategic Managing of Human Resources*, Harlow: FT Prentice Hall.

Fox, A. (1974) *Beyond Contract: Power and Trust Relations*, London: Faber & Faber.

Francis, H. and Keegan, A. (2006) The changing face of HRM: In search of balance, *Human Resource Management Journal*, 16 (3): 231–49.

Franklin, A. L. and Pagan, J. F. (2006) Organization culture as an explanation for employee discipline practices, *Review of Public Personnel Administration*, 26 (1): 52–73.

Fredman, S. (2001) Equality: A new generation? *Industrial Law Journal*, 30 (2): 145–68.

French, J. R. P. and Raven, B. (1959) The bases of social power, in D. Cartwright (ed.), *Studies in Social Power*, Ann Arbor, MI: University of Michigan.

French, P. E. and Emerson, M. C. (2015) One size does not fit all: Matching the reward to the employee's motivational needs, *Review of Public Personnel Administration*, 35 (1): 82–94.

French, S., Kubo, K. and Marsden, D. (2000) *Why Does Performance Pay De-motivate? Financial Incentives Versus Performance Appraisal*, Discussion Paper 476, London: Centre for Economic Performance, London School of Economics and Political Science.

Frenkel, S. J., Korczynski, M., Shire, K. A. and Tam, M. (1998) Beyond bureaucracy? Work organization in call centres, *International Journal of Human Resource Management*, 9 (6): 957–79.

Friedman, A. (1977) Responsible autonomy versus direct control over the labour process, *Capital and Class*, 1: 43–57.

Fuller, A. and Unwin, L. (2003) Learning as apprentices in the contemporary UK workplace: Creating and managing expansive participation, *Journal of Education and Work*, 16 (4): 407–26.

Galagan, P. A. (1993) The search for the poetry of work, *Training and Development*, 47 (10): 33–7.

Gamble, J. (2003) Transferring human resource practices from the United Kingdom to China: The limits and potential for convergence, *International Journal of Human Resource Management*, 14 (3): 369–87.

Ganster, D. C. and Perrewé, P. L. (2011) Theories of occupational stress, in J. C. Quick and L. E. Tetrick (eds), *Handbook of Occupational Health Psychology* (2nd edn), Washington, DC: American Psychological Association.

Ganster, D. C. and Rosen, C. C. (2013) Work stress and employee health: A multidisciplinary review, *Journal of Management*, 39 (5): 1085–122.

Garavan, T. N. (1991) Strategic human resource development, *Journal of European Industrial Training*, 15 (1): 17–30.

Garavan, T. N. (1997) The learning organization: A review and an evaluation, *Learning Organization*, 4 (1): 18–29.

Garavan, T. N. (2007) A strategic perspective on human resource development, *Advances in Developing Human Resources*, 9 (1): 11–30.

Garavan, T. N. and McGuire, D. (2010) Human resource development and society: Human resource development's role in embedding corporate social responsibility, sustainability, and ethics in organizations, *Advances in Developing Human Resources*, 12 (5): 487–507.

Garavan, T. and Morley, M. (1997) The socialization of high-potential graduates into the organization: Initial expectations, experiences and outcomes, *Journal of Managerial Psychology*, 12 (2): 118–37.

Garg, P. and Rastogi, R. (2005) New model of job design: Motivating employees' performance, *Journal of Management Development*, 25: 572–87.

Gatrell, C. and Swann, E. (2008) *Gender and Diversity in Management: A Concise Introduction*, London: Sage.

GCCIJ (German Chamber of Commerce and Industry in Japan) (2010) *Silver Business in Japan: Implications of Demographic Change for Human Resource Management and Marketing*, Tokyo: GCCIJ.

Geary, J. F. (1994) Task participation: Employee's participation enabled or constrained?, in K. Sisson (ed.), *Personnel Management*, Oxford: Blackwell.

Georgopoulos, B. S., Mahoney, G. M. and Jones, N. W. (1957) A path-goal approach to productivity, *Journal of Applied Psychology*, 41 (6): 345–53.

Geppert, M., Matten, D. and Williams, K. (2003) Change management in MNCs: How global convergence intertwines with national diversities, *Human Relations*, 56 (7): 807–38.

Gerhart, B. (2008) Cross-cultural management research: Assumptions, evidence and suggested directions, *International Journal of Cross Cultural Management*, 8 (3): 259–74.

Gibb, S. (2002) *Learning and Development: Process, Practices and Perspectives at Work*, Basingstoke: Palgrave.

Gibb, S. (2011) *Human Resource Development: Foundations, Process, Context* (3rd edn), Basingstoke: Palgrave Macmillan.

Gillen, T. (2002) *Leadership Skills for Boosting Performance*, London: CIPD.

Gilley, K. M., Greer, C. R. and Rasheed, A. A. (2004) Human resource outsourcing and organizational performance in manufacturing firms, *Journal of Business Research*, 57 (3): 232–40.

Gold, J. (2007) Human resource development, in J. Bratton and J. Gold (eds), *Human Resource Management: Theory and Practice* (4th edn), Basingstoke: Palgrave.

Gold, J., Holden, R., Iles, P., Stewart, J. and Beardwell, J. (2009) *Human Resource Development: Theory and Practice*, Basingstoke: Palgrave Macmillan.

Gold, J., Holden, R., Iles, P., Stewart, J. and Beardwell, J. (2013) *Human Resource Development: Theory and Practice* (2nd edn), Basingstoke: Palgrave Macmillan.

Golding, N. (2007) Strategic human resource management, in J. Beardwell and T. Claydon (eds), *Human Resource Management: A Contemporary Approach* (5th edn), London: FT Prentice Hall.

Goleman, D. (1995) *Emotional Intelligence*, New York: Bantam Books.

Gollan, P. J. and Wilkinson, A. (2007) Contemporary developments in information and consultation, *International Journal of Human Resource Management*, 18 (7): 1133–44.

Gooderham, P. and Brewster, C. (2003) Convergence, stasis, or divergence? Personnel management in Europe, *Scandinavian Journal of Business Research*, 1: 6–18.

Gooderham, P., Nordhaug, O. and Ringdal, K. (1999) Institutional and rational determinants of organizational practices: Human resource management in European firms. *Administrative Science Quarterly*, 44: 507–31.

Goodman, J., Earnshaw, J., Marchington, M. and Harrison, R. (1998) Unfair dismissal cases, disciplinary procedures, recruitment methods and management styles, *Employee Relations*, 20 (6): 536–50.

Goss, D. (1994) *Principles of Human Resource Management*, London: Paul Chapman.

Gould-Williams, J. (2003) The importance of HR practices and workplace trust in achieving superior performance: A study of public-sector organisations, *International Journal of Human Resource Management*, 14 (1): 28–54.

Gourlay, S. (2006) Towards conceptual clarity for 'tacit knowledge': a review of empirical studies, *Knowledge Management Research and Practice*, 4 (1): 60–9.

Grant, D. (1999) HRM, rhetoric and the psychological contract: A case of 'easier said than done', *International Journal of Human Resource Management*, 10 (2): 327–50.

Gray, A. (2004) *Unsocial Europe: Social Protection or Flexploitation*, London: Pluto.

Green, A. (2002) The many faces of lifelong learning: Recent education policy trends in Europe, *Journal of Educational Policy*, 17 (6): 611–26.

Green, F. (2006) *Demanding Work*, Princeton, NJ: Princeton University Press.

Green, F. and Tsitsianis, N. (2005) An investigation of national trends in job satisfaction in Britain and Germany, *British Journal of Industrial Relations*, 43 (3): 401–29.

Greene, R. J. (2012) Scenario-based reward management, *Compensation & Benefits Review*, 44 (3): 126–7.

Greene, R. J. (2014) The role of employee ownership in the total rewards strategy, *Compensation & Benefits Review*, 46 (1): 6–9.

Grey, C. (2007) *A Very Short, Fairly Interesting and Reasonably Cheap Book about Studying Organisations*, London: Sage.

Griffin, B., Hesketh, B. and Grayson, D. (2004) Applicants faking good: Evidence of item bias in the NEO-PI-R, *Personality and Individual Differences*, 36 (7): 1545–54.

Griffin, M. A. and Clarke, S. (2011) Stress and well-being at work, in S. Zedeck (ed.), *APA Handbook of Industrial and Organizational Psychology*, vol. 3, Washington, DC: American Psychological Association.

Griffiths, J. (2005) Masculine wiles, *People Management*, 11: 20–1.

Grimshaw, D. and Miozzo, M. (2009) New human resource management practices in knowledge-intensive business services firms: The case of outsourcing with staff transfer, *Human Relations*, 62 (10): 1521–50.

Grimshaw, D., Beynon, H., Rubery, J. and Ward, K. (2002) The restructuring of career paths in large service sector organisations: 'Delayering', upskilling and polarisation, *The Sociological Review*, 50 (1): 89–116.

Grimshaw, D., Ward, K., Rubery, J. and Beynon, H. (2008) Organisations and the transformation of the internal labour market, *Work, Employment and Society*, 15 (1): 25–54.

Grint, K. (1993) What's wrong with performance appraisals? A critique and a suggestion, *Human Resource Management Journal*, 3 (3): 61–77.

Grint, K. (2005) *The Sociology of Work* (3rd edn), Cambridge: Polity Press.

Grote, G. and Raeder, S. (2009) Careers and identity in flexible working: Do flexible identities fare better? *Human Relations*, 62 (2): 219–44.

Grugulis, I. and Stoyanova, D. (2011) Skill and performance, *British Journal of Industrial Relations*, 49 (3): 515–36.

Grugulis, I., Warhurst, P. and Keep, E. (2004) What's happening to skill?, in C. Warhurst, I. Grugulis and E. Keep (eds), *The Skills that Matter*, Basingstoke: Palgrave Macmillan.

Gruman, J. A. and Saks, A. M. (2011) Performance management and employee engagement, *Human Resource Management Review*, 21: 123–36.

The Guardian (2012a) Job cuts 'could leave MoD lacking the staff it needs to run itself', 9 February.

The Guardian (2012b) Political divide as Tories shy away from harsh judgement on Rupert Murdoch, 1 May.

The Guardian (2012c) Executive pay is out of control – shareholders must step up, 1 May.

Guerci, M., Bartezzaghi, E. and Solari, L. (2010) Training evaluation in Italian corporate universities: A stakeholder-based analysis, *International Journal of Training and Development*, 14 (4): 291–308.

Guest, D. E. (1987) Human resource management and industrial relations, *Journal of Management Studies*, 24 (5): 503–21.

Guest, D. E. (1990) Human resource management and the American dream, *Journal of Management Studies*, 27 (4): 377–97.

Guest, D. (1998) Is the psychological contract worth taking seriously? *Journal of Organisational Behaviour*, 19 (S1): 649–64.

Guest, D. (2002) Human resource management, corporate performance and employee wellbeing: Building the worker into HRM, *Journal of Industrial Relations*, 44 (3): 335–58.

Guest, D. (2004) The psychology of the employment relationship: An analysis based on the psychological contract, *Applied Psychology*, 53 (4): 541–55.

Guest, D. and Baron, A. (2000) Piece by piece, *People Management*, 20 July.

Guest, D. and Conway, N. (1997) *Employee Motivation and the Psychological Contract*, London: IPD.

Guest, D. and Conway, N. (1999) Peering into the black hole: The downside of the new employee relations in the UK, *British Journal of Industrial Relations*, 37 (3): 367–89.

Guest, D. and Conway, N. (2002) Communicating the psychological contract: An employer perspective, *Human Resource Management Journal*, 12 (2): 22–38.

Guest, D. and Conway, N. (2004) *Employee Well-being and the Psychological Contract*, Research Report, London: CIPD.

Guest, D. and Hoque, K. (1994) The good, the bad and the ugly: Employment relations in the new non-union workplaces, *Human Resource Management Journal*, 5: 1–14.

Guest, D. and King, Z. (2004) Power, innovation and problem-solving: The personnel manager's three steps to heaven? *Journal of Management Studies*, 41 (3): 402–23.

Guest, D. E. and Peccei, R. (1998) *The Partnership Company*, London: IPA.

Guest, D. E. and Peccei, R. (2001) Partnership at work: Mutuality and the balance of advantage, *British Journal of Industrial Relations*, 39 (2): 207–36.

Guest, D., Michie, J., Conway, N. and Sheehan, M. (2003) Human resource management and corporate performance in the UK, *British Journal of Industrial Relations*, 41 (2): 291–314.

Hackett, T. (2003) *Training Practice*, CIPD: London.

Hall, D. (1996) Protean careers of the 21st century, *Academy of Management Review*, 10 (4): 8–16.

Hall, D. (2002) *Careers In and Out of Organizations*, London: Sage.

Hall, D. (2009) Managing performance, in S. Gilmore and S. Williams (eds), *Human Resource Management*, Oxford: Oxford University Press.

Hamel, G. and Prahalad, C. (1994) *Competing for the Future*, Boston, MA: Harvard Business School Press.

Handy, C. (1976) *Understanding Organisations*, London: Penguin.

Harney, B. and Jordan, C. (2008) Unlocking the black box: Line managers and HRM-Performance in a call centre context, *International Journal of Productivity and Performance Management*, 75 (4): 275–96.

Harper, S. and Vilkinas, T. (2005) Determining the impact an organisation's performance management system, *Asia Pacific Journal of Human Resources*, 43 (1): 76–97.

Harrington, J. M. (2001) Health effects of shift work and extended hours of work, *Occupational Health and Environmental Medicine*, 58: 68–72.

Harris, L. (2000) Procedural justice and perceptions of fairness in selection practice, *International Journal of Selection and Assessment*, 8 (3): 148–57.

Harris, L., Doughty, D. and Kirk, S. (2002) The devolution of HR responsibilities: Perspectives from the UK's public sector, *Journal of European Industrial Training*, 25 (5): 218–29.

Harrison, R. (2005) *Learning and Development* (4th edn), London: CIPD.

Harrison, R. and Kessels, J. W. M. (2004) *Human Resource Development in a Knowledge Economy: An Organizational View*, New York: Palgrave Macmillan.

Harvey, L., Moon, S. and Geall, V. (1997) *Graduates' Work: Organisational Change and Students' Attributes*, Birmingham: Centre for Research into Quality/AGR.

Harvey, M. (2009) Bosses crack down on social networks amid leaks, *The Times*, 19 August.

Harvey, M. G., Heames, J. T., Richey, R G. and Leonard, N. (2006) Bullying: From the playground to the boardroom, *Journal of Leadership & Organizational Studies*, 12 (4): 1–11.

Hasle, P., Limborg, H. J., Kallehave, T., Klitgaard, C. and Andersen, T. R. (2012) The working environment in small firms: Responses from owner-managers, *International Small Business Journal*, 30: 622–39.

Hay Group (2007) *Matching Supply to Demand: A Strategic Approach to Talent Management*, London: Hay Group.

Hay Group (2010) *The Changing Face of Reward*, London: Hay Group.

Hayter, S., Fashoyin, T. and Kochan, T. A. (2011) Collective bargaining for the 21st century, *Journal of Industrial Relations*, 53 (2): 225–47.

Heavey, A. L., Holwerda, J. A. and Hausknecht, J. P. (2013) Causes and consequences of collective turnover: A meta-analytic review, *Journal of Applied Psychology*, 98 (3): 412–53.

Heckscher, C. (1995) *White-Collar Blues: Management Loyalties in an Age of Corporate Restructuring*, New York: Basic Books.

Heery, E. (1997a) Performance-related pay and trade union de-recognition, *Employee Relations*, 19 (3): 208–21.

Heery, E. (1997b) Performance-related pay and trade union membership, *Employee Relations*, 19 (4): 430–42.

Heffernan, M., Haney, B., Cafferkey, K. and Dundon, T. (2009) Exploring the relationship between HRM, creativity climate and organisational performance: Evidence from Ireland, paper presented at 2009 Academy of Management Conference, Chicago, August 7–11.

Hempel, P. S. (2004) Preparing the HR profession for technology and information work, *Human Resource Management*, 43 (2/3): 163–77.

Hencke, D. (2006a) Asda under threat of prosecution for union busting, *The Guardian*, 13 June.

Hencke, D. (2006b) Good shop, bad shop? *The Guardian*, 1 July.

Hendrickson, A. (2003) Human resource management systems: Backbone technology of contemporary human resources, *Journal of Labor Research*, 24 (3): 382–94.

Hendry, C. and Perkins, S. (2000) Performance and rewards: Cleaning out the stables, *Human Resource Management Journal*, 10 (3): 46–62.

Herriot, P., Gibbons, P., Pemberton, C. and Jackson, P. R. (1994) An empirical model of managerial careers in organisations, *British Journal of Management*, 5: 113–21.

Herzberg, F. (1966) *Work and the Nature of Man*, Cleveland, OH: World Publishing Company.

Herzberg, F., Mausner, B. and Snyderman, B. B. (1959) *The Motivation to Work*, New York: John Wiley.

Heywood, J. S. and Wei, X. (2006) Performance pay and job satisfaction, *Journal of Industrial Relations*, 48: 523–40.

Hirsh, W. and Jackson, C. (2004) *Managing Careers in Large Organizations*, London: The Work Foundation.

Hislop, D. (2005) *Knowledge Management in Organizations: A Critical Introduction*, Oxford: Oxford University Press.

Hislop, D. (2009) Knowledge management, in T. Redman and A. Wilkinson (eds), *Contemporary Human Resource Management* (3rd edn), Harlow: FT Prentice Hall.

Hite, L. and MacDonald, K. (2008) A new era for career development and HRD, *Advances in Developing Human Resources*, 10 (1): 3–7.

HM Treasury (2011) *The Plan for Growth*, London: HM Treasury.

Hodson, R. (2001) *Dignity at Work*, Cambridge: Cambridge University Press.

Hofstede, G. (2001) *Culture's Consequences: International Differences in Work-Related Values* (2nd edn), Thousand Oaks, CA: Sage.

Hogarth, T., Hasluck, C. and Pierre, G. (2001) *Work–Life Balance 2000: Results from the Baseline Study*, Research Report RR249, Norwich: Department for Education and Employment.

Holton, E. (1996) The flawed four-level evaluation model, *Human Resource Development Quarterly*, 7 (1): 5–21.

Holton, E. and Naquin, S. (2005) A critical analysis of HRD evaluation models from a decision-making perspective, *Human Resource Development Quarterly*, 16 (2): 257–80.

Honey, P. and Mumford, A. (1992) *The Manual of Learning Styles*, Maidenhead: Peter Honey.

Hope Hailey, V., Farndale, E. and Truss, C. (2005) The HR department's role in organisational performance, *Human Resource Management Journal*, 15 (3): 49–66.

Hoque, K. (1999) Human resource management and performance in the UK hotel sector, *British Journal of Industrial Relations*, 37: 419–43.

Hoque, K. (2000) *Human Resource Management in the Hotel Industry: Strategy, Innovation and Performance*, London: Routledge.

Hoque, K. and Noon, M. (2004) Equal opportunities policy and practice in Britain: Evaluating the 'empty shell' hypothesis, *Work, Employment and Society*, 18: 481–506.

Horwitz, F. M., Heng, C. T. and Quazi, H. A. (2003) Finders, keepers? Attracting, motivating and retaining knowledge workers, *Human Resource Management Journal*, 13(4): 23–44.

Horwitz, F. M., Bowmaker-Falconer, A. and Searll, P. (1996) Human resource development and managing diversity in South Africa, *International Journal of Manpower*, 4 (5): 134–51.

House, R. J., Hanges, P. J., Javidan, M., Dorfman, P. W. and Gupta, V. (eds) (2004) *Leadership, Culture and Organizations: The GLOBE Study of 62 Societies*, Thousand Oaks, CA: Sage.

Howard, L. W. and Dougherty, T. W. (2004) Alternative reward strategies and employee reactions, *Compensation & Benefits Review*, 36 (1): 41–51.

HSE (Health and Safety Executive) (2009) *How to Tackle Work-related Stress: A Guide for Employers on Making the Management Standards Work*, Sudbury: HSE Books.

HSE (Health and Safety Executive) (2011a) *Annual Statistics Report 2010/11*, Bootle: HSE.

HSE (Health and Safety Executive) (2011b) *European Comparisons: Summary of GB Performance*, Bootle: HSE.

HSE (Health and Safety Executive) (2012a) *What Are the Management Standards for Work-related Stress?*, www.hse.gov.uk/stress/standards/index.htm (accessed 18 October 2012).

HSE (Health and Safety Executive) (2012b) *What Is Stress?*, www.hse.gov.uk/stress/furtheradvice/what_is_stress.htm (accessed 18 October 2012).

HSE (Health and Safety Executive) (2012c) *Working Days Lost*, www.hse.gov.uk/statistics/dayslost.htm (accessed 1 May 2012).

HSE (Health and Safety Executive) (2014) *Stress-related and Psychological Disorders in Great Britain 2014*, Bootle: HSE.

Huang, T.-C. (1999) Who shall follow? Factors affecting the adoption of succession plans in Taiwan, *Long Range Planning*, 32 (6): 609–16.

Huang, X. (2008) Guanxi networks and job searches in China's emerging labour market: A qualitative investigation, *Work, Employment and Society*, 22 (3), 467–84.

Huo, Y. P. and Glinow, M. A. (1995) On transplanting human resource practices to China: A culture-driven approach, *International Journal of Manpower*, 16: 3–15.

Huselid, M. A. (1995) The impact of human resource management practices on turnover, productivity, and corporate financial performance, *Academy of Management Journal*, 38 (3): 655–72.

Huselid, M. A., Jackson, S. E. and Schuler, R. S. (1997) Technical and strategic human resource management as determinants of firm performance, *Academy of Management Journal*, 40 (1): 171–88.

Hutchinson, J. (2012) Rethinking workplace bullying as an employment relations problem, *Journal of Industrial Relations*, 54 (5): 637–52.

Hutchinson, S. and Purcell, J. (2007) *Learning and the Line: The Role of Line Managers in Training, Learning and Development*, London: CIPD.

Hutchinson, S., Purcell, J. and Kinnie, N. (2000) Evolving high commitment management and the experience of the RAC call centre, *Human Resource Management Journal*, 10 (1): 63–78.

Hwang, J., Lee, J. J., Park, S., Chang, H. and Kim, S. S. (2014) The impact of occupational stress on employee's turnover intention in the luxury hotel segment, *International Journal of Hospitality & Tourism Administration*, 15 (1): 60–77.

Hyde, P., Boaden, R., Cortvriend, P., Harris, C., Marchington, M., Pass, S., Sparrow, P. and Sibbald, B. (2006) *Improving Health through Human Resource Management: Mapping the Territory*, London: CIPD.

Hyman, J. and Summers, J. (2003) Lacking balance? Work–life employment practices in the modern economy, *Personnel Review*, 33 (4): 418–29.

Hyman, J., Scholarios, D. and Baldry, C. (2005) Getting on or getting by? Employee flexibility and coping strategies for home and work, *Work, Employment and Society*, 19 (4): 705–25.

Hyman, R. (1987) Strategy or structure? Capital, labour and control, *Work, Employment and Society*, 1 (1): 25–55.

IAS (Institute of Alcohol Studies) (2009) *Alcohol and the Workplace Factsheet*, St Ives: IAS.

Ichijo, K., Krogh, G. and Nonaka, I. (1998) Knowledge enablers, in G. Krogh, J. Roos and D. Kleine (eds), *Knowing in Firms*, London: Sage.

Ichniowski, C., Shaw, K. and Prennushi, G. (1997) The effects of human resource management practices on productivity: A study of steel finishing lines, *The American Economic Review*, 87 (3): 297–313.

IDS (Income Data Services) (2002) Implementing a new HR system, *IDS Studyplus*, Summer.

IDS (Income Data Services) (2003) taking out costs, *IDS Studyplus*, Spring.

IDS (Income Data Services) (2006a) Overhaul of the HR function at the National Trust, *IDS HR Studies*, 835, December.

IDS (Income Data Services) (2006b) Survey of flexible working practices, *IDS HR Studies Update*, 834, November.

IDS (Income Data Services) (2008a) Talent management, *IDS HR Studies*, 869, May.

IDS (Income Data Services) (2008b) Flexible benefits, *IDS HR Studies Plus*, 883, December.

IDS (Income Data Services) (2008c) employee assistance programmes, *IDS HR Studies Plus*, 870, May.

IDS (Income Data Services) (2008d) Reward, *IDS HR Studies*, 871, June.

IDS (Income Data Services) (2009) Centralising HR service provision, *IDS HR Studies*, 888, February.

IDS (Income Data Services) (2010) IBM: Internet & e-mail policies, *IDS Case Study*, July.

IDS (Income Data Services) (2011a) Outsourcing HR, *IDS HR Studies*, 940, April.

IDS (Income Data Services) (2011b) HR technology: Virgin Media case study, *IDS HR Studies*, 954, November.

IDS (Income Data Services) (2011c) HR best practice and benchmarking: Managing stress, *IDS HR Studies*, 945, July.

IDS (Income Data Services) (2013) Performance management case study: Marie Stopes International, *IDS HR Studies*, April.

IDS (Income Data Services) (2014) HR best practice and benchmarking: Diversity, *HR in Practice*, August.

Inkson, K. (2008) Are humans resources? *Career Development International*, 13 (3): 270–9.

Inkson, K. and King, Z. (2010) Contested terrain in careers: A psychological contract model, *Human Relations*, 64 (1): 37–57.

Inkson, K., Gunz, H., Ganesh, S. and Roper, J. (2012) Boundaryless careers: Bringing back boundaries, *Organization Studies*, 33 (3): 323–40.

Innocenti, L., Pilati, M. and Peluso, A. M. (2011) Trust as moderator in the relationship between HRM practices and employee attitudes, *Human Resource Management Journal*, 21 (3): 303–17.

Institute of Directors (2007) *Leading Health and Safety: Leadership Actions for Directors and Board Members*, www.iod.com/intershoproot/eCS/Store/en//pdfs/hse_guide.pdf (accessed 31 December 2009).

International Labour Organisation (ILO) (2009) *World Day for Safety and Health at Work 2009: Facts on Safety and Health at Work*, Geneva: ILO.

IPA (Involvement and Participation Association) (1997) *Towards Industrial Partnership New Ways of Working in British Companies*, London: IPA.

IRS (Industrial Relations Service) (2000) Holding the line, *IRS Employment Trends*, 707.

IRS (Industrial Relations Service) (2004) Welcome the new multitasking all-purpose management expert, *IRS Employment Review*, 793: 8–13.

IRS (Industrial Relations Service) (2005) Verdict on appraisals: Good but could be made to work better, *IRS Employment Review*, 827, www.xperthr.co.uk/survey-analysis/verdict-on-appraisals-good-but-could-be-made-to-work-better/55306/ (accessed 18 September 2015).

IRS (Industrial Relations Service) (2009) Managing learning and development in a recession: The 2009 IRS Survey, *IRS Employment Review*, 929, www.xperthr.co.uk/survey-analysis/managing-learning-and-development-in-a-recession-the-2009-irs-survey/96399/ (accessed 28 September 2015).

Ishida, H. (1986) Transferability of Japanese human resource management abroad, *Human Resource Management*, 25: 103–21.

Jackson, C. A. and Cox, T. (2006) *Health and Well-being of Working Age People*, ESRC Seminar Series, London: Economic and Social Research Council.

Jackson, C., Arnold, J., Nicholson, N. and Watts, A. G. (1996) *Managing Careers in 2000 and Beyond*, IES Report 304, Brighton: Institute of Employment Studies.

Jacques, E. (1990) In praise of hierarchy, *Harvard Business Review*, January–February: 127–33.

Jacques, M. (2005) East is east – get used to it, *The Guardian*, 20 May.

James, P. and Walters, D. (2002) Worker representation in health and safety: Options for regulatory reform, *Industrial Relations Journal*, 33 (2): 141–56.

James, S., Warhurst, C., Tholen, G. and Commander, J. (2013) What we know and what we need to know about graduate skills, *Work, Employment and Society*, 27 (6): 952–63.

James, W. B. and Galbraith, M. W. (1985) Perceptual learning styles: Implications and techniques for the practitioner, *Lifelong Learning*, 3 (2): 20–3.

Janssens, M. and Steyaert, C. (2009) HRM and performance: A plea for reflexivity in HRM studies, *Journal of Management Studies*, 46 (1): 143–55.

Janssens, M., Sels, L. and van den Brande, I. (2003) Multiple types of psychological contracts: A six-cluster solution, *Human Relations*, 56 (11): 1349–78.

Jewson, N. and Mason, D. (1986) The theory and practice of equal opportunity policies: Liberal and radical approaches, *Sociological Review*, 34 (2): 307–34.

Johnson, G., Scholes, K. and Whittington, R. (2007) *Exploring Corporate Strategy: Text and Cases*, Harlow: Pearson.

Johnstone, S., Ackers, P. and Wilkinson, A. (2010) Better than nothing? Is non-union partnership a contradiction in terms? *Journal of Industrial Relations*, 52 (2): 151–68.

Jones, D. C., Kalmi, P. and Kauhanen, A. (2010) How does employee involvement stack up? The effects of human resource management policies on performance in a retail firm, *Industrial Relations*, 49 (1): 1–21.

Jonsen, K., Maznevski, M. and Schneider, S. (2011) Diversity and its not so diverse literature: An international perspective, *International Journal of Cross Cultural Management*, 11 (1): 35–62.

Jütting, J. P. and Laiglesia, J. R. (2009) Employment, poverty reduction and development: What's new?, in J. P. Jütting and J. R. Laiglesia (eds), *Is Informal Normal? Towards More and Better Jobs in Developing Countries*, Paris: OECD.

Kahn-Freund, O. (1977) *Labour and the Law* (2nd edn), London: Stevens.

Kalleberg, A. L. (2003) Flexible firms and labor market segmentation: Effects of workplace restructuring on jobs and workers, *Work and Occupations*, 30 (2): 154–75.

Kalleberg, A. L., Reskin, B. F. and Hudson, K. (2000) Bad jobs in America: Standard and non-standard employment relations and job quality in the United States, *American Sociological Review*, 65 (April): 256–78.

Kandola, R. and Fullerton, J. (1994) *Managing the Mosaic: Diversity in Action*, London: IPD.

Kang, S. C. and Snell, S. A. (2009) Intellectual capital architectures and ambidextrous learning: A framework for human resource management, *Journal of Management Studies*, 46 (1): 65–92.

Kanter, R. (1989) Careers and the wealth of nations: A macro-perspective on the structure and implications of career forms, in M. Arthur, D. Hall and S. Lawrence (eds), *Handbook of Career Theory*, Cambridge: Cambridge University Press.

Kanter, R. M. and Corn, R. I. (1994) Do cultural differences make business difference? *Journal of Management Development*, 13 (2): 5–23.

Kaplan, R. and Norton, D. (1992) The balanced scorecard: Measures that drive performance, *Harvard Business Review*, 70 (1): 71–9.

Kashefi, M. (2011) High performance work organizations and job rewards in manufacturing and service economies, *International Sociology*, 26 (4): 547–70.

Katou, A. A. and Budhwar, P. S. (2010) Causal relationship between HRM policies and organisational performance: Evidence from the Greek manufacturing sector, *European Management Journal*, 28 (1): 25–39.

Katou, A. A. and Budhwar, P. S. (2012), The link between HR practices, psychological contract fulfillment, and organizational performance: The case of the Greek service sector, *Thunderbird International Business Review*, 54 (6): 793–809.

Kaufman, B. (2004) 'Employment relations and the employment relations system: A guide to theorizing', in B. Kaufman (ed.), *Theoretical Perspectives on Work and the Employment Relationship*, Champaign, IL: Industrial Relations Research Association.

Keep, E. and Mayhew, K. (1997) British education and training policies and competitive performance, in T. Buxton, C. Chapman and P. Temple (eds), *Britain's Economic Performance*, London: Routledge.

Keep, E. and Mayhew, K. (2004) The economic and distributional implications of current policies on higher education, *Oxford Review of Economic Policy*, 20 (2): 298–314.

Kelly Services (2005) UK employees face high levels of stress in the workplace, Media Release, 18 October, www2-1.kellyglobal.net/web/uk/services/en/pages/about_press05_oct18.html (accessed 8 July 2008).

Kersley, B., Alpin, C., Forth, J., Bryson, A., Bewley, H., Dix, G. and Oxenbridge, S. (2006) *Inside the Workplace: Findings from the 2004 Workplace Employment Relations Survey*. London: Routledge.

Kessler, I. (2005) Remuneration systems, in S. Bach (ed.), *Managing Human Resources: Personnel Management in Transition* (4th edn), Oxford: Blackwell.

Kessler, I. (2007) Reward choices: Strategy and equity, in J. Storey (ed.), *Human Resource Management: A Critical Text* (3rd edn), London: Thomson Learning.

Kessler, I. and Purcell, J. (1992) Performance-related pay: Objectives and application, *Human Resource Management Journal*, 2 (3): 16–33.

Kettley, P. and Reilly, P. (2003) *e-HR: An Introduction*, Report 398, Institute for Employment Studies, Brighton: IES.

Khan, A. S. and Ackers, P. (2004) Neo-pluralism as a theoretical framework for understanding HRM in sub-Saharan Africa, *International Journal of Human Resource Management*, 15 (7): 1330–53.

Kidd, J. M. (2002) Careers and career management, in P. B. Warr (ed.), *Psychology at Work* (5th edn), Harmondsworth: Penguin.

Kidger, P. and Allen, M. (2006), Employment in a global context, in R. Lucas, B. Lupton and H. Mathieson (eds), *Human Resource Management in an International Context*, London: CIPD.

Kikoski, J. F. (1999) Effective communication in the performance appraisal interview: Face-to-face communication for public managers in the culturally-diverse workplace, *Public Personnel Management*, 28: 301–23.

Kim, N. (2012) Towards the use of human resource development for societal development: Issues, challenges and opportunities, *Advances in Developing Human Resources*, 14 (3): 345–54.

Kim, S. and McLean, G. (2012) Global talent management: Necessity, challenges and the roles of HRD, *Advances in Developing Human Resources*, 14 (4): 566–85.

King, Z. (2003) New or traditional careers? A study of UK graduates' preferences, *Human Resource Management Journal*, 13 (1): 5–26.

King, Z. (2004) *Career Management: A Guide*, London: CIPD.

Kinnie, N., Hutchinson, S., Purcell, J. and Swart, J. (2006) Human resource management and organisational performance, in T. Redman and A. Wilkinson (eds), *Contemporary Human Resource Management* (2nd edn), Harlow: FT Prentice Hall.

Kirkpatrick, D. L. (1987) Evaluation of training, in C. R. Bittel (eds), *Training and Development Handbook*, New York: McGraw–Hill.

Kirton, G. and Greene, A. M. (2004) *The Dynamics of Managing Diversity: A Critical Approach* (2nd edn), Oxford: Elsevier Butterworth-Heinemann.

Klaas, B., McClendon, J. A. and Gainey, T. (2001) Outsourcing HR: The impact of organizational characteristics, *Human Resource Management*, 40 (2): 125–38.

Kluckholn, C. and Strodtbeck, F. (1961) *Variations in Value Orientations*, Evanston, IL: Row Peterson.

Knudsen, H., Markey, R. and Simpkin, G. (2013) Work environment and participation: The case of teachers in Denmark and New Zealand, *Industrial Relations Journal*, 44 (1): 38–56.

Kobayashi-Hillary, M. (2007) *India Faces Battle for Outsourcing*, http://news.bbc.co.uk/1/hi/business/6944583.stm (accessed 13 June 2008).

Koch, M. J. and McGrath, R. G. (1996) Improving labor productivity: Human resource management policies do matter, *Strategic Management Journal*, 17 (5): 335–54.

Kochan, T. and Osterman, P. (1994) *The Mutual Gains Enterprise*, Boston, MA: Harvard Business School Press.

Kochan, T., McKersie, R. and Cappelli, P. (1984) Strategic choice and industrial relations theory, *Industrial Relations*, 23: 16–39.

Kochan, T., Bezrukova, K., Ely, R., Jackson, S., Joshi, A., Jehn, K., Leonard, J., Levine, D. and Thomas, D. (2003) The effects of diversity on business performance: Report of the Diversity Research Network, *Human Resource Management*, 42 (1): 3–21.

Kohn, A. (1993) Why incentive plans cannot work, *Harvard Business Review*, 71 (5): 54–63.

Kolb, D. A. (1984) *Experiential Learning: Experience as the Source of Learning and Development*, Englewood Cliffs, NJ: Prentice Hall.

Konstantiou, E. and Fincham, R. (2011) Not sharing but trading: Applying a Maussian exchange framework to knowledge management, *Human Relations*, 64 (6): 823–42.

Kosnik, T., Wong-MingJi, D. J. and Hoover, K. (2006) Outsourcing vs insourcing in the human resource supply chain: A comparison of five generic models, *Personnel Review*, 35 (6): 671–83.

Kotey, B. and Slade, P. (2005) Formal human resource management practices in small growing firms, *Journal of Small Business Management*, 43 (1): 16–40.

Kotter, J. P. (1995) Leading change: Why transformation efforts fail, *Harvard Business Review*, 73 (2): 59–67.

Kovach, K. A. and Cathcart, C. E. (1999) Human resource information systems (HRIS): Providing business with rapid data access, information exchange and strategic advantage, *Public Personnel Management*, 28 (2): 275–82.

Kuijpers, M. and Scheerens, J. (2006) Career competencies for the modern career, *Journal of Career Development*, 32 (4): 303–19.

Kulik, C. T. and Bainbridge, H. T. J. (2006) HR and the line: The distribution of HR activities in Australian organisations, *Asia Pacific Journal of Human Resources*, 44 (2): 240–56.

Kydd, C. T. and Oppenheim, L. (1990) Using human resource management to enhance competitiveness: Lessons from four excellent companies, *Human Resource Management*, 29 (2): 145–66.

Lambert, S. J. (2008) Passing the buck: Labor flexibility practices that transfer risk onto hourly workers, *Human Relations*, 61 (8): 1203–27.

Larsen, H. H. and Brewster, C. (2003) Line management responsibility for HRM: What is happening in Europe? *Employee Relations*, 25 (3): 228–44.

Latornell, J. (2007) The relationship between the 'Psychological Contract' and 'Employment Relations', *Journal of Industrial Relations*, 49 (2): 277–86.

Laursen, K. and Foss, N. J. (2003) New human resource management practices, complementarities and the impact on innovation performance, *Cambridge Journal of Economics*, 27 (2): 243–63.

Lave, J. and Wenger, E. (1991) *Situated Learning: Legitimate Peripheral Participation*, Cambridge: Cambridge University Press.

Lawler, E. E., Benson, G. S. and McDermott, M. (2012) What makes performance appraisals effective?, *Compensation & Benefits Review*, 44 (4): 191–200.

Lazarova, M. and Taylor, S. (2009) Boundaryless careers, social capital, and knowledge management: Implications for organizational performance, *Journal of Organizational Behavior*, 30: 119–39.

Leach, J. L. and Chakiris, B. J. (1988) The future of jobs, work and careers, *Training and Development Journal*, April.

Ledford, G. E. Jr (2014) The changing landscape of employee rewards: Observations and prescriptions, *Organizational Dynamics*, 43: 168–79.

Le Doux, J. (1996) *The Emotional Brain*, London: Weidenfeld and Nicolson.

Lee, C. H. and Bruvold, N. T. (2003) Creating value for employees: Investment in employee development, *International Journal of Human Resource Management*, 14 (6): 981–1000.

Legge, K. (1978) *Power, Innovation and Problem-Solving in Personnel Management*, London: McGraw-Hill.

Legge, K. (1995a) *Human Resource Management: Rhetorics and Realities*, Basingstoke: Macmillan.

Legge, K. (1995b) HRM: Rhetoric, reality and hidden agendas, in J. Storey (ed.), *Human Resource Management: A Critical Text*, London: Routledge.

Lelliott, P., Tulloch, S., Boardman, J., Harvey, S., Henderson, M. and Knapp, M. (2006) *Mental Health and Work*, London: Royal College of Psychiatrists.

Lengnick-Hall, M. and Moritz, S. (2003) The impact of e-HR on the human resource management function, *Journal of Labour Research*, 24 (3): 365–79.

Lengnick-Hall, M. L., Lengnick-Hall, C. A., Andrade, L. S. and Drake, B. (2009) Strategic human resource management: The evolution of the field, *Human Resource Management Review*, 19: 64–85.

Leonard, D. (1998) *Wellsprings of Knowledge: Building and Sustaining the Sources of Innovation*, Boston, MA: Harvard Business School Press.

Lepak, D. P. and Snell, S. A. (1998) Virtual HR: Strategic human resource management in the 21st century, *Human Resource Management Review*, 8 (3): 215–34.

Levenson, A. R., Van der Stede, W. A. and Cohen, S. G. (2006) Measuring the relationship between managerial competencies and performance, *Journal of Management*, 32 (3): 360–80.

Levinson, D. (1978) *The Seasons of a Man's Life*, New York: Knopf.

Lewis, C. (1985) *Employee Selection*, London: Hutchinson.

Lewis, D. and Rayner, C. (2003) Bullying and human resource management: A wolf in sheep's clothing?, in S. Einarson, H. Hoel, D. Zapf and C. L. Cooper (eds), *Bullying and Emotional Abuse in the Workplace: International Perspectives in Research and Practice*, London: Taylor and Francis.

Lewis, D. and Sargeant, M. (2009) *Essentials of Employment Law* (10th edn), London: CIPD.

Lewis, P. (2006) Reward management, in T. Redman and A. Wilkinson (eds), *Contemporary Human Resource Management* (2nd edn), Harlow: FT Prentice Hall.

Lewis, P., Thornhill, A. and Saunders, A. (2003) *Employee Relations: Managing the Employment Relationship*, Harlow: FT Prentice Hall.

Liff, S. (1997) Two routes to managing diversity: Individual differences or social group characteristics, *Employee Relations*, 19 (1): 11–26.

Liff, S. (1999) Diversity and equal opportunities: Room for a constructive compromise? *Human Resource Management Journal*, 9 (1): 65–75.

Liff, S. and Wajcman, J. (1996) 'Sameness' and 'difference' revisited: Which way forward for equal opportunity initiatives? *Journal of Management Studies*, 33 (1): 79–94.

Lindsey, C. (2003) *A Century of Labour Market Change: 1900 to 2000*, London: Office for National Statistics.

Linstead, S. and Grafton-Small, R. (1992) On reading organizational culture, *Organization Studies*, 13: 331–55.

Lloyd, C. and Newell, H. (2001) Changing management–union relations: Consultation in the UK pharmaceutical industry, *Economic and Industrial Democracy*, 22 (3): 357–82.

Locke, E. A. and Latham, G. P. (1990) *A Theory of Goal Setting and Task Performance*, London: Prentice Hall.

López, S. P., Montes Peón, J. M. and Vazquez Ordás, C. J. (2005) Human resource practices, organizational learning and business performance, *Human Resource Development International*, 8 (2): 147–64.

Lowry, D. (2009) Ethics and strategic human resourcing, in J. Leopold and L. Harris (eds), *The Strategic Managing of Human Resources* (2nd edn), Harlow: FT Prentice Hall.

Lucas, R. and Curtis, S. (2006) Human resource management, in R. Lucas, B. Lupton and H. Mathieson (eds), *Human Resource Management in an International Context*, London: CIPD.

Lucas, R., Lupton, B. and Mathieson, H. (2006) *Human Resource Management in an International Context*, London: CIPD.

Lupton, B. and Woodhams, C. (2006) Employment equality, in R. Lucas, B. Lupton and H. Mathieson (eds), *Human Resource Management in an International Context*, London: CIPD.

MacDuffie, J. P. (1995) Human resource bundles and manufacturing performance, *Industrial Relations Review*, 48 (2): 199–221.

Macey, W. H. and Schneider, B. (2008) The meaning of employee engagement, *Industrial and Organizational Psychology*, 1: 3–30.

Machin, S. and Vignoles, A. (2001) *The Economic Benefits of Training to the Individual, the Firm and the Economy: The Key Issues*, London: The Cabinet Office.

Maclagan, P. (2007) Hierarchical control or individuals' moral autonomy: Addressing a fundamental tension on the management of business ethics, *Business Ethics: A European Review*, 16 (1): 48–61.

MacNeil, C. M. (2003) Line managers: Facilitators of knowledge sharing in teams, *Employee Relations*, 25 (3): 294–307.

Malhotra, Y. (1998) Knowledge management, knowledge organizations & knowledge workers: A view from the front lines, *Maeil Business Newspaper*, 19 February, www.brint.com/interview/maeil.htm (accessed 18 September 2015).

Mallon, M. and Cohen, L. (2001) Time for a change? Women's accounts of the move from organisational careers to self-employment, *British Journal of Management*, 12 (3): 217–30.

Mamman, A., Baydoun, N. and Adeoye, B. (2009) Transferability of management innovation to Africa: A study of two multinational companies' performance management systems in Nigeria, *Global Business Review*, 10 (1): 1–31.

Mander, P. (2013) A rare case of staff reinstatement after unfair dismissal, *People Management*, 6 June.

Marchington, M. and Wilkinson, A. (2005) *Human Resource Management at Work* (3rd edn), London: CIPD.

Marchington, M. and Wilkinson, A. (2008) *Human Resource Management at Work* (4th edn), London: CIPD.

Marchington, M., Goodman, J., Wilkinson, A. and Ackers, P. (1992) *New Developments in Employee Involvement*, Department of Employment Research Series No. 2, London.

Marchington, M., Wilkinson, A., Ackers, P. and Goodman, J. (1994) Understanding the meaning of participation: Views from the workplace, *Human Relations*, 47 (8): 867–94.

Markey, R. (2007) Non-union employee representation in Australia: A case study of the Suncorp Metway Employee Council Inc. (SMEC), *Journal of Industrial Relations*, 49 (2): 187–209.

Markey, R. and Townsend, K. (2014) Contemporary trends in employee involvement and participation, *Journal of Industrial Relations*, 55 (4): 475–87.

Marler, J. H. (2009) Making human resources strategic by going to the net: Reality or myth? *International Journal of Human Resource Management*, 20 (3): 515–27.

Martin, G. (2005) *Technology and People Management, the Opportunity and the Challenge*, London: CIPD.

Martin, G. and Beaumont, P. (1998) Diffusing 'best practice' in multinational firms: Prospects, practice and contestation, *International Journal of Human Resource Management*, 9 (4): 671–95.

Martin, G., Reddington, M. and Kneafsey, M. B. (2009) *Web 2.0 and Human Resource Management: Groundswell or Hype?* London: Chartered Institute of Personnel and Development.

Martinez-Lucio, M. and Stuart, M. (2002) Assessing the principles of partnership: Workplace trade union representatives' attitudes and experiences, *Employee Relations*, 24 (3): 305–20.

Maslow, A. (1954/1970) *Motivation and Personality*, New York: Harper.

Matthews, B. and Redman, T. (1998) Managerial recruitment advertisements – just how market-oriented are they? *International Journal of Selection and Assessment*, 6 (4): 240–48.

Mavin, S. and Girling, G. (2000) What is managing diversity and why does it matter? *Human Resource Development International*, 3 (4): 419–33.

Maxwell, G. (2004) Minority report: Taking the initiative in managing diversity at BBC Scotland, *Employee Relations*, 26 (2): 182–202.

Mayson, S. and Barrett, R. (2006) The 'science' and 'practice' of HRM in small firms, *Human Resource Management Review*, 16: 447–55.

McColgan, A. (2000) Family friendly frolics? The maternity and parental leave etc. Regulations 1999, *Industrial Law Journal*, 29 (2): 125–44.

McConville, T. (2006) Devolved HRM responsibilities, middle managers and role dissonance, *Personnel Review*, 35 (6): 637–53.

McCormack, A. and Scholarios, D. (2009) Recruitment, in T. Redman and A. Wilkinson (eds), *Contemporary Human Resource Management* (3rd edn), Harlow: FT Prentice Hall.

McCracken, M. and Wallace, M. (2000) Towards a redefinition of strategic HRD, *Journal of European Industrial Training*, 24 (5): 281–90.

McGovern, P., Hope-Hailey, V. and Stiles, P. (1998) The managerial career after down-sizing: Case studies from the 'leading edge', *Work Employment and Society*, 12 (3): 457–77.

McGovern, P., Smeaton, D. and Hill, S. (2004) Bad jobs in Britain: Non-standard employment and job quality, *Work and Occupations*, 31 (2): 225–49.

McGovern, P., Stiles, P. and Hope, V. (1996) The flexible psychological contract? Career management in an era of insecurity, *Management Research News*, 19 (4/5): 81–4.

McGregor, D. C. (1960) *The Human Side of Enterprise*, New York: McGraw–Hill.

McGuire, D. (2010) Foundations of human resource development, in D. McGuire and K. M. Jørgensen (eds), *Human Resource Development: Theory and Practice*, London: Sage.

McKenna, E. and Beech, N. (2008) *Human Resource Management: A Concise Analysis* (2nd edn), Harlow: FT Prentice Hall.

McKenna, F. (1980) *The Railway Workers, 1840–1890*, London: Faber and Faber.

McLean, G. N. and McLean, L. (2001) If we can't define HRD in one country, how can we define it in an international context?, *Human Resource Development International*, 4 (3): 313–26.

McLoughlin, I. and Gourlay, S. (1994) *Enterprise without Unions: Industrial Relations in the Non-union Firm*, Buckingham: Open University Press.

McSweeney, B. (2002) Hofstede's model of national cultural differences and their consequences: A triumph of faith – a failure of analysis, *Human Relations*, 55 (1): 89–118.

McWhorter, R. R. (2010) Exploring the emergence of virtual human resource development, *Advances in Developing Human Resources*, 12 (6): 623–31.

Megginson, D. and Whittaker, V. (2007) *Continuing Professional Development* (2nd edn), London: CIPD.

Merritt, A. (2000) Culture in the cockpit: Do Hofstede's dimensions replicate? *Journal of Cross-Cultural Psychology*, 31 (3): 283–301.

Mesner Andolsek, D. and Stebe, J. (2005) Devolution or (de)centralization of HRM function in European organizations, *International Journal of Human Resource Management*, 16 (3): 311–29.

Miller, J. (2003) High tech and high performance: Managing appraisals in the information age, *Journal of Labour Research*, 24 (3): 409–24.

Minbaeva, D., Foss, N. and Snell, S. (2009) Guest Editors' Introduction: Bringing the knowledge perspective into HRM, *Human Resource Management*, 48 (4): 477–83.

Mintzberg, H. (1973) *The Nature of Managerial Work*, New York: Harper and Row.

Mintzberg, H. (1976) Planning on the left side and managing on the right side, *Harvard Business Review*, 54 (4): 49–58.

Mintzberg, H. (1987) Crafting strategy, *Harvard Business Review*, July–August: 66–75.

Mintzberg, H. (1994) The fall and rise of strategic planning, *Harvard Business Review*, January–February: 107–14.

Mirvis, P. H. and Hall, D. T. (1994) Psychological success and the boundaryless career, *Journal of Organisational Behaviour*, 15: 365–80.

Mishel, L. and Davis, A. (2014) CEO pay continues to rise as typical workers are paid less, Economic Policy Institute, Issue Brief 380, 12 June.

Moore, G. (2004) Football rules: You must not drink and must eat what you're told. Still want to be a professional? *The Independent*, 2 December.

Mor Barak, M. E. (2011) *Managing Diversity: Towards a Globally Inclusive Workforce* (2nd edn), London: Sage.

Morley, M., Gunnigle, P., O'Sullivan, M. and Collings, D. (2006) New directions in the roles and responsibilities of the HRM function, *Personnel Review*, 35 (6): 609–17.

Morris, J. (2004) The future of work: Organisational and international perspectives, *International Journal of Human Resource Management*, 15 (2): 263–75.

Morris, J. A. and Feldman, D. C. (1996) The dimensions, antecedents and consequences of emotional labor, *Academy of Management Review*, 21 (4): 986–1010.

Mosley, E. (2013) The power of the crowdsourced performance review, *Compensation & Benefits Review*, 45 (6): 320–23.

Mulholland, G., Ozbilgin, M. and Worman, D. (2005) *Managing Diversity: Linking Theory and Practice to Business Performance*, London: CIPD.

Muller, M. (1998) Human resource and industrial relations practices of UK and US multinationals in Germany, *International Journal of Human Resource Management*, 9 (4): 732–49.

Muller, M. (1999) HRM under institutional constraints: The case of Germany, *British Journal of Management*, 10: 31–44.

Muller-Camen, M., Crucher, R. and Leigh, S. (2008) *Human Resource Management: A Case Study Approach*, London: CIPD.

Mulligan, J. R. and Bull Schaefer, R. A. (2011) A new hope for rank and yank, *Journal of Leadership & Organizational Studies*, 18 (3): 385–96.

Mullins, L. (1993) *Management and Organisational Behaviour* (3rd edn), London: Pitman.

Munro-Fraser, J. (1958) *A Handbook of Employee Interviewing*, London: MacDonald and Evans.

Murphy, K. R. (2008) Explaining the weak relationship between job performance and ratings of job performance, *Industrial and Organizational Psychology*, 1: 148–60.

Myloni, B., Harzing, A. K. and Mirza, H. (2004) Host country specific factors and the transfer of human resource management practices in multinational companies, *International Journal of Manpower*, 25 (6): 518–34.

Mylonopoulos, N. and Tsoukas, H. (2003) Technological and organizational issues in knowledge management, *Knowledge and Process Management*, 10 (3): 139–43.

Nabi, G. and Bagley, D. (1998) Graduates' perceptions of transferable personal skills and future career preparation in the UK, *Career Development International*, 3 (1): 31–9.

Nadler, L. (1970) *Developing Human Resources*, Austin: Learning Concepts.

Nadler, L. and Nadler, Z. (1989) *Developing Human Resources* (3rd edn), San Francisco: Jossey-Bass.

Nankervis, A. R. and Compton, R.-L. (2006) Performance management: Theory in practice? *Asia Pacific Journal of Human Resources*, 44: 83–101.

Neal, A. and Griffin, M. A. (1999) Developing a model of individual performance for human resource management, *Asia Pacific Journal of Human Resources*, 37 (2): 44–59.

Newcombe, T. (2013) Employees spend up to half the working day surfing the internet for personal use, says K3 Managed Services, *HR Magazine*, 2 January.

Newell, S. (2006) Selection and assessment, in T. Redman and A. Wilkinson (eds), *Contemporary Human Resource Management* (2nd edn), Harlow: FT Prentice Hall.

Newell, S. and Rice, C. (1999) Assessment, selection and evaluation, in J. Leopold, L. Harris and T. Watson (eds), *Strategic Human Resourcing: Principles, Perspectives and Practices*, London: Pitman.

Newell, S., Robertson, M., Scarbrough, H. and Swan, J. (2002) *Managing Knowledge Work*, London: Palgrave.

Newell, S., Robertson, M., Scarbrough, H. and Swan, J. (2009) *Managing Knowledge Work and Innovation* (2nd edn), London: Palgrave.

Ng, E. S. W. and Burke, R. J. (2005) Person–organisation fit and the war for talent: Does diversity management make a difference? *International Journal of Human Resource Management*, 16 (7): 1195–210.

Nickson, D., Warhurst, C., Cullen, A. and Watt, A. (2003) Bringing in the excluded? Aesthetic labour, skills and training in the 'new' economy, *Journal of Education and Work*, 16 (2): 185–203.

Nikandrou, I., Apospori, E. and Papalexandria, N. (2005) Changes in HRM in Europe: A longitudinal comparative study among 18 European countries, *Journal of European Industrial Training*, 29 (7): 541–60.

Nohria, N. and Ghoshal, S. (1994) Differentiated fit and shared values: Alternatives for managing headquarters–subsidiary relations, *Strategic Management Journal*, 15 (6): 491–502.

Nonaka, I. and Takeuchi, H. (1995) *The Knowledge Creating Company: How Japanese Companies Create the Dynamics of Innovation*, Oxford: Oxford University Press.

Nonaka, I., Noburo, K. and Ryoko, T. (2001) The emergence of 'Ba', in I. Nonaka and T. Nishiguchi (eds), *Knowledge Emergence: Social, Technical, and Evolutionary Dimensions of Knowledge Creation*, Oxford: Oxford University Press.

Noon, M. (2007a) Equality and diversity, in J. Beardwell and T. Claydon (eds) *Human Resource Management* (5th edn), Harlow: Pearson.

Noon, M. (2007b) The fatal flaws of diversity and the business case for ethnic minorities, *Work, Employment and Society*, 21 (4): 773–84.

Noon, M. and Blyton, P. (2007) *The Realities of Work* (3rd edn), Basingstoke: Palgrave Macmillan.

Nord, W. R. and Riggs Fuller, S. (2009) Increasing corporate social responsibility through an employee-centred approach, *Employee Responsibilities and Rights Journal*, 21 (4): 279–90.

Norman, N. (2011) Mobile learning made easy, *T+D*, 65 (12): 52–5.

Nyhan, B., Cressey, P., Tomassini, M., Kelleher, M. and Poell, R. (2004) European perspectives on the learning organisation, *Journal of European Industrial Training*, 28 (1): 67–92.

Obembe, D. (2012) Knowledge sharing, sustained relationships and the habitus, *Management Learning*, 44 (4): 355–72.

O'Connell, D. J., McNeely, E. and Hall, D. T. (2008) Unpacking personal adaptability at work, *Journal of Leadership & Organizational Studies*, 14 (3): 248–59.

O'Donohue, W. and Nelson, L. (2009) The role of ethical values in an expended psychological contract, *Journal of Business Ethics*, 90: 251–63.

OECD (Organisation for Economic Co-operation and Development) (2006) *Education at a Glance 2006*, Paris: OECD.

OECD (Organisation for Economic Co-operation and Development) (2012) *Closing the Gender Gap: Act Now*, Paris: OECD.

OECD (2014) Hours worked: Average annual hours actually worked, *OECD Employment and Labour Market Statistics* (database). DOI: http://dx.doi.org/10.1787/data-00303-en (accessed 17 September 2015).

OECD (Organisation for Economic Co-operation and Development) (2015) *Trade Union Density*, http://stats.oecd.org/Index.aspx?DataSetCode=UN_DEN (accessed 15 May 2015).

Ohemeng, F. L. K. (2009) Constraints in the implementation of performance management systems in developing countries: The Ghanaian case, *International Journal of Cross Cultural Management*, 9 (1): 109–32.

O'Leary, L. (2012) Regulating the employment relationship in professional team sports, *Industrial Law Journal*, 41 (2): 1–27.

Oliver, N., Delbridge, R. and Lowe, J. (1996) Lean production practices: International comparisons and the auto-components industry, *British Journal of Management*, 7 (Special Issue): S29–S44.

O'Neill, G. (1995) Framework for developing a total reward strategy, *Asia Pacific Journal of Human Resources*, 33 (2): 103–17.

ONS (Office for National Statistics) (2008) *Social Trends 38*, Basingstoke: Palgrave Macmillan.

ONS (Office for National Statistics) (2012a) *Population Ageing in the United Kingdom, Its Constituent Countries and the European Union*, Newport: ONS.

ONS (Office for National Statistics) (2012b) *Labour Market Statistics: January 2012*, Newport: ONS.

ONS (Office for National Statistics) (2012c) *Migration Statistics Quarterly Report*, February, Newport, ONS.

ONS (Office for National Statistics) (2012d) *Statistical Release: Labour Market Status for Young People by Ethnicity*, March.

ONS (Office for National Statistics) (2013a) *National Population Projections*, 2012–based Statistical Bulletin, 6 November.

ONS (Office for National Statistics) (2013b) *Women in the Labour Market*, Newport: ONS.

ONS (Office for National Statistics) (2014) *Sickness Absence in the Labour Market*, Newport: ONS.

ONS (Office for National Statistics) (2015a) *Migration Statistics Quarterly Report*, February, Newport: ONS.

ONS (Office for National Statistics) (2015b) *Labour Disputes Annual Article 2014*, July, Newport: ONS.

Ordonez, L. D., Schweitzer, M. E., Galinsky, A. D. and Bazerman, M. H. (2009) Goals gone wild: The systematic side effects of over-prescribing goal setting, Harvard Business School Working Paper, 09–083.

Ortlieb, R. and Sieben, B. (2013) Diversity strategies and business logic: Why do companies employ ethnic minorities?, *Group & Organization Management*, 38 (4): 480–511.

Oshri, I., Kotlarsky, J., Rottman, J. W. and Willcocks, L. L. (2009) Global sourcing: recent trends and issues, *Information Technology and People*, 22 (3): 192–200.

Osterman, P. (2000) Work reorganisation in an era of restructuring: Trends in diffusion and effects on employee welfare, *Industrial and Labor Relations Review*, 53 (2): 179–97.

Overell, S. (1998) All things not being equal, *People Management*, 4 (23): 32–6.

Paauwe, J. (2009) HRM and performance: Achievements, methodological issues and prospects, *Journal of Management Studies*, 46 (1): 129–42.

Parker, L. and Bevan, S. (2011) *Good Work and Our Times: Report of the Good Work Commission*, London: The Work Foundation.

Parker, P. and Inkson, K. (1999) New forms of career: The challenge to human resource management, *Asia Pacific Journal of Human Resources*, 37 (1): 76–85.

Parry, E. and Tyson, S. (2007) Technology in HRM: The means to become a strategic partner?, in J. Storey (ed.), *Human Resource Management: A Critical Text*. London: Thomson Learning.

Parzefall, M.-J. and Salin, D. M. (2010) Perceptions of and reactions to workplace bullying: A social exchange perspective, *Human Relations*, 63 (6): 761–80.

Paton, N. (2007) Continental shifts, *The Guardian*, 24 November.

Paton, N. (2008) Strike 2.0, *The Guardian*, 10 May.

Patterson, M., West, M., Lawthorn, R. and Nickell, S. (1997) *The Impact of People Management Practices on Business Performance*, London: IPD.

Paul, R., Niehoff, B. P. and Turnley, W. H. (2000) Empowerment, expectations, and the psychological contract: Managing the dilemmas and gaining the advantage, *Journal of Socio-Economics*, 29: 471–85.

Payne, S. C., Culbertson, S. S., Lopez, Y. P., Boswell, W. R. and Barger, E. J. (2015), Contract breach as a trigger for adjustment to the psychological contract during the first year of employment, *Journal of Occupational and Organizational Psychology*, 88 (1): 41–60.

Pedler, M., Burgoyne, J. and Boydell, T. (1991) *The Learning Company: A Strategy for Sustainable Development*, London: McGraw–Hill.

People Management (2012) *Eight ways to reward staff without giving them a pay rise*, 29 October.

People Management (2015a) Mental health: 'I thought about jumping in front of a bus so I didn't have to go to work', July.

People Management (2015b) 'Prioritise workforce skills to tackle productivity puzzle, urges CIPD', 2 July.

Peiperl, M. A. and Baruch, Y. (1997) Back to square zero: The post-corporate career, *Organizational Dynamics*, 25 (4): 7–22.

Perkins, S. and White, G. (2010) Modernising pay in the UK public services: Trends and implications, *Human Resource Management Journal*, 20 (3): 244–57.

Perkins, S., White, G. and Cotton, C. (2008) A ripping yarn, *People Management*, 30 October.

Perlmutter, H. V. (1969) The tortuous evolution of the multinational corporation, *Columbia Journal of World Business*, 4: 9–18.

Personnel Management (2012a) HR outsourcing deal at MoD sparks job loss concern, 2 March, www.

peoplemanagement.co.uk/pm/articles/2012/03/hr-outsourcing-deal-at-mod-sparks-job-loss-concern.htm (accessed 7 March 2012).

Personnel Management (2012b) Co-operatives Bill to encourage formation of worker co-ops, 19 January.

Peters, T. J. and Waterman, R. H. (1982) *In Search of Excellence*, New York: Harper and Row.

Pettigrew, A. M. and Whipp, R. (1991) *Managing Change for Competitive Success*, Oxford: Blackwell.

Pfeffer, J. (1994) *Competitive Advantage Through People: Understanding the Power of the Workforce*, Boston, MA: Houghton Mifflin.

Pfeffer, J. (1998) *The Human Equation: Building Profits by Putting People First*, Boston, MA: Harvard Business School Press.

Philips, L. (2006) Be on your guard for online test cheats, *People Management*, 12: 15.

Pilbeam, S. and Corbridge, M. (2006) *People Resourcing* (3rd edn), Harlow: FT Prentice Hall.

Pilbeam, S. and Corbridge, M. (2010) *People Resourcing* (4th edn), Harlow: FT Prentice Hall.

Pincus, F. L. (1996) Discrimination comes in many forms: Individual, institutional, and structural, *American Behavioral Scientist*, 40 (2): 186–94.

Piore, M. J. and Sabel, C. F. (1984) *The Second Industrial Divide*, New York: Basic Books.

Ployhart, R. E. (2006) Staffing in the 21st century: New challenges and strategic opportunities, *Journal of Management*, 32 (6): 868–97.

Poell, R. F., van Dam, K. and van der Berg, P. T. (2004) Organising learning in work contexts, *Applied Psychology: An International Review*, 53 (4): 529–40.

Polanyi, M. (1962) *Personal Knowledge*, London: Routledge and Kegan Paul.

Pollert, A. (1988) The 'flexible firm': Fixation or fact, *Work, Employment and Society*, 2 (3): 281–316.

Pollert, A. and Charlwood, A. (2009) The vulnerable worker in Britain and problems at work, *Work, Employment and Society*, 23 (2): 343–62.

Pollitt, D. (2004) Alliance Unichem uses 360-degree feedback to improve performance, *Human Resource Management International Digest*, 12 (2): 27–9.

Porter, M. (1985) *Competitive Advantage*, New York: Free Press.

Porter, M. E. (1986) *Competition in Global Industries*, Boston, MA: Harvard Business School Press.

Preuss, L., Haunschild, A. and Matten, D. (2009) The rise of CSR: Implications for HRM and employee representation, *International Journal of Human Resource Management*, 20 (4): 953–73.

Price, A. (2007) *Human Resource Management in a Business Context* (3rd edn), London: Thomson Learning.

Pringle, J. K. and Mallon, M. (2003) Challenges for the boundaryless career odyssey, *International Journal of Human Resource Management*, 14 (5): 839–53.

Proctor, S. and Ackroyd, S. (1998) British manufacturing organisation and workplace industrial relations: Some attributes of the new flexible firm, *British Journal of Industrial Relations*, 36 (2): 163–83.

Proctor, S. and Rowlinson, M. (2011) From the British worker question to the impact of HRM: Understanding the relationship between employment relations and economic performance, *Industrial Relations Journal*, 43 (1): 5–21.

Prowse, P. and Prowse, J. (2010) Whatever happened to human resource management performance? *International Journal of Productivity and Performance Management*, 59 (2): 145–62.

Pulakos, E. and O'Leary, R. (2011) Why is performance management broken? *Industrial and Organizational Psychology*, 4: 146–64.

Purcell, J. (1999) Best practice and best fit: Chimera or cul-de-sac? *Human Resource Management Journal*, 9 (3): 26–41.

Purcell, J. and Ahlstrand, B. (1994) *Human Resource Management in the Multi-Divisional Company*, Oxford: Oxford University Press.

Purcell, J. and Hutchinson, S. (2007a) Front-line managers as agents in the HRM–performance causal chain: Theory, analysis and evidence, *Human Resource Management Journal*, 17 (1): 3–20.

Purcell, J. and Hutchinson, S. (2007b) *Rewarding Work: The Vital Role of Line Managers*, London: CIPD.

Purcell, J. and Sisson, K. (1983) Strategies and practice in the management of industrial relations, in G. S. Bain (ed.), *Industrial Relations in Britain*, Oxford: Basil Blackwell.

Purcell, J., Kinnie, N., Hutchinson, S., Rayton, B. and Swart, J. (2003) *Understanding the People and Performance Link: Unlocking the Black Box*, London: CIPD.

Purcell, K., Elias, P. and Wilton, N. (2006) *Looking Through the Glass Ceiling: A Detailed Investigation of the Factors that Contribute to Gendered Career Inequalities*, Report to the European Social Fund, Liverpool: ESF.

Purcell, K., Hogarth, T. and Simm, C. (1999) *Whose Flexibility? The Costs and Benefits of Non-standard Working Arrangements and Contractual Relations*, York: Joseph Rowntree Foundation.

Purcell, K., Rowley, G. and Morley, M. (2002) *Recruiting from a Wider Spectrum of Graduates*, London: Council for Industry and Higher Education.

Purcell, K., Wilton, N., Davies, R. and Elias, P. (2005) *Education as a Graduate Career: Entry and Exit from Teaching as a Profession*, Department for Education and Skills, RR690, London: DfES.

Rainnie, A. (1989) *Industrial Relations in Small Firms*, London: Routledge and Kegan Paul.

Ram, M. (1991) Control and autonomy in small firms: The case of the West Midlands clothing industry, *Work, Employment and Society*, 5 (4): 601–19.

Ramsay, H. (1980) Phantom participation: Patterns of power and conflict, *Industrial Relations Journal*, 11 (3): 46–59.

Ramsay, H., Scholarios, D. and Harley, B. (2000) Employees and high-performance work systems: Testing inside the black box, *British Journal of Industrial Relations*, 38 (4): 501–31.

Reddington, M. (2012) Technology as an agent for transformation, in H. Francis, L. Holbeche and M. Reddington (eds.) *People and Organisational Development: A New Agenda for Organisational Effectiveness*, London: CIPD.

Redman, T. (2006) Performance appraisals, in T. Redman and A. Wilkinson (eds), *Contemporary Human Resource Management* (2nd edn), Harlow: FT Prentice Hall.

Redman, T. and Wilkinson, A. (2006) Human resource management: A contemporary perspective, in T. Redman and A. Wilkinson (eds), *Contemporary Human Resource Management* (2nd edn), Harlow: FT Prentice Hall.

Reid, M., Barrington, H. and Brown, M. (2004) *Human Resource Development: Beyond Training Interventions*, London: CIPD.

Reilly, P. A. (1998) Balancing flexibility – meeting the interests of employer and employee, *European Journal of Work and Organisational Psychology*, 7 (1): 7–22.

Reilly, P., Tamkin, P. and Broughton, A. (2007) *The Changing HR Function: Transforming HR? Research into Practice*, London: CIPD.

Renwick, D. (2009) Line managers, in T. Redman and A. Wilkinson (eds), *Contemporary Human Resource Management* (3rd edn), Harlow: FT Prentice Hall.

Renwick, R. (2003) Line manager involvement in HRM: An insider view, *Employee Relations*, 25 (3): 262–80.

Restubog, S. L. D., Zagenczyk, T. J., Boardia, P., Bordia, S. and Chapman, G. J. (2015) If you wrong us, shall we not revenge? Moderating roles of self-control and perceived aggressive work culture in predicting responses to psychological contract breach, *Journal of Management*, 41 (4): 1132–54.

Ribiere, V. and Sitar, A. (2003) Critical role of leadership in nurturing a knowledge-supporting culture, *Knowledge Management Research and Practice*, 1 (1): 39–48.

Ridder, H.-G., McCandless Baluch, A. and Piening, E. P. (2012) The whole is more than the sum of its parts? How HRM is configured in nonprofit organizations and why it matters, *Human Resource Management Review*, 22: 1–14.

Risher, H. (2005) Refocusing performance management for high performance, *Compensation & Benefits Review*, 35 (5): 20–30.

Risher, H. (2011) Getting performance management on track, *Compensation & Benefits Review*, 43 (5): 273–81.

Risher, H. (2012) Employers need to focus on improving performance management, *Compensation & Benefits Review*, 44 (4): 188–90.

Ritzer, G. (2007) *The McDonaldization of Society* (5th edn), Thousand Oaks, CA: Pine Forge Press.

Rivera, L. A. (2012) Diversity within reach: Recruitment versus hiring in elite firms, *Annals of the American Academy of Political and Social Science*, 639: 71–90.

Roberts, S. J. and Roach, T. (2009) Social networking websites and human resource personnel: Suggestions for job searches, *Business Communication Quarterly*, 72: 110–14.

Roberts, K., Kossek, E. E. and Ozeki, C. (1998) Managing the global workforce: Challenges and strategies, *Academy of Management Executive*, 12 (4): 93–106.

Robertson, M. and O'Malley Hammersley, G. (2000) Knowledge management practices within a knowledge-intensive firm: The significance of the people management dimension, *Journal of European Industrial Training*, 24 (2): 241–53.

Robertson, M. and Swan, J. (2003) 'Control – what control?' Culture and ambiguity with a knowledge intensive firm, *Journal of Management Studies*, 40 (4): 831–58.

Robinson, A. and Smallman, C. (2006) The contemporary British workplace: A safer and healthier place? *Work, Employment and Society*, 20 (1): 87–107.

Robinson, D., Perryman, S. and Hayday, S. (2004) *The Drivers of Employee Engagement*, Report 408, Brighton: Institute of Employment Studies.

Robinson, S. L. and Rousseau, D. M. (1994) Violating the psychological contract: Not the exception but the norm, *Journal of Organisational Behaviour*, 15: 245–59.

Rocha, R. S. (2009) Changing the (im)balance of power: High-performance work systems in Brazil, *Employee Relations*, 32 (1): 74–88.

Rodger, A. (1952) *The Seven-point Plan*, London: National Institute of Industrial Psychology.

Rodrigues, R. A. and Guest, D. (2010) Have careers become boundaryless? *Human Relations*, 63 (8): 1157–75.

Roehling, M. V., Boswell, W. R., Caligiuri, P., Feldman, D., Graham, M. E., Guthrie, J. P., Morishima, M. and Tansky, J. W. (2005) The future of HR management: Research needs and directions, *Human Resource Management*, 44 (2): 207–16.

Rollinson, D. and Dundon, T. (2007) *Understanding Employment Relations*, Maidenhead: McGraw–Hill.

Ronen, S. and Shenkar, O. (1985) Clustering countries on attitudinal dimensions: A review and synthesis, *Academy of Management Review*, 10 (3): 435–54.

Roscigno, V. J., Hodson, R. and Lopez, S. H. (2009) Workplace incivilities: The role of interest conflicts, social closure and organizational chaos, *Work, Employment and Society*, 23 (4): 747–73.

Rose, E. (2008) *Employment Relations* (3rd edn), Harlow: FT Prentice Hall.

Rose, M. (2003) Good deal, bad deal? Job satisfaction in occupations *Work, Employment, and Society*, 17 (3): 503–30.

Rosenfeld, P., Giacolone, R. A. and Riordan, C. A. (1995) *Impression Management in Organizations*, London: Routledge.

Ross, R. and Schneider, R. (1992) *From Equality to Diversity – A Business Case for Equal Opportunities*, London: Pitman.

Rousseau, D. M. (1989) Psychological and implied contracts in organisations, *Employee Responsibilities and Rights Journal*, 2: 121–39.

Rowley, G., Purcell, K., Howe, S., Richardson, M., Shackleton, R. and Whiteley, P. (2000) *Employers Skill Survey: Case Study Hospitality Sector*, Nottingham: Department for Education and Employment.

Royle, T. (1995) Corporate versus societal culture: A comparative study of McDonald's in Europe, *International Journal of Contemporary Hospitality Management*, 7 (2/3): 52–6.

Ruddick, G. (2013) *Tesco sale of Fresh & Easy wins City backing*, The Telegraph, 11 September.

Ruhemann, C. (2010) Trade union negotiating officials' use and non-use of Acas conciliation in industrial disputes, Acas Research Paper 07/10, London: Acas.

Ruona, W., Lynham, S. and Chermack, T. (2003) Insights on emerging trends and the future of human resource development, *Advances in Developing Human Resources*, 5 (3): 272–82.

Russell, J. (2009) Anger as top bosses' pay keeps rising, *Daily Telegraph*, 23 May.

Saha, B. (2006) Labour institutions in China and India: A tale of two nations, *Journal of South Asian Development*, 1 (2): 179–205.

Saks, A. M. (2006) Antecedents and consequences of employee engagement, *Journal of Managerial Psychology*, 21 (7): 600–19.

Salin, D. (2003) Ways of explaining workplace bullying: A review of enabling, motivating and precipitating structures and processes in the work environment, *Human Relations*, 56 (10): 1213–32.

Saridakis, G., Sen-Gupta, S., Edwards, P. and Storey, D. J. (2008) The impact of enterprise size on employment tribunal incidence and outcomes: Evidence from Britain, *British Journal of Industrial Relations*, 46 (3): 469–99.

Saundry, R., Jones, C. and Antcliff, V. (2011) Discipline, representation and dispute resolution: Exploring the role of trade unions and employee companions in workplace discipline, *Industrial Relations Journal*, 42 (2): 195–211.

Sayer, A. (2007) Dignity at work: Broadening the agenda, *Organization*, 14 (4): 565–81.

Scarbrough, H. (1999) Knowledge as work: Conflicts in the management of knowledge workers, *Technology Analysis and Strategic Management*, 11 (1): 5–16.

Schaufeli, W. B., Salanova, M., Gonzalez-Roma, V. and Bakker, A. B. (2002) The measurement of engagement and burnout: a two-sample confirmatory factor analytic approach, *Journal of Happiness Studies*, 3: 71–92.

Schein, E. H. (1978) *Career Dynamics: Matching Individual and Organizational Needs*, Reading, MA: Addison-Wesley.

Schein, E. (1980) *Organizational Psychology*, Englewood Cliffs, NJ: Prentice Hall.

Schein, E. H. (1985) *Organizational Culture and Leadership*, San Francisco, CA: Jossey-Bass.

Schein, E. (1990) *Career Anchors*, San Diego, CA: Pfeiffer.

Schein, E. (1996) Career anchors revisited: Implications for career development in the 21st century, *Academy of Management Executive*, 10 (4): 80–8.

Schein, E. (2004) *Organizational Culture and Leadership* (3rd edn), San Francisco, CA: Jossey-Bass.

Schmitt, M. (2003) Deregulation of the German industrial relations system via foreign direct investment: Are the subsidiaries of Anglo-Saxon MNCs a threat for the institutions of industrial democracy in Germany? *Economic and Industrial Democracy*, 24 (3): 349–77.

Schneider, R. (2001) Variety performance, *People Management*, 7 (9): 26–31.

Schneider, S. and Barsoux, J.-L. (2008) *Managing Across Cultures* (2nd edn), Harlow: FT Prentice Hall.

Schuler, R. (1989) Strategic human resource management and industrial relations, *Human Relations*, 42 (2): 157–84.

Schuler, R. S. (1992) Strategic human resource management: Linking the people with the strategic needs of the business, *Organisational Dynamics*, Summer: 18–31.

Schuler, R. S. and Jackson, S. E. (1987) Linking competitive strategies and human resource management practices, *Academy of Management Executive*, 1 (3): 207–19.

Schulten, T. (1996) European works councils: Prospects for a new system of European industrial relations, *European Journal of Industrial Relations*, 2 (3): 303–24.

Scott, A. (2008) Barclays outsources its recruitment, *People Management*, 30 July.

Scullion, H., Collings, D. G. and Gunnigle, P. (2007) International human resource management in the 21st century: Emerging themes and contemporary debates, *Human Resource Management Journal*, 17 (4): 309–19.

Scullion, H., Collings, G. D. and Caligiuri, P. (2010) Global talent management. *Journal of World Business*, 45: 105–8.

Sels, L., De Winne, S., Maes, J., Delmotte, J., Faems, D. and Forrier, A. (2006) Unravelling the HRM–performance link: Value-creating and cost-increasing effects of small business HRM, *Journal of Management Studies*, 43 (2): 319–42.

Semple, E. (2011) The evolving face of social media: Tools of the trade for IC, *Strategic Communication Management*, 15 (5): 40–2.

Senge, P. (2006) *The Fifth Discipline: The Art and Practice of the Learning Organization* (2nd edn), London: Random House.

Sewell, G. (2005) Nice work? Rethinking managerial control in an era of knowledge work, *Organization*, 12 (5): 685–704.

Shanawaz, M. G. and Goswami, K. (2011) Effect of psychological contract violation on organizational commitment, trust and turnover intention in private and public sector Indian organizations, *Vision: The Journal of Business Perspective*, 15 (3): 209–17.

Sharma, A. N. (2006) Flexibility, employment and labour reforms in India, *Economics and Political Weekly*, 27 May: 2078–85.

Shaw, J. D. (2011) Turnover rates and organizational performance: Review, critique, and research agenda, *Organizational Psychology Review*, 1: 187–213.

Sheehan, C. (2009) Outsourcing HRM activities in Australian organisations, *Asia Pacific Journal of Human Resources*, 47 (2): 236–53.

Sheehan, M. (2012) Developing managerial talent: Exploring the link between management talent and perceived performance in multinational corporations (MNCs), *European Journal of Training and Development*, 36 (1): 66–85.

Sheehan, M. (2014) Human resource management and performance: Evidence from small and medium-sized firms, *International Small Business Journal*, 32 (5): 545–70.

Shen, J. (2005) Effective international performance appraisals: Easily said, hard to do, *Compensation & Benefits Review*, 37: 70–9.

Shen, J. and Benson, J. (2014) When CSR is a social norm: How socially responsible human resource management affects employee work behavior, *Journal of Management*, 1–24.

Shepherd, J. (2009) Teachers campaign against code of conduct, *The Guardian*, 2 September.

Shields, J. (2007) *Managing Employee Performance and Reward: Concepts, Practices, Strategies*, Cambridge: Cambridge University Press.

Shipper, F., Hoffman, R. C. and Rotundo, D. M. (2007) Does the 360 feedback process create actionable knowledge equally across cultures?, *Academy of Management Learning and Education*, 6 (1): 33–50.

Simmonds, D. (2009) The evaluation of learning and development interventions, in D. Mankin (ed.), *Human Resource Development*, Oxford: Oxford University Press.

Simons, G. (2002) *Eurodiversity: A Business Guide to Managing Difference*, Woburn: Butterworth-Heinemann.

Simpson, M. R. (2009) Engagement at work: A review of the literature, *International Journal of Nursing Studies*, 46: 1012–24.

Sinclair, A. (1991) After excellence: Models of organisational culture for the public sector, *Australian Journal of Public Administration*, 50 (3): 321–30.

Singh, J. P. (1990) Managerial culture and work-related values in India, *Organization Studies*, 11 (1): 75–101.

Singh, P. and Finn, D. (2003) The effects of information technology on recruitment, *Journal of Labour Research*, 24 (3): 395–408.

Singh, V. and Point, S. (2004) Strategic responses by European companies to the diversity challenge: An online comparison, *Long Range Planning*, 37 (4): 295–318.

Sisson, K. (1990) Introducing the *Human Resource Management Journal*, *Human Resource Management Journal*, 1 (1): 1–11.

Sisson, K. (1993) In search of HRM, *British Journal of Industrial Relations*, 31 (2): 201–10.

Skills Advisory Group (SAG) (2004) Management skills in the UK, www.regionalobservatories.org.uk/sag_management_skills.pdf (accessed 1 December 2006).

Skinner, B. (1968) *The Technology of Teaching*, New York: Appleton–Century–Crofts.

Sloman, M. (2005) Learning in knowledge-intensive organisations: Moving from training to learning, *Development and Learning in Organizations*, 19 (6): 9–10.

Smith, A. and Elliott, F. (2012) The demands and challenges of being a retail store manager: 'Handcuffed to the front doors', *Work Employment & Society*, 26 (4), 676–684

Smith, A. D. and Rupp, W. T. (2004) 'Managerial challenges of e-recruiting: extending the life cycle of new economy employees', *Online Information Review*, (1): 61–74.

Smith, A., Wadsworth, E., Moss, S. and Simpson, S. (2004) *The Scale and Impact of Illegal Drug Use by Workers*, Research Report 193, Norwich: Health and Safety Executive.

Smith, C. (2014) Employment tribunal claims almost halved over the past year, *People Management*, 11 August.

Smith, P., Dugan, S., Peterson, M. and Leung, K. (1998) Individualism, collectivism and the handling of disagreement: A 23 country study, *International Journal of Intercultural Relations*, 22 (3): 351–67.

Snape, E. and Redman, T. (2010) HRM, practices, organisational citizenship behaviour, and performance: A multi-level analysis, *Journal of Management Studies*, 47 (7): 1219–47.

Sparrow, P. and Hiltrop, J. M. (1994) *European Human Resource Management in Transition*, London: Prentice Hall.

Spector, P. E., Cooper, C. L. and Sparks, K. (2001) An international study of the psychometric properties of the Hofstede values survey module 1994: A comparison of individual and country/province level results, *Applied Psychology: An International Review*, 50 (2): 269–81.

Spell, C. (2001) Organizational technologies and human resource management, *Human Relations*, 54: 193–213.

Spence, J. R. and Keeping, L. M. (2013) The road to performance ratings is paved with intentions: A framework for understanding managers' intentions when rating employee performance, *Organizational Psychology Review*, 3 (4): 360–38.

Spicer, D. P. and Sadler-Smith, E. (2006) Organizational learning in smaller manufacturing firms, *International Small Business Journal*, 24 (2): 133–58.

Squire, K. (2008) Video game-based learning: An emerging paradigm for instruction, *Performance Improvement Quarterly*, 21 (2): 7–36

Stanton, J. M. and Coovert, M. D. (2004) Turbulent waters: The intersection of information technology and human resources, *Human Resource Management*, 43 (2–3): 121–5.

Starbuck, W. (1992) Learning by knowledge-intensive firms, *Journal of Management Studies*, 29: 713–40.

Starkey, K. and Madan, P. (2001) Bridging the relevance gap: Aligning stakeholders in the future of management research, *British Journal of Management*, 12 (Special Issue): 3–26.

Stavrou, E. T. and Brewster, C. (2005) The configurational approach to linking strategic human resource management bundles with business performance: Myth or reality? *Management Revue*, 16 (2): 186–202.

Stavrou, E. T., Brewster, C. and Charalambous, C. (2010) Human resource management and firm performance in Europe through the lens of business systems: Best fit, best practice or both?, *International Journal of Human Resource Management*, 21 (7): 933–62.

Stevens, M. (2012) Michelin succeeds by managing employees' careers, *People Management*, 27 April.

Stewart, J. and Knowles, V. (1999) The changing nature of graduate careers, *Career Development International*, 4 (7): 370–83.

Stewart, J. and Knowles, V. (2000) Graduate recruitment and selection: Implications for HE, graduates, and small business recruiters, *Career Development International*, 5 (2): 65–80.

Stewart, J. and Rigg, C. (2011) *Learning and Talent Development*, London: CIPD.

Stewart, R., Barsoux, J. L., Kieser, A., Ganter, H. D. and Walgenbach, P. (1994) *Managing in Britain and Germany*, Basingstoke: Macmillan.

Stiles, P., Gratton, L., Truss, C., Hope-Hailey, V. and McGovern, P. (1997) Performance management and the psychological contract, *Human Resource Management Journal*, 7 (1): 57–66.

Stone, D. L., Stone-Romero, E. F. and Lukaszewski, K. (2006) Factors affecting the acceptance and effectiveness of electronic human resource systems, *Human Resource Management Review*, 16: 229–44.

Storey, D. J., Saridakis, G., Sen-Gupta, S., Edwards, P. K. and Blackburn, R. A. (2010) Linking HR formality with employee job quality: The role of firm and workplace size, *Human Resource Management*, 49 (2): 305–29.

Storey, J. (ed.) (1995) *Human Resource Management: A Critical Text*, London: Thomson.

Storey, J. (ed.) (2007) *Human Resource Management: A Critical Text* (3rd edn), London: Thomson.

Storey, J. and Barnett, E. (2000) Knowledge management initiatives: Learning from failure, *Journal of Knowledge Management*, 4 (2): 145–56.

Storey, J. and Quintas, P. (2001) Knowledge management and HRM, in J. Storey (ed.), *Human Resource Management: A Critical Text,* London: Thomson Learning.

Strauss, G. (2006) Worker participation: Some under-considered issues, *Industrial Relations*, 45 (4): 778–803.

Strunk, G. Mayrhofer, W. and Schiffinger, M. (2004) New careers, more complex careers? Empirical and methodological results concerning the 'complexity hypothesis' in career research, paper presented at European Group for Organizational Studies (EGOS) conference, Ljubljana, July.

Stuart, M., Cook, H., Cutter, J. and Winterton, J. (2010) *Evaluation of the Union Learning Fund and unionlearn: Preliminary findings*, unionlearn: London.

Stumpf, S. A., Doh, J. P. and Tymon Jr, W. G (2010) The strength of HR practices in India and their effective on employee career success, performance and potential, *Human Resource Management*, 49 (3): 353–75.

Subramony, M. (2009) A meta-analytic investigation of the relationship between HRM bundles and firm performance, *Human Resource Management*, 48: 745–68.

Sullivan, S. (1999) The changing nature of careers: A review and research agenda, *Journal of Management*, 25 (3): 457–84.

Sung, J. and Ashton, D. (2006) *Achieving Best Practice in Your Business – High Performance Work Practices: Linking Strategy and Skills to Performance Outcome*, London: Department for Trade and Industry/Chartered Institute of Personnel and Development.

Super, D. (1957) *The Psychology of Careers*, New York: Harper.

Sutherland, S. (2007) *Irrationality* (2nd edn), London: Pinter and Martin.

Sutton Trust (2014) *Internship or Indenture?*, Research Brief, November.

Suzuki, H. (2010) Employment relations in Japan: Recent changes under global competition and recession, *Journal of Industrial Relations*, 52 (3): 387–401.

Swanson, R. A. and Holton, E. F. (2001) *Foundations of Human Resource Development, San Francisco,* CA: Berret-Koehler.

Swart, J. and Kinnie, N. (2003) Sharing knowledge in knowledge-intensive firms, *Human Resource Management Journal*, 13 (2): 60–75.

Swart, J., Kinnie, N. and Purcell, J. (2003) *People and Performance in Knowledge Intensive Firms*, CIPD Research Report, London: CIPD.

Szabó, K. and Négyesi, A. (2005) The spread of contingent work in the knowledge-based economy, *Human Resource Development Review*, 4 (1): 63–85.

Tansley, C. (2011) What do we mean by the term 'talent' in talent management? *Industrial and Commercial Training*, 43 (5): 266–74.

Tansley, C., Harris, L., Stewart, J. and Turner, P. (2007) *Talent Management: Strategies, Policies and Practices*, London: CIPD.

Tayeb, M. (1987) Contingency theory and culture: A study of matched English and Indian manufacturing firms, *Organization Studies*, 8: 241–62.

Tayeb, M. (1992) *The Global Business Environment*. London: Sage.

Tayeb, M. (1998) Transfer of HRM practices across cultures: An American company in Scotland, *International Journal of Human Resource Management*, 9 (2): 332–58.

Tayeb, M. (2003) *International Management*, Harlow: Pearson.

Tayeb, M. (2005) *International Human Resource Management: A Multinational Company Perspective*, Oxford: Oxford University Press.

Taylor, P. and Bain, P. (1999) 'An assembly line in the head': Work and employee relations in the call centre, *Industrial Relations Journal*, 30 (2): 101–17.

Taylor, P., Baldry, C., Bain, P. and Ellis, V. (2003) A unique working environment: Health, sickness and absence management in UK call centres, *Work, Employment and Society*, 17 (3): 435–58.

Taylor, P., Mulvey, G., Hyman, J. and Bain, P. (2002) Work organization, control and the experience of work in call centres, *Work Employment and Society*, 16 (1): 133–50.

Taylor, S. (2008) *People Resourcing* (4th edn), London: CIPD.

Taylor, S., Beechler, S. and Napier, N. (1996) Towards an integrative model of strategic human resource management, *Academy of Management Review*, 21 (4): 959–85.

Tempel, A. (2001) *The Cross-national Transfer of Human Resource Management Practices in German and British Multinational Companies*, Munich: Rainer Hampp Verlag.

Terpstra, V. and David, K. (1991) *The Cultural Environment of International Business*, Cincinnati, OH: South-Western.

Thite, M. (2001) Help us but help yourself: The paradox of contemporary career management, *Career Development International*, 6 (6): 312–17.

Thomas, D. C. (2008) *Cross-Cultural Management: Essential Concepts* (2nd edn), London: Sage.

Thomas, D. C., Au, K. and Ravlin, E. C. (2003) Cultural variation and the psychological contract, *Journal of Organisational Behavior*, 24: 451–71.

Thompson, P. (2003) Disconnected capitalism: Or why employers can't keep their side of the bargain, *Work Employment and Society*, 17 (2): 359–78.

Thompson, P. (2004) *Skating on Thin Ice: The Knowledge Economy Myth*, Glasgow: University of Strathclyde/Big Thinking.

Thompson, P. and McHugh, D. (2002) *Work Organisations* (3rd edn), Basingstoke: Palgrave.

Thompson, P. and Warhurst, C. (2003) Doubt is the key to knowledge: Problems in mapping and measuring a 'knowledge-driven' economy and work, paper presented at European Sociological Association conference, Murcia, Spain, 23–26 June.

Tissen, R. J., Lekanne Deprez, F. R. E., Burgers, R. G. B. M and van Montfort, K. (2010) 'Change or hold: Reexamining HRM to meet new challenges and demands': The future of people at work: A reflection on diverging human resource management policies and practices in Dutch organizations, *International Journal of Human Resource Management*, 21 (5): 637–52.

Tomlinson, J. (2004) Perceptions and negotiations of the 'business case' for flexible careers and the integration of part-time work, *Women in Management Review*, 19 (8): 413–20.

Tomorrowtoday (2013) The future of recruitment, a paper prepared for the AGRG Annual Conference 2013, www.agr.org.uk/CoreCode/Admin/ContentManagement/MediaHub/Assets/FileDownload.ashx?fid=87959&pid=12689&loc=en-GB&fd=False (accessed 20 June 2015).

Torrington, D., Hall, L. and Taylor, S. (2008) *Human Resource Management* (7th edn), Harlow: FT Prentice Hall.

Trade Union Congress (TUC) (1999) *Partners for Progress*, London: TUC.

Tregaskis, O., Edwards, T., Edwards, P., Ferner, A. and Marginson, P. (2010) Transnational learning structures in multinational firms: Organizational context and national embeddedness, *Human Relations*, 63 (4): 471–99.

Tribunals Service (2011) *Employment Tribunal and EAT Statistics (GB), 1 April 2010 to 31 March 2011*, www.justice.gov.uk/statistics/tribunals/employment-tribunal-and-eat-statistics-gb (accessed 18 June 2012).

Tribunals Service (2012) *Employment Tribunal and EAT Statistics (GB), 1 April 2011 to 31 March 2012*, www.justice.gov.uk/statistics/tribunals/employment-tribunal-and-eat-statistics-gb (accessed 15 November 2012).

Trompenaars, F. (1994) *Riding the Waves of Culture: Understanding Diversity in Global Business*, New York: McGraw–Hill.

Trompenaars, F. and Hampden-Turner, C. (1998) *Riding the Waves of Culture: Understanding Diversity in Global Business* (2nd edn), New York: McGraw–Hill.

Tsai, C.-H, Chen, S.-J., and Fang, S.-C. (2009) Employment modes, high-performance work practices, and organizational performance in the hospitality industry, *Cornell Hospitality Quarterly*, 50 (4): 413–31.

Tsoukas, H. and Vladimirou, E. (2001) What is organizational knowledge?, *Journal of Management Studies*, 38 (7): 973–93.

Tuselmann, H., McDonald, F. and Heise, A. (2003) Employee relations in German multinationals in an Anglo-Saxon setting: Towards a Germanic version of the Anglo-Saxon approach, *European Journal of Industrial Relations*, 9 (3): 327–49.

Tyson, S. (1995) *Human Resource Strategy: Towards a General Theory of Human Resource Management*, London: Pitman.

UKCES (UK Commission for Employment and Skills (2015) *Growth through People: Evidence and Analysis*, London: UKCES.

Ulrich, D. (1997) *HR Champions*, Boston MA: Harvard Business School Press.

Ulrich, D. (1998) A new mandate for HR, *Harvard Business Review*, January–February: 124–34.

Ulrich, D. (2015) The future of HR is about relationships, *People Management*, 24 March.

Ulrich, D. and Brockbank, W. (2005) *The HR-Value Proposition*, Boston MA: Harvard Business School Press.

Ulrich, D., Younger, J. and Brockbank, W. (2008) The twenty-first-century HR organization, *Human Resource Management*, 47 (4): 829–50.

UNISON (2011) *Bullying and Harassment at Work: A Guide*, www.unison.org.uk/file/B6082.pdf (accessed 12 November 2012).

Vaiman, V. and Collings, D. G. (2013) Talent management: Advancing the field, *International Journal of Human Resource Management*, 24 (9): 1737–43

Valverde, M., Ryan, G. and Soler, C. (2006) Distributing HRM responsibilities: A classification of organisations, *Personnel Review*, 35 (6): 618–36.

van den Berg, N., Meijers, F. and Sprengers, M. (2006) More vocational education and supplementary training: An analysis of a training and development fund in the Netherlands, *Human Resource Development International*, 9 (1): 5–24.

van der Veen, R. (2006) Human resource development: Irreversible trend or temporary fad? *Human Resource Development Review*, 5 (1): 3–7.

van de Voorde, K., Paauwe, J. and van Veldhoven, M. (2010) Predicting business unit performance using employee surveys: Monitoring HRM-related changes, *Human Resource Management Journal*, 20 (1): 44–63.

van de Voorde, K., Paauwe, J. and Van Veldhoven, M. (2012) Employee well-being and the HRM–organizational performance relationship: A review of quantitative studies, *International Journal of Management Reviews*, 14 (4): 391–407.

Van Dyke, M. and Ryan, M. (2013) Changing the compensation conversation and the growing utility of noncash rewards and recognition, *Compensation & Benefits Review*, 44 (5): 276–79.

van Wanrooy, B., Bewley, H., Bryson, A., Forth, J., Freeth, S., Stokes, L. and Wood, S. (2013) *Employment Relations in the Shadow of Recession: Findings from the 2011 Workplace Employment Relations Study*, London: Palgrave Macmillan.

Vaughan, R. H. and Wilson, M. C. (1994) Career management using job trees: Charting a path through the changing organization, *Human Resource Planning*, 17 (3): 43–55.

Verreynne, M.-L., Parker, P. and Wilson, M. (2011) Employment systems in small firms: A multilevel analysis, *International Small Business Journal*, 31 (4): 405–31.

Von Glinow, M. A., Drost, E. A. and TeaGarden, M. B. (2002) Converging on IHRM best practices: lessons learnt from a globally distributed consortium on theory and practice, *Human Resource Management*, 41 (1): 123–40.

Vroom, V. H. (1964) *Work and Motivation*, New York: Wiley.

Walker, B. and Hamilton, R. T. (2011) The effectiveness of grievance processes in New Zealand: A fair way to go?, *Journal of Industrial Relations*, 53 (1): 103–21.

Wall, T. D. and Wood, S. J. (2005) The romance of human resource management and business performance, and the case for big science, *Human Relations*, 58: 429–62.

Walsh, K. and Taylor, M. S. (2007) Developing in-house careers and retaining management talent: What hospitality professionals want from their jobs, *Cornell Hotel and Restaurant Administration Quarterly*, 48 (2): 163–82.

Walters, D., Nichols, T., Connor, J., Tasiran, A. C. and Cam, S. (2005) *The Role and Effectiveness of Safety Representatives in Influencing Workplace Health and Safety*, Research Report 363, Norwich: Health and Safety Executive.

Walton, R. E. (1985) From control to commitment in the workplace, *Harvard Business Review*, March–April: 77–84.

Waples, E. P. and Friedrich, T. L. (2011) Managing creative performance: Important strategies for leaders of creative efforts, *Advances in Developing Human Resources*, 13 (3): 366–85.

Warhurst, C. and Thompson, P. (1998) Hands, hearts and minds: Work and workers at the end of the century, in P. Thompson and C. Warhurst (eds), *Workplaces of the Future*, London: Macmillan.

Warr, P., Bird, M. and Rackham, N. (1970) *Evaluation of Management Training: A Practical Framework with Cases for Evaluating Training Needs and Results*, Gower Press, London.

Warren, R. C. (1996) The empty raincoat: Morality and job security, *Personnel Review*, 25 (6): 41–53.

Wasti, S. A. (1998) Cultural barriers in the transferability of Japanese and American human resources practices to developing countries: The Turkish case, *International Journal of Human Resource Management*, 9 (4): 608–31.

Watson, T. J. (2008) *Sociology, Work and Industry* (5th edn), London, Routledge.

Watson, T. (2009) Organisations, strategies and human resourcing, in J. Leopold and L. Harris (eds), *The Strategic Managing of Human Resources* (2nd edn), Harlow: FT Prentice Hall.

Watts, J. (2006) Wal-Mart backs down and allows Chinese workers to join union, *The Guardian*, 11 August.

Webster, S., Buckley, P. and Rose, I. (2007) *Psychosocial Working Conditions in Britain in 2007*, London: Health and Safety Executive.

Weinstein, C. E. and Mayer, R. E. (1986) The teaching of learning strategies, in M. C. Wittrock (ed.), *Third Handbook of Research on Teaching*, New York: Macmillan.

Weiss, R. and Bass, S. (2002) *Challenges of the Third Age: Meaning and Purpose in Late Life*, Oxford: Oxford University Press

Welbourne, T. M. and Andrews, A. O. (1996) Predicting the performance of initial public offerings: Should human resource management be in the equation? *Academy of Management Journal*, 39 (4): 891–919.

Wentling, R. M. (2000) Evaluation of diversity initiatives in multinational corporations, *Human Resource Development International*, 3 (4): 435–50.

West, M., Borrill, C., Dawson, J., Scully, J., Carter, M., Anelay, S., Patterson, M. and Waring, J. (2002) The link between the management of employees and patient mortality in acute hospitals, *International Journal of Human Resource Management*, 13 (8): 1299–310.

Westwood, R., Sparrow, P. and Leung, A. (2001) Challenges to the psychological contract in Hong Kong, *International Journal of Human Resource Management*, 12 (4): 621–51.

White, M., Hill, S., McGovern, P., Mills, C. and Smeaton, D. (2003) 'High performance' management practices, working hours and work–life balance, *British Journal of Industrial Relations*, 41 (2): 175–95.

Whittaker, S. and Marchington, M. (2003) Devolving HR responsibility to the line: Threat, opportunity or partnership, *Employee Relations*, 25 (3): 245–61.

Whittington, R. (2001) *What Is Strategy and Does It Matter?* (2nd edn), London: Thomson.

Whymark, K. and Ellis, S. (1999) Whose career is it anyway? Options for career management in flatter organisational structures, *Career Development International*, 4 (2): 101–7.

Wilcox, T. (2006) Human resource development as an element of corporate social responsibility, *Asia Pacific Journal of Human Resources*, 44 (2): 184–96.

Wilcox, T. and Lowry, D. (2000) Casual workers and the human centred organisation, *Business and Professional Ethics Journal*, 19 (3/4): 29–54.

Wilensky, H. L. (1960) Careers, life-styles, and social integration, *International Social Science Journal*, 12: 553–8.

Wilkinson, A. (1999) Employment relations in SMEs, *Employee Relations*, 21 (3): 206–17.

Wilkinson, A., Dundon, T., Marchington, M. and Ackers, P. (2004) Changing patterns of employee voice: Case studies from the UK and Republic of Ireland, *Journal of Industrial Relations*, 46 (3): 298–322.

Willcocks, L. L. and Lacity, M. (2009) *The Practice of Outsourcing: From ITO to BPO and Offshoring*, London: Palgrave Macmillan.

Williams, C. (2014) Out of the shadows: A classification of economies by the size and character of their informal sector, *Work, Employment and Society*, 28 (5): 735–53.

Williams, K. and Geppert, M. (2006) The German model of employee relations on trial: Negotiated and unilaterally imposed change in multi-national companies, *Industrial Relations Journal*, 37 (1): 48–63.

Williams, S. and Adam-Smith, D. (2005) *Contemporary Employment Relations: A Critical Introduction*, Oxford: Oxford University Press.

Williams, S. and Rumbles, S. (2009) Grievance, discipline and absence in organizations, in S. Gilmore and S. Williams (eds), *Human Resource Management*, Oxford: Oxford University Press.

Wilson, E. M. and Iles, P. A. (1999) Managing diversity: An employment and service delivery challenge, *International Journal of Public Sector Management*, 12 (1): 2–4.

Wilson, T. and Davies, G. (1999) The changing career strategies of managers, *Career Development International*, 4 (2): 101–7.

Wilton, N. (2006) Strategic choice and organisational context in HRM in the hotel sector, *The Service Industries Journal*, 26 (8): 1–17.

Wilton, N. (2007) The early career paths of business and management graduates in a changing labour market, unpublished PhD thesis, University of the West of England, Bristol.

Wilton, N. (2008) The path of least resistance? Choice and constraint in HRM strategy in the UK hotel sector, in D. Tesone (ed.), *Handbook of Hospitality Human Resource Management*, Oxford: Elsevier.

Wilton, N. (2012) Do employability skills really matter in the graduate labour market? The case of business and management graduates, *Work, Employment and Society,* 25 (1): 85–100.

Wilton, N. and Purcell, K. (2010) The impact of partnership and family-building on the early careers of female graduates in the UK, *Equality, Diversity and Inclusion*, 29 (3): 271–88.

Windolf, P. (1986) Recruitment, selection, and internal labour markets in Britain and Germany, *Organization Studies*, 7 (3): 235–54.

Winstanley, D. and Stuart-Smith, K. (1996) Policing performance: The ethics of performance management, *Personnel Review*, 25 (6): 68–84.

Winstanley, D. and Woodall, J. (2000) The ethical dimension of human resource management, *Human Resource Management Journal*, 10 (2): 5–20.

Winterton, J. (2004) A conceptual model of labour turnover and retention, *Human Resource Development International*, 7 (3): 371–90.

Winterton, J., Parker, M., Dodd, M., McCraken, M. and Henderson, I. (2000) *Future Skills Needs of Managers*, Research Brief 182, Nottingham: DfEE.

Wintour, P. (2008) Agency and temporary workers win rights deal, *The Guardian*, 21 May.

Wocke, A. and Heymann, M. (2012) Impact of demographic variables on voluntary labour turnover, *International Journal of Human Resource Management*, 23 (16): 3479–94.

Wolf, A. (2002) *Does Education Matter? Myths about Education and Economic Growth*, London: Penguin Education.

Wolff, C. (2014) *Xperthr Learning Budgets Survey 2014: Employer Spending Trends*, www.xperthr.co.uk/survey-analysis/xperthr-learning-budgets-survey-2014-employer-spending-trends/153561/ (accessed 18 September 2015).

Women and Work Commission (2009) *Shaping a Fairer Future: A Review of the Recommendations of the Women and Work Commission Three Years On*, London: Government Equalities Office.

Wood, R. and Payne, T. (1998) *Competency-based Recruitment and Selection*, Chichester: Wiley.

Woodall, J. and Winstanley, D. (1998) *Management Development: Strategy and Practice*, Oxford: Blackwell.

Worren, N. and Koestner, R. (1996) Seeking innovating team players: Contextual determinants of preferred applicant attributes, *International Journal of Human Resource Management*, 7 (2): 521–33.

Wright, C. (2008) Reinventing human resource management: Business partners, internal consultants and the limits to professionalization, *Human Relations*, 61: 1063–86.

Wright, C. F. (2011) What role for trade unions in future workplace relations?, Acas discussion paper, September

Wright, P. M. and Nishii, L. H. (2007) *Strategic HRM and Organizational Behavior: Integrating Multiple Levels of Analysis*, CAHRS Working Paper Series, Paper 468.

Wright, P. M., Dunford, B. B. and Snell, S. A. (2001) Human resources and the resource based view of the firm, *Journal of Management*, 2: 701–21.

Wright, P. M., Gardner, T. M. and Moynihan, L. M. (2003) The impact of HR practices on the performance of business units, *Human Resource Management Journal*, 13 (3): 21–36.

Yahya, S. and Goh, W.-K. (2002) Managing human resources towards achieving knowledge management, *Journal of Knowledge Management*, 6 (5): 457–68.

Yanow, D. (2000) Seeing organizational learning: A 'cultural' view, *Organization*, 7 (2): 247–68.

Youndt, M. A., Snell, S. A., Dean, J. W. and Lepak, D. P. (1996) Human resource management, manufacturing strategy and firm performance, *Academy of Management Journal*, 39 (4): 836–66.

Zaleska, K. J. and de Menezes, L. M. (2007) Human resources development practices and their association with employee attitudes: Between traditional and new careers, *Human Relations*, 60: 987–1018.

Zanoni, P. and Janssens, M. (2004) Deconstructing difference: The rhetoric of human resource managers' diversity discourses, *Organization Studies*, 24 (1): 55–74.

Zhang, M., Macpherson, A. and Jones, O. (2006) Conceptualizing the learning process in SMEs, *International Small Business Journal*, 24 (3): 299–323.

Zielinski, D. (2012) Group learning: use social media to engage employees in knowledge sharing, *HR Magazine*, 57(5): 49–52.

Zingheim, P. K. and Schuster, J. R. (2005) The next decade for pay and rewards, *Compensation & Benefits Review*, 37 (1): 26–32.

INDEX